'It is a remarkable fact that our Victorian forebears worked out that health and planning were inextricably linked. The great schemes of sanitation and urban improvement which had such tangible beneficial effects on the health of the population stand as a monument to their vision and practical problem solving. How did we lose our way? How did we arrive at a situation where planning and public health became so disjoined? In this excellent new book the authors point us in a direction which shows what can and could be achieved in the contemporary age. It is a landmark text which will be highly influential in the years to come.'

Mike Kelly, Institute of Public Health, University of Cambridge, UK,
and former Director of the Centre for Public Health at NICE

'This is a manifesto for how we should plan our neighbourhoods, towns and cities. It champions the objectives of health and well-being – time-honoured values in the history of planning – as the core means to achieving well-made, rich, beautiful and happy places. I'd like to see every politician, planner and developer given a copy. I'd like every household in the country to understand its message.'

Kevin McCloud MBE

THE ROUTLEDGE HANDBOOK OF PLANNING FOR HEALTH AND WELL-BEING

Urban planning is deeply implicated in both the planetary crisis of climate change and the personal crises of unhealthy lifestyles. Worldwide health issues such as obesity, mental illness, growing health inequalities and climate vulnerability cannot be solved solely by medicines; the social, economic and environmental determinants must also be tackled. At a time when unhealthy and unsustainable conditions are being built into the physical fabric of cities, a new awareness and strategy is urgently needed to put health and well-being at the heart of planning.

The *Routledge Handbook of Planning for Health and Well-Being* authoritatively and comprehensively integrates health into planning, strengthening the hands of those who argue and plan for healthy environments. With contributions from international leaders in the field, the *Handbook of Planning for Health and Well-Being* provides context, philosophy, research, processes and tools of experienced practitioners through case studies from four continents.

Hugh Barton is Emeritus Professor of Planning, Health and Sustainability at the University of the West of England, Bristol, UK. Until 2012 he was Director of the WHO Collaborating Centre for Healthy Urban Environments. He is a recognised international expert in the field, and lead author of key texts on sustainability and health, including *Healthy Urban Planning* (for the WHO Healthy Cities programme; Taylor & Francis 2000), *Sustainable Communities* (Earthscan 2000) and *Shaping Neighbourhoods* (Routledge 2010). His research, teaching and consultancy work has been about building bridges between disciplines, professions, stakeholders, spatial scales and policy areas. He has made a particular study of energy-efficient urban form, neighbourhood design, inclusive decision processes and health-integrated planning.

Susan Thompson is Professor of Planning and Associate Director (Healthy Built Environments) at the City Futures Research Centre, UNSW Australia (The University of New South Wales, Australia). Susan has worked in urban planning for over 30 years focusing on cross-disciplinary research, teaching and practice. She has qualifications in urban planning, geography and education. Her areas of expertise encompass cultural diversity in urban planning, meanings of home and the use of qualitative research methodologies in the built environment disciplines. For the last decade Susan's work has focused on healthy urban planning. In 2012 Susan was elected Fellow of the Planning Institute of Australia and she is widely published in urban planning and health.

Sarah Burgess is a qualified planner specialising in urban design and planning policy. She has experience in public and private practice in both Australia and the United Kingdom, working on projects and policies at local and strategic levels. Sarah is a Senior Lecturer in Health and Urban Planning at the University of the West of England, UK. Her research interests include urban form and the quality of the urban environment and the integration of health into planning policies and processes. She is a Built Environment Expert with the Commission for Architecture and the Built Environment and an Academician of the Academy of Urbanism.

Marcus Grant has been exploring questions at the interface of human flourishing, sustainability and land use since the mid-1980s. He has working experience of the consultancy, academic and public policy worlds and is concerned with accessing their inherent, but untapped, synergies to make better places. Recently, he has been active in this field as Deputy Director of the WHO Collaborating Centre for Healthy Urban Environments and Associate Professor in the Department of Planning and Architecture at the University of the West of England, UK. Marcus holds a degree in ecology, is a Chartered Landscape Architect, a Fellow of the Faculty of Public Health and an Associate Fellow of the National Institute for Health Research.

THE ROUTLEDGE HANDBOOK OF PLANNING FOR HEALTH AND WELL-BEING

Shaping a sustainable and healthy future

Edited by Hugh Barton, Susan Thompson,
Sarah Burgess and Marcus Grant

Routledge
Taylor & Francis Group

LONDON AND NEW YORK

First published 2015
by Routledge
2 Park Square, Milton Park, Abingdon, Oxon OX14 4RN

and by Routledge
711 Third Avenue, New York, NY 10017

Routledge is an imprint of the Taylor & Francis Group, an informa business

British Library Cataloguing in Publication Data
A catalogue record for this book is available from the British Library

Library of Congress Cataloging in Publication Data
The Routledge handbook of planning for health and well-being : shaping a sustainable and healthy future / edited by Hugh Barton, Susan Thompson, Sarah Burgess, and Marcus Grant.
p. ; cm.
Handbook of planning for health and well-being
Includes bibliographical references and index.
I. Barton, Hugh, editor. II. Thompson, Susan, 1954- , editor. III. Grant, Marcus, 1958- , editor. IV. Burgess, Sarah, editor. V. Title: Handbook of planning for health and well-being.
[DNLM: 1. Urban Health. 2. Architecture as Topic. 3. City Planning. 4. Environment Design. WA 380]
RA566.7
362.1′042—dc23
2014042458

ISBN: 978-1-13802-330-7 (hbk)
ISBN: 978-1-31572-826-1 (ebk)

Typeset in Bembo Std
by Swales & Willis Ltd, Exeter, Devon, UK

Printed and bound in the United States of America by Publishers Graphics, LLC on sustainably sourced paper.

DEDICATION

The book is for all those practitioners involved in the production of the built environment, and all those concerned – as professionals, commentators, researchers or students – with the need for humane, inclusive, healthy and ecologically sustainable towns and cities.

CONTENTS

Contents

Contents

Contents

FIGURES

Part I: Perspectives

Part III: The human habitat

Part IV: Processes and tools

Part V: Healthy planning in global practice

CONTRIBUTORS

Carl Abbott has taught urban studies, planning and history at Portland State University, USA, over the course of five decades. He has published over a dozen books on US urban history, urban planning and science fiction. His recent publications include *Portland in Three Centuries: The Place and the People* (Oregon State University Press 2011) and the North America chapter in *The Oxford Handbook of Cities in World History* (Oxford University Press 2013).

Lynda Addison has worked in both the public and private sector. She was a Director of Planning & Transport before establishing an award winning consultancy and subsequently advising national and local Government on all aspects of planning, specialising in management and the integration of planning and transport. She received an OBE for services to planning in 2006. She is a Visiting Professor at University of Westminster, UK, an English Heritage Commissioner, sits on the Planning Committee of LLDC and Chairs the Sustainable Transport Panel for CIHT.

Jessica Allen is a Deputy Director of the Institute of Health Equity. Her main activities are working to embed a social determinants approach to health inequalities in England and globally. She was co-director of the Review of Social Determinants of Health and the Health Divide in the World Health Organization (WHO) European Region and was previously Project Director of the Strategic Review of Health Inequalities in England post-2010 (the Marmot Review). She has worked closely with national and local governments, third sector organisations and the National Health Service (NHS) and published widely on social determinants of health. She holds a doctorate from the University of London, UK.

Matilda Allen is a Research Fellow for the Institute of Health Equity. She has been involved in researching and writing Institute reports, disseminating the work of the Institute through presenting at conferences and events, and running programmes of work for the Institute. She has also published a number of articles and other publications on the social determinants of health. She has an MSc in Philosophy and Public Policy from LSE and a BA in Politics from the University of Manchester, UK.

Emily Ballantyne-Brodie is Director of Urban Reforestation and principal consultant at Sustainable Everyday. Through a design-led approach she enables innovative ventures in local food and urban agriculture movements. Emily was a finalist in the United Nations of Australia

Sustainability Entrepreneur award 2011 and was nominated for the Telstra Business Woman of the Year award in 2014.

Hugh Barton is Emeritus Professor of Planning, Health and Sustainability at the University of the West of England, Bristol, UK. Until 2012 he was Director of the WHO Collaborating Centre for healthy urban environments. He is a recognised international expert in the field, and lead author of key texts on sustainability and health, including *Healthy Urban Planning* (for the WHO Healthy Cities programme; Spon Press 2000), *Sustainable Communities* (Earthscan 2000) and *Shaping Neighbourhoods* (Routledge 2010). His research, teaching and consultancy work has been about building bridges between disciplines, professions, stakeholders, spatial scales and policy areas. He has made a particular study of energy-efficient urban form, neighbourhood design, inclusive decision processes and health-integrated planning.

Brenda Boardman is an Emeritus Fellow of the University of Oxford, UK, having previously led the Lower Carbon Futures group at the Environmental Change Institute there. In 2012 she wrote *Achieving Zero: Delivering Future-Friendly Buildings* (Environmental Change Institute, University of Oxford) which considers the policies required to get all energy, in all UK buildings to zero carbon emissions by 2050, primarily through demand reduction.

Sarah Burgess is a qualified planner specialising in urban design and planning policy. She has experience in public and private practice in both Australia and the United Kingdom, working on projects and policies at local and strategic levels. Sarah is a Senior Lecturer in Health and Urban Planning at the University of the West of England, Bristol, UK. Her research interests include urban form and the quality of the urban environment and the integration of health into planning policies and processes. She is a Built Environment Expert with the Commission for Architecture and the Built Environment and an Academician of the Academy of Urbanism.

Libby Burton was Professor of Sustainable Building Design and Wellbeing and founder director of the WISE (Wellbeing in Sustainable Environments) research unit at the University of Warwick, UK. Her research investigated the social aspects of sustainability and how the built environment influences people's well-being. She had particular expertise in ageing research, including dementia-friendly design. Very sadly Libby died before the book was published. Her chapter was the last major thing that she wrote.

Anthony Capon directs the International Institute for Global Health at United Nations University, based in Kuala Lumpur. His research focuses on urban futures, sustainability and human health. Since 2008, he has been working with the International Council for Science to develop the global interdisciplinary science programme on health and well-being in the changing urban environment using systems approaches.

Ben Cave has specialised in Health Impact Assessment for the last 15 years. He runs a specialist consultancy which works across the UK, in mainland Europe and further afield with policy-makers, public health academics, environment scientists and spatial planners. He is also an active member of the International Association for Impact Assessment.

Tzu-Yuan Stessa Chao is Assistant Professor in the Department of Urban Planning at National Cheng Kung University, Taiwan. Her research mainly focuses on demographic change and the urban planning system in terms of planning mechanisms and legal systems. She was the first project leader of the National Age-Friendly Cities Program in Taiwan in 2010–2011 and has been highly involved in Healthy/Age-Friendly Cities research in Taiwan.

Jason Corburn is an Associate Professor in the School of Public Health and the Department of City and Regional Planning at the University of California, Berkeley, USA. He directs Berkeley's Center for Global Healthy Cities and Berkeley's joint public health and city planning degree programme. He has been a visiting scholar at the University of Paris, Nanterre, University of Nairobi, and the State University of Rio de Janeiro.

Linda Corkery is an Associate Professor and Discipline Director for Landscape Architecture in the Faculty of Built Environment at UNSW Australia (The University of New South Wales). Her research and teaching focuses on planning and design of urban parklands and open space, design of the public domain, people/place relationships, and interdisciplinary service learning. Linda is a Fellow of the Australian Institute of Landscape Architects.

Paul Cozens is an environmental criminologist and expert in Crime Prevention Through Environmental Design (CPTED). He is a Senior Lecturer at Curtin University's Department of Urban and Regional Planning and a co-director of the Design Out Crime Research Centre in Western Australia. His recently published book is entitled *Think Crime! Using Evidence, Theory and Crime Prevention Through Environmental Design (CPTED) for Planning Safer Cities* (Praxis Education 2014).

Adrian Davis is a public health and transport consultant who is internationally recognised as an expert in the field, consulting for local, regional and national governments and the World Health Organization. He is a Visiting Professor at the University of the West of England, Bristol, UK, and is an Editor of the *Journal of Transport & Health*.

Jane Dixon, Senior Fellow, National Centre for Epidemiology and Population Health, Australian National University undertakes research at the intersection of food systems sociology and public health. A particular focus of her research concerns the socio-cultural determinants of health, and this is reflected in two recent books: *Weight of Modernity* (Springer 2012) and *When Culture Impacts Health* (Elsevier 2013).

Nicholas Falk is an urbanist and economist, and set up his own company, URBED, in London in 1976. Some four decades later, with colleague David Rudlin who runs the Manchester office, he won the 2014 Wolfson Economics Prize for their submission for a fictional town, Uxcester Garden City. Nicholas is co-author, with David Rudlin, of *Sustainable Urban Neighbourhood: Building the 21st Century Home* (Routledge 2009) and worked with Sir Peter Hall on *Good Cities Better Lives: How Europe Discovered the Lost Art of Urbanism* (Routledge 2014).

Nalan Fidan worked for 10 years in the Planning Department of Bursa Metropolitan Municipality, and in 2005 took a leadership role in the establishment of the Turkish Healthy Cities Association where she worked as Director until 2014, whilst at the same time working as Head of the Projects Department of Bursa Metropolitan Municipality. In 2014 she was appointed Head of the Environmental Protection and Inspection Department.

Sarah Foster is a Research Fellow at the Centre for the Built Environment and Health, based at The University of Western Australia. Her work focuses on the impact of the built environment on a range of health and well-being outcomes. She has a particular interest in the interplay between suburban neighbourhood design, crime and residents' feelings of 'safety' and walking behaviours.

Jacinta Francis is a public health researcher at the McCaughey VicHealth Centre for Community Wellbeing, The University of Melbourne, Australia, and The Centre for the Built Environment and Health, The University of Western Australia. Her research interests include neighbourhoods and public space, parks and restorative environments, positive mental health and psychosocial outcomes such as sense of community, social support and sense of place.

Robert Freestone is Professor of Planning and Associate Dean (Research) in the Faculty of Built Environment at UNSW Australia (The University of New South Wales). He is a former President of the International Planning History Society. His latest book is *Exhibitions and the Development of Planning Culture* (Ashgate Publishing Ltd 2014).

Rachel Gallo trained in Public Health Nutrition and Town Planning and specialises in Obesogenic Environment research. Rachel's PhD focuses on the influence of the neighbourhood environment on health outcomes (diet and physical activity) in young people within the North East of England.

Billie Giles-Corti is Director of the McCaughey VicHealth Centre for Community Wellbeing, The University of Melbourne, Australia. She has published over 200 articles and reports and, in 2014, was included in Thomson Reuters' list of Highly Cited Researchers, ranking her among the top 1 per cent of researchers globally in her field.

Herbert Girardet, Hon FRIBA, is a cultural ecologist, working as a writer and international consultant. Herbert is a member of the Club of Rome, honorary member of the World Future Council, and former chairman of the Schumacher Society UK. He is a recipient of a UN Global 500 award for outstanding environmental services.

Marcus Grant has been exploring questions at the interface of human flourishing, sustainability and land use since the mid-1980s. He has working experience of the consultancy, academic and public policy worlds and is concerned with accessing their inherent, but untapped, synergies to make better places. Recently, he has been active in this field as Deputy Director of the WHO Collaborating Centre for Healthy Urban Environments and Associate Professor in the Department of Planning and Architecture at the University of the West of England, Bristol, UK. Marcus holds a degree in ecology, is a Chartered Landscape Architect, a Fellow of the Faculty of Public Health and an Associate Fellow of the National Institute for Health Research.

Cliff Hague is Emeritus Professor of Planning and Spatial Development at Heriot-Watt University, Edinburgh, UK, and a freelance researcher and author. He is a Past President of the Royal Town Planning Institute and also of the Commonwealth Association of Planners, a former Chair of Built Environment Forum Scotland, and a Fellow of the Academy of the Social Sciences.

James de Havilland has over 20 years' experience in both the public and private sectors including 14 years creating sustainable, mixed use masterplans and providing urban design advice to the private sector. His recent experience ranges from large urban extension projects to quarry/heavy industry regeneration schemes, pioneering a new approach to the layout of mixed use sustainable neighbourhoods.

Enda Hayes is an environmental resource management researcher and practitioner specialising in air quality and carbon management. He has worked with local authorities, and national governments in the UK, European Member States and South Africa and more recently with the European Commission providing research and advice on technical and policy issues. He is a member of the Institution of Environmental Sciences and the Institute of Air Quality Management.

Peter Headicar worked as a transport planner in local government in the UK for 20 years, and from 1989 to 2010 held the post of Reader in Transport at the Department of Planning at Oxford Brookes University, UK, where he led teaching on the Master's degree in Transport Planning and wrote the textbook *Transport Policy and Planning in Great Britain* (Routledge 2009). In 2012 he received the Planning and Transport, Research and Computation (PTRC) Lifetime Achievement Award.

Paula Hooper is a Research Fellow on the National Health and Medical Research Council's (NHMRC's) Centre for Research Excellence in Healthy, Liveable Communities at the Centre for the Built Environment and Health, The University of Western Australia. Paula's research has focused on the role of the built environment and planning policy in the promotion of physical activity and walking behaviours.

Zafar Iqbal has worked in senior public health in the West Midlands, UK, since the mid-1990s. During this time he has covered the full spectrum of public health functions ranging from programmes influencing the determinants of health to prioritisation of health resources. He is a Board Member (Assistant Registrar) of the UK Faculty of Public Health and has honorary posts at both Staffordshire and Keele Universities, UK.

Jennifer Kent is a Post-Doctoral Fellow in the Faculty of Architecture, Design and Planning at the University of Sydney, Australia. Jennifer's research interests lay primarily in the intersections between planning and health, including planning for active transport and attachments to the private car as a form of mobility.

Val Kirby is a landscape architect, town planner and cultural geographer, with much experience in landscape and cultural heritage policy and strategy. She has worked for local and central government agencies in England, and has also held academic posts in England and New Zealand. She is currently a research associate in the Countryside and Community Research Institute at the University of Gloucestershire, UK.

Mohammad Javad Koohsari holds joint Research Fellow appointments at the McCaughey VicHealth Centre for Community Wellbeing, The University of Melbourne, Australia, and the Baker IDI Heart and Diabetes Institute in Melbourne, Australia. As an urban designer, his research interests focus on understanding the influence of the built environment on health outcomes, with a specific emphasis on relationships between urban form, physical activity and sedentary behaviour.

Leo Kosonen is an architect and worked as a city planner in Finland for 40 years. His concept of three urban fabrics led to new practices and several major projects at the City of Kuopio, Finland. Now he works as a researcher on the new Theory of Urban Fabrics together with Professor Peter Newman, who is based in Australia.

Judy Kurth has worked for many years as a senior public health practitioner and has been influential in developing regional, national and international public health partnerships. As Strategic Manager for healthier and safer communities in Stoke-on-Trent City Council, Judy is the City Council WHO Healthy City Co-co-ordinator and is a member of the European WHO Healthy Cities Advisory Committee.

Amelia A. Lake is a Lecturer in Knowledge Exchange in Public Health at the Centre for Translational Research in Public Health (Fuse). Amelia's current work is to explore the Obesogenic Environment. She has a particular interest in the food environment, the environments of young people and the workplace environment. Amelia is a Dietitian by background and is a registered Public Health Nutritionist.

Jessica Lamond is Senior Research Fellow in the Centre for Floods, Communities and Resilience at the University of the West of England, Bristol, UK. Jessica's research focuses on structural and non-structural responses to flood risk and climate adaptation in urban settings. She is currently studying the impacts of flooding in frequently flooded communities and the delivery and benefits of Blue Green Cities.

Martin Large works as a facilitator, land reformer, publisher and co-op developer. He lectured in Behavioural Science for 18 years at what is now the University of Gloucestershire, UK, chaired the Community Land Trust (CLT) National Demonstration Project 2007–2009, founded the Biodynamic Farm Land Trust and Gloucestershire Land for People CLT which developed Stroud's groundbreaking Cashes Green CLT with Kevin McLeod of Grand Designs.

Roderick J. Lawrence is Director of the Global Environmental Policy Programme at the University of Geneva, Switzerland, in partnership with the United Nations Environment Programme (UNEP). In January 1997 he was nominated to the New York Academy of Science, and since September 2014 he is also Visiting Professor at the United Nations University for two years.

Lamine Mahdjoubi trained as an architect and urban designer. His work focuses on the role of planning design aspects of the built environment in the promotion of healthy lifestyles. He recently led a multidisciplinary and inter-professional team, which examined the effects of planning design of the built environment on outdoor play that is conducive to regular physical activities.

Elena Marco is an architect and educator who built a strong profile in sustainable design at Feilden Clegg Bradley Studios working on many pioneering and award winning projects. Now Head of Department for Architecture at the University of the West of England, Bristol, UK, she continues to develop her research interests which focus on the crossover between health, sustainability and architecture.

Louise McKenzie is a PhD candidate in the Healthy Built Environments Program at UNSW Australia (The University of New South Wales). She has a Master's degree in the Built Environment (Sustainable Development) and Bachelor of Landscape Architecture. Her focus is on interdisciplinary approaches to creating healthy cities and neighbourhoods in response to a warming climate. Her PhD research explores the influence of urban heat on the everyday use of public space and implications for public health.

Moriah McSharry McGrath is Assistant Professor of Public Health in the Department of Sociology, Anthropology, Social Work, and Public Health at Pacific University in Forest Grove, Oregon, USA. She has spent over a decade working at the intersection of urban planning and public health.

Bruce McVean is a principal strategy planner at Transport for London. Previous roles include associate director at Beyond Green and senior policy advisor at the Commission for Architecture and the Built Environment (CABE). Bruce is a trustee of Living Streets and has advised the National Institute for Health and Care Excellence (NICE) on physical activity and the built environment.

Ove Christen Mørck is the co-founder and director of Cenergia Energy Consultants (Cenergia), and has worked with planning and implementation of energy conservation and renewable energy integration in buildings and environmental issues since 1978. Ove has a profound knowledge of energy conservation and renewable energy technologies suitable for the built environment.

John Parkin worked for consulting engineers before joining academia, and he is now Professor of Transport Engineering at the University of the West of England, Bristol, UK. He has been involved in all stages of the promotion of transport schemes including policy formulation, modelling and forecasting, operational analysis and economic appraisal, design and construction. He has experience across all modes of transport and has a particular specialism in cycling.

Mala Rao is Professor and Senior Clinical Fellow, Department of Primary Care and Public Health, Imperial College London and Honorary Consultant, Public Health England. She has extensive experience of working in public health practice, research and policy, and was previously Head of Public Health Workforce at the Department of Health for England. Mala is a globally recognised champion of climate change action and has been raising awareness of the links between health, urbanisation and sustainable development for many years.

Charlotte Robinson started her career as a Planning Policy Officer at the City of Lincoln Council. She is a member of the Royal Town Planning Institute with over 12 years of experience in local government and currently works for the Central Lincolnshire Local Plan Team, responsible for preparing a joint Local Plan for three district councils.

Lucy Saunders is the Public Health Specialist in Transport and Public Realm for Transport for London and the Greater London Authority. She is a National Institute for Health and Care Excellence (NICE) Scholar and Academician of the Academy of Urbanism. Recently Transport for London became the first transport authority in the world to publish a Health Action Plan and Lucy leads on its implementation.

Paul Southon leads a team tackling the social determinants of health and is the author of the Sandwell Joint Health and Wellbeing Strategy. Since 2010 Paul has co-ordinated the Sandwell Healthy Urban Development Unit. He is also chair of the West Midlands Health and Planning Group and a member of the Spatial Planning and Health Group.

Ben Spencer is an urban designer studying the relationship between public open spaces and the benefits that they can provide. Ben completed his PhD on *Playful Public Places for Later Life* in 2013. He is currently working on *cycle BOOM*, researching older people's cycling and its health and well-being benefits.

Maheep Singh Thapar is the Managing Director at Adapt Technologies & Consultancy Services India Pvt Ltd employing urban planners and Geographical Information Systems (GIS) experts. He has led numerous planning assignments, especially Master Plans for Hyderabad Core City and other projects. Ongoing consulting assignments include the Revised Master Plan for Bangalore City. Maheep is a regular speaker at national and international conferences and a visiting lecturer at educational institutions. He is also a jury member for colleges of architecture and planning.

Susan Thompson is Professor of Planning and Associate Director (Healthy Built Environments), City Futures Research Centre at UNSW Australia (The University of New South Wales, Australia). Susan has worked in urban planning for over 30 years focusing on cross-disciplinary research, teaching and practice. She has qualifications in urban planning, geography and education. Her areas of expertise encompass cultural diversity in urban planning, meanings of home and the use of qualitative research methodologies in the built environment disciplines. For the last decade Susan's work has focused on healthy urban planning. In 2012 Susan was elected Fellow of the Planning Institute of Australia and is widely published in urban planning and health.

Paddy Tillett grew up in rural Scotland, completing his formal education in Oxford and Liverpool. He practised architecture and planning in London and many other parts of the world before settling in Portland, Oregon, USA in 1982. He is a principal with ZGF Architects LLP focusing on planning and urban design.

Tim Townshend is Director of Planning and Urban Design at the School of Architecture, Planning and Landscape, Newcastle University, UK. He has a national/international profile in urban design research and has published on a wide range of topics addressing the impact of the design of the built environment in relation to contemporary social concerns.

Suzanne Vallance is a Senior Lecturer in the Department of Environmental Management at Lincoln University, New Zealand. Her work focuses on exploring ways in which we can collectively make cities and settlements better, safer and healthier places in which to live under conditions of uncertainty. Her research interests include the co-production and collaborative deployment of risk reduction strategies as they pertain to housing, food security, urban renewal and public space.

Chris Weston is a Consultant in Public Health and Fellow of the Faculty of Public Health. Initially based in the National Health Service (NHS), Chris is currently working in local government in the County of Lincolnshire, UK. He has a long association and interest in working to promote health and spatial planning at a local, regional and national level.

Andrew Wheeler is an urban planner and researcher with interests in metropolitan strategic planning, urban policy and healthy built environments. He is a casual academic in the Faculty of Built Environment at UNSW Australia (The University of New South Wales), a specialist consultant in healthy urban planning and a director of the Planning Institute of Australia. His work in the non-profit, academic and public sectors has been instrumental in raising the profile of health in planning policy and practice in Australia.

Ercüment Yilmaz graduated from Bilkent University Translation and Interpretation Department in 2001. In his career at Bursa Metropolitan Municipality's Healthy Cities Project Office, he has focused on distributing and disseminating knowledge and experiences of local governments in Turkey and around the world. He has also worked as a deputy coordinator in various projects on social cohesion, economic and social integration of migrants, tourism and cultural heritage.

ACKNOWLEDGEMENTS

First, many thanks to all our chapter authors for their remarkable enthusiasm, depth of knowledge and sustained commitment. In addition to those listed in the contents, and in the list of contributors, we would like to thank Laurence Carmichael, of UWE, for her draft of the overview of Part 5, and Lynne Mitchell, of Warwick University, for assisting with references for Libby Burton.

Great appreciation goes to our two help-mates: Gillian Evans, book administrator, and Bruce Winslade, graphic artist, both of Stroud, England. Without them this book might never have seen the light of day.

Thanks to Alex Hollingsworth, previously of Routledge, England, who believed in the book at the outset; and subsequently to Judith Newlin and Nicole Solano, in New York, who have carried the book through to completion.

Thanks, too, to all the colleagues, friends and students over the years who have helped to refine and sometimes challenge the concepts and principles in the book. This relates in particular to Agis Tsouros of WHO and the members of the Healthy Urban Planning Sub-network of the European Healthy Cities programme, which included planners and healthy cities co-ordinators from across the continent, some represented here.

Finally we have to express our gratitude to our nearest and dearest, who have tolerated and supported us through the long process of book gestation: Val, David, Peter and Vicky.

FOREWORD

Agis Tsouros

I welcome this book as a major step in taking forward the implementation of the healthy cities vision. Worldwide health issues such as obesity, mental illness, growing health inequalities and climate vulnerability cannot be solved by medicines, but by tackling the social, economic and environmental determinants. The broad sphere of urban planning and design is critical. Some planners and public health professionals have begun to understand this. But across the globe the key urban decision-makers – politicians and developers as well as professionals – still tend to treat health and well-being as secondary issues, or even irrelevant. It is vital that all the built environment professions, and those who employ them, take urgent action to stop building unhealthy human environments.

This book offers a fresh perspective. It redefines the purpose of planning, putting people, their health and well-being at the heart of spatial decision-making. It builds on and brings together valuable knowledge and experience from the WHO European Healthy Cities movement. The book provides a wealth of evidence which could motivate and inform policy. Half the book is about the science of 'healthy planning', the other half about the art of planning, with studies from different parts of the globe where action has begun. Thus it bridges the gulfs between theory and reality, and between the health professionals, planners and urbanists. This landmark book signifies healthy urban planning coming of age.

The *Handbook of Planning for Health and Well-Being* is a discipline-defining publication. It is the first in this field oriented around the needs of planning professionals and academics. It is extensive and authoritative, yet accessible in style and language. If you believe in a proper ethical and truly inspiring basis for planning, read it. Use it.

Dr Agis D. Tsouros
Director, Policy and Governance for Health and Wellbeing
WHO, Regional Office for Europe

INTRODUCTION

*Hugh Barton, Susan Thompson, Sarah Burgess
and Marcus Grant*

This book is about urban planning as a positive force for change in the twenty-first century. It places concern for health at the heart of planning. It is clear that many aspects of city and town planning across the world compromise health and well-being. In many ways we are quite literally building unhealthy conditions into human settlements. So the fundamental question is: how do we plan and design our settlements to promote health and well-being? How do we create the conditions for healthy behaviour, equitable environments, and resilience in the face of climate change?

The entrepreneurial planners and social reformers a century ago, reacting to the unsanitary and inhumane conditions prevailing in the industrial cities of Europe and America, saw health as central. Promoting a healthy environment was not viewed in opposition to economic development. Rather, it was seen as a prerequisite for it, increasing creativity and productivity. However, having conquered the prevailing communicable diseases, partly through better town planning, there is now a rising economic burden from non-communicable diseases. To rely heavily on health care to address these issues is both misjudged, as to their origins, and misguided in terms of economic realities. The UN Habitat report 'Hidden Cities' (WHO 2010) sees the health threat facing urban populations as one that could cripple global health care systems.

The urban environment is implicated in this crisis. The early planning ideals of healthy towns were blown away over the latter part of the twentieth century. The segregation of professional and institutional responsibilities, the pressures of technological change (particularly motorisation), and the triumph of neo-liberal economics have meant that holistic principles were submerged. With some notable exceptions, a selection reported in our book, silo decision-making predominates. Health planning is all about providing services for those who are ill, while tacitly ignoring the many societal factors, including environmental conditions, that are tending to make them ill. Income inequality has grown even in the maelstrom of worldwide recession. Health inequality has followed suit, reinforced by social exclusion in housing, transport and access to facilities. The worldwide obesity epidemic is at least partially due to an environment that prejudices healthy physical activity. Parallel rises in mental illness, stress-related cardiac morbidity and respiratory diseases – usually dealt with in separate clinical silos – are similarly related when considered from a spatial planning perspective.

The public and political debate on planning is, in most places, at kindergarten level. Vested interests, political dogma and public ignorance sideline rational response to human problems. Plans may offer the rhetoric of sustainability and health, while actual investment decisions by private and public sectors are taken in a disjointed, unconnected way. Planners, working to fulfil the conflicting aspirations of politicians, investors and communities, have become acclimatised to making the best of a bad job. But this is not good enough. Our book aims to re-energise built environment professionals, providing an ethical base for planning, informed by good science and an integrated strategic vision.

There are some welcome signs of change. The World Health Organization (WHO) Healthy Cities Programme has, since 2000, been actively promoting the idea of 'healthy urban planning'. Some cities across the globe have begun to re-orientate their spatial policy-making and design principles towards health and well-being. The research community has embraced the healthy planning agenda. Over the last decade the depth and breadth of evidence linking spatial decisions to human behaviour and health has expanded exponentially. We are now in a position to be clear about the kind of environment that promotes health. What we need is a sea-change in attitudes and action.

The characteristics of a healthy urban environment are clean air and pure water, contact with nature, a wide choice of good quality affordable housing, safe and convenient active travel networks, a full range of accessible local facilities, varied and safe opportunities for outside play, convivial meeting places free from excessive noise, and – overriding all of these – a location that gives excellent access to a wide range of jobs, high-level facilities and wider social networks without necessary recourse to the car.

The purpose and scope of the book

This book aims to re-orientate the debate on both urban planning and health, so that their intimate relationship is fully exposed. The purpose is to strengthen the hand of those who argue and plan for healthy environments, drawing agnostic researchers and practitioners into engagement. The book sets out the context, the philosophy, the science, the processes, together with many examples of places working to achieve healthy planning. It builds a bridge between the separate worlds of academia and practice, across disciplines and professions, looking for health-promoting synergies in urban planning, responding to calls from the WHO (for example, WHO 2008). In this rapidly emerging trans-disciplinary field, it is the most comprehensive text available.

The book is international in scope. We have brought together 40 different authors, from academia and practice, across four continents. Our focus is the planning of human settlements as a *generic* activity – not about the legal systems and procedures which are distinct in each country, but the spatial planning principles, understandings and skills which apply irrespective of the institutional context. The concern for health is about physical, mental, social and cultural health. Healthy towns promote healthy individuals, and work towards a sustainable global future.

Much of the book is devoted to providing the evidence of the multiple influences of the environment on health and well-being. It becomes clear that health is not in opposition to other primary purposes of planning – sustainable development, economic growth, social justice, cultural identity and aesthetic quality – each of which has its constituency of support. On the contrary, planning for health offers a lens through which the relevance, importance and practical interplay of all these goals can be better understood.

Even more fundamental than science is *will*. The WHO Healthy Urban Planning initiative in Europe shows one way that political and professional will to act can be galvanised. This book emerges from 15 years of involvement in the Healthy Cities movement and related research. The key is integrated programmes, across departments and agencies, with commitment from political and commercial decision-makers and engagement with local communities. If public health and planning departments can form a genuine alliance under the banner of human well-being and quality of life, it will be a powerful force for good.

It is our hope that this book will give added impetus to the international move to plan cities as if people, their health and well-being, really mattered. The book is for all those professions involved in the production of the built environment, and all those concerned – as commentators, researchers or students – with the need for humane, inclusive, healthy and ecologically sustainable towns and cities.

The book is organised in five parts.

Part I: Perspectives orientates the reader in relation to the background, the history, and critical issues of health inequality, urbanisation, global ecology and organisational inertia. Chapter 1 provides an introduction to the themes addressed throughout the book.

Part II: The human experience takes the needs of people as its starting point. It presents our scientific understanding of the relationship between physical and mental well-being, healthy physical activity, diet and the environment. The twenty-first century has seen an explosion of knowledge in these fields, with an increasing focus on health equity.

Part III: The human habitat continues with the presentation of scientific evidence and its implications for policy and design – but in this part, examining the nature of the environment itself. The early chapters review the form and structure of city regions, neighbourhoods and greenspace in relation to health. The later chapters study the fundamentals of excessive heat and cold, air quality and water management.

Part IV: Processes and tools turns to the way decisions are taken and implemented. The common thread is the recognition that the achievement of healthy environments relies on working in partnership and recognising the potential multiple benefits of action. Most of the contributors are practitioners, experienced in their field.

Part V: Healthy planning in global practice is a series of case studies by practitioners from widely differing contexts in four continents, demonstrating that where there is political will and technical ability, real progress can be made. While the places are at different stages of application, it is striking that comparable strategies and processes are pursued. Essential ingredients are cross-sector, inter-agency co-operation, and long-term commitment to an environment that supports healthy physical activity, community cohesion, access to nature, viable local services and ecological balance.

References

WHO. 2010. *Unmasking and overcoming health inequities in urban settings. Evolutionary ecology* (Vol. 10, pp. 1–145). World Health Organization; UN–HABITAT. doi:10.1373/clinchem.2011.163634

WHO. 2008. *International public health symposium on environment and health research; science for policy, policy for science: bridging the gap, Madrid, Spain, 20–22 October 2008, report.* Copenhagen, WHO Regional Office for Europe (online www.euro.who.int/symposium2008, accessed 3 July 2014).

PART I

Perspectives

Overview by Hugh Barton

The purpose of this first group of chapters is to provide a series of varied perspectives on the subject of planning and health, with the object of helping readers to orientate their thinking. The perspectives range from the theory of planning to the need for professional bridge-building, from the central issue of health inequalities to that of climate change, from the history of health and planning in the West to the current plight of unhealthy environments in poorer countries. It becomes evident that, despite *planning for health* being in general a new field of study, it reaches back in time, and across many of the fundamental social, economic, environmental and political concerns of today. The authors – from England, Australia, the USA, Scotland, Wales and Switzerland – are all leaders in their fields, and internationally respected.

Health and well-being at the heart of planning

Chapter 1 serves as an introduction to the whole book. Hugh Barton sets the context by defining both health and planning broadly, making clear that health policy is not just the concern of doctors, and planning not just of town planners. He explains the 'time-bomb' of public health, and the role that spatial planning plays in shaping unhealthy or healthy urban environments. The core of the chapter reviews the way that planners look at themselves: the move from an early focus on health to an increasing concern with means not ends, culminating in the principles of collaborative planning. Barton argues that promoting health and well-being should be re-instated as the prime purpose of planning. He presents a conceptual framework – the *Settlement Health Map* – as an aid to integrating health, planning and sustainable development.

The history of planning in relation to health

Chapter 2, by Robert Freestone and Andrew Wheeler, traces the history of planning through a public health lens, from the late nineteenth century to the present day. They show that the trajectory of health integration into planning is neither simple nor consistent. While early planners were concerned about basic living conditions – effective sanitation, healthy housing, access to greenspace – there was subsequently fragmentation of responsibility and regulation that made integrated strategies problematic. Public health became oriented around the medical view of health, while planning was caught up in the rush to motorisation. The market re-asserted its position (if it had ever lost it) and the increasing pluralism of built environment decision-making impeded coherent strategies.

In the later twentieth century the United Nations and the World Health Organization were at the forefront of moves to re-affirm the centrality of people, and their health, in planning decisions. The authors talk about rebirth of the nexus, and the beginning of the healing of the rift.

Urban inequities, population health and spatial planning

In Chapter 3, Jason Corburn examines the central issue of health inequity, tracing its persistence through the twentieth century. Modern planning often involved the renewal of unhealthy neighbourhoods, yet by late in the century environmental inequality remained. The problem has shifted from communicable to non-communicable disease, and the policies designed to tackle the former are no longer a sufficient basis for healthy planning. There are winners and losers in the political and economic struggles of place making. Corburn advocates an adaptive planning style, working with stakeholders, that recognises cumulative disadvantage and does not wait for absolute proof of causality, but emphasises action in the face of uncertainty.

Rapid urbanisation, health and well-being

Cliff Hague, in Chapter 4, amplifies the equity theme in relation to rapid urbanisation in the developing world. As president of the Commonwealth Association of Planners he has studied the housing and health problems of the poor, especially in slums and informal settlements. The sheer speed of urban growth has outpaced the ability of governments to manage the situation, and planning has sometimes become part of the problem, not the solution – including when planning full motorisation for the rich at the expense of the poor. Hague argues for better targeted regulation, aimed at participatory upgrading of the slums. The chapter provides a welcome corrective to the general emphasis in the book on richer countries – but the solutions proposed have a general relevance.

Healthy cities, healthy planet

Chapter 5, by Herbert Girardet, picks up the theme of urbanisation and relates it to questions of global sustainability. Cities depend for their survival on the exploitation of scarce resources, and tend to pollute both their immediate hinterland and the water and atmosphere of the earth, threatening life and health. The current linear approach to urban metabolism is unsustainable, and needs to be replaced with circular systems. Girardet illustrates a move from what he calls *Petropolis* to *Ecopolis*, with the aims of moderating the rate of climate change and regenerating the human habitat. People's health depends on global health. Technology, he says, is not the problem. Rather it is the short-term, patchwork approach to problems by decision-makers.

Bridging the divide between knowledge and practice

In the final chapter, Roderick Lawrence takes up the governance issues raised by Corburn, Hague and Girardet. He explores the difficulties of bridging two divides: that between professionals, politicians and the public; and that between different disciplines and professions. The prevailing approach of public and private decision-makers is to recognise direct impacts of their decisions (especially if monetised), but sideline the indirect and complex longer-term impacts. The persistence of the construction of urban environments that compromise health is illustrative of this. Business as usual needs to be replaced by interdisciplinary and transdisciplinary processes that apply a human ecology perspective, working with stakeholders through open and critical inquiry.

1

PLANNING FOR HEALTH AND WELL-BEING

The time for action

Hugh Barton

Introduction: scope and purpose

Planning and public health are siblings, born of the same concerns. The history of town planning, from the era of Hippocrates and Hippodamus in classical Greece to the present, is full of examples of towns designed with the well-being and health of residents a primary concern.[1] Modern planning emerged in the late nineteenth century largely in reaction to the unsanitary, overcrowded and inhumane conditions of industrial cities. It was recognised then, and it is increasingly recognised now, that there is an umbilical link between environmental conditions and human health. This link is not only a matter of the direct physical impacts – for example of foul air or contaminated water – but also of indirect social and behavioural effects, on the exercise we take, the people we meet, on equity of access to essential services and to nature.

Yet the environment we have been creating around us compromises health and well-being in many ways. Fundamental issues of housing, sewage treatment and water supply – the concerns of nineteenth-century policy-makers – still prevail in the slums of many great cities in poor and middle income countries. Air pollution is a recognised health problem in most major cities, rich and poor. High car ownership and road construction in many city regions has led to the progressive dispersal of key functions and of population, increasing carbon emissions, undermining the practicality of daily walking and cycling to get to facilities, contributing to the obesity epidemic. Health inequalities, largely due to income, education and status differentials, have been reinforced by spatial inequities (CSDH 2008; WHO 2013).

The concepts of both 'health' and 'planning' can be interpreted narrowly or broadly. In common parlance 'health planning' means the provision of health services – hospitals, clinics and doctors' surgeries. In-as-much as prevention *is* pursued, public health programmes focus on infectious diseases, addiction (tobacco, alcohol, drugs) and poor nutrition rather than healthy environments. The emphasis is on the provision of services for people who are ill with acute or chronic conditions, while sidelining the many societal factors that are tending to make them ill. The holistic definition of health formulated by the World Health Organization (WHO) when it was founded in 1946, in the period of determined idealism that followed the Second World War, offers a radical alternative perspective:

> Health is a state of complete physical, mental and social well-being and not merely the absence of disease or infirmity. The enjoyment of the highest attainable standard of

health is one of the fundamental rights of every human being, without distinction of
race, religion, political belief, economic or social condition.

(WHO 1948)

This definition makes it clear that health policy is not only a matter for health care professionals, but for the many powers and professions that affect the social, economic and environmental
determinants of health. In that context planners, designers and developers have responsibility for
promoting healthy settlements.

Planning also needs defining in an inclusive way. It is not simply the bureaucratic process of
land use control. We use the term 'spatial planning' to indicate a broad concern with all aspects
of the human habitat and human settlements that impinge on physical space. The aims of spatial
planning are social, economic, ecological and aesthetic. The means are the planning, design, construction and management of the environment. As such it is not the preserve of one profession,
the town planner or *urbaniste*, but embraces the roles of urban designers, architects, landscape
architects, transport engineers, land surveyors, economic development officers and other sectoral
planners. All these professionals are of course duty bound to satisfy their clients' demands, be they
elected representatives, commercial firms or charitable organisations. But they also have a professional responsibility to the *users* of the environment they plan and design. The responsibility to
users should logically include responsibility for the health impact of their actions.

The rest of this chapter, and the book as a whole, take the broad understanding of health and
of spatial planning as given. The chapter first summarises the scope of the relationship between
health and the physical environment, highlighting current and emerging crises, and then the
level of influence that planning exerts on that environment. It then reviews the evolving theories that have interpreted the role and purpose of planning, arguing for a revived ethical stance
that prioritises people's health and well-being. This leads to the presentation of a framework for
thinking about healthy spatial planning that integrates the social determinants of health with an
ecological understanding of human settlements. This framework, known as the *Settlement Health
Map* (Barton and Grant 2006), provides the conceptual underpinning for the book.

The time-bomb of public health

On a cursory examination, worldwide trends in health and well-being are positive. Life expectancy
is increasing in poor, medium and high income countries. Child mortality has fallen dramatically.
These trends are expected to continue. Nevertheless, a series of factors are interacting to create
a 'perfect storm', threatening the ability of nations and communities to cope. Increased longevity
means a growing elderly population dependent on a falling proportion of wage earners. And
while people are living longer, many are subject to disability as a result of chronic conditions
such as heart disease, cancer, diabetes and mental illness. Some places exhibit alarming characteristics. In the most deprived neighbourhoods in England at the turn of the century people
experienced almost 30 per cent of life with a physical or mental disability (Marmot et al. 2010).
Recent data suggests the situation is worsening.[2]

At the same time increased affluence, technological changes and lifestyle choices are contributing to an epidemic of obesity, evident to varying degrees in almost all countries across the
world. In the US, obesity rates increased dramatically between 1990 and 2010, now affecting
a third of adults, and being overweight has become the norm (Butland et al. 2007). According
to the UK Foresight Report, by 2050 Britain could be a mainly obese society (ibid.). Research
suggests that there is a direct relationship between obesity and modal choice: in the US each
additional kilometre walked per day is associated with a 5 per cent reduction in the likelihood

of obesity, while each extra hour in a car is associated with a 6 per cent increase (Frank et al. 2004). In China the likelihood of being obese is 80 per cent higher for adults in households with vehicles (Davis et al. 2007). In India 50 per cent of those who travel to work by private vehicle are overweight or obese, double the figure for those who walk or cycle. The longer the cycling trips the greater reduction in obesity, diabetes and hypertension (Millett et al. 2013).

Health inequality is a central concern in this emerging crisis. Wilkinson and Pickett, in their seminal book *The Spirit Level* (2009), demonstrate that, for rich countries, health is unrelated to national income per head, but is strongly related to income inequality. The analysis of the 'health gradient' between rich and poor in London is salutary: 40 per cent of the poorest groups suffer from a long-term limiting illness, while for the richer groups it is around 5 per cent (Wilkinson and Pickett 2009). We are recognising that the varied prevalence of non-communicable diseases is a reflection of societal values, economic structures and environmental conditions.

The increasing cost of looking after those who are sick is experienced across the world. In the US health care expenditure is claiming a larger and larger share of gross domestic product (GNP) – up from 5 per cent in 1960 to 18 per cent in 2010.[3] The annual cost of the 'obesity epidemic' is predicted to reach $344 billion by 2018.[4] Seventy-five per cent of US health expenditure is attributed to treating chronic disease. With the coincidence of an ageing population, increasing obesity and the remorseless rise of chronic illnesses, the ability of services to cope, and society to pay, is increasingly problematic. The WHO concludes that the triple threat to urban health from infectious diseases, injuries and violence, and non-communicable diseases have the potential to cripple health care services – yet most countries give scant attention to the social and environmental determinants of health (WHO and UN-HABITAT 2010).

Environmental determinants of health

The scope of environmental impacts on health is remarkably broad. The WHO European Healthy Cities programme identified 12 key health determinants and related them to planning policy areas. They range from the influence on lifestyle and physical activity to the threat of climate change, and in between include social cohesion; housing quality; access to work, services, healthy food and open space; safe and equitable environments; healthy air, water and soils (Barton and Tsourou 2000). Subsequently, other authors taking a holistic, ecological approach have strongly reinforced this message (for example Corburn 2009; Dannenburg et al. 2011). Research in new fields such as mental well-being and place, health and nature, active travel and urban form, as well as in traditional fields such as air quality, have blossomed this century, providing a wealth of substantiating evidence. It has become clear that human health and well-being relate to all facets of spatial planning and design. Health cannot be treated as a separate, independent issue, but is linked to other social, economic and environmental goals. Given the importance and cross-cutting nature of health equity, this issue is used below to illustrate the evidence available.

Social justice, place equity and health

Social inclusion is critical for health, and is related to place equity. Accessibility, inclusive transport, affordable housing and safe neighbourhoods each play a crucial role in shaping social inclusion and therefore health (Marmot 2004). Location, urban form and environmental characteristics are important for good or ill. For example, American research suggests that urban sprawl has a malign effect on levels of physical activity, obesity and chronic disease (McCann and Ewing 2003). A survey of New York residents shows that – after adjustments for age, ethnicity, sex, individual and neighbourhood income – people living in neighbourhoods characterised by poor housing quality and poor maintenance were much more likely to report both recent and lifetime depression, than respondents living in neighbourhoods with better environments (Galea et al. 2005). Several studies show the detrimental effects of individual poverty on health are reduced when poor people live in a socially mixed neighbourhood with more affluent, and better educated, people (Wen et al. 2003; Ellaway et al. 2012).

It is not only the built environment and related social variables that help support health and well-being. The natural environment, as managed by humans, is also critical. Living close to green space increases the likelihood of recreational physical activity and improves mental well-being, particularly for low income groups (Mitchell and Popham 2008). Air quality in Britain is responsible for 29,000 premature deaths, 5 per cent of the total every year, with an average 11 year shortening of life (COMEAP 2010). While the rich tend to be the main air polluters through their greater use of vehicles, the poor tend to live in the areas most exposed to polluted air (Jephcote and Chen 2012). The inequities globally are even starker: every year more than 2.1 million die prematurely in Asia from poor air quality. Air pollution in 180 Indian cities is more than six times higher than WHO standards, and is the country's fifth biggest killer (IPCC 2014).

This is just a very small sample of studies. It is possible in these fields and others to show that the environment – particularly the urban environment – has an impact on health. In many places we are literally building unhealthy conditions into the physical fabric of settlements. However, the *degree* of influence is often a matter of contention, with differential results from different studies. This is partly to do with transferability: cultural norms in relation to walking and cycling in the US, Britain and the Netherlands, for example, are so fundamentally different that findings in one country are often not applicable in another. Social, cultural, economic and governance factors interact in complex ways with the physical environment and health. That complexity needs to be better understood (Rydin et al. 2012). The chapters in Parts II and III of the book seek to reduce the uncertainties, and provide a more consistent platform on which to build policy.

Does planning control the environment?

The environment influences health, but how far can planning influence the environment? This question returns us to the way we define planning. The land use planner in the public sector normally has limited control, but nevertheless has responsibilities for the co-ordination of diverse agencies involved in spatial decision-making. But the varied professionals in our inclusive definition, taken together, working for the private and community sectors as well as the state, employ a wide range of mechanisms and decision areas:

- land use policies such as countryside and parkland protection, conservation areas, housing and employment zoning, mixed use centres, density guidelines, design codes, affordable housing and open space requirements;
- local and national infrastructure investments in relation to transport, energy, water, health and education;
- land division and building controls, including plot size (a critical factor in housing in North America and Australasia);
- site selection and appraisal for investors and developers;
- the design of buildings, streets and landscape, the master-planning of estates and neighbourhoods;
- the management of land, especially public spaces, streets, parks, playgrounds, and semi-natural landscapes.

Spatial planning professionals thus have a huge role and responsibility, but clearly they do not have a free hand. They are working to the briefs set by clients and politicians. Those briefs have economic or political objectives that do not generally prioritise the long-term health and well-being of the population. Commercial and institutional investors normally make decisions on the basis of profit maximisation, minimum cost, operational efficiency and pragmatism. It is obvious that the problems of achieving consensus around healthy, sustainable spatial strategies are manifold. Parts IV and V of the book – on effective processes and case studies from around the world – give hope that, given the will, and better understanding, huge progress can nevertheless be achieved.

However, planners in pluralist societies are in an invidious position: expected to deliver economic growth, environmental quality and 'sustainable development', in line with the rhetoric of the powerful – but faced by the reality of globalisation, high carbon lifestyles, and the commodification of space. Adding *health* into the mix can seem like adding insult to injury. There are fundamental questions that need asking about the way society sees the role of planning, and the way spatial planners see themselves.

Planning at the crossroads

'Planning' means different things in different cultures and political contexts. In countries that experienced the excessive control exercised by communist governments, planning is a contaminated principle. This is also the case in many parts of the USA where the sanctity of private land ownership, and of private development rights, dominate political decision-making. Conversely, in European countries such as Denmark and Sweden, the social democratic model means that urban planning is an essential tool of social, economic and environmental policy. In the Netherlands, much of which is below sea level, planning is essential for survival. In many countries planning is primarily pursued in the interests of supporting economic growth and conserving built and natural environmental assets. In the last few decades the rhetoric of the free market, and the purely economic valuing of land – sidelining social, cultural and ecological value – has tended to compromise traditional planning approaches. Decisions on land development are seen through the lens of 'economic development' not 'sustainable development', let alone 'health and well-being'.[5]

The future role of spatial planning is therefore contentious. On the one hand there are hopes that planning will prioritise healthy and sustainable living environments (fulfilling international obligations on biodiversity, climate change and pollution; responding to issues of population change, obesity and health inequalities; satisfying public aspirations in relation to environmental quality and heritage). On the other hand there are powerful societal neo-liberal trends, placing the land rights of firms and private individuals above the rights of the wider community or the health of whole populations.

Planning has reached a crossroads. Should it move further towards the light touch, privatised, business-supporting mode, consistent with neo-liberal principles? Or should it attempt to shift the spatial behaviour of populations and businesses towards health, equity and ecological sustainability, with the implication of greater community intervention in land markets, land use and urban design? Should planning be instrumental or normative?

The purpose of planning: ends and means

The arrival at this crossroads raises fundamental questions about the purpose of planning. The philosophy of the planning profession has evolved in response to changing external pressures and developments in knowledge. It has moved from a situation where health was central, to one where it was almost forgotten, and now just beginning to return. The trajectory of planning thought is examined below, in order to understand the professional context and underpin the case for health-integrated planning.

In the early years of modern planning, from the pioneers such as Howard and Geddes through to the post-war era, the emphasis was on physical design solutions to the recognised health and environmental problems of industrial cities: key ideas included garden suburbs, neighbourhood units, land use zoning, green belts, road hierarchies. Different pundits proposed startlingly different images of towns (contrast Le Corbusier, Abercrombie, Lynch and Cullen). But planning was seen by all as essentially about town and civic design in order to achieve assumed ends. To a significant extent the ends became submerged, and the means (that is the policies and designs) became ends in themselves (Taylor 1998). Practice and related theory became focused more on the physical *product* of planning than on outcomes.

The approach was heavily criticised in the 1960s. Writers such as Jane Jacobs (1962), Herbert Gans (1968) and Melvin Webber (1969) argued that design-based planning formulae were being imposed irrespective of the way they actually affected the behaviour and well-being of people. Planning was accused of being socially and politically naïve. Non-designer planners therefore started to apply more rational, scientific methods, with greater involvement of the people directly affected, in order to ensure better understanding. Town planning started moving, in other words, from being an art to being a science.

Planning theorists in the 1960s and 1970s developed a heady sequence of theories about the best way to make good decisions. Part of this was the conceptualisation of the city. Instead of seeing plans as pictures or blueprints of reality, the new systems approach, building on earlier work in transport planning, viewed plans as staging posts in city evolution, based on an understanding of economic processes and human behaviour. In principle this was a huge advance: recognition of the complex interaction between land use, transport and behaviour over a city region. But it led to increasingly technocratic ('black box') approaches, including land use/transport models and cost–benefit analyses, which tend to conceal critical assumptions, and distance planners from reality.

Many theories of rational decision-making were advanced. Focus on *process* took over from focus on product. Chapin (1965), Friedmann (1965), McLoughlin (1969), Lindblom (1969) and Friend and Jessop (1969) all devised different ways of working through to good and acceptable solutions, trying to combine logic and creativity with practicality. These rational processes remain embedded in the stated requirements of many planning systems. They are reflected (to a greater or lesser extent) in current international standards for environmental impact assessment and strategic environmental assessment.

By the 1980s many theorists and practitioners moved to a greater recognition of the complexity of putting plans into practice – and the need to fuse policy-making and action (Barrett and Fudge 1981). Ambitious modelling and technical processes did not, it was observed, guarantee implementation. In a pluralist society spatial decisions are made by many different agencies, public and private. In this context the planner was seen as entrepreneurial, negotiating between different interests, an advocate for coherent outcomes. Rather than being a technical expert, the planner is an operator of, and in, the system.

This focus on implementation in a complex pluralist world was a necessary corrective. Nevertheless, in the context of increasingly market-oriented politics there is the danger that the planners concentrate on the legal, administrative and commercial processes, serving either political or commercial interests, unable to fulfil broader social goals. Awareness of this danger led to further evolution of planning theory.

Communicative planning

Successful implementation relies heavily on public/political engagement, and the active involvement of stakeholders in the process of decision-making. Forrester, in his seminal work *Planning in the Face of Power* (1989), argued that the key skills needed by the action-oriented planner are communication and negotiation. As planning became more obviously instrumental, engagement gave a new legitimacy to planning in a pluralistic society. Communicative (and collaborative) planning sees the planner as facilitating and informing effective debate (Healey 1997). The planner has a clear normative role:

- To reach out to stakeholders and try to draw them in, especially 'hard to reach' groups, forging networks and helping to build alliances.
- To increase community and institutional capacity to participate effectively, and avoid domination by powerful groups.
- To provide technical input to assist mutual understanding of issues raised by the stakeholders, and inform the process of devising options.
- To work towards consensus between parties on the substantive objectives and means of achieving them.

Many planners are actively engaged now as facilitators and negotiators, working to achieve sensible consensus on planning policies and the design of development. Their role is not to impose their own values, but to enable stakeholders to realise *their* values. Communicative planning is not only

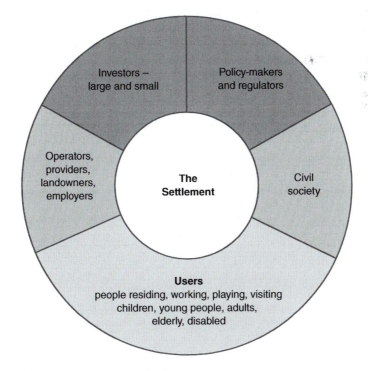

Figure 1.1   Stakeholders in the planning of settlements

Source: Based on Barton et al. 2010, Figure 2.3.

all about process, but states that the process *is* the outcome. However, critics point to its unrealistic expectations. Fainstein, in her influential book *The Just City* (2010), challenges the assumption that open participation will of itself lead to better decisions. This is because participants are far from equal in their propensity to get involved and their ability to put their case. Powerful vested interests, including private and public sector landowners, house builders, government departments and municipal agencies, will ensure their message gets across and seek to negotiate from strength. Articulate resident groups will promote their own, often defensive, interests. Difficult issues, lacking champions, are likely to be avoided. For example the interests of teenagers, wanting somewhere to socialise in the urban environment, are often forgotten or treated as problematic (Shaftoe 2008). More generally, public health, in the absence of strong advocates, is often treated as irrelevant.

Human well-being as the purpose of planning

A collaborative approach is necessary, Fainstein argues, but not sufficient. The substance of debate is crucial. If planners focus primarily on the *manner* of decision-making not the *matter*, then the implication is that planners are abrogating their responsibility. She advocates an explicit normative stance based on the concept of social justice. Planners should see their job as trying to foster a more equal and inclusive environment, not simply a more equal and inclusive process.

This stance echoes earlier theorists who developed 'critical theory' of the status quo. Harvey, for example, in his influential book *Social Justice and the City* (1973), pointed to the coincidence of interest between big development companies and local planning authorities, at the expense of poorer people. It becomes clear that the social justice and health equity agendas have much in common.

Harvey, Fainstein and many others are concerned with *outcomes*. The focus of planning theory and practice on *process* – often reinforced by government priorities – is part of the reason why critical issues of health and well-being, as well as social justice, have been ignored. There is though a basic problem with the concept of social justice. It appeals to some people, and to some political parties, but is anathema to others. It is often perceived as being anti-free market. In the context of neo-liberalism, social justice is pejoratively aligned with socialist and Marxist dogma. So it is essential to adopt a prime goal for planning which appeals to all, has a chance of achieving consensus across political divides, of building bridges towards a sustainable future.

We believe that prime goal is *health*, the achievement of a healthy human environment. Following the WHO lead, health embraces the concepts of *well-being*, *happiness* and *quality of life*. It is difficult for politicians or others to argue for an *unhealthy* environment. It is not a question of sacrificing economic development or environmental sustainability on the altar of health. Both are critically important to achieving healthy communities. Equally, healthy people are necessary for economic vitality, and to reduce the long-term burden of ill-health on the public purse. The apparently divisive rhetoric of social justice – and of untrammelled free markets – can be sidestepped, and replaced with *health for all*.

Planning is at a crossroads. In one direction, favoured by many commercial and political interests, is deregulation of land use and design. In the other direction is 'healthy urban planning', intentionally creating environments that foster well-being. Given the complexity of the relationships between planning, the environment and the health of people, we need a framework of thinking to advance understanding across professions and sectors. One such approach is described below.

Framing the debate: the Settlement Health Map

The *Settlement Health Map* (Figure 1.2; Barton and Grant 2006) provides the conceptual framework for this book. Since it first appeared, the Map has been widely adopted by

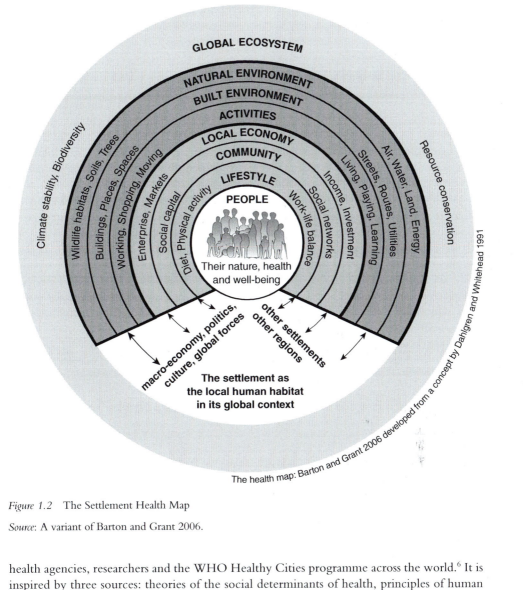

Figure 1.2   The Settlement Health Map

Source: A variant of Barton and Grant 2006.

health agencies, researchers and the WHO Healthy Cities programme across the world.[6] It is inspired by three sources: theories of the social determinants of health, principles of human ecology, and understanding of the constituent disciplines of planning. For those familiar with health literature, the Map has obvious and intentional antecedents: Hancock's (1985) 'mandala of health' linked health and the human ecosystem; more specifically Whitehead and Dahlgren's (1991) model of 'the social determinants of health'. To those with a 'sustainability' training, the Map reflects the dependence of human settlements on the surrounding global environment.

The Settlement Health Map's value is as a dynamic tool that provides a basis for dialogue and provokes enquiry. *People* are at its heart, emphasising that the purpose of a settlement – and of settlement planning – is to provide a healthy human habitat. This reflects Brundtland's anthropogenic definition of sustainable development (WCED 1987). The sequence of spheres moves through the social, economic and environmental variables of a settlement, linked to broader social, political and economic forces, placed within the all-encompassing sphere of the earth. Each sphere also relates to a constituent discipline of spatial planning: public health, behavioural sciences, sociology, economics, geography, environmental sciences and ecology. Equivalently professionals can locate their sphere of influence.

Planning professionals have their most *direct* influence on the 'built environment' sphere, through the planning, design, construction and management of 'spaces and channels' (McLoughlin 1969). Working inwards on the diagram, the purpose of the spaces and channels is to provide for human activities and movement, to support the economy, to facilitate social interaction and healthy lifestyles. Changes in the built environment stem from demands placed on it by the inner spheres, and investment provided by economic activity. The lifestyles, social networks, employment opportunities, activities and built environment are all determinants of mental and physical well-being.

Working outwards on the diagram, the built environment sphere (and the human activities within it) profoundly affect the natural environment, and vice versa: settlements are dependent on the ecological processes of nature, at both local and global scales. Good health depends on clean air, pure water, effective drainage, fresh food, access to nature, freedom from climatic extremes and flood. The outer parts of the Map and the inner are directly related. When people walk rather than rely on the car they reduce greenhouse emissions, and thus help to moderate the threat of climate change. The microcosm of personal behaviour and health and the macrocosm of global ecology are linked. The diagram encourages recognition of symbiosis: healthy people; healthy places; healthy planet.

The Map encourages a holistic approach to policy evaluation. Figure 1.3 illustrates the appraisal of a new town bypass, changing the built environment. The *direct* (or primary) impacts are on:

- the jobs in construction;
- the landscape, farms and habitats through which the bypass goes;
- travel patterns and modal choices that results, notably increased car use.

Secondary impacts are on:

- the pattern of accessibility and consequent changes in land values;
- the locational choices of businesses, institutions, developers and households;
- possible attraction of new employment opportunities;
- cumulative travel patterns, including less active travel, as people switch to car and use more distant facilities that are now accessible;
- the viability of local and district centres, and related social networks;
- air pollution and noise increased in the outer areas but reduced in town centres;
- higher carbon emissions overall.

Thus there are effects on every sphere of the Map. Each of those in turn has positive or negative implications for health and well-being. The Map encourages a rounded assessment.

Conclusions: health at the heart of planning

In spite of emerging health crises across the world, it is arguable that both spatial planning and public health too easily fall down the political agenda. Yet there is strong evidence 'that health is societally determined, that public health is high in the public's notion of what a good society is, and that health underpins economics' (Lang and Rayner 2012, p. 1). The Commission on the

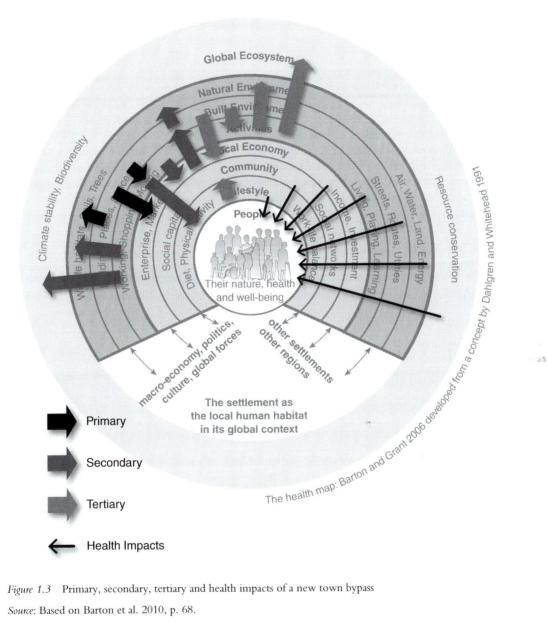

Figure 1.3 Primary, secondary, tertiary and health impacts of a new town bypass

Source: Based on Barton et al. 2010, p. 68.

Social Determinants of Health puts as top priority the improvement of daily living conditions: healthy places, healthy people (CSDH 2008). Another WHO report, *Health 2020*, allies the creation of environments that support health, including health equity, with the need for climate resilient communities (WHO 2013). There is no longer any doubt that spatial planning has a critical role to play in promoting health and well-being.

Planning, however, has to overcome the legacy of its estrangement from the healthy environment focus established by the early twentieth-century planning pioneers. This legacy is about the loss of clarity in relation to spatial outcomes. While some professions – such as civil engineers – have established an effective professional bottom line (in terms of structural safety for example), spatial planners have in general failed to do so. If health is reinstated as the core purpose of planning, and the growing wealth of health–environment–planning evidence is used effectively to influence decision-makers, then human settlements will become progressively more health-giving and sustainable.

The Settlement Health Map offers an integrated ecological model of the urban environment. The Map encourages holistic analysis, and allows varied professionals and other stakeholders to locate their own sphere of influence within its context. In particular, health professionals see their concerns at its heart, while built environment professionals see the significance, but also the limits, of their influence on the whole. The focus on *people*, their health and well-being, cuts through traditional political battle lines, being pro-job creation, social justice and environmental sustainability. Health provides a clear ethical stance for spatial planners, so that in the context of communicative planning, they have something very positive to contribute now and into the future.

Notes

1 In researching the history of town planning from earliest times for a new textbook, I have been struck by the convincing evidence for this statement. Even when the prime motive for town development was commercial or imperial, the best examples demonstrate fundamental understanding of planning for well-being of the population.
2 Office for National Statistics, 2014, as reported in the *I* newspaper, 2 May 2014: in Manchester and Liverpool, England, men on average live 56 years before developing a major life-limiting condition, but then live on to 78. So over a third of life is physically or mentally disabled.
3 US Centers for Medicare and Medicaid Services, quoted in Urban Land Institute 2013.
4 US Centers for Disease Control and Prevention, quoted in Urban Land Institute 2013.
5 In Britain this observation is commonplace.
6 The Settlement Health Map article from 2006 remains, after eight years, one of the most consistently downloaded articles on the University of the West of England website. Copies of the Map for use can be obtained by searching for 'download settlement health map barton and grant' on the internet. It is available in over 30 different languages with a free to use and adapt creative commons licence.

References

Barrett, S. and Fudge, C. 1981. *Policy and action: essays on the implementation of public policy*. London: Methuen.
Barton, H. and Grant, M. 2006. A health map for the local human habitat. *Journal of the Royal Society for the Promotion of Health* 126(6): 252–253.
Barton, H. and Tsourou, C. 2000. *Healthy urban planning: a WHO guide to planning for people*. Copenhagen: WHO Regional Office for Europe, and London: Spon Press.
Barton, H., Grant, M. and Guise, R. 2010. *Shaping neighbourhoods: for local health and global sustainability*. Abingdon: Routledge.
Butland, B., Jebb, S., Kopelman, P., McPherson, K., Thomas, S., Mardell, J. and Parry, V. 2007. *Foresight tackling obesities: future choices – project report*. London: Government Office for Science.
Chapin, S. 1965. *Urban land use planning: second edition*. Urbana: University of Illinois Press.
COMEAP (Committee on the Medical Effects of Air Pollutants). 2010. *The mortality effects of long-term exposure to particulate air pollution in the UK*. London: HMSO.
Corburn, J. 2009. *Towards the healthy city: people, places and the politics of urban planning*. Cambridge, MA: MIT Press.
CSDH (Commission on the Social Determinants of Health). 2008. *Closing the gap in a generation*. Geneva: WHO.
Dannenburg, A., Frumkin, H. and Jackson, R. (eds). 2011. *Making healthy places*. Washington, DC: Island Press.
Davis, A., Valsecchi, C. and Fergusson, M. 2007. *Unfit for purpose: how car use fuels climate change and obesity*. London: Institute for European Environmental Policy.

Ellaway, A., Benzeval, M., Green, G., Leyland, A. and Macintyre, S. 2012. Getting sicker quicker: does living in a more deprived neighbourhood mean your health deteriorates faster? *Health and Place* 18: 132–137.

Fainstein, S. 2010. *The just city*. Ithaca, NY: Cornell University Press.

Forrester, J. 1989. *Planning in the face of power*. Berkeley, CA: University of California Press.

Frank, L., Anderson, M. and Schmid, T. 2004. Obesity relationships with community design, physical activity and time spent in cars. *American Journal of Preventive Medicine* 27(2): 87–96.

Friedmann, J. 1965. A response to Altshuler: comprehensive planning as a process. *Journal of the American Institute of Planners* 31, August. (Reprinted in Faludi, A. 1973. *A reader in planning theory*. Oxford: Pergamon, pp. 211–215.)

Friend, J. and Jessop, W. 1969 *Local government and strategic choice*. London: Tavistock Publications.

Galea, S., Ahern, J., Rudenstine, S., Wallace, Z. and Vlahov, D. 2005. The relationship between characteristics of the neighbourhood internal and external built environment, and depression. *Journal of Epidemiology Community Health* 59: 1219–1229.

Gans, H. 1968. Planning for people, not buildings. *Environment and Planning A* 1: 33–46.

Hancock, T. 1985. The mandala of health: a model of the human ecosystem. *Family & Community Health* 8(3): 1–10.

Harvey, D. 1973. *Social justice and the city*. London: Verso.

Healey, P. 1997. *Collaborative planning: shaping places in fragmented societies*. (2nd edition 2006.) Basingstoke: Palgrave Macmillan.

IPCC (Intergovernmental Panel on Climate Change). 2014. *Climate change 2014: impacts, adaptation and vulnerability*. Geneva: IPCC. www.ipcc.ch/report/ar5/wg2

Jacobs, J. 1962. *The death and life of great American cities*. Harmondsworth: Penguin.

Jephcote, C. and Chen, H. 2012. Environmental injustices of children's exposure to air pollution from road transport. *Science of the Total Environment* 414: 140–151.

Lang, T. and Rayner, G. 2012. Ecological public health: the 21st century's big idea? *British Medical Journal* 345: e5466 doi: 10/1136/bmj

Lindblom, C. 1969. The science of muddling through. *Public Administration Review* Spring. (Reprinted in Faludi, A. 1973. *A reader in planning theory*. Oxford: Pergamon Press, pp. 151–170.)

Marmot, M. 2004. *The status syndrome: how social standing affects our health and longevity*. London: Times Books.

Marmot, M., Allen, J., Goldblatt, P., Boyce, T., McNeish, D., Grady, M. and Geddes, I. 2010. *Fair society, healthy lives: strategic review of health inequalities in England post 2010*. London: Public Health England.

McCann, B. and Ewing, R. 2003. *Measuring the health effects of sprawl: a national analysis of physical activity, obesity and chronic disease*. Washington, DC: Surface Transportation Policy Project.

McLoughlin, B. 1969. *Urban and regional planning: a systems approach*. London: Faber and Faber.

Millett, C., Agrawal, S., Sullivan, R., Vaz, M., Kurpad, A., Bharathi, A., Prabhakaran, D., Reddy, K., Kinra, S., Smith, G. and Ebrahim, S. 2013. Associations between active travel to work and overweight, hypertension and diabetes in India: a cross-sectional study. *PLOS Medicine*. e1001459, doi: 10.1371/journal.pmed 1001459.e5466, 1–11.

Mitchell, R. and Popham, F. 2008. Effect of exposure to natural environment on health inequalities and observational population health. *Lancet* 372: 1655–1660.

Rydin, Y., Bleahu, A., Davies, M., Dávila, J.D., Friel, S., De Grandis, G., Groce, N., Hallal, P.C., Hamilton, I., Howden-Chapman, P., Lai, K.-M., Lim, C.J., Martins, J., Osrin, D., Ridley, I., Scott, I., Taylor, M., Wilkinson, P. and Wilson, J. 2012. Shaping cities for health: complexity and the planning of urban environments in the 21st century. *The Lancet* 379: 2079–2108.

Shaftoe, H. 2008. *Convivial urban spaces*. London: Earthscan.

Taylor, N. 1998. *Urban planning theory since 1945*. London: Sage Publications.

Urban Land Institute. 2013. *Intersections: health and the built environment*. Washington, DC: Urban Land Institute.

WCED (World Commission on Environment and Development). 1987. *Our common future* (the Brundtland Report). Oxford: Oxford University Press.

Webber, M. 1969. Planning in an environment of change, part 2: permissive planning. *Town Planning Review* XX(1): 277–295.

Wen, M., Browning, C. and Cagney, K. 2003. Poverty, influence and income inequality: neighbourhood economic structure and its implications for health. *Social Science and Medicine* 57: 843–860.

Whitehead, M. and Dahlgren, G. 1991. 'The main determinants of health model', version accessible in: Dahlgren, G. and Whitehead, M. (2007) *European strategies for tackling social inequities in health: levelling up part 2*. Copenhagen: WHO Regional Office for Europe.

WHO (World Health Organization). 1948. *Preamble to the constitution of WHO, as adopted by the International Health Conference*. Geneva: WHO.

WHO Regional Office for Europe. 2013. *Health 2020: a European policy framework for the 21st century*. Copenhagen: WHO Regional Office for Europe.

WHO and UN-HABITAT. 2010. *Hidden cities: unmasking and overcoming health inequities in urban settings*. Geneva: World Health Organization Press.

Wilkinson, R. and Pickett, K. 2009. *The spirit level: why equality is better for everyone*. London: Penguin.

2

INTEGRATING HEALTH INTO TOWN PLANNING

A history

Robert Freestone and Andrew Wheeler

Introduction: a cyclical relationship

This chapter traces the history of town planning through a public health lens from the late nineteenth century to the present day. While the planning and public health professions grew out of and were united in their joint efforts to improve living conditions in the polluted, unsanitary cities of the nineteenth century, their subsequent relationship proved less symbiotic than cyclical. Others have written insightfully on these historical linkages from both planning (for example, Hebbert 1999; Sloane 2006; Corburn 2009; Lopez 2012) and public health (for example, Duhl and Sanchez 1999; Perdue et al. 2003; Frumkin et al. 2011) perspectives. Our interest lies with the evolution of healthful planning within the context of evolving mainstream planning concerns. The discussion draws on an extensive review of major planning and public health journals, significant scholarly monographs, and general reports. The chapter is focused on the western, and predominantly Anglo-American, experience.

Our analysis has been organised into a historical narrative divided into several key phases, their characteristics and chronology determined by a distinctive interplay of different cultural, ideological, political and physical criteria. These are recorded in Figure 2.1, which provides the overall framework and detailed backdrop for our treatment. During the more than 100 years considered here, there has usually been some degree of common purpose between planning and public health. At times, however, the relationship has declined, becoming more symbolic than actual. Periods of effective and productive collaboration have tended to coincide with landmark research and reporting. The relationship is currently experiencing another period of close re-alignment, about which we have the least to say here since it provides the *raison d'être* for this entire volume. We would argue, nevertheless, that the success of the planning–health dialogue will be critical in meeting future challenges for improved urban health outcomes (Rydin et al. 2012).

The nineteenth century: sanitising space

Planning as town design and the negotiation of property rights is of great antiquity. In the global 'north', however, modern planning emerged from the maelstrom of the Industrial

	Theme	Foci	Major Influences	Key People	Landmark Publications
19TH CENTURY	Sanitising space	Sanitary and housing reform Water supply Overcrowding Pollution and odour Street layout and design Public health legislation Open space Communicable diseases Settlement House movement	Select Committee on the Health of Towns (1840) British Royal Commission on the Health of Towns 1843 Health of Towns Association (1844) British Public Health Acts (1848, 1875) British Local Government Acts (1858, 1894) New York City Metropolitan Board of Health (1866) American Public Health Association (APHA) (1872)	Edwin Chadwick William Farr Johann Peter Frank John Griscom Octavia Hill Henry Littlejohn FL Olmsted Benjamin Richardson Lemuel Shattuck John Simon Stephen Smith Thomas Smith John Snow	*A Complete System of Medical Policy* (Frank 1779–1827) *Report from the Select Committee on the Health of Towns* (1840) *Report on the Sanitary Condition of the Labouring Population of Great Britain* (Chadwick 1842) *The Sanitary Condition of the Labouring Population of New York* (Griscom 1845) *Report of the Sanitary Commission of Massachusetts* (Shattuck 1850) *Report on the Sanitary Condition of the City of Edinburgh* (Littlejohn 1865) *Hygeia* (Richardson 1876) *How the Other Half Lives* (Riis 1890) *To-morrow: A Peaceful Path to Reform* (Howard 1898)
EARLY 20TH CENTURY (1900s–1910s)	Healthy houses and communities	Town planning legislation Slum clearance Housing Garden City movement Planned suburbs Environmentalism	Garden City Association (1899) New York Tenement House Act (1901) Letchworth Garden City (1905) British Town Planning Act (1909) Canadian Commission of Conservation (1909) First National Conference on City Planning and the Problems of Congestion (Washington 1909) Congress of the Royal Institute of Public Health (Birkenhead 1910) New York City Committee on Congestion of Population (1910) Imperial Health Conference (London 1914) British Unhealthy Areas Committee (1919)	Thomas Adams Patrick Geddes Ebenezer Howard William Lever Benjamin Marsh Raymond Unwin	*Garden Cities of To-morrow* (Howard 1902) *An Introduction to City Planning* (Marsh 1909) *Town Planning in Practice* (Unwin 1909) *Cities in Evolution* (Geddes 1915) *Manual on Unfit Houses and Unhealthy Areas* (British Ministry of Health 1919)
INTER-WAR (1920s–1930s)	Local regulation and regional planning	Land use zoning Community design Suburban development Regional planning	British Ministry of Health (1919) League of Nations (1919) American Society of Planning Officials (1934) APHA Committee on the Hygiene of Housing (1937)	Frederick Adams John Clarke Norman Macfayden George Pepler CEA Winslow	*Basic Principles of Healthful Housing* (APHA 1938)

Period	Theme	Key concepts	Organizations/events	People	Publications
POST-WAR (mid-1940s–1960s)	Planning places versus curing patients	Neighbourhood planning; Community health services; Environmental health; Mental health; Air pollution	United Nations (UN) (1945); World Health Organization (WHO) (1848)	Bernard Frieden; Jane Jacobs	*Housing for Health* (APHA 1941); *Planning the Neighbourhood* (APHA 1948); *The Death and Life of Great American Cities* (Jacobs 1961); *The Urban Condition* (Duhl 1963); *Environmental Health Aspects of Metropolitan Planning and Development* (WHO 1965)
LATE 20TH CENTURY (1970s–1990s)	New movements and programmes	Public health facilities; Environmentalism; Sustainable development; Pollution (air, water, noise); Community participation; New Urbanism; Smart Growth	UN World Commission on Environment and Development (1983); First International Conference on Health Promotion (1986); WHO Healthy Cities Program (1986); The Rio Earth Summit (1992)	John Ashton; Leonard Duhl; Jan Gehl; Michael Greenberg; Trevor Hancock; Ilona Kickbusch; Elliott Sclar; Agis Tsouros	*Development of Environmental Health Criteria for Urban Planning* (WHO 1972); *Our Common Future* (UN 1987); *Ottawa Charter for Health Promotion* (WHO 1986); *Promoting Health in the Urban Context* (Hancock and Duhl 1988); *Agenda 21* (UN 1992); *Healthy Cities* (Ashton 1992)
EARLY 21ST CENTURY (2000s–2010s)	Rebirth of nexus	Compact cities; Transit-oriented development; Liveability; Obesity; Sustainability; Climate change; Mixed-use development; Non-communicable diseases; Health Impact Assessment	WHO; US Centres for Disease Control and Prevention (CDC); Joint Planning/Health university appointments and courses; Interdisciplinary conferences; 'Designing Healthy Communities' TV/DVD series	Hugh Barton; Jason Corburn; Andrew Dannenberg; Lawrence Frank; Howard Frumkin; Richard Jackson	*Healthy Urban Planning* (Barton & Tsourou 2000); *Health and Community Design* (Frank et al. 2003); *Urban Sprawl and Public Health* (Frumkin et al. 2004); *Toward the Healthy City* (Corburn 2009); *Making Healthy Places* (Dannenberg et al. 2011); *Building American Public Health and The Built Environment and Public Health* (Lopez 2012); *Healthy City Planning* (Corburn 2013)

Figure 2.1 A timeline of western town planning and public health

Source: Freestone/Wheeler.

Revolution and its impact on the urbanisation process. Developing through the nineteenth century, there was growing awareness of inadequate governance structures for managing the pressures of population growth, prompted by a suite of interdependent reform movements – from utopianism through urban aesthetics to pragmatic campaigns for better housing, open space and infrastructure. A ubiquitous challenge for government was overcrowding and poor sanitation, and the resultant physical and moral ill health. The collective responses were strongly environmentalist, with an emergent focus on regulating the physical environment through street layout, building regulation and more generous space standards (Hall 2014).

The British experience

Great Britain's experience during the nineteenth century was representative and influenced events in many other places. Industrialisation triggered the rapid expansion of towns and cities as they transformed into new loci for technologically driven economic development. By the end of the nineteenth century London was the world's most populous city, burgeoning to over 6.5 million (Cherry 1974). Such unprecedented growth resulted in widespread overcrowding and strain on the public infrastructure required to ensure liveability. This in turn triggered and exacerbated outbreaks of infectious diseases, including cholera, yellow fever, tuberculosis, measles and diphtheria. Unhealthy living conditions, particularly in London's tenement districts, had a dramatic impact on morbidity and mortality rates. By the 1830s 'public opinion had begun to realise, although only vaguely, that something would have to be done about the terrible conditions which existed' (Bradbury 1951, p. 47). Public health rapidly became a – if not *the* – principal social and economic problem of the day.

Physicians and sanitarians soon pioneered new methods for understanding the aetiology of disease, and their collective efforts progressively improved living conditions. Three British physicians instrumental in these developments were Thomas Southwood Smith, Edwin Chadwick and Henry Littlejohn, all of whom published analytical reports of far-reaching significance. Chadwick's belief in miasma theory – the spread of disease by 'bad air' – was ultimately disproved by William Farr and John Snow (Figure 2.2). Nevertheless, Chadwick's *Report on an Inquiry into the Sanitary Condition of the Labouring Population of Great Britain* (1842) and founding of the Health of Towns Association (1844) were ground-breaking. The Royal Commission on the Health of Towns which he chaired led to the first Public Health Act in 1848. This Act explicitly recognised the connection between the built environment and public health, placing particular emphasis on housing, water and sanitation (Fee and Brown 2005). Subsequent legislation gave governments extended powers over physical layouts. Action on public health also foreshadowed and underscored reforms to the structure of local government and the provision of housing.

A wider problem

Similar reforms were also taking place in other western nations. The growing concern with the cleanliness of towns and cities was underpinned by research with global reach, including an exhaustive nine-volume treatise, *System einer Vollständigen Medicinischen Polizey* (*A Complete System of Medical Policy*) (1779–1827), by German physician Johann Peter Frank. Continental advances in town extension planning, zoning, land tenure reform, and affordable housing became beacons for British and American urban reformers. The growth of American

Figure 2.2   The John Snow pub in London's West End[1]

Source: Freestone/Wheeler.

concern with municipal sanitation and civic administration paralleled the British experience (Adams 1952). Research by physicians like John Griscom and Lemuel Shattuck began to link poor population health to industrialisation and unsanitary living conditions. Pioneering public health legislation followed. Building on these advances, the American Public Health Association (APHA), founded in 1872, 'began its career with a clear recognition of the importance of housing as a public health problem' (Winslow 1939, p. 25).

Early town planning formulations

By the latter half of the nineteenth century, integrative manifestos and decisive municipal interventions conscious of public health improvements were beginning to point the way forward for the nascent planning profession. Benjamin Ward Richardson extended Chadwick's work, and his *Hygeia: A City of Health* (1876) demonstrated how a model healthy city might be organised. Ebenezer Howard similarly proffered a solution to the evils of the big city in *To-morrow: A Peaceful Path to Reform* (1898). His garden city ideas proved enduringly influential on a global scale. In the search for alternatives to the baneful and baleful influences of unplanned cities, they provided new community forms at once both compact and spacious: 'the combination of town and country is not only healthful, but economic' (Howard 1898, p. 25). Minus the radical economic underpinnings of Howard's manifesto, progressive industrialists such as planning benefactor William Lever at Port Sunlight and social reformers like Henrietta Barnett would advance these ideas in tangible form in their housing experiments.

21

Sanitary and housing reform paved the way for planning innovations at even larger scales. In the United States (US), Frederick Law Olmsted influenced urban policy as Secretary of President Lincoln's Sanitary Commission in the 1860s and went on to design numerous public places, parks and open space systems (Twombly 2010). In Europe, administrators including Georges-Eugène Haussmann in Paris and designers such as Ildefons Cerdà in Barcelona decisively synthesised health and other concerns in dramatic urban transformations. Cerdà advocated good connectivity and accessibility, greenspace, effective waste management, and well-lit and ventilated homes at very different densities to the emergent Anglo-American preference for house-and-garden environments (Neuman 2011).

Synthesis and fragmentation

The union between planning and public health in the nineteenth century was thus driven at different levels and in various places by reformers in both the medical and built environment professions. With the approach of a new century, health was on the public policy agenda and something resembling modern planning was emerging. This new discipline encouraged a holistic approach to urban environments so far lacking in traditional disciplines such as architecture, surveying and engineering. Nevertheless, there were limits to integration. At the turn of the century, for example, the sanitary impulse was already being deflected into technical-engineering directions where it would have 'little bearing on the overall shaping of great cities' (Peterson 2003, p. 39).

The early twentieth century: healthy houses and communities

At the dawn of the new century, the planning movement – given different labels in different countries – was gaining traction. The first two decades provided a heady mix of evangelism and innovation, as planning was promoted by mainly middle class advocates through a variety of channels – conferences, public lectures, exhibitions, books, journals, films, study visits and, in some countries, through the beginnings of professional education, usually as an adjunct to architectural training. During the first decade of the twentieth century, the spirit of collaboration between planning and public health strengthened and formalised, with both professions focusing on improving housing quality and the health of entire communities.

Discourses intertwined

Health concerns underpinned the birth of organised planning movements in many countries and became a central focus of new professional associations and interdisciplinary conferences. For example, the Congress of the Royal Institute of Public Health, held at Birkenhead, England, in 1910, included a special section on town planning. In his presidential address, William Lever highlighted the need for planning and public health to work together to raise living standards, particularly through provision of good housing (Lever 1910). Four years later the Imperial Health Conference in London drew representatives from all British dominions to advance understanding of the interrelationship between planning, housing and public health. Speakers included leading planner-architects Raymond Unwin and Herbert Baker (Victoria League 1914).

In the US, the early planning movement was also driven in part by similar concerns for human health and an equally distinctive social justice agenda. In 1909 Benjamin Marsh chaired the first National Conference on City Planning and the Problems of Congestion, which centred on these issues. Marsh was Executive Secretary of the Committee on Congestion of Population in New York and his book, *An Introduction to City Planning*, published the same year as the conference, identified government-led planning interventions as 'the most important factor in securing good living conditions and preserving the life, health and well-being of all citizens' (Marsh 1909, p. 1).

A feature of early planning research and publications was statistical and graphical comparisons of the mortality and morbidity of planned and unplanned communities, usually denoting healthy and unhealthy places respectively (Aldridge 1915) (Figure 2.3). Public health concerns intensified with the outbreak of the First World War, with large numbers of volunteers rejected as medically unfit. This was also accompanied by moral panic; unsanitary conditions, it was feared, would breed revolutionary resentment. Such anxiety also helped the case for town planning at the national political level.

Legislative and policy responses

The passing of new laws to remedy unhealthy living conditions in cities accompanied and inspired the rise of the planning movement. Legislation such as the New York State Tenement House Act of 1901, and the UK Town Planning Acts of 1909 and 1919, ushered in a forensic focus on regulating the room, the dwelling and the street – their size, dimensions and orientation. These statutes placed growing responsibility on government, strengthening 'the powers of state and local governments to protect the health, safety, and welfare of the general public' (Schilling and Linton 2005, p. 98). In addition to their focus on housing, early planning laws also attempted to minimise human exposure to infectious diseases and industrial hazards, whilst promoting healthy behaviours through the provision of public open space for physical and social activity (Kochtitzky et al. 2006).

Housing remained the dominant unifying force connecting planning and health. In Britain, the Ministry of Health's Unhealthy Areas Committee (1919–1921), chaired by Neville Chamberlain, provided detailed policy guidance on housing density and design, recommending that housing blocks be limited to three storeys in the inner city (Ministry of Health 1919). Health concerns continued to drive urban renewal programmes, including widespread slum clearance, although the redevelopment potential of land for new transport arteries and employment areas also influenced government decision-making; health-driven policy was only one component of the eclectic planning agenda. Housing development on the outskirts of cities was guided by garden city ideals, which promoted basic residential amenities such as open space and safe streets at relatively low densities (Foley 1962). In Continental Europe, however, with a longer tradition of higher density living, there was a notable emphasis on reforming the design standards of perimeter housing apartment blocks (Sonne 2009).

Different paradigms

Despite the common origins of planning and public health, and their joint efforts to improve quality of life in the late nineteenth and early twentieth centuries, the professions slowly began to drift apart as they pursued different agendas following the First World War. Public

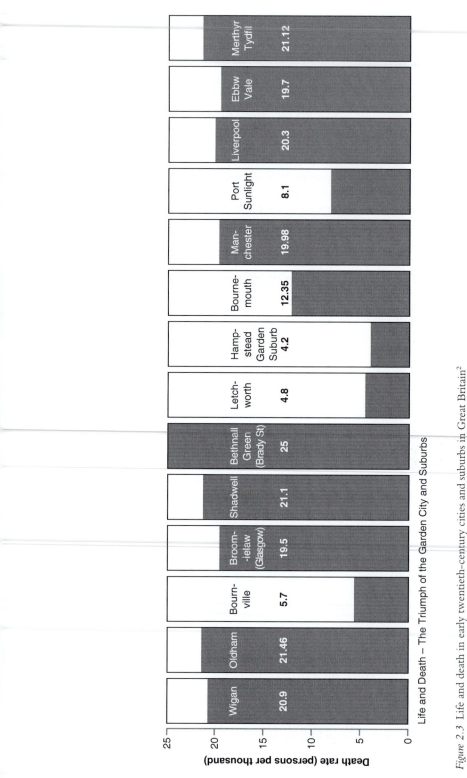

Life and Death – The Triumph of the Garden City and Suburbs

Figure 2.3 Life and death in early twentieth-century cities and suburbs in Great Britain[2]

Source: Redrawn from Aldridge (1915).

health adhered almost exclusively to a biomedical model, concentrating on the individual at the expense of broader physical and social influences such as the built environment. Meanwhile, in an attempt to find its own voice, the town planning movement professionalised its activities, squeezing out fringe members of the early coalition which had coalesced around the challenge of creating healthy communities. The fate of Benjamin Marsh in the US is a case in point. While his goals were compelling, the remedy embedded in his 'philosophical maxims' was deemed radical: 'to open the door of opportunity for health, we must close the door for exploitation of land' (Marsh 1909, p. 2). Pragmatic first generation city planners, led by Frederick Law Olmsted Jr., baulked at this prescription, which challenged conventional notions of private property ownership (Peterson 2003). Instead, comprehensive planning ideals converged around spatial orderliness, convenience, community and aesthetics.

Many modernist influences inherited from the nineteenth century – open space, density, housing, beautification, transit, zoning – remained strong themes during this period and were still being assembled conceptually as interdependent elements of the new science of town planning. However, this very process was already sowing the seeds for fragmentation, as these elements separated into distinct 'specialisms'. Some planning 'missionaries' like polymath Patrick Geddes advocated a united vision based on place, but otherwise the profession became increasingly focused on specialised technical problems (Goist 1974).

The inter-war period: local regulation and regional planning

Planning shifted in focus and scale during the inter-war period as prosperity initially returned and issues of growth management and infrastructure provision came to the fore. In the US this was the heyday of the 'city functional' movement, which not only downplayed earlier aesthetic goals but shifted planning's gaze to an emergent urban science of efficiency (Scott 1969). While health and planning remained bedfellows in the 1920s, encouraged by major events such as international congresses on urbanism and hygiene on the Continent (for example, Strasbourg in 1923), the health agenda as an inspiration for planning reform became more muted. In part this resulted from the institutionalisation and day-to-day implementation of earlier reform ideas for regulating urban spaces. In particular, aspirations for affordable, spacious garden suburbs and apartments were increasingly being met, at least for middle-income earners. But when the 'roaring 20s' gave way to the Great Depression in the early 1930s there were signs of renewed interest in explicit engagement with community health.

Health and urban governance

Although collaboration between planning and public health was limited in the 1920s, the two professions were connected through prescriptive statutory legislation, including sweeping measures to separate or eliminate unhealthy land uses through the practice of zoning. Driving this convergence in Britain was the assimilation of earlier reforms into the machinery of the Ministry of Health, which oversaw planning during the inter-war years. In the US, zoning ordinances deemed constitutional by the Supreme Court in 1926 became the key statutory instrument for pursuing varied and sublimated planning goals, albeit with an increasing focus on the protection of private property rights (Schilling and Linton 2005). This form of spatial regulation was successful 'in limiting health and safety risks caused by inappropriate mixing of land uses' (Kochtitzky et al. 2006, p. 34). The conventional wisdom of a mosaic of mono-functional land use precincts was nonetheless sowing the seeds for future health problems associated with dispersed, car-dependent cities.

In the 1920s, planning innovation also shifted away from the micro-scale to the city region. In Britain, advocates of regional planning, including the eminent planning academic-consultant, Patrick Abercrombie, and the Chief Town Planning Inspector at the British Ministry of Health, George Pepler, believed this was an important step if the profession was to address the full range of macro-scale problems impinging upon the well-being and future orderly growth of cities (Abercrombie 1959; Essex and Brayshay 2005). While home and neighbourhood were not entirely neglected, 'economic' health emerged as a major preoccupation amidst an ever-expanding agenda that further diluted the historic connections between planning and public health.

The 1930s

In the 1930s, all western nations experienced severe curtailment of living standards that had been rising steadily through the preceding decades. Growing unemployment had a nega-tive impact on working class communities still often concentrated in the same slums and tenements of concern at the turn of the twentieth century. As a result, health re-emerged as an explicit theme for planning and public policy. In 1938, Norman Macfadyen, the first medical officer at Letchworth, reiterated the importance of the good physical and social environment exemplified in British garden cities (Macfadyen 2013). A key figure in the US, although his work was influential globally, was C.E.A. Winslow, a public health expert and past-president of the APHA. From 1937, Winslow was also inaugural chairman of the APHA's Committee on the Hygiene of Housing. This interdisciplinary committee was established at the request of the League of Nations – later the United Nations (UN) – and its membership included prominent Massachusetts Institute of Technology (MIT) plan-ning professor Frederick Adams. In his role as Committee chairman, Winslow observed an important shift in attitudes to planning, as planners began to turn away from 'the superficial trappings of city growth' and back towards 'the central problem of human living' (Winslow 1939, p. 27).

The Committee on the Hygiene of Housing issued several authoritative publications. Its first report, *Basic Principles of Healthful Housing* (1938), outlined 30 fundamental principles of 'healthful housing', covering issues as wide-ranging as the provision of open space and access to essential services such as shops, schools and medical centres. The report provided detailed guidance on how urban environments could be designed to promote positive physical and mental health outcomes, and its recommendations were widely endorsed 'by authorities in housing, city planning and environmental sanitation' (Solow and Twichell 1947, p. 24). The Committee's work proved an invaluable resource worldwide as plan-ning authorities began to exert more influence on the overall form and structure of cities through extensive urban development programmes (Figure 2.4). Meanwhile, as public health principles were being recodified they also began to reappear in planning education. Under the direction of Frederick Adams, for example, students in the internationally rec-ognised programme at MIT received supplementary instruction in public health (Adams 1949).

Figure 2.4   Greenbelt, Maryland[3]

Source: Freestone/Wheeler.

The post-war period: planning places versus curing patients

As prosperity returned after the Depression and the war, the planning profession was largely preoccupied with accommodating and facilitating urban and regional growth. Driven by the idealistic ethos of post-war reconstruction, the planning agenda expanded to include comprehensive blueprint plans intended to address an array of social, economic and environmental problems. Land use planning was the ascendant paradigm, and looked to implementation strategies through zoning and physical development controls. Health was relevant to these concerns, and the need for community and neighbourhood planning was a notable theme into the 1950s. In the US, for example, the APHA Committee on the Hygiene of Housing continued to act as an authoritative voice. The release of *Planning the Neighborhood* (APHA 1948), the first report in the Standards for Healthful Housing series, armed authorities with 'the basic health criteria which should guide the planning of [the] residential neighborhood environment' (APHA 1948, p. v). But the wider alliance between planning and public health remained sluggish.

The chasm reappears

Notwithstanding the notable efforts of organisations such as the APHA and, on a global scale, the UN and World Health Organization (WHO), by the mid-twentieth century health was in decline as a central planning objective. To some degree planning had become a victim of its own success: 'infectious disease had been brought under control, and as a result the layout and planning of cities came to be viewed as a matter of esthetics or economics, but not health' (Perdue et al. 2003, p. 1390). The planning profession was caught up in a period of unprecedented growth and auto-oriented development with few alarm bells anticipating the later health consequences of urban sprawl (Figure 2.5). At the same time, and closely mirroring events following the First World War, public health professionals focused their attention on modifying human behaviour rather than broader social determinants of health (Corburn 2004). A divide thus emerged again between 'planning places' and 'curing patients' as the planning and public health professions pursued different agendas linked, if at all, by responsiveness to immediate concerns rather than truly forward-looking programmes.

In this vacuum, the market again reaffirmed its dominance in guiding land use decision-making in western capitalist economies, and planning receded into isolated specialisms that failed to grasp the complex and multifaceted relationship between people and place. The *Town Planning Review* described these trends as 'the two great errors of the "feeble fifties"' (Anon 1964, p. 180). While some health professionals recognised the need to adopt a more collaborative and strategic approach to growth management that would include health factors in urban development (for example, Brown 1964; Prindle 1968), the planning profession was generally unresponsive. This left an unenviable legacy that has endured to this day:

> The loss of close collaboration between urban planning and public health professionals that characterized the post-World War II era has limited the design and implementation of effective interventions and policies that might translate into improved health for urban populations.
>
> *(Northridge et al. 2003, p. 557)*

Figure 2.5   Incipient urban sprawl in the south-western suburbs of Sydney, Australia in the early post-war years[4]

Source: Cumberland County Council (1948).

New perspectives and pressures

Although health was marginalised as a planning concern in the 1950s and 1960s, new health-related problems were being identified and research into environmental issues, such as air and water pollution, was increasing. The WHO began to take an active interest in these issues, linking them to urbanisation (WHO 1965). This period also saw a rekindling of interest in the relationship between cities and mental health. Viennese psychiatrist Hans Strotzka, for example, undertook research into the socio-psychological dimensions of city planning, observing that housing quality, land use density, traffic conditions, commuting distances and recreational facilities all had important bearings on mental health outcomes (Strotzka 1957). Like Strotzka, two prominent American planners, Harvey Perloff and Lowdon Wingo, warned that the future of planning would depend on its ability to connect with other broad movements. On the topic of planning and mental health, they noted:

> This is a critically important link to be forged, for if city planning yields up its concern for the emotional welfare of the urbanite, it may find itself reduced to the service of a few dusty canons of urban design.
>
> *(Perloff and Wingo 1962, pp. 68–69)*

A year later, Leonard Duhl, a psychiatrist at the National Institute of Mental Health in the US, and the intellectual father of the Healthy Cities movement, explored these issues in *The Urban Condition* (1963). Others began to challenge the received wisdoms guiding contemporary planning. In *The Death and Life of Great American Cities* (1961), Jane Jacobs critiqued many of the fundamental tenets of planning, including the notion that higher densities were detrimental to human health. Her visionary ideas – on urban renewal, neighbourhood design and community participation – underpin many contemporary planning principles, particularly those centring on human health and community well-being.

Health planning

From the late 1960s, attempts were made to revive moribund links between planning and health, but with limited success. The WHO continued to drive change, calling for 'greater co-operation and co-ordination on a much wider scale between planners and environmental health workers' (WHO 1965, p. 13). The Organization established an expert committee on environmental health aspects of planning, and drafted new guidelines to help planners raise the profile of health in policy and practice. More broadly, interdisciplinary forums such as the Greek Delos Symposia organised by planner-architect Constantinos Doxiadis, and the Harvard Urban Design Conferences in the 1950s and 1960s, encouraged planners to adopt a more collaborative and humanistic approach to contemporary practice (Shoshkes and Adler 2009). Ultimately, however, these initiatives had little impact on reunifying planning and health at a strategic level. With the approach of the 1970s, activity between the two professions focused almost exclusively on 'health planning' – the planning of health and medical services – rather than the built environment's role in promoting healthy lifestyle choices. Even within this context, a survey of more than 200 American city planning agencies revealed that only one-sixth of these agencies spent more than 2 per cent of their time on 'health planning' (Frieden and Peters 1970).

The late twentieth and early twenty-first centuries: rebirth of the nexus

The late twentieth century was a turbulent time in urban environments, with planning pulled in different directions as the post-war consensus on the benefits of growth unravelled. The reverberations of this era are still being felt today. The closing decades were distinguished by increasingly direct environmental interventions under the banner of sustainability as well as a strengthening alliance between economic development goals and planning instruments. Other trends were economic and cultural globalisation, challenges to mainstream design paradigms initially under the guise of post-modernism, and shifts to more inclusive governance structures. It is difficult to single out any one dominant paradigm; in theory as with practice it was a 'jigsaw puzzle of urban growth policy' (Beckman 1972, p. 231). Within this pluralistic environment public health concerns received only limited attention in planning up until the late 1990s.

Sustainable development and the new public health

The final decades of the twentieth century were, nevertheless, marked by several key events that helped to gradually restore the historical connections between planning and health. In the early 1980s, for example, New Urbanist ideals advocating pedestrian-friendly, transit-oriented neighbourhoods as the basis of sustainable communities encouraged planners to address health at the community planning scale. Similarly, the parallel concept of 'smart growth' gave planners a framework within which they could advance alternatives to urban sprawl that would be both sustainable and healthy (Frumkin et al. 2004). Indeed, a groundswell of activity in this period around the multifaceted concept of sustainability was helping to re-cast the very meaning of health 'away from the absence of disease and towards a more holistic definition' (Barton 2005a, p. 282). This shift was captured by Hancock and Perkins (1985) in their 'mandala of health' (Figure 2.6) as well as influential prescriptions such as *Agenda 21*, which emerged from the UN Conference on Environment and Development (the Rio Earth Summit) in 1992. *Agenda 21* recognised that 'health ultimately depends on the ability to manage successfully the interaction between the physical, spiritual, biological and economic/social environment' (UN 1993, p. 42). The guiding principle emerging for urban and regional planning was that 'healthy places nurture healthy people, and that public policies should aim at sustaining both healthy people and healthy places, not one or the other' (Lucy 1994, p. 305).

The WHO Healthy Cities Programme

The most important global force linking planning and health from the mid-1980s was the WHO Healthy Cities Programme. This Programme was initiated by two health physicians, Canadian Trevor Hancock and American Leonard Duhl, with the goal of raising the profile of public health among decision-makers, and empowering local authorities and communities to create healthier urban environments (Hancock and Duhl 1988; Ashton 1992). In 1997, the WHO European Healthy Cities Network launched the 'healthy urban planning' initiative, which was accompanied by landmark publications including *Healthy Urban Planning: A WHO Guide to Planning for People* (Barton and Tsourou 2000), and played a central role in reintegrating health into planning policy and practice (Barton et al. 2003). Meanwhile, growing concern about the health consequences of urban sprawl and 'obesogenic environments' was also renewing interest in the relationship between planning and health, particularly among medical and health professionals (Larkin 2003).

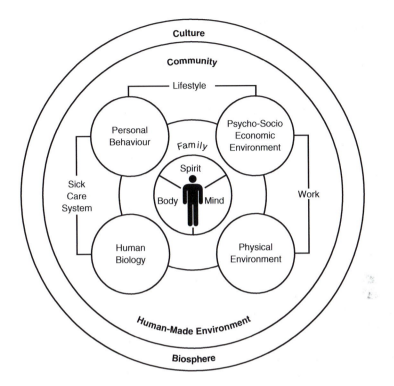

Figure 2.6 The mandala of health[5]

Source: Hancock and Perkins (1985).

Where are we now?

Despite a multiplicity of competing goals for planning, health has gradually established or at least reclaimed its direction-setting credentials over the last two decades. The disconnection between the planning and public health professions that prevailed through the latter half of the twentieth century has slowly healed and the alliance has been reinvigorated. It is now widely accepted that health should be one of the prime considerations in determining planning policy, by providing a coherent and evidence-based foundation for assessing the health implications of planning and development decisions. In a similar manner to the 'mandala of health', Barton's (2005b) 'health map' offers a conceptual framework for integrating health into spatial decision-making by unifying planning's economic, environmental and social aspirations around a central humanistic concern for health and well-being. Nagging questions remain, however, about healthy urban planning's position within the broader concerns of planning, since the latter show no signs of narrowing. Some observers consider a single paradigm of planning practice impracticable, given the variety of issues which contemporary urban planning must address (Myers and Banerjee 2005, p. 121). Nonetheless, the number of cities achieving a good level of understanding and activity in healthy urban planning has risen demonstrably since the turn of the century, and this is particularly so for those achieving effective strategic integration of health and planning (Barton and Grant 2013).

Conclusions: opportunities for
re-integration

This chapter has considered the relationship between planning and health from a historical perspective arguing, in agreement with Sloane (2006, p. 10), that the ties between them have been strongest 'when upheld by converging theories and commonly perceived problems'. The bonds were strongest in the mid-nineteenth century, the early twentieth century, the 1940s and over the last two decades. Indeed, the current era, as this book testifies, has seen a remarkable resurgence of research and policy interest in healthy built environments. Health has never disappeared as a high-level concern but has always had to vie with other priorities shaped by broader societal forces, with economic development – often regarded as a panacea for many ills – currently in the ascendant.

Notwithstanding this continuity, what emerges is a remarkably paradoxical evolution for health considered from a planning perspective. The agenda in the affluent cities of both eastern and western hemispheres examined here has shifted radically over the past century, representing the life-span of modern planning. In the early 1900s, for example, the major concerns were communicable diseases, high mortality rates, emaciated children, and the challenge of securing space and sunlight in overcrowded environments. Today, the primary concerns are non-communicable diseases associated with unsafe, uninviting, automobile-oriented and socially isolating, mono-functional environments. The transition from a sanitation-led to an eco-logically framed perspective represents a profound shift in orientation (Ashton and Ubido 1991). The ultimate irony, perhaps, is that for some observers high-density now connotes a healthy environment, while low-density suburban environments have become increasingly problematic (Chakrabarti 2013). The current focus on physical activity, connecting and strengthening communities, and providing equitable access to healthy food also has roots in the past but very different implications today (Kent and Thompson 2014).

In efforts to address these concerns, future challenges and opportunities are already evident across policy, research and education. A key challenge for policy is to develop planning frameworks which advance public health concerns in a spatial policy context driven increasingly by market forces (Barton and Grant 2013). The reinstatement of health into city and metropolitan planning objectives provides a starting point, just as the mainstreaming of Health Impact Assessment (HIA) is helping to institutionalise operational awareness (Wheeler and Thompson 2010; Ross et al. 2014). More broadly, a 'Health in All Policies' approach could further enhance policy integration between health and planning (Hensgen 2009; Kamper-Jørgensen 2010). Research, a second factor, has also been vital to recent progress. More collaborative research and practice across the built environment, public health and medical sectors can be built on this foundation, especially through identifying and emphasising shared values (Dannenberg et al. 2003; Cohen and Schuchter 2013). Expanding the evidence base is crucial to inform and guide health-focused built environment interventions, as is education, which plays a key role for planning and health professionals, politicians, and the community (Wheeler et al. 2011). The recent spate of joint medical/planning appointments in universities is a promising trend, and strengthens interdisciplinary professional bonds. Further development of courses straddling planning and public health will be especially effective in addressing the health implications of the built environment. In doing so, as we have seen, there will be every reason to stress again the interconnected histories of these fields back over nearly two centuries.

Acknowledgement

We would like to thank Andrew Dannenberg, University of Washington, and Iain Butterworth, University of Melbourne, for their comments on an earlier version of this chapter.

Notes

1 The pub is a popular commemoration of epidemiological research undertaken by its namesake, physician John Snow. In the 1850s, Snow traced an outbreak of cholera to a contaminated public water pump located nearby. His discovery helped disprove the 'miasma' theory of bad air as a carrier of disease and highlighted the importance of proper urban sanitation.
2 The health aspects of good housing and proper community planning were frequently depicted by statistical comparisons of birth, death and sickness rates between big industrial cities and new communities, many of which were planned on garden city lines. In the early 1900s, the death rate (shown in persons per thousand) was markedly lower in planned communities such as Hampstead Garden Suburb, Letchworth and Port Sunlight.
3 This planned community was developed as a satellite town of Washington, DC during the American New Deal programme of the early 1930s. Its planning attributes of compactness, playgrounds, walkways, civic amenities and active living in a landscaped setting anticipated later New Urbanist ideals.
4 This image captures the low-density scatter facilitated by and ultimately dependent on rising car ownership. Captioned 'No Man's Land' in a 1948 metropolitan planning report, the major concern was 'yards and yards of road per house' as an uneconomic development pattern rather than the looming lack of walkability.
5 As a 'model of the human ecosystem', the mandala exemplifies the move towards more holistic thinking about influences on health in the 1980s.

References

Abercrombie, P. 1959. *Town and country planning*. 3rd Edn. London: Oxford University Press.
Adams, F.J. 1949. The planning schools: I. Massachusetts Institute of Technology. *Town Planning Review*. 20(2): 144–149.
Adams, J.W.R. 1952. *Modern town and country planning*. London: J. and A. Churchill.
Aldridge, H.R. 1915. *The case for town planning*. London: National Housing and Town Planning Council.
Anon. 1964. Editorial notes. *Town Planning Review*. 35(3): 179–182.
APHA (American Public Health Association), Committee on the Hygiene of Housing. 1938. Basic principles of healthful housing: preliminary report. *American Journal of Public Health and the Nations Health*. 28(3): 351–372.
APHA (American Public Health Association), Committee on the Hygiene of Housing. 1948. *Planning the neighborhood*. Chicago: Public Administration Service.
Ashton, J. 1992. *Healthy cities*. Milton Keynes: Open University Press.
Ashton, J. and Ubido, J. 1991. The healthy city and the ecological idea. *Journal of the Society for the History of Medicine*. 4(1): 173–181.
Barton, H. 2005a. Healthy urban planning: setting the scene. *Built Environment*. 31(4): 280–287.
Barton, H. 2005b. A health map for urban planners: towards a conceptual model for healthy, sustainable settlements. *Built Environment*. 31(4): 339–355.
Barton, H. and Grant, M. 2013. Urban planning for healthy cities: a review of the progress of the European Healthy Cities Programme. *Journal of Urban Health*. 90(1) Suppl: 129–141.
Barton, H. and Tsourou, C. 2000. *Healthy urban planning: A WHO guide to planning for people*. London: Spon Press.
Barton, H., Mitcham, C. and Tsourou, C. (eds.) 2003. *Healthy urban planning in practice: experience of European cities*. Copenhagen: WHO Regional Office for Europe.

Beckman, N. 1972. Toward development of a national urban growth policy: legislative review 1971. *Journal of the American Institute of Planners.* 38(4): 231–249.

Bradbury, R. 1951. The technique of municipal housing in England: with particular reference to Liverpool. *Town Planning Review.* 22(1): 44–71.

Brown, R.M. 1964. Urban planning for environmental health. *Public Health Reports.* 79(3): 201–204.

Chadwick, E. 1842. *Report to Her Majesty's principal secretary of state for the home department, from the poor law commissioners, on an inquiry into the sanitary condition of the labouring population of Great Britain.* London: W. Clowes and Sons.

Chakrabarti, V. 2013. *A country of cities.* New York: Metropolis Books.

Cherry, G.E. 1974. *The evolution of British town planning: a history of town planning in the United Kingdom during the 20th century and of the Royal Town Planning Institute, 1914–74.* New York: Wiley.

Cohen, A.K. and Schuchter, J.W. 2013. Revitalizing communities together: the shared values, goals, and work of education, urban planning, and public health. *Journal of Urban Health.* 90(2): 187–196.

Corburn, J. 2004. Confronting the challenges in reconnecting urban planning and public health. *American Journal of Public Health.* 94(4): 541–546.

Corburn, J. 2009. *Toward the healthy city: people, places, and politics of urban planning.* Cambridge: MIT Press.

Cumberland County Council. 1948. *Report on the planning scheme for the County of Cumberland, New South Wales.* Sydney: Cumberland County Council.

Dannenberg, A.L., Jackson, R.J., Frumkin, H., Schieber, R.A., Pratt, M., Kochtitzky, C. and Tilson, H.H. 2003. The impact of community design and land-use choices on public health: a scientific research agenda. *American Journal of Public Health.* 93(9): 1500–1508.

Duhl, L.J. (ed.) 1963. *The urban condition: people and policy in the metropolis.* New York: Basic Books, Inc.

Duhl, L.J. and Sanchez, A.K. 1999. *Healthy cities and the city planning process: a background document on links between health and urban planning.* Copenhagen: WHO Regional Office for Europe.

Essex, S. and Brayshay, M. 2005. Town versus country in the 1940s: planning the contested space of a city region in the aftermath of the Second World War. *Town Planning Review.* 76(3): 239–264.

Fee, E. and Brown, T.M. 2005. The Public Health Act of 1848. *Bulletin of the World Health Organization.* 83(11): 866–867.

Foley, D.L. 1962. Idea and influence: the Town and Country Planning Association. *Journal of the American Institute of Planners.* 28(1): 10–17.

Frank, J.P. 1779–1827. *System einer Vollständigen Medicinischen Polizey* [*A Complete System of Medical Policy*]. Various Publishers.

Frieden, B.J. and Peters, J. 1970. Urban planning and health services: opportunities for cooperation. *Journal of the American Institute of Planners.* 36(2): 82–95.

Frumkin, H., Frank, L. and Jackson, R. 2004. *Urban sprawl and public health: designing, planning and building for healthy communities.* Washington: Island Press.

Frumkin, H., Wendel, A.M., Abrams, R.F. and Malizia, E. 2011. An introduction to healthy places. In A.L. Dannenberg, H. Frumkin and R.J. Jackson (eds.). *Making healthy places: designing and building for health, well-being, and sustainability.* Washington: Island Press, pp. 3–32.

Goist, P.D. 1974. 'Patrick Geddes and the city'. *Journal of the American Institute of Planners.* 40(1): 31–37.

Hall, P. 2014. *Cities of tomorrow: an intellectual history of urban planning and design since 1880.* 4th Edn. Hoboken, NJ: Wiley-Blackwell.

Hancock, T. and Duhl, L. 1988. *Promoting health in the urban context.* WHO Healthy Cities Papers No. 1. Copenhagen: FADL Publishers.

Hancock, T. and Perkins, F. 1985. The mandala of health: a conceptual model and teaching tool. *Health Education.* 24(1): 8–10.

Hebbert, M. 1999. A city in good shape: town planning and public health. *Town Planning Review.* 70(4): 433–453.

Hensgen, S. 2009. *Planning and health: a study on the integration of health and planning in South Australia.* Adelaide: SA Health.

Howard, E. 1898. *To-morrow: a peaceful path to reform.* London: Swann Sonnenschein.

Jacobs, J. 1961. *The death and life of great American cities.* New York: Random House.

Kamper-Jørgensen, F. 2010. The healthy city. *Scandinavian Journal of Public Health.* 38(2): 113–114.

Kent, J.L. and Thompson, S. 2014. The three domains of urban planning for health and well-being. *Journal of Planning Literature.* 29(3): 239–256.

Kochtitzky, C.S., Frumkin, H., Rodriguez, R., Dannenberg, A.L., Rayman, J., Rose, K., Gillig, R. and Kanter, T. 2006. Urban planning and public health at CDC. *Morbidity and Mortality Weekly Report*. 55 Suppl: 34–38.

Larkin, M. 2003. Can cities be designed to fight obesity? Urban planners and health experts work to get people up and about. *The Lancet*. 362(9389): 1046–1047.

Lever, W.H. 1910. *Royal Institute of Public Health, Birkenhead Conference: inaugural address by the president*. Port Sunlight: Lever Brothers.

Lopez, R. 2012. *Building American public health: urban planning, architecture, and the quest for better health in the United States*. New York: Palgrave Macmillan.

Lucy, W.H. 1994. If planning includes too much, maybe it should include more. *Journal of the American Planning Association*. 60(3): 305–318.

Macfadyen, N. 2013. Health and garden cities. Tomorrow Series Paper 14 (originally published 1938). *Town and Country Planning*. 82(3): 1–8.

Marsh, B.C. 1909. *An introduction to city planning: democracy's challenge to the American city*. New York: privately published.

Ministry of Health, Great Britain. 1919. *Manual on unfit houses and unhealthy areas*. London: His Majesty's Stationery Office.

Myers, D. and Banerjee, T. 2005. Toward greater heights for planning: reconciling the differences between profession, practice, and academic field. *Journal of the American Planning Association*. 71(2): 121–129.

Neuman, M. 2011. Ildefons Cerdà and the future of spatial planning: the network urbanism of a city planning pioneer. *Town Planning Review*. 82(2): 117–144.

Northridge, M.E., Sclar, E.D. and Biswas, P. 2003. Sorting out the connections between the built environment and health: a conceptual framework for navigating pathways and planning healthy cities. *Journal of Urban Health*. 80(4): 556–568.

Perdue, W.C., Stone, L.A. and Gostin, L.O. 2003. The built environment and its relationship to the public's health: the legal framework. *American Journal of Public Health*. 93(9): 1390–1394.

Perloff, H.S. and Wingo, L. 1962. Planning and development in metropolitan affairs. *Journal of the American Institute of Planners*. 28(2): 67–90.

Peterson, J.A. 2003. *The birth of city planning in the United States, 1840–1917*. Baltimore, MD: John Hopkins University Press.

Prindle, R.A. 1968. Health aspects of the urban environment. *Public Health Reports*. 83(7): 617–621.

Richardson, B.W. 1876. *Hygeia: a city of health*. London: Macmillan and Co.

Ross, C.L., Orenstein, M. and Botchwey, N. 2014. *Health impact assessment in the United States*. New York: Springer.

Rydin, Y., Bleahu, A., Davies, M., Dávila, J.D., Friel, S., De Grandis, G., Groce, N., Hallal, P.C., Hamilton, I., Howden-Chapman, P., Lai, K.M., Lim, C.J., Martins, J., Osrin, D., Ridley, I., Scott, I., Taylor, M., Wilkinson, P. and Wilson, J. 2012. Shaping cities for health: complexity and the planning of urban environments in the 21st century. *The Lancet*. 379(9831): 2079.

Schilling, J. and Linton, L.S. 2005. The public health roots of zoning: in search of active living's legal genealogy. *American Journal of Preventive Medicine*. 28(2) Suppl 2: 96–104.

Scott, M. 1969. *American city planning since 1890*. Berkeley, CA: University of California Press.

Shoshkes, E. and Adler, S. 2009. Planning for healthy people/healthy places: lessons from mid-twentieth century global discourse. *Planning Perspectives*. 24(2): 197–217.

Sloane, D.C. 2006. From congestion to sprawl: planning and health in historical context. *Journal of the American Planning Association*. 72(1): 10–18.

Solow, A.A. and Twichell, A.A. 1947. Housing objectives in terms of health. *Journal of the American Institute of Planners*. 13(3): 22–25.

Sonne, W. 2009. 'Dwelling in the metropolis: reformed urban blocks 1890–1940 as a model for the sustainable compact city. *Progress in Planning*. 72(2): 53–149.

Strotzka, H. 1957. Man, health and city structure: socie-medical and socio-psycholegical views en city and land planning. *Journal of the American Institute of Planners*. 23(1): 9–12.

Twombly, R. (ed.) 2010. *Frederick Law Olmsted: essential texts*. New York: W.W. Norton.

UN (United Nations). 1993. *Agenda 21: The United Nations Programme of Action from Rio*. New York: United Nations Department of Public Information.

Victoria League. 1914. *Report of proceedings of the Imperial Health Conference held at the Imperial Institute, London May 18th to 21st, 1914*. London: Victoria League.

Wheeler, A. and Thompson, S. 2010. The future health and environmental sustainability of South East Queensland: an evaluation of the regional plan. *Australian Planner.* 47(3): 152–161.

Wheeler, A., Kent, J. and Thompson, S. 2011. A pathway for practice: translating research evidence into healthy planning policy. *Proceedings of the 3rd World Planning Schools Congress.* Perth: The University of Western Australia.

WHO (World Health Organization). 1965. *Environmental health aspects of metropolitan planning and development: report of a WHO expert committee.* Technical Report Series No. 297. Geneva: WHO.

Winslow, C.E.A. 1939. Opportunities and responsibilities of the health officer in connection with the Federal Housing Acts. *Journal of the American Institute of Planners.* 5(2): 25–29.

3

URBAN INEQUITIES, POPULATION HEALTH AND SPATIAL PLANNING

Jason Corburn

Introduction: health in cities vs healthy cities

The twenty-first century is the century of the city, as the world's population now lives predominantly in urban areas. Where you live and how that place is governed can determine when and if you get sick, receive medical treatment and die prematurely. City living can be beneficial for human health, since urban areas generally offer greater economic and educational opportunities, medical services, political and gender rights, affordable housing and cultural, political and religious expression. This holds true in both rich and poor cities of the global North and South. Yet, not everyone in cities can take advantage of these socially produced resources and the poor and socially marginalised often experience health inequities, or differences in access to health promoting resources that are unnecessary, avoidable and unfair.

Today, most urban health interventions are focused on bringing social services, primary care, economic opportunities and physical improvements to urban residents or their neighbourhoods. Interventions tend to focus either on people or places, but rarely both at the same time. Interventions are generally conceptualised and led by experts, and focused on one disease, one risk factor, one hazardous exposure, one population group, or one suspected 'cause' of poor health, such as poverty (Corburn 2009). More care, more places offering care, more prevention and more services tend to be intervention targets. This is the *health in cities* approach, and while life has become better for most urban residents using this approach, the strategy has largely failed to address the spatial (and ethnic/racial) inequities in health (EU 2013). In this chapter, I set the context for today's efforts to reconnect policy fields to address rising health inequities, by first exploring some public health and planning history. I then review some of the connections between planning and human health that suggest the built and social environments matter, as well as the governance of cities and places, for understanding the complex ways place gets into our bodies. I close with some approaches for more healthy urban governance that includes an attention to new science and politics in the twenty-first century. This healthy urban governance framework embraces complexity science, uses processes of ecological adaptive management, and emphasises the expertise of city residents as problems solvers and beneficiaries of healthy city planning.

The rise of urban health inequities

Sanitation, germs and spatial segregation

A dominant narrative in the history of urban public health, as set out in the previous chapter, is that sanitary interventions during the nineteenth century arrested epidemics of infectious disease and helped clean-up dirty and unhealthy cities. As nineteenth- and early twentieth-century urban populations increased across Europe and North America, improvements in physical infrastructure, particularly housing, water and sanitation did not keep pace. Buildings were quickly overcrowded as rooms were divided to house more workers and their families. Animal, human and industrial wastes accumulated dramatically in cities without systems for their removal. Common methods of waste disposal in cities, such as cesspools, regularly overflowed and contaminated water supplies and wells. Human and animal waste heaps were infested with flies and vermin, had unbearable odours and, when combined with the thousands of animals brought into the city for slaughter to feed the growing population, were logically seen as the culprit for infectious disease (Duffy 1990). Edwin Chadwick's *Report on the Sanitary Condition of the Labouring Population in Great Britain in 1842*, documenting unsanitary living conditions afflicting the urban poor across Britain, led to the subsequent Royal Commission on the Health of Towns concluding that physical changes to the city were necessary to improve population health and particularly the well-being of the poor.

While the movement for urban sanitation and health gained momentum, others would point to economic and political inequities as the reasons behind inadequate life-supporting infrastructure for the poor. Friedrich Engels would point to economic and social inequalities that he claimed produced the physical squalor and diseases of the poor in *The Conditions of the Working Class in England in 1844* (Engels 1891). After an epidemic of typhus broke out in Upper Silesia, an economically depressed Prussian province inhabited by a large Polish minority, the pathologist Rudolf Virchow was hired to investigate and issue a report. Virchow (1848) concluded, in what would become a classic of social medicine, that eliminating epidemics in the future would not require more palliation but the 'politics of prophylaxis' – unlimited democracy, devolution of decision-making, universal education, disestablishment of the church, taxation reform, and industrial development in the poorest regions. Yet, by 1848, the arguments of Chadwick and the Health of Towns Commission, not Engels, would help to establish the first British Public Health Act.

Sanitary engineers emerged to take a prominent role in city management and governance. The British physician and sanitarian Benjamin Ward Richardson would advocate in 1876 for the utopian vision of *Hygeia: A City of Health*, where he outlined the site selection, street layout, water and sewerage, park system and housing design that together could reduce mortality. Engineers laid claim to having the knowledge for designing healthy water delivery, street networks, and sewer systems – the 'arteries of the city'.

By the end of the nineteenth century and into the early twentieth, modern city planning and public health were using physical interventions to respond to urban public health crises. While planning and public health both addressed sanitation and housing reforms during this time, the driving ideology was physical removal, of both 'environmental miasmas' – garbage, wastewater, slum housing, 'swamp' land, and so forth – and 'undesirable and sick' people. These interventions rarely addressed urban poverty or other social inequalities that also contributed to disease and premature death. As the driving theory of disease causation in public heath shifted from miasma – filth and dirty air – to germ theory, urban health interventions would move even further away from addressing social inequities and instead focus on the cell, or pathogens, as bacteriology took hold.

Germs, labs and city management

Bacteriology stimulated laboratory research that developed vaccines to immunise the poor, rather than clean up their neighbourhoods, workplaces and improve their economic status. Laboratory public health research also treated drinking water, milk and food for disease-carrying microbes. This research led to compulsory vaccinations for school-age children and the chlorination of municipal drinking water supplies. Clearly, these non-specific urban health strategies helped reduce the spread of infectious diseases.

The model of laboratory science seen as producing definitive, apolitical knowledge also contributed to a view of city management during this time. City planners interested in improving health were often confronted with finding ways to pay for politically and economically controversial infrastructure projects that often wouldn't produce results for a decade or more. Planners and engineers turned to the prestige of laboratory science for a model of city management, since in the lab results were often unquestioned as researchers were viewed as neutral and detached from the social context where investigations were taking place, inputs into lab experiments were highly controlled and restricted, and analytic techniques were mechanical and standardised, so that results from a lab anywhere could be applied everywhere. City managers demanded political autonomy in the interest of the city's health, and used new 'efficiency' technologies such as benefit–cost analyses, land use zoning and long-range comprehensive planning, to radically alter urban governance.

A least two urban design schemes from the early twentieth century highlight the laboratory-like claims of city planners, engineers and managers: the Garden City and the Neighbourhood Unit. In Britain, Ebenezer Howard (1965) aimed to integrate a regional perspective with principles from ecology to improve well-being in his Garden City designs. The Garden City, he claimed, could create 'slumless and smokeless' cities and merge the best of the country into the city, while eliminating the features of each that were unhealthy. Clarence Perry (1929) proposed the Neighbourhood Unit in 1922 as a design scheme intended to provide order, liveable scale and health-promoting rationality to urbanisation. The Garden City and the Neighbourhood Unit offered a physical ideal that tended to ignore the often contested, gendered, variegated and value-laden characteristics of cities. By leaving out the distinctive virtues of particular places in a bid for universal applicability, these representations of the city were intended to be credible and capable of being applied regardless of time and place, social and physical geography, or political and administrative organisation – much like results from laboratory science.

Perry's Neighbourhood Unit idea took hold with planners, developers, and the American Public Health Association's (APHA) Committee on the Hygiene of Housing. The APHA Committee adopted the Neighbourhood Unit design scheme as the basis for two reports; one, in 1938, *Basic Principles of Healthful Housing* (APHA 1938), and a second in 1948, *Planning the Neighborhood* (APHA 1948). The *Planning the Neighborhood* guidelines were increasingly used to justify state-sponsored slum clearance in American cities, with municipal public health agencies using the guide as justification for labelling poor neighbourhoods blighted. In the UK in 1944, the Ministry of Health, Central Housing Advisory Committee, published guidelines on the design of dwellings and a *Housing Manual* (commonly referred to as the 'Dudley Report') to guide post-war reconstruction, both of which were based on the design standards of the Neighbourhood Unit and Garden City (Ministry of Health 1944).[1]

Rise of modern planning and razing of unhealthy neighbourhoods

Modern city planning had taken hold by the early 1920s in both Europe and North America, with societies, conferences and new academic training programmes. European zoning, or the segregation of space by categorising land uses, would emerge as a key tool for planners to separate 'unhealthy' spaces – such as industry – from residences. In the US, neighbourhood health centres also emerged at this time as one way to connect planning and health, since they were one-stop locations in poor, often immigrant urban areas, where ambulatory health services were combined with community participation in development and planning decisions. A federal policy, the Sheppard-Towner Maternity and Infancy Protection Act of 1921, funded a network of community health centres in urban and rural areas.

Federal housing policies, such as urban renewal in North America, encouraged the razing of what were viewed by both planning and public health professionals as blighted, unhealthy neighbourhoods. The idea was to rebuild these neighbourhoods with modern high-rise social housing. However, urban renewal also displaced thousands of urban poor residents, largely African-Americans and new immigrants, from their social and financial networks and is viewed as a key reason why the health of these populations rapidly declined during this period. Federal home-loan policies accompanied urban renewal programmes, but loan guarantees were limited to new single-family homes, giving rise to the American suburb and a subsequent auto-centred development pattern in and around metropolitan regions. Federal highway policies and road-building subsidies also emerged in the 1950s, as national and metropolitan planning was oriented toward road building, not transit, helping entrench an auto-centred development pattern that would come to dominate the landscape for much of the latter half of the twentieth century.

By the mid- to late twentieth century, the driving ideology in public health had shifted again to the biomedical model, which attributes morbidity and mortality to molecular-level pathogens brought about by individual lifestyles, behaviours, hereditary biology or genetics. Urban health interventions shifted to the 'health in cities' approach, aiming to change unhealthy behaviours such as drinking alcohol, smoking tobacco and poor diets (Corburn 2013). Yet, urban health activists continued to challenge medical and planning professionals for why, in the face of rising economic prosperity and advancements in medical technologies, inequalities in health persist for the urban poor and people of colour? The fields of urban public health and city planning were in crisis at the turn of the twenty-first century, as reports from governments around the world and the World Health Organization noted the rise in health inequalities and declining health for some urban populations living in the poorest areas (cf. 'Black Report' (Townsend and Davidson 1980), and 'Targets for health for all' (WHO Regional Office for Europe 1985)).

How twenty-first century urbanisation shapes health

Cities in the twenty-first century are more diverse than their nineteenth-century counterparts in terms of their built environments, social characteristics and governance schemes. Further, the health outcomes that afflict urban dwellers are different than those of 150 years ago; non-communicable diseases are more prevalent as are issues of mental health. Finally, people in cities are living longer, so ageing and associated functional and independence limitations have become core twenty-first-century urban health, design and planning issues. Thus, nineteenth-century urban health solutions focused almost exclusively on physical improvements to the urban environment will be insufficient to address the complex contributors to twenty-first-century urban health inequities. Below, we review some of the complex ways the twenty-first-century city impacts health inequities.

Physical and built environments

The physical environments of cities still matter for health, such as whether there is access to safe and affordable drinking water, sanitation, drainage and garbage collection. Urban air and noise pollution remain critical health determinants in highly industrialised cities of Europe and Latin America as well as developing cities in China and Sub-Saharan Africa (Harpham 2009). Urban air pollution is linked to up to 1 million premature deaths each year. Over 90 per cent of air pollution in cities in these countries is attributed to vehicle emissions brought about by high numbers of older vehicles coupled with poor vehicle maintenance, inadequate infrastructure and low fuel quality (UNEP 2014). Urban particulate matter is associated with cardiovascular death and asthma. Noise pollution, a common urban nuisance, is associated with hearing impairment, hypertension and ischemic heart disease. Exposure to environmental pathogens in urban air and water can contribute to both infectious (i.e. parasitic, diarrhoeal, intestinal, etc.) and non-infectious diseases.

Pedestrian conflicts with motor vehicles are one of the leading causes of injuries in urban areas. When a new development project includes new housing and commercial activity, pedestrian activity increases and this can lead to an increase in injuries. However, greater pedestrian activity can promote physical activity that reduces heart disease, stroke and mental illness and increase functional status and the longevity of independence among the elderly. Creating new opportunities for pedestrian activity can also improve well-being by increasing the likelihood of social interactions that can reduce feelings of isolation. However, the construction of highways contributes to vehicular air pollution and suburban sprawl, while the lack of or inadequate transport inhibits access to employment and health promoting services, especially for the urban poor. Highways and streets can limit green open space, which can act as a site for physical activity, social interactions, and an urban heat sink, reducing the likelihood of adverse human health impacts from climate change induced urban heat islands.

Social environment and urban health

The physical and social environments of cities frequently interact and cannot be disassociated when trying to understand and improve urban health inequities. The urban social environment includes the institutions that shape the structure and characteristics of relationships and opportunities among people and different population groups within a given community (Healey 1999). Perhaps the most well researched aspect of the social environment that influences health is economic status or class. While debate continues whether absolute or relative poverty matter more for influencing health, there is agreement that being poor in any city increases one's likelihood of a range of health risks across the life-course, from infant mortality and low birth weight, to stunted physical and cognitive development to early on-set chronic illnesses and higher rates of infections (Marmot et al. 2012).

The economic 'environment' also influences well-being. Neighbourhoods with high concentrations of liquor stores also have high rates of addiction. However, local businesses can act as a source for employment and culturally appropriate food and other services. Displacement of local businesses can adversely impact health by altering the availability and affordability of essential goods and services and the type of local employment possibilities. Business displacement can also contribute to physical blight – the tooth-gaped landscape all too common in poor neighbourhoods where widespread property abandonment has taken hold. Property abandonment can adversely influence health by increasing the likelihood of illegal dumping of garbage and hazardous wastes.

The social environment also influences health through a variety of other pathways, including the support of individual or group behaviours that affect health, buffering or enhancing the impact of stressors, and providing access to goods and services that influence health (for example housing, food, informal health care). Limited social supports may predispose persons to poorer coping and adverse health. High levels of social stressors, such as social isolation and violence, are also known to adversely impact the health of urban residents. In cities, the greater spatial proximity of one's social networks may accentuate their role in shaping individual and population health (Friel et al. 2011).

Perhaps the most crucial social and political force in cities that influences health is spatial segregation. Many cities worldwide are highly segregated with discrimination against certain racial, ethnic, caste or tribal groups often acting as justification. Spatial segregation can have multiple effects, including the enforcement of homogeneity in resources and social network ties and suppressing diversity that may benefit persons of lower socioeconomic status. Persons who live in segregated communities may have disproportionate exposure, susceptibility and response to economic and social deprivation, toxic substances and hazardous conditions. The physical and social factors that influence health in cities are summarised in Figure 3.1.

Health resource	Urban physical and social influences on health (examples)
Environmental quality, including noise, air, soil and water pollution	Vehicle emissions exacerbate respiratory disease and increase cardio-pulmonary mortality, while indoor allergens exacerbate asthma
	Chronic noise exposure adversely harms sleep, temperament, hearing and blood pressure, all of which can lead to developmental delays in children
	Trees and green space remove air pollution from the air and mitigate the urban heat island effect
Access to high quality transit and safe roadways, sidewalks and bicycle lanes	Vehicle/pedestrian injuries are most severe where sidewalks and crosswalks are non-existent
	Sidewalks and bicycle lanes facilitate physical activity, reducing heart disease, diabetes, obesity, blood pressure, osteoporosis and symptoms of depression.
	Public transit provides access to employment, education, parks and health care services
Access to quality childcare, education and health care facilities	Quality childcare can build disease immunities and increase likelihood of future educational attainment and earnings
	Education can enhance health literacy about preventative behaviors and services
	Timely access to primary health services prevents serious illness
Affordable, safe, stable and socially integrated housing	Crowded and substandard housing conditions increase risks for infections, respiratory disease, fires and stress
	Unaffordable rents or mortgages result in trade-offs between housing, food and medical care
	Racial residential segregation limits economic and educational opportunities, concentrates disadvantage and increases social distance between racial/ethnic groups
Access to safe and quality open space, parks, cultural and recreational facilities	Clean and safe parks can increase the frequency of physical activity
	Cultural activities can promote cross-cultural understanding, decrease violence and enhance social cohesion
Employment providing meaningful, safe and living wage jobs	Higher income is associated with better overall health, reduced mortality and higher emotional stability
	Unemployment is a source of chronic stress, while job autonomy increases self-esteem

Access to affordable and quality goods and services	Neighbourhood grocery stores support nutritious diets
	Local financial institutions help families create and maintain wealth
Protection from crime and physical violence	Indirect effects of violence and crime include fear, stress, anxiety and unhealthy coping behaviors, over-eating, smoking and alcohol/drug abuse
	Fear of crime can force children to stay indoors, increasing exposure to toxic indoor air and allergens, and limiting physical activity outside
Social cohesion and political power	Physical and emotional support buffers stressful situations, prevents isolation, contributes to self-esteem and reduces the risk of early death
	Stress from severed/lack of social ties/support can contribute to low birth weight, which increases risk of infant death, slow cognitive development, hyperactivity, breathing problems, overweight and heart disease.

Figure 3.1 Urban health resources and risks

Source: Corburn (2009).

Politics, urban governance and health

The physical and social characteristics and dynamics in cities that influence health do not happen randomly or by accident. Cities and metropolitan regions more generally are not shaped by faceless forces of natural succession and competition. Social movements and citizens make urban places through activism, generating economic and cultural opportunities (i.e. markets, community centres, places of worship, etc.), building homes and play spaces, using these spaces in certain ways, maintaining their spaces (or not) and making the environment open and hospitable to others/outsiders (or not). There are real winners and losers in the *political struggles* of place making, and static definitions of physical and social variables rarely captures this dynamic of places. The political processes of urban place making and remaking are what I refer to as 'urban governance'.

The term governance is broadly understood as attentive to the relationships between the overlapping spheres of political, economic and social life, as each aim to influence collective action. Governance is not government, but is inherently about the struggle and conflict between formal institutions and organisations and informal norms and practices.[2] Urban governance includes a complex mix of different contexts, actors, arenas and issues, where struggles over power can be manifested in public discourses or tacit day-to-day routines. An urban governance approach to healthy planning is attentive to both processes and outcomes, and must ask questions such as: what conditions lead to planners using or abusing power, responding to or even resisting market forces, working to empower some groups and dis-empower others, promoting multi-party consensual decision-making discourses or simply rationalising decisions already made? The governance approach views urban planning as a process that includes the shaping of public agendas and attention, available evidence and norms of inquiry, inclusive or exclusive deliberations, and responses (or lack thereof) to bias, discrimination, inequality and a recalcitrant state. An attention to governance moves health equity planning away from only focusing on vulnerable people or places to also include altering the political processes and institutions that work to maintain the social inequities driving urban health inequities.

Toward a twenty-first-century science for healthy city planning

A new urban science for healthy cities ought to capture the combination of physical, social and political forces, and their interactions across space and time. This is what we could call a 'relational' view of healthy place making. A relational view of place is crucial for understanding healthy urban planning because social processes, such as power, inequality and collective action, are often revealed through the construction and reconstruction of the material forms and social meanings of places (Cummins et al. 2007).

Consider the now well-documented idea that social stress can be toxic to the human body, especially when place-based stressors are chronic and cumulative across one's lifetime (McEwen 2007). In toxic stress situations, the constant chemical release of 'fight or flight' hormones does not properly regulate or shut off, and wears away at the immune system as it overworks to manage the hormonal releases, contributing to a host of chronic diseases such as overweight and obesity, diabetes, hypertension, cardiovascular disease, stroke, asthma and other immune-related illnesses. Since populations in many deprived and impoverished areas of cities are likely experiencing multiple 'toxic stressors', planners must be attentive to the physical and social stressors that they may help co-produce, such as institutional responses to poverty and discrimination, housing instability, or neighbourhood exposure to violence. The toxic stress idea suggests that a twenty-first-century science for the healthy city can no longer view a person as, for example, one day an African immigrant, another day born low birth weight, another day raised in a home bearing remnants of lead paint, another day subjected to racial discrimination at work, and still another day living in a racially segregated neighbourhood without a supermarket or access to transport. Just as the body does not neatly partition these experiences – all of which may serve to increase risk of uncontrolled hypertension and related morbidity and premature mortality – the urban planner aiming to improve health in the twenty-first-century city can no longer separate these spheres and sectors in research or practice (Corburn 2013).

We suggest how a relational view of place can differ from a built environment and health view in Figure 3.2. We suggest that geographic scales must explore the interactions between local and global decisions, not just static administrative boundaries. Distance under the relational view ought to include physical and social relations and view populations and places embedded within networks. Importantly, in a relational view of place population groups are not treated as static but rather as dynamic and heterogeneous, so that, for instance, the slum dweller in Nairobi's Kibera settlement is not assumed to be afflicted by the same toxic stressors as their neighbour in an adjacent village or a slum dweller in the Mathare settlement on the other side of town. The biographies of people and the histories of places matter for understanding and acting to improve health in the relational view. Importantly, governance and political power are essential features that are investigated, analysed and incorporated in the relational approach, not 'controlled for' as confounding or ignored in urban health research and practice.

Adaptive urban health science

The discussion here has suggested that cities and urban health are complex 'systems' problems; they have multiple historical and contemporary inputs and no one linear pathway of cause and effect. Adaptive ecosystem management offers a model of scientific research and practice for healthy urban planners (Corburn 2013). Adaptive management acknowledges the failures of linear processes where narrow disciplinary scientists have aimed to develop complex models, predict long-term outcomes and suggest one-time policy standards. Instead, adaptive management begins with an acknowledgement of the inherent complexity and uncertainty within

	Built environment	*Relational view of place*
Geography	Boundaries at specific scale (i.e., census tract); distinct scales	No dichotomy between local and global
Distance	Fixed physical distance	Physical and social location; networks
Populations	Static in time/space; differences between	Contingent and mobile; differences within and between
Resources	Physical and social in specific locations; culturally neutral	Physical and social plus culturally specific meanings assigned to them
Political power	Not addressed	Relations among populations in place and held by institutions that shape places

Figure 3.2 A built environment and relational definition of place

Source: Corburn (2009).

systems, that this complexity demands an iterative, ongoing learning process among a range of expert stakeholders, and policy interventions must be adjusted to reflect newly acquired knowledge (Lee 1999). Another difference between adaptive management and conventional science policy is that adaptive management does not postpone actions until definitive causality is known about a system, but rather emphasises the importance of action in the face of uncertain science and couples these decisions tightly to rigorous monitoring.

The adaptive management approach begins by articulating, often with a range of stakeholders, the overall management objectives. In the case of health and planning, this might be to reduce or eliminate intra-urban health inequities. Second, a baseline model of change for the urban system needs to be described. Again, for urban health inequities, an adaptive urban health approach might begin with the 'toxic stressors' model of cumulative disadvantages. Next, a range of management choices are considered, prioritised, and a monitoring and evaluation strategy is developed for each management strategy. The prioritised strategies are implemented and monitored. An important feature of adaptive management is that the process does not end with decision analysis, but rather results from ongoing monitoring feedback into management processes as a form of social learning. Stakeholders consider the effectiveness of early interventions, learn from monitoring data and adjust decisions based on whether interventions are or are not approaching the original objectives.

Conclusions: prioritising health equity

While far from ideal, adaptive urban health management offers a framework for planners interested in linking research and practice to meet the twenty-first-century challenges of urban health equity. Planners must still do the hard work of getting 'inside' urban neighbourhoods to understand the interactions of physical and social forces that are influencing human health. Yet, the adaptive approach offers a robust model of participatory democracy, since the management team must be comprised of a range of interested stakeholders in order for the process to represent the varieties of expertise necessary to address complex problems. Planners may be ideally suited to facilitate these inclusionary processes, rather than just exert their 'expert' analyses into complex urban health problem solving. As the world continues to urbanise, planners must take a leading role in offering new models for understanding and improving the place-based characteristics that influence health equity. We have offered some ideas here that aim to prioritise health equity for planning in the twenty-first-century city.

Notes

1 Importantly, the UK housing standards based on the neighbourhood unit were not viewed as unquestionably health promoting. In 1948, Lord Silkin (1948), then Minister of Town and Country Planning, addressed the Town Planning Institute, noting: 'In every plan now it is fashionable to provide neighbourhoods. The assumption is that by dividing up your population into groups of 10,000 to 20,000 and surrounding them by open spaces, railways and main roads you will get nice little communities living happily and sociably together. On what evidence is that based? . . . Do we really get a good life that way? What steps do you take to ensure that people inside these little areas do mix freely together and do all the things one thinks it good for them to do? I would like more thought to be given to the question of neighbourhoods, even to the whole conception of the idea. I have fallen for it myself, but I would like to think it out again.'

2 The United Nations Human Settlements Programme (UN-HABITAT), as part of its 'Inclusive City' declaration in 2000, emphasised the continual struggle and conflicts inherent in urban governance, defining it as: 'the sum of the many ways individuals and institutions, public and private, plan and manage the common affairs of the city. It is a continuing process through which conflicting or diverse interests may be accommodated and cooperative action can be taken. It includes formal institutions as well as informal arrangements and the social capital of citizens' (http://ww2.unhabitat.org/campaigns/governance/docs_pubs.asp#Inclusive%20Cities).

References

APHA (American Public Health Association). 1938. *Basic principles of healthful housing*. Committee on the Hygiene of Housing. Chicago, IL: Public Administration Service.

APHA. 1948. *Planning the neighborhood: standards for healthful housing*. Committee on the Hygiene of Housing. Chicago, IL: Public Administration Service.

Chadwick, E. 1842. *Report on the sanitary condition of the labouring population of Great Britain: supplementary report on the results of special inquiry into the practice of interment in towns*. Volume 1. London: HMSO.

Corburn, J. 2009. *Toward the healthy city: people, places and the politics of urban planning*. Cambridge, MA: MIT Press.

Corburn, J. 2013. *Healthy city planning: from neighbourhood to national health equity*. London: Routledge.

Cummins, S., Curtis, S., Diez-Roux, A.V. and Macintyre, S. 2007. Understanding and representing 'place' in health research: a relational approach. *Social Science & Medicine* 65(9): 1825–1838.

Duffy, J. 1990. *The sanitarians: a history of American public health*. Chicago, IL: University of Illinois Press.

Engels, F. 1891. *The conditions of the working class in England in 1844*. London: Oxford University Press.

European Union (EU). 2013. Health inequalities in the EU: final report of a consortium. http://ec.europa.eu/health/social_determinants/docs/healthinequalitiesineu_2013_en.pdf, accessed 4 January 2014.

Friel, S., Akerman, M., Hancock, T., Kumaresan, J., Marmot, M., Melin, T., Vlahov, D. and GRNUHE members. 2011. Addressing the social and environmental determinants of urban health equity: evidence for action and a research agenda. *Journal of Urban Health* October; 88(5): 860–874.

Harpham, T. 2009. Urban health in developing countries: what do we know and where do we go? *Health & Place* 15: 107–119.

Healey, P. 1999. Institutionalist analysis, communicative planning, and shaping places. *Journal of Planning Education and Research* 19: 111–121.

Howard, E. 1965. *Garden cities of tomorrow*. Cambridge, MA: MIT Press.

Lee, K.N. 1999. Appraising adaptive management. *Conservation Ecology* 3(2): 3. www.consecol.org/vol3/iss2/art3, accessed 23 July 2013.

Marmot, M., Allen, J., Bell, R., Bloomer, E. and Goldblatt, P.; Consortium for the European Review of Social Determinants of Health and the Health Divide. 2012. WHO European review of social determinants of health and the health divide. *Lancet* 380(9846): 1011–1029.

McEwen, B. 2007. Physiology and neurobiology of stress and adaptation: central role of the brain. *Physiological Review* 87(3): 873–904.

Ministry of Health. 1944. *Housing manual.* London: Ministry of Works.

Perry, C.A. 1929. City planning for neighborhood life. *Social Forces* 8(1): 98–100.

Richardson, B.W. 1876. *Hygeia: a city of health.* Alexandria: Library of Alexandria.

Silkin, L. 1948. Planning Act of 1947. *Journal of the Town Planning Institute,* v. 35.

Townsend, P. and Davidson, N., eds. 1982. Inequalities in health: the Black report. Harmondsworth: Penguin.

UNEP (United Nations Environment Programme). 2014. Urban environmental issues. www.unep.org/urban_environment/issues/urban_air.asp, accessed 9 January 2014.

Virchow, R. 1848. *Report on the typhus epidemic in Upper Silsea.* Reprinted in *Social Medicine,* originally published as: *Archiv fur Pathologie. Anotomie u Physiologie ur flur klin Medicin,* 1848, Vol. II. www.social-medicine.info/index.php/socialmedicine/issue/view/5/showToc, accessed 8 April 2015.

WHO Regional Office for Europe. 1985. Targets for health for all. www.euro.who.int/__data/assets/pdf_file/0006/109779/WA_540_GA1_85TA.pdf, accessed 8 April 2015.

4

RAPID URBANISATION, HEALTH AND WELL-BEING

How informal settlements, slums and sprawling suburbs are globalising health problems

Cliff Hague

Introduction: refreshing the approach

Urbanisation, health and town planning have a long and complex relationship. Across nineteenth-century northern and central Europe and the northern states of the USA, industrialisation sent a siren call to those working on farms and in forests. Jobs, money, opportunities; an escape from dependence on fickle harvests, the prospect of gainful employment all the year round (Griffin 2014). Millions made the momentous move, but death and disease stalked the 'dreadful habitations' of the world's early industrial cities. Manchester, the archetypal city of the age, grew from 77,000 people in 1801 to over 316,000 in 1851. Only 45 per cent of the 401,000 inhabitants of the Manchester–Salford city at mid-century had been born locally (Douglas et al. 2002 p. 237).

A combination of statistical evidence and ethical vision made possible the containment of the lethal effluents and contagions of urban living. Regulation of the built environment played a key role in the transition. Average life expectancy in Manchester 1881–1900 was 29 for males and 33 for females (Taylor 1962 p. 176). However, before the end of the nineteenth century there was wide understanding of the formula for engineering healthier cities. Basic sanitation, a clean water supply, and a bit of fresh air and daylight could stem many, and eliminate some, of the bearers of early mortality. Public parks could help disperse the foul vapours and provide places for exercise, recreation, sports and for communities to gather by floral displays or bandstands.

People living in planned new settlements and garden cities began to grow taller and be healthier than their cousins crowded in the tenements and back-to-back houses of a nearby city. Cherry (1973 p. 31) reported, for example, on a comparison of the height and weight of children between the ages of 6 and 12 living in the planned town of Bourneville and an area in nearby Birmingham.

The world has continued urbanising, but in different places and in different ways. On average urban dwellers enjoy better health than their rural counterparts. This is because cities generally have better health services than rural areas, and offer better educational opportunities. However, averages must be treated with caution. If we disaggregate averages, and look separately at the statistics for men and for women, for rich and for poor people, for slum dwellers and those in other parts of a city, the stories that are hidden by an overall average are revealed. Tragically, the association of urban growth with ill health and premature death has been reaffirmed for many people. Why has the formula for healthy urban living been misplaced or disregarded? Safe water and sanitation demonstrably improved urban health in the developed world, yet almost half of city dwellers in Africa, Asia and Latin America still suffer from at least one disease caused by lack of safe water and sanitation (World Health Organization/UNICEF Joint Monitoring Programme for Water Supply and Sanitation 2005).

The pace and scale of urbanisation

For the first time a majority of people on the planet now live in urban areas. In the next generation that proportion will continue to rise. The absolute numbers of urban dwellers will increase still further given global population growth. As it was in nineteenth-century England, so today urbanisation is fundamental to the transition from an agricultural to an industrial/service-based economy. By the middle of this century, it is expected that out of every ten people on the planet, seven will be living in urban areas. This contemporary surge of urbanisation is adding 200,000 people a day to the world's urban population (UN-Habitat 2013 p. 25). It will impact on all parts of the Settlement Health Map (see Chapter 1, Figure 1.2; Barton and Grant 2006). Rapid urbanisation is of central importance to global health.

Box 4.1 China: rapid urbanisation can deliver health benefits

China's urban population increased from 17 per cent to 39 per cent between 1963 and 2003. To appreciate the speed of this transformation, the same change in urban population took 120 years in Great Britain and 80 years in the USA (UN-Habitat 2013 p. 51). During this period Shenzhen was one of the world's fastest growing cities. The urban growth was both cause and effect of a phenomenal growth in Shenzhen's gross domestic product (GDP). This new prosperity funded, amongst other things, a new social security and public health system (UN-Habitat 2013 p. 52). Rapid urbanisation can bring health benefits.

Over 90 per cent of the growth in urban population now takes place in developing countries. There are three components to urban growth. Natural increase accounts for roughly 60 per cent, rural to urban migration makes up 20 per cent, as does reclassification of settlements, which happens when what were villages outside the urban area become urbanised (UN-Habitat 2013 p. 25). Cities such as Phnom Penh, Cambodia; Tijuana, Mexico; Marrakesh, Morocco; and Lagos, Nigeria are expected to grow at annual rates of around 4 per cent, effectively doubling their populations within the next 17 years. Some cities in China, such as Shenzhen and Xiamen, will experience annual growth rates of more than 10 per cent, doubling their populations roughly every seven years (World Health Organization and UN-Habitat 2010 p. ix).

In Asia there are 0.88 million new urban dwellers every week. In Africa the weekly increase is 0.23 million; in Latin America and the Caribbean 0.15 million (UN-Habitat 2013 p. 29). These figures partly reflect the overall population numbers of these different regions, but also the existing levels of urbanisation. Africa will still only have 45 per cent of its population living in urban centres by 2025 (UN-Habitat 2013 p. 30). However, regional averages conceal significant differences between countries within a global region. For example, Africa's urban population growth rate was on average 3.3 per cent per year in 2010, but in 30 poor African countries the rate was over 4 per cent, whereas in nine countries classed as 'upper middle-income' the annual rate from 2005 to 2010 was 2 per cent (UN–Habitat 2013 p. 33). This evidence suggests that stage of development is a key influence on how rapidly urbanisation happens. Put another way, rapid urbanisation is particularly associated with countries that have a low GDP per capita.

The dynamics of informal settlements

Low-income countries have been urbanising since the 1960s, but in many cases their GDP per capita has not grown; indeed between 1970 and 2000 it even decreased (UN–Habitat 2013 p. 43). Here people are 'pushed' to the cities, to escape rural poverty, or from areas adversely affected by conflicts or environmental disasters. Rapid urban growth that is not matched by GDP growth imposes fiscal pressures on national and local governments. Professionals with skills in urban management tend to be thin on the ground, and concentrated in the capital cities, national ministries or the private sector. Many local authorities simply do not have the financial or human resource capacities effectively to manage rapid urbanisation. Regulation is often weak, information haphazard.

Thus, while poverty in the developing world was traditionally associated with rural areas, it has become increasingly urbanised. Furthermore, urban living is more expensive than living in the countryside, so income-based comparisons may underestimate the extent of the urbanisation of poverty. In cities, the poor lack access to adequate shelter. A billion people, one in three urban dwellers, are in slums and shanty towns (World Health Organization and UN–Habitat 2010 p. iv). Informal settlements differ from one country to another in terms of their construction, and are given different names (for example shanty towns, *favelas*, *bidonvilles*, *katchi abadis* or *campamentos*). These places are defined by their (il)legal status.

Moving towards the core of the Settlement Health Map in an effort to understand the spread of informal settlements, we can note that while urban populations are growing, the supply of land

Figure 4.1   Informal housing next to formal development, Lagos, Nigeria

Source: Hague.

Figure 4.2   Informal housing squeezed into a small site fronting a dangerous main road, East Port of Spain, Trinidad

Source: Hague.

for development is finite. Land that is seen as underused is likely to be occupied and developed through self-build using locally available materials. Government-owned or public land is often a target, as is land adjacent to railway lines, though there are obvious safety risks (Figure 4.2). Similarly, land not previously developed because of environmental hazards such as risk of landslides, flooding or pollution may be taken. While some informal settlements are created by spontaneous actions of discrete households, in other cases a landowner may be complicit in the development. This seems particularly to be the case in Asia, with owners renting sites to families, even if the tenancy has no formal legal status. Similarly, once an informal settlement is established, patterns of landlordism can develop, again taking varied forms from a household renting out-houses on their plot to criminals operating protection rackets.

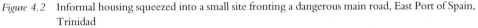

Box 4.2 Life inside the slums: Nairobi

Deepsea is one of around 200 informal settlements and slums in Nairobi. In 2007 it was one of the newer ones, with only 3,000 people, but no electricity. I interviewed Rosemary, a young woman living there, who was born in the countryside. 'Deepsea is built on somebody else's land, so the government regularly demolishes our houses. The Catholic church gives us tents and we live in those until we can rebuild the shanties', she told me. Rents were only 200 (£1.60) to 500 shillings a month, although a hut with a concrete floor cost about 1,500 shillings. A typical day's earnings for a man from Deepsea able to get work would be 200 shillings.

(continued)

(continued)

Deepsea had no public lighting and no paved roads. Emergency vehicles cannot get through the narrow alleys. Health services amount to over-the-counter purchases of medicines from a local shop.

I also interviewed Rosemary's friend, Nancy who grew up in Huruma, home to some 300,000 people, which is part of the larger Mathare slum on the east of Nairobi. Her parents came from the countryside. Huruma is part shanty town of mud huts and part slum. The mud huts literally dissolve in heavy rain. The slum is where the better-off poor live, crammed in small flats in unauthorised seven-storey buildings. Sanitation is open drains running through the maze of streets.

Nancy told me, 'There is one communal bathroom and toilets in a seven-storey block, used by 60 to 70 households. Water is available on tap, but only from midnight to 5a.m., and it does not reach the top floor. We are lucky: we have electricity. You hire an electrician to connect you (illegally) to the supply, but it only works for the TV and the lights, and goes off during the day. Landlords fit circuit breakers so you can't use an iron, for example. At night the whole family sleeps in one room. Rents are about 2,000 shillings a month, collected by agents: but nobody knows who their landlord is.'

The lack of legal title to land influences many of the health characteristics of informal settlements. The degree of insecurity, and consequent stress, will vary. At best, over time the 'illegal' houses become legalised; at worst there can be repeated phases of eviction and demolition, followed by re-occupation, as the example of Deepsea shows.

The minimum standards for services and infrastructure which operate in the better off neighbourhoods do not apply in the informal areas, because of their illegal status. Water, sanitation and electricity are the most obvious deficiencies that impact on health, though health centres are also typically lacking. In many cities in the developing world, slums and informal settlements are the predominant mode of settlement today: they are not just a few, isolated neighbourhoods (Figure 4.3).

Figure 4.3   Finding somewhere to live: Kibera in Nairobi, a long established slum area where lack of sanitation combines with poor nutrition to leave residents vulnerable to illnesses and diseases

Source: Hague.

Rapid urbanisation means urban plans quickly get out of date, so that the legally identified supply of land for new houses often fails to keep pace with the needs of the people. In addition, one of the legacies of the planning systems handed down by colonial powers has been a belief in urban containment. In theory this helps to protect the natural environment from encroachment by the built environment. In practice it criminalises the efforts by people to find somewhere to live in rapidly growing cities.

Cities, slums and health

There are a number of ways in which cities by their very nature present health risks for their residents. The concentration of people – a definitive feature of cities – increases the risks of exposure to infectious diseases. Similarly, the concentration of activities means that urban dwellers inhale air polluted by the emissions from factories and vehicles. Waste is generated in greater volumes because there are more people and activity than in villages, and its disposal is also inherently more problematic in a built-up area than in the countryside. This is true for solid waste as well as for the challenges of sanitation. Access to clean water is also likely to be more problematic.

None of these problems is insurmountable: cities might not have grown in the way they have if there were no solutions. However, the costs of overcoming such urban challenges mean that the impacts of inequality on health and well-being are more acute in the cities. Across the urban world, but especially in rapidly urbanising countries, we witness cities that are divided internally in terms of health outcomes. While poverty and social exclusion from adequate health services fundamentally shape these outcomes, the built environment is a significant influence also. Informality is the process, slums are the condition.

UN-Habitat (2006 p. 21) defines a slum household as a group of individuals living under the same roof in an urban area who lack one or more of the following:

1. Durable housing of a permanent nature that protects against extreme climate conditions.
2. Sufficient living space, which means not more than three people sharing the same room.
3. Easy access to safe water in sufficient amounts at an affordable price.
4. Access to adequate sanitation in the form of a private or public toilet shared by a reasonable number of people.
5. Security of tenure that prevents forced evictions.

It is easy to see the causal connections between slums and poor health. Contamination of water supplies, inadequate sanitation and problems of solid waste disposal are particularly severe influences on child mortality rates. As the World Health Organization/UN-Habitat report noted:

> Pneumonia and diarrhoeal diseases are the leading causes of childhood death globally, and can be a particular problem in urban settings due to crowding, indoor air pollution and poor access to health care in urban slums. For similar reasons, children in urban areas are susceptible to death from malaria and vaccine-preventable illnesses such as measles.
> *(World Health Organization and UN-Habitat 2010 p. 13)*

In Africa, Asia and the Americas:

> . . . children from the poorest urban families are roughly twice as likely to die as children from the richest urban families . . . In each of the 42 low- and middle-income

countries for which data (from 2000 onwards) are available, the poorest urban children are twice as likely as the richest urban children to die before the age of five years.

(World Health Organization and UN-Habitat 2010 p. 41)

Overcrowding is a feature of slums. It contributes to stress and family violence. Consequences include child maltreatment, partner violence and sexual violence, and elder abuse. Poor housing, overcrowding and urban noise (for example, from traffic), along with pollution, unemployment, poverty and cultural dislocation can also create or make worse a range of mental health problems, including anxiety, depression, insomnia and substance abuse (World Health Organization and UN-Habitat 2010 p. 29).

The result is that:

> Throughout the world, slum dwellers have less access to health resources, have more illness and die earlier than people in any other segment of the population. These unfair health gaps are growing in spite of unprecedented global wealth, knowledge and health awareness. Despite the relatively good health services in urban areas, the urban poor seem to have lower health status than their rural counterparts.
>
> *(World Health Organization and UN-Habitat 2010 p. 5)*

However, it is surprisingly difficult to get reliable statistical information about urban health inequalities. In part this is because informal settlements are often officially regarded as temporary and illegal, and thus public health authorities simply do not collect information about the health of people living in them. The absence of such information is then a further barrier to remedial actions.

Hazards

Rapid urbanisation and slum-led urban growth is also one of the main reasons for the staggering increase in disaster death tolls over recent decades. The number of people affected by natural hazards each year nearly quadrupled from 1975–1984 to 1996–2005 (Brecht et al. 2013 p. 2). The main cause is the growing concentration of people living in vulnerable locations. The processes and forms of rapid urbanisation are increasing the numbers of people at risk. The urban poor typically occupy the most hazardous locations and live in buildings that are not capable of withstanding extreme environmental events. In the last 30 years, the global population living in flood plains increased by 114 per cent and in cyclone prone coastlines by 192 per cent (Brecht et al. 2013 p. 3). Almost 80 per cent of deaths from disasters in the first decade of this century were in developing nations (Brecht et al. 2013 p. 3).

Researchers have computed the countries most at risk of mortality from the main natural hazards (Brecht et al. 2013 p. 21). The results show that rapidly urbanising countries figure prominently in the countries ranked highest. India, for example, is ranked number one for cyclones, two for floods, and three for both earthquakes and landslides.

Metro Manila in the Philippines is one of the world's most disaster-prone cities. In 2010 its population was around 12 million, an increase of almost 2 million since 2000. Urban inequality is high, with the rich living in gated communities and the poor in slums and informal settlements. Located on a flood plain and with a monsoon climate, Manila is highly at risk from earthquakes, floods and landslides. In 2012 it experienced devastating floods with almost two thirds of the city area being submerged after a week of torrential rains.

Figure 4.4 Natural hazards: in 2004 a tsunami triggered by an earthquake killed some 230,000 people in 14 countries around the Indian Ocean. The damage to this house on the west coast of Sri Lanka illustrates its devastating impact

Source: Hague.

Although the mega-cities such as Metro Manila are understandably the focus of most attention, there are also rapidly growing smaller cities which are located in places where there is significant exposure to natural hazards. Toluca in Mexico and Conakry in Guinea are identified as examples (Brecht et al. 2013 p. 22). Many such cities are expected to become large cities over the next 30–40 years.

Climate change is likely to exacerbate the risks. Examples of health-related impacts anticipated are heat waves, air pollution, severe storms and infectious diseases, while rising seas levels are associated with salinisation of water supplies in some places, which combined with increased demand linked to rapid urbanisation could adversely affect access to safe water.

Once again, solutions exist, but is there the economic capacity and political will to implement them? Between 1980 and 2006, Pakistan and the USA both experienced nineteen major earthquakes (>5.0 on the Richter scale). While in Pakistan 74,112 people died during these earthquakes, in the USA only 145 people were killed (Brecht et al. 2013 p. 18). This enforces the concept that tragedies are not caused by the earthquake itself, but rather by poor construction practices and failures of public policy. What can be done?

The perils of affluence

There are other less obvious hazards associated with urban living and the greater affluence that it can create for some. One is traffic and the risk of accidents, especially if there is poor provision for pedestrians and cyclists and inadequate traffic management – a typical condition of rapid urbanisation.

Figure 4.5 Failures of regulation: illegal addition of storeys to properties in Nairobi, Kenya, creates a potential hazard

Source: Hague.

Box 4.3 Risks to women's safety and health in stations: India

Jagori (which means 'Awaken, women') is a women's non-governmental organisation (NGO) in India. Jagori has undertaken safety audits of three stations in Kolkata. These revealed that women experienced not only harassment on the trains, but a catalogue of risks in and around the stations. For example, they highlighted the lack of access to drinking water, toilets and waiting areas, along with poorly lit spaces and passages, so that people prefer to cross the tracks rather than use the bridges over the tracks. Meanwhile, the Delhi Development Authority has described fly-overs and grade-separated junctions as 'rape dens' (Hague 2013).

Rapid urbanisation is typically associated with fast growing motorisation. Inevitably this prompts road building, which in turn generates further motorisation and increases problems such as traffic congestion, air pollution and traffic accidents. China demonstrates this transition. When I first went there in 1997 bicycles dominated the urban roads, which typically were lined with trees providing shelter from the summer sun. Today, the bicycles are much less evident, the trees have been felled, roads are wider and traffic jams and air pollution is worse. However, there are some positive signs. The 12th Five-Year Plan for China's Economic and Social Development in 2011–15 is the first such plan to include a special section on developing comprehensive public transport networks in cities. In addition, three national agencies, that is, the Ministry of Housing and Urban-Rural Development, the National Development and Reform Commission, and the Ministry of Finance, have jointly promulgated a guidance note on promoting the development of pedestrian and bicycle transport in Chinese cities (World Bank 2013).

Another threat comes from lifestyles, which tend to be different in cities than in rural areas. For example, there is likely to be easier access to tobacco, drugs and alcohol. The greater anonymity of the city also increases the risk from sexually transmitted diseases and also the dangers of assault. Urban residence may also be associated with less energetic lifestyles than are necessary for those working the land, and there is also likely to be greater reliance on processed foods than in the countryside. Thus urbanisation is associated with a shift towards calorie-dense diets, characterised by high levels of fat, sugar and salt (World Health Organization and UN-Habitat 2010 p. 29).

Across urban Africa, Asia and Latin America, as well as the increase in slums and informal settlements, we are also seeing the rise of an urban middle class that is increasing in numbers and in wealth. Average household size is already declining in most of these cities, so that the rate of increase in households exceeds the rate of population increase. In cities generally population density is inversely correlated with wealth. Cities of over two million in the richer countries rarely have population densities exceeding 3,000 inhabitants per square kilometre, while there are 60 cities of that size with densities over 10,000, and all are in developing countries (Ortiz 2014 p. 14).

We can expect that as people become more affluent they will opt to have more space about the house, and so urban areas will spread at a greater rate. It is anticipated that Chinese and South Asian cities alone will construct residential floor space equivalent to the land area of the Netherlands by 2025 (McKinsey Global Institute 2012).

The aspiration of many if not most of these new consumers is for car ownership and suburban living on a North American model. This is embedding a set of health problems. In India, for example, there was a 38-fold increase (3 to 115 million) in the number of registered motor vehicles between 1981 and 2009 (Millett et al. 2013 p. 2). A comparison of travel characteristics and health, comparing urban and rural residents, found that bicycling was the commonest mode of travel to work among the rural dwellers (68.3 per cent), followed by private vehicle (12.5 per cent), walking (11.9 per cent) and public transport (7.3 per cent). In contrast, the commonest mode of travel to work in urban dwellers was private vehicle (44.5 per cent), 15.9 per cent bicycled to work and 12.5 per cent walked (Millett et al. 2013 pp. 3–5). The study found (p. 6) that those who used any mode of active travel to work were significantly less likely to be overweight or obese than those who travelled by private vehicle. After adjusting for a range of social, employment and health-influential factors (for example smoking), the research demonstrated that those bicycling to work were significantly less likely to have hypertension or diabetes. Seen globally, urbanisation on the current model is literally driving the world to an obesity problem on a scale far greater than we currently have.

Conclusions: health, rapid urbanisation and urban planning

The health and well-being problems associated with rapid urbanisation, the urbanisation of poverty, but also urban affluence, present a major challenge to the idea and practice of urban planning. Statutory town or urban planning emerged as a response to the health problems created by rapid urban industrial growth in the nineteenth and early twentieth centuries. While the rules and procedures varied between different countries, the solutions and practices associated with planning were similar and not particularly contentious. Development should be regulated by local government to ensure that it complied with minimum standards in terms of infrastructure, and so delivered adequate housing in a tolerable living environment with access to essential services. Slums needed to be replaced by broad streets, green spaces and fresh air, places that would enable residents to live a healthier and longer life. Infrastructure – above and below ground – needed to be planned and provided by the public sector to meet demand.

This was the model of urban planning that empires bequeathed to their largely rural colonies along with independence from the 1950s onwards. As the pace of urbanisation quickened and former colonies began to struggle with debt repayments in the 1970s, the model broke down. Governments were unable to supply houses, sewers or roads in the numbers or of the quality that the model expected, and the private sector knew that building good housing for people on low and irregular incomes was one of the least attractive investment opportunities. The minimum standards prescribed in plans were simply too expensive for the poor to afford, and so enforcement meant evictions and relocation for the poor, and their replacement by better off people.

In the 1960s and 1970s, led by the writings of Charles Abrams and John Turner, town planning became the problem not the solution, while informal settlements became the solution not the problem. In a seminal article for the United Nations, Turner (1969 p. 526) argued:

> There are many good reasons for the existence of these slums, and it is inevitable that they will continue for as long as the poor remain poor. The basic problem of the slums is not how to eradicate them, but how to make them liveable.

This view has infused the practice of people involved in low-income housing and community-based development projects over the last half century, though planners and politicians have been more reluctant to embrace it, as evidenced by demolitions and forced evictions such as those in Deepsea that were described earlier. If urban planning is to become a positive tool for improving the health of people who are driving slum-led urbanisation, then it needs a new outlook and new practices.

There is a role for regulation, but it needs to be realistic in relation to the place and the capacities for enforcement. Less but better regulation is what is required. It is reasonable to prevent development on hazardous sites, provided that adequate land is made available to meet needs and in accessible locations. It is futile to imagine, as some plans do, that the population of a city can be capped in an arbitrary manner. A land supply with secure title and basic infrastructure enables new householders to then construct the dwellings that they can afford, an approach known as 'sites and services'. This could help reduce some of the health risks of slum-led rapid urbanisation, and enhance well-being by reducing insecurities and forced evictions.

Participatory upgrading is needed in existing slum areas. The major resource in such areas is the people themselves, and to be agents for positive change planners need a community development approach, not a bureaucratic mindset or a preconceived urban design 'vision' for the place. Basic improvements could make real differences – for example provision of pavements and adequate lighting can reduce accidents. Participatory safety audits have proved valuable tools enabling women and girls to identify places where they feel at risk of harassment and assault (Hague 2013). Across the Global South there are many bottom-up initiatives that seek to upgrade slums and install and maintain essential infrastructure (Hague et al. 2006; Satterthwaite and Mitlin 2013). Planners need to be aware of these and the lessons from them – for example, the ways in which finance can be raised, and how to network and scale up the benefits from a successful initiative.

Box 4.4 Bottom-up slum upgrading: India

The Indian Alliance is an umbrella body linking three major NGOs representing the poor (the National Slum Dwellers Federation, the Society for the Promotion of Area Resource Centres and a network of women's collectives called Mahila Milan). Through its involvement, the Oshiwara housing scheme is housing over 3,000 families over two phases.

Private landowners in Mumbai approached the Alliance seeking help in developing their land. The Alliance had experience and expertise that the owners lacked when it came to dealing with resettlement of people from slum areas. The Alliance also knew their way through the government bureaucracy. The Alliance could access subsidies from the World Bank's Mumbai Urban Infrastructure Project, which provides subsidies to the landowner giving their land for resettlement, and to the developer.

The Alliance negotiated with private contractors and employed them on parts of the housing scheme. It also negotiated contracts that a proportion of labour or sub-contracting had to be drawn from local slum communities. The contracts also required development to standards approved by slum communities during previous projects. One of the largest banks in India agreed to invest £2.4m into the second phase of the work. Homeless International, a UK-based NGO, guaranteed the loan.

In both phases of the development a small percentage of the houses were sold on the open market. This provided an element of cross-subsidy to the slum dwellers, and added to the private sector involvement (Hague et al. 2011 p. 195).

Urban planning is also needed to address the creation of car dependency that is accompanying rapid urbanisation, with deleterious health consequences. Strategic long-term planning of big infrastructure networks such as water, sewers, public transport systems and roads offers the best hope of steering development into forms that encourage walking, cycling and use of public transport, for example by creating transit-oriented development opportunities. It won't be easy to sell this vision to consumers or to politicians. Just as developing countries 'skipped a technology' in embracing mobile phones when landlines were few, might the dynamics of rapid urbanisation create innovative solutions, enabling them to leap over the age of the car-based suburb?

A final word

In terms of the Settlement Health Map, the macro-economy, politics and global forces structure the built environment and its relation to the natural environment, and so also shape activities, local economies and people's lifestyles. If the urban lifestyles and health issues from the Global North are now being embedded in the Global South, so too aspects of the urbanism of the

Global South are also being intruded into the cities of the North. As cheap, flexible labour becomes an increasingly significant part of metropolitan economies, and welfare states are being deconstructed, so we are seeing the growth in rich countries of informal and unregulated housing in bed sheds, 'hot bedding' in which people use the same beds in shifts, illegal squatting, homelessness or trailer parks. Health gaps are widening in rich cities. Yet we know how to build safe, healthy, sustainable and equitable settlements, and urban growth can produce the wealth to create better health for all. Time to act.

References

Barton, H. and Grant, M. 2006. A health map for the local human habitat. *Journal of the Royal Society for the Promotion of Health*, 126(6), 252–253.

Brecht, H., Deichmann, U. and Wang, H.G. 2013. A global urban risk index. *Policy Research Working Paper 6506*, Washington, DC: The World Bank, http://www-wds.worldbank.org/servlet/WDS ContentServer/WDSP/IB/2013/06/25/000158349_20130625133954/Rendered/PDF/WPS6506. pdf, downloaded 2 January 2014.

Cherry, G.E. 1973. *Town planning in its social context*. Aylesbury: Leonard Hill Books, Student Edition.

Douglas, I., Hodgson, R. and Lawson, N. 2002. Industry, environment and health through 200 years in Manchester, *Ecological Economics*, 41, 235–255.

Griffin, E. 2014. *Liberty's dawn: a people's history of the Industrial Revolution*. New Haven, CT: Yale University Press.

Hague, C. 2013. *Women's safety in India*, Planning Resource, http://cliffhague.planningresource. co.uk/2013/01/08/womens-safety-in-india/#more-671, downloaded 2 January 2014.

Hague, C., Hague, E. and Breitbach, C. 2011. *Regional and local economic development*. Basingstoke and New York: Palgrave Macmillan.

Hague, C., Wakely, P., Crespin, J. and Jasko, C. 2006. *Making planning work: a guide to approaches and skills*. Rugby: Practical Action.

McKinsey Global Institute. 2012. *Urban world: cities and the rise of the consuming class*, www.mckinsey.com/ insights/urbanization/urban_world_cities_and_the_rise_of_the_consuming_class, downloaded 3 January 2014.

Millett, C., Agrawal, S., Sullivan, R., Vaz, M., Kurpad, A., Bharathi, A.V., Prabhakaran, D., Srinath Reddy, K., Kinra, S., Davey Smith, G. and Ebrahim, S. 2013. Associations between active travel to work and overweight, hypertension, and diabetes in India: a cross-sectional study, *PLoS Med* 10(6): e1001459. doi: 10.1371/journal.pmed.1001459, www.plosmedicine.org/article/fetchObject. action?uri=info per cent3Adoi per cent2F10.1371 per cent2Fjournal.pmed.1001459&representation= PDF, downloaded 3 January 2014.

Ortiz, P. 2014. *The art of shaping the metropolis*. New York: McGraw Hill.

Satterthwaite, D. and Mitlin, D. 2013. *Reducing urban poverty in the global south*. Abingdon: Routledge.

Taylor, W. 1962. Social statistics and social conditions of greater Manchester, in C.F. Carter (ed.) *Manchester and its region: a survey prepared for the British Association*, Manchester: Manchester University Press, pp. 171–186.

Turner, J.F.C. 1969. Uncontrolled urban settlement: problems and policies in G. Breese (ed.) *The city in newly developing countries: readings on urbanism and urbanization*, London: Prentice-Hall, pp. 507–531.

UN-Habitat. 2006. *State of the world's cities 2006–2007: The Millennium Development Goals and urban sustainability: 30 years of shaping the Habitat Agenda*. London: Earthscan.

UN-Habitat. 2013. *State of the world's cities 2012/2013: prosperity of cities*. New York: Routledge.

World Bank. 2013. *Project appraisal document on a proposed loan in the amount of US$120 million to the People's Republic of China for the Qinghai Xining Urban Transport Project*, http://www-wds.worldbank.org/external/ default/WDSContentServer/WDSP/IB/2013/12/10/000461832_20131210111836/Rendered/ PDF/PAD4470PAD0P12010Box379877B00OUO090.pdf, downloaded 18 February 2014.

World Health Organization and UN-Habitat. 2010. *Hidden cities: unmasking and overcoming health inequities in urban settings*. Kobe, Japan: WHO.

World Health Organization/UNICEF Joint Monitoring Programme for Water Supply and Sanitation. 2005. *Water for life: making it happen*. Geneva, www.who.int/water_sanitation_health/monitoring/ jmp2005/en/index.html, downloaded 1 January 2014.

5

HEALTHY CITIES, HEALTHY PLANET

Towards the regenerative city

Herbert Girardet

Introduction: the global ecology of cities

As cities become the primary human habitat, three interconnected questions need an urgent answer:

1. Can a world of cities be a healthy habitat for their ever growing populations?
2. Can it be compatible with maintaining a healthy global environment?
3. How can the healthy cities and the healthy planet agendas be merged?

Never before in history have so many people – some 3.7 billion people and rising in 2014 – lived closely together in urban settlements across the world. This development poses unprecedented challenges for urban communities and policy makers concerned with both human health and planetary health. According to John Ashton, one of the founders of the healthy cities movement, 'the concept of a healthy city implies that the city is a place which shapes human possibility and experiences and has a crucial role to play in determining the health of those living in it'.[1]

It is well established that human coexistence in urban environments has major health implications – for the transmission of pathogens, exposure to air pollutants and the occurrence of injuries. The creation of healthy homes, life-enhancing physical environments and clean water and air is therefore critical to the emergence of healthy cities. Following on from the public health disasters of the nineteenth and twentieth centuries, much public policy effort has been made in many countries to prevent the occurrence of infectious disease, premature death and accidents. The World Health Organization (WHO) Healthy City initiative is the primary example of international collaboration in this context. But do such initiatives also contribute to the health of our planet?

According to John Ashton,

> it is important to consider the impact of urban living on the health of the planet as a whole. . . . Cities take in nature's bounty and spew our rubbish and waste. They behave as though there was an infinite supply of resources and as though the natural ecosystems had an infinite capacity for regeneration . . . Without a healthy planet there can be no community health . . .

61

The emergence of humanity as a predominantly urban species represents a fundamental, systemic change in the relationship between humans and nature. This is the case, above all else, because cities are the centres of human economic activity, accounting for 55 per cent of gross national product (GNP) in the least developed countries, 73 per cent in middle income countries and 85 per cent in the most developed countries (UN Habitat 2007). According to McKinsey (2011), some 70 per cent of all worldwide economic activity takes place in the world's 600 largest cities which accommodate 1.5 billion people, or 22 per cent of the global human population.

A key systemic problem in this context is that cities have developed a habit of absorbing vast amounts of non-renewable resources from nature and discharging wastes without taking responsibility for the consequences. Human impacts on the world's ecosystems and landscapes are dominated by the ecological footprint of cities which now cover much of the Earth's surface. They can be hundreds of times larger than the cities themselves.

The concentration of economic activities and intense human interaction is also reflected in high average levels of personal consumption.

One estimate suggests that a North American city with 650,000 people requires some 30,000 square kilometres of land to meet domestic needs, without even including the environmental demands of its industries. In comparison, an Indian city of this size would require just 2,800 square kilometres, or less than 10 per cent of an American city.[2] But meanwhile cities across the world, including India, are in the process of catching up with the consumption patterns of European and North American cities.

The World Wide Fund for Nature (WWF) states in its *Living Planet Report* (Pollard et al. 2010) that in the last 30 years a third of the natural world has been obliterated. Forty to 50 per cent of Earth's ice-free land surface has been heavily transformed or degraded by human activities, 66 per cent of marine fisheries are either overexploited or at their limit, and atmospheric carbon dioxide (CO_2) has increased more than 30 per cent since the advent of industrialisation (Vitousek et al. 1997).

Cities as economic and consumer hubs, then, are characterised by a huge throughput of resources. Apart from a near monopoly on the use of fossil fuels, metals and concrete, an urbanising humanity now consumes nearly *half* of nature's annual photosynthetic capacity as well.

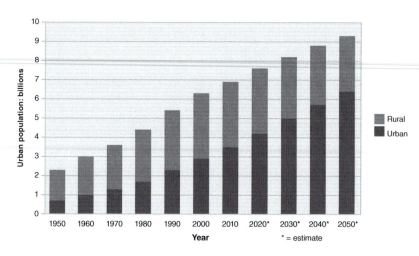

Figure 5.1   World urban population

Source: Derived from data from UN Department of Economic and Social Affairs, Population Division.

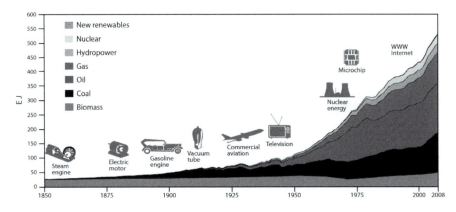

Figure 5.2   World energy sources

Source: Girardet.

All this has enormous consequences for all life on Earth, including the long-term prospects of human life.

Urbanists tend to hail cities as places where poverty is being tackled most effectively. Policy makers are at ease with the idea of creating productive and liveable urban environments but rarely concern themselves with the effects of this on the health of the planet: assuring local well-being is a vote winner, but maintaining a healthy planet much less so.

Cities and entropy

Modern cities are entropy accelerators. They are vast interconnected systems designed for turning energy into 'work' or motion, flowing along their roads, rails, wires and pipes. As fossil energy is used and raw materials are processed, their quality inevitably deteriorates. Order, which is established in the form of cities, causes disorder elsewhere in nature. So concentrating on ordering human activities in high-energy cities means increasing entropy: disorder, waste and pollution for the planet as a whole.

To improve our understanding of the beneficial linkages between healthy cities and a healthy planet, it is useful to analyse cities as 'eco-technical organisms', or super-organisms (Girardet 2014). They have a quantifiable metabolism. Whereas nature has an essentially circular zero-waste metabolism – every output by an organism replenishes and sustains the whole living environment – modern cities have an essentially linear metabolism, with resources flowing through the urban system without much concern about their origin, and about the destination of wastes.

Inputs and outputs are considered as largely unrelated. Fossil fuels are extracted from rock strata, refined and burned, and the waste gases are discharged into the atmosphere. Raw materials are extracted, combined and processed into consumer goods that ultimately end up as rubbish which cannot be beneficially reabsorbed into living nature. In distant forests, trees are felled for their timber or pulp, but all too often forests are not replanted.

Similar processes apply to food: nutrients and carbon are taken from farmland as food is harvested, processed and eaten. The resulting sewage, with or without treatment, is then discharged into rivers and coastal waters downstream from population centres, and usually not returned to farmland. Rivers and coastal waters all over the world are 'enriched' both with sewage and toxic effluents, as well as the run-off of mineral fertiliser applied to the farmland used for feeding cities.

In an urbanising world aiming for long-term viability this approach cannot continue. The environmental externalities of urban resources use can no longer be ignored. Unless we learn from nature how to create *circular systems*, an urbanising world will continue to be an agent of global environmental decline and, ultimately, the demise of cities. Urban resource use, as currently practised, is fundamentally undermining ecosystems across the world on whose integrity cities ultimately depend.

On a predominantly urban planet, cities will need to adopt circular metabolic systems to assure their own long-term viability and quality of life, as well as that of the rural environments on which they depend. Outputs will need to become inputs into the local and regional production system. Whilst in recent years a very substantial increase in recycling of paper, metals, plastic and glass has occurred, much more needs to be done. Most importantly, it is crucial to convert organic waste into compost, and to return plant nutrients and carbon to farmland feeding cities, to assure its long-term fertility.

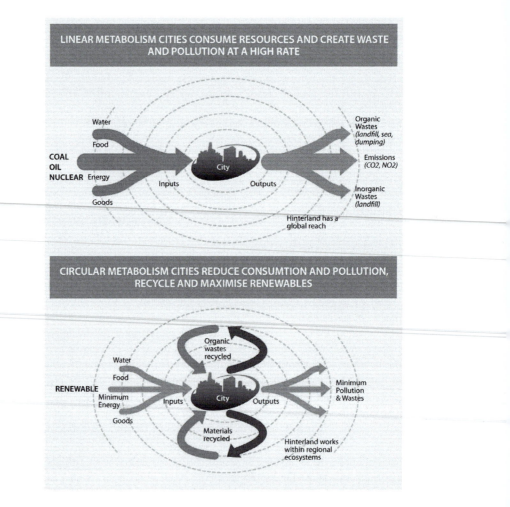

Figure 5.3 City metabolism

Source: Girardet.

Resource efficiency

A critical issue today, as cities become the primary human habitat, is whether urban living stand-ards can be maintained whilst the local and global environmental impacts of cities are brought down to a minimum. To get a clearer picture of the 'performance' of cities, it helps to draw up balance sheets comparing urban resource flows across the world. It is becoming apparent that similar-sized cities supply their needs with a greatly varying throughput of resources.

Most large cities have been studied in considerable detail and usually it won't be very diffi-cult to compare their use of resources. In developed country cities, disposability and built-in obsolescence still permeates collective behaviour. In contrast, in developing countries large cities have a much lower per capita resource throughput and much higher recycling rates, since recycling and reuse are an essential part of local economies.

Does the healthy city agenda invariably overlap with the quest for a healthy planet? Not necessarily so: here are two examples.

From air pollution to climate change

The WHO says air pollution in many of the world's cities is breaching its guidelines. In a survey of 1,600 cities in 1991 nearly 90 per cent of people in urban centres breathe air that fails to meet levels deemed safe. About half of the world's urban population is exposed to pollution at least 2.5 times higher than it recommends. Air quality is poorest in cities in Asia, followed by those in South America and Africa. In 2010 seven million people around the world died as a result of air pollution. The WHO calls it the world's single largest environmental health risk, with close links to heart disease, respiratory problems and cancer.[3]

Urban air pollution, of course, is nothing new. For instance, until the 1950s London was noto-rious for its smog – from local factory and power station chimneys, and from coal fires burning in millions of rooms across the city. Things came to a head in early December 1952. The thick air pollution at that time was so toxic it was even reported to have choked cows to death in fields close to London. In some places people could not see their own feet, and it brought road, air and rail transport to a virtual standstill. At least 4,000 people died as a result of the smog.

A direct response to 1952 London smog was the UK Clean Air Act of 1956. To reduce air pollution, 'smoke control areas' were introduced in London and other cities in which only smokeless fuels could be burned. Use of cleaner coal, and of electricity and gas heating reduced the amount of smoke pollution from household fires. Power stations were moved away from cities, and the height of their chimneys was increased.

The Clean Air Act helped to create healthier cities, but it actually had significant detrimental effects on the natural environment: the production of electricity by power stations outside cit-ies was highly inefficient, requiring more fuel to be burned per unit of energy. Tall chimneys discharged toxic fumes across longer distances. Within a couple of decades the death of forests and lakes in Scandinavia from acidic fumes discharged from UK power stations became a major bone of contention. The UK Clean Air act externalised the problems of air pollution, making British cities healthier, but increasing the damage to the regional or global environment.

As long as people experience pollution directly as a significant local health problem they demand efforts to clean it up. But the detrimental effects of acid fumes such as sulphur and nitro-gen oxides on forests and farm crops downwind from cities and power stations is outside most people's every day experience. And, beyond this, greenhouse gas emissions affecting the global climate require an even greater shift of concern from impacts on local *human health* to dealing with impacts on *planetary health*, which is even more difficult to face up to.

Recent reports about the accelerated loss of ice from the Arctic and Antarctic lend particular urgency to the need to curtail the fossil fuel dependence of modern cities.

The rapid increase of CO_2 in the atmosphere is closely linked to combustion in and on behalf of the world's cities. Until recently it was widely assumed that we could get away with a doubling of pre-industrial concentrations of CO_2. But the Arctic regions, in particular, have been found to be exceedingly sensitive to anthropogenic CO_2 emissions. According to the Intergovernmental Panel on Climate Change 'Arctic temperatures have increased at almost twice the global average rate in the last 100 years . . . Temperatures at the top of the permafrost layer have generally increased since the 1980s . . . by up to 3°C.'[4]

This could trigger the release of other greenhouse gases into the atmosphere, particularly methane which has been locked up in Arctic permafrost, fuelling global warming even more.[5]

The CO_2 output of cities is far too large for trees within their territories to be able to absorb. Every year we are now discharging nearly 10 billion tonnes of carbon per year of which 4 to 5 billion tonnes are not being reabsorbed into the world's ecosystems but which are accumulating in the atmosphere. This is the primary cause of the climate change problem that we are faced with.

All this has huge implications for the way we design and manage our cities, where we locate them and how we power them. Communicating the dangers of such *boomerang effects*, which could soon undermine the very existence of our modern cities, is a huge challenge for educators and policy makers.

The most dramatic population growth has been occurring in giant coastal cities. Of the 17 megacities of over 10 million people around the globe, 14 are located in coastal areas. Forty per cent of the world's cities of 1–10 million people are also located near coastlines. Careless development practices have caused important habitats such as wetlands, coral reefs, sea grasses and estuaries to be degraded or destroyed.[6] And with substantial sea level rises expected by the end of the twenty-first century, major northern coastal megacities and greenhouse gas emitters, such as London, New York and Shanghai, could well become the primary victims, and southern low-lying megacities such as Calcutta, Dhaka and Lagos could also be affected.[7]

The challenge is to clean up local air pollution whilst assuring that global air pollution is tackled at the same time.

Water and sewage

The London sewage story is similar: in 1853–4, a cholera epidemic killed nearly 11,000 Londoners. Eventually, in a pioneering feat of environmental detective work, a medical doctor, John Snow, traced the outbreak to a well in Soho whose water was contaminated with human excrement. Then, in 1858, sewage pollution of the river became an overwhelming problem. In the notorious year of the 'great stink', the members of the House of Parliament were forced to come up with a solution. How could the sewage produced by millions of people be dealt with? A passionate debate ensued and various schemes were proposed. One was a recycling system consisting of metal pipes arranged like the spokes of a wheel through which the sewage would be transported to fields on the urban fringe to be used for growing crops for Londoners.

But after much debate, the engineer Joseph Bazalgette was commissioned to build 82 miles of large sewers along the Thames and a network of smaller sewage pipes criss-crossing London. From 1865, 20,000 men worked for 13 years to construct the world's most extensive and expensive sewage collection and disposal system. The 1866 Sanitary Act mandated the connection of all London's buildings to Bazalgette's sewage network which ended downriver at Crossness and Beckton. From there the sewage was flushed into the Thames estuary – out of sight, out of mind. When the system was up and running, the exposure of Londoners to their own sewage ended for good and cholera became a thing of the past.

London had become a healthier city, but much of its night soil was no longer returned to the farmland on the edge of the city, but was flushed away instead.

At first guano and then, increasingly, artificial fertilisers were used to replace the use of human urine and faeces as fertiliser. Today, both human sewage and artificial fertilisers contaminate coastal waters across the world. The plant nutrients contained in urban sewage are flushed into rivers and coastal waters, or intercepted in sewage systems, never to be returned to the land. Sewage technology has helped to make cities healthier whilst contributing to the deterioration of the health of soils, and thus the health of the planet.

There are certainly instances when measures to create healthy cities are also good for the global environment, but contemporary sewage technology is not one of them.

Creating regenerative cities

The challenge today is not just to create sustainable cities, as is widely argued, but to create truly *regenerative* cities: to implement *strategies for an environmentally enhancing, restorative relationship between cities and ecosystems, of benefit to both people and planet.*

The concept of *regenerative cities* seeks focuses on the relationship between cities and the territories that supply them with vital resources. It is all about creating new local economies from cleaning up the urban environment whilst enhancing the relationship between cities and the ecosystems on which they depend.

Types of urban system: Agropolis and Petropolis

To get to grips with these issues it may be worth looking at historic changes in the relationship between cities and the world around them. Towns and cities do not exist in splendid isolation.

In his book *The Isolated State* the prominent nineteenth-century economist Johann Heinrich von Thünen described the way in which traditional human settlements, in the absence of major transport systems, are systemically tied into the landscape surrounding them through various logically arranged modes of cultivation.[8] In fact, they have an active, symbiotic relationship to it: they also assure its continuing productivity and fertility by returning appropriate amounts of organic waste to it. I use the term 'Agropolis' to describe this traditional type of human settlement.

Von Thünen describes how isolated communities are surrounded by concentric rings of varying land uses. Market gardens and milk production are located closest to the town since vegetables, fruit and dairy products must get to market quickly. Timber and firewood, which are heavy to transport but essential for urban living, would be produced in the second ring. The third zone consists of extensive fields for producing grain which can be stored longer and can be transported more easily than dairy products, and can thus be located further from the city. Ranching is located in the fourth zone since animals can be raised further away from the city because they are 'self-transporting' on their own legs. Beyond these zones lies uncultivated land of less economic relevance to urban living.

In many parts of the world traditional towns and cities, in the absence of efficient transport systems, had these kinds of systemic relationships to the landscapes from which they emerged, depending on nearby market gardens, orchards, forests, arable and grazing land and local water supplies for their sustenance. Until very recently, many Asian cities were still largely self-sufficient in food as well as fertiliser, using human and animal wastes to sustain the fertility of local farms (King 2004). Are these traditional arrangements still relevant in the twenty-first century?

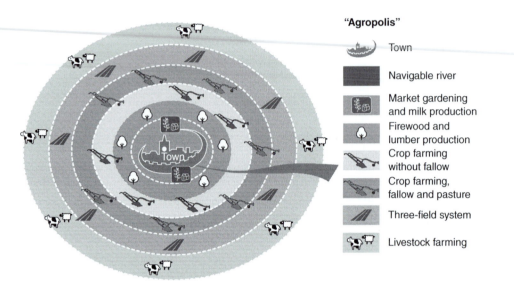

Figure 5.4 'Agropolis'

Source: Girardet/Lawrence.

Of course, life within traditional cities was highly precarious at times. Sanitation was often sorely lacking. Typhoid, cholera, the plague and many other infectious diseases could cause traditional urban settlements to be less healthy than cities even if they often existed in a relatively healthy local environment.

The rise of Petropolis

The industrial revolution of the last 250 years largely obliterated Agropolis. It fuelled a virtual explosion of urban growth and the unprecedented concentration of industrial activities in urban centres. Cities increasingly cut the umbilical cord between themselves and their local hinterland and became global economic and transport hubs. Cities became centres of *mobilisation* rather than civilisation, with access to global resources as never before.

The modern city could be described as 'Petropolis': all its key functions – production, consumption and transport – are powered by massive injections of non-renewable fossil fuels. But the resulting dependencies are ecologically, economically and geopolitically precarious – above all else because the fossil fuel supplies on which modern cities depend are, most definitely, finite. The associated problems of air pollution have already been discussed.

There is an ever growing awareness that we live on a finite planet, but infinite economic and urban growth is still taken for granted. While the world's population has grown fourfold in the twentieth century, urban populations and global resource consumption have increased sixteen fold and are still rising. Cities are central to this: despite taking up only 3 to 4 per cent of the world's surface area they use approximately 80 per cent of its resources and also discharge similar proportions of waste.

Whilst most of the 'easy' coal, oil and gas is now used up, new kinds of highly problematic extraction methods have come to underpin the existence of our urban systems. Fracking for gas and oil across the US, tar sand mining in Canada and off-shore deep sea oil extraction are symbols of the struggle to maintain fossil fuel supplies.

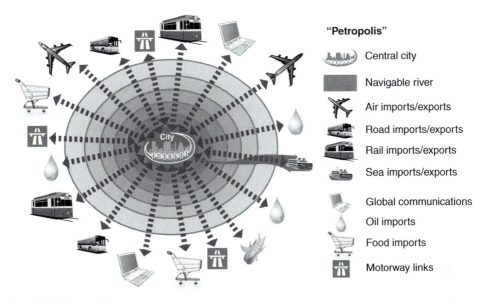

"Petropolis"

Central city

Navigable river

Air imports/exports

Road imports/exports

Rail imports/exports

Sea imports/exports

Global communications

Oil imports

Food imports

Motorway links

Figure 5.5 'Petropolis'

Source: Girardet/Lawrence.

Cities have become globalised centres of production as well as consumption, with through-puts of unprecedented quantities of resources and industrial products becoming the norm in the wealthier countries. In developing countries, too, the process of urbanisation is closely associated with ever increasing per-capita use of fossil fuels and with impacts on ever more distant ecosystems.

It has become clear that the concept of Petropolis needs to be challenged fundamentally as its systemic flaws become increasingly evident.

These are some of the dominant trends: demand for fossil fuels, energy costs, carbon emissions, climate instability and sea levels are increasing, whilst global reserves of natural resources and the time left for action is steadily decreasing. But, crucially and hopefully, so is the cost of renewable energy (RE)!

Conclusions: towards Ecopolis

Can modern cities that are the product of fossil fuel-based technologies be powered by renewable energy instead? The living planet we inhabit derives its energy supply from the sun and the Earth's core and, ultimately, these two primary energy sources need to be used to power our cities. The good news is that in the last few years rapid strides have been made with a wide spectrum of renewable energy technologies.

The technological breakthroughs in the field of RE have been facilitated by government policies. In many countries RE is making rapid strides. For instance, in the Thames Estuary the first phase of the 'Thames Array' of 175 turbines was completed in 2013, which has the capacity to supply some 30 per cent of London's domestic electricity.[9] In combination with energy efficiency measures, a dramatic reduction in the dependence on fossil fuels can be achieved.

Meanwhile transport technologies are also changing. Just 10 years ago car manufacturers could barely imagine making cars that did not run on petrol or diesel. Today, all mainstream manufacturers are working on hybrid or electric or fuel cell powered cars which are promising to become the norm in a matter of years.

The argument for increasing urban density has been gaining much credence as well. Transport energy efficiency can be greatly enhanced by designing for *proximity*. We need to get people walking and cycling rather than driving their cars wherever possible and in this we have much to learn from the compact layout of traditional cities.

Traffic calming, pedestrianisation and measures to encourage cycling feature prominently in this context. The same is true of all measures that encourage the greening of the urban environment – tree planting, and the creation of parks small and large.

All of these measures, taken together, can dramatically change urban production and consumption patterns, creating major new local economic sectors whilst enhancing the prospects for urban health at the same time.

Food for cities

In many parts of the world, urban growth has been directly linked with mechanisation of farming and rural depopulation. Food is supplied to cities by ever more energy intensive production systems. For example, in the US one farmer, with his complex array of fossil fuelled equipment, typically feeds 100 urban people. But ten times more fossil fuel energy goes into this type of food production system than the calories that are actually contained in the food we get to eat.[10]

We need a new emphasis on local food production. It is well documented that in Cuba, 'intra-urban' organic agriculture now supplies large amounts of food to cities such as Havana. According to Cuba's Ministry of Agriculture, some 150,000 acres of land is being cultivated in urban and suburban settings, in thousands of community farms, ranging from modest courtyards to production sites that fill entire city blocks.[11] China still has a national policy of surrounding its cities with belts of cultivated land. Such 'peri-urban' food growing systems are also reappearing in the US where farmers' markets supplied by local growers are becoming popular again.

In the US significant 'intra-urban' agriculture initiatives are also under way. Cities that have lost a significant part of their economy are at the forefront. Detroit, once a city of 2 million people, has contracted to less than 900,000 people, with vast areas of land now lying derelict. The American Institute of Architects came to this conclusion in a recent report: 'Detroit is particularly well suited to become a pioneer in urban agriculture at a commercial scale.' Similar options are now being considered for New Orleans, St. Louis, Cleveland and Newark. Whilst local produce may sometimes be more expensive than imported produce stocked in supermarkets, farmers markets are enjoying ever increasing popularity.

Even very large cities can source substantial amounts of the vegetables and fruit they require from the urban territory and the surrounding countryside. However, grain supplies require much larger areas of land and most will have to be supplied from farmland further afield.

The ecosystems beyond

But renewable energy, urban agriculture and resource efficient redevelopment are only part of the story of truly creating Ecopolis. Above all else we need to address the relationship between cities and the ecosystems beyond their boundaries on which they will continue to depend even if major redevelopment initiatives are taken within cities (Girardet 2014).

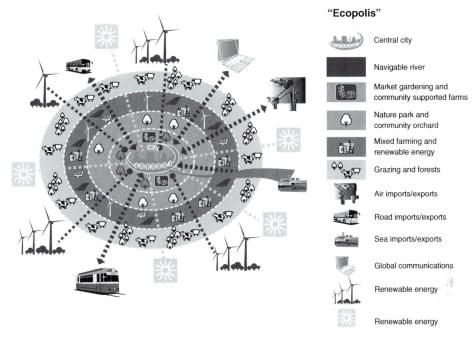

Figure 5.6 'Ecopolis'

Source: Girardet.

The regenerative development of cities is a comprehensive approach that goes beyond established concepts of sustainable development. Cities need to proactively contribute to the replenishment of the run-down ecosystems – including farm soils, forests and marine ecosystems – from which they draw resources for their survival. And while cities continue to burn fossil fuels, they also need to find ways of assuring that their CO_2 emissions are reabsorbed through 'bio-sequestration' in soils and forests (Girardet and Mendonca 2009).

This is where the concept of 'Ecopolis', the regenerative city, needs to assert itself, drawing together the various themes discussed in this text into one comprehensive concept. Policy makers, the commercial sector and the general public need to jointly develop a much clearer understanding of how cities can develop a restorative relationship to the natural environment on which they ultimately depend and how city people can benefit from this. The underlying incentive is that positive outcomes are likely to be beneficial for both global ecology as well as the local urban economy.

To initiate projects for restoring the health of forests, soils and aquatic ecosystems that have been damaged by urban resource demands certainly goes beyond strictly urban policy initiatives. Creating parameters for appropriate action will involve both political and business decisions – with a spectrum ranging from transnational to national and to urban levels of decision making. It involves drawing up novel legal frameworks and addressing the profit logic of companies involved in natural resource extraction.

From Petropolis to Ecopolis: the regenerative city

The new task facing urban decision makers and communities is to create spatial structures that satisfy the needs of city people whilst also assuring their ecological and economic resilience and a healthy global environment.

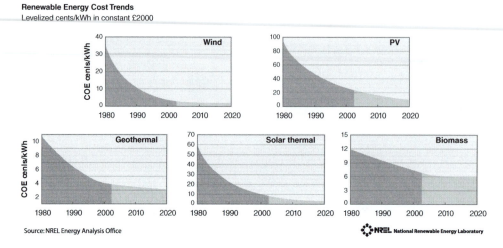

Figure 5.7   Renewable energy cost trends

Source: NREL Energy Analysis Office.

New approaches have to be developed to ensure that cities implement renewable energy strategies and actively contribute to the comprehensive restoration of damaged ecosystems on whose efficient 'services' they ultimately depend.

We need to provide secure habitats that allow us to move about our cities efficiently, and we want them to provide pleasant spaces for work, recreation and human interaction. We want urban environments that are free from pollution and waste accumulation. But we also need to get to grips with the impacts of cities beyond their boundaries.

Most importantly, the transformative changes that are required to create regenerative cities call for far-reaching strategic choices and long-term planning as compared to the short-term compromises and patchwork solutions that characterise political decision making systems at all spheres of government.

A wide range of solutions towards the goal of creating regenerative cities are already available, but implementation has to be speeded up by assuring that it is seen as part

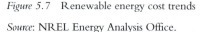

- of the remit of city authorities and urban planners,
- and of the mental horizons of urban citizens.

Unless we can develop settlements that are ecologically resilient, both global health and local health will be severely compromised. Internationally, cities need to work closely together to develop and implement policies for regenerating regions across the world that have been damaged and depleted by urban consumption patterns. One or two organisations have made a tentative start at creating truly regenerative cities but implementation has barely begun.

Notes

1 www.healthycities.org.uk/uploads/files/healthy_cities___the_new_public_health_in_action.pdf
2 The International Institute for Sustainable Development, Urban and Ecological Footprints, www.gdrc.org/uem/footprints
3 www.bbc.co.uk/news/science_and_environment-27313349
4 www.ipcc.ch/assessment-report/ar4/.../ar4-wg1-spm.pdf

5 findarticles.com/p/articles/mi_m1272/is_2651.../ai_55500436
6 findarticles.com/p/articles/mi_m0CYP/is.../ai_95527025
7 www.timesonline.co.uk/tol/news/environment/article6938356.ece
8 en.wikipedia.org/wiki/Johann_Heinrich_von_Thünen
9 London Array, www.londonarray.com
10 http://blogs.scientificamerican.com/plugged-in/2011/08/11/10-calories-in-1-calorie-out-the-energy-we-spend-on-food
11 www.i-sis.org.uk/OrganicCubawithoutFossilFuels.php

References

Girardet, H. 2014. *Creating regenerative cities*. London: Routledge.

Girardet, H. and Mendonca, M. 2009. *A renewable world: energy, ecology and equality*. A report for the World Future Council. Totnes, UK: Green Books & Resurgence Books.

King, F.H. 2004. *Farmers of forty centuries: organic farming in China, Korea, and Japan*. New York: Courier Dover Publications.

McKinsey Global Institute. 2011. Urban world: mapping the economic power of cities. New York: McKinsey Global Institute.

Pollard, D., Almond, R., Duncan, E., Grooten, M., Hadeed, L., Jeffries, B. and McLellan, R. 2010. *Living planet report 2010*. Switzerland: World Wide Fund for Nature.

UN Habitat. 2007. *The state of the world's cities 2006/7, Nairobi*. New York: United Nations.

Vitousek, P.M., Mooney, H.A., Lubchenco, J. and Melillo, J.M. 1997. Human domination of earth's ecosystems. *Science*, 277(5325), 494–499.

6

MIND THE GAP

Bridging the divide between knowledge, policy and practice

Roderick J. Lawrence

Introduction: reframing the issues

Economic, health, environmental and land use policies and projects implicitly have a shared goal of improving the living conditions of people. Nonetheless, not all cities, or citizens within a specific city benefit equally (Hardoy et al. 2001). The impacts of economic and urban policies on the health and well-being of human populations and the environmental constituents of their habitat are neither neutral nor symmetrical. The policies have a wide range of effects but many do not have intentional or predictable outcomes (Lawrence 1996). The diverse kinds of interrelations between environmental, health and economic policies should be identified and incorporated into decision-making. Today one challenge in this field is to integrate environmental, health and socio-economic equity dimensions into mainstream policy formulation and implementation across national, regional and local levels.

Planning for health and well-being in urban, suburban or rural localities raises complex questions that do not have simple answers as shown by the chapters in this book. Nonetheless, too frequently, urban administrators, scientific researchers and planners have identified specific problems and considered them too narrowly. Therefore, they have ignored complexity, especially the interrelated nature of the natural and built environments and how these can influence health and well-being (Dannenberg et al. 2011). The 'one problem—one solution' approach cannot achieve policy goals or respond to complex questions by identifying and applying 'the best solution'. Uses of hypotheses, pilot projects and scenarios remain rare. The limitations of fragmented approaches, even those that have led to short-term incremental improvements, in domains such as mobility and transport, are still common today. For example, from the 1950s, urban planners and traffic engineers developed programmes and projects for public transportation that frequently gave a higher priority to private vehicles than diverse kinds of public transport systems. In many cities, extensive networks of tramways were removed and vast urban development projects based largely on spatial segregation by zoning land uses were planned. These included hectares of roads and parking allotments for commuters who were compelled to travel between neighbourhoods that accommodated specified and segregated urban activities (Rodwin and Sanyal 2000). These programmes and projects not only changed the biological, ecological and human components of urban environments but they have also been self-defeating in some respects. For example, despite the large increase in the volume of roads, traffic congestion is a daily dilemma experienced by many commuters around the world. Moreover, high levels of air pollution and noise nuisance are unintended outcomes which have both short- and long-term consequences on the health of citizens, the local economy and the sustainability of urban ecosystems.

This example illustrates that, in countries with either market or socialist economies, urban planning has increasingly become the province of design professions, public administrators, politicians, property owners and investors. Concurrently, technocratic, rationalistic and bureaucratic approaches coupled with monetary values and econometric calculations have commonly become dominant or exclusive (Lawrence 1996). Although advocacy planning and community action did receive a hearing in a few countries during the 1960s and 1970s, their innovative contribution still remains a beacon for change. Recurrent approaches still create a social divide between professionals, politicians and the public. They continue to apply ad hoc piecemeal approaches to serve narrowly defined, short-term interests, based largely on short-term sector-based approaches that are meant to yield monetary returns.

Today, too few public and private institutions are examining the full range of costs and benefits of urban development for specific communities, regional and national populations, or the global environmental. Despite the fact that urban administrators and design professionals have been surprised by the unintended consequences of some recent policies and projects, one of the great anomalies of the conduct of these professions is that systematic evaluation of policies and projects is not considered to be their responsibility (Rodwin and Sanyal 2000). This limitation could be overcome, at least partly, by a democratisation of decision-making, by the decentralisation of control and expertise, as well as by a redefinition of current uses of knowledge and different kinds of information in both the public and private sectors.

This chapter will argue that if planning for health and well-being is to achieve desired goals then it is essential to replace business as usual by innovative interdisciplinary and transdisciplinary contributions that address the complexity of the topic. These approaches are defined later in this chapter. They endorse the application of a human ecology perspective that applies an interdisciplinary interpretation of health and well-being in architectural and urban planning projects (Lawrence 2002). This perspective can be enlarged to include stakeholders in local communities in decision-making processes about the future of their habitat. This approach will be illustrated by ongoing action research on whether the provision of green public spaces can be a catalyst for health promoting behaviours of different population groups (for example, children, adolescents or elderly citizens) that effectively leads to positive health outcomes.

Confronting complexity and diversity

The formulation and implementation of traditional sector-based contributions in housing, building and land use planning can be challenged on several accounts, not least their unexpected negative impacts on health and quality of life. Incremental improvements (in sectors such as road traffic circulation) are often achieved in tandem with unintended consequences, which may include negative impacts on environmental conditions in urban agglomerations, the urban economy and the health of citizens. These unforeseen outcomes are partly due to the number and complexity of all those factors that policy decision-makers need to consider (Rittel and Webber 1973). They are also due to the recurrent lack of coordination in the field of urban development policies, which can be associated with the following conditions:

1. The number and the complexity of all those factors that researchers, practitioners and policy decision-makers ought to consider.
2. The uncertainties and the unpredictability of the interrelations between many of these factors which are rarely admitted.
3. The segmented knowledge of researchers, public administrators and practitioners who may be experts on specific subjects but do not have an integrated perspective of what they consider.
4. The lack of coordination between actors in different sectors and between people working at different administrative levels.
5. The lack of systematic monitoring and feedback within sectors (such as housing or transport) and especially across different local, regional and national levels.
6. The non-conformity between the goals, priorities and values of policy decision-makers and of citizens in relation to their interpretation and use of human settlements and the characteristics of their habitat.

A fundamental rethinking of the relationships between social, economic and health inequalities and other kinds of problems is urgently required (Lawrence 2002). The interrelations between housing markets, land use planning, health systems, social development and environmental policies have been poorly articulated until now. However, it is crucial to acknowledge the important role of cities as localities for the management of resources, as places for accommodating diverse cultures and lifestyles, and as significant forums for economic development at both the national and regional levels. Although housing and land use policies have rarely been a high priority in the manifestos of governments, or political parties, the author of this chapter argues that there are reasons why health, social, housing and environmental policies should become important components of domestic agendas in order to promote social cohesion and quality of life.

The ecological definition of health

The word health is derived from the old English word *hal* meaning whole, healed and sound. Health is a difficult concept to define and, therefore, it is not surprising that it has been interpreted in diverse ways (Lawrence 2002). Health has an intrinsic value which cannot be quantified only in monetary units. This stems from that fact that health is fundamentally different from other attributes of human life owing to the unique status of the human body. Unlike other objects, the body is not only possessed by an individual but it also constitutes that person. Each individual may be a consumer of, and an object to which, health services are directed. Simultaneously, each person is also an active producer of her/his health by following habits of diet, exercise and hygiene, as well as other lifestyle traits, which may or may not be conducive to promoting health.

The ancient Greeks believed that *Asclepios*, the god of medicine, had two daughters: *Hygieia* was responsible for prevention, whereas *Panacea* was responsible for cure (Loudon 1997). This long-standing distinction between prevention and the cure or treatment of illness and disease corresponds closely to the difference between public health interventions intended for entire populations and clinical interventions for individuals and specific groups. The exception to this generalisation can be prevention by immunisation which is applied to individuals, but it does not necessarily involve the whole population in a country, city or any precise geographical area. One key public policy issue should be to establish the appropriate scope and range of preventive and curative interventions to deal with specific health issues in precise localities. This is a crucial challenge for all research on the positive health effects of architecture and urban planning.

Health is defined in this chapter as a condition or state of human beings resulting from the interrelations between them and their biological, chemical, economic, physical and social environment as shown in Figure 6.1. Hence, health is place based and should be considered as locality specific not just population specific. All the components of human habitats should be compatible with their basic human needs and full functional activity including biological reproduction over a long period (Lawrence 2001). Health is the result of both the direct pathological effects of chemicals, some biological agents and radiation, and the influence of physical, psychological and social dimensions of daily life including housing, transport and other characteristics of metropolitan areas shown in Figure 6.2. For example, improved access to medical services is a common characteristic of urban neighbourhoods that is rare in many rural areas.

In the field of health promotion, health is not considered as an abstract condition, but as the ability of an individual to achieve her/his potential and to respond positively to the challenges of daily life. Hence, health is an asset or a resource for everyday life, rather than a standard or goal that ought to be achieved. This redefinition is pertinent for studies of the interrelations between health, human behaviour and built or natural environments because the environmental and social conditions in precise localities do impact on human relations, they may induce stress, and they can have positive or negative impacts on the health status of groups and individuals (Hartig and Lawrence 2003). It also implies that the capacity of the health sector to deal with

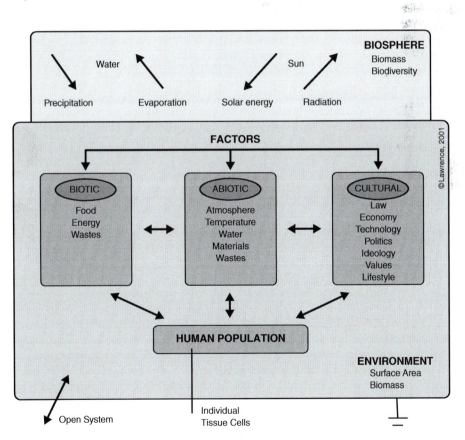

Figure 6.1 Holistic framework of a human ecology perspective

Source: Lawrence.

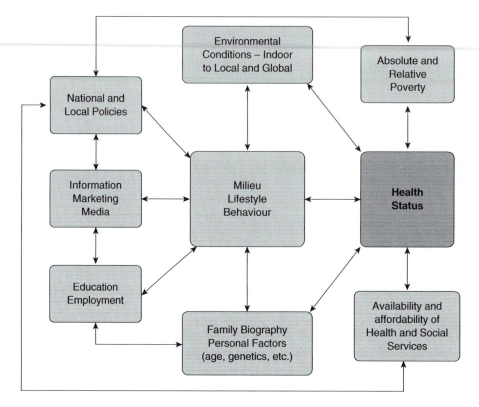

Figure 6.2 Eight classes of factors ('determinants') of health. These classes of factors are multidimensional and the interrelations between them can be direct or indirect. Interdisciplinary and inter-sector collaboration are necessary in order to understand health status in precise localities

Source: Lawrence.

health promotion and prevention is limited and that collaboration with other sectors would not only be beneficial but is necessary in order to improve health status.

The distinction between biomedical models and ecological interpretations of health is fundamental (Rayner and Lang 2012). The germ theory, for example, is an incomplete explanation of human illness and disease because it ignores the contribution of numerous physical and social dimensions of the environment that can influence health. Ecological interpretations maintain that the presence of a germ is a necessary but not a sufficient condition for an individual to become ill. These interpretations note that some individuals become more susceptible to certain illnesses because of their differential exposure to numerous environmental and social variables that can promote or be harmful to health and well-being. This interpretation does not ignore the influence of genetics, individual behaviour or primary health care. However, it maintains that, alone, these do not address possible relations between social problems and illness (for example, inadequate nutrition of households living in poverty) or positive social dimensions and health promotion (for example, health promoting behaviour such as regular physical activity). This chapter stresses that the distinction between potential and actual health status can be the foundation of interdisciplinary and transdisciplinary interpretations of health which can be applied to improve current understanding of the multiple interrelations between local environmental conditions, human behaviour and health status.

Beyond disciplinary confinement: barriers to change

It has been common practice for scientific researchers to produce studies that are passed on to architectural and environmental professionals who are meant to read them and make informed decisions. This caricature of the relations between research and professional practice is representative of applied research in many fields including housing and urban planning (Lawrence 1987). At the same time, the lack of effective collaboration between scientists and professional practitioners has been discussed in these and many other sectors. The so-called applicability gap has led to criticisms of researchers by professional practitioners. These criticisms stem from sector-based and disciplinary perspectives that illustrate misunderstandings about the different contexts of research, programme definition and implementation.

Applicability gap in architecture and urban planning

Four decades ago there were a number of criticisms about the relationship between social research, the practice of architecture, and urban design and planning (Zeisel 1981). At that time authors including Reizenstein (1975) and Heath (1984) contested the lack of application of the findings of social research in architectural and urban design processes. This schism between knowledge and professional practice led to criticisms of architects and urban planners who were challenged because they did not apply the empirical findings of research in their projects and plans. At the same time, there were also criticisms of psychologists and sociologists who were accused of misunderstanding the nature of architectural and urban design (Pressman and Tennyson 1983). This debate warrants further consideration in relation to current concern about evidence based design (Hamilton and Watkins 2009).

From about the 1960s social research about topics including housing, building and urban planning included numerous social surveys of extant living and working conditions in many cities and towns around the world. For example, household surveys of residential satisfaction, user preferences and the personalisation of domestic space were completed mainly by academic researchers, sometimes by public authorities. It is noteworthy that the health of residents was rarely included (see Lawrence 2002). The purpose of many of these contributions was to establish guidelines for the construction of new residential buildings and neighbourhoods. The underlying assumption was that architects and urban designers could use the findings of empirical knowledge from these surveys by incremental improvement (Zeisel 1981). This is also the assumption of evidence based design which should, however, be treated with caution for two reasons. First, the context dependent nature of housing, building and urban planning should not be ignored as was commonly the case in the 1960s and 1970s when standardised and rationalised housing policies and building construction methods were widely applied in many countries. Hence cultural, geographical and social diversity was commonly disregarded even though we know that each architectural and urban design project has a specific geographical, cultural, economic and social and political context which should be taken into account (Lawrence 1987). This means that social researchers and design professionals should identify and understand what is contextually specific and what is variable between different localities.

The second reason is that reviews show that many empirical studies of people in their daily surroundings ignore subjectivity and, therefore, they do not consider how data and information can be interpreted and used by professionals and lay-people in different ways before, during and after a design and planning process (Heath 1984). This misunderstanding of the epistemology of design and planning processes has been attributed to those who challenge the non-application of findings from social research (Zeisel 1981).

This chapter rejects those claims that functional requirements and deterministic relationships exist between people and their built environments. Instead of social engineering, or rational standards and prescriptive rules, a different approach is necessary. Given that there is no pre-determined relationship between people and their built environment, this chapter argues for a reconsideration of both architectural and urban design as processes that are meant to decipher and understand the multiple relationships and uses that people attribute to their immediate environment. In order to promote more effective collaboration between scientists and professional practitioners, it is necessary to build bridges between researchers in different disciplines, and then between them and decision-makers in government and the community. One way to do this is to consider decision-making on complex issues as open critical inquiry (Zeisel 2006).

Building bridges over barriers

It is noteworthy that there appears to be no methodological reasons for the lack of collaboration between researchers and professional practitioners. Nonetheless, academics, professionals and politicians have created conceptual and institutional barriers that hinder effective partnerships between them. Three sets of these barriers are:

1. Conceptual barriers such as inapt analogies, metaphors and models used by academics and professionals which do not address the complexity of the human–made environment but promote rational, utilitarian approaches to interpret the layout, use and management of human habitats.
2. Institutional barriers stemming from professional specialisation, and the segmentation and bureaucratisation of expertise and knowledge. 'Experts' apply technocratic knowledge in order to apply instrumental rationalism based largely on quantitative proposals at the expense of qualitative dimensions including the tacit know-how of citizens.
3. Social barriers produced by human differentiation and compounded by shortcomings in formal education and a lack of information transfer between professionals, politicians and the public. The consequent lack of communication between interest groups means that basic democratic practices, such as residents being informed about architectural and urban projects that will influence their lives, are still not common. Consequently, citizens are frequently unaware of policy decision-making about their city and their local neighbourhood.

This chapter argues that conceptual barriers are more influential than the institutional and social barriers, which reflect and reinforce the conceptual ones.

At the outset it is necessary to challenge the common interpretation of design as either a product (for example, the material composition of housing units) or as a process (for example, furnishing activities of households). This dual interpretation of design hinders the application of more integrated concepts that can be used to promote health and well-being (Lawrence 2002). In contrast, design can be reinterpreted as the intentional organisation of both natural and built environments, a setting for human activities and a longer-term project to achieve desired objectives. This integrated definition of design underlines the principle that architecture and urban planning always occur in a human context. It also highlights the principle that they are intentional rather than being haphazard because professionals choose between several options in order to achieve preferred outcomes. Therefore, architecture and urban planning are much more than aesthetic and spatial composition.

Interdisciplinary and transdisciplinary bridge-building

In this chapter, disciplinarity refers to the specialisation and fragmentation of academic disciplines especially since the nineteenth century. Each discipline has its own concepts, definitions and methodological protocols for the study of its precisely defined domain of competence (Lawrence 2010). For example, in the domain of the built environment, different definitions and interpretations of density coexist in architecture, building construction, demography and geography. This means that collaboration across disciplinary boundaries is not easy until a common understanding can be achieved.

Multidisciplinary refers to an additive research agenda in which each researcher remains within his/her discipline and applies its concepts and methods without necessarily sharing a common goal with other researchers (Lawrence 2010). This approach is still common in the environmental sciences today and it is frequently applied in environmental impact assessment (EIA) of large-scale urban projects.

Interdisciplinary contributions are those in which concerted action and integration are accepted by researchers in at least two different disciplines as a means of achieving a shared goal that usually is a common subject of study. Pinson (2004) argues that urban planning is an 'undisciplined discipline' because it usually involves collaboration between professionals trained in different disciplines such as architecture, civil engineering, building construction, geology and landscape planning.

In contrast to interdisciplinary contributions, transdisciplinary contributions incorporate a combination of concepts and knowledge not only used by academics and researchers but also other actors, including representatives of the private sector, public administrators and civil society (Lawrence 2010). These contributions enable the cross-fertilisation of knowledge and experiences from diverse groups of people that can promote an enlarged vision of a subject, as well as new explanatory theories. Rather than being an end in itself, this kind of research is a way of achieving innovative goals, enriched understanding and a synergy of new methods.

Multidisciplinarity, interdisciplinarity and transdisciplinarity are complementary rather than being mutually exclusive (Lawrence 2010). Both interdisciplinary and transdisciplinary research and practice require a common conceptual framework and analytical methods based on shared terminology, mental images and common goals. Without specialised disciplinary studies there would be no in-depth knowledge and information about the built environment. The following section will illustrate how such disciplinary competences can be coordinated and integrated in order to deal with the complexity of urban land use planning that can enable healthy lifestyles and promote quality of life.

Building bridges between health, behaviour and public greenspaces

Experimental and epidemiological studies have assessed the impacts of the built and natural environments on human health and well-being. Although interest in this domain has grown rapidly in recent decades, few empirical studies on the benefits of greenspaces for human beings with both objective and subjective measures have produced cumulative findings (Bowler et al. 2010; Lee and Maheswaran 2010). Furthermore, the diversity of the study design, health outcomes and population groups has meant that the comparison between the results is difficult. This partly explains the current applicability gap between knowledge in public health and practices in urban planning.

Our review of publications found that a restricted disciplinary interpretation of health has hindered the development of a broad understanding of the multiple relations between human behaviour, environmental conditions and positive health effects. These contributions rarely refer to theories or conceptual frameworks. A conceptual framework is interpreted as a way of thinking about a subject in order to interpret empirical evidence about it. Hence alternative conceptual frameworks can exist. These frameworks can be derived from literature reviews, observational studies or other kinds of empirical research. A broad conceptual framework is proposed in Figure 6.3 (on the right side) and is meant to replace the piecemeal approach represented on the left side. Without this kind of framework empirical contributions on this topic will continue to be completed without cumulative knowledge production.

In principle, a conceptual framework like that shown on the right of Figure 6.3 can be used to generate two explanatory models. A model refers to a description or representation of a phenomenon, such as the plausible pathways between the provision of public greenspace, health promoting behaviour and positive health outcomes. A conceptual model like that presented by Hoehner et al. (2003) represents the multiple processes and pathways between those key variables that should be taken into account in order to understand the multiple relations between health promoting behaviours in natural settings and possible positive health outcomes. This approach is explicitly interdisciplinary involving epidemiology, human ecology, medical sciences, psychology and sociology. A different model like that proposed by Morris et al. (2006) can be formulated for policy decision-makers and professional practitioners in health promotion, landscape architecture and greenspace management order to show how their decisions can promote health in precise localities. These two kinds of models are the concern of numerous research groups in several countries including the consortium of the PHENOTYPE project.[1]

Using the second kind of model it will be possible to involve different types of stakeholders during the project lifespan with the objective to integrate three different kinds of knowledge:

1. Knowledge from scientific research.
2. Knowledge/know-how of professional practitioners.
3. The tacit knowledge of stakeholders and citizens.

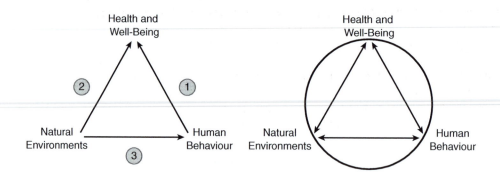

Figure 6.3   The relations (shown as 1) between the positive health impacts of certain human behaviours (physical activity, social interaction, leisure) on health have been established by a large number of empirical studies. The positive impact of nature on human health (shown as 2) has been assumed and studied by numerous uncoordinated studies in the social and psychological sciences but the accumulated evidence remains unclear. There is very little coordinated empirical research (shown as 3) which has concluded that natural environments are the catalysts of health promoting human behaviours that do lead to positive health outcomes. An integrated conceptual framework (shown on the right) should replace the piecemeal approach (shown on the left) that has dominated contributions to date

Source: Lawrence.

This is an explicit way of bridging the divide between scientists, professionals and the public in order to generate recommendations and guidelines for landscape architecture, greenspace management, urban planning and health promotion.

Conclusions: synthesis

This chapter has argued and illustrated that current shortcomings of traditional scientific research and professional practice are not necessarily the result of the lack of political commitment, or financial resources, or viable solutions. They are, above all, the logical outcome of the narrow vision of so-called experts who do not address fundamental issues but only topics isolated from their societal context. In order to deal with these limitations, various sets of obstacles need to be revised or dismantled. First, ontological frameworks or world-views that do not embrace the complexity of the natural and built environment should be challenged. Second, knowledge that only values rational, utilitarian approaches to interpret the layout, use and management of human and natural ecosystems should be questioned. Third, the specialisation, segmentation and bureaucratisation of knowledge and expertise need to be replaced by more collaboration. And finally, the lack of transfer and communication between researchers, professionals, politicians, interest groups and the public needs to be overcome.

There is a need to reconsider the knowledge base that made possible the twentieth-century revolution in health in order to deal not only with many kinds of infectious diseases but also the increasing burden of non-communicable diseases (Rayner and Lang 2012). In order to move towards this goal, this chapter has argued that there is a need for conceptual clarification, and methodological rigour using a combination of qualitative and quantitative approaches. It has also argued that there is an urgent need for more coordination between disciplines and professions, because health and well-being are not limited to health services or the medical sciences. In addition, a major barrier to the design and construction of built environments that support health is the strong tendency for architects, planners and policy makers to focus too narrowly on aesthetic and technical criteria without referring to a holistic framework, without understanding the contextual conditions of the site location, and without considering the dialectics of people–health–environment relations at the local and regional levels.

This chapter has also shown that interdisciplinary and transdisciplinary contributions can contribute to broaden current understanding because they enable the cross-fertilisation of different contributions that can promote an enlarged vision of architecture and urban planning for health and well-being. Transdisciplinarity is a way of achieving innovative goals, enriched understanding and a synergy of new methods, which are essential if current understanding of healthy human habitats is to be applied in policy definition and during the implementation of urban planning.

Note

1 www.phenotype.eu

References

Bowler, D.E., Buyung-Ali, L.M., Knight, T.M. and Pullin, A.S. 2010. A systematic review of evidence for the added benefits to health of exposure to natural environments. *BMC Public Health*, Vol. 10, No. 1, p. 456.

Dannenberg, A., Frumkin, H. and Jackson, R. (eds.) 2011. *Making healthy places: designing and building for health, well-being, and sustainability*. Washington, DC: Island Press.

Hamilton, D. and Watkins, D. 2009. *Evidence-based design for multiple building types*. Hoboken, NJ: John Wiley.

Hardoy, J., Mitlin, D. and Satterthwaite, D. 2001. *Environmental problems in an urbanizing world*. London: Earthscan.

Hartig, T. and Lawrence, R. 2003. Introduction: the residential context of health. *Journal of Social Issues*, Vol. 59, pp. 455–473 (special issue).

Heath, T. 1984. *Method in architecture*. Chichester, UK: John Wiley.

Hoehner, C.M., Brennan, L.K., Brownson, R.C., Handy, S.L. and Killingsworth, R. 2003. Opportunities for integrating public health and urban planning approaches to promote active community environments. *American Journal of Health Promotion*, Vol. 18, No. 1, pp. 14–20.

Lawrence, R. 1987. *Housing, dwellings and homes: design theory, research and practice*. Chichester, UK: John Wiley.

Lawrence, R. 1996. Urban environment, health and the economy: cues for conceptual clarification and more effective policy implementation. In C. Price and A. Tsouros (eds.) *Our cities, our future: policies and action plans for health and sustainable development*. Copenhagen: World Health Organization Regional Office for Europe, pp. 38–64.

Lawrence, R. 2001. Human ecology. In K. Tolba (ed.) *Our fragile world: challenges and opportunities for sustainable development, vol. 1*. Eloss: Oxford, pp. 675–693.

Lawrence, R. 2002. Healthy residential environments. In R. Bechtel and A. Churchman (eds.) *Handbook of environmental psychology*, New York: John Wiley, pp. 394–412.

Lawrence, R. 2010. Deciphering interdisciplinary and transdisciplinary contributions. *Journal of Engineering and Science*, Vol. 1, No. 1, pp. 125–130.

Lee, A. and Maheswaran, R. 2010. The health benefits of urban green spaces: a review of the evidence. *Journal of Public Health*, Vol. 33, No. 2, pp. 212–222.

Loudon, I.S. (ed.) 1997. *Western medicine: an illustrated history*. Oxford: Oxford University Press.

Morris, G., Beck, S., Hanlon, P. and Robertson, P. 2006. Getting strategic about the environment and health. *Public Health*, Vol. 120, pp. 889–907.

Pinson, D. 2004. Urban planning: an 'undisciplined' discipline? *Futures*, Vol. 36, No. 4, pp. 503–513.

Pressman, N. and Tennyson, J. 1983. Dilemmas facing social scientists and designers. *Journal of Architectural Education*, Vol. 36, No. 4, pp. 16–21.

Rayner, G. and Lang, T. 2012. *Ecological public health: reshaping the conditions of good health*. Abingdon, UK and New York: Routledge.

Reizenstein, J. 1975. Linking social research and design, *Journal of Architectural Research*, Vol. 4, No. 3, pp. 26–38.

Rittel, H.W. and Webber, M.M. 1973. Dilemmas in a general theory of planning. *Policy Sciences*, Vol. 4, pp. 155–169.

Rodwin, L. and Sanyal, B. 2000. *The profession of city planning: changes, images and challenges, 1950–2000*. New Brunswick, NJ: Rutgers University Press.

Zeisel, J. 1981. *Inquiry by design: tools for environment-behavior research*. Belmont, CA: Brooks/Cole Publishing.

Zeisel, J. 2006. *Inquiry by design: environment/behavior/neuroscience in architecture, interiors, landscape and planning*. New York: W.W. Norton.

PART II

The human experience

Overview by Susan Thompson

This section of the book examines the human experience of place, unpacking the health implications of the physical and socio-cultural qualities of the settlements that planners plan and manage. Authors from both sides of the globe present the latest research on how health is supported, and conversely hindered, by where we live, work, recreate and the spaces in between. Design for active lives is a key component, particularly how we travel from place to place, as well as the neighbourhoods in which we make our homes. And this is not just about the utilitarian activities of daily living – it is also about creating playful environments for enjoyment and pleasure across the generations. In addition, our surroundings are critical in supporting good mental health. Being and feeling safe in the places we inhabit on a daily basis is foundational to the healthy city. So too is being able to access nutritious and culturally appropriate food grown and harvested in ways that sustain planetary systems to produce adequate food for future generations. And underpinning all of these is equity – those with the greatest needs in our communities are the ones who suffer the most adverse health impacts.

Health inequalities and the role of the physical and social environment

In the opening chapter Matilda Allen and Jessica Allen focus our attention on equity. There are stark health contrasts between rich and poor countries, as well as regional differences within nations, relating both to life expectancy, and the number of 'disability-free' years that people can expect to enjoy as they age. The environmental conditions in which people grow up, live and work, together with their access to power, money and resources, are all key predictors in determining an individual's health trajectory over the life course. Allen and Allen examine the latest research evidence in five key areas in considering how this plays out. Housing conditions – especially temperature control, overcrowding and affordability – have serious implications for physical and mental health. So too does access to different modes of active transport, the ability to purchase sufficient nutritious food and enjoyment of adequate greenspace in the local neighbourhood. The social environment, particularly as it relates to community cohesion, isolation and social capital, is also scrutinised. Suggested policy interventions to address health inequities are presented. Allen and Allen's chapter sets the scene for many of the discussions throughout this book, giving the reader a solid basis from which to consider how access to resources impacts on health in multiple ways for all.

Active travel: its fall and rise

In this chapter Adrian Davis and John Parkin give the reader a broad overview of active travel as one of the most important aspects of a healthy built environment. They begin by reminding us that transport involves movement and consequently just how important travel modes are on human health. The dangers of insufficient activity levels are well known, as are the health benefits of regular cycling and walking, the rates of which vary across cities and nations. Getting people physically active on a daily basis, as part of their transport to and from work, school and other activities, is critical for good health. With the use of sophisticated social and psychological models of behaviour we are gaining a better understanding of how to encourage this to occur. Healthier travel patterns also underpin environmental sustainability which can be a further motivation for their uptake – both by the individual and the policy maker. Recognising the different disciplinary backgrounds of those with interests in active transport, Davis and Parkin explore current arguments around the nature of research evidence and, importantly, its translation into policy. This sets the scene for much of the detailed planning and design issues explored in the following chapter.

The influence of urban design and planning on physical activity

Billie Giles-Corti, Sarah Foster, Mohammad Javad Koohsari, Jacinta Francis and Paula Hooper come together to present Chapter 9. This team from Australia provides the key research evidence about how specific urban design interventions and planning policies encourage and support active lifestyles across different population groups. A range of built environment attributes are associated with higher levels of physical activity, including walking for transport and recreation. Connected streets, environments safe from traffic and crime, and a well maintained network of footpaths and cycle paths are all part of the picture. So too are walkable destinations where it is easy to access nearby shops, services and public transport. In combination with higher density housing, the research shows that such environments encourage short trips undertaken on foot which are important for physical and mental health. Active recreation is influenced by neighbourhood aesthetics, as well as a network of local public open spaces, but other factors such as convenience play a role as well. The chapter concludes with an example from Western Australia of how these environmental attributes are being implemented in residential neighbourhoods to support healthy behaviour as part of everyday living.

Healthy play for all ages in public open spaces

Play is an activity we often associate with children and leave behind when we become adults. Lamine Mahdjoubi and Ben Spencer show that this need not be the case. Indeed, we can all enjoy playful activities across the life course, together with the resultant physical and mental health benefits. For children, play has an important role in their motor skill and social development. For older people, play can enhance cognitive function, fitness and community belonging. Play involves physical activity and social interaction. It is a state of mind encompassing an engagement in the moment, either alone or in company, where happiness is experienced and contributes to good health. The role of public spaces in supporting play and the importance of spaces, such as streets, for informal play, are explored. So too are the environmental, land use and cultural restrictions on play – the latter particularly related to risk aversion by care takers. The chapter concludes with an overview of design considerations for policy makers to use in ensuring that we have places across our cities for playfulness to thrive.

Mental well-being and the influence of place

How do the places we inhabit affect our mental health, which in turn impacts on our physical well-being? Libby Burton provides us with a comprehensive overview in this chapter. She considers a range of mental health issues from happiness, comfort and relief from mental fatigue, to stress, anxiety, depression and dementia. Burton discusses the research on aspects of the built environment exploring both the positive and negative impacts for mental health. Her coverage highlights different mechanisms that explain the indirect relationships between the built environment and mental well-being. The list includes physical activity, social engagement, privacy, contact with nature, accessibility, attachment and belonging, autonomy and independence and equity. There is a wide range of built environment characteristics that influence mental well-being either directly or indirectly. Research evidence is presented in relation to residential density, the mix of uses, including proximity to services and facilities, and street configuration and design. Issues related to housing form, including spaces in dwellings, adequacy of daylight and the ability to keep homes warm or cool and insulated against excessive noise, are all explored. The incorporation of greenery is a critical factor in enhancing mental health, as is the safety of the environment, which is explored in the next chapter.

Crime and community safety: challenging the design consensus

It has been argued that safety is the foundation of a healthy city. If citizens are worried about their safety as they move about local neighbourhoods and beyond, they will curtail their activities, reducing the extent of their physical activity and interaction with others. This will be detrimental to health. Paul Cozens contends that planners need to have a better understanding of environmental criminology theories and research, which challenge the assumption that high-density, mixed-use and permeable developments always reduce crime. He engages with the concepts of first and second generation of Crime Prevention Through Environmental Design (commonly known as CPTED), showing how it is often misinterpreted and misapplied. The chapter considers how an environmental criminology perspective can assist in promoting well-being, as well as the planning, design and management of safer, healthier and more sustainable cities. Cozens concludes that the incidence of crime is most likely to be reduced if planners are better educated about its complex nature. In turn this will enhance the opportunity to create a healthy built environment.

The role of planning and design in advancing a bio-nutrition-sensitive food system

The final chapter in this section focuses on food, diet and health. Jane Dixon and Emily Ballantyne-Brodie do this in a fascinating way with their examination of 'food systems' which they link to human health and environmental sustainability. They define a health promoting food system as one that guarantees food and nutrition security. In addition, the health of the environment must be protected so that future generations can be guaranteed their food security. This is a 'bio-nutrition-sensitive' food system, which contrasts to a 'food yield driven' system that functions irrespective of health and environmental impacts. Dixon and Ballantyne-Brodie argue that industrial food systems are creating three public health problems: malnutrition; inferior mental well-being/psycho-social anxiety; and bio-physical degradation. They then unpack the planning policy and practice dimensions of each. And while it is acknowledged that urban planning is part of the problem, the chapter shows how it contributes to the solution. There are three planning domains here – planning for food system diversity; planning for social inclusion and participation; and planning for agri-environmental sustainability. The chapter concludes with a design-led food community approach that has at its core an integrative methodology.

7

HEALTH INEQUALITIES AND THE ROLE OF THE PHYSICAL AND SOCIAL ENVIRONMENT

Matilda Allen and Jessica Allen

Introduction: health inequalities and the social determinants of health

The places where people live have significant effects on the quality of their lives, and consequently their health. Indeed, physical and social environments are important determinants of health. The quality of environments also closely relates to inequalities across population health status. This chapter sets out how physical and social environments shape health outcomes and inequalities in five key areas – housing, transport, social environment, healthy food and greenspace. While these are not the only areas where environments impact on health, they are critical.

In 2008, *Closing the Gap in a Generation* (Commission on the Social Determinants of Health) reported on global health inequalities and priorities for action. Two years later this analysis was followed by reviews for England – 'The Marmot Review' (The Marmot Review Team 2010) – and in 2013, for the World Health Organization (WHO) European region (The Institute of Health Equity 2013).

These reports describe the avoidable and unnecessary inequalities in health and life expectancy both within and between countries. For example, there is a difference of 36 years between the life expectancy of Sierra Leone (47 years) and Japan (83 years) (WHO 2013b). There is a difference of 17 years in male life expectancy between the richest and poorest countries in Europe (The Institute of Health Equity 2013). In many nations, there are even larger differences in 'disability-free' or 'healthy' life expectancy – the number of years a person can expect to live in good health.

Inequities in health and mortality are not simply the results of genetic variation, or access to health care. They are influenced by the conditions in which people are born, grow, live, work and age. They are also impacted by inequities in power, money and resources.

Improving health and reducing inequalities requires effective action on the social determinants of health. The Marmot Review (The Marmot Review Team 2010) set out the responses needed, defined in reference to six broad policy areas as follows:

1. Ensure every child has the best start in life.
2. Enable all children, young people and adults to maximise their capabilities and have control over their lives.
3. Create fair employment and good work for all.

4.   Ensure a healthy standard of living for all.
5.   Create and develop healthy and sustainable places and communities.
6.   Strengthen the role and impact of ill health prevention.

The social gradient and proportionate universalism

There is a clear relationship between income and health. This means that everyone, except the wealthiest members of a society, is likely to experience slightly worse health than those who are marginally better off. This is known as the 'social gradient' in health and is observable within most countries. Figure 7.1 illustrates the 'social gradient' of health in England in 2003. It also shows the steeper social class gradient in disability-free life expectancy. Not only are most people dying sooner than the wealthiest, they are spending more of their shorter life with life limiting disabilities.

Proportionate universalism refers to the strategy of implementing interventions and strategies at a population level, but with an intensity proportionate to need. Where this is done effectively, it can help to 'level up' the social gradient by having the greatest impact on those who need it most. Simply targeting minimal groups, or those who are most deprived, neglects the 'middle sections' who are also experiencing some degree of health inequity.

The environment as a social determinant of health

The physical and social environments in which people live are key determinants of health. The 2013 Review of Social Determinants and the Health Divide in the WHO European Region (The Institute of Health Equity 2013, p. 94) stated that:

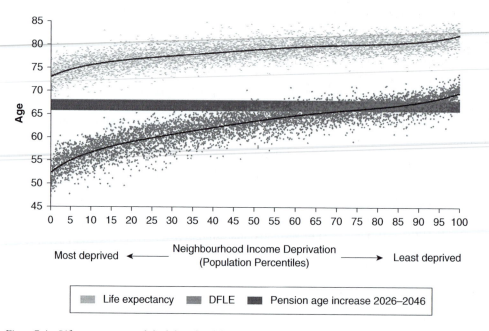

Figure 7.1   Life expectancy and disability-free life expectancy at birth, persons by neighbourhood income level, England, 1999–2003

Source: Office for National Statistics (www.nationalarchives.gov.uk/doc/open–government–licence).

. . . people who are poor and powerless are more likely than those who are better off to live in a poor-quality environment. Their lack of control over where they live exposes them to conditions of daily living that further reduce the control they can exercise over their lives, consequently posing increased risks to their health.

Those living in areas of deprivation are more likely to be exposed to a variety of adverse conditions which negatively affect health. These include:

- biological and chemical contamination;
- air pollution;
- flooding;
- poor sanitation and water scarcity;
- noise pollution;
- road traffic;
- hazardous waste sites;
- places that feel unsafe, unwelcoming and uncongenial;
- scarcity of green space;
- unsafe transport;
- fewer opportunities for healthy activities.

(The Institute of Health Equity 2013)

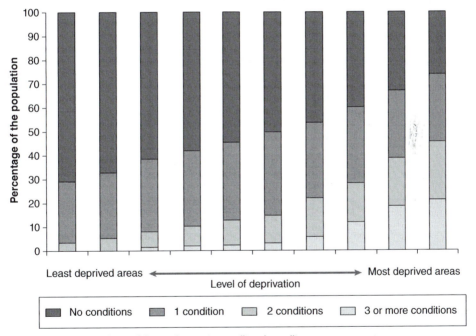

Figure 7.2 Populations living in areas with, in relative terms, the least favourable environmental conditions, 2001–2006

Source: Department for Environment, Food and Rural Affairs (www.nationalarchives.gov.uk/doc/open-government-licence).

Figure 7.2 shows that in the UK, these factors occur more frequently in communities that are more deprived. In the most deprived areas, over 70 per cent of the population experience one or more adverse environmental conditions. These are low river water and air quality, insufficient green space and habitat favourable to biodiversity, flood risk, litter, unsuitable housing conditions, road accidents, and sites used for hazardous purposes. Similar inequities in environmental conditions can also be seen in other countries.

The cumulative health impact of these negative environmental conditions is significant, resulting in shorter and less healthy lives. Poor environmental conditions are a contributor to health inequalities across the world. The evidence linking environmental conditions and health is presented in the rest of this chapter, commencing with housing.

Housing

The buildings in which people live have an immediate and significant effect on their physical and mental well-being. In the WHO European Region alone, inadequate housing is responsible for more than 100,000 deaths each year (Braubach et al. 2011). Housing factors that impact on health include residential location, dwelling type and design (which is important in protecting inhabitants from heat, cold or damp), adequate construction and ongoing maintenance, internal features, crowding, and feeling secure in one's home (The Institute of Health Equity 2013). Affordability is also an issue forcing some to accept less suitable accommodation due to an inadequate supply of good quality affordable housing (Crew 2007). Similarly, high housing costs can increase poverty. At the most extreme, those who are homeless or living in slums are likely to experience significantly worse health outcomes than the rest of the population. The life expectancy of a homeless woman in England is just 47, which is 30 years less than the average of 77 years (Crisis 2011).

To better understand the ways in which housing affects health, we explore the evidence on inequalities and health in two areas – housing design and overcrowding.

Housing design

Housing design is important for keeping houses warm in cold climates and seasons, as well as keeping them cool in hot weather, and reducing damp.

Inequalities

How adequately people's homes protect them from external temperatures is influenced by a variety of factors. These include household income, housing and energy costs in the area, type of ownership (for example private renters may be constrained in making needed adaptations to their housing), energy efficiency of the home (for example insulation), location of residence (for example rural or urban) and country of residence.

There are clear inequalities in the prevalence of fuel poverty. This is where inhabitants are not able to sufficiently heat their home due to the price of energy, limited income, and/or poor energy efficiency of the dwelling. Figure 7.3 shows that amongst the richest households in England, fuel poverty is almost non-existent, whereas nearly 35 per cent of the poorest quintile of households experience fuel poverty. Other at-risk populations include older people, children, those with long-term illnesses and disabilities, and people who spend their days at home such as carers, unemployed and those who are ill (UCL Institute of Health Equity 2011).

Keeping homes cool is also often problematic – globally, there are higher proportions unable to keep their houses comfortably cool in summer than those unable to keep the house warm

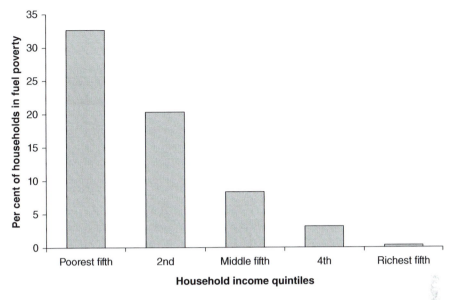

Figure 7.3   The risk of fuel poverty according to household income, 2009

Source: English House Conditions Survey, Department of Communities and Local Government (www. nationalarchives.gov.uk/doc/open–government–licence).

Note: Per cent in fuel poverty relates to households in fuel poverty after deducting housing costs.

in winter (WHO Regional Office for Europe 2012). Extreme heat has an unequal effect, with those on low incomes being more likely to live in areas that are hotter during the summer months (Stern 2006). There is also a gradient in the ability to keep a home cool in summer according to income, as can be seen in Figure 7.4.

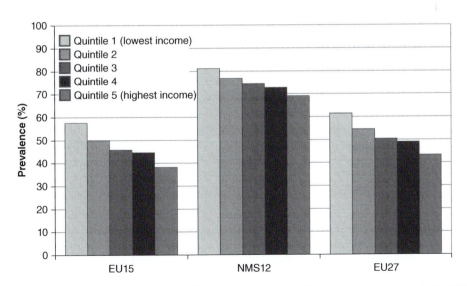

Figure 7.4   Prevalence of inability to keep the home adequately cool in summer by income quintile, 2007

Source: Eurostat.

Health effects

In England and Wales, each centigrade degree reduction in outdoor winter temperature corresponds to an extra 3,500 deaths (Laake and Sverre 1996). This is partly due to cold homes, which are believed to be a principle factor in causing the winter increase in respiratory and circulatory conditions (Power et al. 2009).

A pan-European study found that the most important predictive factors in seasonal variations in mortality rates are differences in indoor temperatures, health care spending and socio-economic circumstances (Healy 2003). Further, international evidence shows that improvements to energy efficiency and reductions of fuel poverty have positive impacts on the mental health of adults and adolescents. These improvements also have significant effects on the physical health of the young, including reduced hospital admissions and assisting sufficient infant weight gain (Liddell and Morris 2010).

Children in bad housing conditions, including cold and damp homes, are more likely to experience poor mental health, contract meningitis, have respiratory problems, and have slow physical growth and cognitive development (Harker and Shelter 2006).

The impact of cold on mental health is particularly disturbing. Residents with bedroom temperatures of 21 degrees centigrade are 50 per cent less likely to suffer depression and anxiety than those with bedroom temperatures of 15 degrees centigrade. This does not, however, control for other potential causes, such as deprivation (Green and Gilbertson 2008). Children in poor quality housing have more psychological distress, and lower motivation, compared to those in better quality housing (Evans et al. 2001).

Similarly, homes that are not adequately ventilated or cooled, and therefore subject residents to damaging high temperatures, can adversely impact health. Uncomfortably high temperatures can reduce mental concentration, elevate stress levels, and increase accident rates. They can also cause fatigue and put an extra burden on heart and other body functions. Those who are over 45, in poor general health, or with a low level of fitness, are most vulnerable to adverse reactions in hot temperatures (Canadian Centre for Occupational Health and Safety 2008).

Overcrowding

Inequalities

Families on lower incomes are more likely to live in overcrowded conditions as they are less likely to be able to afford a home of sufficient size. What is defined as 'overcrowding' varies between countries. In the UK, for example, the law defines overcrowded conditions in relation to room size and occupancy rates (Shelter 2013). In England, 3 per cent of homes are defined as overcrowded. However, in houses headed by an ethnic minority, this rises to 12 per cent (Department for Communities and Local Government 2013).

Figure 7.5 shows that the overcrowding rate varies dramatically between European countries. Further, and most importantly, there is an increased rate of overcrowding amongst those defined as 'at risk of poverty'.

Health effects

Overcrowding is associated with a range of negative health outcomes. For example, an ecological study in several London boroughs between 1982 and 1991 found that for every 1 per cent increase in the number of people living in overcrowded accommodation, the average notification rate for tuberculosis increased by 12 per cent (Mangtani et al. 1995). Overcrowding has also been linked to increased mortality rates, meningitis, respiratory infections, poorer self-rated health and increased stress (Krieger and Higgins 2002).

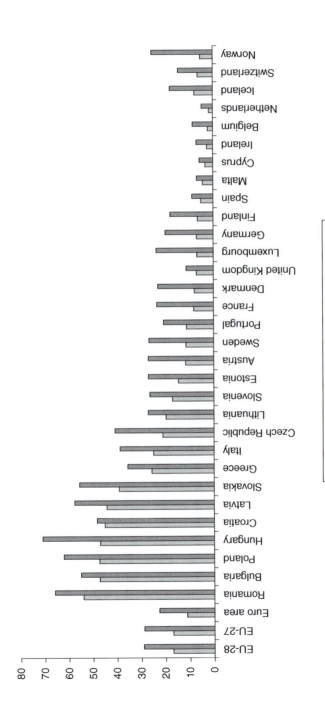

Figure 7.5 Overcrowding rate, 2011 (% of specified population), European countries

* Population below 60 per cent of median equivalised income.

Source: Eurostat 2011.[1]

As well, there are adverse effects of overcrowding on children. Evidence from Brazil shows that when four or more children share a bedroom, they are 2.5 times more likely to suffer from acute respiratory infections (The Acute Respiratory Infections Atlas 2013). Emergency hospital admissions in London for respiratory illness amongst children have been shown to have a strong link to overcrowded conditions (Kyle et al. 2011). Overcrowded housing can also have a negative impact on child development and school performance (Jackson and Roberts 2001).

Box 7.1 Example intervention: improvements to energy efficiency

An important measure to reduce adverse health impacts of cold homes is to improve the energy efficiency of housing stock. Energy improvements for low income households significantly enhance social functioning, and physical and emotional well-being (Raw et al. 2001). Targeting low income populations is likely to be particularly beneficial as it improves their life chances and removes choices such as 'heat or eat'. This is when people have to choose whether to spend limited income on heating costs or other essentials such as food or clothing (Power et al. 2009). American research found poor families reduced spending on food by a similar amount to the extra needed for fuel bills during winter. This resulted in both children and adults consuming 200 less calories a day. In comparison, richer families show increased spending on food during winter (Bhattacharya et al. 2003).

Improving energy efficiency can also have impacts on energy usage, thereby contributing to reduced carbon emissions and potentially mitigating climate change. In Germany, for example, energy use was reduced by 80 per cent in pilot retrofit housing schemes, and the government has plans to retrofit all pre-1983 properties by 2020. This scheme has also been shown to increase jobs, particularly in deprived areas (Lee 2010).

Transport

The availability and quality of different types of transport in a neighbourhood can affect local population health. Here we show how this relationship works in three areas – active travel, public transport and car traffic.

Active travel

Active travel refers to forms of travelling which involve exercise – usually walking and cycling.

Inequalities

Walking and cycling would seem to be universally accessible compared with more 'expensive' forms of travel such as that by private car. However, a range of factors act as barriers to active travel in deprived areas. These include higher (perceived or actual) crime rates; less attractive streets; a lack of walkways, pavements or pedestrianised areas; or the inaccessibility of amenities, services, education and employment within walking or cycling distance. For both walking and cycling, 'lack of time' has also been cited as a barrier to taking part (Kent et al. 2011).

Figure 7.6 shows that the proportion of people cycling in England follows a clear social gradient. While there have been increases in cycling rates, this has not reduced the gradient. Social grade A is the highest socio-economic status, whereas social grade E is the lowest.

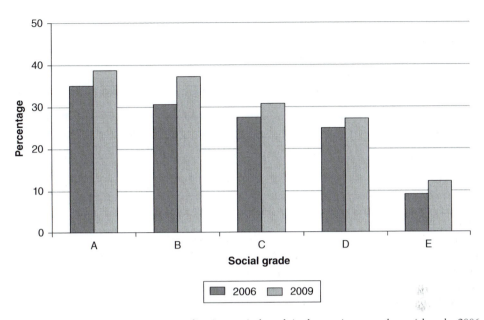

Figure 7.6   Proportion reporting any cycling in a typical week in the previous year, by social grade, 2006 and 2009

Source: Department for Transport.

Health effects

Active travel has a number of health benefits. It can contribute to reductions in overweight and obesity, with consequent improvements in conditions such as heart disease and diabetes. Further, being active reduces the risk of chronic conditions including stroke, cancer and musculoskeletal conditions (Department of Health 2011). Since active travel involves being outside, some of the benefits of spending time in greenspace, outlined below, are also relevant.

Active travel has also been shown to improve mental health and reduce premature death (BMA Science and Education Department 2012). Active commuting, where employees walk or cycle to work, has been shown to reduce sick leave and increase employee loyalty (NICE 2008). Increased walking and cycling have positive social effects, including providing support to local businesses; reducing car travel, pollution and congestion; reducing road danger and noise; and increasing social interaction (Public Health England and Local Government Association 2013).

Public transport

Inequalities

There is not a clear social gradient in public transport use. In developed countries, many of those from lower income groups cannot afford to own a car, and therefore use public transport more than wealthier segments of the population. In some cases, this varies according to type of public transport. For example, a large scale survey in America found that 21 per cent of journeys on rail were made by those on low incomes, compared to 43 per cent of those on buses (American Public Transportation Association 2007). However, for some people, low income and high travel costs can prevent them from using public transport. Figures 7.7a and 7.7b show how transport use varies by income in Great Britain.

In many countries, those living in rural areas are likely to have difficulties accessing good local transport connections. This can increase social isolation, as well as reduce access to jobs and other important destinations. In England, for example, 79 per cent of rural trips are in a car or other private transport, compared to 42 per cent in London (Department for Transport 2010). In Germany, the Netherlands, Denmark and Switzerland, bus and train schedules are synchronised so those in rural areas can more easily commute (Transport 2003). Disabled people are also likely to be particularly disadvantaged by insufficient public transport links or quality (WHO 2011).

Health effects

Effective and affordable public transport systems can have a positive effect on health. Public transport can provide opportunities to work, and access education and other services (UNL Transport Research Consultancy 2000). Effective public transport can allow people to improve social interactions and community cohesion (The Marmot Review Team 2010). It can also

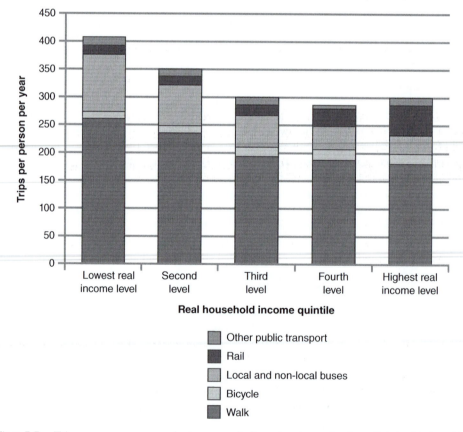

Figure 7.7a   Trips per person per year by income quintile and main mode, Great Britain, 2012: public transport and active travel

Source: Department for Transport 2013.

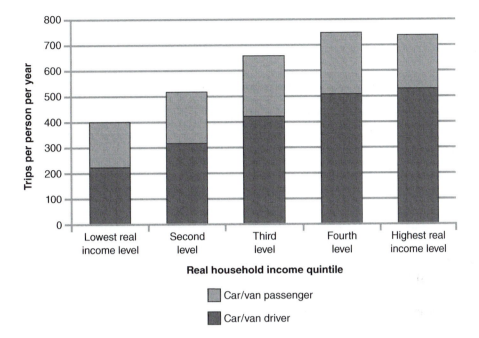

Figure 7.7b   Trips per person per year by income quintile and main mode, Great Britain, 2012: car/van passenger and driver

Source: Department for Transport 2013.

increase physical activity – people are often willing to walk to get to good public transport links, such as light rail stations. However, where transport is expensive or difficult to access, social isolation can be exacerbated, further burdening those already in poverty. Further, there is some evidence that investment in public transit and support for sustainable modes of transport tend to reduce inequities in health (Gorman et al. 2003).

Car traffic

There are three main elements of car traffic that can be detrimental to health – higher levels of pollution, road traffic accidents and reduced active travel rates. This section addresses these elements in relation to inequalities and health.

Inequalities

Pollution follows a social gradient, with poorer communities on average experiencing higher concentrations of pollution. In the UK for example, 66 per cent of carcinogenic chemicals emitted into the air are released in the 10 per cent most deprived areas (The Marmot Review Team 2010). Noise pollution often adds to the environmental burden in more deprived and highly urbanised areas. It has also been shown to be worse in neighbourhoods with high density housing and rented accommodation (Geddes et al. 2011).

Road traffic accidents are also unequally distributed. Children who live in the most deprived localities in the UK are four times more likely to be hit by a car than those who live in the least deprived areas (Grayling and Institute for Public Policy Research 2002). Road traffic injuries and deaths are therefore a major contributor to health inequalities. In particular, the single major avoidable cause of death for children over five is unintentional injury on the roads. The social class gradient in injury across all ages is steeper than for any other cause of death or long-term disability (Gorman et al. 2003).

Health effects

There is clear evidence of the adverse effects of outdoor air pollution, especially for cardio-respiratory mortality and morbidity (Heinrich et al. 2005; Pope 2007). Studies also show that reductions in traffic to reduce air pollution are successful in improving health (Boyce et al. 2009). Further, it has been demonstrated that noise pollution negatively impacts on mental and physical health. Outcomes include increased stress levels and reduced educational attainment by children, as well as increased stress and hypertension in adults (Gorman et al. 2003).

Road traffic accidents create an increase in injury and mortality. In areas where road traffic accidents are particularly frequent, such as areas of high deprivation, life expectancy can decline. In 2010, road traffic injuries caused an estimated 1.24 million deaths worldwide. Deaths from road traffic accidents vary considerably – the death rate per 100,000 that can be attributed to road traffic accidents varies from 53.4 in Namibia to 2.4 in the Maldives (WHO 2013a).

Box 7.2 Example intervention: reduce the car speed limit

Traffic interventions which reduce the density and speed of vehicles can diminish road accidents (Boyce et al. 2009). Many English studies have suggested a 20 miles per hour (mph) speed limit in residential areas (British Academy 2014; Insall 2007; Power et al. 2009; The Marmot Review Team 2010). At this speed, most adults and children survive collisions (British Academy 2014; Richards 2010).

Since it is disproportionately those in more disadvantaged areas who are negatively affected by road traffic accidents, reducing vehicular speed is likely to have a greater impact lower down the social gradient, thereby 'levelling up' outcomes. It has been estimated that, within the UK, there would be 600 fewer deaths nationally if all adults were as likely to be involved in a road traffic collision as those in the highest social class (Christie et al. 2010).

In addition, lower local speed limits are likely to lead to increased active travel due to improved road safety and where appropriate infrastructure is provided, greater uptake of cycling and walking. This then reduces air and noise pollution, as well as increasing neighbourhood connectivity (British Academy 2014).

In Sweden, a speed limit of 18.5 mph is common in residential areas. This has resulted in a significant reduction in road traffic accidents. In contrast, in the USA, road traffic accidents are comparatively high. Residential speed limits vary by state, ranging from 24 to 89 mph. The difference is so significant that, alongside homicides, rates of deaths on the road 'explain a large part of the difference in mortality rates between Sweden ... and the USA' (British Academy 2014).

Social environment

The social environment in which people live has a clear impact on their lives. A good 'social environment' includes community cohesion and a high level of social contacts, strong social capital, and a lack of social isolation. The social environment of an area depends, in part, on its physical design. For example, if places of employment, education, leisure, shopping and other destinations are within a small area, providing easy access for residents, they are more likely to have contact with their local community (Geddes et al. 2011).

Inequalities

The relationship between the social environment and inequalities is not straightforward, as many areas of higher deprivation have thriving communities. However, there is some evidence to show that community capital is lower in areas of deprivation. This includes reduced socialising and low levels of trust in others, particularly in areas that are perceived to be unsafe (Attwood et al. 2003; see Figure 7.8). Lack of money can undermine social activity as some people feel a sense of shame about their environment, increasing social isolation. High relative costs of transport (particularly private car transport) can also deter people from making trips, which is again likely to increase social isolation.

Health outcomes

Social isolation, and a lack of community contact, are themselves important indicators of well-being. However, there is also evidence that shows links between the social environment and physical and mental health. Low levels of social integration and loneliness have been shown to significantly increase mortality – those who are socially isolated are between two and five times more likely to die prematurely compared to those who have strong social ties (Bennett 2002). Social isolation can cause depression and stress, particularly for parents of young people and the elderly population (Allen 2008). Social participation appears to act as a protective factor against dementia and cognitive decline in people over 65 years of age (Bassuk et al. 1999). Social connection can also aid recovery after periods of illness (Halpern 2004).

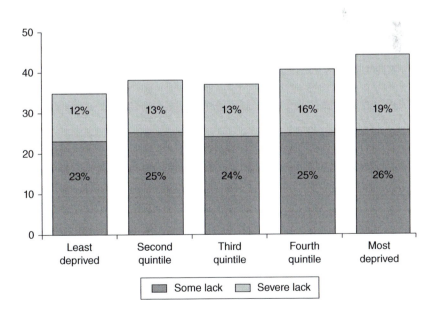

Figure 7.8 Percentage of those lacking social support, by deprivation of residential area, 2005

Source: Health Survey of England (www.nationalarchives.gov.uk/doc/open-government-licence).

Box 7.3 Example intervention: designing local areas to increase social interaction and reduce crime

The design of local areas can have a positive impact on social interactions. Alongside mixed land use, measures that improve safety, such as car traffic control, can make it easier for people to leave their home and interact with the community. This is particularly so for the elderly, disabled and other vulnerable residents (Allen 2008). Similarly, making neighbourhoods easier to get around, and providing good quality, safe greenspace is likely to increase community contact.

The promotion of alternative spaces of contact can be positive for social interaction, for example, 'third places', described as 'places that provide for informal and unorganised social interaction' (Kent et al. 2011). Examples include children's playgrounds, cafes, shopping malls, town squares and transport stops. Third places are areas where social interaction does not depend on predefined roles unlike, for example, more formally defined places where people work or go to school.

Accessibility of healthy food options

Inequalities

Low income and area deprivation are both barriers to purchasing fresh and nutritious foods (Dowler and Dobson 1997), and lower income households are the harder hit by food price fluctuations. The combination of economic and spatial barriers means that people living in areas of deprivation are less likely to have access to healthy diets (Cummins and Macintyre 2006; Friel et al. 2006; Kent et al. 2011). For example, hot food takeaways are generally high in fat and salt, and low in fibre, fruit and vegetables (London Food Board and CIEH 2012). There tends to be a correlation between an area's deprivation and the concentration of fast food outlets (Public Health England, CIEH and Local Government Association 2013). One study showed that per capita provision of McDonald's outlets was four times higher in the most deprived localities compared to those with the least deprivation (Cummins et al. 2005). A study in Melbourne, Australia, revealed that those living in areas with the lowest socio–economic status (SES) had access to two and a half times the number of fast food restaurants than those in the highest SES neighbourhoods (Reidpath et al. 2002).

Health effects

Healthy diets are associated with reduced prevalence of chronic diseases, including diabetes and cancer (Public Health England 2013). Part of the reason for this is that healthy diets are an essential component of reducing obesity, which is a clear cause of chronic disease and early death (The Information Centre 2013).

Further research is needed on the direct links between the food environment and health, although there is some evidence of a relationship (Kent et al. 2011). For example, some American studies have reported a relationship between closer proximity of convenience stores and higher body mass index (BMI) or metabolic syndrome (Dengel et al. 2009; Galvez et al. 2009). Zenk et al. (2009) have showed that those who have access to a large grocery store in their neighbourhood tend to eat more fruit and vegetables each day.

Box 7.4 Example intervention: changing the food environment around schools

A study of middle and high school students in California found that children whose schools were within the vicinity of fast food restaurants were more likely to be overweight or obese, and eat less fruit and vegetables (Daniel et al. 2010). This applied even after controlling for student and school level characteristics. Obese children are more likely to become obese adults (Serdula et al. 1993), and obesity in both child- and adulthood is related to a range of negative health outcomes. For this reason, it is important to consider the food environment around schools, particularly those where students tend to leave the premises to buy lunch (Public Health England et al. 2013). These considerations, and their likely impact on health, have been recognised by the UK-based National Institute for Health and Care Excellence (NICE) guidance *Prevention of Cardiovascular Disease*, which states that planning authorities should 'restrict planning permission for takeaways and other food retail outlets in specific areas (for example, within walking distance of schools)' (NICE 2010). This may also have other positive effects, as a greater prevalence of hot food takeaways or fast food outlets can increase litter and food waste, potentially attracting animals and pests. There is also an increase in night time noise and traffic congestion (Public Health England et al. 2013).

Greenspace

Inequalities

Research indicates there is an association between proximity to greenspace and inequalities. Twenty per cent of the most affluent neighbourhoods in England have five times the amount of greenspace than the most deprived 10 per cent neighbourhoods (CABE 2010b). Income deprivation related health inequalities were found to be lower in populations living in the greenest areas (Mitchell and Popham 2008).

There may also be a decreasing use of greenspace across the social gradient. A survey of over 4,500 people across nine countries found that 29 per cent of respondents reported spending less time in parks than they did five years previously. Fifty-seven per cent thought this generation of children spent less time in parks than they did when they were youngsters. Eighty-nine per cent of respondents considered access to greenspace a human right (Husqvarna Group 2013).

Health effects

Numerous studies point to the direct benefits of greenspace to both physical and mental health and well-being (Croucher et al. 2007; Greenspace Scotland 2008; Pretty et al. 2007).

Reduced hospital admissions for mental illness have been associated with access to higher levels of greenspace, even after controlling for deprivation and population density (Wheater et al. 2007). There is evidence of preventive, psychological, physical and social benefits of engagement with the natural environment for people suffering from mental illness and dementia (Clark et al. 2013). Less greenspace in a living environment is associated with greater risk of anxiety and depression, feelings of loneliness and perceived shortage of social support (Maas et al. 2009). Contact with nature is linked with improved mood, and reduced stress, anxiety and severity of attention deficit hyperactivity disorder (ADHD) symptoms in children (CABE 2010a).

Additionally, people living in urban areas with greater amounts of greenspace show significantly lower mental distress and higher well-being when compared to those in neighbourhoods lacking greenspace (White et al. 2013).

A Dutch study of over 10,000 people showed that those who lived in a greener environment reported better physical and mental health (de Vries et al. 2003). Other research found that access to greenspaces can reduce all-cause mortality in low income communities (Mitchell and Popham 2008). Evidence from Japan shows that the longevity of older people increased by having walkable greenspace near their home. This applied independently of SES (Takano et al. 2002).

Conclusions: towards an equitable planning system

The physical and social environments in which people live have a clear and direct impact on their physical and mental health. This is not distributed fairly. Those living in areas of deprivation and/or poverty are more likely to be exposed to environmental conditions and circumstances that negatively impact upon their health. In this chapter, inequities in distribution or quality, and consequent health effects, have been discussed in relation to five topics – housing, transport, the social environment, food access and greenspace. Example interventions to demonstrate and motivate action at a local and national level are also presented.

Good planning systems that emphasise equity are essential in reducing the negative impact of health-damaging environments so that health inequalities are addressed and ameliorated. Equitable planning systems, which include multiple sectors, can also help to reduce poverty. This can occur through improving access to employment and services, decreasing the amount of money spent on domestic temperature control by insulating homes, and fostering cheap accessible transport systems. Action is needed by a range of organisations in order to ensure that the environments in which people live have a positive impact on their health and well-being.

Note

1 EU-28 refers to the current 28 EU Member States. EU-27 refers to the 27 EU Member States before Croatia joined in 2013.

References

Allen, J. 2008. *Older people and well-being*. London: IPPR.

American Public Transportation Association. 2007. *A profile of public transportation passenger demographics and travel characteristics reported in on-board surveys*. Washington DC: APTA.

Attwood, C., Singh, G., Prime, D., Creasey, R. and Great Britain Home Office Research Development Statistics Directorate. 2003. *2001 Home Office citizenship survey: people, families and communities*. London: Home Office Research and Statistics Directorate.

Bassuk, S.S., Glass, T.A., and Berkman, L.F. 1999. Social disengagement and incident cognitive decline in community-dwelling elderly persons. *Annals of Internal Medicine, 131*(3), 165–173.

Bennett, K.M. 2002. Low level social engagement as a precursor of mortality among people in later life. *Age and Ageing, 31*(3), 165–168.

Bhattacharya, J., DeLeire, T., Haider, S. and Currie, J. 2003. Heat or eat? Cold weather shock and nutrition in poor American families. *American Journal of Public Health, 93*(7), 1149–1154.

BMA Science and Education Department. 2012. *Healthy transport = healthy lives*. London: British Medical Association.

Boyce, T., Patel, S. and The Kings Fund. 2009. *The health impacts of spatial planning decisions*. London: The King's Fund.

Braubach, M., Jacobs, D. and Ormandy, D. 2011. *Environmental burden of diease associated with inadequate housing: a method guide to the quantification of health effects of selected housing risks in the WHO European region*. Copenhagen: WHO Regional Office for Europe.

British Academy. 2014. 'If you could do one thing . . .' Nine local actions to reduce health inequalities. Retrieved 07/04/2014, from www.britac.ac.uk/policy/Health_Inequalities.cfm

CABE. 2010a. *Community green: using local spaces to tackle inequality and improve health*. London: Chartered Association of Building Engineers.

CABE. 2010b. *Urban green nation: building the evidence base*. London: Chartered Association of Building Engineers.

Canadian Centre for Occupational Health and Safety. 2008. Hot environments: health effects. Retrieved 19/01/2014, from www.ccohs.ca/oshanswers/phys_agents/heat_health.html

Christie, N., Ward, H., Kimberlee, R., Lyons, R., Towner, E., Hayes, M., Robertson, S. and Rana, S. 2010. *Road traffic injury risk in disadvantaged communities: evaluation of the neighbourhood road safety initiative*. London: Department for Transport.

Clark, P., Mapes, N., Burt, J. and Preston, S. 2013. *Greening dementia: a literature review of the benefits and barriers facing individuals living with dementia in accessing the natural environment and local greenspace*. Worcester: Natural England.

Commission on the Social Determinants of Health. 2008. *Closing the gap in a generation: health equity through action on the social determinants of health. Final report of the Commission on Social Determinants of Health*. Geneva: World Health Organization.

Crew, D. 2007. *The Tenants' Dilemma – Warning: your home is at risk if you dare complain*. Liverpool: Citizen Advice Bureau.

Crisis. 2011. Homelessness: a silent killer – a research briefing on mortality amongst homeless people. Retrieved 19/01/2014, from www.crisis.org.uk/data/files/publications/Homelessness%20-%20a%20 silent%20killer.pdf

Croucher, K., Myers, L. and Bretherton, J. 2007. *The links between greenspace and health: a critical literature review*. Stirling: Greenspace Scotland.

Cummins, S. and Macintyre, S. 2006. Food environments and obesity: neighbourhood or nation? *International Journal of Epidemiology, 35*(1), 100–104.

Cummins, S., McKay, L. and Macintyre, S. 2005. McDonald's restaurants and neighborhood deprivation in Scotland and England. *American Journal of Preventive Medicine, 29*(4), 308–310.

Daniel, M., Paquet, C., Auger, N., Zang, G. and Kestens, Y. 2010. Association of fast-food restaurant and fruit and vegetable store densities with cardiovascular mortality in a metropolitan population. *European Journal of Epidemiology, 25*(10), 711–719.

de Vries, S., Verheij, R.A., Groenewegen, P.P. and Spreeuwenberg, P. 2003. Natural environments – healthy environments? An exploratory analysis of the relationship between greenspace and health. *Environment and Planning A, 35*(10), 1717–1731.

Dengel, D.R., Hearst, M.O., Harmon, J.H., Forsyth, A. and Lytle, L.A. 2009. Does the built environment relate to the metabolic syndrome in adolescents? *Health Place, 15*(4), 946–951.

Department for Communities and Local Government. 2013. *English housing survey: households. Annual report on England's households, 2011–2012*. London: Department for Communities and Local Government.

Department of Health. 2011. *Start active, stay active: a report on physical activity from the four home countries' chief medical officers*. London: Department of Health.

Department for Transport. 2010. Travel in urban and rural areas: personal travel factsheet – March 2010. Retrieved 20/01/2014, from www.gov.uk/government/uploads/system/uploads/attachment_data/file/230556/Travel_in_urban_and_rural_areas_personal_travel_factsheet___March_2010.pdf

Department for Transport. 2013. National travel survey 2012: NTS0705. Retrieved 20/01/2014, from www.gov.uk/government/publications/national-travel-survey-2012

Dowler, E.A. and Dobson, B.M. 1997. Nutrition and poverty in Europe: an overview. *Proceedings of the Nutrition Society, 56*(1A), 51–62.

Eurostat. 2011. Overcrowding rate, European Commission. Retrieved 19/01/2014, from http://epp.eurostat.ec.europa.eu/statistics_explained/index.php?title=File:Overcrowding_rate,_2011_%28%25_of_specified_population%29_YB14.pngandfiletimestamp=20131210161924

Evans, G., Saltzman, H. and Cooperman, J. (2001). Housing quality and children's socioemotional health. *Environmental Behaviour, 33*(3), 389–399.

Friel, S., Walsh, O. and McCarthy, D. 2006. The irony of a rich country: issues of financial access to and availability of healthy food in the Republic of Ireland. *Journal of Epidemiology and Community Health, 60*(12), 1013–1019.

Galvez, M.P., Hong, L., Choi, E., Liao, L., Godbold, J. and Brenner, B. 2009. Childhood obesity and neighborhood food-store availability in an inner-city community. *Academic Pediatriatrics, 9*(5), 339–343.

Geddes, I., Allen, J., Allen, M. and Morrisey, L. 2011. The Marmot Review: implications for spatial planning. Retrieved 19/01/2014, from www.nice.org.uk/nicemedia/live/12111/53895/53895.pdf

Gorman, D., Douglas, M.J., Conway, L., Noble, P. and Hanlon, P. (2003). Transport policy and health inequalities: a health impact assessment of Edinburgh's transport policy. *Public Health, 117*(1), 15–24.

Grayling, T. and Institute for Public Policy Research. 2002. *Streets ahead: safe and liveable streets for children.* London: IPPR.

Green, G. and Gilbertson, J. 2008. *Warm front: better health – health impact evaluation of the warm front scheme.* Sheffield: Sheffield Hallam University, Centre for Regional Social and Economic Research.

Greenspace Scotland. 2008. *Green space and quality of life: a critical literature review.* Stirling: Greenspace Scotland.

Halpern, D. 2004. *Social capital.* Cambridge: Polity.

Harker, L. and Shelter. 2006. *Chance of a lifetime: the impact of bad housing on children's lives.* London: Shelter.

Healy, J.D. 2003. Excess winter mortality in Europe: a cross country analysis identifying key risk factors. *Journal of Epidemiology and Community Health, 57*(10), 784–789.

Heinrich, J., Schwarze, P.E. and Stilianakis, N. 2005. Studies on health effects of transport-related air pollution. In M. Krzyzanowski, B. Kuna-Dibbert, J. Schneider and World Health Organization Regional Office for Europe (Eds.), *Health effects of transport-related air pollution*: Copenhagen: World Health Organization Europe.

Husqvarna Group. 2013. Global green space report. Retrieved 19/01/2014, from http://greenspacereport.com/pdf/Husqvarna_Global_Green_Space_Report_2013.pdf.html

Insall, P. 2007. Walking and cycling. In N. Cavill and F. National Heart (Eds.), *Building health: creating and enhancing places for healthy active lives: what needs to be done?* London: National Heart Forum.

Jackson, A. and Roberts, P. 2001. Physical housing conditions and the well-being of children. Background paper. Ottawa, ON: Canadian Council on Social Development. Retrieved 19/01/2014, from www.ccsd.ca/pubs/2001/pcc2001/housing.htm

Kent, J., Thompson, S.M. and Jalaludin, B. 2011. *Healthy built environments: a review of the literature.* Sydney: Healthy Built Environments Program, City Futures Research Centre, UNSW.

Krieger, J. and Higgins, D.L. 2002. Housing and health: time again for public health action. *American Journal of Public Health, 92*(5), 758–768.

Kyle, R.G., Kukanova, M., Campbell, M., Wolfe, I., Powell, P. and Callery, P. 2011. Childhood disadvantage and emergency admission rates for common presentations in London: an exploratory analysis. *Archives of Disease in Childhood, 96*(3), 221–226.

Laake, K. and Sverre, J.M. 1996. Winter excess mortality: a comparison between Norway and England plus Wales. *Age Ageing, 25*(5), 343–348.

Lee, M. 2010. LSE's Anne Power: My recipe for 80 per cent energy savings in your home. Retrieved 08/14/2014, from www.theecologist.org

Liddell, C. and Morris, C. 2010. Fuel poverty and human health: a review of recent evidence. *Energy Policy, 38*(6), 2987–2997.

London Food Board and CIEH. 2012. *Takeaways toolkit.* A London Food Board and Chartered Institute of Environmental Health publication based on a consultancy report by Food Matters. London.

Maas, J., Verheij, R.A., de Vries, S., Spreeuwenberg, P., Schellevis, F.G. and Groenewegen, P.P. 2009. Morbidity is related to a green living environment. *Journal of Epidemiology and Community Health, 63*(12), 967–973.

Mangtani, P., Jolley, D.J., Watson, J.M. and Rodrigues, L.C. 1995. Socioeconomic deprivation and notification rates for tuberculosis in London during 1982–91. *BMJ, 310*(6985), 963–966.

Mitchell, R. and Popham, F. 2008. Effect of exposure to natural environment on health inequalities: an observational population study. *Lancet, 372*(9650), 1655–1660.

NICE. 2008. *Promoting physical activity in the workplace.* Manchester: National Institute for Health and Care Excellence.

NICE. 2010. *Prevention of cardiovascular disease.* Manchester: National Institute for Health and Care Excellence.

Pope, C.A. 2007. Mortality effects of longer term exposures to fine particulate air pollution: review of recent epidemiological evidence. *Inhalation Toxicology, 19*, 33–38.

Power, A., Davis, J., Plant, P. and Kjellstrom, T. 2009. *The built environment and health inequalities. Task group submission to the Marmot Review.* London: The Marmot Review.

Pretty, J., Peacock, J., Hine, R., Sellens, M., South, N. and Griffin, M. 2007. Green exercise in the UK countryside: effects on health and psychological well-being, and implications for policy and planning. *Journal of Environmental Planning and Management, 50*(2), 211–231.

Public Health England. 2013. About obesity. Retrieved 19/01/2014, from www.noo.org.uk/NOO_about_obesity/lifestyle

Public Health England, CIEH and Local Government Association. 2013. *Obesity and the environment: regulating the growth of fast food outlets*. London: Public Health England.

Public Health England and Local Government Association. 2013. *Obesity and the environment: increasing physical activity and active travel*. London: Public Health England.

Raw, G., Aizlewood, C.E. and Hamilton, R.M. 2001. *Building regulation health and safety*. Watford, UK: Building Research Establishment and Department for the Environment, Transport and the Regions.

Reidpath, D.D., Burns, C., Garrard, J., Mahoney, M. and Townsend, M. 2002. An ecological study of the relationship between social and environmental determinants of obesity. *Health Place, 8*(2), 141–145.

Richards, D. 2010. Relationship between speed and risk of fatal injury: pedestrians and car occupations. Road Safety Web Publication No. 16. Retrieved 19/01/2014, from http://assets.dft.gov.uk/publications/pgr-roadsafety-research-rsrr-theme5-researchreport16-pdf/rswp116.pdf

Serdula, M.K., Ivery, D., Coates, R.J., Freedman, D.S., Williamson, D.F. and Byers, T. 1993. Do obese children become obese adults? A review of the literature. *Preventative Medicine, 22*(2), 167–177.

Shelter. 2013. Overcrowding. Retrieved 19/01/2014, from http://england.shelter.org.uk/get_advice/repairs_and_bad_conditions/home_safety/overcrowding

Stern, N. 2006. *The economics of climate change: the Stern Review*. London: Cabinet Office and HM Treasury.

Takano, T., Nakamura, K. and Watanabe, M. 2002. Urban residential environments and senior citizens' longevity in megacity areas: the importance of walkable green spaces. *Journal of Epidemiology and Community Health, 56*(12), 913–918.

The Acute Respiratory Infections Atlas. 2013. Overcrowding. Retrieved 19/01/2014, from www.ariatlas.org/drivers_of_aris/overcrowding

The Information Centre. 2013. *Statistics on obesity, physical activity and diet*. England: Health and Social Care Information Centre.

The Institute of Health Equity. 2013. *Review of the social determinants and the health divide in the WHO European region*. Copenhagen: WHO Europe.

The Marmot Review Team. 2010. *Fair society, healthy lives: strategic review of health inequalities in England post-2010*. London: Marmot Review Team.

Transport. 2003. *Rural transport futures: summary*. London: Transport 2000.

UCL Institute of Health Equity. 2011. The health impacts of cold homes and fuel poverty. Retrieved 08/12/2014, from www.instituteofhealthequity.org/projects/the-health-impacts-of-cold-homes-and-fuel-poverty

UNL Transport Research Consultancy. 2000. *Social exclusion and the provision and availability of public transport*. London: Department of the Environment, Transport and the Regions.

Wheater, C., Potts, E., Shaw, E., Perkins, C., Smith, H., Casstles, H., Cook, P. and Bellis, M. 2007. *Returning urban parts to their public health roots*. Manchester: Department of Environmental and Geographical Sciences, Manchester Metropolitan University.

White, M.P., Alcock, I., Wheeler, B.W. and Depledge, M.H. 2013. Would you be happier living in a greener urban area? A fixed-effects analysis of panel data. *Psychological Science, 24*(6), 920–928.

WHO (World Health Organization). 2011. *World report on disability*. Geneva: WHO.

WHO. 2013a. *Global status report on road safety 2013: supporting a decade of action*. Geneva: WHO.

WHO. 2013b. Life expectancy: life expectancy by country. Retrieved 02/08/2013, from http://apps.who.int/gho/data/node.main.688?lang=en

WHO Regional Office for Europe. 2012. Environmental health inequalities in Europe. Retrieved 08/12/2014, from www.euro.who.int/__data/assets/pdf_file/0010/157969/e96194.pdf

Zenk, S.N., Lachance, L.L., Schulz, A.J., Mentz, G., Kannan, S. and Ridella, W. 2009. Neighborhood retail food environment and fruit and vegetable intake in a multiethnic urban population. *American Journal of Health Promotion, 23*(4), 255–264.

8

ACTIVE TRAVEL

Its fall and rise

Adrian Davis and John Parkin

Introduction: what is active travel?

Transport, by definition, involves movement. As well as the two predominant physically active methods of walking and cycling (using either conventional or electrically assisted bicycles), physically active journey making can embrace the use of roller-blades, skate-boards and scooters (often used by children and propelled by one leg).

Different methods of movement exhibit different periods and intensities of physical activity. Physical effort can occur for parts of a journey – for example, shorter or longer walks at either end of a trip in a car or on public transport. There may also be limited or prolonged periods of standing involved.

The intensity of activity will depend principally on the speed of cycling or walking. It is generally found that walking provides physical activity at largely a moderate level, whereas some cycle users will experience more and longer periods of vigorous activity (Vuori et al. 1994). Vigorous activity provides significantly greater protection from disease, and poor health and well-being.

Walking is, by far, more common than cycling across much of the developed world. Walking is a rhythmic, dynamic, aerobic activity of large skeletal muscles that confers multifarious benefits with minimal adverse effects (Morris and Hardman 1997). Walking is the most basic form of physical activity humans can undertake to maintain good health. Regular walking reduces the risk of deaths from all causes and, in particular, death from cardiovascular and respiratory diseases, type 2 diabetes and some cancers. Regular walking also helps to counter depression and maintain mental well-being.

A useful definition of 'physically active transport' is one where some outcome from the physically active nature of the transport is manifest. Physical activity itself is a broad term used to describe 'any force exerted by skeletal muscle that results in energy expenditure above resting level' (Casperson et al. 1985). Thus the term 'physical activity' includes any form of human movement including walking, cycling, play, active hobbies or manual occupations, as well as structured exercise or sport. It is important to understand that sport and exercise are subsets of physical activity. International guidance recommends for adults (from 19 to 64 years of age) a minimum of 150 minutes per week of moderate physical activity in bouts of ten minutes or more across the week. Activity duration has to be a minimum of ten minutes on each occasion, with some of the 150 minutes being vigorous. This is defined as a heart rate elevated to at least 60 per cent of its theoretical maximum. An alternative recommendation is for 75 minutes of vigorous activity spread across the week. Promoting physical activity is as much the role of the transport and town planner, ensuring that there is good provision for safe walking and cycling possibilities, as it is for those providing facilities for people to be active (Start Active, Stay Active 2011).

This chapter firstly reviews the important matter of travel decision-making behaviour and goes on to note trends in travel making currently emerging in developed economies. We then explore the interconnected relationships between transport, health and the environment. Recognising the different disciplinary backgrounds of those with interests in active transport, we go on to explore current contentions around the nature of evidence and its use in policy. Finally, we draw the threads together to provide an holistic understanding of transport and health.

Travel decision-making behaviour

In the main, people travel in order to undertake activity at the end of the journey. Sometimes they may engage in activity such as working during a journey, and sometimes they travel for the intrinsic enjoyment of the journey itself. The choices people make about how they travel are varied and complex. Traditionally, transport activity has been modelled, albeit largely for the movement of motorised transport, and schemes for infrastructure improvement have been appraised, mainly based on an account of the time and cost savings to the user. Such modelling approaches assume a perfect market with perfect knowledge, which is unlikely to subsist at any level of aggregation.

Better appreciation of motivations and choices in relation to travel are developing through wider application of a range of social and psychological models of behaviour (for example the theory of planned behaviour, Ajzen 1981). Advances in both theory and application of behavioural change science has led to more sophisticated ways in which motivation towards voluntary behaviour change can be targeted, and which draw on a taxonomy of possible intervention approaches (Abraham and Michie 2008; Michie et al. 2009; Bird et al. 2013).

The household is the traditional 'unit' generating transport demand. In large land use and transportation models the production factors are reduced to household size (number of people), household structure (related to numbers in employment), income and car ownership. Decision making about transport is, however, more complex. It is related not only to the modes available, but especially in more complex households, to the interrelated needs for transport of the inhabitants. There are general issues about the way households make decisions. Further, there is a growing literature on the specific influences of different household members, including the varying contributions of children, mothers and fathers.

Household decision making is clearly complex. The mechanisms vary across cultures, particularly where the position of women is different, perhaps related to religious belief. The processes of decision making will likely vary as the household matures, either through the ageing of children, or simply via different relationships emerging over time.

There is also the issue of habit. This has been examined, for example, in the context of choice between cycling and car use as part of a model using the theory of planned behaviour (Bamberg and Schmidt 1994). Fresh choices will not be made every day because of the cognitive load, the time available and previous experiences. Hence habit will be used to short-cut to the 'assumed' most appropriate option. Another barrier is the image of cycling, with cycle users being regarded as members of an 'out group' as a result of social norms. Considering the image of cyclists Daley and Rissel (2011) found that respondents did not consider cycling as a mainstream method of transport. Their study also revealed that media reporting on cyclists, and cycling in locations with low cycling levels, portrays the activity as extreme (for example, cycling long distances for charity) with cyclists being portrayed as 'problem' road users (Rissel et al. 2010; Busse 2012). Such research suggests that affecting social norms is likely to be an important task in enabling more people to choose cycling. Moreover, the research connects understanding about habits with norms and cultural change (Schwanen et al. 2012).

By way of contrast to a focus on active travel, travel by private motorised transport has been seen increasingly as the normative mode of travel in many wealthier societies. There has, however, been a hidden cost to motorisation which has been impacting on individual users' health in a number of ways, and little recognised until recently. This includes the risk of habitual sedentary behaviour, not least because, for the commute, the choice of a private motorised mode reduces the opportunities available elsewhere in the day to be physically active. To this is added strong evidence for weight gain with the attendant risks of ill health with habitual car use (Frank et al. 2004; Bassett et al. 2008; Suigiyama et al. 2013).

The quality of the networks and infrastructure provided for different modes also plays a significant part in choice. Keeping with an econometric view of the world, the UK government provides monetised values for 'journey ambience' of cycle lanes and tracks of different levels of separation from motor traffic (DfT 2012). This rather limited methodology for accounting for the nature of the transport system in travel behaviour is contestable and a range of literature is emerging which takes a wider view of the determinants of travel behaviour.

Handy (2005) reviewed studies which considered the relationship between transport, land use and physical activity. This review suggests a strong inverse correlation between active travel and distance between origin and destination, as well as a strong correlation with measures for density of development and population. These relations are clearly explicable and have significant policy implications for spatial planning as a tool for establishing the background against which physically active travel could flourish. Additionally, there are relationships between active travel and a variety of transport system variables including the nature of the road network, the presence of walking and bicycle paths, motor traffic speed, and the availability of parking.

Extending the work, at least for cycling, into a meta-analysis Robertson et al. (2013) suggest significant relationships between bicycle use and measures for distance, land use, the transportation system, safety, and neighbourhood characteristics, with distance having the largest effect. Heinen et al. (2010) believe more research is required, however, to understand issues connected with the density of the network and surrounding land uses, contiguity of infrastructure and the provision of facilities separate from those provided for motor traffic. Pucher et al. (2010) found positive and significant relationships between cycling levels and infrastructure from aggregate studies, but the picture was more mixed from individual level studies.

In all of this work, there remain, however, two broad issues. The first is around causality. This asks whether the presence of cycling and walking has encouraged the development of an environment that is compatible to these activities, or whether the reverse is true. That is, investment in infrastructure has had the effect of encouraging walking and cycling. It could also be the case that effects are working 'both ways'. The second scenario is around the operationalisation of variables, such as journey ambience and feelings of security, which appropriately measure built environment factors. This has been tackled to some extent for walking by Ewing and Handy (2009), but more needs to be known.

Trends in transport

Levels of walking and cycling vary between developed countries, and have generally shown declines over the decades since the 1970s. A survey in 27 European countries shows that currently the main mode of transport in daily activities is private motorised transport, that is, the car and motorbike – 53 per cent and 2 per cent respectively (Eurobarometer 2011). Public transport accounts for 22 per cent, with walking at 13 per cent and cycling at 7 per cent (with the balance of 3 per cent comprising respondents who do not travel regularly and those who travel by other modes). Figure 8.1 provides data on trends and compares the countries in Europe with some of the largest shares of cycling and walking (The Netherlands, Germany and Denmark) with the United Kingdom, France and the United States of America.

Pucher and Buehler (2010), in putting these data together, note the disparity of sources and the fact that data collection differences limit comparability of the figures. Combined cycling and walking shares vary from around 10 per cent to almost 50 per cent. France and the UK show the greatest declines over the three decades, with lesser downward trends evident in The Netherlands, Denmark and Germany. These latter three countries also have the larger cycling mode shares. Other developed nations generally fit a pattern somewhere within the extremes as shown in Figure 8.1.

There is variability in use within countries, with some cities demonstrating much larger mode shares than other areas. Figure 8.2 provides a picture of that variability by showing the cities with the largest and smallest cycling mode shares for six countries reported in Pucher and Buehler (2008).

Pucher and Buehler conclude that the differences in levels of bicycle use relate to the provision of separate facilities for cycle traffic. Policy interventions relating to transport have to forecast the future. They will do so based on observations of behaviour in the present day, coupled with future forecasts of population and other factors such as wealth. These types of models do not include variables linked with the built environment or the more subtle decision-making processes discussed above. Choice parameters that exist in the present day will be replicated in the future in such models because normally there is no better assumption to make.

There are, however, other interesting trends becoming evident suggesting that average per capita growth of travel has stopped in some places. This may be linked with smaller benefits of even more travel (Metz 2013), and, as far as car use is concerned, a lower proportion of young

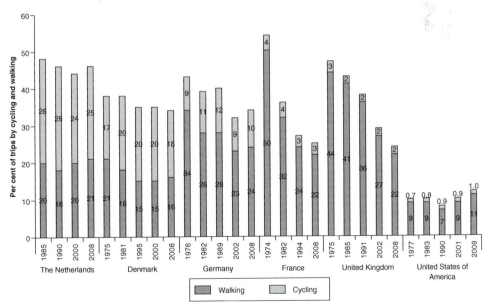

Figure 8.1   Trends in percentage of trips by cycling and walking in six developed countries

Source: Source data from Pucher and Buehler (2010).

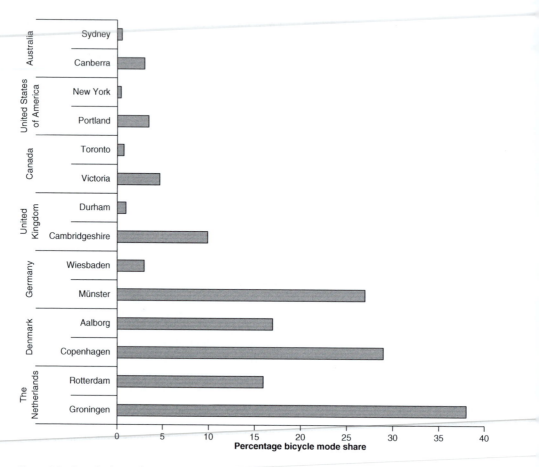

Figure 8.2   Bicycle share of trips in cities in six countries

Source: Source data from Pucher and Buehler, 2008.

people acquiring driving licences (Delbosc and Currie 2013). Further, there is a trend towards population movement in urban rather than suburban areas (Headicar 2013).

So now, with an understanding of decision-making behaviour and trends in transport, we move on to explore the relationships between transport, health and the environment in more detail.

Transport, health and the environment

In this section we review the relationships between transport and health, and explore the co-benefits of physically active travel on health and the environment. Finally, we discuss health economics and health equity.

Relationship of transport to health

The primary function of transport is in providing the connection between people and the goods and services they require. Transport also affords access to the built and natural environment from which people gain material and non-material wealth, health and well-being. When distances are short, as in urban areas, the opportunities for active travel are potentially large. The health benefits of physical activity have been extensively documented since the first studies in the 1950s. These showed that adults who are physically active during the course of employment suffered less than half the coronary events of those with sedentary occupations, while controlling for lifestyle factors such as smoking and alcohol consumption (Morris et al. 1953; Paffenbarger et al. 1978).

Early references to the interrelationship between transport and health focused almost exclusively on the acute impacts of negative outcomes such as air and noise pollution, and traffic casualties (for example, MoT 1963). Benefits were viewed in terms of high levels of mobility, principally for car occupants. As scientific understanding of impacts has developed and subtle and chronic impacts are better researched, it has become clear that the relationships between transport and health are substantive and have economic, social and environmental consequences. There are therefore important interrelationships with relevance to a range of public policy.

One of the most significant changes in understanding is transport's potential contribution to total physical activity time in order to reduce the disease burden causally related to physical activity deficiency (WHO 2000). More recently, this understanding has been extended to include well-being benefits. This is both through the intrinsic physical health benefits of active travel, and the ways that transport often facilitates social connectivity, which itself has beneficial health impacts (Environment Canterbury 2010; Betts Adams et al. 2011; Nordbakke and Schwanen 2013). Beyond the physical benefits of activity, active travel-friendly neighbourhood designs facilitate incidental contacts between neighbours and appear to foster social capital (that is social networks, norms and trust). Numerous studies show positive associations between social capital and physical and mental health, and health promoting behaviours (Putnam 1999; Leyden 2003). Meaningful social activities reduce the harmful effects of stress by enhancing the body's immune response function. Social capital may promote positive social norms while simultaneously controlling anti-social behaviours that can fuel feelings of insecurity. Greener environments, including quality greenspace such as parks, are also important for health (for example, Sugiyama et al. 2008; Sallis et al. 2009).

Another negative health consideration is the stress of driving, most especially for the daily home-to-work commute. In contrast, active travellers tend to be least dissatisfied with their commute (Paez and Whalen 2010), if not in fact actually deriving enjoyment from the journey. Car commuters find their journey more stressful than other mode users. The main sources of this stress are reported to be delays and other road users. Users of public transport also 'complain' about delays; however, this results in boredom as well as stress. Walking and cycling journeys are the most relaxing and exciting and therefore seem the most optimal form of travel from an affective perspective (Gatersleben and Uzzle 2007). Explanatory factors include desirable physical exercise from walking and cycling, and the provision of a psychological 'buffer' between the spheres of work and non-work. Negative feelings during the work commute increase with the length of the commute (Olsson et al. 2013).

Co-benefits of health and the environment and other benefits

There is urgency for moving towards lower carbon futures. The fifth assessment report of the International Panel on Climate Change states that it is 'extremely likely that human influence has been the dominant cause of the observed warming since the mid-20th century', and that 'continued emissions of greenhouse gases will cause further warming and changes in all components of the climate system' (IPCC 2013, p. 17 and p. 19). The report suggests that 'substantial and sustained' reductions of greenhouse gas emissions will be required to 'limit' future climate change. Transport is presently a fossil fuel intensive industry and moves towards physically active travel will bring with it benefits for the climate more generally.

Relatively recently, and initially through recognition of the impact of successful climate change mitigation strategies, an understanding of what have become termed co-benefits has developed (Woodcock et al. 2009). In the case of such strategies applied to road transport, co-benefits occur when, for example, carbon reduction measures result in an increase in human energy expenditure.

The economics of health benefits

The volume of economic literature on active travel, especially that addressing health economics, has risen significantly in the first decade of the new millennium. There is also more evidence applying a cost–benefit analysis approach, and more so for cycling than walking interventions. Further, the growth of research reveals that the economic justification for investments to facilitate cycling and walking had previously been under-rated or even ignored (Davis 2010). Much of the benefit is derived from reductions in premature deaths (through the 'value of a statistical life') with large health savings and consequent benefits to the economy. The financial benefits of active travel that result are often large (Cavill et al. 2008), and have mostly been left out of economic assessments. Moreover, the majority of the recorded benefits accrue from health gains despite the fact that morbidity (illness) costs are generally excluded from studies: the World Health Organization (2007) suggests that the economic benefits of active travel attributable to health gains would be even larger than those from reductions in mortality alone if morbidity costs were included.

A recent review for the UK Department for Transport found that almost all infrastructure and behaviour change studies report economic benefits of walking and cycling interventions that are highly significant. In terms of value for money, the UK Department of Transport values 'very highly' any scheme that returns more than £4 for every £1 invested. The mean benefit-to-cost ratio for all schemes identified in the review was 6.28 : 1 (Davis 2014).

Changes to neighbourhood design could also produce benefits for the local micro-economy. Increasing population densities and boosting local pedestrian and cycling traffic flows can increase the economic viability of cafes and corner stores, as well as improving access to jobs and services without increasing congestion or vehicle emissions. For example, researchers report that in Toronto people who bike and walk to Bloor Street, a commercial locality, reported they spent more money in the area per month than those who drove there (Clean Air Partnership 2009).

Health and health equity

The World Health Organization defines health as a state of complete physical, mental and social well-being and not merely the absence of disease or infirmity (WHO 1946). Health equity relates to the social determinants of health, that is the conditions in which people are born, grow, live, work and age.

Road transport contributes to health inequity through a number of pathways. In terms of active travel health, inequity is increased not least by the deterrent effect whereby people who would choose active modes, at least for some trips, do not do so due to the perceived road danger. Using an economic word, this is the 'externalisation' of traffic danger by those using motorised transport modes onto other road users. As we noted earlier, distance can also deter active modes, partly due to poor land use such as out of town superstores and business parks. Cultural norms also influence travel mode choice when potential active travel mode users see that the norm is to drive a car. Cultural norms have strong influences on travel behaviour. Such barriers result in the forfeiture of the health benefits that would have accrued.

Additionally, there are possible amplification effects whereby some of those denied the use of the active travel modes do not have access to alternative modes (e.g. through cost or age) and so have their access opportunities restricted. This can include lack of access to employment, health and other facilities, with serious economic and health consequences. Still others may be forced to walk but find the experience unpleasant if not stressful (Bostock 2001; Ekkekakis et al. 2008). Such outcomes themselves can be seen as products of unequal power relationships and the economic forces in which they originate and unfold. From this viewpoint, health inequities are the result of unequal power relations, both in terms of social structures including, for example, social class, patriarchy and racism, and their manifestations in terms of car-oriented developments that are beneficial to the wealthy at the expense of the less powerful.

Evidence and policy making

The supportive role of the built environment for human health has been, at least since the new millennium, a growing area of interdisciplinary research, evidence-based policy development, and related practice. Nevertheless, despite closely linked origins, the contemporary professions of public health and urban planning largely operate within a neo-liberal framework of academic, political and policy silos (Kent and Thompson 2012). A similar disconnect has been identified between public health and transport planning (Litman 2003; Davis 2003).

There is an increasing breadth and strength to the evidence base in relation to active travel. Since about the year 2000, there has been a rapid growth of evidence around active travel and the built environment. Yet ironically, the built environment disciplines are engaging in more demand-driven research, that is to say research which is commissioned to inform a particular policy decision which may already have been taken.

In this section, we briefly explore the contested nature of evidence and its relation to policy making. The very meaning of evidence is highly contestable and it has been repeatedly and cogently argued that evidence is socially constructed (Krieger 1992; Chan and Chan 2000). So, what is accepted as evidence, how much is it valued, and how does this differ across professions and policy makers? What counts as evidence, and the rules and criteria for assessing evidence, and whether evidence is valued at all, are all negotiated phenomena and contested within and across professions. Rychetnik and Wise (2004, p. 248) note that:

> concepts of evidence vary among professionals, disciplinary and social groups: for example, scientists have traditionally adopted different standards of evidence to lawyers. Since the advent of evidence-based medicine in the early 1990s, health professionals, managers and consumers have been debating (and negotiating) what is considered as valuable and credible evidence to support decisions about health services, public health, health promotion and health policy.

A complete meeting of minds on the nature of evidence and its use in policy making is possibly some way off. However, at a programme level, there are opportunities for synthesis between policy makers and researchers. A synthesis approach could work through prior engagement whereby policy makers and researchers actively work together in framing the nature of the problem (if indeed new research is needed) and hence in determining forms of analysis that could be applied. In England, for example, we may have the opportunity to make progress in this regard because of the return of public health as a function to top tier local government since April 2013.

A specific issue in relation to understanding evidence is the methodology of its genesis. Public health adopts the well-established hierarchy of evidence as noted below.

1. Systematic reviews and meta-analysis.
2. Randomised controlled trials (RCTs) with definitive results.
3. Randomised controlled trials (RCTs) with non-definitive results.
4. Cohort studies.
5. Case-controlled studies.
6. Cross sectional surveys.
7. Case reports.

The most robust methodological approaches are systematic reviews, meta-analyses and RCTs and the weakest, cross sectional studies and case reports. As a result of closer collaboration, it is much more possible to introduce an evidence hierarchy into transport practice, and this will help to reduce bias in decision making and improve cost-effectiveness.

A longer term approach to improving engagement is through the development of courses for the built environment professionals of the future. Although still exceptions, courses have been developed to stimulate interdisciplinary learning around the built environment and public health and are likely to go some way to help develop greater understanding as to the benefits of a shared understanding as to the meaning of evidence (Botchwey et al. 2009).

It is also important to provide design guidance that supports engineers and urban planners in achieving a better balance between the movement and place functions of the urban realm (see, for example, DfT 2007). Since the turn of the millennium, there has been a growing literature on transport, health and the built environment which has resulted in additional and generally complementary guidance on the need for human movement through personal energy expenditure especially focused on the effectiveness of interventions to increase active travel modes (e.g. NICE 2008, 2012).

McClintock provided an early study focusing on barriers to the take up of guidance and utilisation of research findings among transport professionals in the UK addressing bicycle and pedestrian planning (McClintock 2001). Here he touched on the understanding of meanings of knowledge and the plurality of meaning in the context of in-career learning and 'keeping abreast of relevant guidance and research findings'. Through a survey of transport practitioners the findings in terms of accessing new knowledge were that this was largely sought through trade magazines and journal articles and little use of the internet. The survey was conducted in 1999 so it might be that internet use is a major conduit to such knowledge well over a decade later. McClintock noted that one of the obstacles to more effective take up of guidance and research findings was the reluctance of some, especially senior and more experienced professionals, to accept that cycling and walking were to be taken seriously. This appears to underlie personal values and experiences which may reflect their life experiences in growing up and working in an age when the dominance of the motor car has been seen as the cultural norm.

Evidence is clearly contested, often by vested interests, mediated and assessed in terms of alignment of values and social norms by those who have power to make decisions. What is accepted, adopted and taken for use in public policy making consequently varies considerably from the initial evidence input (Juntti et al. 2009). This 'filtering' means that the logic of championing, financing and implementing active travel interventions has most often been blocked and sometimes before it reaches the decision table of politicians.

Conclusions: a holistic understanding and future directions

In terms of road transport, the need for movement results from the distance between the places where activities occur. The planning of activity location, that is to say land use planning, is therefore a mechanism that has direct influence on travel. A paradigm of planning with an assumed solution based on the flexibility of the motor car has allowed for the creation of patterns of set-tlement where distance, so long as the capacity and speed have been appropriately high, is not a problem. For reasons linked with the finite availability of 'space', it appears as though patterns of land use are intensifying with the natural consequence that, at least for some people and for some journey purposes, distances to undertake activities are not now extending as they once were.

The engineering community has made an excellent job, over post-war generations, of adapting as much space as they have been allowed by policy makers to maximise the capacity and speed of motor traffic. This has, from early days, been assisted by technology, for example in the form of traffic signal control, and, more latterly, particularly on inter-urban routes in the form of comprehensive management of the route as a 'system'. This engineering led, systems-based approach has, however, had little regard for the social, environmental and health consequences of motorised transport and the unequal distributional impacts on those who may be adversely affected by the movement of others.

The evidence suggests that there are already some indications of deviation away from con-tinued growth in motorisation. The need to do so is evident to combat climate change and to enhance public health.

Broadband internet is also dramatically changing the way people access goods and services, with the burden of individual travel being replaced by an ever expanding logistics industry. Quality of service provision to the end user (for example, in terms of slots for delivery of perish-able goods) is a prime issue. Similarly, the internet is having an impact on the daily and weekly patterns of travel activity in terms of commutes and business travel.

We conclude that the tide may well be turning towards a more sustainable transport future. We hope that, if we are correct, the speed of change will be much faster than that which evolved to support a car-based society.

References

Abraham, C. and Michie, S. 2008. A taxonomy of behaviour change techniques used in interventions. *Health Psychology*. 27, 379–387.

Ajzen, I. 1991. The theory of planned behaviour. *Organisation and Human Decision Processes*. 50(x) 179–211.

Bamberg, S. and Schmidt, P. 1994. Auto oder Fahrrad? Empirischer Test einer Handlungstheorie zur Erklärung der Verkehrsmittelwahl. [Car or bicycle? An empirical test of theory of mode choice.] *Kölner Zeitschrift für soziologie und social psychologie*. 46(1), 80–102. March.

Bassett, D., Pucher, J., Buehler, R., Thompson, D. and Crouter, S. 2008. Walking, cycling, and obesity rates in Europe, North America and Australia. *Journal of Physical Activity and Health*. 5, 795–814.

Betts Adams, K., Leibrandt, S. and Moon, H. 2011. A critical review of the literature on social and leisure activity and well-being in later life. *Ageing and Society*. 683–712. doi:10.1017\S0144686X10001091.

Bird, E., Baker, G., Mutrie, N., Ogilvie, D., Sahlqvist, S. and Powell, J. on behalf of the iConnect Consortium. 2013. Behaviour change techniques used to promote walking and cycling: a systematic review. *Health Psychology*. 32(8), 829–838.

Bostock, L. 2001. Pathways of disadvantage? Walking as a mode of transport among low-income mothers. *Health Society and Community Care*. 9(1)11–18.

Botchwey, N., Hobson, S., Dannenberg, A.L., Mumford, K.G., Contant, C.K., McMillan, T.E., Jackson, R.J., Lopez, R. and Winkle, C. 2009. A model curriculum for a course on the built environment and public health: training for an interdisciplinary workforce. *American Journal of Preventive Medicine*. 36(2), S63–S71.

Busse, H. 2012. Healthy but dangerous: the representation of cycling and cyclists in the print media. Master's of Health Psychology Dissertation. University of Bath.

Casperson, C., Powell, K. and Christnesen, G. 1985. Physical activity, exercise and physical fitness: defini-tions and distinctions of health-related research. *Public Health Reports*. 100, 126–131.

Cavill, N., Kahlmeier, S., Rutter, H., Racioppi, F. and Oja, P. 2008. Economic analysis of transport infrastructure and policies including health effects related to cycling and walking: a systematic review. *Transport Policy*. 15: 291–304.

Chan, J. and Chan, J. 2000. Medicine in the millennium: the challenge of postmodernism. *Medical Journal of Australia*. 17, 332–334.

Clean Air Partnership. 2009. Bike lanes, on-street parking and business: a study of Bloor Street in Toronto's Annex neighbourhood. www.cleanairpartnership.org/pdf/bike-lanes-parking.pdf, accessed 8 April 2015.

Daley, M. and Rissel, C. 2011. Perspectives and images of cycling as a barrier or facilitator of cycling. *Transport Policy*. 18(1), 211–216.

Davis, A. 2003. Can the health sector influence transport planning for better health? In Sidell, M., Jones, L., Katz, G., Peberdy, A. and Douglas, J. (Eds). *Debates and dilemmas in promoting health: a reader*. 2nd Edition. Basingstoke: Palgrave Macmillan.

Davis, A. 2010. *Value for money: an economic assessment of investment in walking and cycling*. Bristol: Department of Health. www.healthyweight4children.org.uk/resource/item.aspx?RID=90422, accessed 21 July 2013.

Davis, A. 2014. Claiming the health dividend: a summary and discussion of value for money estimates from studies of investment in walking and cycling. London: Department for Transport. www.gov.uk/government/uploads/system/uploads/attachment_data/file/371096/claiming_the_health_dividend.pdf, p. 6, accessed 8 April 2015.

Delbosc, A. and Currie, G. 2013. Causes of youth licensing decline: a synthesis of evidence. *Transport Reviews*. 33(3), 271–290.

DfT (Department for Transport). 2007. *Manual for streets*. Department for Transport, Department of Communities and Local Government, Welsh Assembly Government. London: Thomas Telford.

DfT. 2012. *Guidance on the appraisal of cycling and walking schemes*. Transport Analysis Guidance TAG Unit 3.14.1. Department for Transport. www.dft.gov.uk/webtag/documents/expert/pdf/u3_14_1-walking-and-cycling-120723.pdf, accessed 22 November 2013.

Ekkekakis, P., Backhouse, S., Gray, C. and Lind, E. 2008. Walking is popular among adults but is it pleasant? A framework for clarifying the link between walking and affect as illustrated in two studies. *Psychology of Sport and Exercise*. 9, 246–264.

Environment Canterbury Regional Council. 2010. *Wider health and well-being impacts of transport planning: literature review*. Canterbury: Environment Canterbury Regional Council/Canterbury District Council/Christchurch City Council.

Eurobarometer. 2011. Future of transport: analytical report. Brussels: European Commission.

Ewing, R. and Handy, S. 2009. Measuring the unmeasureable: urban design qualities related to walkability. *Journal of Urban Design*. 14(1), 65–84.

Frank, L., Andersen, M. and Schmid, T. 2004. Obesity relationships with community design, physical activity, and time spent in cars. *American Journal of Preventive Medicine*. 27(2), 87–96.

Gatersleben, B. and Uzzle, D. 2007. Affective appraisals of the daily commute: comparing perceptions of drivers, cyclists, walkers, and users of public transport. *Environment and Behaviour*. 39(3), 416–431.

Handy, S. 2005. *Critical assessment of the literature on the relationships among transportation, land use, and physical activity*. Transport Research Board Special Report 282. http://onlinepubs.trb.org/onlinepubs/archive/downloads/sr282papers/sr282Handy.pdf, accessed 8 April 2015.

Headicar, P. 2013. The changing spatial distribution of the population in England: its nature and significance for 'peak car'. *Transport Reviews*. 33(3), 310–324.

Heinen, E., van Wee, B. and Mart, K. 2010. Commuting by bicycle: an overview of the literature. *Transport Reviews*. 30(1), 59–96.

IPCC. 2013. Working Group 1 contribution to the fifth assessment report of the Intergovernmental Panel on Climate Change. www.climatechange2013.org/images/report/WG1AR5_ALL_FINAL.pdf, accessed 8 April 2015.

Juntti, M., Russell, D. and Turnpenny, J. 2009. Evidence, politics and power in public policy for the environment. *Environmental Science and Policy*. 12, 207–215.

Kent, J. and Thompson, S. 2012. Health and the built environment: exploring foundations for a new inter-disciplinary profession. *Journal of Environmental and Public Health*. doi:10.1155/2012/958175

Krieger, N. 1992. The making of public health data: paradigms, politics, and policy. *Journal of Public Health Policy*. 13, 412–427.

Leyden, K. 2003. Social capital and the built environment: the importance of walkable neighbourhoods. *American Journal of Public Health*. 93(9), 1546–1551.

Litman, T. 2003. Integrating public health objectives in transportation decision-making. *American Journal of Health Promotion*. 18(1), 103–108.

McClintock, H. 2001. Practitioners' take-up of professional guidance and research findings: planning for cycling and walking in the UK. *Planning Practice and Research*. 16(2), 193–203.

Metz, D. 2013. Peak car and beyond: the fourth era of travel. *Transport Reviews*. 33(3), 255–270.

Michie, S., Abraham, C., Whittington, C., McAteer, J. and Gupta S. 2009. Effective techniques in healthy eating and physical activity interventions: a meta-regression. *Health Psychology*. 28, 690–701. doi:10.1037/a0016136

Morris, J. and Hardman, A. 1997. Walking to health. *Sports Medicine*. 23(5), 306–332.

Morris, J., Heady, J., Raffle, P. and Parks, J. 1953. Coronary heart disease and physical activity at work. *The Lancet*. 265, 1111–1120.

MoT (Ministry of Transport). 1963. *Traffic in towns: a study of the long term problems of traffic in urban areas*. London: HMSO.

NICE (National Institute for Health and Care Excellence). 2008. Promoting and creating built or natural environments that encourage and support physical activity. PHG 8. www.nice.org.uk/PH008, accessed 8 April 2015.

NICE. 2012. Walking and cycling: local measures to promote walking and cycling as forms of travel or recreation. PHG 41. http://guidance.nice.org.uk/PH41, accessed 8 April 2015.

Nordbakke, S. and Schwanen, T. 2013. Wellbeing and mobility: a theoretical framework and literature review focusing on older people. *Mobilities*. 9(1), 104–129.

Olsson, L.E., Gärling, T., Ettema, D., Friman, M. and Fujii, S. 2013. Happiness and satisfaction with work commute. *Social Indicators Research*. 111, 255–263.

Paez, A. and Whalen, K. 2010. Enjoyment of commute: a comparison of different transportation modes. *Transportation Part A: Policy and Practice*. 44(7), 537–549.

Paffenbarger, R., Wing, A. and Hyde, R. 1978. Physical activity as an index of heart attack risk in college alumni. *American Journal of Epidemiology*. 108(3), 161–175.

Pucher, J. and Buehler, R. 2008. Making cycling irresistible: lessons from the Netherlands, Denmark and Germany. *Transport Review*. 28(4), 495–528.

Pucher, J. and Buehler, R. 2010. Walking and cycling for healthy cities. *Built Environment*. 36(4), 391–414.

Pucher, J., Dill, J. and Handy, S. 2010. Infrastructure, programs, and policies to promote cycling: an international review. *Preventive Medicine*. 50 (Supplement), S106–S125.

Putnam, R. 1999. *Bowling alone: the collapse and revival of American community*. New York: Simon & Schuster.

Rissel, C., Bonfiglioli, C., Emilsen, A. and Smith, B.J. 2010. Representations of cycling in metropolitan newspapers: changes over time and differences between Sydney and Melbourne, Australia. *BMC Public Health* 10, 371.

Robertson, K., Bamberg, S., Parkin. J. and Fyhri, A. (2013) *Bicycle-friendly cities: the relevance of urban form and infrastructure*. (Swedish with English summary) VTI Report 769. Linköping, Sweden. ISSN 0347-6030.

Rychetnik, L. and Wise, M. 2004. Advocating evidence-based health promotion: reflections and a way forward. *Health Promotion International*. 19(2), 247–257.

Sallis, J., Bowles, H.R., Bauman, A., Ainsworth, B.E., Bull, F.C., Craig, C.L., Sjöström, M., De Bourdeaudhuij, I., Lefevre, J., Matsudo, V., Matsudo, S., Macfarlane, D.J., Gomez, L.F., Inoue, S., Murase, N., Volbekiene, V., McLean, G., Carr, H., Heggebo, L.K., Tomten, H. and Bergman, P. 2009. Neighbourhood environments and physical activity among adults in 11 countries. *American Journal of Preventive Medicine*. 36(6), 484–490.

Schwanen, T., Banister, D. and Anable, J. 2012. Rethinking habits and their role in behaviour change: the case of low carbon mobility. *Journal of Transport Geography*. 24, 522–532.

Start Active, Stay Active. 2011. A report on physical activity for health from the four home countries' chief medical officers. London: Department of Health.

Sugiyama, T., Leslie, E., Giles-Corti, B. and Owen, N. 2008. Association of neighbourhood greenness with physical and mental health: do walking, social coherence and local social interaction explain the relationships? *Journal of Epidemiology and Community Health*. 62, e9.

Suigiyama, T., Ding, D. and Owen, N. 2013. Commuting by car: weight gain among physically active adults. *American Journal of Preventive Medicine*. 44(2), 169–173.

Vuori, I., Oja, P. and Paronen, O. 1994. Physically active commuting to work: testing its potential for exercise promotion. *Medicine and Science in Sports and Exercise*. 26(7), 844–850.

WHO (World Health Organization). 1946. Preamble to the Constitution of the World Health Organization as adopted by the International Health Conference, New York, 19–22 June, 1946; signed on 22 July 1946 by the representatives of 61 States (Official Records of the World Health Organization, no. 2, p. 100) and entered into force on 7 April 1948.

WHO. 2000. *Road transport and health*. Dora, C. and Phillips, M. (Eds). Copenhagen: Regional Office.

WHO. 2007. *Economic assessment of transport infrastructure and policies: methodological guidance on the economic appraisal of health effects related to walking and cycling*. Copenhagen: Denmark. www.euro.who.int/en/health-topics/environment-and-health/Transport-and-health/publications/2011/health-economic-assessment-tools-heat-for-walking-and-for-cycling.-methodology-and-user-guide, accessed 2 December 2013.

Woodcock, J., Edwards, P., Tonne, C., Armstrong, B.G., Ashiru, O., Banister, D., Beevers, S., Chalabi, Z., Chowdhury, Z., Cohen, A., Franco, O.H, Haines, A., Hickman, R., Lindsay, G., Mittal, I., Mohan, D., Tiwari, G., Woodward, A. and Roberts, I. 2009. Public health benefits of strategies to reduce greenhouse-gas emissions: urban land transport. *The Lancet*. 374(9705), 1930–1943.

9

THE INFLUENCE OF URBAN DESIGN AND PLANNING ON PHYSICAL ACTIVITY

Billie Giles-Corti, Sarah Foster, Mohammad Javad Koohsari, Jacinta Francis and Paula Hooper

Introduction: the scale of the problem

Why should urban designers and planners be concerned about creating environments to keep people active? After all, keeping people physically active is a public health priority. Physical inactivity is an independent risk factor for the major preventable chronic diseases currently crippling health systems, as well as their associated risk factors (United Nations 2011). Globally some five million people die annually because they are physically inactive (Lee et al. 2012). It is estimated that worldwide, around 60 per cent of people do insufficient physical activity to benefit their health. 'Sufficient activity' is defined as undertaking *30 minutes* of daily moderate activity, including walking. Apart from the direct impact on chronic disease, this is important because around 20 million children (aged five and under) and 1.3 billion adults are now either overweight or obese (World Health Organization 2006). Thus, even a modest increase in the number of physically active people could produce significant societal benefits, with substantial savings to global health systems (Stephenson and Bauman 2000).

The potential impact of chronic disease on global economies is considered to be so large that a 2011 high level meeting of the United Nations concluded that this is not a problem that the health sector can fix alone. Rather, an effective response requires engagement of multiple sectors including urban and transport planning (United Nations Population Fund 2011). This is because creating environments that facilitate, foster and protect health, including those that encourage and support increased physical activity, extends well beyond the health sector's remit. The health sector can (and does) treat the ill and promote the benefits of being physically active. However, it is the decisions made daily by built environment policy-makers and practitioners – urban, transport and recreational planners and designers – that determine the conditions for good or bad health, and whether healthy choices are easy choices (Milio 1986). From a public health perspective, this is a profound responsibility.

Traditionally, the link between public health and urban planning has focused on issues of environmental health, such as the provision of sanitation, clean water and housing. These remain critical basic building blocks of healthy urban development. However, in the twenty-first century healthy urban design and planning requires going beyond these basic foundations in order to create neighbourhoods that encourage active healthy lifestyles with the aim of preventing and controlling chronic disease (Koohsari et al. 2013).

What does the evidence tell us about the impact of urban design and planning on levels of physical activity?

Over the last 15 years, there has been a plethora of studies demonstrating that a range of built environment attributes are associated with physical activity outcomes generally, as well as walking for transport and recreation (Sallis et al. 2012; Sugiyama et al. 2012; Kent and Thompson 2014). Here we provide an overview of recent evidence and consider the implications for urban design and planning.

A physical activity supportive transportation network

A supportive transportation network is essential for active living. This network includes connected streets, managed vehicle traffic to provide safe environments for walking, cycling and other physical activities, as well as a system of footpaths and cycle paths. These need to link residents to a variety of proximate and accessible local destinations (for example, public open space, recreational facilities, shops, services and schools).

Street connectivity is defined as 'the directness and availability of alternative routes from one point to another within a street network' (Transportation Research Board 2005, p. 104). Figure 9.1 shows the difference between connected (that is, a grid pattern, Figure 9.1a) and disconnected (that is, more cul-de-sacs, Figure 9.1b) street networks. A connected street network influences travel behaviour in two ways. It facilitates direct routes to destinations, as well as determining the number of 'potential routes' between destinations within a locality (Handy et al. 2003).

Figure 9.1a   Traditional connected network. Predominantly grid-style street pattern demonstrating a high level of connectivity

Source: Authors.

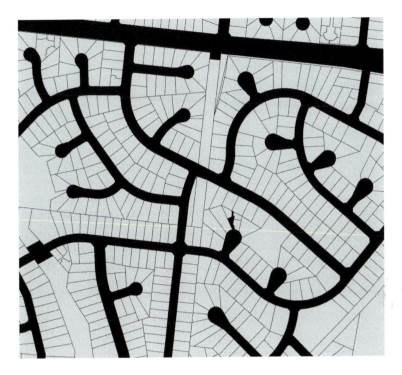

Figure 9.1b   A disconnected street network. Predominantly hierarchical and non-grid street pattern –
typically includes many cul-de-sacs and demonstrates low connectivity

Source: Authors.

Connected street networks have been shown to facilitate walking for transport in most age
groups (Frank et al. 2007; Sugiyama et al. 2012) and promote recreational walking in adult and
elderly populations (Li et al. 2008; Sugiyama et al. 2009). Similarly, for adolescents with some
level of independence, having a connected street network facilitates their mobility in the same
way that it does for adults. However, the evidence for younger children is less clear (Kerr et al.
2007; Carver et al. 2010; Veitch et al. 2010). Neighbourhoods with fewer connected streets
and more cul-de-sacs provide additional spaces for young children's active play and they are
often perceived by parents as safer (Figure 9.2) (Carver et al. 2008). Yet children are more likely
to walk to school (Giles-Corti et al. 2011; Trapp et al. 2012), and to be more independently
mobile (Villanueva et al. 2013) where there is high street connectivity and low traffic volumes.
Conversely, in neighbourhoods with a combination of high street connectivity and high traffic
volumes, children are less likely to walk to school (Giles-Corti et al. 2011), and boys are less
likely to cycle (Trapp et al. 2011). Hence, creating a street network that supports physical activity across the life course requires consideration of street connectivity together with other aspects
of the transportation network, particularly traffic management.

Traffic volume is a major issue influencing children's use of active modes of transport, as well
as their levels of independent mobility – that is, children being allowed to walk or cycle without
an adult present (Villanueva et al. 2013). Studies repeatedly show that traffic volume and safety,
together with the presence of suitable road crossings, are important factors affecting children's
and adolescents' physical activity (Panter et al. 2008). Indeed, the likelihood of younger children using active modes of transport declines if they must cross a busy road (Timperio et al.

Figure 9.2   A cul-de-sac provides a shared area for neighbours separated from main road traffic

Source: Google Maps.

2006), and presence of suitable road crossings is positively associated with older children's and adolescents' physical activity levels, particularly active transport (Boarnet et al. 2005; Ziviani et al. 2006; Carver et al. 2010). These studies highlight the importance of road modifications such as street narrowing and providing safe crossing points to facilitate getting from one side of the road to the other.

The evidence associating traffic volume and safety, and suitable road crossings with adults' physical activity is inconsistent. Some research shows associations in the anticipated direction – heavy traffic deters physical activity; traffic safety and road crossings promote physical activity (Panter et al. 2008; Strath et al. 2012). Other evidence is counter-intuitive indicating that higher perceived traffic is associated with more physical activity (Cao et al. 2006). It is possible that adults who do more walking and cycling are more conscious of traffic volumes and safety. However, it is also likely that pedestrian-friendly areas with more destinations are attractive to drivers as well as pedestrians and cyclists, and consequently additional traffic may well be present.

Traffic calming, along with other supportive infrastructure, is likely to increase physical activity levels. The presence of footpaths, for example, is consistently shown to be associated with physical activity in all pedestrian groups (Kerr et al. 2006; Titze et al. 2010). This is particularly so for vulnerable groups such as children, adolescents and older adults (Burton et al. 2005; Kerr et al. 2006).

Neighbourhood aesthetics are repeatedly shown to be important for physical activity (Sugiyama et al. 2012). Few studies have explored the independent role of street trees in promoting physical activity, but trees are an essential component of a neighbourhood's 'aesthetic' quality. Street trees are deserving of particular mention, as there is some evidence that their presence promotes active transport in both adults and adolescents, creating convivial and safer routes (Sugiyama et al. 2012). In addition, in cities with hotter climates, street trees that provide shade are particularly important to support being physically active.

In summary, a supportive transportation network underpins urban designs that enhance physical activity. Careful consideration needs to be given to creating a transportation network with connected street and pedestrian networks that increase the proximity and variety of routes to local destinations, as well as the aesthetic qualities of these pedestrian networks. For destinations frequented by children and older adults – schools, retirement housing, public open space – it is also critical to reduce and manage traffic. This includes avoiding locations on heavily trafficked roads and implementing traffic management measures as discussed above.

Local access to shops, services and transit

Walking for transport is largely dependent on the availability of walkable destinations – that is, a mix of shops, services and public transport stops. A Western Australian study found that for every additional transport-related destination present (for example, a postbox, a delicatessen, a newsagent), walking as a means of transport increased by around six minutes per destination (McCormack et al. 2008). Accordingly, an area rich with local destinations will encourage short trips undertaken by foot. In terms of walking for recreation, residential density and land use mix are also important. They contribute to a varied and interesting environment that entices walkers into the neighbourhood. However, walking for recreation is influenced mainly by neighbourhood aesthetics as discussed below.

The evidence regarding destinations is consistent: the physical activity levels of residents are enhanced in neighbourhoods with access to a mix of proximate destinations. Proximity is particularly important for children, whose independent mobility is hindered when destinations are near their homes. The likelihood of a child using destinations declines beyond about 800 metres. This also applies to sporting and recreational facilities (Cohen et al. 2006a; Epstein et al. 2006).

Commonly, researchers combine residential density and land use mix measures with street connectivity to create 'walkability' indices. These summarise the capacity of the built environment to promote walking for transport (Frank et al. 2007). They highlight the importance of a combination of measures in creating environments that support physical activity. Moreover, having a mix of destinations available also appears to be important (McCormack et al. 2008).

In contrast to adults, less is known about the mix of neighbourhood destinations that promote children's active transport. Nevertheless, numerous studies underscore the importance of decisions about the presence, proximity and siting of local schools. The distance between students' homes and schools is crucial in determining whether children will walk or cycle to school (Trapp et al. 2011). Evidence indicates that living within an 800 metre threshold of the school is important, with the frequency of walking or cycling dropping when children live beyond 750 metres away (Merom et al. 2006).

However, as previously considered, urban form alone will not promote young peoples' physical activity unless parents perceive their neighbourhood to be safe from traffic (Panter et al. 2008). Ironically, parents who elect to drive their children to school generate considerable traffic congestion around schools, contributing to an unsafe environment for those children who do walk or cycle (Transportation Research Board 2002). As noted, street layout is also important. Schools located in areas with both high street connectivity and traffic volumes reduce the likelihood of children walking or cycling to school (Giles-Corti et al. 2011; Trapp et al. 2011). Siting schools in a way that increases proximity to homes, yet avoids crossing busy roads and reduces exposure to traffic, creates the conditions most suitable to encouraging children's active transport modes. Environmental interventions are enhanced by actively encouraging children and their parents to use alternative active modes of transport to travel to school and other local destinations. Consideration could be given to siting school drop-off zones away from school.

Access to sport and recreational facilities

The presence and proximity of local sporting and recreational opportunities is particularly relevant to those unable to drive, such as low income households, children, adolescents and older adults. There is consistent evidence that young people (aged 8 to 16) are more likely to both use and walk or cycle to parks and sports centres when they are within 800 metres of the home (Cohen et al. 2006b; Epstein et al. 2006). For example, Epstein and colleagues (2006) found that when facilities were within 800 metres of participants' homes, weekly moderate to vigorous physical activity, measured objectively using an activity monitor called an accelerometer, increased from between 17.2 to 38.9 minutes per week. In the same way that proximity and mix of venues are important for adults (McCormack et al. 2007), they also appear to be important for youth. Evenson et al. (2007) found that when adolescent girls had a choice of between 9 to 14 different physical activity destinations close to home, on average their moderate to vigorous physical activity was 84.9 minutes per week higher than girls with fewer local physical activity destinations.

With an ageing, less mobile population, the presence of local physical activity infrastructure serving older adults will become increasingly important. Although the evidence is inconclusive (Michael et al. 2006), a number of studies have found associations between actual or perceived access to local sporting or recreational facilities with older adults' physical activity and sports participation (Michael et al. 2010). The evidence for able-bodied adults with access to a motor vehicle is less compelling. Indeed, there is some suggestion that the convenience, rather than the proximity of physical activity and recreational destinations, is more important (Sallis et al. 1990). Hence, near or en route to work may be more pertinent to adults' physical activity levels than proximity to home.

Finally, in addition to proximity and accessibility, the quality and design of local sports and recreational facilities are also important. A Norwegian study found that the presence of outdoor facilities in secondary schools was associated with students' daily physical activity participation during breaks (Haug et al. 2010). Furthermore, a subsequent Australian study of primary aged children had similar results, suggesting that larger grassed areas and the provision of sports equipment were associated with class-time and recess physical activity (Martin et al. 2012).

In summary, the presence of proximate local sporting and recreational opportunities is associated with increased physical activity, particularly for children, adolescents and older adults. The evidence for able-bodied adults is less clear, and it may be that convenience, rather than geographic proximity, is more important to those with access to a motor vehicle. However, the presence of proximate public open space is consistently shown to be associated with recreational walking. The importance of accessible local public open space is now considered.

A network of public open spaces

Public open space is defined as a 'managed open space, typically green and available and open to all, even if temporally controlled' (Carmona 2010, p. 169). It includes a variety of spaces such as parks, playgrounds, sports fields and urban squares. Access to public open space has numerous community and health benefits, including promoting physical activity as well as mental health (Sugiyama and Ward Thompson 2008; Francis 2010; Coutts et al. 2013). For children and adolescents, public open space is not only a place to play outdoors, but to socialise, explore and escape the constraints of an 'increasingly adult world' (Wood 2009, p. 1). As cities urbanise and become denser, the provision of public open space will become even more important as access to private open space declines (Giles-Corti et al. 2012).

Living in close proximity to public open space is associated with increased physical activity in all age groups (see Figure 9.3) (Li et al. 2005; Cohen et al. 2006a; Coutts et al. 2013).

Figure 9.3   Public open spaces can be either a destination to walk to or a setting to walk within

Source: Authors.

A longitudinal study of adults found that walking for recreation increased by around 18 minutes per week for each type of recreational destination present in the neighbourhood (Giles-Corti et al. 2013). Further, as highlighted earlier, children and adolescents living within 800 metres of local parks and sports centres are more likely to use them, as well as walk or cycle to them (Epstein et al. 2006). Engagement in after-school physical activity is enhanced if the local park contains play or sports equipment (Cohen et al. 2006a).

Aside from proximity, there is evidence that access to large attractive public open space with supportive infrastructure for physical activity promotes recreational walking and other forms of exercise (Giles-Corti et al. 2005; Sugiyama et al. 2010). However, the provision and location of infrastructure requires careful consideration to maximise use by all groups. Conflicts can arise when the needs of different groups are not considered from the outset. For instance, the provision of skate ramps is important for adolescent Australian males as up to 21 per cent of them engage in skating, outnumbering participation rates in some traditional sports (ABS 2009). Yet one study found that while skate parks appeal to teenage boys, their presence may deter girls undertaking physical activity (Cohen et al. 2006a). Furthermore, large gatherings of adolescent boys at skate ramps can render older adults fearful, potentially inhibiting their park use. One solution is to locate skate parks centrally in very popular locations, frequented by the full spectrum of society, that is, children and families, adolescents, adults *and* older adults. In turn this generates natural surveillance, thereby increasing safety (Jacobs 1961), and perhaps avoiding the marginalisation of young people that might stem from siting skate parks in undesirable locations. From a public health perspective it is important to design open space to maximise use by all population groups.

In summary, providing access to a network of proximate, accessible and high quality public open spaces with a variety of supportive infrastructure catering to the needs of multiple user groups is good for physical and mental health. There is consistent evidence that neighbourhoods with well-designed public open space are associated with increased levels of physical activity in all age groups. Well used public open space encourages more users, and enhances natural surveillance thereby creating safer parks and neighbourhoods.

Evaluating higher density housing

Sprawled low density suburban development has become standard in many cities across the globe, particularly on the urban fringe (Bruegmann 2006; Soule 2006). This typically consists of uniform residential dwellings situated on large lots, with curvilinear street patterns and few (if any) destinations within walking distance. Instead, such neighbourhoods are served by large auto-oriented shopping complexes, with most employment and leisure activities undertaken outside the neighbourhood.

Sprawled low density housing development contrasts with the (relatively) higher density developments that have connected grid-pattern street networks and a mix of destinations integrated within close proximity of a variety of residential dwelling types (Duany et al. 2001). There is consistent evidence that these developments are associated with more walking – particularly for transport – across all age groups (Giles-Corti et al. 2012). However, higher residential densities and land use mix are interdependent. As observed by Handy (2005) it is not density per se that increases physical activities such as walking and cycling, rather, density works in combination with other built environment features. Walking for transport (and some forms of walking for recreation) is largely dependent on having somewhere to walk to – that is, a mix of shops, services and transport connections. However, notably, neighbourhoods require sufficient residential density to ensure that destinations are proximate to housing, and that local businesses are viable.

How much density is required to optimise physical activity outcomes? This question is not new – in the 1960s, visionary urbanist Jane Jacobs mused that consideration of appropriate city dwelling densities are a matter of performance and that we 'ought to look at densities in much the same way as we look at calories and vitamins. Right amounts are right amounts because of how they perform. And what is right differs in specific instances' (Jacobs 1961, p. 209).

If the focus of residential density recommendations is viewed through a 'health' lens, then the priority performance criterion for density would be the level that promotes *health and well-being*. More specifically, in the context of this chapter, it would be the *minimum* level of density that would encourage walking and cycling for transport and recreation.

Using a case study approach of compact developments that optimise walking outcomes, Campoli (2012) concluded that the lower end of the optimum range of densities *begins* at eight units of housing per acre or 20 dwellings per hectare. This threshold is consistent with empirical Australian evidence where densities of at least 20 dwellings per hectare were observed to be critical (Learnihan et al. 2011).

In summary, a certain level of density in a neighbourhood is essential because it determines the presence, proximity and viability of local amenities, for example public transport, shops and services. Densities no lower than around 20 dwellings per hectare are required to promote *health and well-being*, principally through walking for transport. However, the creation of higher density compact cities needs to be paired with an understanding of the impacts of increasing urban intensification on crime and residents' feelings of safety. Indeed, one key ingredient that facilitates local physical activity is how safe residents feel. Good urban design can contribute to this.

Crime prevention through environmental design

Numerous personal, social and built environment factors contribute to residents' feelings of safety and perceptions of neighbourhood crime. While some correlates of perceived safety cannot be changed (that is, women and older adults perceive themselves to be vulnerable to crime, and are consequently more fearful), other correlates can be targeted as a means of improving both crime-related safety *and* physical activity outcomes. This is particularly true of attributes of the built environment that encourage natural surveillance, or reflect social control and place attachment (Foster and Giles-Corti 2008). For example, suburban house characteristics that promote natural surveillance (for example, front porches) and reflect the residents' proprietary behaviour (for example, garden upkeep) appear to help contain the incidence of graffiti and disorder in the street – features which both aggravate safety concerns and deter walkers (Foster and Giles-Corti 2008). Further, increased natural surveillance contributes to children's physical activity, and adults' transport and recreational walking (Craig et al. 2002; Panter et al. 2008). This highlights the potential benefit of simple built environment interventions that optimise natural surveillance in suburban areas (Foster et al. 2011).

Although there is some evidence to the contrary (Hoehner et al. 2005), the literature generally suggests that well lit streets, with natural surveillance from surrounding buildings, and minimal physical incivilities can contribute to residents engaging in more physical activity (Chad et al. 2005; Evenson et al. 2007; Velasquez et al. 2009). For example, Foster and colleagues found that the likelihood of walking for recreation in the local neighbourhood almost halved when local parks had higher levels of disorder (Foster et al. 2012; see Figure 9.4). Counter-intuitive positive associations between physical incivilities and physical activity may be because more frequent walkers are exposed to, and therefore aware of, physical incivilities. Furthermore,

Figure 9.4   Graffiti and vandalism may deter walkers

Source: Authors.

incivilities tend to cluster in more populous areas, where there are additional places to walk (King 2008). Nonetheless, on balance, these results highlight the importance of natural surveillance and maintenance as a means of increasing a sense of safety for residents and users of public spaces, with ensuing benefits for physical activity levels.

Combating sprawl: liveable neighbourhoods in Perth, Western Australia

While the principles promoted in this chapter are laudable, the question is: are they achievable and how do they get implemented? By way of example, we offer a case study from Perth, Western Australia. The dominant mode of planning and development in Perth has resulted in a distinct fringe of peripheral suburbs with a widely dispersed population in low density residential development. This is accompanied by rigid spatial separation of homes, shops, daily services and places of employment. However, urban design and planning that promotes walking, cycling and public transport use has for some time been acknowledged and recommended by multiple sectors, including Western Australia's planning authorities.

In February 1998, the Western Australian State Government began trialling the 'Liveable Neighbourhoods Community Design Guidelines' (LNG). This was introduced to replace the conventional design codes and facilitate the development of sustainable suburban communities (Western Australian Planning Commission 2000). The LNG is essentially a local interpretation of New Urbanism, tailored to the Western Australian context. From 1998 to 2008 LNG provided developers and planners with a voluntary alternative to the existing policies that dictated land development practices. LNG has now been formally adopted by the Western Australian Planning Commission. It is now the preferred operational policy for the design and assessment of structure plans (regional, district and local). It is also used for subdivisions, for new urban and suburban (predominantly residential) areas in metropolitan and rural centres, on greenfield and large brownfield and urban infill sites.

A key intended outcome of the LNG has been to reduce suburban sprawl and car dependence and encourage more walking, cycling and public transport use (Western Australian Planning Commission 2000). The LNG consists of six general design topics, four of which provide more compact, self-sufficient, pedestrian-friendly neighbourhoods, with local destinations and public transport links. These design elements are:

- community design;
- movement networks;
- lot layout;
- public parkland.

The introduction of the LNG provided a unique opportunity for a natural experiment. In 2003 the RESIDential Environments (RESIDE) project commenced. The aim was to assess the impact of the policy on the walking, cycling and public transport behaviours of residents moving into new suburban greenfield developments (Giles-Corti et al. 2008). As part of the RESIDE project, a comprehensive process was devised to evaluate the levels of on-ground implementation of 43 LNG requirements across 36 housing developments. Measures were developed in geographic information systems (GIS) to quantify the degree of implementation as envisaged by the policy and to investigate whether greater levels of implementation led to better walking outcomes (Hooper et al. 2014).

The results showed that despite a lack of full implementation of the policy, positive impacts were observed for both transport and recreation walking behaviours (Hooper et al. 2014).

Moreover, there was a dose–response relationship between overall levels of policy compliance as well as the community design, movement network and lot layout elements with walking behaviours. In other words, the change in walking behaviour was associated with increased levels of implementation of the LNG policy after a certain exposure time. Critically, the results highlighted the importance of implementing the community design element, above and beyond that of the movement network and lot layout elements alone. This ensured that residents had a diversity of utilitarian destinations to walk to, thereby supporting walking for transport within the neighbourhood. In practice this suggests that simply providing the transportation networks, or even increasing density without providing local destinations, will be insufficient to increase physical activity. Compliance with the public parkland element in combination with the movement network element was also essential for encouraging recreational walking in the neighbourhood.

Longitudinal analyses from RESIDE provide additional support for the principles of the LNG policy (Christian et al. 2013; Giles-Corti et al. 2013). Participants who gained access to transport-related destinations after moving to their new neighbourhoods increased their transport walking by around six minutes per week for each type of utilitarian destination gained. Recreational walking increased by around 18 minutes per week for each type of recreational destination gained (Giles-Corti et al. 2013).

In general terms, RESIDE's results highlight the importance of policy as a means of achieving pedestrian and physical activity-friendly neighbourhoods. Nevertheless, in order to impact residents' physical activity, the findings highlight that greater attention must be given to policy implementation and compliance. In addition, while the main focus of this chapter has been on neighbourhood planning, this needs to be considered within the context of regional planning. Work from the UK has found that ad hoc small developments have limited effects on travel behaviour (Williams 2001). This results in widespread piecemeal residential developments, all of which are too small to warrant their own provision of a centre. Efforts to increase the walkability of local neighbourhoods will be more successful if achieved within a 'regional framework' focused on providing transit infrastructure and mixed used development (Southworth and Parthasarathy 1997).

Conclusions: the pivotal role of planners and urban designers

Our chapter has provided an overview of the ways in which the design of the built environment supports different groups in the community being physically active. Urban designers and planners have a critical role to play in designing physical activity-friendly communities. If successful, these communities will actively promote participation in varying types of physical activity, contributing to reducing the risk of chronic diseases. The impact of the built environment on health is profound. Professionals who plan and build communities have an enormous responsibility. Together their decisions create the underlying environmental conditions for good (or bad) health.

References

ABS (Australian Bureau of Statistics). 2009. Children's participation in organised sport and leisure activities. Canberra: ABS.

Boarnet, M.G., Anderson, C.L., Day, K., McMillan, T. and Alfonzo, M. 2005. Evaluation of the California Safe Routes to School legislation: urban form changes and children's active transportation to school. *American Journal of Preventive Medicine* 28(2), 134–140.

Bruegmann, R. 2006. *Sprawl: a compact history*. Chicago: University of Chicago Press.

Burton, N.W., Turrell, G., Oldenburg, B. and Sallis, J.F. 2005. The relative contributions of psychological, social and environmental variables to explain participation in walking, moderate-, and vigorous-intensity leisure-time physical activity. *Journal of Physical Activity and Health* 2, 181–196.

Campoli, J. 2012. *Made for walking*. Cambridge, MA: Lincoln Institute of Land Policy.

Cao, X., Handy, S.L. and Mokhtarian, P.L. 2006. The influences of the built environment and residential self-selection on pedestrian behavior: evidence from Austin, TX. *Transportation* 33, 1–20.

Carmona, M. 2010. Contemporary public space, part two: classification. *Journal of Urban Design* 15(2), 157–173.

Carver, A., Timperio, A.F. and Crawford, D.A. 2008. Neighborhood road environments and physical activity among youth: the CLAN study. *Journal of Urban Health: Bulletin of the New York Academy of Medicine* 85(4), 532–544.

Carver, A., Timperio, A., Hesketh, K. and Crawford, D. 2010. Are safety-related features of the road environment associated with smaller declines in physical activity among youth? *Journal of Urban Health: Bulletin of the New York Academy of Medicine* 87(1), 29–43.

Chad, K.E., Reeder, B.A., Harrison, E.L., Ashworth, N.L., Sheppard, S.M., Schultz, S.L., Bruner, B.G., Fisher, K.L. and Lawson, J.A. 2005. Profile of physical activity levels in community-dwelling older adults. *Medicine and Science in Sports and Exercise* 37(10), 1774–1784.

Christian, H., Knuiman, M., Bull, F., Timperio, A., Foster, S., Divitini, M., Middleton, N. and Giles-Corti, B. 2013. A new urban planning code's impact on walking: the Residential Environments Project. *American Journal of Public Health* 103(7), 1219–1228.

Cohen, D.A., Ashwood, J.S., Scott, M.M., Overton, A., Evenson, K.R., Staten, L.K., Porter, D., McKenzie, T.L. and Catellier, D. 2006a. Public parks and physical activity among adolescent girls. *Pediatrics* 118(5), e1381–e1389.

Cohen, D.A. et al. 2006b. Proximity to school and physical activity among middle school girls: the Trial of Activity for Adolescent Girls Study. *Journal of Physical Activity and Health* 3(Suppl 1), S129–S138.

Coutts, C., Chapin, T., Horner, M. and Taylor, C. 2013. County-level effects of green space access on physical activity. *Journal of Physical Activity and Health* 10(2), 232–240.

Craig, C.L., Brownson, R.C., Cragg, S.E. and Dunn, A.L. 2002. Exploring the effect of the environment on physical activity: a study examining walking to work. *American Journal of Preventive Medicine* 23(2), 36–43.

Duany, A., Plater-Zyberk, E. and Speck, J. 2001. *Suburban nation: the rise of sprawl and the decline of the American dream*. New York: Macmillan.

Epstein, L.H., Raja, S., Gold, S.S., Paluch, R.A., Pak, Y. and Roemmich, J.N. 2006. Reducing sedentary behavior: the relationship between park area and the physical activity of youth. *Psychological Science* 17(8), 654–659.

Evenson, K.R., Scott, M.M., Cohen, D.A. and Voorhees, C.C. 2007. Girls' perception of neighborhood factors on physical activity, sedentary behavior, and BMI. *Obesity* 15(2), 430–445.

Foster, S. and Giles-Corti, B. 2008. The built environment, neighborhood crime and constrained physical activity: an exploration of inconsistent findings. *Preventive Medicine* 47(3), 241–251.

Foster, S., Giles-Corti, B. and Knuiman, M. 2011. Creating safe walkable streetscapes: does house design and upkeep discourage incivilities in suburban neighbourhoods? *Journal of Environmental Psychology* 31(1), 79–88.

Foster, S., Giles-Corti, B. and Knuiman, M. 2012. Does fear of crime discourage walkers? A social-ecological exploration of fear as a deterrent to walking. *Environment and Behavior* 46(6), 698–717.

Francis, J. 2010. *The relationship between public open space, sense of community and mental health*, PhD, The University of Western Australia.

Frank, L., Kerr, J., Chapman, J. and Sallis, J. 2007. Urban form relationships with walk trip frequency and distance among youth. *American Journal of Health Promotion* 21(4), 305–311.

Giles-Corti, B., Broomhall, M.H., Knuiman, M., Collins, C., Douglas, K., Ng, K., Lange, A. and Donovan, R.J. 2005. Increasing walking: how important is distance to, attractiveness, and size of public open space? *American Journal of Preventive Medicine* 28(2), 169–176.

Giles-Corti, B., Knuiman, M., Timperio, A., Van Niel, K., Pikora, T.J., Bull, F.C., Shilton, T. and Bulsara, M. 2008. Evaluation of the implementation of a state government community design policy aimed at increasing local walking: design issues and baseline results from RESIDE, Perth, Western Australia. *Preventive Medicine* 46(1), 46–54.

Giles-Corti, B., Wood, G., Pikora, T., Learnihan, V., Bulsara, M., Van Niel, K., Timperio, A., McCormack, G. and Villanueva, K. 2011. School site and the potential to walk to school: the impact of street connectivity and traffic exposure in school neighborhoods. *Health & Place* 17(2), 545–550.

Giles-Corti, B., Ryan, K. and Foster, S. 2012. Increasing density in Australia: maximising the health benefits and minimising harm. Report to the National Heart Foundation of Australia. Melbourne: National Heart Foundation of Australia.

Giles-Corti, B., Bull, F., Knuiman, M., McCormack, G., Van Niel, K., Timperio, A., Christian, H. and Boruff, B. 2013. The influence of urban design on neighbourhood walking following residential relocation: longitudinal results from the RESIDE study. *Social Science & Medicine* 77, 20–30.

Handy, S. 2005. Critical assessment of the literature on the relationships among transportation, land use, and physical activity. Resource paper for TRB Special Report 282. Washington, DC: Transportation Research Board and the Institute of Medicine Committee on Physical Activity, Health, Transportation, and Land Use.

Handy, S., Paterson, R.G. and Butler, K. 2003. *Planning for street connectivity: getting from here to there.* Chicago: American Planning Association.

Haug, E., Torsheim, T., Sallis, J.F. and Samdal, O. 2010. The characteristics of the outdoor school environment associated with physical activity. *Health Education Research* 25(2), 248–256.

Hoehner, C.M., Brennan Ramirez, L.K., Elliott, M.B., Handy, S.L. and Brownson, R.C. 2005. Perceived and objective environmental measures and physical activity among urban adults. *American Journal of Preventive Medicine* 28(2), 105–116.

Hooper, P., Giles-Corti, B. and Knuiman, M. 2014. Evaluating the implementation and active living impacts of a state government planning policy designed to create walkable neighborhoods in Perth, Western Australia. *American Journal of Health Promotion* 28(3 Suppl), S5–S18.

Jacobs, J. 1961. *The death and life of great American cities.* London: Jonathon Cape.

Kent, J.L. and Thompson, S. 2014. The three domains of urban planning for health and well-being. *Journal of Planning Literature*, published online 19 February 2014.

Kerr, J., Frank, L.D., Sallis, J. and Chapman, J. 2007. Urban form correlates of pedestrian travel in youth: differences by gender, race, ethnicity and household attributes. Transportation Research Part D 12: 177–182.

Kerr, J., Rosenberg, D., Sallis, J.F., Saelens, B.E., Frank, L.D. and Conway, T.L. 2006. Active commuting to school: associations with environment and parental concerns. *Medicine and Science in Sports and Exercise* 38(4), 787–793.

King, D. 2008. Neighbourhood and individual factors in activity in older adults: results from the Neighbourhood and Senior Health Study. *Journal of Aging and Physical Activity* 16, 144–170.

Koohsari, M.J., Badland, H. and Giles-Corti, B. 2013. (Re)Designing the built environment to support physical activity: bringing public health back into urban design and planning. *Cities* 35, 294–298.

Learnihan, V., Van Niel, K.P., Giles-Corti, B. and Knuiman, M. 2011. Effect of scale on the links between walking and urban design. *Geographical Research* 49(2), 183–191.

Lee, I.M., Shiroma, E.J., Lobelo, F., Puska, P., Blair, S.N. and Katzmarzyk, P.T. 2012. Effect of physical inactivity on major non-communicable diseases worldwide: an analysis of burden of disease and life expectancy. *Lancet* 380(9838), 219–229.

Li, F., Fisher, K.J. and Brownson, R.C. 2005. A multilevel analysis of change in neighbourhood walking activity in older adults. *Journal of Aging and Physical Activity* 13, 145–159.

Li, F., Harmer, P.A., Cardinal, B.J., Bosworth, M., Acock, A., Johnson-Shelton, D. and Moore, J.M. 2008. Built environment, adiposity, and physical activity in adults aged 50–75. *American Journal of Preventive Medicine* 35(1), 38–46.

Martin, K., Bremner, A., Salmon, J., Rosenberg, M. and Giles-Corti, B. 2012. School and individual-level characteristics are associated with children's moderate to vigorous-intensity physical activity during school recess. *Australian and New Zealand Journal of Public Health* 36(5), 469–477.

McCormack, G.R., Giles-Corti, B. and Bulsara, M. 2007. Correlates of using neighborhood recreational destinations in physically active respondents. *Journal of Physical Activity & Health* 4(1), 39–53.

McCormack, G., Giles-Corti, B. and Bulsara, M. 2008. The relationship between destination proximity, destination mix and physical activity behaviors. *Preventative Medicine* 46(1), 33–40.

Merom, D., Tudor-Locke, C., Bauman, A. and Rissel, C. 2006. Active commuting to school among NSW primary school children: implications for public health. *Health & Place* 12(4), 678–687.

Michael, Y.L., Beard, T., Choi, D., Farquhar, S.A. and Carlson, N. 2006. Measuring the influence of built neighborhood environments on walking in older adults. *Journal of Aging and Physical Activity* 14(3), 302–312.

Michael, Y.L., Perdue, L.A., Orwoll, E.S., Stefanick, M.L. and Marshall, L.M. 2010. Physical activity resources and changes in walking in a cohort of older men. *American Journal of Public Health* 100(4), 654–660.

Milio, N. 1986. *Promoting health through public policy.* Ottawa: Canadian Public Health Association.

Panter, J., Jones, A. and van Sluijs, E. 2008. Environmental determinants of active travel in youth: a review and framework for future research. *International Journal of Behavioral Nutrition and Physical Activity* 5, 34.

Sallis, J.F., Hovell, M.F., Hofstetter, C.R., Elder, J.P., Hackley, M., Caspersen, C.J. and Powell, K.E. 1990. Distance between homes and exercise facilities related to frequency of exercise among San Diego residents. *Public Health Reports* 105(2), 179–185.

Sallis, J.F., Floyd, M.F., Rodríguez, D.A. and Saelens, B.E. 2012. Role of built environments in physical activity, obesity, and cardiovascular disease. *Circulation* 125(5), 729–737.

Soule, D.C. 2006. *Urban sprawl: a comprehensive reference guide.* Westport, CT: Greenwood Publishing Group.

Southworth, M. and Parthasarathy, B. 1997. The suburban public realm II: Eurourbanism, new urbanism and the implications for urban design in the American metropolis. *Journal of Urban Design* 2(1), 9–34.

Stephenson, J. and Bauman, A. 2000. *The cost of illness attributable to physical inactivity in Australia.* Canberra: CDHAC and Australian Sports Commission.

Strath, S.J., Greenwald, M.J., Isaacs, R., Hart, T.L., Lenz, E.K., Dondzila, C.J. and Swartz, A.M. 2012. Measured and perceived environmental characteristics are related to accelerometer defined physical activity in older adults. *International Journal of Behavioral Nutrition and Physical Activity* 9, 40.

Sugiyama, T. and Ward Thompson, C. 2008. Associations between characteristics of neighbourhood open space and older people's walking. *Urban Forestry an Urban Greening* 7(1), 41–51.

Sugiyama, T., Leslie, E., Giles-Corti, B. and Owen, N. 2009. Physical activity for recreation or exercise on neighbourhood streets: associations with perceived environmental attributes. *Health & Place* 15(4), 1058–1063.

Sugiyama, T.P., Francis, J.M., Middleton, N.B., Owen, N.P. and Giles-Corti, B.P. 2010. Associations between recreational walking and attractiveness, size, and proximity of neighborhood open spaces. *American Journal of Public Health* 100(9), 1752.

Sugiyama, T., Neuhaus, M., Cole, R., Giles-Corti, B. and Owen, N. 2012. Destination and route attributes associated with adults' walking: a review. *Medicine & Science in Sports & Exercise* 44(7), 1275–1286.

Timperio, A., Ball, K., Salmon, J., Roberts, R., Giles-Corti, B., Simmons, D. and Baur, L.A. 2006. Personal, family, social, and environmental correlates of active commuting to school. *American Journal of Preventive Medicine* 30(1), 45–51.

Titze, S., Giles-Corti, B., Knuiman, M., Pikora, T., Timperio, A., Bull, F. and van Niel, K. 2010. Associations between intrapersonal and neighborhood environmental characteristics and cycling for transport and recreation in adults: baseline results from the RESIDE Study. *Journal of Physical Activity and Health* 7, 423–431.

Transportation Research Board. 2002. *The relative risks of school travel.* Washington, DC, Transportation Research Board.

Transportation Research Board. 2005. *Does the built environment influence physical activity? Examining the evidence.* Washington, DC: Transportation Research Board.

Trapp, G., Giles-Corti, B., Christian, H., Bulsara, M., Timperio, A., McCormack, G. and Villanueva, K. 2011. On your bike! A cross-sectional study of the individual, social and environmental correlates of cycling to school. *International Journal of Behavioral Nutrition and Physical Activity* 8, 123.

Trapp, G.S.A., Giles-Corti, B., Christian, H.E., Bulsara, M., Timperio, A.F., McCormack, G.R. and Villanueva, K.P. 2012. Increasing children's physical activity: individual, social, and environmental factors associated with walking to and from school. *Health Education & Behavior* 39(2), 172–182.

United Nations. 2011. Sixty seventh session political declaration of the high level meeting of the General Assembly on the prevention and control of non-communicable diseases. From www.un.org/ga/search/view_doc.asp?symbol=A/66/L.1

United Nations Population Fund. 2011. *State of world population 2010.* New York: UNFPA.

Veitch, J., Salmon, J. and Ball, K. 2010. Individual, social and physical environmental correlates of children's active free-play: a cross-sectional study. *International Journal of Behavioral Nutrition and Physical Activity* 7(11): doi 10.1186/1479-5868-7-11

Velasquez, K., Holahan, C. and You, X. 2009. Relationship of perceived environmental characteristics to leisure-time physical activity and meeting recommendations for physical activity in Texas. *Preventing Chronic Disease* 6(1), A24.

Villanueva, K., Giles-Corti, B., Bulsara, M., Timperio, A., McCormack, G., Beesley, B., Trapp, G. and Middleton, N. 2013. Where do children travel to and what local opportunities are available? The relationship between neighborhood destinations and children's independent mobility. *Environment and Behavior* 45(6), 679–705.

Western Australian Planning Commission. 2000. *Liveable neighbourhoods: a Western Australian government sustainable cities initiative.* Perth: Western Australian Planning Commission.

Williams, K. 2001. Does intensifying cities make them more sustainable? In Williams, K., Burton, E. and Jenks, M. (Eds) *Achieving sustainable urban form*. London: E & FN Spon Press, pp. 30–45.

Wood, L. 2009. Parks and open space: for the health and wellbeing of children and young people. Action for Young Australians Report. Perth: Australian Research Alliance for Children and Youth (ARACY).

World Health Organization. 2006. *Obesity and overweight*. Geneva: WHO.

Ziviani, J., Kopeshke, R. and Wadley, D. 2006. Children walking to school: parent perceptions of environmental and psychosocial influences. *Australian Occupational Therapy Journal* 53(1), 27–34.

10

HEALTHY PLAY FOR ALL AGES IN PUBLIC OPEN SPACES

Lamine Mahdjoubi and Ben Spencer

Introduction: play throughout the life course

Play in outdoor environments can make a positive contribution to the well-being of all – from children to those in later life. This chapter will establish the benefits of play in public urban environments such as streets and open spaces. It will show how play can increase levels of physical fitness across different age and social groups, improving and sustaining people's quality of life and independence well into older age. To date, this field of study has been dominated by a piecemeal age and gender specific approach. We seek to provide a more holistic appreciation focusing on the characteristics of urban environments that are conducive to outdoor play and the many health and well-being benefits that result. In this context, play is something possible throughout the course of a person's life.

This chapter examines relevant health issues, policy and practice before exploring the nature of play and leisure in more depth. To illustrate the interaction of the environment with play across the life course, a case study of play by groups of people of different ages is then examined, before final conclusions for policy and practice are drawn.

Background

A sustainable urban environment is one where the environmental quality of streets, parks and outdoor space both supports and encourages healthy lifestyles for all. The importance of 'age friendly' cities providing suitable outdoor spaces for older people to age in a place with a good quality of life has been promoted by the World Health Organization (WHO 2007). The right of the child to play and recreation was endorsed by the United Nations Declaration on the Rights of the Child in 1959 and strengthened by the United Nations Committee on the Rights of the Child (UN CRC) in 2013. More specifically the local neighbourhood is the urban environment that is particularly important for those in early and later life where opportunities for movement further afield can be more limited. This has been recognised in the development of UK policy such as Lifetime Neighbourhoods which emphasises that it is 'the neighbourhoods where we live that have a significant role in keeping us well and independent as we grow old' (DCLG 2011 p. 7) and the place where older people want to see change to support healthy ageing (Age-Friendly New York City 2012).

The increasing incidence of chronic non-communicable disease, such as heart disease, stroke, diabetes and cancer due to poor diet and lack of exercise, has been acknowledged (WHO 2009). In the face of such challenges, people's play in attractive and accessible outdoor areas is seen as potentially contributing to the population's health and well-being. Play in outdoor environments has the potential to enhance levels of physical activity, both formal and informal, encourage independence and social interaction, particularly in children and older adults, as well as contribute to better mental health and relief from depression and stress (Morris 2003). Access outdoors and use of public open space can also increase social networks and build social capital. In addition, playing in natural settings has been identified as a way to reduce bullying among children (Malone and Tranter 2003). Yet several factors have paved the way for a decline in the use of the outdoors. In an international review of children's contemporary play opportunities Lester and Russell (2010) identify a number of environmental 'stressors' in modern urban life including traffic, environmental hazards, parental overprotection and risk aversion. Amongst these factors, fear of victimisation has been recognised as a major obstacle for outdoor activity, especially by children, women and older people (Pantazis 2000), along with a lack of suitable spaces and facilities (Cole-Hamilton 2011). The results of a study carried out in the US showed that children were physically active for an extra 49 minutes a week in neighbourhoods perceived as safe, compared to their counterparts in neighbourhoods considered unsafe (Molnar et al. 2004).

Definitions of play

Opportunities for play throughout the life course are emerging as an area of interest across many disciplines. Within urban design the playfulness of the Situationists has grown into explorations of the ludic, or playful, city (Stevens 2007). The benefits of good emotions associated with play are also found in the current research and policy interest in positive psychology (New Economics Foundation 2011).

Play is, however, an ambiguous concept (Sutton-Smith 1997) and hard to define (Whitebread 2012). Within the realm of children's play a clear and generally understood definition is lacking. Nevertheless, the UN CRC (2013) states that play by children (those aged under 18 or the country's age of majority) is 'any behaviour, activity or process initiated, controlled and structured by children themselves'. Further, play by children is

> . . . non-compulsory, driven by intrinsic motivation and undertaken for its own sake, rather than as a means to an end. Play involves the exercise of autonomy, physical, mental or emotional activity, and has the potential to take infinite forms, either in groups or alone . . . The key characteristics of play are fun, uncertainty, challenge, flexibility and non-productivity. Together, these factors contribute to the enjoyment it produces and the consequent incentive to continue to play.
>
> *(UN CRC 2013, pp. 4–5)*

Following an extensive review of the literature on play and children, Lester and Russell (2008) concluded that the dominant paradigm for understanding play is centred on child development. This views children's play as preparation for adulthood and can be understood as utilitarian (Woodyer 2012) with immediate and deferred benefits for children's cognitive, emotional and social development (Cohen 2006). It has been argued that adults, as well as children, play in many ways (Sutton-Smith 1997; Stevens 2007; Brown 2008) and that play is vitally important for adults too (Huizinga 1955; Whitebread 2012).

This chapter adopts the premise that play is a state of mind where thoughts and actions are perceived to be freely chosen, personally directed and intrinsically motivated in the pursuit of positive affect. Play can be understood as a non-serious engagement in the moment with the real and imagined social and physical environment, with thoughts and activities undertaken for their own sake (Spencer et al. 2013). This means that it is possible to play throughout one's life, even if the expression of playfulness is not as prevalent in adults as it is in children (Millar 1968). Historically, play has been identified as a lifelong phenomenon (Whitebread 2012) and is increasingly being recognised as such (see for example Play Scotland in Cole-Hamilton 2011).

The state of mind underpinning play is different to that which is commonly found in functional everyday life. Nevertheless, it can still be present in such instrumental activities (Sutton-Smith 1997). A playful state of mind may lead to playful physical activity and expression, such as smiles and laughter. In this way shared acknowledgement that play is happening occurs. Play in public spaces can also involve spontaneity, creativity, self-expression and the seeking out of physical and emotional risk, along with the flexible, experimental and adaptive use of objects, relationships and rules (Lester and Russell 2008). Play can be experienced individually, but public spaces have particular potential to enable social play by adults (Stevens 2007; Hayllar and Griffin 2009) and between generations (Spencer 2013) – a shared experience that resonates even after play has finished (Huizinga 1955).

Impact of play on physical activity, social interaction and development

The benefits of play across the life course can be summarised as the experiencing of enjoyment, social interaction and bonding, a sense of freedom and control, physical activity, the satisfaction and enjoyment of supporting the development of others, the maintenance and development of self-identity, and of new activities. However, opportunities for benefiting from play are often limited. The following section outlines the key factors involved.

Physically active play, particularly in the early years, can lead to the development of bodily attributes including strong bones and muscles and good lung capacity, providing endurance and co-ordination. Physical exercise and other activities in natural surroundings have been shown to be particularly effective in reducing blood pressure, stress and mental fatigue, and improving cognitive functioning (Hartig et al. 2003). There is some evidence that patterns of activity established when young relate to adult activity levels (Matthews et al. 2011).

The health benefits of physical activity from walking, running or playing formalised sport are well understood. While there is an extensive literature on the benefits of exercise for older people in public open space, the physical benefits of play for older people have not been researched in detail. Play can offer opportunities throughout the life course for individuals to develop attachment to people and place (Lester and Russell 2008). This is particularly important in terms of the development of children's friendships (Panksepp 2007). Physical skills such as running and climbing, together with co-ordination, can be developed through active play. Unaccompanied activities by children are particularly important as over time these independent experiences result in a feeling of competence (Huttenmoser 1995). Agency allows children to learn negotiation skills and to be creative (Parker 1998; Lester and Russell 2010). Play provides opportunities for developing and testing relationships with peers and people of other ages, learning negotiation skills, experiencing different roles, and developing language and comprehension. Play is an important tool not only for developing these social skills, but also for nurturing the wider culture of a community (Hart 1994).

While the literature on adults and play is much more limited, the potential contribution of play to adult mental and physical health, adaptability, creativity and sense of well-being has also been identified (Kane 2004; Stevens 2007; Brown 2009), along with increased social capital and thus better quality of life.

When considering the benefits of play for adults research from positive psychology is relevant. Enjoyment is an important aspect of play. It brings short-term positive affect which, it can be argued, is sufficient on its own to justify encouraging play (Lester and Russell 2010). On balance, having more positive than negative emotions contributes to long term well-being (Diener et al. 1991). Positive affect has also been linked to the development of resilience in adults (Fredrickson 2004) with positive emotions playing an important role in helping people to cope with negative events (Tugade et al. 2004). Fredrickson argues that 'positive emotions prompt individuals to engage with their environments and partake in activities' (2004, p. 1368) and that playful activity has a longer-term social impact as shared amusement and smiles create social bonds.

The benefits of humour and laughter, which are often involved in play, have been identified as the initiation and regulation of social interaction, signalling that play is currently happening and improving longer term resistance to health risks (Pressman and Cohen 2005). It has also been suggested that cognitive function and emotional growth may be maintained and encouraged by playfulness in later life (Elder et al. 2003).

In their study of older women Yarnal et al. (2008, p. 235) concluded that play is a 'context for fun, laughter, and feeling good'. They found that older women appreciate the opportunity to be 'silly and goofy' around each other in an unstructured context that offers freedom from the grind of everyday life, enabling participants to think and behave in unusual ways. Short term enjoyment can produce longer term well-being, and providing opportunities for play in public open space is an important way of facilitating this to happen. We now go on to discuss how different environments support play.

Play and developing a relationship with the environment

Experimentation with the environment through exploration, testing and influencing a range of environments provides experiences of surprise which help the development of emotional regulation (Lester and Russell 2010). The importance of play in natural environments has received much recent interest. Play in such settings can provide children with opportunities for personal development, emotional resilience, increased cognitive functioning, a sense of freedom and chances for self-discovery (Pretty et al. 2009; Louv 2009). Outdoor play allows children to explore their local neighbourhood, learn the rules of everyday life and discover the different textures and elements in the world (Clements 2004).

There is evidence to suggest that children value and prefer natural environments to urban and built environments. The former are associated with adventure, risk and the challenge of being outdoors (Titman 1994). In the US, it was found that publicly owned natural spaces are an ideal resource to support various aspects of human health and well-being (Maller et al. 2006). Healthy therapeutic affect is experienced by children who are directly exposed to nature (Wells and Evans 2003). Natural environments are also associated with the cognitive development of children through opportunities for exploration, experimentation and play (Hart 1994). Active learning in outdoor settings stimulates all aspects of child development more readily than indoor environments (Moore and Wong 1996).

The dynamic relationship between person and place

The relationship between an individual and their physical and social environment is dynamic. There is the potential for the experience of play in public space to provide benefits to the individual, as well as the wider community. This can come about in terms of the quality of public open space and the realisation of the right to the city for all (Harvey 2008). These benefits of play in the public sphere are summarised in Figure 10.1.

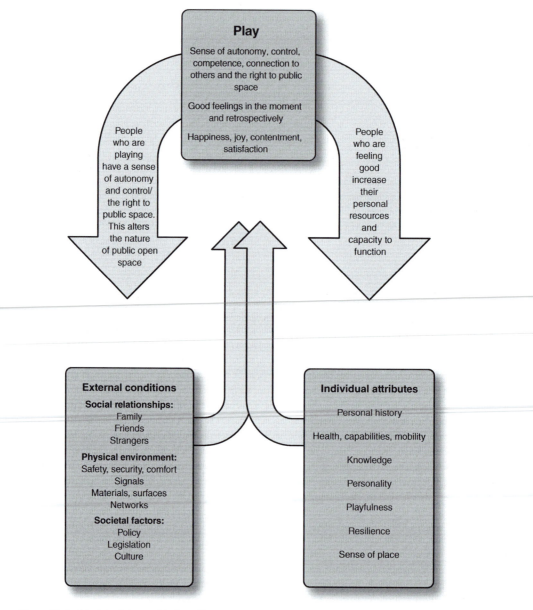

Figure 10.1   Model of play and its benefits

Source: Adapted from Spencer (2013) based on New Economics Foundation (2011) model of well-being.

Restrictions on play

The types and location of play, as well as who participates, can vary widely between communities depending on what is culturally acceptable (Gaskins et al. 2007). The different experiences of play by children across the globe have also been contrasted (Lester and Russell 2010) and common factors identified that restrict children's access to play in cities. These factors include the danger of traffic, pollution and other environmental hazards, lack of natural environments and public open spaces that can be appropriated for play, and risk aversion by parents which can lead to overprotection and limited opportunities for children to travel independently. The outcome is an 'islanding' of the experiences of children as they are transported around the city by adults (Furedi 2001; Gill 2007; Freeman and Tranter 2011). In essence this is a spatial ghettoisation of children's urban involvement. Freeman and Tranter argue that 'children have become increasingly relegated to "child spaces" in the city and are increasingly unwelcome in others' (2011, pp. 10–11) – a contradiction to the recognised benefits of independent mobility and free play.

Children's opportunities for play depend on many interacting variables. The UN CRC (2013) identifies particular concerns for children from poor backgrounds, those with disabilities, children belonging to minorities and indigenous children. There are also concerns about play opportunities for girls for whom play may be seen by some as inappropriate or a waste of time. In addition, girls generally have fewer opportunities to play outdoors and travel very far (Lester and Russell 2010). In socio-economic terms, Lester and Russell (2010) identify a tendency for middle class children to participate in activities structured by adults and not to play in public space. Older people are similarly affected in accessing public spaces for play. This can be related to mental and physical health and poverty, as well as loneliness and isolation. It terms of the urban environment, adult participation in play can be limited by simple factors such as a lack of seating or public toilets. Conversely, access can be encouraged by good quality and enjoyable paths (Sugiyama et al. 2009).

To examine the relationship between the urban environment and play, we use the following case study which focuses on research carried out in Bristol, England. The first study was an examination of children's play in their neighbourhood using Global Positioning System (GPS) devices and parental questionnaires. The second was a qualitative study of the meaning and nature of play for people over 65. This case study illustrates issues relating to play across the life course discussed in the subsequent section of the chapter.

Environmental characteristics and children's play: case study

The quality of play taking place in formal places (playgrounds), informal places (front gardens, streets and open spaces) and private gardens was studied in a neighbourhood in north Bristol (see Figure 10.2). The research involved 64 children, aged between seven and ten years old, and their parents/guardians (Rowhani 2011).

Each child's play in the outdoor environment and after school hours was examined over a seven day week.

The study showed that the typology of play spaces (informal, formal and private) are related to the levels of interaction among children. The levels of interaction between peers are higher among those children who play in informal spaces. The passive supervision of these informal spaces supported more interaction among children. A positive relationship was also found between the level of friendship and frequency of play in informal spaces. This confirms that informal places in Bristol, such as streets, support and nurture social interaction amongst

Figure 10.2   Children play in informal spaces

Source: Mahdjoubi.

children. Children tended to play longer and more frequently in informal areas that are hard landscaped (that is, tarmac and block paving). These spaces, particularly streets, are often closer to children's homes (Figure 10.3).

In relation to playgrounds, children spent relatively longer periods of time per visit, but the frequency of these visits was rare, compared to play in neighbourhood informal spaces. A positive association was also found between playing in informal play spaces and children's levels of physical activity.

In addition, the study showed that children who regularly played in informal spaces had almost double the independent mobility range when compared to children who did not play in such spaces. Further, accompaniment of children by adults adversely affected the duration and

Location	% Frequency	% duration 60 minutes plus
Neighbourhood streets	78	51
Neighbourhood playgrounds	23	59
Home gardens	73	53

Figure 10.3   Frequency of play episodes and duration of outdoor play

Source: Mahdjoubi in Rowhani (2011).

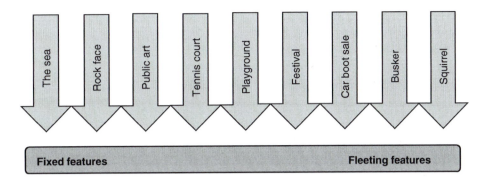

The sea · Rock face · Public art · Tennis court · Playground · Festival · Car boot sale · Busker · Squirrel

Fixed features · **Fleeting features**

Figure 10.4   A range of examples of playful temporal features in public open space

Source: Spencer (2013, p. 198).

frequency of the children's outdoor play. Parents' perceptions of neighbourhood safety and on-site supervision were also associated to children's levels of physical activity.

In summary, the results of this study suggest that play in informal spaces within the neighbourhood is significantly and positively associated with higher levels of play frequency, physical activity, sociability and independent mobility among children.

The second study involved 33 people aged over 65 from a wide range of socio-economic backgrounds. They lived in different areas of Bristol and participated in focus groups exploring their understanding of play. The interviewees tended not to relate the term 'play' to their own experiences, but enthusiastically reported doing a variety of activities that can be understood as playful. They also talked about a constrained desire to undertake more playful activities and how being with their grandchildren provided them with a 'glorious excuse' for such behaviour. The permission provided through signs, trails and the behaviour of other people were important in encouraging their playful behaviour. The participants also found pleasure in watching other people being playful, particularly their own offspring, but also strangers.

Subsequent walking interviews, where the researcher accompanied the participant on a walk and discussed their experience *in situ*, revealed a variety of positive experiences in different public open spaces. These included activities such as observing wildlife, plants, public art, performers and other details of the built environment along different routes. As well, participants spoke about relating personal and historical knowledge about the environment, and other enjoyable pursuits including car boot sales. Playful activities embraced a range of temporal features as shown in Figure 10.4.

Participants were adamant that basic amenities, particularly public toilets and seating, had to be in place before playfulness could occur. They also needed to feel safe, secure and free from intimidation by other users of the outdoor space to be able to express their playfulness. Play for the older people in this study was associated less with the commercialised landscapes of consumption, such as shopping centres, even with their toilets, cafes and other places to rest, but was more closely associated with informal spaces.

Places for playfulness to thrive

We now turn to examining the requirements of the built and social environments that can enable play. Most factors apply equally across all ages and groups, but there are some conditions essential for specific needs. Burghardt (2005, quoted in Lester and Russell 2010) identifies four conditions that are necessary, but not sufficient, for play:

1. enough bodily energy after basic survival needs are satisfied for both a playful disposition, as well as its realisation;
2. a 'relaxed field' where more urgent survival needs have been met;
3. stimulation in the form of physical and social affordances; and
4. a style of life that involves complex sequences of behaviour in varying conditions.

Globally there are severe problems of poverty and deprivation affecting basic human needs that are beyond the scope of this chapter. The focus here is on how to create a 'relaxed field' with varying physical and social features that can enable play. As Lester and Russell argue: 'Being able to play will not alleviate poverty and hardships, but it may help to act as a buffer against associated stress' (2010, p. 47).

Urban experience depends on a range of factors at varying scales from the city to the street, public space and building (Freeman and Tranter 2011). Detailed design of these spaces is critical. The majority of design guidance on play has, to date, focused on play facilities for children. A critique of the preponderance of what have been termed 'KFC' playgrounds (Kit, Fence and Carpet) in the UK has questioned the play value of standard equipment placed on a plastic safety surface and surrounded by a fence to keep children in and dogs out. There is a sense that these are frequently provided more to fulfil planning obligations rather than fulfilling the play needs of the community.

Beyond simple physical activity, playgrounds offer little in terms of imaginative and social play (Freeman and Tranter 2011). This lack has contributed to the development of the concept of 'playable space' for children (Shackell et al. 2008). Defined as places where youngsters are free to play, these spaces have features with potential play value integrated into the landscape, as well as a social setting and wider culture that supports children's play. The broader concept of a multifunctional space that enables play (Sanson et al. 2012, p. vi) is 'a "shared" public space or communal space, which offers a range of leisure and recreation opportunities for users of all ages'. This supports the vision of Lifetime Neighbourhoods (DCLG 2011) where people of all ages have access to places near their homes. Such spaces are comfortable and relaxing, and provide a range of opportunities for social contact and physical activity.

What is crucially important is independent mobility. This need is demonstrated by our case study and other research. The studies of McKendrick et al. (2000) and Furedi (2001) relate children's independent mobility to free play in neighbourhood outdoor spaces. These findings also support Wheway and Millward (1997), who found that travelling from one place to another constitutes a significant amount of time spent outdoors by children.

Improvements in the street network connectivity for pedestrians, along with a reduction in traffic volume, tend to facilitate children's access to informal neighbourhood spaces. Enabling children's ease of independent movement within the neighbourhood is positively associated with higher levels of physical activity and sociability. Similarly, for older people, connectivity along pleasant routes is important for supporting and encouraging access to the neighbourhood (Sugiyama et al. 2009). This needs to be supported by sufficient seating, which can be viewed as 'staging posts', as well as reliable availability of decent toilets at frequent intervals.

Our case study suggests that a richness of opportunities for playfulness should be integrated throughout the urban realm rather than simply at leisure destinations. These 'playable spaces' should also be suitable for intergenerational play where both direct opportunities, together with the chance to observe others playing, can be afforded. While older people may not be able to always engage in the range of physical playful activities, they can relish 'play-form' social interaction (Simmel and Hughes 1949). Playful public open space can support this by providing a focus for social contact and stimulation for interaction. In addition, this has the potential to improve the daily experience of local neighbourhoods from a less commercial perspective.

In this way, although play is non-instrumental, opportunities for it to occur can be integrated into more functional aspects of everyday life, such as trips to the local shops. This may enhance older people's playful activities, which are often short-lived and fleeting (Stevens 2007), yet such 'micro-flow' experiences (Nakamura and Csikszentmihalyi 2001) are highly valued.

Informal spaces provide a good context for playful activity by older people as well as children. Spaces that are highly controlled do not encourage playful responses. Having a wide range of possible affordances for different types of play for people of varying ages means that participants will not get bored during repeated experiences of the same place, nor as they progress through the life course. However, a balance is required between routine and spontaneity. A familiar 'safe frame' is needed within which play can happen, together with opportunities for challenge, surprise and spontaneity.

A range of temporal interventions can animate places – from the fleeting view of a squirrel to temporary musical events, car boot sales and public art installations – encouraging the happy expectation of the unexpected. Care should be taken to review successful and unsuccessful elements of a space with users, including children and older people, before significant, and possibly more permanent, changes are made. It can be easy to undervalue the playful uses, emotional engagement and appreciation of existing places, particularly informal ones, by the community.

The qualities of play provision include flexibility of physical elements to enhance the play experience. These elements can include different natural elements. Sensory experiences for sight, touch and smell are also important. Varieties of play spaces are essential to give children and others the opportunities for different physical, social and emotional experiences. Play environments should cater for people to meet and socialise, as well as creating opportunities for being solitary. Spaces for play should provide somewhere to explore and take risks, offering opportunities for climbing and balancing and a chance for children to test themselves and each other. Appropriate play environments offer excitement, movement and colour. They include equipment or landscaping with different textures, materials, heights and levels that permit fantasy and imaginative play as well as more traditional activities. These are spaces in which to be noisy, boisterous and energetic (Coffin and Williams 1989).

While there are many commonalities about the environments that can support and encourage play there are some important special considerations. First, both children and older people need to feel that they have a right to public space and are not marginalised. There are some uses of public open space that benefit from separation. These comprise spaces for the frail and vulnerable – not necessarily those who are very old or young – and spaces suitable for higher levels of physical activity (Freeman and Tranter 2011, p. 101) including more specialised sports facilities. Children have also called for the differentiation of play facilities for varying levels of challenge, suitable for a range of ages and abilities (Cole-Hamilton 2011). A balance needs to be struck between the opportunities for adults to sit and watch children playing, with the spatial separation of different types of activity. Lester and Russell (2010, p. 45) warn that 'adults should . . . be careful not to colonise or destroy children's own places for play through insensitive planning or the pursuit of other adult agendas, or through creating places and programmes that segregate children and control their play'. The potential for intergenerational play is also important with adults both providing a level of support for children's play, getting involved in play themselves, and gaining enjoyment from witnessing others playing while still allowing independence, risk taking and experimentation by children and young people (UN CRC 2013).

It is inevitable that there will be some tensions in designing and enabling play for all. This is due in part to the experimental and exploratory nature of play in public space (Stevens 2007). It is also due to the current cultural expectations about what play is, who can play and what they 'should' be doing where and when.

Design principles		Realisation
Enable autonomy and control for all ages and abilities	Provides safety and security	People present. Informal oversight of spaces. Lighting.
	Offers comfort	Clean, open toilets nearby. Cafes/restaurants nearby. Away from traffic. Responds to microclimate by providing shelter from sun, wind, rain, cold with shelter close at hand.
	Ensures ease of access	Conveniently located and integrated with wider facilities/environment. Safe, convenient, enjoyable choice of routes by foot, cycle, public transport. Free to access at varied times.
Enable engagement and stimulation for all ages and abilities	Contains 'signals' that this is a place to play	Place is welcoming and like other places where play happens. There is evidence of people playing previously/now. Organised activities such as music, sport, games, tours occur. Written sign/poster/information board/trail.
	Offers interest, variety, challenge and excitement	Things/people to observe and interact with – for example, great/grand/children, family, friends, dogs. Multi-sensory richness. Differing levels of predictability and unpredictability. Range of scale of different design elements. Flexible elements/loose parts – that is, things for playing with or watching: water/sand/snow/sticks/leaves/boulders/trees. Public art with which people can interact. Specific facilities and equipment, for example, outdoor gyms, ball courts, pitches. Quiet places away from busy and noisy areas.
	Enhances sense of place and local identity	Elements linked to memory/history/culture/environment.
	Provides opportunities for looking at and looking out from	Seating. Walls, steps, slopes, changes in height and level. Viewpoints. Gathering and performance spaces.
	Appropriate surfaces and levels	Variety of natural, smooth, level surfaces and slopes to enable use of wheels, balls etc.
	Includes community involvement	In policy development, the planning, development and management of public spaces recognises the importance of play.

Figure 10.5 Summary of design principles and how they can be realised to support play for all

Source: Based on Spencer (2013, p. 212) and a summary in Freeman and Tranter (2011, p. 206).

Conclusions: creating a more playful city

The ability for all to play, particularly in local streets and other informal neighbourhood spaces, should be enhanced. In terms of the wider culture there is a need to educate policy makers, parents and guardians of the benefits of regular outdoor play to children's health, development and well-being. Older people also have a right to the city and their potential enjoyment of public space can be enabled by simple measures such as the provision of seating and public toilets (Handler 2014).

In addition, there is a need to shift the debate about risk and safety for children playing independently. The benefits of accommodating a tolerable level of risk and challenge in children's outdoor environments have to be acknowledged. Parents and guardians should be made aware of the benefits of unaccompanied play. Chaperoning children everywhere and seeking to protect them from every potential risk may lead to adverse consequences for their health, development and well-being. There is a need to avoid diverting scarce resources to soft surfacing to reduce injury risk and overreliance on commercial play equipment in parks.

On-site supervision of spaces within close proximity to residential areas should be maximised. The role of 'eyes on the street' (Jacobs 1961) could be improved by good design. This includes maximising the number of windows overlooking the informal areas where play can occur, encouraging pedestrian flow in the neighbourhood and enabling people to dwell for longer in informal public spaces. The promotion of street activities and social interaction among neighbours of all ages can in itself contribute to informal supervision. There a need to foster and sustain children's interaction with peers and their range of independent mobility. Encouraging play in informal spaces, reducing speeds and volumes of traffic in residential streets, and providing continuous footpath networks that connect the whole neighbourhood are key aspects here.

What is important is the creation of places where people want to spend time, where they feel safe and relaxed, where there is interest, excitement and physical features that can be used at different times in varied ways and by different types of people. We propose a framework of design principles and examples of how they can be realised to support play for all (Figure 10.5).

Play has many potential instrumental benefits for wider society – most importantly improving and enhancing the health and well-being of the population. Play is not only 'swings and roundabouts' for children (Children's Play Council 2002), nor bowling, card playing or chess for older people. It is about creating a truly playable city where the inherent playfulness of people of all ages can be expressed. Play is intrinsically enjoyable in itself and can be justified and encouraged on that basis alone – so together with the many health benefits of play, there is ample evidence for policy makers and practitioners to incorporate play for everyone everywhere.

References

Age-Friendly New York City. 2012. *Aging improvement districts.* Office of the Mayor, New York City Council, The New York Academy of Medicine. www.nyam.org/agefriendlynyc/initiatives/current/aging-improvement-districts.html, accessed 8 April 2015.

Brown, S. 2008. Play is more than fun it's vital. TED (Technology, Entertainment and Design). www.ted.com/talks/stuart_brown_says_play_is_more_than_fun_it_s_vital.html, accessed 31 January 2013.

Brown, S. 2009. *Play: how it shapes the brain, opens the imagination, and invigorates the soul.* New York: Avery.

Burghardt, G.M. 2005. *The genesis of animal play: testing the limits.* Cambridge, MA: MIT Press.

Children's Play Council. 2002. *More than swings and roundabouts: planning for outdoor play.* London: Children's Play Council.

Clements, R. 2004. An investigation of the status of outdoor play. *Contemporary Issues in Early Childhood* 5(1), 68–80.

Coffin, G. and Williams, M. 1989. *Children's outdoor play in the built environment*. London: The National Children's Play and Recreation Unit.

Cohen, D. 2006. *The development of play*. 3rd ed. Hove: Routledge.

Cole-Hamilton, I. 2011. Getting it right for play – the power of play: an evidence base., Roslin, Scotland: Play Scotland. www.playscotland.org/wp-content/uploads/assets/Power-of-Play.pdf, accessed 8 April 2015.

DCLG (Department for Communities and Local Government). 2011. *Lifetime neighbourhoods*. London: DCLG. www.gov.uk/government/uploads/system/uploads/attachment_data/file/6248/2044122.pdf, accessed 8 April 2015.

Diener, E.D., Sandvik, E. and Pavot, W. 1991. Happiness is the frequency, not the intensity, of positive versus negative affect. In Strack, F. (ed.) *Subjective well-being: an interdisciplinary perspective*. Oxford: Pergamon Press, p. 119.

Elder, G., Johnson, M. and Crosnoe, R. 2003. The emergence and development of life course theory. In Anon. *Handbook of the life course*. New York: Kluwer Academic/Plenum Publishers, p. 3.

Fredrickson, B. 2004. The broaden-and-build theory of positive emotions. *Philosophical Transactions. Royal Society London B*. 359, 1367–1377.

Freeman, C. and Tranter, P.J. 2011. *Children and their urban environment: changing worlds*. Abingdon, UK: Routledge.

Furedi, F. 2001. *Paranoid parenting: abandon your anxieties and be a good parent*. London: Allen Lane.

Gaskins, S., Haight, W. and Lancy, D.F. 2007. The cultural construction of play. In Göncü, A. and Gaskins, S. (eds.) *Play and development: evolutionary, sociocultural and functional perspectives*. Mahwah, NJ: Lawrence Erlbaum.

Gill, T. 2007. *No fear: growing up in a risk-averse society*. London: Calouste Gulbenkian Foundation.

Handler, S. 2014. *A research & evaluation framework for age-friendly cities*. Manchester: UK Urban Ageing Consortium.

Hart, R. 1994. *The right to play and children's participation*. Presented at: Article 31: the child's right to play. Birmingham, England.

Hartig, T., Evans, G.W., Jamner, L.D., Davis, D.S. and Gärling, T. 2003. Tracking restoration in natural and urban field settings. *Journal of Environmental Psychology* 23(2), 109–123.

Harvey, D. 2008. The right to the city. *New Left Review*, 53, 23.

Hayllar, B. and Griffin, T. 2009. Urban tourist precincts as places of play. In Maciocco, G. and Serreli, S. (eds.) *Enhancing the city: new perspectives for tourism and leisure*. Netherlands: Springer.

Huizinga, J. 1955. *Homo ludens: a study of the play-element in culture*. Boston, MA: Beacon Press.

Huttenmoser, M. 1995. Children and their living surroundings: empirical investigations into the significance of living surroundings for the everyday life and development of children. *Children's Environments* 12(4), 403–413.

Jacobs, J. (1961) *The death and life of great American cities*. New York: Random House.

Kane, P. 2004. *The play ethic: a manifesto for a different way of living*. London: Macmillan.

Lester, S. and Russell, W. 2008. *Play for a change: play, policy and practice, a review of contemporary perspectives*. London: Play England / National Children's Bureau.

Lester, S. and Russell, W. 2010. Children's right to play: an examination of the importance of play in the lives of children worldwide. Working Paper No. 57. The Hague, The Netherlands: Bernard van Leer Foundation.

Louv, R. 2009. *Last child in the woods: saving our children from nature-deficit disorder*. London: Atlantic Books.

Maller, C., Townsend, M., Pryor, A., Brown, P. and St Leger, L. 2006. Healthy nature healthy people: 'contact with nature' as an upstream health promotion intervention for populations. *Health Promotion International* 21(1), 45–54.

Malone, K. and Tranter, P. 2003. Children's environmental learning and the use, design and management of schoolgrounds. *Children, Youth and Environments* 13(2), 87–137.

Matthews, N., Kilgour, L., De Rossi, P. and Crone, D. 2011. Literature review to investigate the evidence underpinning the role of play for holistic health: final report. Gloucester, England: University of Gloucestershire.

McKendrick, J., Bradford, M. and Fielder, A. 2000. Kid customer? Commercialization of playspace and the commodification of childhood. *Childhood* 7, 295–314.

Millar, S. 1968. *The psychology of play*. Harmondsworth: Penguin.

Molnar, B.E., Gortmaker, S.L., Bull, F.C. and Buka, S.L. 2004. Unsafe to play? Neighborhood disorder and lack of safety predict reduced physical activity among urban children and adolescents. *American Journal of Health Promotion* May/June 18(5), 378–386.

Moore, R. and Wong, H. 1996. *Natural learning: the life history of an environmental schoolyard*. Berkeley, CA: MIG Communications.

Morris, N. 2003. *Health, well-being and open space*. Edinburgh: OPENspace Research Centre.

Nakamura, J. and Csikszentmihalyi, M. 2001. The concept of flow. In Snyder, C.R. and Lopez, S.J. (eds.) *Handbook of positive psychology*. Oxford: Oxford University Press, pp. 89–105.

New Economics Foundation. 2011. *Measuring our progress: the power of well-being*. London: New Economics Foundation.

Panksepp, J. 2007. Can play diminish ADHD and facilitate the construction of the social brain? *Journal of the Canadian Academy of Child and Adolescent Psychiatry* 16(2), 57–66.

Pantazis, C. 2000. Fear of crime, vulnerability and poverty. Evidence from the British crime survey. *British Journal of Criminology* 40, 414–436.

Parker, K. 1998. *School kids haven't outgrown recess*. Lexington: Kentucky Connect.

Pressman, S. and Cohen, S. 2005. Does positive affect influence health? *Psychological Bulletin* 131(6), 925–971.

Pretty, J., Angus, C., Bain, M., Barton, J., Gladwell, V., Hine, R., Pilgrim, S., Sandercock, G. and Sellens, M. 2009. *Nature, childhood, health and life pathways*. Colchester: University of Essex.

Rowhani, S. 2011. An investigation of the role of informal play environments for quality outdoor play. Unpublished PhD, University of the West of England, UWE, Bristol, UK.

Sanson, H., Carlsen, J. and Newitt, M. 2012. *Shaping neighbourhoods: play and informal recreation – supplementary planning guidance*. London: Greater London Authority.

Shackell, A., Butler, N., Doyle, P. and Ball, D.J. 2008. *Design for play: a guide to creating successful play spaces*. London, England: Play England, The Department for Children, Schools and Families (DCSF) and the Department for Culture, Media and Sport (DCMS).

Simmel, G. and Hughes, E.C. 1949. The sociology of sociability. *American Journal of Sociology* 55(3), 254–261.

Spencer, B. 2013. Playful public places for later life: how can neighbourhood public open space provide opportunities for improving older people's quality of life by enabling play? PhD thesis, University of the West of England, Bristol, UK.

Spencer, B., Williams, K., Mahdjoubi, L. and Sara, R. 2013. Third places for the third age: the contribution of playable space to the well-being of older people. In Coles, R. and Milman, Z. (eds.) *Landscape, well-being and the environment*. Abingdon: Routledge.

Stevens, Q. 2007. *The ludic city: exploring the potential of public spaces*. Oxford: Routledge.

Sugiyama, T., Ward Thompson, C. and Alves, S. 2009. Associations between neighborhood open space attributes and quality of life for older people in Britain. *Environment and Behavior* 41(1), 3.

Sutton-Smith, B. 1997. *The ambiguity of play*. Cambridge, MA: Harvard University Press.

Titman, W. 1994. *Special places special people*. Winchester: Learning Through Landscapes Trust.

Tugade, M.M., Fredrickson, B.L. and Feldman-Barrett, L. 2004. Psychological resilience and positive emotional granularity: examining the benefits of positive emotions on coping and health. *Journal of Personality* 72(6), 1161–1190.

UN CRC (United Nations Committee on the Rights of the Child). 2013. General comment No. 17 (2013) on the right of the child to rest, leisure, play, recreational activities, cultural life and the arts (Article 31). www.refworld.org/docid/51ef9bcc4.html, accessed 8 April 2015.

Wells, N.M. and Evans, G.W. 2003. Nearby nature: a buffer of life stress among rural children. *Environment and Behavior* 35(3), 311–330.

Wheway, R. and Millward, A. 1997. *Child's play: facilitating play on housing estates*. London: Chartered Institute of Housing.

Whitebread, D. 2012. *The importance of play*. Brussels, Belgium: Toy Industries of Europe.

WHO (World Health Organization). 2007. *Global age-friendly cities: a guide*. Geneva, Switzerland: WHO.

WHO. 2009. *Interventions on diet and physical activity: what works*. Summary Report. Geneva, Switzerland: WHO.

Woodyer, T. 2012. Ludic geographies: not merely child's play. *Geography Compass* 6(6), 313–326.

Yarnal, C.M., Chick, G. and Kerstetter, D.L. 2008. 'I did not have time to play growing up . . . so this is my play time. It's the best thing I have ever done for myself': what is play to older women? *Leisure Sciences* 30, 235.

11

MENTAL WELL-BEING AND THE INFLUENCE OF PLACE

Libby Burton

Introduction: renewing our focus

This book is testament to the renewed interest in environmental influences on human health. In contrast with the nineteenth century, ill health now stems, at least in the developed world, from chronic rather than infectious diseases. And, although obesity has received the most attention in environmental research, there is now an understanding that where we live and work affects not just our physical health but also our mental health, and our general well-being (Jackson et al. 2013). Depression has been ranked among the ten leading contributors to the global burden of disease and is projected to be among the top three by 2020. Mental illness in general plays a large part in loss of productivity through days off work. So it is vital that it is addressed.

At the same time, there has been a growing realisation that 'well-being' or 'happiness' is important. It can influence how healthy we are physically (Veenhoven 2010). In the UK, the well-being of the population is being used as a measure of success in national policy. Evidence suggests that it is related only weakly to wealth/income, above a certain level, but it is influenced significantly by having strong social networks, which protect against both mental and physical illness (Gale et al. 2011). Other influences, including the built environment, are being explored (the key book in this field is Halpern 1995). Instinctively, it makes sense to believe that the environments around us affect how we feel. We all know places that lift our spirits, perhaps those holiday destinations we regularly visit. We also know places that depress us or make us feel claustrophobic.

The purpose of this chapter is to outline the key ways in which places affect our mental well-being and to discuss the aspects of the built environment that appear to be either positive or negative. The content is based on the latest research and evidence.

Overview of research

Research in the field of mental health and the built environment is growing. To date, most researchers have come from non-built environment disciplines: usually public health, epidemiology, environmental psychology and geography, which means that some of the research investigates neighbourhood socio-economic status or general built environment quality rather than the presence of specific built environment features. In general, there is a paucity of research in this field, certainly in comparison with research on physical activity and greenery. There are weaknesses in study designs – often inevitable given the complexity of the subject. The research tends to be cross-sectional, so it is difficult to establish causal relationships. Studies often lack a good understanding of the built environment and its design and creation, making it difficult to apply the findings through guidance. Further, many studies use subjective measures of the built environment (ratings of quality) or measures of incivilities, rather than objective measures. To date, in the built environment, there has been little demand for the type of evidence normally found in health. This is because architecture and urban design are professions based on creativity and originality rather than empirical evidence. Consequently, most design guidance lacks an evidence base and tends to contain objectives rather than solutions (for example design safe, attractive places).

Aspects of mental well-being influenced by the built environment

Mental well-being is a broad concept and embraces many disparate aspects, not all of which are relevant when thinking about the built environment. Nevertheless, there are some key aspects that have come under scrutiny in research on the built environment. These are:

- stress/anxiety;
- ability to recover from stress;
- depression;
- general mood/happiness;
- attention restoration and recovery from mental fatigue;
- ability to cope with the symptoms of mental disorders such as dementia, Attention Deficit Hyperactivity Disorder (ADHD) and autism;
- general comfort (whether people are warm or cool enough, have sufficient light);
- ability to live well in older age;
- successful childhood development; and
- quality of life/satisfaction with life.

Pathways of influence

When considering how the built environment affects mental well-being, the relationship is rarely direct. A direct impact would result from an environment altering our mood (for example making us feel down or claustrophobic, or happy and/or stimulated) or causing stress (for example through noise pollution). Most impacts, however, are indirect. There are a number of different mechanisms or pathways that potentially explain these indirect relationships between the built environment and mental well-being. These pathways, outlined below, have been identified through a review of the literature.

- *Physical activity*: this can be promoted or limited by the built environment. Lack of physical activity/exercise has been linked to poor mental well-being, especially depression and anxiety.
- *Social engagement* (or similar concepts such as social capital and networks): the built environment can provide opportunities for social interaction, which in turn protects against social isolation, mental illness and general unhappiness.
- *Privacy* (from external and internal noise, visual intrusion): this can be compromised by the way the environment is designed, which often leads to social withdrawal, tension and conflicts with neighbours or other family members, thus creating stress.

- *Biophilia* (or the benefits accruing from contact with nature – Wilson, 1984): the environment can optimise contact with nature through the incorporation of greenery and water.
- *Accessibility*: the design/layout of urban areas can affect people's ability to access services and facilities, which in turn can influence their quality of life in a variety of ways – for example long commuting times to work add to stress, but being able to walk to shops and restaurants brings positive benefits.
- *Attachment and belonging*: this can be affected by the character of people's neighbourhoods. For example, it is thought that using local traditions/styles and incorporating distinctive features promotes attachment (Butina Watson and Bentley 2007; Madanipour 1996). This feeling of attachment/belonging is generally thought to be important for mental well-being, particularly for children as they grow up.
- *Safety and security*: people are more likely to be depressed and anxious and are less likely to get out and about and meet people if they feel unsafe in their immediate residential environment.
- *Competence/accomplishment*: environments can help us to learn skills and stretch our abilities. For example, children can develop physical prowess climbing trees, and people can learn spatial skills finding their way around.
- *Autonomy and independence*: research has shown the value of 'ageing in place' – that is, older people remaining in their own homes for as long as possible. Environments can help or hinder older people's ability to manage when they become frail. Also, environments differ in terms of how much they can be altered and controlled by people, or how far they allow people to pursue their individual goals.
- *Equality/inequality*: environments can exacerbate the differences between those well off and not so well off. Mental ill health is higher in countries where inequalities are high (Wilkinson and Pickett 2009).

Elements of the built environment that influence mental well-being

There is a wide range of built environment characteristics that influence mental well-being either directly or indirectly via the pathways outlined above. These are discussed below.

Residential density

The evidence is mixed and sometimes contradictory for this element of the built environment (Dempsey et al. 2012). In general, access to services and facilities is better in higher-density environments, and there is a higher proportion of walking trips, with benefits to mental well-being (Calve-Blanco 2013). However, where there are higher-density forms, such as terraced housing and flats, privacy is sometimes compromised, which means that social engagement is lower. Higher-density environments also tend to be associated with restricted access to nature. This is arguably more a matter of good urban design. My conclusion would be that higher densities can be made to work if they are designed well – that is, higher-density housing restricted to terraced forms with front doors onto the street; street layouts which incorporate grass verges and street trees, roof terraces and so on.

Mix of uses or proximity to services/facilities

Again, this is not straightforward. On the whole, a mix of uses in urban areas appears to be positive for mental well-being. It is easier for people to access the services and facilities they need

Figure 11.1 Higher-density housing has to be designed well and give residents easy access to useable and well maintained greenspace – these developments in Sydney offer varying open space access and design quality

Source: Thompson.

(Feng et al. 2010), and it also tends to encourage people to walk more as they have a reason to go out (Sarkar et al. 2013). A mix of uses can encourage social interaction as people meet at local facilities such as shops and pubs (Jacobs 1961). However, to be positive the mix of uses has to be the right mix (Wood et al. 2010). Certain uses, such as industrial ones, or nightclubs/late night bars, may cause stress through noise annoyance. Having too many commercial properties in a residential area can cause concern for safety when they are shut up at night and there are no 'eyes on the street'. A study by Foster et al. (2013) showed that perceived safety is lower in more mixed neighbourhoods. So, again, a mix of uses is good, but it needs to be designed well, avoiding blank facades and ensuring adequate sound insulation for noisy premises.

Incorporation of greenery

On the face of it, it would seem obvious that incorporation of greenery would always be a positive feature in an urban area, but, yet again, there are caveats. It is possible that places can have too much greenery. There is a fine balance between the incorporation of open spaces and the maintenance of sufficiently high residential densities to support local shops and restaurants, with the promotion of walking. Greenspaces also need to be designed well. Quality is more important than quantity (Francis et al. 2012). The modernists, such as Le Corbusier, had plans to raise the city up on 'pilotis' (columns) so that the whole city was in effect a park with buildings positioned like pavilions within it. This was a noble, well-meaning vision. But we know now that it would have been a disaster in practice. Space that is not 'owned' by people becomes uncared for and unsafe. Greenspaces need clear boundaries and demarcation of public, semi-public and private space. Small to medium areas of open greenspace are valuable if they are well defined. They provide destinations for people to walk to in the neighbourhood and sources of exercise in their own right (for example tennis courts, bowling greens, running tracks, play and exercise equipment). Fresh air and exercise are beneficial in turn for well-being. Parks and greenspaces also provide opportunities for social interaction, whether informal gatherings of friends or local events and festivals (Kazmierczak 2013). Social interaction has a significant impact on well-being.

Greenspaces are by no means the only form of greenery to be found in urban areas. It can be provided in the more immediate residential or work environment, through grass verges, street trees, roof terraces and 'living walls'/green balconies. Such greenery appears to be almost universally beneficial for well-being (de Vries et al. 2013). The benefits arise not only from spending time in this greenspace but also from viewing it from inside. Research by the author found that older people's well-being was better if they had a view of greenery from their living rooms (I'DGO 2012). Previous research found many benefits from having a view of greenery (Kaplan 2001; Velarde et al. 2007). Even in high-density housing, with little space for private gardens, a green view is readily achievable. In work environments, access to, or views of greenery provide the opportunity to recover from mental fatigue (Lottrup et al. 2013). In hospitals, those with a view of greenery from their ward are more likely to get better quickly, with less need for pain relief (Beukeboom et al. 2012; Ulrich et al. 1991).

Street configuration and design

Street layouts have been studied in relation to walking in neighbourhoods. It makes sense that grid layouts, as opposed to cul-de-sac or 'lollipop' layouts, are easier to walk around as there are more choices in getting from one place to another and distances tend to be less. Research supports this – people walk more in neighbourhoods with well-connected street layouts. Walking in the local neighbourhood makes people feel better because they are getting exercise and fresh air, and they are also more likely to meet people and feel attached to the area (Leyden 2003; Sarkar et al. 2013). However, there is some evidence that people living in cul-de-sacs feel safer (from crime) – they tend to know their neighbours and there is informal monitoring of 'strangers' and unusual activity. Traffic levels are low so they are safe streets in which children can play. An ideal scenario would be grid layouts that include some low depth cul-de-sacs, or crescents. Research on design for dementia suggests that a distorted grid is better than a regular one (Burton and Mitchell 2006). A distorted grid staggers junctions to create T-junctions, limiting the number of cross-roads, which is where people with dementia tend to lose their way. Distorted grids also incorporate bends and curves in roads, which relieves the monotony of long, straight streets. People with dementia maintain their concentration better in gently curving streets which gradually open up before them. This makes it more likely they remember where they are and what they are doing. Bends and curves also help slow down traffic, leading to safer neighbourhoods for children to play and more opportunities for social interaction (Appleyard and Lintell 1974).

Figure 11.2 Small parks and street gardens make an important contribution to greenspace in urban areas. A small street park in Seattle, USA; another in Adelaide, Australia

Source: Thompson.

Housing form

People living in high-rise and multi-family housing (apartments/flats) are more likely to be depressed and less likely to report good community spirit (Evans et al. 2003). Children tend to do less well, both academically and behaviourally. This may be because of a lack of privacy (quiet space for doing homework) and safe outdoor places to play. Play areas may be at some distance from apartments so parents are unwilling to allow children out. It seems that people interact less, perhaps because their need for privacy is not being met, leading to withdrawal. Perhaps some of the negative impacts of high-rise, multi-family living could be avoided through good design, such as adequate sound insulation between dwellings, and avoidance of certain layout types. Research by the author, for example, found that people were more likely to be depressed if they lived in flats with 'deck' access – that is, outdoor corridors (Weich et al. 2002). This is probably because privacy is compromised when people have to pass directly in front of doors and windows to access other flats.

There may, again, be limits to the positive impacts of lower-density housing. People living in very low-density detached housing, set back far from the street, are less likely to report good community spirit and feel attached to their neighbourhood. They are unlikely to meet or encounter their neighbours as they come and go (normally by vehicle), especially if they have high gates, hedges and fences. Semi-detached and terraced (row) housing are ideal (Sarkar et al. 2013), especially if they incorporate small front gardens (Figure 11.3). Research by the author found that older people's sense of community was best among those living in housing with front gardens (I'DGO 2012). This is probably because these front gardens act as a buffer zone between the private area inside the home and the public domain of the street. When people's need for privacy is satisfied they are more inclined to socialise (see the section on 'soft edges' below). Another reason why conventional semi-detached and terraced housing contributes positively to well-being is that it achieves a clear differentiation of public and private space (see below).

Figure 11.3   Historic terraced housing in Newcastle, UK

Source: Thompson.

Space in housing

There have been a plethora of studies, from as far back as the 1960s, investigating the impacts of lack of space or overcrowding in housing. It can lead to depression, stress and anxiety, and poor behaviour, social skills and academic performance in children (Evans et al. 2003). This may be because there is insufficient space for different activities to take place at once in the home – doing homework, eating and watching television, causing conflicts and tensions between family members. Lack of space can be ameliorated to some extent by good design. For example, the incorporation of discrete rooms rather than open plan layouts and adequate sound insulation between spaces/rooms. In the UK, there is pressure on the government, from, for example, the Royal Institute of British Architects, to reintroduce space standards for housing. However, there are worries that these might discourage the building of new housing by developers at a time of critical shortage.

Presence of 'soft edges', or transition zones

There are types of space, often called 'soft edges' (Gehl 1986) or semi-private zones, that appear to promote social interaction. These tend to be spaces where people come and go, but also linger (Brown et al. 1998). Research by the author found that overall sense of community and actual interaction with neighbours were greater among residents living in homes with a front garden (I'DGO 2012). We can speculate about why this space is effective. The front garden constitutes a 'soft edge' or transition zone in the housing environment. It provides a buffer between the private area inside the home and the public domain of the street. It is a space where people come and go, where they can observe their neighbours and see what is happening on the street without being noticed themselves, where they can control the environment and engage with people on their own terms (Spokane et al. 2007). Urban design theorists have long extolled the virtues of soft edges – that is, areas or facades within which people linger, gather, engage with others and are generally active (Alexander 1979; Gehl 2011). Residents may spend considerable time in their front gardens, perhaps just sitting in the sun or watching the world go by, or tending to gardening chores. Where front doors open directly onto the street, informal encounters with neighbours as they come and go is possible, but what is lacking is space in which people can linger.

Soft edges also help to provide privacy for people inside their homes or workplaces – a buffer zone between private and public space. Having sufficient privacy is an important aspect of mental well-being and often a precursor to social engagement which in itself contributes to well-being.

'Eyes on the street'

It is important to people's well-being that they feel safe in their homes and neighbourhoods. The built environment can contribute to a sense of safety in a number of ways but perhaps the most significant is through 'eyes on the street' – that is, windows and doors and other glazed areas that face the footway/pavement outside (Brown et al. 2009). These openings provide a form of surveillance in the neighbourhood and a deterrent to crime. People feel safer when they are walking along a street that is overlooked – by people in their homes, workplaces or other active spaces. A mix of uses in a neighbourhood can ensure that buildings are occupied 24 hours a day for constant surveillance. Sometimes the balance is wrong, leading to long stretches of street that are shut up at night – for example, commercial buildings that are unoccupied after about six o'clock in the evening. These areas can feel unsafe. Flats/apartments over the commercial premises can reduce the sense of threat.

Figure 11.4   Higher density housing in Rouse Hill in Sydney which provides front gardens for residents

Source: Emily Mitchell, Faculty of the Built Environment, UNSW, Australia.

Clear differentiation of public/private space (defensible space)

In the 1960s and 1970s, architects experimented with space, creating new, exciting forms. However, in practice, many modernist housing developments became unpleasant, unsafe places to live, failing to promote well-being. It may have seemed a good idea to provide plenty of open/greenspace around housing, rather like positioning homes in parkland, but, in reality, such swathes of outdoor space felt windswept, unsafe and neglected. This was mostly because nobody had any formal ownership of this space. Traditionally, housing has public fronts facing the street and private backs. Where backs of housing face onto fronts, problems arise as privacy is eroded. Often, high walls are built to preserve privacy but then people walking along the street feel unsafe because there are no eyes on the street. Alice Coleman (1985) and Oscar Newman (1972) observed this phenomenon in the 1960s/1970s/1980s and coined the term 'defensible space'. Generally, people feel better and have a good quality of life when they have their own private outdoor space and a buffer zone of semi-private space between their home and the street (Gehl 2011). They benefit from a clear differentiation between public and private space as they know what is expected and allowed in the different spaces. This space preserves privacy and promotes social engagement. It also promotes a sense of 'ownership', even when the housing is rented. If people consider space belongs to them they will look after and take care of it. If not, it tends to be neglected, unkempt and can attract crime such as vandalism, graffiti and drug dealing.

Daylighting

Now we have the luxury of electricity and artificial lighting, architects and developers can be less careful in designing buildings. The Victorians were brilliant at bringing natural light into homes and institutional buildings. They believed it was important for health. The traditional terrace design with the 'kitchen extension' is an example of how they used a number of techniques to maximise light. By rights such a deep plan design should be gloomy and dark, but large windows, the 'L' shaped rear, and skylights, bring lots of natural light into the home. Nowadays, large window openings can be seen as problematic in colder countries because a lot of heat is lost through glazing, and in hotter climates because of over-heating. However, natural lighting has been shown to be very important for well-being (Andersen et al. 2013). People tend to feel more depressed in dark environments. Patients recover more quickly from surgery when their hospital ward has plenty of natural light (Joarder and Price 2013). Large windows in buildings are also beneficial because they provide views to the outside. This is especially true for older and disabled people who are less able to go outside. Views of the outside keep them in touch with the seasons and the time of day (see the section on 'greenery' above)

Ability to keep homes warm or cool

Energy-efficient housing is beneficial not just for physical health but also for mental health and general well-being (Howden-Chapman et al. 2007). When people can afford to keep their whole house warm in winter, they use more of the space, which leads to fewer conflicts between family members and greater ability to pursue desired activities. Children are able to complete homework in comfort. When people are cold, they become tense and irritable. Conversely, when people are warm they are more relaxed. Therefore, to maximise well-being it is important that homes are easy to heat. This means they are well insulated. However, some energy efficient homes have been found to be unhealthy – this is usually because they are so airtight there is insufficient ventilation, leading to poor air quality, condensation and mould. Well insulated homes should also be well ventilated. Another problem is that, in many climates, buildings are exposed not just to very cold temperatures, but also to very hot ones. The same building needs to keep people warm in winter and cool in summer and that is tricky. It is helpful if buildings can be naturally ventilated (for example through cross-ventilation, wind-catchers) and shaded in summer.

Sound insulation

In general, sound insulation in newly built housing is not as good as that found in older dwellings of solid wall construction. Lightweight, timber-framed walls lend themselves to high levels of insulation and responsive heating systems, but do not so easily create sound privacy. For well-being, adequate sound insulation in buildings, both from external and internal noise, is crucial. People exposed to high levels of noise, either from outside traffic or overhead planes, have high levels of stress and poorer health (Gee and Takeuchi 2004; Haines et al. 2001). Children can grow up with behavioural and developmental problems. Within the home, people need privacy from each other, otherwise tension grows between household members. Trees and other forms of greenery can also mitigate the effect of noise annoyance (Li et al. 2012).

Attractiveness

People are wary of discussing attractiveness because 'beauty is in the eye of the beholder'. It cannot be defined or pinned down for many reasons, including cultural elements. Since ancient times, people have pondered the nature of beauty and tried to come up with 'rules' to create or measure it. In architecture it was thought that certain proportions were innately beautiful (Alexander et al. 2012). We have not progressed in our understanding of what makes buildings beautiful. Nevertheless several recent studies have pointed to the importance of aesthetics for well-being (for example Bond et al. 2012). 'Ugly' environments tend to make us feel depressed and 'attractive' environments tend to make us feel happy. Aesthetics also affect how attached we feel to where we live. We could contribute much towards our well-being if we knew how to create universally attractive places, albeit with cultural differences. The sense of 'attractive-ness' is probably related to our memories and associations – buildings that remind us of happy holidays are likely to be perceived as attractive. Buildings should also have human scale – details that we can relate to such as balconies and window panes. They may also be seen as attractive if they incorporate greenery – either in small front gardens or growing up walls/on window sills and balconies (White and Gatersleben 2011). People also seem to respond well to depth in building facades. They like windows to be recessed and details to be layered on top through steps and porches and other projecting devices. Completely flat facades are generally disliked. All this needs more research but I do think it is possible to identify some common ground when it comes to attractiveness, certainly in housing.

Conclusions: environments for human flourishing

So what is a happy place to live? What environments will help us to flourish? As this chapter shows, the answer is not straightforward with many caveats of various types. Different envi-ronments will suit some people but not others, depending on their personality and cultural background. Some environments will suit people at certain times of their lives but not at oth-ers. However, in general, we have to design places that suit everyone. It seems, at least in the UK context, the best sort of environment would be one which is moderately dense, compris-ing a mix of terraces and semi-detached houses, all with front doors facing onto the street and small front gardens with terraces, porches and steps. Without a doubt, this perfect environment should incorporate as much greenery as possible, mostly in the immediate vicinity. There should be well-defined open greenspaces or parks but also plenty of grass verges, street trees, living walls and roof terraces. Streets layouts should be well connected with curving streets and T-junctions rather than crossroads (an irregular grid). Space should be given to footways at the expense of roads in order to slow traffic. Housing should be carefully designed and easy to keep warm, with views of greenery from the living areas, private areas at the back, plenty of ventilation and day-light and very good sound insulation in walls and floors. There is scope for designers to be more inventive when it comes to public buildings and special places such as galleries and museums, but there is an art to the design of housing and neighbourhoods. This art should be based on knowledge of what works best. We know this from both history and research.

Undoubtedly, more research is needed as there are still big gaps in our understanding (Kim 2008). This is particularly the case when it comes to difficult-to-define aspects of housing such as attractiveness. Nevertheless, we know enough to start making a difference in practice. We have made much progress in sustainable housing – energy-efficiency standards are high in new development in many countries. We now need to realise that it is just as important to design for mental well-being, and that this can be consistent with design for sustainability. We need places that make us happy, and, more than that, help us to flourish.

References

Alexander, C. 1979. *The timeless way of building*. Oxford: Oxford University Press.
Alexander, C., Neis, H.J. and Alexander, M.M. 2012. *The battle for the life and beauty of the earth: a struggle between two world-systems*. Oxford: Oxford University Press.
Andersen, M., Gochenour, S.J. and Lockley, S.W. 2013. Modelling 'non-visual' effects of daylighting in a residential environment. *Building and Environment* 7: 138–149.

Appleyard, D. and Lintell, M. 1974. Environmental quality of city streets: the residents' viewpoint. *Journal of the American Institute of Planners* 38: 84–101.

Beukeboom, C.J., Langeveld, D. and Tanja-Dijkstra, K. 2012. Stress-reducing effects of real and artificial nature in a hospital waiting room. *Journal of Alternative and Complementary Medicine* 18: 329–333.

Bond, L., Kearns, A., Mason, P., Tannahill, C., Egan, M. and Whitely, E. 2012. Exploring the relationships between housing, neighbourhoods, and mental wellbeing for residents of deprived areas. *BMC Public Health* 12(48).

Brown, B.B., Burton, J.R. and Sweaney, A.L. 1998. Neighbors, households, and front porches: new urbanist community tool or mere nostalgia? *Environment and Behavior* 30: 579–600.

Brown, S.C., Mason, C.A., Lombard, J.L., Martinez, F., Plater-Zyberg, E., Spokane, A.R., Frederick, L. Newman, F.L., Pantin, H. and Szapocznik, J. 2009. The relationship of built environment to perceived social support and psychological distress in Hispanic elders: the role of 'eyes on the street'. *Journal of Gerontology: Social Sciences* 64B(2): 234–246.

Burton, E. and Mitchell, L. 2006. *Inclusive urban design: streets for life.* Oxford: Architectural Press.

Butina Watson, G. and Bentley, I. 2007. *Identity by design.* Oxford: Architectural Press.

Calve-Blanco, T. 2013. *The social value of local facilities and its impact on residents' well-being.* Draft PhD, University of the West of England, Bristol.

Coleman, A. 1985. *Utopia on trial: vision and reality in planned housing.* London: Hilary Shipman.

de Vries, S., van Dillen, S., Groenewegen, P. and Spreeuwenberg, P. 2013. Streetscape greenery and health: stress, social cohesion and physical activity as mediators. *Social Science and Medicine* 94: 26–33.

Dempsey, N., Brown, C. and Bramley, G. 2012. The key to sustainable urban development in UK cities? The influence of density on social sustainability. *Progress in Planning* 77: 89–141.

Evans, G., Wells, N. and Moch, A. 2003. Housing and mental health: a review of the evidence and a methodological and conceptual critique. *Journal of Social Issues* 59(3): 475–500.

Feng, J., Glass, T., Curriero, F., Stewart, W. and Schwartz, B. 2010. The built environment and obesity: a systematic review of the epidemiologic evidence. *Health and Place* 16: 175–190.

Foster, S., Wood, L., Christian, H., Knuiman, M. and Giles-Corti, B. 2013. Planning safer suburbs: do changes in the built environment influence residents' perceptions of crime risk? *Social Science and Medicine* 97: 87–94.

Francis, J., Wood, L., Knuiman, M. and Giles-Corti, B. 2012. Quality or quantity? Exploring the relationship between public open space attributes and mental health in Perth, Western Australia. *Social Science and Medicine* 74: 1570–1577.

Gale, C.R., Dennison, E.M., Cooper, C. and Sayer, A.A. 2011. Neighbourhood environment and positive mental health in older people: the Hertfordshire Cohort Study. *Health and Place* 17: 867–874.

Gee, G.C. and Takeuchi, D.T. 2004. Traffic stress, vehicular burden and well-being: a multilevel analysis. *Social Science & Medicine* 59(2): 405–414.

Gehl, J. 1986. 'Soft edges' in residential streets. *Scandinavian Housing & Planning Research* 3: 89–102.

Gehl, J. 2011. *Life between buildings: using public space.* Washington: Island Press.

Haines, M.M., Stansfeld, S.A. and Job, R.F.S. 2001. Chronic aircraft noise exposure, stress responses, mental health and cognitive performance in school children. *Psychological Medicine* 31(2): 265–277.

Halpern, D. 1995. *More than bricks and mortar? Mental health and the built environment.* London: Taylor & Francis Inc.

Howden-Chapman, P., Matheson, A., Crane, J., Viggers, H., Cunningham, M., Blakely, T., Cunningham, C. and Davie, G. 2007. Effect of insulating existing houses on health inequality: cluster randomised study in the community. *British Medical Journal* 334: 460.

I'DGO (Inclusive Design for Getting Outdoors). 2012. Why does the outdoor environment matter? www. idgo.ac.uk/pdf/Intro-leaflet-2012-FINAL-MC.pdf, accessed 8 April 2015.

Jackson, R., Dannenberg, A. and Frumkin, H. 2013. Editorial: health and the built environment 10 years after. *American Journal of Public Health* 103(9): 1542–1544.

Jacobs, J. 1961. *The death and life of great American cities.* New York: Vintage.

Joarder, A.R. and Price, A.D.F. 2013. Impact of daylight illumination on reducing patient length of stay in hospital after coronary artery graft bypass surgery. *Lighting Research and Technology* 45(4): 435–449.

Kaplan, R. 2001. The nature of the view from home: psychological benefits. *Environment and Behaviour* 33(4): 507–542.

Kazmierczak, A. 2013. The contribution of local parks to neighbourhood social ties. *Landscape and Urban Planning* 109(1): 81–96.

Kim, D. 2008. Blues from the neighborhood? Neighborhood characteristics and depression. *Epidemiologic Reviews* 30(1): 101–117.

Leyden, K.M. 2003. Social capital and the built environment: the importance of walkable neighbourhoods. *American Journal of Public Health* 93: 1546–1551.

Li, H.N., Chou, C.K., Tse, M.S. and Tang, S.K. 2012. On the study of the effects of sea views, greenery views and personal characteristics on noise annoyance perception at homes. *Journal of the Acoustical Society of America* 131(3): 2131–2140.

Lottrup, L., Grahn, P. and Stigsdotter, U.K. 2013. Workplace greenery and perceived level of stress: benefits of access to a green outdoor environment at the workplace. *Landscape and Urban Planning* 110: 5–11.

Madanipour, A. 1996. *Design of urban space: an inquiry into a socio-spatial process.* Chichester: John Wiley & Sons.

Newman, O. 1972. *Defensible space: people and design in the violent city.* London: Architectural Press.

Sarkar, C., Gallacher, J. and Webster, C. 2013. Urban built environment configuration and psychological distress in older men: results from the Caerphilly study. *BMC Public Health* 13: 695.

Spokane, A.R., Lombard, J.L., Martinez, F., Mason, C.A., Gorman-Smith, D., Plater-Zyberg, E., Brown, S.C., Perrino, T. and Szapocznik, J. 2007. Identifying streetscape features significant to well-being. *Architectural Science Review* 50(3): 234–245.

Ulrich, R.S., Simons, R.F., Losito, B.D., Fiorito, E., Miles, M.A. and Zelson, M. 1991. Stress recovery during exposure to natural and urban environments. *Journal of Environmental Psychology* 11: 201–230.

Veenhoven, R. 2010. Greater happiness for the greater number? *Journal of Happiness Studies* 11: 605–629.

Velarde, M.D., Fry, G. and Tveit, M. 2007. Health effects of viewing landscapes: landscape types in environmental psychology. *Urban Forestry & Urban Greening* 6: 199–212.

Weich, S., Blanchard, M., Prince, M., Burton, E., Sproston, K. and Erens, R. 2002. Mental health and the built environment: a cross-sectional survey of individual and contextual risk factors for depression. *British Journal of Psychiatry* 180: 428–433.

White, E. and Gatersleben, B. 2011. Greenery on residential buildings: does it affect preferences and perceptions of beauty? *Journal of Environmental Psychology* 31: 89–98.

Wilkinson, R. and Pickett, K. 2009. *The spirit level: why greater equality makes societies stronger.* New York: Bloomsbury Press.

Wilson, E.O. 1984. *Biophilia.* Cambridge, MA: Harvard University Press.

Wood, L., Frank, L.D. and Giles-Corti, B. 2010. Sense of community and its relationship with walking and neighborhood design. *Social Science & Medicine* 70: 1381–1390.

12

CRIME AND COMMUNITY SAFETY

Challenging the design consensus

Paul Cozens

Introduction: an environmental criminology perspective

Crime can seriously affect the health and well-being of citizens. There are significant financial, personal, psychological and emotional costs to individuals and communities. Low levels of crime are crucial to what is regarded as a good place to live. So what are the professions of planning and public health doing to achieve community safety and deliver a safe environment?

Guidelines for 'healthy' communities commonly refer to crime, which is recognised as a threat to health, well-being and liveability. Polices promoting urban consolidation via high density, mixed-use and permeable (walkable) developments close to public transport and infrastructure are assumed to be more sustainable and promote health and well-being. Another assumption these policies make is that increased levels of natural surveillance or 'eyes on the street' enable such environments to promote community safety.

The use of Crime Prevention Through Environmental Design (CPTED) is often a recommended strategy for achieving community safety. This chapter provides an overview of CPTED and introduces the less familiar concept of 2nd Generation CPTED. It is argued that although CPTED is a useful tool to help promote community safety, it is currently being applied as an outcome, rather than a process. A vital part of CPTED is to understand crime risks. I contend that CPTED is often misinterpreted and misapplied. This is particularly so in relation to the assumptions that it universally promotes and supports the use of permeable, mixed-use communities at high densities.

Theories and evidence from environmental criminology, which challenge the assumption that urban consolidation always reduces crime, are explored. The chapter considers how an environmental criminology perspective can assist in promoting well-being, as well as the planning, design and management of safer, healthier and more sustainable cities. The chapter seeks to clarify the relationship between the built form, planning, health and crime.

The costs of crime and fear of crime

The costs of crime are significant and can be divided into four categories (McCollister et al. 2010). First, there are community justice system (CJS) costs. These relate to expenditure on police, courts, prosecutions and prisons. In 2004, globally this was estimated at around US$424 billion, with 62 per cent on policing, 18 per cent on courts, 17 per cent on prisons and 3 per cent on prosecutions (Farrell and Clark 2004). This represents 2.8 per cent of gross domestic product (GDP) in the UK and 2.1 per cent in the USA (Haldenby et al. 2012). These tangible costs do not reflect the more difficult to measure personal, psychological and emotional toll associated with crime. Second, crime career costs are the opportunity costs of an offender's choice to participate in illegal, rather than legal and productive behaviour. Third, victim costs are the direct economic losses of victims of crime and include medical expenses, lost earnings and property damage and destruction. Finally, intangible costs are indirect losses and include pain, suffering, reduced quality of life and psychological stress. These are likely to impact on the well-being of citizens and communities significantly.

Crime can also affect health directly via the physical/psychological impacts on victims and communities. Fear of crime can discourage citizens from using parts, or all, of their neighbourhood and the city beyond. In turn this affects individual well-being and the functioning of urban environments (Stafford et al. 2007). Crime can discourage walking and active recreation, thereby contributing to obesity (Foster and Giles-Corti 2008). Perceptions of anti-social behaviour, such as drunkenness and burglary, have also been associated with less walking (Mason et al. 2013). As well, reduced levels of physical activity and increased fear and worry about crime have been linked to poor mental and physical health (Jackson and Stafford 2009). Fear of crime can affect health indirectly due to an individual's anxiety and concern. This feedback loop is illustrated in Figure 12.1.

Clearly, crime and the fear of crime can impact on health and well-being in diverse and complex ways. Intriguingly, some consider crime as an 'externality' of urban development and as a form of pollution with its own carbon costs (Farrell and Roman 2006; Pease and Farrell 2011). Security and safety from crime are therefore important characteristics of a healthy city in both developed and developing countries (Rydin et al. 2012a).

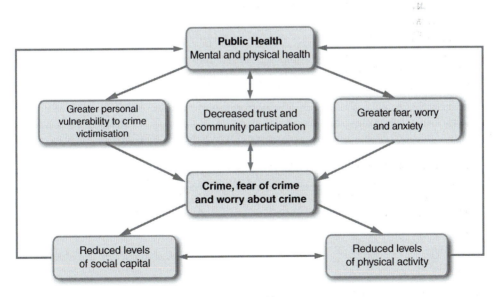

Figure 12.1 A feedback model of crime and public health

Source: Adapted from Jackson and Stafford (2009).

The design and management of the built form is certainly not to blame for all these costs. However, the promotion of high-density, mixed-use and permeable developments as being inherently and routinely crime-reductive is myopic and misleading. It is more complex than that.

Over 60 years ago, Maslow (1943) put forward his hierarchy of needs, which still resonates today. Indeed, it is argued that a healthy and sustainable environment should meet a variety of human needs. These relate to:

1. Self-actualisation (personal growth and fulfilment).
2. Esteem needs (achievement, status, responsibility and reputation).
3. Belongingness and love needs (family, affection, relationships work group, etc.).
4. Safety needs (protection, security, order, law, limits, stability, etc.).
5. Biological and physiological needs (basic life needs – air, food, drink, shelter, warmth, sex, sleep, etc.).

Crime prevention and community safety are clearly located within the 'safety needs' element of the hierarchy.

Crime, sustainability and public health

Today, the prevalence of various public health problems indicates that these needs are not always met. Importantly, crime is a now recognised as a sustainability and health issue (Cozens 2014). In the public health arena, it is accepted that crime reduction, along with economic conditions, housing, education and transport, contribute positively to health and well-being (Shepherd 2001). Indeed, one of the eight elements of a healthy city is 'localities offering security and a sense of community' (Rydin et al. 2012a, p. 554).

Security is an essential part of sustainability. It is necessary for people to realise their potential, and it has been argued that 'a safe environment is the foundation of a healthy city' (Thompson and McCue 2008, p. 9).

An important question to ask is what strategies are planners and public health professionals advocating to achieve such objectives? Significantly, one approach is the promotion of urban consolidation policies. These are assumed to solve many of the problems and issues of the twenty-first-century city, including the incidence of crime (Commonwealth of Australia 1995; Office of the Deputy Prime Minister 2004). It is considered that mixed-use areas with higher residential densities and permeable street networks are safer since there are more citizens out and about providing extra passive surveillance. Commonly termed 'eyes on the street', it is assumed that this is effective in reducing crime. Such an understanding is central to the theoretical perspectives of both urban planning and public health.

Nevertheless, some have questioned the assumption that various features of a quality built environment are always socially beneficial (for example, Dempsey 2008; Barton 2010; Rydin et al. 2012b). Interactions between the built environment, land use, population and morphology are complex and they can affect social cohesion (Rydin et al. 2012b). This can result in crime, violence, injury and poor mental health. This chapter recommends planning and public health should adopt a similarly critical and cautionary approach when it comes to urban consolidation policies and assumptions about community safety from crime.

Whilst there is agreement that safety from crime is essential to the maintenance of a high quality built environment, there is no agreement on how this should be achieved. Planning has at times failed to critically analyse key assumptions within its discipline (Yiftachel 2001).

I argue that this is also the case in terms of assumptions about crime (Cozens 2011, 2014). Accordingly, built environment and health professionals need to know more about crime, and people's fear of crime, before seeking to design it out (Cozens 2011, 2014). 'We have to know more about [crime] to be able to know what to do' and where to do it (Wikstrom 2007, p. 60). Since planning and health professionals do not commonly study the temporal and spatial dimensions of crime, nor the fear of crime, it is necessary to explore the theories and evidence from a discipline which does – the field of environmental criminology. But prior to doing so, it is useful to outline the basics of CPTED.

Crime Prevention Through Environmental Design

1st Generation CPTED

1st Generation CPTED evolved from key contributors including Jane Jacobs (1961), Oscar Newman (1973) and Timothy Crowe (2000). It can be divided into six key elements, with territoriality at its core (Saville and Cleveland 2008). The aim is to maximise territorial control and defensible space, thereby reducing criminal opportunities and the fear of crime (see Figure 12.2). 'Access control' is about managing entrances and exits to encourage legitimate users to regulate who is permitted entry into rooms, buildings and/or neighbourhoods. Surveillance performs a similar role and maximises 'eyes on the street' via good sightlines, adequate lighting and appropriate landscaping and design. 'Image and milieu', promoted by regular maintenance and space management, can enhance territoriality by sending a clear message that someone 'cares' for the space. 'Activity support' encourages different land uses and associated activities into an area to support and enhance the territoriality of the space via increased levels of 'eyes on the street'. Finally, 'target hardening' controls access at the individual building level with

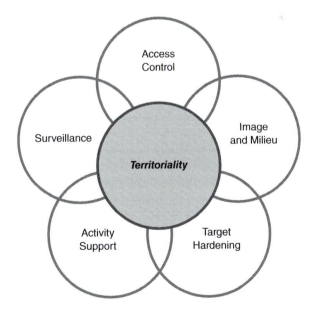

Figure 12.2 1st Generation CPTED

Source: Cozens.

interventions such as secure doors and windows, locks and intruder alarms. These have been discussed at length elsewhere (for example Cozens et al. 2005).

1st Generation CPTED thinking is dominated by the concept of territoriality which some have argued is not universal. Levels of territoriality can differ across and within urban groups (Merry 1981). Spaces possessing good CPTED qualities are not always safe or actively observed by residents (Merry 1981). People may not have the time, inclination or capacity to take up the opportunity to watch and defend their streets or communities. Indeed, 'what is significant about Jacobs' "eyes on the street" are not the sightlines or even the streets, but the eyes' (Saville and Cleveland 1997, p. 1). Such sentiments underpinned the development of 2nd Generation CPTED. Crucially, Jacobs' 'eyes on the street' concept was based on observations of large American cities over 50 years ago. She explicitly cautioned against transferring her ideas into guidelines for towns, small cities or suburbs (Jacobs 1961, p. 26). 'Eyes on the street' may not be as relevant or effective as it once was (Cozens and Hillier 2012).

2nd Generation CPTED

2nd Generation CPTED is the evolution of the opportunity-reducing 1st Generation CPTED concepts with social mechanisms that help reduce the motivation to offend, as well as supporting the design and management of space (Saville and Cleveland 1997, 2008). Significantly, it has been demonstrated that the most effective strategies to reduce crime involve both opportunity *and* motivation reduction (Scott 2000). Broadly, there are four key concepts to 2nd Generation CPTED: social cohesion; community connectivity; community culture; and threshold capacity. These have their origins in pattern language (Alexander et al. 1977). Put simply, they help to encourage community participation in the problem–identification and problem–solving associated with local streets and neighbourhoods.

The bedrock of 2nd Generation CPTED is social cohesion which has two components: social glue and positive esteem. Social glue relates to strategies to bring community members together to take responsibility for their area. It also embraces organising community events where participants come together to learn about 1st Generation CPTED. Positive esteem involves personal characteristics such as conflict resolution, self-confidence skills and emotional intelligence training. These have been used to encourage residents to identify problems in their communities and to attempt to solve them using 1st Generation CPTED.

Community connectivity is when a neighbourhood possesses positive relations and influence with other agencies. This can involve teaching grant-writing skills, setting up web-based communities and promoting community participation. Organisations need to connect outside themselves – to others with similar problems, as well as issues and different levels of government. Well-connected and integrated communities are more empowered and can nurture a sense of place. This can encourage self-policing and discourage crime and deviant behaviour. There is a strong link between community connection, health and crime.

Community culture is how residents come together to share a sense of place and why they bother to display any territoriality. Indeed, it has been suggested that we do not require '. . . neighbourhoods of watchers; we need a sense of community where people care about who they are watching' (Saville and Cleveland 2008, p. 83). This relates to cultural events and festivals, gender and minority equality strategies, celebrations of social and cultural diversity and a sense of pride about local characteristics and community traditions. Youth clubs have long been a crime prevention and community-building strategy, dating back to the 1930s Chicago Area Project in the USA (Shaw and McKay 1942). The absence of youth clubs or similar facilities can lead to boredom and social exclusion, with groups of young people roaming the streets searching for something to do.

Threshold capacity is about promoting human-scale, pedestrian-oriented neighbourhoods where size and density does not promote anonymity. 2nd Generation CPTED sees the neighbourhood as an ecosystem with a finite carrying capacity for specific land–uses and activities, including crime. This 'tipping point' can relate to the over-concentration of bars in a city centre or increasing con-centrations of abandoned and derelict properties (Spelman 1993). This resonates with the notion of neighbourhoods as social ecosystems (Jacobs 1961).

2nd Generation CPTED focuses on supporting and encouraging communities to get involved in identifying and solving crime problems in their neighbourhood using 1st Generation CPTED strategies. Such participation can enhance the effectiveness of CPTED by using it as a participa-tory process, rather than a design outcome (Cozens 2011, 2014).

Delivering effective CPTED strategies

There are various strategies to help practitioners deliver effective CPTED strategies. This includes working with the communities to undertake safety audits of perceived problems in and around their neighbourhoods. Residents can also participate in creating 'fear-of-crime' maps for their localities. Processes can also involve community accords and participatory decision-making processes, together with conflict resolution. These strategies help to enhance community social interactions (Saville and Cleveland 1997). Clearly, CPTED should encompass more than con-temporary design guidelines. It can go well beyond the physical optimisation of surveillance and providing an urban form that encourages 'eyes on the street'.

Figure 12.3 illustrates how this process was used to enable the community to identify crime problems and develop solutions for a local railway station in South Wales (UK). Following the modifications to this station, patronage increased by 33 per cent and a budget of £2.5 million was announced for further investment in infrastructure (Cozens et al. 2004).

A more critical understanding of crime patterns and environmental criminology theory can also assist in improving the application of CPTED to improve health and well-being. In the next section I consider how this can occur.

Environmental criminology

Environmental criminology is 'the study of crime, criminality, and victimisation as they relate first, to particular places, and secondly, to the way that individuals and organisations shape their activities by placed-based or spatial factors' (Bottoms and Wiles 1997, p. 305). Understanding local crime patterns, as part of environmental criminology, should be factored into the CPTED process – before it is applied as a solution (Atlas 2008; Cozens 2014).

Figure 12.3   Railway station before CPTED modifications (left) and after CPTED modifications (right)

Source: Cozens.

The intellectual foundations of environmental criminology lie in the ecology of crime. This evolved from mapping the location of offenders and offences in the nineteenth century (Guerry 1833) and the work of urban sociologists at the 'Chicago School' (for example Shaw and McKay 1942). The ecology of crime and environmental criminology share much in common (see Stark 1987).

Three crime opportunity theories are useful in understanding environmental criminology. These are Routine Activities Theory (Cohen and Felson 1979), Crime Pattern Theory (Brantingham and Brantingham 1981) and Rational Choice Theory (Cornish and Clarke 1986). The key characteristics of each are illustrated in Box 12.1.

Extensive research from the field of environmental criminology reveals that specific types of environmental settings (for example, land uses) are more criminogenic than other settings (Felson and Boba 2010). Among those which can be more criminogenic are industrial, commercial and recreational locations, educational settings (for example, schools and universities), offices, hospitals, retail stores, parks, parking areas and public transport nodes. Different land use types are associated with varying types of crime. For example, the crime of burglary is associated with industrial, commercial and residential settings, while hospitals and bars are often linked to increased incidents of assaults. A further example is how public transport nodes and retail settings provide opportunities for increased levels of theft/robbery. However, not all settings exhibit high crime risks. A minority of each specific setting type (usually around 20 per cent) is likely to be significantly more problematic than others (Clarke and Eck 2007). For example, bars are a land use type which is associated with alcohol-related crime. Commonly, a minority of the bars in an entertainment district will be responsible for the majority of all the problems, while most bars will be relatively safe.

Box 12.1 Crime opportunity theories

Routine Activities Theory (RAT)	Crime Pattern Theory (CPT)	Rational Choice Theory (RCT)
Offenders have routine daily activities in known and used 'awareness spaces'.	Certain locations and pathways between them are linked to crime.	Offenders rationally consider the risks of being seen or apprehended, the effort needed to carry out the offence and the rewards on offer before deciding to offend.
Offenders identify and select their criminal targets.	'Crime attractors' attract large numbers of users and provide opportunities for crime (for example, drug-treatment centres).	
Well-used and familiar locations (usually close to home, leisure, work or friends) are more likely to be targeted as crime opportunities.		Different environmental settings provide varying opportunities for crime.
	'Crime generators' attract large numbers of users and generate specific opportunities for crime (for example, transit stations).	Rationality in offenders can vary. For certain types of crimes and some offenders (for example, when under the influence of alcohol and/or drugs) may show little, if any, rational thinking or decision-making.
At a specific place and time, there must be a motivated offender, a suitable target and the absence of a capable guardian for a crime to take place.	'Crime detractors' lack attractions and may be underused and can encourage offending (for example, vacant or derelict buildings).	

We can look through the lens of environmental criminology and apply these theories to the crime-reductive assumptions made about high-density, mixed-use, permeable developments. Urban planners and public health professionals are largely unaware of this perspective (for a more detailed discussion see Cozens 2011, 2014). Planners therefore need to acknowledge these potential crime risks and balance them against other planning concerns in order to better design, plan and manage more supportive environments for health.

Box 12.2 presents some of the evidence showing how urban consolidation (high densities, mixed uses and permeable streets) does not always mean safety from crime. This evidence reveals how locations with higher densities have been linked to increased crime rates generally, and higher rates of violent crime and pick-pocketing specifically. Offenders are more anonymous in crowded environmental settings and larger numbers of bystanders are less likely to intervene. This needs to be understood in creating safe higher density cities. In order to make a higher density area safer, planners would consider applying all of the CPTED concepts. They would pay particular attention to, and focus on, specific land uses commonly associated with crime, such as crime generators and attractors highlighted in Box 12.1. This approach goes beyond the simplistic assumption that high densities are inherently safe by virtue of increased 'eyes on the street'.

In terms of mixed land uses, research has found burglary rates are higher and crime in general is more likely when compared with single use residential locations. Informal social controls are more difficult to maintain and offender anonymity is also higher. Further, the potential for recognising strangers is diminished. For permeable street layouts, most research has consistently reported increased crime levels when compared to less permeable configurations, particularly in relation to burglaries (Armitage et al. 2010; Johnson and Bowers 2010). Permeable streets provide increased access to criminals, as well as to law-abiding citizens. Offenders can be present and can legitimately be travelling through these areas.

A limited body of research (for example see Hillier and Shu 2000) contradicts the extensive research on crime in permeable locations, but has been widely criticised as being unconvincing (for example Schneider and Kitchen 2007; Cozens and Love 2009). Over 40 studies linking permeability with increased crime are highlighted by Cozens and Love (2009). In spite of this evidence, the permeability debate continues to generate conflict. For example, in the UK, many architects, planners and urban designers advocating permeability are challenged by the perspective of police architectural liaison officers (ALOs) who advocate less permeability (for example, via cul-de-sacs). The ALOs work closely on the 'Secured By Design' scheme (SBD). This is an initiative developed in 1989, and applies CPTED strategies to reduce crime in new housing developments. SBD layouts generally restrict permeability and have consistently demonstrated significant crime reductions (see Teedon et al. 2010; Armitage and Monchuk 2011).

Box 12.2 Urban consolidation and research from environmental criminology

High densities and crime

Higher density areas exhibited higher crime rates than those with lower densities (Harries 2006; Lachapelle and Noland 2013).

(continued)

(continued)

Increased densities have been associated with higher rates of violent crime (Calhoun 1962).

Informal social controls were found to be more difficult to maintain, offenders more anonymous and increased opportunities for crime in dense, mixed-use locations were observed (Stark 1987).

Specific types of crime, such as pick-pocketing, have been reported in crowded locations (Loukaitou-Sideris 1999).

Crime has been associated with higher densities in prisons (Paulus 1988), nightclubs (Macintyre and Homel 1997) and naval ships (Dean et al. 1978).

Larger numbers of residents sharing a common entrance were linked to increased crime rates (Newman 1973).

Larger numbers of onlookers ('eyes on the street') have been linked with less intervention in a crime situation (Barnyard 2008).

Mixed-uses and crime

Informal social controls have been found to be more difficult to maintain in mixed-use locations (Stark 1987).

In mixed-use locations it was easier for offenders to remain anonymous (Stark 1987).

Mixed-use communities have been found to exhibit weaker social cohesion and higher crime rates (Roncek 2000).

Single-use residential environments have revealed lower rates of crime than areas with mixed uses (Greenberg et al. 1982; Greenberg and Rohe 1984).

Increased vehicular and pedestrian flows reduced the potential for interaction and for recognising strangers (Appleyard 1980; Taylor and Harrell 1996).

Proximity to a range of mixed land-uses 'generated' crime (Luedtke 1970; Buck et al. 1993).

Residential burglary was more frequent in properties close to commercial areas (Dietrick 1977).

Businesses in residential areas exhibited increased burglary rates (Wilcox et al. 2004).

Burglaries were more likely in properties located in mixed-use sites (Yang 2006).

In residential areas increases in business activity were linked to more crime (Taylor et al. 1985).

Mixed-use developments have been associated with increased crime risks (Sampson and Raudenbush 1999; Sampson et al. 2002).

Permeability and crime

Increased connectivity has repeatedly been found to increase crime (Bevis and Nutter 1978; Bowers et al. 2005; Johnson and Bowers 2010).

Properties on cul-de-sacs exhibited lower crime levels than those on grid streets (Beavon et al. 1994; Town et al. 2003; Teedon et al. 2010).

Corner houses were more vulnerable to burglary (Taylor and Nee 1988; Hakim et al. 2001).

Modifying grids into cul-de-sacs using road closures reduced crime (Matthews 1992; Newman 1995; Lasley 1998).

New pathways connecting the ends of cul-de-sacs led to increases in crime (Sheard 1991).

Crime was more frequent in accessible areas with commercial land uses (Davison and Smith 2003).

In a study of over 3,000 residential burglaries, lower rates were reported for properties located on less permeable layouts (Yang 2006).

Source: Adapted from Cozens (2011, 2014).

The theories and evidence from environmental criminology clearly challenge the safety assumptions underpinning consolidated urban environments and healthy, walkable communities. Crime is potentially an unintended consequence of urban planning and public health policies that promote high-density, mixed-use and permeable developments. The traditional separated ways-of-working in public health and planning (Barton 2010) might partly explain the reticence to engage with the evidence from environmental criminology and think more critically about how best to promote community safety. The physical and mental health promoting aspects of higher density areas are well established. So how do we balance this with the evidence from criminology in creating healthy and safe cities? An understanding of environmental criminology will hopefully go some way to contributing towards the development of a more holistic approach to promoting health and well-being.

The Settlement Health Map: crime and community safety

When we consider the Settlement Health Map (see Chapter 1, Figure 1.2; Barton and Grant 2006), there are three objectives directly relevant to crime and community safety. They are:

1. facilitating social networks and social cohesion;
2. supporting a sense of local pride and cultural identity;
3. promoting a safe environment.

These objectives are certainly likely to promote community safety and potentially reduce crime. What is missing, however, is *how* to promote a safe environment. Currently, 1st Generation CPTED is the main tool – but its application as a design outcome falls short of this objective. 2nd Generation CPTED provides an obvious link with the first two safety objectives of the Settlement Health Map. Disseminating this understanding of 2nd Generation CPTED to planning and public health practitioners could do much to strengthen synergies between the two approaches and the successful creation of safe and healthy cities.

If we reflect on the Settlement Health Map through the perspective of environmental criminology, it may assist public health professionals and planners in moving beyond the isolated design outcomes of 1st Generation CPTED. Figure 12.4 illustrates a 'dynamic model for designing out crime' (Cozens 2014). It attempts to contextualise 1st and 2nd Generation CPTED. Some key points emerge when we consider the theories and evidence presented in this chapter and how they might inform the Settlement Health Map.

- Crime and fear of crime are not only located within the community sphere – routine activities suggest they transcend all the spheres, as people (victims, offenders and bystanders) move around urban space. There is an ecology of crime, which is interwoven within all legitimate activities.
- At the sphere of 'Built Environment' in some streets, places and buildings, and along different routes, crime risks can be very different to the safety assumptions espoused by urban consolidation policies.
- Physical and social crime prevention (including 1st and 2nd Generation CPTED) should be applied contemporaneously at specific places as a process.
- A temporal perspective is important to extend the times that buildings are occupied so that they are used for working, shopping, living, playing and learning over longer periods of the day and night.

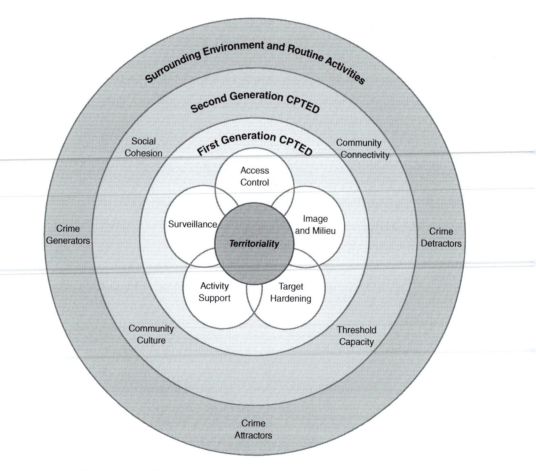

Figure 12.4 A dynamic model for designing out crime

Source: Cozens (2014).

- This temporal dimension can be expanded to consider a 'cradle to the grave' approach. This embraces crime risks associated with the built form from the initial design and construction stages, through to use and reuse, to when the building(s) become disused and derelict and ultimately, demolished. Crime risks will change throughout this lifecycle. CPTED is a dynamic process and is about the design, management and use of the built form – not just its design.

This model will hopefully stimulate discussion and debate, encouraging more critical thinking about crime. Further, it may assist in nurturing a more holistic understanding of what to consider when designing or planning for a safe(r) environment in the promotion of urban sustainability, community safety, health and well-being. This represents a contribution to the development of a form of 'urban environmentalism' for the twenty-first century (Cozens 2002, p. 130).

Conclusions: balancing act

It is crucial to emphasise that crime concerns should not dominate planning and health decision-making. Issues such as the amenity of the physical and social environment, walkability, public health needs, and environmental sustainability all require balanced consideration. This chapter has attempted to shed new light on the concept of CPTED and on the complexity of crime – using theories and evidence from environmental criminology. This complexity relates to crime risks associated with the design, management and use of the built form. The discussion does not necessarily conclude that urban consolidation policies should be avoided. Preventing crime is not the only objective and needs to be considered alongside other important planning objectives. A way through this quandary is to acknowledge that some of these objectives may, at times, work against each other. Trade-offs will have to be made. Balanced thinking and decision-making are paramount. In order to plan and design safer environments, the complex nature of crime needs to be better understood by all stakeholders. It is not as simple as promoting the use of CPTED guidelines as a 'one-size-fits-all' approach. 'Eyes on the street' will not always save the day.

When this complexity is acknowledged, and locations are considered as distinct contexts, mixed-use, high-density and permeable layouts can be designed (or not) as appropriate. When they are designed, CPTED (and other) strategies can then be used in a highly focused and targeted manner. Specific high-risk locations can be identified and CPTED can be applied as a process – not as a design outcome. Local communities can also be part of this participatory process. They can help to identify implementation strategies and solutions appropriate for their local crime problems – while also considering issues such as amenity, walkability, public health and sustainability.

The fourth recommendation of the Lancet Commission on public health was the need to conduct a complexity analysis in order to identify unintended consequences of urban health policies (Rydin et al. 2012b). This chapter has attempted to respond to this recommendation by identifying crime as an unintended consequence of urban consolidation policies. It has highlighted how community safety can be enhanced by considering 2nd Generation CPTED, by understanding the theories and evidence from environmental criminology and using CPTED as a participatory process, not as a design outcome. Understanding crime risks and thinking about crime are not currently common practice in planning and will often challenge the design consensus. A better informed approach to crime and community safety will be more likely to reduce crime, and enhance public health and well-being, contributing towards a healthy built environment.

References

Alexander, C., Ishikawa, S. and Silverstein, M. 1977. *A pattern language*. New York: Oxford University Press.

Appleyard, D. 1980. *Livable streets, protected neighborhoods*. Berkeley, CA: University of California Press.

Armitage, R. and Monchuk, L. 2011. Sustaining the crime reduction impact of designing out crime: re-evaluating the Secured by Design scheme 10 years on. *Security Journal* 24, 320–343. doi: 10.1057/sj.2010.6.

Armitage, R., Monchuk, L. and Rogerson, M. 2010. It looks good, but what is it like to live there? Exploring the impact of innovative housing design on crime. *European Journal on Criminal Policy Research*. doi: 10.1007/s10610-010-9133-8.

Atlas, R. 2008. *21st Century security and CPTED: designing for critical infrastructure protection and crime prevention*. Boca Raton, FL: CRC Press, Taylor & Francis Ltd.

Barnyard, V. 2008. Measurement and correlates of pro-social bystander behaviour: the case of interpersonal violence. *Violence and Victims* 23(1), 83–97.

Barton, H. 2010. Strengthening the roots of planning. *Planning Theory and Practice* 11(1), 95–101.

Barton, H. and Grant, M. 2006. A health map for the local human habitat. *Journal of the Royal Society for the Promotion of Health* 126(6), 252–253.

Beavon, D., Brantingham, P. and Brantingham, P. 1994. The influence of street networks on the patterning of property offenses. In Clarke, R. (ed.). *Crime prevention studies*. Volume 2. Monsey, NY: Criminal Justice Press.

Bevis, C. and Nutter, J. 1978. *Changing street layouts to reduce residential burglary*. Minneapolis: Minnesota Crime Prevention Center.

Bottoms, A.E. and Wiles, P. 1997. Environmental criminology. In Maguire, M., Moran, R. and Reiner, R. (eds.). *The Oxford handbook of criminology*. Oxford: Clarendon Press.

Bowers, K., Johnson, S. and Hirschfield, A. 2005. Closing-off opportunities for crime: an evaluation of alley-gating. *European Journal on Criminal Policy and Research* 10(4), 285–308.

Brantingham, P. and Brantingham, P. 1981. *Environmental criminology*. Beverly Hills, CA: Sage Publications.

Buck, A., Hakim, S. and Spiegel, U. 1993. Endogenous crime victimization, taxes and property values. *Social Science Quarterly* 74(2), 334–348.

Calhoun, J.B. 1962. Population density and social pathology. *Scientific American* 206, 139–148.

Clarke, R. and Eck, J. 2007. Understanding risky facilities: tool guide number 6. Washington, DC: US Department of Justice, Office of Community Oriented Policing Services. www.popcenter.org/tools/risky_facilities.pdf, accessed 6 June 2013.

Cohen, L. and Felson, M. 1979. Social change and crime rate trends: a routine activity approach. *American Sociological Review* 44, 588–608.

Commonwealth of Australia. 1995. *AMCORD: A national resource document for residential development*. Canberra: Commonwealth of Australia, Department of Housing and Regional Development.

Cornish, D. and Clarke, R. 1986. *The reasoning criminal*. New York: Springer-Verlag.

Cozens, P. 2002. Sustainable urban development and crime prevention through environmental design for the British city. 2002. Towards an effective urban environmentalism for the 21st century. *Cities: The International Journal of Urban Policy and Planning* 19(2), 129–137.

Cozens, P. 2011. Urban planning and environmental criminology: towards a new perspective for safer cities. *Planning Practice and Research* 26(4), 481–508.

Cozens, P. 2014. *Think crime! Using evidence, theory and crime prevention through environmental design for planning safer cities*. Praxis Education: Quinns Rock, Western Australia.

Cozens, P. and Hillier, D. 2012. Revisiting Jane Jacobs' 'Eyes on the Street' for the 21st century: evidence from environmental criminology. In Hirt, S. and Zahm, D. (eds.). *The urban wisdom of Jane Jacobs*. Oxfordshire: Routledge, Chapter 13, pp. 196–214.

Cozens, P. and Love, T. 2009. Permeability as a process for controlling crime: a view from Western Australia. *Special Edition of the Built Environment Journal*. Security versus safety: how to deliver less crime and more sustainable design. 35(3), 346–365.

Cozens, P.M., Neale, R.H., Whitaker, J. and Hillier, D. 2004. Tackling crime and fear of crime while waiting at Britain's railway stations. *Journal of Public Transportation* 7(3) 23–41.

Cozens, P.M., Saville, G. and Hillier, D. 2005. Crime prevention through environmental design (CPTED): a review and modern bibliography. *Journal of Property Management* 23(5), 328–356.

Crowe, T. 2000. *Crime prevention through environmental design: applications of architectural design and space management concepts.* 2nd edn. Oxford: Butterworth-Heinemann.

Davison, E. and Smith, W. 2003. Exploring accessibility versus opportunity crime factors. *Sociation Today: The Journal of the North Carolina Sociological Association* 1(1).

Dean, L., Pugh, W. and Gunderson, E. 1978. The behavioural effects of crowding: definitions and methods. *Environment and Behavior* 10, 413–431.

Dempsey, N. 2008. Quality of the built environment in urban neighbourhoods. *Planning Practice and Research* 23(2), 249–264.

Dietrick, B. 1977. The environment and burglary victimization in a metropolitan suburb. Annual Meeting of the American Society of Criminology. Atlanta, USA.

Farrell, G. and Clark, K. 2004. What does the world spend on criminal justice? *Heuni Paper No. 20.* The European Institute for Crime Prevention and Control affiliated with the United Nations, Helsinki. ISSN 1236-8245. http://heuni.fi, accessed 17 January 2014.

Farrell, G. and Roman, J. 2006. Crime as pollution: proposal for market-based incentives to reduce crime externalities. In Moss, K. and Stephens, M. (eds.). *Crime reduction and the law.* London and New York: Routledge, Chapter 8, pp. 14–33.

Felson, M. and Boba, R. 2010. *Crime and everyday life.* 4th edn. Thousand Oaks, London, New Delhi: Sage Publications.

Foster, S. and Giles-Corti, B. 2008. The built environment, neighbourhood crime and constrained physical activity: an exploration of inconsistent findings. *Preventative Medicine* 47(3), 241–251.

Greenberg, S. and Rohe, W. 1984. Neighborhood design and crime: a test of two perspectives. *Journal of the American Planning Association* 50, 48–60.

Greenberg, S., Rohe, W. and Williams, J. 1982. Safety in urban neighborhoods: a comparison of physical characteristics and informal territorial control in high and low crime neighborhoods. *Population and Environment* 5(3), 141–165.

Guerry, A. 1833. *Essai sur la Statistique Morale de la France avec Cartes.* Paris: Crochard.

Hakim, S., Rengert, G. and Shachamurove, Y. 2001. Target search of burglars: a revisited economic model. *Papers in Regional Science* 80, 121–137.

Haldenby, A., Majumdar, T. and Tanner, W. 2012. *Doing it justice: integrating criminal justice and emergency services through police and crime commissioners.* www.reform.co.uk/wp-content/uploads/2012/10/DoingItJustice.pdf, accessed 18 January 2014.

Harries, K. 2006. Property crimes and violence in United States: an analysis of the influence of population density. *International Journal of Criminal Justice Sciences* 1 (2), July. http://cjsjournal.brinkster.net/harries.html, accessed 8 April 2015.

Hillier, B. and Shu, S. 2000. Crime and urban layout: the need for evidence. In Ballintyne, S., Pease, K. and McLaren, V. (eds.). *Secure foundations: key issues in crime prevention, crime reduction and community safety.* London: Institute of Public Policy Research, pp. 224–248.

Jackson, J. and Stafford, M. 2009. Public health and fear of crime: a prospective cohort study. *British Journal of Criminology* 49, 832–847.

Jacobs, J. 1961. *The death and life of great American cities.* London: Jonathon Cope.

Johnson, S. and Bowers, K. 2010. Permeability and burglary risk: are cul-de-sacs safer? *Quantitative Journal of Criminology* 26(1), 89–111.

Lachapelle, U. and Noland, B. 2013. Inconsistencies in associations between crime and walking: a reflection of poverty and density. *International Journal of Sustainable Transportation.* http://dx.doi.org/10.1080/15568318.2012.742947.

Lasley, J. 1998. *Designing out gang homicides and street assaults.* Washington, DC: US National Institute of Justice.

Loukaitou-Sideris, A. 1999. Hot spots of bus stop crime: the importance of environmental attributes. *Journal of the American Planning Association* 65(4), 395–411.

Luedtke, G. and Associates. 1970. *Crime and the physical city: neighborhood design techniques for crime reduction.* Washington, DC: US Department of Justice.

Macintyre, S. and Homel, R. 1997. Danger on the dance floor: a study on interior design, crowding and aggression in nightclubs. In Homel, R. (ed.). *Policing for prevention: reducing crime, public intoxication and injury. Crime prevention studies, Volume 7.* Monsey, New York: Criminal Justice Press, pp. 91–113.

Maslow, A. 1943. *Motivation and personality.* New York: Harper.

Mason, P., Kearns, A. and Livingston, M. 2013. 'Safe going': the influence of crime rates and perceived crime and safety on walking in deprived neighbourhoods. *Social Science and Medicine* 91, 15–24.

Matthews, R. 1992. Developing more effective strategies for curbing prostitution. In Clarke, R. (ed.). *Situational crime prevention: successful case studies*. New York: Harrow and Heston.

McCollister, K., French, M. and Fang, H. 2010. The cost of crime to society: new crime-specific estimates for policy and program evaluation. *Drug and Alcohol Dependence* 108, 98–109.

Merry, S. 1981. Defensible space undefended: social factors in crime prevention through environmental design. *Urban Affairs Quarterly* 16(3), 397–422.

Newman, O. 1973. *Defensible space: people and design in the violent city*. London: Architectural Press.

Newman, O. 1995. Defensible space: a new physical planning tool for urban revitalization. *Journal of the American Planning Association* 61, 2149–2155.

Office of the Deputy Prime Minister. 2004. *Places: the planning system and crime prevention*. London: Office of the Deputy Prime Minister, Home Office.

Paulus, P. 1988. *Prison crowding: a psychological perspective*. New York: Springer-Verlag.

Pease, K. and Farrell, G. 2011. Climate change and crime. *European Journal on Criminal Policy and Research* 17(2), 149–162.

Roncek, D.W. 2000. Schools and crime. In Goldsmith, V., McGuire, P.G., Mollenkopf, J.H. and Ross, T.A. (eds.). *Analyzing crime patterns: frontiers of practice*. Thousand Oaks, CA: Sage Publications, Inc.

Rydin Y., Davies, M., Dávila, J., Pedro, C., Hallal, P., Hamilton, I., Man Lai, K. and Wilkinson, P. 2012a. Healthy communities: local environment. *The International Journal of Justice and Sustainability* 17(5), 553–560.

Rydin Y., Bleahu, A., Davies, M., Dávila, J., Friel, S., De Grandis, G., Groce, N., Hallal, P., Hamilton, I., Howden-Chapman, P., Lai, K., Lim, C., Martins, J., Osrin, D., Ridley, I., Scott, I., Taylor, M., Wilkinson, P. and Wilson, J. 2012b. Shaping cities for health: complexity and the planning of urban environments in the 21st century. *The Lancet* 379(9831), 2079–2108.

Sampson, R., Morenoff, J. and Gannon-Rowley, T. 2002. Assessing 'neighborhood effects': social processes and new directions in research. *Annual Review of Sociology* 28, 443–478.

Sampson, R.J. and Raudenbush, S.W. 1999. Systematic social observation of public spaces: a new look at disorder in urban neighborhoods. *American Journal of Sociology* 105, 603–651.

Saville, G. and Cleveland, G. 1997. 2nd generation CPTED: an antidote to the social Y2K virus of urban design. Paper presented at the 2nd Annual International CPTED Conference, Orlando, FL, 3–5 December, available at: www.cpted.net.

Saville, G. and Cleveland, G. 2008. Second-generation CPTED: the rise and fall of opportunity theory. In Atlas, R. (ed.). *21st Century security and CPTED: designing for critical infrastructure protection and crime prevention*. Boca Raton, FL: CRC Press, Taylor & Francis Ltd, Chapter 7, pp. 79–90.

Schneider, R. and Kitchen, T. 2007. *Crime prevention and the built environment*. London and New York: Routledge.

Scott, M. 2000. *Problem-oriented policing: reflections on the first 20 years*. Washington, DC: US Department of Justice, Office of Community Oriented Policing Services.

Shaw, C.R. and McKay, H.D. 1942. *Juvenile delinquency and urban areas*. Chicago, IL: University of Chicago Press.

Sheard, M. 1991. Report on burglary patterns: the impact of cul-de-sacs. Delta, British Columbia: Delta Police Department.

Shepherd, J. 2001. Criminal deterrence as a public health strategy. *The Lancet* 358(9294), 1717–1722.

Spelman, W. 1993. Abandoned buildings: magnets for crime? *Journal of Criminal Justice* 21(3), 481–495.

Stafford, M., Chandola, T. and Marmot, M. 2007. Association between fear of crime and mental health and physical functioning. *American Journal of Public Health* 97, 2076–2081.

Stark, R. 1987. Deviant places: a theory of the ecology of crime. *Criminology* 25(4), 893–909.

Taylor, M. and Nee, C. 1988. The role of cues in simulated residential burglary. *British Journal of Criminology* 28, 396–401.

Taylor, R.B. and Harrell, A.V. 1996. *Physical environment and crime*. Washington, DC: National Institute of Justice, US Department of Justice.

Taylor, R.B., Shumaker, S.A. and Gottfredson, S.D. 1985. Neighborhood-level links between physical features and local sentiments: deterioration, fear of crime, and confidence. *Journal of Architectural Planning and Research* 2, 261–275.

Teedon, P., Reid, T., Griffiths, P. and McFadyen, A. 2010. Evaluating Secured by Design door and window installations: effects on residential crime. *Crime Prevention & Community Safety* 12(4), 246–262.

Thompson, S. and McCue, P. 2008. The chess principles for healthy environments: an holistic and strategic game-plan. www.pcal.nsw.gov.au/__data/assets/file/0003/27651/chess.pdf, accessed 26 February 2009.

Town, S., Davey, C. and Wooton, A. 2003. *Design against crime: secure urban environments by design.* Salford: The University of Salford.

Wikstrom, P. 2007. Doing without knowing: common pitfalls in crime prevention. In Farrell, G., Bowers, K., Johnson, S. and Townsley, M. (eds.). *Imagination for crime prevention: crime prevention studies.* Monsey, NY: Criminal Justice Press, Volume 21, pp. 59–80.

Wilcox, P., Quisenberry, N., Cabrera, D.T. and Jones, S. 2004. Busy places and broken windows? Towards defining the role of physical structure and process in community crime models. *Sociological Quarterly* 45(2), 185–207.

Yang, X. 2006. *Exploring the influence of environmental features on residential burglary using spatial-temporal pattern analysis.* Gainesville, FL: University of Florida. http://etd.fcla.edu/UF/UFE0013390/yang_x.pdf, accessed 17 February 2010.

Yiftachel, O. 2001. Introduction: outlining the power of planning. In Yiftachel, O., Alexander, I., Hedgcock, D. and Little, J. (eds.). *The power of planning: spaces of control and transformation.* Dordrecht: Kluwer Academic.

13

THE ROLE OF PLANNING AND DESIGN IN ADVANCING A BIO-NUTRITION-SENSITIVE FOOD SYSTEM

Jane Dixon and Emily Ballantyne-Brodie

Introduction: food systems, food security, food habitats

Food systems – national and local – are critical to human health and environmental sustainability. As they currently operate, industrial scale and corporate owned food systems contribute to key human and environmental health problems. In contrast to the food system model that prevails in many countries, a health promoting food system is one that guarantees food and nutrition security – that is, the uninterrupted delivery of sufficient energy and micro-nutrients for all peoples to lead a healthy and productive life – while promoting the health of the environment so that future generations can be guaranteed their food security. This is a 'bio-nutrition-sensitive' food system as opposed to a food yield driven system that operates regardless of health and environmental impacts.

Food security is a complex and multi-faceted concept, with understandings having evolved over time to encompass interconnections between the quality of the food supply, how and where food is distributed and exchanged, and how and why food is consumed (Pinstrup-Andersen 2009). Today, the widely accepted five pillars of food security are availability, accessibility, affordability, appropriateness and acceptability. In this chapter we focus on the interrelationship between 'food habitats', or more specifically bio-nutrition-sensitive habitats, and food security.

We begin by arguing that industrial food systems are generating three public health problems: malnutrition; inferior well-being/psycho-social anxiety; and bio-physical degradation. Each has a planning policy and practice dimension.

While planning is part of the problem, it is part of the solution too. In the second part of the chapter we describe three planning domains which have a role to play. These are planning for food system diversity, planning for social inclusion and participation in order to enhance interactions with food activities, and planning for agri-environmental sustainability. We conclude with a holistic methodology for integrating the planning activities across the domains. This involves a design-led food community approach. The nature of food system problems and planning opportunities which are explored in this chapter apply broadly to high and middle income countries, but especially to those with a long history of public disengagement from food systems.

Three food system problems

Food not only contributes to human health and well-being, but to the converse: to disease and the inability to enjoy and participate in meaningful social activities. Equally, food flora and fauna are integral to the health of natural environments and to bio-diversity, but their production, harvesting and processing can lead to the depletion and destruction of natural resources when methods are inappropriate in scale and intensity. In this section we explore in more detail how food-related activities can be problematic.

The triple burden of malnutrition

Globally, between 800 million to one billion people are undernourished in terms of calorific sufficiency, and so are underweight. A further 1.4 billion are overweight and obese, and possibly two billion people suffer micro-nutrient deficiencies – the most common being anaemia. Globally, diet-related disease is now a leading contributor to premature mortality through wasting, stunting and chronic diseases, including coronary heart disease, type 2 diabetes and cancers. A recent editorial in *Public Health Nutrition* noted that nutrition related non-communicable diseases '. . . once seen as a burden of the affluent classes, now impact every socio-economic group at every level of macro-economic development' (Nazmi and Monteiro 2013, p. 571). The three states of malnutrition co-exist in most middle and high income countries, although underweight is less of an issue. According to The Economist Intelligence Unit (2012), high income countries can be food secure but not necessarily nutritionally secure, with low levels of vegetal iron being a major food supply problem.

Evidence from a broad sweep of the food social sciences reveals that the built environment shapes human food consumption behaviours in one of three ways. First, the contestation over land use, and in particular between land for agricultural and food growing enterprises and other uses (residential, industrial). This influences what foods are locally available and whether foods have to enter the system from elsewhere affecting control over stability of supply, price fluctuations and quality. Second, the local food retail habitat plays its part in what foods and nutrients are available, affordable and accessible. Third, the presence of food-related services and general amenity in the consumption locale can influence dietary behaviours, and what is acceptable in terms of food – the how, when and why food and nutrients are consumed, for example, fast food and take-away outlets when the need is for quick eating; sit-down tables when catching up with friends.

Historically, the typical pattern to human settlements was based on considerations of ready access to potable water and lands suitable for food production or wild food harvesting. It was not until after the Second World War when countries were encouraged by the Food and Agriculture Organization and other international agencies to consider the role of tradable food commodities in their national development and food security. The idea of national food self-sufficiency began to dissipate, and the value of agricultural land was reconsidered as 'land awaiting higher economic development' (Mason and Knowd 2010, p. 64). This was especially so for agricultural lands close to growing cities, allowing for the spread of urbanisation and the associated revaluation of urban land for residential and service developments. As a result, metropolitan planning either ignored or overrode agricultural uses.

In relation to the second habitat, that of food retail, considerable research effort has gone into understanding the impacts of easy access to, and concentration of, fast food outlets. Initially it was thought that there was a relationship between household and school proximity to these outlets and obesity (Reidpath et al. 2002; Davis and Carpenter 2009). While fast food chains have received the greater public health scrutiny, there are good reasons to also question the contribution of supermarket activities to diet-related disease. For instance, supermarkets expose consumers to large amounts of cheap processed foods and more expensive fresh foods relative to that sold in fresh food markets (Hawkes 2008; Banwell et al. 2012). Their land acquisition and holding-for-development ('land-banking') not only erect barriers to entry by competitor firms (Simms 2007), they can change the dynamics and vitality of a shopping street or area which loses an independent food retailer when these become no longer viable for lack of passing customers. Further, siting supermarkets in areas with more affluent populations disadvantages poorer populations (Eisenhower 2001), while sites accessible only by cars compounds the public health effects of car reliance – reduced physical activity, increased greenhouse gas emissions, noise, accidents and traffic congestion (Blythman 2005; Kjellstrom and Hinde 2007).

These factors combine to mean that poorer and less mobile populations are at relatively greater risk of being malnourished. However, rather than criticise any particular retail format, there is some suggestion that the stronger association with nutritionally inferior diets is the nature of the local food environment. This is understood as a composite of factors, including retail outlet mix, product mix, product pricing, food promotions and marketing, and general amenity (White 2007).

In relation to consumption practices which have a spatial component, healthy eating has been shown to result from a particular style of eating. A healthy eating style favours spending more time on a meal in a social setting rather than individual dining. Slow and commensal eating leads to lower energy intake, at least in some cultural settings (Rozin et al. 2003; Sobal and Nelson 2003; Fischler 2011). Slowing down eating allows for early satiety to 'kick in'. In addition, social eating can be more 'mindful' about portion sizes and the content of the meal (Fischler 2011). In social situations, there can be powerful cultural pressures not to consume to excess, although where over-eating is now normalised as in the USA, eating with others can promote excessive consumption (Christakis and Fowler 2007). These findings from a range of research projects in a variety of countries are supported by the conclusion of a meta-review of studies examining the environmental determinants of healthy eating, namely that: 'socio-cultural environmental factors defining what is acceptable, desirable and appropriate to eat may be more important for healthful eating than physical environments that define the availability and accessibility of foods' (Brug et al. 2008, p. 307).

While much social eating takes place in private households, an increasing number of meals are being consumed outside the home in street-side cafes and other food service sector outlets (Huntley 2011). This means that the public food consumption habitat is an important mediator of how food is consumed, with a key nutrition-sensitive feature being spaces which help to slow the eating tempo, as well as create opportunities for social interaction together with eating (Wasnic 2004). Again, retail planning is important, as is cultural planning which we discuss later.

Psycho-social anxieties and social exclusion

As food supply networks have become more complex, and urban customers have become increasingly distanced from food production and processing, a situation of disembedded food systems has been observed (Goodman and DuPuis 2002). Such systems are based on the global trade in foods, the rise of novel foods of unknown provenance, the overriding of seasonal variations through year-long supplies of produce, and the production of foods irrespective of environmental suitability. In this highly industrialised food system model, a 'nutritional cacophony' also prevails causing confusion regarding 'good' and 'bad' nutrition (Fischler 1993). Indeed an increased focus on nutrition values (Dixon 2009), at a time when the food supply is increasingly distanced physically and metaphysically from consumers, has only served to heighten food-related ontological insecurity or 'gastro-anomie' (Fischler 1993). Put another way, citizens in many countries have lost mastery over their diets and the food system more broadly.

The encroachment of psycho-social anxieties into the world of eating is indicated by a series of surveys conducted in the US, France, Japan and Belgium. Somewhat counter-intuitively, eating-for-pleasure appeared from the studies to be health protective compared to individualised eating-for-health (Rozin et al. 1999). This conclusion was arrived at by associating national diet-related disease prevalence with citizen views towards food consumption. For the health-obsessed Americans, diet-related disease was far higher than that among the 'food as pleasure' oriented French. Belgians were closer to Americans, and Japanese closer to the French along the pleasure–health continuum. When pleasure was present, food quantities were smaller (Rozin et al. 2011).

Reducing food-related ontological insecurity and anxiety requires confidence which comes through both familiarity and trust in the food system (Fischler 1993). It is possible to explain the findings above by noting that both France and Japan have durable culinary food cultures (some would say insular culinary cultures) which are very much based on locally grown produce. Their respective population's stronger connections to agriculture may entail lower levels of gastro-anomie, pointing to the importance of experiencing a food system which is embedded within, and familiar to, the society.

More than three decades ago, Jane Jacobs challenged planners to consider how neighbourhood design could be used to foster social solidarity, interdependence and trust: all qualities that underpin the practice of particular lifestyles including those associated with food (Zukin 2003). Building on Jacobs' thinking, Zukin (2003, p. 129) argues the importance of acknowledging the 'connections between the production of physical spaces and symbols and between the built environment, sociability and urban lifestyles'. Meeting this challenge necessarily requires collaborations between spatial and cultural planners.

Environmental degradation

We are at a very early stage of understanding the environmental challenges posed by the demand and supply of different diets, although there is some scientific consensus for the following propositions (McMichael et al. 2007; Lang et al. 2009; Lancet and University College London Institute for Global Health Commission 2009):

- food systems have a range of impacts on the environment, which in turn prejudices the quantity, quality and fair distribution of future food supplies;
- affluent country diets – high in red meat, fish, oils, dairy, fruit and vegetables, and pre-prepared foods which are often imported from low cost producer countries – are not sustainable in environmental health terms;
- flying and shipping foods around the world (referred to as 'food miles') contributes to greenhouse gas emissions;
- the global expansion in dairy production is increasing greenhouse gas emissions and land degradation caused by grazing ruminant animals.

Concerns over the links between climate change, coupled with the dietary demands from an increasingly affluent world population, have encouraged renewed interest in promoting horticultural production and consumption. It is here that land use planning is pivotal because, due to their perishable nature and short growing cycles, fruit and vegetables have been traditionally produced close to the consuming market in cities and towns. Typically this sector has been based on urban market gardens and small, peri-urban farms and the output distributed through extensive networks of independent 'green grocers'.

There is a further dimension to environmental degradation over and above food production methods and locales, and this involves the spatial impacts of food distribution systems (Biggs et al. 2010; Edwards et al. 2011). The 'supermarketisation' of supply chains, with their sophisticated capacity to store and transport foods in temperature controlled ways across the hemispheres (what is referred to as the international cool chain), means that producers can be separated from their markets by thousands of kilometres. This logistical capability contributes to acceptance that fruit and vegetable growing can be pushed into less fertile soils while freeing up land for 'higher-order' land developments. Not only are environmental externalities generated by these long supply chains, but they amplify the disembedded nature of food systems described above.

Ameliorative/restorative approaches involving planning

We have argued that contemporary industrial food systems are not delivering 'good nutrition', well-being or environmental sustainability benefits. We also contend that a quarter of a century's worth of public health interventions aimed at dietary behaviour modification – via education, motivation, skills training and social support – have had minimal success in changing food consumption patterns. Behavioural approaches are limited for several reasons: they reach only small numbers of participants; they perpetuate social inequalities through partial and unequal access to healthy choices; they generally produce weak effects and do not effect sustained changes (Hill et al. 2004). This assessment has led to the conclusion that '[t]here is growing evidence that modifications in the physical environment and in social policies will be required to accomplish the goal [of widespread dietary behaviour modification]' (Hill et al. 2004, p. 111).

If the ultimate goal of food security is access by all people in this and subsequent generations to live a healthy and productive life, three types of nutrition and bio-sensitive food habitat planning interventions are required to counteract the problems identified in the previous section. The interventions involve a range of planning specialisms: spatial, retail, environmental and transport, augmented by a heavy dose of cultural planning and design. Design is understood here as working alongside the statutory planning process to insert the culturally attuned specificity and contextual site detail required in order to understand each population's unique needs.

Over the past few years at Milano Politecnico, researchers have explored and tested the co-design or co-creation process to unlock new forms of value including product innovation, sustainable changes, process efficiency, place development, social innovation or long-term growth (Meroni 2007, 2011; Koskinen 2012; Manzini and Meroni 2014). The innovation in this process is to encourage collaborative exploration among all stakeholders from providers/producers to users to passers-by (Manzini and Rizzo 2011; Koskinen 2012). As in the early days of participatory planning action-led research (Sandercock 1975), the contemporary design field provides an opportunity for social innovators to establish new spatial models of everyday living possibilities, including local food systems (Meroni 2011, 2012; Koskinen 2012).

Now to a description of our three proposed planning interventions.

Planning for health through designing nutrition sensitive habitats to counteract malnutrition

'Nutrition-sensitive' habitats encompass the following aspects:

- what foods are available and their nutrient content;
- what foods are accessible and affordable;
- consumption practices linked to place-based characteristics.

At a minimum, there are three planning considerations. These are statutory planning for food production and processing; retail planning to ensure a diversity of outlets and ready access; and cultural planning to create opportunities for healthy food practices, like taking time to eat and commensal dining. A planning and design approach can optimise these outcomes through harnessing new forms of local food system. We outline this approach in the final section of the chapter.

In terms of what food is available, a healthy food supply needs to give primacy to plant-based foods which have traditionally entered city markets through urban market gardens and peri-urban farms. Planners involved in metropolitan land use policy could consider the multiple public health, economic, environmental and social benefits that come with growing fruit, vegetables, nuts and legumes in metropolises. Mason and Docking (2005) have charted a wide range of economic, social and health values which follow from the multiple, but diminishing, forms of urban agriculture which exist within the Sydney Basin in New South Wales, Australia. For example, they describe the recreational, social cohesion and food access benefits from backyard and community gardens (see Figure 13.1).

There are the environmental benefits of market gardens, orchards and fodder crops as they sequester urban wastes, and contribute to hydrological systems and natural bio-diversity. Further, there are multiplier economic effects for supply and distribution firms and civil society farmers' markets (see Figure 13.2). However, as they note, metropolitan planning strategies need to protect these activities from incompatible and inappropriate uses. Their analysis is widely applicable to all cities.

In addition to protecting food producing lands and 'healthy agriculture' close to population centres, the accessibility and affordability of foods is important to healthy diets. Thus, a second requirement for a nutrition-sensitive environment is a nutrition-sensitive retail experience

Figure 13.1 Community garden in a suburb of Perth, the capital of Western Australia. The garden is integrated within the suburb

Source: Thompson.

Figure 13.2　Farmers' market, Berlin. Such markets offer independent outlets for locally grown and seasonal produce

Source: Thompson.

which is a composite mix of retail outlets (with a range of product choices), an agreeable amenity to the shopping precinct (lighting, personal safety), where exposure to product marketing/advertising is limited, and ease of access/convenience (White 2007; MacDonald et al. 2009). A diversity of outlets and transport options are key, with fresh produce being celebrated as worthy of attention: a feature of so many European towns and cities (see Figure 13.3).

Figure 13.3　Fresh produce market, which sits at the heart of shopping precinct, Saint-Jean d'Angely, western France

Source: Dixon.

A third feature of a nutrition-sensitive food system concerns the food consumption experience. Outer suburban areas of many cities stand in stark contrast to gentrified inner localities, which have evolved to be highly 'convivial' due to their multi-faceted gastronomic possibilities. In a town planning analysis of the gastronomic features of Australian cities, Parham (1990) made suggestions for designing cities that bring people out of their isolation to share interaction and food involvements. She was particularly critical of the role played by regional shopping malls with their food courts: where people drive up in their private 'spaces', rush through someone else's private space and grab a bite to eat from a standardised, speed driven outlet. Once again, citizens become alienated from their food supply and what food offers beyond acting as quickly consumed fuel for the body. European and Asian cities which were established well before the car have prefigured what convivial spaces can look like, with their organic development unfolding over the centuries giving priority to small areas devoted to the sharing of food: whether under a tree (Figure 13.4) or in a square (Figure 13.5). Australia approaches public picnic areas in a similarly minimalist, or uncluttered, manner so that engagement with natural surroundings is possible (Figure 13.6).

Planning for well-being through food system re-engagement

Much of the research on food security focuses on agriculture and related concepts such as food yields, nutrient quality and access. It is problem-centric, as well as production and distribution focused. While there is minimal research on how citizens experience food in emotionally rewarding ways, there is growing awareness that the built environment affects health. It does this by providing opportunities for sufficient physical activity and food, as well as a sense of belonging and opportunities for participation and empowerment (Butterworth 2000; Flourney and Yes 2004).

Even though many cities and urban places have lost their convivial nature, food 'spaces' offer a unique way to re-engage with food and community. Planners recognise the need to build

Figure 13.4   Regular Saturday morning gathering, Montcuq village, central France. The cafe is on the way to the fresh produce market which lines the footpaths of several narrow pedestrian streets

Source: Dixon.

Figure 13.5   Square St Emilion, France, with tables laid out for half a dozen restaurants. The small scale, no advertising and little car traffic focuses the eating experience on the food and conversation

Source: Dixon.

Figure 13.6   A table laid out in Western Park, on the shore of Lake Burley Griffin, Canberra, Australia. Tables and barbecues dot the park, which is 2 kilometres from the central business district (CBD)

Source: Dixon.

resilient communities for health, economic and social reasons. Local food movements and food sovereignty projects can be major catalysts for bringing people together to build resilient and healthy communities (Thompson et al. 2007; Dowler et al. 2009). Local food systems can be a convivial way to foster community capital, or the building of trust and reciprocity (Ballantyne-Brodie et al. 2013a). There is an emerging trend to adopt participatory approaches in the development of convivial food places, including community gardens,[1] food hubs[2] and even whole-of-community food systems.[3]

The participatory process of designing a food space can create convivial places through the simple act of social connection. In turn, socially connected individuals can become motivated to organise 'alternative' food systems and to practise principles of food sovereignty. This is defined as 'the right of peoples to . . . define their own food and agriculture systems' (Declaration of Nyéléni 2007).[4] Many countries now host highly active food sovereignty movements. These operate at international, national and local levels. Local food sovereignty can be observed when provincial or city governments develop local food plans providing regulatory and capacity building support to local agriculture and sites of food exchange, as in food hubs which we describe in the next section. Spatial planners can play a central role in making food hubs possible (see Figure 13.7).

Planning for bio-sensitive agriculture (rural and urban) to counteract environmental degradation

Food systems are most appropriately conceived of as bio-complex systems. They emerge from 'the interplay of behavioural, biological, chemical, physical, and social interactions that affect, sustain, or are modified by living organisms, including humans' (Michener et al. 2001, p. 1018). In a public health ecology critique of industrial food systems, Lang (2005) distinguished between a productionist paradigm of food and nutrition with what he termed an 'ecologically integrated' paradigm. The productionist approach is characterised by industrial scale operations, mono-culture farming, lack of consideration of environmental costs and consumer

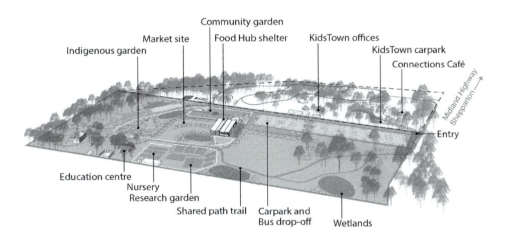

Figure 13.7 Pictorial representation of plan for Shepparton Food Hub. Shepparton lies at the heart of horticultural production in rural Victoria, Australia

Source: Pollen Studio.

autonomy from what is on-offer, and resignation to the inevitable diet-related diseases. In contrast, an ecological approach favours one based on the principle of 'the right to be well; [with] the entire food supply geared to deliver health' (Lang 2005, p. 735). The ecological approach rests on diverse systems of food production and care of food producing environments (Dahlberg 2008). From this perspective, agricultural lands perform multiple functions beyond food production, including landscape amenity, eco-cultural tourism and environmental protection from over-development. The stewardship of lands by people with a deep knowledge of its capabilities is integral to planning for future food security. This occurs through safeguarding the condition of agricultural lands, as well as providing food producers with incomes to maintain their own futures by being able to adapt to changing environmental conditions and emerging market opportunities.

Depending on their environmental resource use approach, urban food system activities can renew bio-physical environments. This is done with the vegetation cover afforded by plant foods, which in turn ameliorates heat extremes, absorbs and holds water, and through their root systems retains soils in place. Agri-environmental renewal can also be enhanced through methods which return vital chemical elements via waste recycling and organic fertiliser use. Community gardens can 'give back' to the environment in a similar fashion but on a much smaller scale. At the same time, they can deliver health co-benefits given evidence that contacts with the natural world can benefit mental and physical health (Thompson et al. 2007; Townsend and Weerasuriya 2010) (see Figure 13.8).

As to planning reforms in regard to distribution, few would question the remarkable efficiencies introduced into modern food systems especially by supermarket chains. These efficiencies have been largely due to increasing scales of operation and the technological sophistication of large producers, processors and logistics enterprises. However, whether a few big players at each

Figure 13.8 A neighbourhood shared allotment garden, Newcastle, New South Wales

Source: Thompson.

stage of the food system are good for environmental sustainability and food system resilience is questionable (Larsen et al. 2008, p. 11; Whitelegg 2005).

In order to support small and medium sized food enterprises, there has been an explosion in interest in independent and alternative food hub models. A food hub can be described as a place that provides the social and physical infrastructure to connect local buyers and sellers, offers facilities for farmers to store and process their produce, and for others to market and distribute food. The operations of a food hub can stem from a place, through a website, or via existing food services. Food hubs can be local, city or regional, with the latter defined as 'a business or organisation that actively manages the aggregation, distribution, and marketing of source identified food products primarily from local and regional producers to strengthen their ability to satisfy wholesale, retail, and institutional demand' (USDA 2012, p. 9). Food hubs can act as a catalyst to spark a local food economy, culture and spatial community (Ballantyne-Brodie et al. 2013a).

Food hubs have many different functions, but they usually focus on coordinated marketing and distribution of local fresh produce. They provide the 'missing local middleman' in local food infrastructure (Larsen 2014). Food hubs range in scale from volunteer-run buying groups using temporary spaces for receipt and packing of goods (like community or school halls, churches and garages), to permanent and well-established firms offering a variety of business, educational and/or food access services. Findings from an American Food Hubs survey showed that they are broadening the distribution infrastructure for local food across the nation (Michigan State University Center for Regional Food Systems 2013). It was found that 62 per cent of food hubs began operations within the last five years, 31 per cent of food hubs had $1,000,000 or more in annual revenue and the majority of food hubs were supporting their businesses with little or no grant assistance. Financially, the most successful tended to be for-profit and cooperative in structure, in operation for more than 10 years and working with a relatively large number of producers. The values-based nature of food hubs makes it hard to judge many of them solely on their level of financial success.

Research undertaken for the Sydney City Farm (City of Sydney 2010) revealed that food hubs in Australia take numerous forms. They range from what is described as the *Articulated Model* – involving a permanent headquarters that coordinates a programme of activities, which grow and expand to other sites in the region as new compatible offerings arise – to a *Mobile Model* which is described as a transitional approach where infrastructure, activities and programmes are based on temporary sites and move to locations as they become available. The creativity being shown by the food hub movement exemplifies the cross-fertilisation taking place between design and planning professions, as we go on to explain.

The design-led food community approach

One approach to tackling the three food system problems described above must involve making existing statutory planning tools better attuned to food security through safeguarding agricultural lands (Noble 2008). However given the multi-faceted nature of bio-nutrition-sensitive food habitats, statutory and land use planning alone cannot deliver food security or environmental sustainability. What is required is a more holistic approach to a case-by-case food habitat.

In this context, we argue that the design field can augment the statutory and strategic services planning field. In one such example, Australia's National Heart Foundation launched the Food-Sensitive Planning and Urban Design framework and toolkit in 2011. FSPUD, as it is known, was developed within the context of Victoria's State and Local Planning Policy Frameworks to create opportunities for planners and urban designers to consider Food in the decisions they make. It can be woven into decision-making processes, enabling informed consideration of: supply and access to Food; whether created environments foster enjoyment of Food; and the potential of careful design to enable people to meet their other needs while meeting their Food needs.

(Donovan et al. 2011, p. 10)

FSPUD challenges strategic planners, statutory planners and 'designers of the urban public realm' to reorient food systems towards health and sustainability objectives.

The inclusion of place-based designers is highly relevant given the specificity of agro-ecological, geo-spatial and socio-cultural conditions which influence the viability of different approaches to national food supplies and food distribution systems. Having multiple unique environmental and social conditions precludes any one generalisable response to growing food sustainably. Instead, the response has ideally to be based on an agro-ecology approach. Agro-ecology not only acknowledges the specificities of local natural conditions, but historical approaches to food production and producer practices that are most suited to the natural and social environment.

Evolving out of the co-design principles described earlier, and complemented by an approach called Design Led Innovation (Behrendorff et al. 2011; Bucolo and Matthews 2011), Design-led Food Communities (DFC) is a novel approach to achieve public re-engagement in food systems (Ballantyne-Brodie et al. 2013b). The DFC approach recognises diverse actors and operations, including social enterprises, local governments and commercial firms. DFC was developed through five years of research and development on food system projects to assist in generating solutions collaboratively between government, business and citizens. Thus far, the approach has been used to develop four major projects in Australia and Italy over 2009–2014.[5] Case studies have been integral to developing the appropriate tools and process principles to assist a diverse array of communities with varying contexts and issues.

Out of this experience, DFCs have been observed to emerge through the synergies of four mechanisms (see Figure 13.9).

1. *Via the economy, manufacturing and new business models*: with the aim to encourage established and emerging food businesses and social enterprises to develop innovative business models and ventures for growing, processing, distributing and retailing food.
2. *Via communities and participation models*: to unite communities to develop creative social innovation projects and drive the social economy through volunteer programmes and sharing schemes.
3. *Via policy and innovative governance models*: to redesign governance and local government strategies to facilitate entrepreneurial food production and distribution models.
4. *Via action research to steer academic institutions*: toward creating societal changes for local communities and food systems.

All DFC work is reflected upon through a rigorous action-research agenda based at this stage at the Design-Led Innovation Lab at the Queensland University of Technology, Brisbane, Australia, and the Design for Sustainability Laboratory at Politecnico di Milano, Italy.

Conclusions: planning healthy and robust food systems

Population growth is combining with major social trends, including changing dietary habits, to predispose more people to diet-related diseases. As well, the capacity of bio-physical food

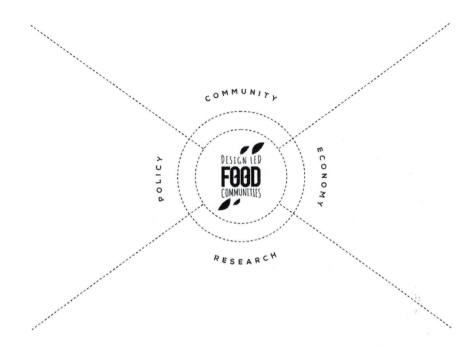

Figure 13.9   Design-led Food Communities approach

Source: Ballantyne Brodie.[6]

environments is diminishing. The health and well-being of populations and environments, now and into the future, require healthy and sustainable food systems, with bio-nutrition-sensitive habitats sitting at their centre. From a public health perspective, new planning policies and practices are required in three domains. First, built and natural food environments require a mix of regulations and design approaches to ensure that they provide access to afford-able dietary diversity (with a predominance of plant foods). Second, place, community and business models all need to be redesigned to minimise ontological food insecurity. This has to occur through providing first-hand engagement in food-related activities, including food growing and processing, cooking, food exchange, waste disposal, and access to slow and convivial eating opportunities. Third, there is an urgency to promote the most environmen-tally sustainable forms of agriculture, in both rural and urban localities. In short, a holistic approach led by planners and designers, and involving businesses, governments and citizens, is pivotal to the co-evolution of food systems which contribute to positive population and environmental health.

Notes

1   www.urbanreforestation.com/what-we-do/docklands-community-garden
2   www.urbanreforestation.com/what-we-do/shepparton-food-hub
3   European Union Sustainable Food for Urban Communities Policy Design Project: www. sustainable-everyday-project.net/urbact-sustainable-food/; the City of Greater Dandenong Design-led Food Strategy: http://fieldinstitute.co/dandenong
4   www.nyeleni.org/spip.php?article290
5   www.urbanreforestation.com
6   www.sustainableeveryday.com

References

Ballantyne-Brodie, E., Fassi, D. and Simone, G. 2013a. Coltivando: making a university convivial garden. European Academy of Design. Sweden.

Ballantyne-Brodie, E., Wrigley, C., Ramsey, R. and Meroni, A. 2013b. Design led innovation to rejuvenate local food systems and healthy communities: an emerging research agenda. In 2013 Tsinghua International Design Management Symposium. 1–2 December 2013. Shenzhen, China.

Banwell, C., Dixon, J., Seubsman, S.-A., Pangsap, S., Kelly, M. and Sleigh, A. 2012. Evolving food retail environments in Thailand and implications for the health and nutrition transition. *Public Health Nutrition*. 16(4): 608–615.

Behrendorff, C., Bucolo, S. and Miller, E. 2011. Designing disruption: linking participatory design and design thinking in technology orientated industries. In *Proceedings of the 2011 Conference on Designing Pleasurable Products and Interfaces* (p. 53). New York: ACM.

Biggs, C., Ryan, C. and Wiseman, J. 2010. Distributed systems. A design model for sustainable and resilient infrastructure. VEIL Distributed Systems Briefing Paper N3. Melbourne: University of Melbourne. www.ecoinnovationlab.com/wp-content/attachments/305_VEIL.Resilient-Systems-Briefing-Paper. pdf, accessed 8 April 2015.

Blythman, J. 2005. *Shopped: the shocking power of British supermarkets*. London: HarperPerennial.

Brug, J., Kremers, S., van Lenthe, F., Ball, K. and Crawford, D. 2008. Environmental determinants of healthy eating: in need of theory and evidence. *Proceedings of the Nutrition Society*. 67: 307–316.

Bucolo, S. and Matthews, J. H. 2011. Design led innovation: exploring the synthesis of needs, technologies and business models. In *Proceedings of Participatory Interaction Conference 2011*. Sønderborg, Denmark.

Butterworth, I. 2000. *The relationship between the built environment and wellbeing: a literature review*. Melbourne: Victorian Health Promotion Foundation.

Christakis, N. and Fowler, J. 2007. The spread of obesity in a large social network over 32 years. *The New England Journal of Medicine*. 357(4): 370–379.

City of Sydney. 2010. City farm feasibility study. http://sydneyyoursay.com.au/document/show/44, accessed 8 April 2015.

Dahlberg, K. 2008. Pursuing long-term food and agricultural security in the United States: decentralization, diversification and reduction of resource intensity. In Lyson, T., Stevenson, G. and Welsh, G. (Eds). *Food and the mid-level farm*. Cambridge, MA: The MIT Press, pp. 23–34.

Davis, B. and Carpenter, C. 2009. Proximity of fast-food restaurants to schools and adolescent obesity. *American Journal of Public Health*. 99(3): 505–510.

Dixon, J. 2009. From the imperial to the empty calorie: how nutrition relations underpin food regime transitions. *Agriculture and Human Values*. 26(4): 321–331.

Donovan, J., Larsen, K. and McWhinnie, J. 2011. *Food sensitive planning and urban design*. David Lock Associates, University of Melbourne and National Heart Foundation of Australia. www.heartfoundation. org.au/SiteCollectionDocuments/Food-sensitive-planning-urban-design-full-report.pdf, accessed 8 April 2015.

Dowler, E., Kneafsey, M., Cox, R. and Holloway, L. 2009. 'Doing food differently': reconnecting biological and social relationships through care for food. *The Sociological Review*. 57: 200–221.

Edwards, F., Dixon, J., Friel, S., Hall, G., Larsen, K., Lockie, S., Wood, B., Lawrence, M., Hanigan, I., Hogan, A. and Hattersley, L. 2011. Climate change adaptation at the intersection of food and health. *Asia-Pacific Journal of Public Health*. 23(2): 91–104.

Eisenhower, E. 2001. In poor health: supermarket redlining and urban nutrition. *GeoJournal*. 53(2): 125–133.

Fischler, C. 1993. A nutritional cacophony or the crisis of food selection in affluent societies. In Leatherwood, P., Horisberger, M. and James, W. (Eds). *For a better nutrition in the 21st century*. New York: Vervey/Raven Press, pp. 57–65.

Fischler, C. 2011. Commensality, society and culture. *Social Science Information*. 50(3–4): 1–21.

Flourney, R. and Yes, I. 2004. The influence of community factors on health: an annotated bibliography. A PolicyLink Report, Los Angeles: The California Endowment.

Goodman, D. and DuPuis, M. 2002. Knowing food and growing food: beyond the production consumption debate in the sociology of agriculture. *Sociologia Ruralis*. 42(1): 5–22.

Hawkes, C. 2008. Dietary implications of supermarket development: a global perspective *Development Policy Review*. 26(6): 657–692.

Hill, J., Sallis, J. and Peters, J. 2004. Economic analysis of eating and physical activity: a next step for research and policy change. *American Journal of Preventive Medicine*. 27(3S): 111–116.

Huntley, R. 2011. *Main meal repertoires: how Australians plan, purchase and choose main meals*. Sydney: Meat & Livestock Australia.

Kjellstrom, T. and Hinde, S. 2007. Car culture, transport policy and public health. In Kawachi, I. and Wamala, S. (Eds). *Globalization and health*. New York: Oxford University Press, pp. 98–121.

Koskinen, 2012. *Design research in field and practice and showroom*. Waltham, MA: Morgan Kaufmann.

Lancet and University College London Institute for Global Health Commission. 2009. Managing the health effects of climate change. *The Lancet*. 373: 1693–1731.

Lang, T. 2005. Food control or food democracy? Re-engaging nutrition with society and the environment. *Public Health Nutrition*. 8(6A): 730–737.

Lang, T., Barling, D. and Caraher, M. 2009. *Food policy: integrating health, environment and society*. Oxford: Oxford University Press.

Larsen, K. 2014. Australian Food Hubs Network website. www.foodhubs.org.au, accessed May 2014.

Larsen, K., Ryan, C. and Abraham, C. 2008. *Sustainable and secure food systems for Victoria: what do we know? What do we need to know?* Melbourne: Victorian Eco-Innovation Lab (VEIL) and Australian Centre for Science, Innovation and Society, University of Melbourne.

MacDonald, L., Ellaway, A. and Macintyre, S. 2009. The food retail environment and area deprivation in Glasgow City, UK. *International Journal of Behavioral Nutrition and Physical Activity*. 6: 52: doi: 10.1186/1479–5868–6–52.

McMichael, A., Powles, J., Butler, C. and Uauy, R. 2007. Food, livestock production, energy, climate change, and health. *The Lancet*. 370(9594): 1253–1263.

Manzini, E. and Rizzo, F. 2011. Small projects/large changes: participatory design as an open participated process. *CoDesign: International Journal of CoCreation in Design and the Arts*. 7: 3–4, 199–215.

Manzini, E. and Meroni, A. 2014. Catalysing social resources for sustainable changes: social innovation and community centred design. In Vezzoli, C., Kohtala, C. and Srinivasan, A. (Eds). *Product-service system design for sustainability*. Sheffield: Greenleaf Publishing, pp. 362–379.

Mason, D. and Docking, A. 2005. *Agriculture in urbanising landscapes: a creative planning opportunity*. Planning Institute of Australia Congress, Melbourne.

Mason, D. and Knowd, I. 2010. The emergence of urban agriculture: Sydney, Australia. *International Journal of Agricultural Sustainability*. 8(1–2): 62–71.

Meroni, A. (ed.) 2007. *Creative communities: people inventing sustainable ways of living*. Milano: Edizioni Polidesign.

Meroni, A. 2011. Design for services and place development: interactions and relations as ways of thinking about places. In Lou Y. and Zhu X. (Eds). *Cumulus proceedings: Shanghai young creators for better city & better life*. Helsinki: University of Art and Design, pp. 234–240.

Meroni, A. 2012. Designing for social innovation. The project 'Feeding Milano. Energy for change'. In Bartolo R. and Cipolla C. (Eds). *Inovação social e sustentabilidade. Desenvolvimento local, empreendedorismo e design*. Rio de Janeiro: E-papers, pp. 155–174

Michener, W., Baerwald, T., Firth, P., Palmer, M., Rosenberger, R., Sandlin, E. and Zimmerman, H. 2001. Defining and unravelling biocomplexity. *BioScience*. 51(12): 1018–1023.

Michigan State University Center for Regional Food Systems and The Wallace Center at Winrock International. 2013. *Findings of the 2013 National Food Hubs survey*. http://foodsystems.msu.edu/resources/2013-food-hub-survey, accessed 8 April 2015.

Nazmi, A. and Monteiro, C. 2013. The nutrition transition: the same, but different. *Public Health Nutrition*. 16(4): 571–572.

Noble, M. 2008. Gastronomic planning policy: planning for food in Sydney. Honours Thesis. University of New South Wales. www.be.unsw.edu.au/sites/default/files/upload/pdf/cf/hbep/research/Theses/MNoble_Thesis.pdf, accessed 8 April 2015.

Parham, S. 1990. The table in space: a planning perspective. *Meanjin*. 49: 213–219.

Pinstrup-Andersen, P. 2009. Food security: definition and measurement. *Food Security*. 1: 5–7.

Reidpath, D., Burns, C., Garrard, J., Mahoney, M. and Townsend, M. 2002. An ecological study of the relationship between social and environmental determinants of obesity. *Health & Place*. 8(2): 141–145.

Rozin, P., Fischler, C., Imada, S., Sarubin, A. and Wrzesniewski, A. 1999. Attitudes to food and the role of food in life in the U.S.A., Japan, Flemish Belgium and France: possible implications for the diet–health debate. *Appetite*. 33(2): 163–180.

Rozin, P., Kabnick, K., Pete, E., Fischler, C. and Shields, C. 2003. The ecology of eating. *Psychological Science*. 14(5): 450–454.

Rozin, P., Remick, A. and Fischler, C. 2011. Broad themes of difference between French and Americans in attitudes to food and other life domains: personal versus communal values, quantity versus quality, and comforts versus joys. *Frontiers in Psychology*. 2. doi: 10.3389/fpsyg.2011.00177

Sandecock, L. 1975. *Public participation in planning*. Adelaide, South Australia: Government Printer.

Simms, A. 2007. *Tescopoly: how one shop came out on top and why it matters*. London: Constable.

Sobal, J. and Nelson, M. 2003. Commensal eating patterns: a community study. *Appetite*. 41(2): 181–190.

The Economist Intelligence Unit. 2012. *Global food security index*. The Economist Intelligence Unit Ltd. http://foodsecurityindex.eiu.com, accessed 8 April 2015.

Thompson, S., Corkery, L. and Judd, B. 2007. The role of community gardens in sustaining healthy communities. Paper presented at the State of Australian Cities National Conference, Adelaide.

Townsend, M. and Weerasuriya, R. 2010. Beyond blue to green: the benefits of contact with nature for mental health and well-being. Melbourne, Victoria: Beyond Blue Limited.

USDA. 2012. *USDA regional food hub resource guide*. Washington, DC: USDA. http://dx.doi.org/10.9752/MS046.04-2012

Wasnic, B. 2004. Environmental factors that increase the food intake and consumption volume of unknowing consumers. *Annual Review of Nutrition*. 24: 455–479.

White, M. 2007. Food access and obesity. *Obesity Reviews*. 8(Suppl. 1) 99–107.

Whitelegg, J. 2005. London sustainable food hub: opportunities for a sustainable food logistics centre in London. London: Sustain. www.lowhub.com/Lowhub/Resources_files/London%20Sustainable%20Food%20Hub(LDA).pdf, accessed 8 April 2015.

Zukin, S. 2003. Urban lifestyles: diversity and standardisation in spaces of consumption. In Clarke, D., Doel, M. and Housiaux, K. (Eds). *The consumption reader*. London: Routledge, pp. 127–131.

PART III

The human habitat

Overview by Marcus Grant

While Part II explored the field from the stance of human experience, this part examines the nature of the places where we live. Each chapter is concerned with the impacts on health and health equity that can be ascribed to the intimate blend between natural and built environment that we have created as our urban habitat. They describe research relevant to a range of scales from streets and neighbourhoods to whole conurbations and regions in relation to individual and population health. The first four chapters review the form and structure of city regions, neighbourhoods and greenspace. The final four study the fundamental topics of excessive heat and cold, air quality and water management. Each author was asked to provide key pointers for policy stemming from research.

Together these chapters provide valuable insights into how our health, and health equity, is influenced by the places we build; how we research those interactions; and where policy-makers need to focus their attention.

There are two overarching messages from this section. First, planning policy and city design both need to be more adept in responding to insights arising from research. Second, with the plethora of risks and challenges to health from poor urban development, compounded with worrying future trends of climate change and resource depletion, we simply can not afford to go ahead fixing one problem at a time. Healthy urban design, healthy urban planning, sustainable urban development – call it what you will – needs to be soundly based on a systemic understanding of the interrelated nature of the human habitat.

Obesogenic built environment: concepts and complexities

The first chapter provides a link between Parts I and II. Townshend, Gallo and Lake explore an issue of global concern, the rising level of obesity in developed and developing cities. Both sides of the energy equation – the food ingested and the physical exercise taken – are looked at from a habitat perspective. Evidence is examined with a view to its robustness, correlation studies are separated from those showing causal relationships and the issue of self-selection in residential locations is discussed. The core of the chapter develops our understanding through discussing a research project which captures the complexities inherent when examining obesity in the multifactorial urban environment.

Settlement patterns, urban form and travel

In the next chapter, Headicar has provided an elegant and accessible synthesis of a huge area of research. He begins with a historical synopsis of how the modern urban realm arrived at its current state. In doing so he carefully distinguishes physical form, transport modes and population behaviour, an approach to the subject that permeates the chapter. Headicar unwraps the problems, and not just in terms of health, but looking more broadly at function and dysfunction in urban conurbations. He examines the research evidence about healthy, sustainable environments in relation to all key spatial parameters of urban systems, ranging from urban densities, housing balance and neighbourhood configuration, through issues of modal mix to carrot and stick policies for behaviour change. Whereas the review of studies, from contrasting international contexts, does not always provide unambiguous results, his own empirical work in Oxfordshire, England, demonstrates the great significance of location.

Retrofitting suburbia for health: scenarios for neighbourhood planning

Continuing with the theme of physical form, Barton and Grant discuss neighbourhood design in depth. The concept and importance of the 'neighbourhood' as a setting for health is presented. Spatial patterning of urban growth fits into a number of archetypes, dictated by either market forces or different 'theories' of planning. Each archetype is described together with the characteristics of the resultant neighbourhoods. In terms of the spatial determinants of health, some archetypes support health through more active travel, better access to local facilities and reduced social exclusion; others frustrate these objectives. The balance between factors such as housing density, public transport and culturally determined travel preferences is explored through local trip data from 12 suburban neighbourhoods. The conclusions demonstrate that the challenge in developing healthier neighbourhoods is not just a technical issue but a matter of institutional priorities and public policy.

Beyond the park: linking urban greenspaces, human well-being and environmental health

This chapter adds to our developing understanding of neighbourhood form through turning the reader's attention to urban greenspace. The focus is the interactions between urban nature and people's health. As an essential component of the urban ecosystem, Corkery reviews the critical role of greenspace and its contribution to individual and collective human health. Through providing the evidence from a variety of disciplines, she establishes the important contribution that greenspace and nature provide for physical and mental health. The challenges of protecting and planning greenspace are then explored, followed by a valuable examination of the health benefits of greenspace for selected vulnerable sub-populations. The final sections pose a number of challenges as provocations for greenspace planning to be better informed by research findings.

Hotter cities: climate change and planning for resilient, healthy urban environments

The World Health Organization acknowledges that climate change presents one of the biggest challenges to future global health. With the inclusion of a stark but all too real account of a heatwave, McKenzie then provides a framework through which to view vulnerability and heat-related public health risk against a background of increasing global temperatures. A number of issues are discussed such as ageing and chronic illness, physical activity and community resilience, raising important questions for urban planning. With the knowledge, skills and technology now available to model, measure and monitor urban heat, decision-makers have less excuse for inaction.

Housing, energy efficiency and fuel poverty

Boardman deals with the issue of fuel poverty, a problem that exacerbates health inequalities. It is most prevalent in countries where there is a demand for heating in winter and a stock of poor quality, energy-inefficient homes. Fuel poverty occurs when a household has difficulty in paying for the energy services that it needs. The chapter examines a range of policy mechanisms employed in different countries to tackle fuel poverty and the associated health impact, including excess winter deaths. Factors determining energy efficiency are outlined, followed by an example from the UK where area-based approaches are proving valuable. Despite a clear link between cold weather and hospital admissions, there are few links as yet between the value of a property and its thermal performance.

The spatial determinants of air quality

Hayes explores the spatial determinants of air quality, a key issue for urban quality of life. Starting with the definition of air pollution, the chapter swiftly moves on to examine the sources and technical parameters of airborne pollutants. The health effects of poor air quality are outlined and a distinction made between chronic and acute exposure. The distribution of air pollution raises the issue of social equity and Hayes argues that air quality management needs to be considered in the context of wider environmental justice. The majority of cities have very ineffectual air quality management approaches. A list of urban policy initiatives to combat or ameliorate air pollution is discussed, setting the context for a description, and call for a comprehensive risk management approach.

Water management, urban development and health

Water is central to health and well-being. In this chapter, Lamond unpacks issues inherent in our need to build human habitats with access to water resources in an era of climate extremes and sea level change. Through historic location and current population pressure, many countries now have examples of flooding disasters that have led to adverse health impact and often loss of life. Knock-on effects through financial losses compound these impacts. In this chapter the health and well-being implications of both flooding and drought are explained. Lamond reviews traditional engineering approaches that have exacerbated the problems and then explores new systemic approaches that point to a way forward. These examples, selected from several countries, outline whole catchment management practices and blue-green techniques. The chapter ends with pertinent lessons, and challenges, for future policy and practice.

14

OBESOGENIC BUILT ENVIRONMENT

Concepts and complexities

Tim Townshend, Rachel Gallo and Amelia A. Lake

Introduction: obesity is a global concern

Obesity is an issue of global concern. Obesity rates have risen rapidly in the recent past with an associated increase in a number of related serious health conditions. While the basic equation behind human obesity seems simple – too much energy consumed, too little energy expended – the causes are complex and multifactorial, including biological, psychological, sociological and economic influences. Swinburn et al. (1999) coined the term 'obesogenic environment' as the 'sum of influences, opportunities, or conditions of life' that promote obesity in individuals or populations, an all-encompassing concept that includes the built environment. While establishing causal pathways between the built environment and obesity has been notoriously difficult, the Foresight report (2007) suggested there was enough expert evidence to implicate the built environment in the obesity crisis – calling for greater consideration of the issue in urban planning.

This chapter will review the evidence around the concept of an obesogenic built environment and explore why the evidence has been so difficult to capture, why it is time to act on the evidence we have (even if partial) and how urban planning might contribute to amelioration of the obesity crisis.

A complex issue

Before looking at the evidence that links the built environment and obesity, it is important to briefly outline why obesity is a significant concern and what the complexities of the issue are. Obesity was highlighted by the World Health Organization as a 'global epidemic' at the start of the twenty-first century (WHO 2000). It is significant because it is recognised as a major risk factor in a number of serious health conditions, such as type 2 diabetes, coronary heart disease and certain cancers. The most common way to measure a state of being overweight or obese is based on body mass index (BMI), using the equation weight (kg) / [height (m)]^2. For adults, a BMI of over 25 is considered overweight and over 30 is classified as obese.[1] Obesity in children and adolescents is of particular concern, since weight problems at a younger age tend to 'track' through to adulthood.

In the UK in 2007 a key report by Foresight highlighted that while people had not altered biologically by comparison with previous generations, the ways we live – for example work patterns, transportation, food production and the way we purchase food – have changed radically over the past five decades (Foresight 2007). Many of these changes have exposed people to an underlying, often inherent, biological tendency, that is, to gain weight. However, underlying this seemingly simple problem is a complex set of interrelationships between a myriad of variables, both individual and environmental. This complexity is captured in Foresight's obesity 'system map', a conceptual representation which was constructed using available evidence from experts in relevant disciplines. The system map is useful in many ways, not least in that it demonstrates that trying to establish simple cause and effect relationships within the system is unlikely to be possible. This creates an epistemological challenge around what can be established with certainty, what we treat as 'evidence' and how we respond to it. This is important not least because both public health and planning policy increasingly call for evidence to underpin them (with different interpretations of what evidence should demonstrate) – we will return to this important issue in the concluding section.

While this chapter uses the UK situation and the way the planning system in the UK might respond to the country's obesity problem as an example, this is very much a part of the global crisis (Delpeuch et al. 2009) and generic conclusions can be drawn that are universally applicable. Of particular concern are soaring obesity rates, particularly among the newly established middle classes, in large parts of the rapidly developing and newly industrialised world over the past decade. As personal wealth has increased, individuals' diets in countries such as India and China have changed, with higher meat and dairy content, while at the same these countries have increasingly adopted developed world approaches to transport and urban development. Active travel (walking and cycling) has declined as ownership of private vehicles has burgeoned, and suburban built forms more usually associated with western countries have become the norm (Bell et al. 2002; Reynolds et al. 2007; James et al. 2010).

Food and the built environment: current evidence

Importantly, the built environment has the potential to influence both sides of the energy (im)balance that leads in humans to becoming overweight and obese. The places we live, work, go to school and so on can either provide, or constrain, opportunities for physical activity and for healthy and unhealthy food access. The Foresight report cited above found that there was enough expert evidence to implicate the built environment in the obesity crisis; the rest of this section will review current evidence.

The way in which we obtain food has changed radically in recent decades. The 'food environment' includes any opportunity to obtain food and is influenced by socio-economic, cultural and policy factors at all levels (Lake and Townshend 2006). On an everyday level, therefore, the food environment encompasses a mixture of shops and supermarkets, where we buy food for home consumption; as well as cafes, takeaways and restaurants and even vending machines at our schools, places of work and leisure venues – where food for consumption mainly outside the home is purchased. Food environments therefore encompass what food is available, what it costs, how it is promoted and so on (Figure 14.1) (Lake et al. 2015).

The types of food implicated in health problems are well-established – those high in saturated fats, sugars and salt (WHO 2003). However, the exact pathways between the availability of these types of food, our propensity to consume them and, therefore, their health consequences, are actually less well understood. The evidence that can help to unpick the environmental influence on individual diet is very much in its infancy. Furthermore, the food environments in different countries can be vastly different, so that findings from one country are not easily translated to other contexts. Examples of this are so-called 'food deserts' – areas where affordable healthy

Figure 14.1　The food environment includes availability and promotion

Source: Authors.

food is difficult to obtain: research in the US found a clear link between the existence of food deserts, diet and health, but these relationships have not been found in the UK.

A recent review of 38 studies that looked at the evidence of a relationship between food environments and diet (mostly examining the consumption patterns for certain food groups – such as fruits and vegetables) suggested there is moderate evidence to support the hypothesis that food environments influence dietary health (Caspi et al. 2012). Caspi et al. suggest that evidence relating to fast food was weakest; however, evidence is mounting. In England research has reported that the availability of fast-food outlets around secondary schools can be an obstacle to establishing healthy eating habits (Smith et al. 2013). Recent research has established that there is a link between fast-food availability and obesity in older children (Cetateanu and Jones 2014).

Some studies have attempted to measure weight status in relation to food access and neighbourhood. Black and Macinko's review of 37 studies pre-2007, while finding there to be inconsistency in the relationship between obesity and the availability of healthy and unhealthy food, also noted that the measures used to assess local food environments were generally inadequate (Black and Macinko 2008). Another issue with many studies (including those examined by Black and Macinko) is that they only explore food access and availability around address of residence – however, these don't take into account the other places where people spend large amounts of time, such as work, leisure or the environments they pass through when travelling to and from work (Burgoine and Monsivais 2013).

Some local authorities have attempted interventions to tackle the proliferation of takeaway food outlets in the built environment. For example, the London Borough of Barking and Dagenham's 'Saturation Point' policy includes exclusion zones for new takeaways within 400m of a primary or secondary school, restricting clustering by allowing no more than 5 per cent of units as takeaways within retail centres and no more than two adjacent to one another. In addition, where takeaways are granted planning permission, a one off £1,000 charge is levied from them to go towards obesity amelioration initiatives, such as improving children's play areas (London Borough of Barking and Dagenham 2009). Since its adoption, the policy has had some success, including the refusal for a well-known pizza chain to open a premises in a retail location, on the grounds that it was both within a 400m exclusion zone and would result in exceeding the acceptable amount of shop frontage allowed for takeaways. The decision to refuse was upheld on appeal. However, this policy and similar ones adopted by other councils have not always been upheld during the planning appeals procedure. This suggests that the UK Planning Inspectorate is giving less weight to these kinds of policies than to other planning considerations, for example, policies for maintaining retail frontage (Lake et al. 2015). This is of concern and an issue we return to at the end of this chapter.

In comparison to the built environment's role in providing exposure to unhealthy food choices, opportunities to provide healthy food exposure are even less well researched. For example there is evidence from the US that adults with access to an allotment, or community garden, consume more fruit and vegetables (Alaimo et al. 2008) (Figure 14.2) and community gardens have been used to improve the diet of poor communities, particularly in the developing world. More generally there is evidence to suggest allotments and community gardens increase social capital among communities and therefore benefits accrued to diet may spread beyond immediate gardeners and their families as friends and families share in excess produce. Allotments also promote active lifestyles and mental well-being (van den Berg et al. 2010) which are in turn linked to better diet (McCormack et al. 2010). There are no known studies that

Figure 14.2 Adults with access to a community garden or allotment consume more fruit and vegetables

Source: Authors.

link these opportunities to weight management/obesity prevention and other health outcomes; however, some local authorities are linking allotment provision with health aspirations. The London Borough of Brent's (2012) food and allotments strategy, for example, links promoting the benefits of food growing and healthy eating through school cookery classes.

In summary, environmental exposures in terms of the availability and accessibility of food interact with our individual food preferences to drive food choice. The relationship between the food environment and obesity is complex; however, understanding the relationship between what we eat and the environmental context in which food choices are made is essential to the development of sustainable obesity prevention strategies. In parallel we need to develop our understanding of how the built environment fits into the obesity equation through providing or hindering food access. As stated earlier, achieving either of these objectives will not be an easy task and may be many years away. In the meantime, further damage to communities' health may be caused if action is not taken. We need to take planning decisions/create policy on the evidence base we have, an issue that we return to in our final discussion and conclusion section.

Physical activity and the built environment: the evidence

The built environment can either provide opportunities for, or place constraints upon, physical activity. This has two aspects: 'active travel' – that is, travel which involves human effort (walking, cycling, skateboarding and so on) as opposed to motorised transportation (see also Chapter 8, Active Travel); and active leisure, such as gardening or playing sports. If someone lives in a neighbourhood where the daily requirements of life, shops, services, schools, workplaces and so on are nearby, this may encourage them to opt for active travel. Having access to greenspaces, parks, riverside walks, nature reserves and similar places is likely to encourage walking and cycling for leisure, as well as other physical activity, such as playing games and sports (Giles-Corti et al. 2005). The fact that the built environment provides opportunities for physical activity is therefore significant since we know exercise is important to help individuals maintain a healthy weight.

As with food environments, however, causal networks between the built environment and health outcomes are extremely complex. Research suggests that living in greener neighbourhoods is correlated with greater well-being and lower levels of ill health. One suggested mechanism is that greener neighbourhoods encourage more active travel and greater physical activity in leisure time (Giles-Corti et al. 2005; Tilt et al. 2007), though not all studies have shown this relationship. Again there is a huge amount of complexity around this issue and research is ongoing (De Vries 2010).

There has been a raft of studies that attempted to *correlate* neighbourhood level factors to walking – mostly it should be noted from the US. These have generally associated 'walkability' with higher residential density, mixed land uses, well-connected street patterns, good access to public transport and a safe, comfortable and attractive public realm (Townshend 2014a). A number of studies have further attempted to correlate walkability in the built environment with weight status (mostly BMI). Black and Macinko's (2008) review of pre-2007 studies found that neighbourhoods which displayed barriers to physical activity were associated with increased BMI. However, a more recent review, while finding increased physical activity in walkable neighbourhoods, counter-intuitively found that BMI was generally unaffected (Durand et al. 2011).

While useful, the reviews mainly draw on research that was, as stated, located in North America, or Australia. More useful for discussion here is evidence from Europe. A key study is provided by Barton et al. (2012) which presented evidence from 12 suburban/commuter locations in four English city regions: London, Newcastle, Cambridge and Bristol. This study generally supported earlier findings, in that where local facilities are provided within walking distance, they are used and, moreover, contrary to common belief people walked considerable distances in these areas. However, a key point the researchers emphasised is that mode of travel varied hugely between areas – for example active travel even for local trips ranged between 29 per cent and 64 per cent of trips. This modal breakdown reflected a diversity of local area factors: accessibility of facilities, the quality of the public realm, the socio-demographic profile of the local population, along with local cultural and behavioural norms. It drew the researchers to conclude that the unique nature of places could not be 'reduced to one or two convenient variables' to explain differences in behaviour (ibid.: 196). There were shared patterns for active travel, for example, proximity of shops and services was clearly important in generating trips, but there were also many complex exceptions, meaning that making generalisations about 'suburban' or any other type of area may be very misleading; this particular aspect of complexity is returned to below in relation to work undertaken at Newcastle University.

Another key finding of the research reviewed above was that more recent suburbs – those developed in the last 20–30 years – displayed more car dependence than older ones (Figure 14.3), suggesting that while planning policy in the recent past has promoted neighbourhoods which are more sustainable and healthy, what has been delivered on the ground seems to be very different. These points are made elsewhere (Townshend and Lake 2009): that, first, although many new housing developments are built to densities that would support local shops and services, in practice these are often lacking; and, second, even if land uses are mixed, land uses such as warehousing or drive-through restaurants may not generate much active travel.

The picture across older suburbs is also complex. Over the past two decades our shopping habits have transformed. In wealthier suburbs traditional grocers, butchers and bakers have been

Figure 14.3 Great Park, Newcastle, is largely car dependent

Source: Authors.

replaced by coffee shops, delis and shops selling upmarket 'knick-knacks'. However, in many lower socio-economic status (SES) neighbourhoods the situation is very different. Declining traditional retailing has given way to a toxic mix of fast-food takeaways, 'pay-day' loan outlets and betting shops. Therefore, the problems of fast food outlined in the first part of 'Food and the built environment: current evidence' above are compounded by other unhealthy services associated with mental and physical health problems (Townshend 2014b). The benefits of generating active travel in such areas may therefore be outweighed by the unhealthy nature of what is on offer there: this is an issue planning urgently needs to address in the UK and should be a warning to other countries following a similar trajectory.

Self-selection

No review of obesogenic environments would be complete without some commentary on the issue of self-selection. Self-selection is the notion that any correlation found between active travel and certain residential characteristics is likely to result from the choices made by people who enjoy being active to live in places that support their lifestyle preferences. In other words, higher active travel behaviours reflect lifestyle preference more than other drivers (it should be noted self-selection has only been raised in relation to physical activity, that is, no known studies have thus far suggested people who like fast food move to areas where there is a ready supply!). There is evidence that some self-selection probably does exist (Boone-Heinonen et al. 2011). However, the concept itself is not without considerable problems. It assumes people have a large amount of choice about where they live and make rational decisions based on in-depth prior knowledge of potential neighbourhoods; both issues are debatable. In the UK residential choice, particularly for many in society, for example those on lower incomes or those seeking to enter the housing market for the first time, is very limited. Furthermore, other factors such as access to good schools (for families with school age children) or social networks are potentially more important in housing choice.

Some people will pursue a sedentary lifestyle no matter how supportive of an active lifestyle their neighbourhood happens to be. However, this misses the point: there is compelling evidence that people in the UK will walk considerable distances, even where conditions are far from ideal, to use local shops, services and open spaces (Townshend and Lake 2011; Barton et al. 2012). How much more walking people would do if their neighbourhoods were made *more* supportive of walking might only be guessed at, but this cannot be ignored in future development.

Capturing complexity: environmental factors affecting children's weight

In 2010 a research project was established at Newcastle University which sought to examine the relationship between the prevalence of being overweight and obese and factors within the broad environment (land use, school, home etc.), for children aged 10–11 years. The study explored the ways in which environmental factors affect energy balance and adiposity among the target age group, taking into account dietary behaviour (the acquisition of, types and amounts of foods eaten) and physical activity behaviour (leisure activity, within education and commuting).

Methods

A mixed methods approach was employed in the study, with quantitative analysis of behaviours and environmental features (using validated tools) and qualitative analysis to provide explanatory description. After an initial pilot study to test the efficacy of methods, eight primary schools were recruited to the main study, the Children's Neighbourhood Environment Study (CNES), based on obesity rates (National Obesity Observatory 2011) and Index of Multiple Deprivation (IMD) scores, divided into quintiles. Four schools each representing the highest and lowest quintiles by obesity prevalence and IMD score were recruited to the study during two phases – winter (2011) and summer (2012). Fifteen randomly selected children (aged 10–11) were then recruited to the study from each school. The children self-reported physical activity and dietary intake using a four day diary that was designed and tested during the pilot study phase. The diary recorded activity type, intensity, location and any companions. In relation to food intake, the diary recorded items, time consumed and food source (the participants also photographed their activity and food). Participants' anthropometric measurements were taken. Participant and parental perceptions of their neighbourhood environments, physical activity, home food environment and diet were assessed, using questions adapted from validated surveys (Birch et al. 2001; Davison et al. 2003; Saelens et al. 2003; Davison and Jago 2009; Lake et al. 2009; Rosenberg et al. 2010; Davison et al. 2011). The participants' neighbourhood environment was subjected to a standardised audit within a 400m buffer of participants' homes. Details were recorded of parks and greenspaces, sports facilities, non-food shops and services, food outlets, food advertising, roads and streets (length, safety, quality) and cyclability.

Findings

Associations between BMI and neighbourhood parks and green spaces, shops and services, road length and safety and street length were in the direction expected (that is, favourable neighbourhood features correlated with lower BMIs). However, neighbourhood sports facilities, cycling facilities and street quality showed a counter-intuitive direction of association with BMI, that is, higher BMI measurements. The direction of association between physical activity and neighbourhood greenspace, road and street length, sports facilities (not leisure centres) and cycling facilities was in the direction expected (that is, favourable neighbourhood environment features and higher physical activity). Conversely neighbourhood shops and services, leisure centres, road safety and street quality showed counter-intuitive direction of association with physical activity. Dietary intake showed no significant associations with neighbourhood environment.

The participant and parent perceptions of the neighbourhood environment, comprising shops and services, leisure facilities, food outlets and walkability, did not consistently correlate with each other or objective measurement.

Group level analysis was complex and potentially skewed due to the high level of complexity of neighbourhood environments. In the existing obesogenic environment literature there is an at times unwritten assumption that neighbourhoods fall into inherent 'types', comprising an (un)healthy food environment, high/low walkability and the (non)promotion of leisure pursuits. What this study found was that 'types' are, in most cases, neither *fully*, nor even *scaled along a continuum between*, healthy and unhealthy across all measures within that type (for example, a neighbourhood may contain predominately healthy food outlets but the closest outlet is an unhealthy outlet – the measure used would consequently result in differing conclusions). And 'types' are not mutually exclusive (for example, a neighbourhood may be highly walkable but contain no leisure facilities).

The 400m buffers fail to capture the highly complex nature of neighbourhood environments which may have pockets of similarity, but taken holistically may not represent the sum of their parts; for example see Figure 14.4 which contains four distinct areas or types: industrial, out-of-town shopping, traditional housing with dispersed access to shops and services, and a traditional high street. These issues of *type* and *buffer* are compounded by the incoherence between *perception* and objective environment audit. This issue may be attributable to the varying understanding and

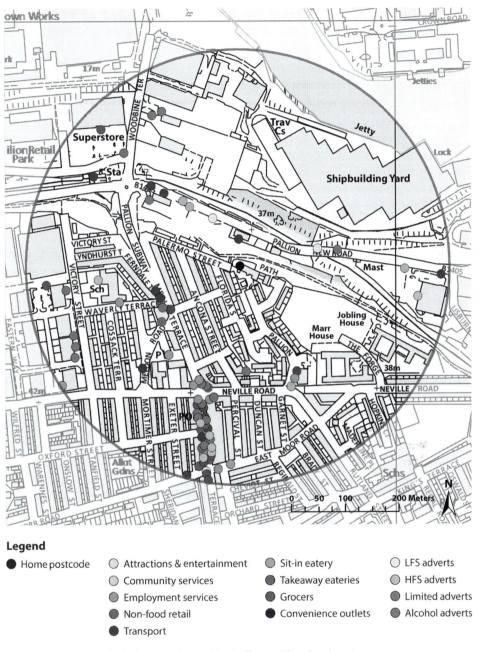

Legend

● Home postcode	○ Attractions & entertainment	◐ Sit-in eatery	○ LFS adverts
	○ Community services	● Takeaway eateries	◐ HFS adverts
	◐ Employment services	● Grocers	● Limited adverts
	● Non-food retail	● Convenience outlets	◐ Alcohol adverts
	● Transport		

Figure 14.4 Overweight female participant 400m buffer neighbourhood environment

Source: Authors.

definition of what constitutes a 'neighbourhood', in which case it could be mitigated by taking alternate measures of the neighbourhood environment, that is, using Global Positioning System (GPS) loggers[2] which track actual environmental exposure. We would therefore recommend such approaches for further investigation.

The overall conclusion from the Newcastle study is that there is much research that needs to be undertaken to better comprehend the multifaceted nature of environmental influence on both health behaviours and outcomes.

Conclusions: the role for planning

The key message from this chapter is that the role of the built environment in the obesity crisis is multifactorial and highly complex. Obesity is a very complex condition in itself; the built environment is even more complex in its variety – places are by definition unique and no matter how similar, no two are exactly the same. Drawing out the links between obesity and the built environment is, therefore, extremely difficult. However, as stated at the opening to this chapter, Foresight suggests there is enough evidence to implicate the built environment (2007). We would accept this and note the importance of Lawrence's concept of trans-disciplinarity (see Chapter 6). However, this concept is undoubtedly challenging to those academics who are too deeply enmeshed within their planning or public health silos.

Reuniting health and planning, through the new public health responsibility for local authorities and the requirement for planners to work with public health organisations to address local health priorities, *should* bring the opportunity to look at the issue of evidence *across* the disciplines *and* at the local level. However, this will be dependent on the capacities of each partner to reach out and grasp the perspective of the other – strong leadership and commitment will be required.

New policies which are emerging around fast-food outlet proliferation are an encouraging first step. The fact that planning decisions made in line with these policies in England have been over-turned at appeal, however, brings the evidence debate sharply into focus. It suggests that authorities with planning responsibilities need to be meticulous about how such policies are worded, evidenced, applied in practice and the weight these policies carry in any particular planning system. Policies should, therefore, be as robust as possible, be *core* to planning aims and objectives, and statutory, wherever possible, rather than supplementary, or dispensed in optional 'guidance'.

More generally, planning policy needs to translate the promotion of healthy and sustainable places into an on-the-ground reality. This needs a holistic and comprehensive approach and while obesity is not the *only* contemporary health issue of concern, what holds true for obesity amelioration is likely to have other health benefits, both physical and mental. We are entering the realm here of co-benefits; this is not a zero-sum game. There are other drivers promoting the need to support active travel, provide local shops and services as well as adequate greenspace and general 'greenery' in neighbourhoods – while at the same time tackling those toxic services that have embedded themselves in many traditional shopping areas. As outlined in this chapter, this is much more easily said than done; however, planning policy and practice must be reviewed and looked at in terms of how it can support this public health imperative. Where concerns are found planning must change now if further harm is to be avoided. For even if those influences of the built environment are small at the individual level, taken over whole communities and across generations, they are decidedly significant.

Notes

1 Other measures have included hip to waist ratio and adiposity (body fat), and as a consequence, comparisons between research using different measures can be difficult to interpret, particularly for non-specialists.
2 That is, GPS devices worn by participants to show exactly where and what they access.

References

Alaimo, K., Packnett, E., Miles, R.A. and Kruger, D.J. 2008. Fruit and vegetable intake among urban community gardeners. *Journal of Nutrition Education and Behavior.* 40(2), pp. 94–101.

Barton, H., Horswell, M. and Millar, P. 2012. Neighbourhood accessibility and active travel. *Planning Practice and Research.* 27(2), pp. 177–201.

Bell, A.C., Ge, K. and Popkin, B.M. 2002. The road to obesity or the path to prevention: motorized transportation and obesity in China. *Obesity Research.* 10(2), pp. 277–283.

Birch, L.L., Fisher, J.O., Grimm-Thomas, K., Markey, C.N., Sawyer, R. and Johnson, S.L. 2001. Confirmatory factor analysis of the child feeding questionnaire: a measure of parental attitudes, beliefs and practices about child feeding and obesity proneness. *Appetite.* 36(3), pp. 201–210.

Black, J.L. and Macinko, J. 2008. Neighborhoods and obesity. *Nutrition Reviews.* 66(1), pp. 2–20.

Boone-Heinonen, J., Gordon-Larsen, G., Guilkey, D.K., Jacobs, D.R. and Popkin, B.M. 2011. Environment and physical activity dynamics: the role of residential self-selection. *Psychology of Sport and Exercise.* 12, pp. 54–60.

Burgoine, T. and Monsivais, P. 2013. Characterising food environment and exposure at home, at work, and along commuting journeys using data on adults in the UK. *International Journal of Behavioural Nutrition and Physical Activity.* 10.

Caspi, C.E., Sorensen, G., Subramanian, S.V. and Kawachi, I. 2012. The local food environment and diet: a systematic review. *Health and Place,* 18, pp. 1172–1187.

Cetateanu, A. and Jones, A. 2014. Understanding the relationship between food environments, deprivation and childhood overweight and obesity: evidence from a cross sectional England-wide study. *Health & Place.* 27, pp. 68–76.

Davison, K., Cutting, T. and Birch, L. 2003. Parents' activity-related parenting practices predict girls' physical activity. *Medicine and Science in Sports and Exercise.* 35(9), pp. 1589–1595.

Davison, K.K. and Jago, R. 2009. Change in parent and peer support across ages 9 to 15 yr and adolescent girls' physical activity. *Medicine and Science in Sports and Exercise.* 41(9), pp. 1816–1825.

Davison, K.K., Kaigang, L., Baskin, M.L., Cox, T. and Affuso, O. 2011. Measuring parental support for children's physical activity in white and African American parents: the Activity Support Scale for Multiple Groups (ACTS-MG). *Preventive Medicine.* 52, pp. 39–43.

De Vries, S. 2010. Nearby nature and human health: looking at mechanisms and their implications. In Ward Thompson, C., Aspinall, P. and Bell, S. (eds.) *Innovative approaches to researching landscape and health.* Abingdon: Routledge.

Delpeuch, F., Maire, B., Monnier, E. and Holdsworth, M. 2009. *Globesity: a planet out of control.* London: Earthscan.

Durand, C.P., Andalib, M., Dunton, G.F., Wolch, J. and Pentz, M.A. 2011. A systematic review of built environment factors related to physical activity and obesity risk: implications for smart growth urban planning. *Obesity Reviews.* 12, pp. e173–e182.

Foresight. 2007. *Tackling obesities: future choices – project report.* London: Government Office for Science.

Giles-Corti, B., Broomhall, M.H., Kniuman, M., Collins, C., Douglas, K., Ng, K., Lange, A. and Donovan, R.J. 2005. How important is distance to, attractiveness, and size of public open space? *American Journal of Preventive Medicine.* 28(2S2), pp. 169–176.

James, W.P.T., Jackson-Leach, R. and Rigby, N. 2010. An international perspective on obesity and obesogenci environments. In Lake, A.A., Townshend, T.G. and Alvanides, A. (eds.) *Obesogenic environments: complexities, perceptions and objective measures.* Oxford: Wiley-Blackwell.

Lake, A. and Townshend, T. 2006. Obesogenic environments: exploring the built and food environments. *The Journal of the Royal Society for the Promotion of Health.* 126(6), pp. 262–267.

Lake, A., Tyrrell, R. and Greenhalgh, F. 2009. *7th international conference on diet and activity methods.* Washington, DC, 5–7 June.

Lake, A.A., Townshend, T.G. and Burgoyne, T. 2015. *Obesogenic environments.* In Lanham-New, S. (ed.) Public Health Nutrition Second Edition: The Nutrition Society Textbook Series. Oxford: Wiley-Blackwell.

London Borough of Barking and Dagenham. 2009. *Saturation point: addressing the health impacts of hot food takeaways. Draft supplementary planning document.* London.

London Borough of Brent. 2012. *Food for thought: a food growing and allotments strategy for the London Borough of Brent.* London.

McCormack, L.A., Laska, M.N., Larson, N.I. and Story, M. 2010. Review of the nutritional implications of farmers' markets and community gardens: a call for evaluation and research efforts. *Journal of the American Dietetic Association*. 110(3), pp. 399–408.

National Obesity Observatory. 2011. *Child obesity and its determinants: single map e-atlas. Middle super output area (MSOA) level data.* Available at: www.sepho.nhs.uk/noo/msoa/singleatlas/atlas.html, accessed 11 May 2011.

Reynolds, K., Gu, D., Whelton, P.K., Wu, X., Duan, X., Mo, J., He, J. and A.C.G. 2007. Prevalence and risk factors of overweight and obesity in China. *Obesity*. 15(1), pp. 10–18.

Rosenberg, D., Ding, D., Sallis, J.F., Kerr, J., Norman, G.J., Durant, N., Harris, S.K. and Saelens, B.E. 2010. Neighborhood Environment Walkability Scale for Youth (NEWS-Y): reliability and relationship with physical activity. *Preventive Medicine*. 49(2–3), pp. 213–218.

Saelens, B.E., Sallis, J.F., Black, J.B. and Chen, D. 2003. Neighborhood-based differences in physical activity: an environment scale evaluation. *American Journal of Public Health*. 93(9), pp. 1552–1558.

Smith, D., Cummins, S., Clark, C. and Stansfield, S. 2013. Does the local food environment around schools affect diet? Longitudinal associations in adolescents attending secondary schools in East London. *BMC Public Health*. 13(70).

Swinburn, B., Egger, G. and Raza, F. 1999. Dissecting obesogenic environments: the development and application of a framework for identifying and prioritizing environmental interventions for obesity. *Preventive Medicine*. 29(6), pp. 563–570.

Tilt, J.H., Unfried, T.M. and Roca, B. 2007. Using objective and subjective measures of neighborhood greenness and accessible destinations for understanding walking trips and BMI in Seattle, Washington. *American Journal of Health Promotion*. 21(4), pp. 371–379.

Townshend, T.G. 2014a. Walkable neighbourhoods principles, measures, and health impacts. In Cooper, R., Burton, E. and Cooper, C.I. (eds.) *Wellbeing and the environment: wellbeing: a complete reference guide, volume II*. Chichester: John Wiley & Sons.

Townshend, T.G. 2014b. Warning! Toxic high street. *Town and Country Planning*. 83(4), pp. 107–109.

Townshend, T.G. and Lake, A.A. 2009. Exploring obesogenic urban form: theory, policy and practice. *Health and Place*. 15(4), pp. 909–916.

Townshend, T.G. and Lake, A.A. 2011. Relationships between 'Wellness Centre' use, the surrounding built environment and obesogenic behaviours, Sunderland, UK. *Journal of Urban Design*. 16(3), pp. 351–367.

van den Berg, A.E., van Winsum-Westra, M., de Vries, S. and van Dillen, S. 2010. Allotment gardening and health: a comparative survey among allotment gardeners and their neighbors without an allotment. *Environmental Health* 9(74).

WHO. 2000. *Obesity: preventing and managing the global epidemic. Technical report series 894*. Geneva.

WHO. 2003. *Diet, nutrition and the prevention of chronic disease. Technical report series 916*. Geneva.

15

SETTLEMENT PATTERNS, URBAN FORM AND TRAVEL

Peter Headicar

Introduction: transport mobility and evolving urban form

From earliest times the growth of settlements has been influenced by the connectivity they enjoy with other places through natural or man-made transport routes. The form of settlements themselves has undergone profound changes with the development of successive transport technologies. Bicycles, trams, buses and commuter railways overcame the constraints of walking and – coupled with population growth – introduced 'suburbia' as the dominant urban form surrounding the densely developed core of formerly compact towns and cities.

The physical manifestation of these earlier eras remains in the development patterns of most urban areas even though the buildings themselves (and sometimes the activities they house) have often undergone subsequent change. The *functioning* of these areas has, however, been transformed by the revolution of the last half century brought on by mass car ownership. The greater freedom available to car owners has meant that these people are able to travel further and combine where they live, work, take their children to/from school etc. in ways that would be difficult or impossible by other modes. Commercial and public services have responded to this greater mobility by exploiting economies of scale and investing in fewer, better equipped outlets at a more limited number of locations. The overall effect is for more travel – and much more vehicle mileage – to be incurred in fulfilling a similar number of journeys. Traffic congestion and the environmental degradation of streets are two of the most conspicuous consequences.

For the individual motorist, or for businesses which rely on access by car-borne customers, the mobility provided by the private car offers almost unlimited flexibility. It opens up the possibility of development in 'greenfield' areas where householders and businesses can enjoy spacious surroundings and unconstrained provision for car parking. This is a major factor underlying the shifts which have taken place in business activity towards 'out of town' locations and in population movements from conurbations and cities to smaller towns and rural areas (so-called 'counter-urbanisation').

But the private car is a very space-hungry mode and operates best where travel demands are diffused over wide areas and between scattered origins and destinations – the very opposite of the traditional town or city. Urban forms predicated on car dependence invoke problems of land-take (loss of countryside), of high energy use, pollution and CO_2, of deterring active travel (walking and cycling) and of severely restricting opportunities amongst groups within

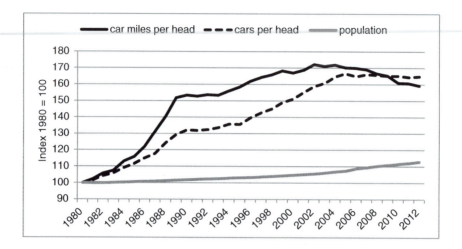

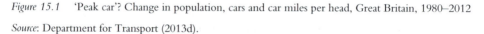

Figure 15.1   'Peak car'? Change in population, cars and car miles per head, Great Britain, 1980–2012

Source: Department for Transport (2013d).

the population who do not or cannot have use of a car. Planning policy is thus faced with the conundrum of how to fulfil the mobility expectations of a society which has become accustomed to widespread car use whilst combating its adverse repercussions – or, put more positively, how to maintain and enhance travel opportunities whilst lessening the need for car use. As already implied this is not simply a matter of transport policy or traffic management but invites debate on the very form and character of urban areas themselves.

For much of the twentieth century it seemed as though increased car ownership and use was the inevitable counterpart of economic growth. But over the last 15 years (and well before the post-2008 economic recession) there has been a slowing and even a decline in car use per person in several of the world's advanced economic nations (Millard–Ball and Schipper 2011). This has given rise to speculation about a possible 'peak car' phenomenon (Figure 15.1).

However, a stabilisation in car use per person – if indeed this is maintained over the longer term – does not signify a cessation in traffic growth. For one thing categories of traffic other than private cars (notably light vans) continue to increase. In addition population growth in Britain is currently occurring at historically high levels and its significance as a factor in future traffic forecasts is much increased. For example in 1997 the 30-year forecasts generated by the Department for Transport's National Traffic Model ascribed a mere 3 per cent increase in traffic to population growth. In the latest forecasts this figure is 20 per cent (Department for Transport 2013b). Exactly where and how the additional population is to be accommodated therefore assumes much greater importance than hitherto.

Opportunities for promoting sustainable travel through town planning

The location and design of development are important factors in influencing the volume of car use through the resulting length of journeys and the proportion made by car. (Just how important is, however, very difficult to determine – see Box 15.1.) More obviously, development characteristics (from settlement patterns to neighbourhood design) define the opportunities available for people without access to a car, the scope for engaging in active travel and the potential for less car use generally. Hence contemporary planning is concerned not merely with creating environments which produce a desired set of travel outcomes on 'day one' but with creating the conditions in which it is practicable (and attractive) for people subsequently to change their behaviour and adopt more sustainable habits. Once built, physical developments are 'fixed' but the travel patterns associated with them continue to change. Virtuous circles can be created. Developments which foster the use of public transport, for example, enable higher standards of service to be provided which in turn generate additional patronage. The willingness of people to walk and cycle in an area is affected by the number of other people in an area doing the same (Pooley et al. 2011).

Box 15.1 Researching the relationship between spatial characteristics and travel behaviour

There is no automatic relationship between a particular set of spatial or development features and the travel behaviour of the people living and working amongst them. Decisions about when, where and how to travel are strongly influenced by the pattern of opportunities available, that is, by *accessibility* (how long fulfilling a particular type of journey purpose will take, how much it will cost, how convenient, comfortable or reliable the journey is likely to be). These attributes are a product of the pattern of land use and transport networks *in combination*. Hence trying to account for travel behaviour in terms of development characteristics alone would be to look at only half the picture.

In addition every individual will perceive and respond to these opportunities in a different way. Some of these differences can be analysed in terms of 'standard' socio-economic variables such as age, gender, income etc. since these will tend to determine what sorts of journey people make and their propensity for using the various transport modes. (These variables are generally regarded as the principal source of variation in observed patterns of travel behaviour – see Stead 2001.) But some individual attributes are more idiosyncratic – and unpredictable. Attitudes to travel in general and car ownership and use in particular are very significant and will result in otherwise similar individuals faced with the same options making different choices (Anable 2005). That said it has been possible to produce a segmentation model in the UK utilising socio-economic and geographical variables which identifies nine main groups within the population according to their current volume of car use and, via their level of environmental concern, the likelihood of this changing (Thornton et al. 2011).

Given the complexity of the subject it is inevitable that most researchers tend to focus on the impact of individual development features on particular aspects of travel behaviour and to control for socio-economic variations as far as practicable (Ewing and Cervero 2010). Unfortunately the vast majority of empirical research has been conducted in the USA and the transferability of its findings to the very different conditions and traditions of European cities is problematic (van de Coevering and Schwanen 2006). Even with specific development features the issue of 'self-selection' can be a complicating factor (Cao et al. 2009), that is, the fact that particular individuals have the propensity to undertake more or less travel and have pre-set preferences between modes. The effect of the spatial variable then becomes difficult to determine. If, for example, people living near to a railway station are seen as more likely to commute by rail, is that evidence of the effect of the station's proximity or a by-product of the fact that those people predisposed to using rail are more likely to choose to live close to a station?

For much of second half of the twentieth century the dynamic processes operated in the opposite direction. Town planning was preoccupied with accommodating the growing volume of vehicle traffic in ways which overcame safety, congestion and pollution problems characteristic of traditional urban forms and street patterns. The ancillary consequences in terms of worsening conditions for other modes and the decline in their use were generally overlooked or viewed as 'inevitable'.

The cost and disruption involved in the physical restructuring of towns to accommodate projected traffic volumes – plus the evident unattractiveness of the resulting environments – led to changes in transport policy applied to town centres and inner urban areas. Road-building was curtailed, car use limited through traffic management and parking controls, and public transport promoted. Pedestrianisation was introduced into traditional high streets and not merely within purpose-built shopping developments. However, these changes plus continued road-building around and between towns fostered decentralisation of business uses to more car-friendly locations – adding to the overall volume of car use. During the 1980s, as part of a wider economic strategy, planning policies in Britain were relaxed to facilitate 'out of town' commercial development. Large, car-dependent shopping centres and business parks in peripheral locations are the unfortunate legacy which most towns have to contend with today.

Publication of the Brundtland Report in 1987 and official acknowledgement of the need for 'sustainable development' highlighted the adverse effects of traffic growth as a contributor to global warming. In response the European Commission advocated the concept of the 'compact city' (Commission of the European Communities 1990) and this provided the stimulus for a wave of new research (Jenks et al. 1996).

In the UK the government commissioned its own research to examine the scope for reducing CO_2 emissions from transport through planning (ECOTEC 1993). This led to an important change in national planning policy whereby the location and design of development were to be geared to 'reducing the need to travel' and 'ensuring a choice of modes' (UK Departments of Environment and Transport 1994). In the period since, greater insight has been gained through research and practice about the opportunities and constraints involved in promoting sustainable travel.

Domestic and international experience was comprehensively reviewed for the UK Commission for Integrated Transport (Halcrow Ltd 2009). The resulting report and practitioner guide was structured around a number of themes – being 'domains' at various spatial scales in which influence could be exerted through planning policy. This same structure is adopted here, partly so that readers can readily follow up the guide online to obtain further information, viz.

- settlement size and jobs/housing balance;
- strategic development location and strategic transport networks;
- density;
- accessibility of key facilities and mixed uses;
- development site location;
- neighbourhood design and street layout.

In each case there is a brief commentary on:

- how travel behaviour is influenced by the particular aspect of urban form;
- the treatment of this aspect in British planning policy and practice;
- the planning principles needed to promote sustainable travel.

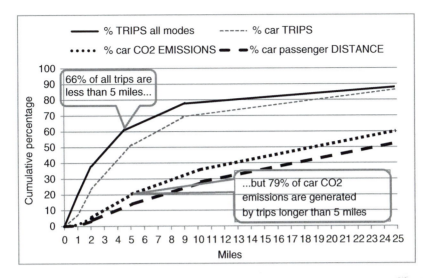

Figure 15.2 Cumulative percentage of trips and car CO_2 emissions by trip length, Great Britain

Source: Department for Transport (2009a).

These themes are discussed individually although in practice they are interrelated. However, as far as reducing car use is concerned it is decisions at the *strategic* level which are the most important. This is because whereas the majority of trips take place over short distances the majority of car mileage and associated CO_2 emissions are incurred on longer ones – principally those involving journeys to or between urban areas (Figure 15.2). This is salutary since in practice it is at the *local* level that the traffic consequences of development tend to be most 'visible' and hence receive the most public attention.

Elements of urban form

Settlement size and jobs/housing balance

Each field of human activity (education, retailing, health care etc.) tends to operate in the form of a hierarchy with larger and/or more specialised facilities located in larger urban areas accessible to a greater pool of workers, customers or clients. Smaller settlements can only fulfil a proportion of the requirements of their residents. To access others (or to exercise greater choice) it is necessary to travel to other – usually larger – settlements, that is, to undertake 'between-town' journeys. These are inevitably longer, often impracticable for walking and cycling, and (because of relatively low levels of demand) with only a limited public transport service.

Unsurprisingly, therefore, there is a clear overall relationship between settlement size and car use per head (Figure 15.3). Higher volumes of car use in smaller towns and rural settlements are a product of longer average journey lengths and a greater proportion of journeys by car. Some of it is also a product of socio-economic differences between the populations of the various-sized settlements but a clear overall gradient remains even when these differences are accounted for (WSP and Arup 2005).

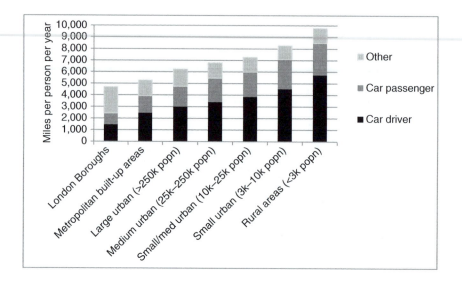

Figure 15.3 Distance travelled per person per year by area-type and mode, Great Britain, 2011/12

Source: Department for Transport (2013a).

All other things being equal, therefore, the bulk of new development should be located in and around the *largest* urban areas within a region. This principle is reinforced by the desirability of securing a broad numerical balance between jobs and workers in the vicinity of individual urban areas in order to avoid the creation of dormitory towns and enforced longer-distance commuting. Larger towns usually contain a disproportionate share of employment within a subregion and their greater pool of job opportunities means that residents are less likely to choose to commute elsewhere.

Throughout the period of statutory development control in Britain there has been a general presumption against development in the open countryside and only limited development permissible within smaller rural settlements. However, the distribution of development between urban areas of various sizes is more problematic. Antipathy to the uncontrolled sprawl experienced in the 1930s has led to 'urban containment' being a dominant feature of British planning policy ever since, implemented most forcefully through the designation of green belts around many larger cities. From London downwards this has required overspill to smaller free-standing settlements resulting in large volumes of longer-distance commuting.

In addition to green belt constraints residential dispersal within city-regions may be prompted by house price gradients around favoured cities (for example London, Oxford, Bath) or by consumer preference for smaller/non-industrial towns to escape the perceived social and environmental ills of core cities (for example North Yorkshire in relation to Leeds/Bradford). However, there is evidence that in recent decades planning policies of urban regeneration, reuse of previously developed ('brownfield') land and higher development densities have contributed to a stemming of long-term 'counter-urbanisation' trends (Figure 15.4).

Strategic development location/strategic transport networks

Much research has been conducted on the desirable forms of individual urban areas. But as noted earlier the bulk of traffic is generated by movements between them. Hence the *relationship*

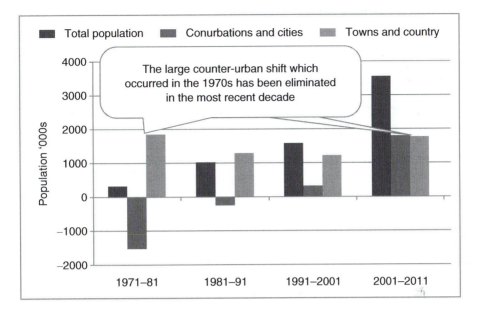

Figure 15.4   Change in England's population and its spatial distribution, 1971–2011

Source: Headicar (2013).

of settlements to one another is a critical dimension to be considered in strategic planning. This can be conceived both in purely spatial terms and in terms of the standard and configuration of transport networks.

Data on per capita travel associated with settlements of different sizes represents an average across very different spatial settings. In practice a small town of 10,000 people, for example, is likely to be much more 'self-contained' if it is a service centre within an extensive rural area than if it is located within a more urbanised region where alternative opportunities relatively close by will prompt a higher proportion of external journeys.

In city-regions where there is a strong 'pull' towards the core city (and where expansion of the city itself is constrained) it does not follow therefore that distributing new development to secondary towns in the region on the basis of settlement size will necessarily minimise travel generation. In relation to commuting (for which local patterns can be analysed from data within the Population Census) it is possible to explore the *combined* effect of the proportion of residents in a town who work outside it with the distance these people travel. In this context a smaller settlement within a 'green belt' ring or similar may represent a more favourable prospect than a larger one beyond it.

On top of purely spatial relationships, the effect of transport networks needs to be super-imposed. The standard and configuration of main routes will alter the pattern of accessibility measured by time rather than distance. This will extend commuting areas along the corridors concerned and place a premium in terms of development potential on locations which offer ready access points (for example major highway interchanges or principal rail stations). Although commercially attractive, developments in motorway corridors conflict with sustainable travel objectives since they facilitate a disproportionate share of longer-distance, car-based journeys. Conversely rail-served locations may represent a sustainable option. However, this can be misleading if the location would not otherwise be favoured since in practice only a minority of external journeys will actually be made by rail.

Oxfordshire demonstrates relationships between spatial features and travel in a particularly striking manner (Figure 15.5). The principal source of variation (as between the main urban areas) in the amount of car mileage incurred in journeys made regularly has been shown to be due to differences in commuting (Headicar 2000). Part of this is attributable to settlement size and job/worker ratio which together prompt wide variations in the proportion of residents working in their home town. However, the bulk of car mileage is incurred on 'external' journeys and in this case the key factors are distance to alternative major sources of employment and the relative accessibility to them by car and public transport. These differences can be seen in Figure 15.6 where the net outcome is for car mileage per commuter to vary by a factor of 2.6 (that is, 8.7/3.4) between urban areas within the same subregion.

Oxford City has innate characteristics conducive to sustainable travel, complemented by a progressive transport management regime. Three quarters of residents have workplaces within the city and fewer than a quarter of these drive to work.

Banbury and Abingdon, both established medium-sized towns, generate similar averages of commuting mileage but for different reasons. Banbury is relatively isolated regionally and has a high proportion of people working locally (with very short commuting distances) but the average of those commuting externally is inevitably high. By contrast Abingdon has a more

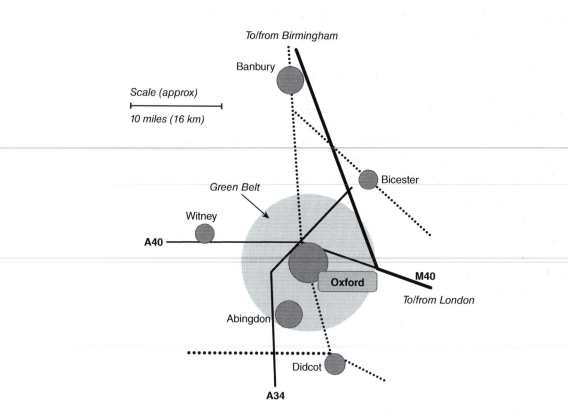

Figure 15.5 Settlement size and location relative to major centres and transport routes: the example of Oxfordshire

Source: Headicar.

Town	Population 000's	Job/ worker ratio*	% working in home town*	Average distance** external journeys (miles)	% external journeys as car driver	Average commute distance** (miles)	Average car miles per commuter**
Oxford	134.2	1.47	75%	19.2	69%	6.3	**3.4**
Banbury	41.8	1.31	67%	19.0	78%	7.2	**5.3**
Abingdon	31.3	0.99	37%	11.2	75%	7.5	**5.5**
Bicester	28.7	0.67	36%	16.7	79%	11.1	**8.7**
Didcot	23.5	0.58	29%	12.6	74%	9.3	**6.3**
Witney	26.6	0.95	43%	13.7	79%	8.2	**6.4**

Figure 15.6   Oxford region towns and their work travel patterns

Source: Population Census (2001).

Notes: *excludes people working at or from home   ** per single one-way journey

dormitory character with a much lower proportion of residents working in the town. Commuting distances to Oxford or other external workplaces in central Oxfordshire are, however, comparatively short.

Bicester, Didcot and Witney are smaller towns historically which have been expanded greatly in recent decades as a counterpart to green belt restriction on the growth of Oxford. Although planned as 'balanced communities' the majority of their residents in fact commute out. Differences between the towns are partly attributable to opportunities available for long-distance commuting by motorway (Bicester) and Intercity rail (Didcot). These differences are much more marked in new housing developments whose residents come disproportionately from outside the town. Recent re-surveys of estates 20 years after construction show that this distinction between 'indigenous' and 'in-coming' residents remains a prominent feature of commuting behaviour (Headicar 2015).

Within city regions the accessibility afforded by rail or principal bus routes is much more tightly concentrated spatially than is the case with the car. In terms of strategic development location settlements along inter-urban public transport routes represent particularly valuable opportunities to achieve levels of service which offer realistic alternatives to the car (but which are not available in similar sized settlements away from these routes). Expanding smaller settlements of this kind (in 'beads on a string' fashion) may also be preferable to the more usual peripheral expansion of larger ones where, away from main radial routes, bus services typically serve the local town centre only. Again, in assessing possible development locations, it is the combination of distance and likely modal share for the different types of journey which requires examination.

Density

There are huge differences between the densities characteristic of cities in different parts of the world and these can be linked with per capita amounts of car travel (see Figure 15.7 where the relationship with urban density is shown in terms of transport-related energy consumption). In North America and Australia where the bulk of development has occurred during the era of motorisation and extensive tracts of open land are available, low densities and high levels of car

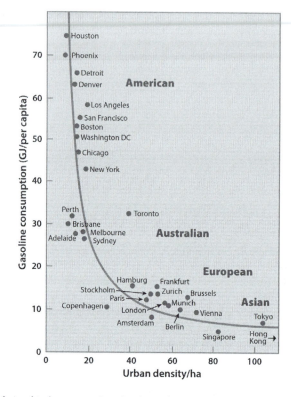

Figure 15.7   The relationship between urban density and transport-related energy consumption

Source: Newman and Kenworthy (1989).

use are pervasive. By contrast, within Western European countries there is both a physical and cultural legacy of higher development densities. Typically there is a relationship between settlement size and average density and in each settlement a 'density gradient' falling from (older) inner areas to (newer) outer suburbs.

In the early years of town planning there were strongly divergent views over the densities that should be sought and the built form that developments should take. 'Modernists' argued for high density blocks of flats set in areas of public open space whilst promoters of the 'garden city' advocated the lower density model of mainly individual dwellings with their own private gardens. In Great Britain during the post-war decades something of a compromise emerged with higher density terraces and flats characterising new developments originally built as public (social) housing and lower density detached and semi-detached houses continuing to characterise private developments. More recently, since the end of large-scale house building by local authorities, public policy has shifted towards larger developments comprising a mix of housing types and tenures with overall densities significantly higher than the traditional suburban norm.

The longer journey distances which typify low density suburbia and the accompanying sparseness of public transport result in personal dependence on car use which is the antithesis of sustainable travel. Against this can be contrasted the merits of the 'compact city' in which higher densities reduce average journey distances and hence the overall volume of travel. A larger proportion of destinations fall within convenient walking or cycling distance and the greater intensity of travel demand creates the conditions for more frequent and commercially viable bus services. In combination, therefore (that is, via shorter distances and greater use of non-car modes), car use per head is much lower.

Higher densities coupled with the spatial concentration of facilities do, however, invoke traffic congestion which heightens fuel consumption, air pollution and CO_2 emissions and worsens conditions for non-car modes. This has been termed the 'paradox of intensification' (Melia et al. 2011). In practice, therefore, delivery of the benefits offered by the compact city is dependent on complementary policies concerning the location of facilities and, in larger centres, on forms of traffic demand management to limit car use to the available highway capacity (see below).

Accessibility of key facilities/mixed uses

Facilities of various kinds can be categorised in the form of a hierarchy reflecting the catchment population they require, the proportion of the general population who use them and the frequency with which they do so. Facilities which fall into a similar category are best located in 'centres' (local, district, town, etc.) so that people can conveniently fulfil more than one purpose with a single trip. At the local level this principle was recognised in the English New Towns which were typically planned around the concept of 'neighbourhoods' such that day-to-day facilities were available in centres within convenient walking distance of people's homes.

More recently the concept of the 'urban village' has been advanced which is less formally structured but is characterised by relatively high densities, a mix of uses and high standards of urban design – features which were taken up in official planning policy guidance in the mid-1990s (Department of the Environment 1997). In addition to promoting sustainable travel such places offer variety and vitality in contrast to the 'barren' quality which characterises low density suburbs. At a larger scale the growth of service employment means that, compared with the days of manufacturing industry generating pollution and heavy goods traffic, businesses no longer need to be segregated into (relatively remote) sectors or zones of a city.

The principle of centres accommodating employment and other 'attraction' uses is also important in creating the conditions in which an attractive network of bus services can be operated. (To be viable these are dependent on a concentration of passenger flows.) However, in larger settlements the concentration of movements to and from a single town or city centre can also be problematic because of the resulting congestion on highways and public transport alike. The development of suburban centres, therefore, has an important role to play in spreading overall travel demands and in mitigating excessive 'tidal' flows. These centres may include larger 'out-of-town' shopping or business parks originally conceived as car-dependent and major hospitals or higher education establishments which have decentralised to more spacious suburban locations.

Not all attraction uses can be accommodated in established centres. Locations along well-served bus corridors or in the vicinity of rail stations or other transport interchanges are therefore other options which need to be utilised. This has the twin benefits of ensuring good standards of personal accessibility without the need for car use and promoting patronage on principal public transport routes so as to foster high levels of service and commercial viability. In outer urban areas nodes on the public transport network are also potentially useful locations for facilities which serve peri-urban settlements in the same corridor.

Development site location (residential)

In addition to the strategic considerations highlighted earlier (of settlement size and location relative to major centres and transport networks) there are important accessibility issues relating to site selection for residential development in or adjacent to any given urban area. Proximity to local facilities is a prerequisite for minimising the traffic generated by these commonplace journeys and for maximising the proportion of trips by non-motorised modes.

The conditions experienced in making walking and cycling journeys is also a material factor. This is not simply a matter of design within the development itself (see below) but in the provision of safe and attractive routes across trafficked roads surrounding the site and through established areas to the relevant destination. Ideally such routes should form part of a network which serves the town as a whole and which offers access to places further afield including parks and nearby countryside to promote active recreation.

Proximity to facilities and network characteristics were two of the most important factors noted in research which identified the use of non-motorised modes for local activities varying between 19 per cent and 65 per cent across a range of neighbourhoods types (Barton et al. 2011).

Accessibility by public transport is also critical in serving places beyond convenient walking and cycling distance and in meeting the needs of people with limited physical mobility. This is dependent on the frequency and configuration of services and – for longer journeys – the scope for convenient interchange. These are not attributes which can be gauged merely from looking at a map. Care needs to be exercised to avoid the pitfall of interpreting 'public transport accessibility' simply in terms of distance to the nearest bus stop or railway station. Such access is a necessary but not sufficient condition. The time and monetary cost involved in actually travelling to destinations, including the effects of interchange where necessary, needs to be assessed. In England the government sponsors the publication of data which enables the accessibility of locations to key facilities to be identified relative to specified travel time standards (Department for Transport 2013c).

Neighbourhood design and street layout

With the growth of traffic the conflict arising in traditional streets between activities associated with frontage development on the one hand and the interests of moving vehicles on the other became a major concern. In Great Britain government guidance advocated a distinction between 'distributor' roads of various grades (forming a network to serve through and circulating traffic) and 'access' roads branching off the local distributors to serve properties within the residential cells. The access roads – many in cul-de-sac form – would inevitably have low traffic volumes and speeds were typically contained by short road lengths and curving alignments. The characteristic 'maze-like' outcome was deliberately designed to prevent through traffic movement.

Unfortunately the 'impermeable' nature of such layouts also had a barrier effect on movements by other modes. Journeys of short crow-fly distance potentially suitable for walking and cycling were rendered circuitous and unattractive. Even where 'cut-throughs' were provided (e.g. to create more direct links within an estate) these are typically narrow, not overlooked, poorly lit and with overgrown vegetation. Movements which involve travelling or across distributor roads have to contend with environments geared to the requirements of motor traffic – visually unattractive, lacking the variety and humanity of frontage properties and with traffic moving at higher speeds. These are the roads which also have to be utilised by local bus services, resulting in circuitous routes and uninviting waiting areas.

In recent years official planning guidance in the UK has recommended a radically different model with more permeable layouts and streets designed and managed to slow traffic and create a more attractive public realm (Department for Transport 2007). A purpose-built network of walk and cycle ways and direct bus routes with easily accessed stopping places needs to form the backbone of neighbourhood design – not shoehorned in as an afterthought. The layout of development and incidental public open space can be arranged to overcome the visual impression of car use being the default mode of travel. Higher densities close to bus stops and railway stations reduce the average distance involved in walking to them and foster public transport use. However, as with the links between spatial features and travel behaviour more generally, research has identified a complex mix of relationships between personal attitudes, neighbourhood design features and individual travel behaviour (Susilo et al. 2012).

Conclusions: carrots, sticks and lifestyles

The principles set out above seek to ensure that patterns of development reduce the need to travel and facilitate the use of sustainable modes. However, except in special circumstances (e.g. pedestrianised areas) development characteristics alone cannot determine that sustainable travel outcomes will result. For this to happen requires a complementary regime of transport demand management incorporating a mix of what are popularly referred to as 'carrot' and 'stick' measures. 'Stick measures' act as restraints on car use and include physical traffic management restrictions and controls on the amount and price of parking (on- and off-street). In theory they could also include direct charging for road use, varied by time and place – often referred to as 'congestion charging'. 'Carrot' measures include improvements in facilities for sustainable modes, including priority allocation of road space, and information and marketing campaigns promoting their use. In Great Britain all proposed major developments are required to produce Travel Plans demonstrating how their operation is to be managed to promote sustainable travel outcomes (Department for Transport 2009b).

Although planning and transport policy in Great Britain has made some moves in the direction of sustainability over the last 20 years the impact has not been dramatic. (Much of the observed 'peaking' in individual car use noted earlier can be attributed to other socio-economic factors.) Current travel behaviour and resulting traffic and environmental conditions remain a very long way from what is desirable. Physically and culturally, private car ownership and use has established a very forceful inertia over the last century which it is now extremely difficult to overcome politically. A 'catch-22' situation arises whereby in order to address the adverse effects of motorisation in general the development forms, transport or fiscal measures needed to promote sustainable travel typically involve some corresponding compromise or perceived detriment on the part of the individual motorist. They also challenge traditional norms concerning the pattern of individual settlements in what are now highly interconnected city-regions.

Over the coming decades improved vehicle technology and changing forms of energy supply will reduce pollution and CO_2 emissions, although not to levels commensurate with UK government targets. They will also not address the other ills of a car-dependent society. Given the requisite ambition, however, it is possible that the transition to low-carbon motoring could be planned and managed in a way which encourages greater use of car hire and car club vehicles for occasional use (in preference to wholesale private vehicle ownership) in circumstances where attractive and reliable alternatives are available for the bulk of day-to-day journeys. A lifestyle involving a mix of transport modes (including some tele-substitution for particular journeys) is the model which needs to be promoted to partner the development forms advanced in this chapter to achieve the desired holistic sustainable outcome.

References

Anable J (2005) Complacent car addicts versus aspiring environmentalists? Identifying travel behaviour segments using attitude theory. *Transport Policy* 12(1) 65–78.

Barton H, Grant M and Horswell M (2011) Suburban solutions: the other side of the story. *Town and Country Planning* 80(7/8) 339–345.

Brundtland G (1987) *Our common future: report of World Commission on Environment and Development.* Oxford: Oxford University Press.

Cao X, Mokhtarian P and Handy S (2009) Examining the impacts of residential self-selection on travel behavior: a focus on empirical findings. *Transport Reviews* 29(3) 359–395.

Commission of the European Communities (1990) Green paper on the urban environment. Brussels: European Commission.

Department for Transport (2007) Manual for streets. www.gov.uk/government/uploads/system/uploads/attachment_data/file/341513/pdfmanforstreets.pdf, accessed 8 April 2015.

Department for Transport (2009a) Low carbon transport: a greener future. Cm 7682. http://webarchive.nationalarchives.gov.uk/+/http:/www.dft.gov.uk/pgr/sustainable/carbonreduction/low-carbon.pdf, accessed 8 April 2015.

Department for Transport (2009b) Good practice guidelines: delivering travel plans through the planning system. http://webarchive.nationalarchives.gov.uk/20120214193900/http://dft.gov.uk/pgr/sustainable/travelplans/tpp/goodpracticeguidelines-main.pdf, accessed 8 April 2015.

Department for Transport (2013a) National travel survey 2012. www.gov.uk/government/uploads/system/uploads/attachment_data/file/225735/nts2012-technical.pdf, accessed 8 April 2015.

Department for Transport (2013b) Road traffic forecasts 2013. www.gov.uk/government/uploads/system/uploads/attachment_data/file/260700/road-transport-forecasts-2013-extended-version.pdf, accessed 8 April 2015.

Department for Transport (2013c) Transport connectivity and key services guidance. www.gov.uk/government/publications/transport-connectivity-and-accessibility-of-key-services-statistics-guidance, accessed 8 April 2015.

Department of Transport (2013d) Transport statistics Great Britain 2013. www.gov.uk/government/uploads/system/uploads/attachment_data/file/264679/tsgb-2013.pdf, accessed 8 April 2015.

Department of Environment and Transport (1994) Planning policy guidance: transport (PPG13). London: HMSO.

Department of the Environment and Welsh Office (1997) Planning policy guidance: general policy and principles (PPG 1). London: HMSO.

ECOTEC Research and Consultancy Ltd (1993) Reducing transport emissions through planning, report for UK Departments of Environment and Transport. London: HMSO.

Ewing R and Cervero R (2010) Travel and the built environment: a meta-analysis. *Journal of the American Planning Association* 76(3) 265–294.

Halcrow Ltd et al. (2009) Planning for sustainable travel research report and practitioner guide, prepared for the UK Commission for Integrated Transport London. www.plan4sustainabletravel.org, accessed 8 April 2015.

Headicar, P (2000) The exploding city-region: should it, can it, be reversed? In Williams K, Burton E and Jenks M (eds) *Achieving sustainable urban form.* London: E & FN Spon.

Headicar P (2013) The changing spatial distribution of the population in England: its nature and significance for 'peak car'. *Transport Reviews* 33(3) 310–324.

Headicar P (2015) Homes, jobs and commuting: development location and travel outcomes. In Banister D et al. (eds) *Transport and development handbook.* Camberley: Edward Elgar.

Jenks M, Burton E and Williams K (eds) (1996) The compact city: a sustainable urban form. London and New York: E & FN Spon.

Melia S, Barton H and Parkhurst G (2011) The paradox of intensification. *Transport Policy* 18(1) 46–52.

Millard-Ball A and Schipper L (2011) Are we reaching peak travel? Trends in passenger transport in eight industrialised countries. *Transport Reviews* 31(3) 357–378.

Newman P and Kenworthy J (1989) Cities and automobile dependence: an international sourcebook. Aldershot: Gower.

Pooley C et al. (2011) Understanding walking and cycling: summary of key findings and recommendations. Lancaster: Lancaster University.

Stead D (2001) Relationships between land use, socio-economic factors and travel patterns in Britain. *Environment and Planning B:* 28(4) 499–528.

Susilo Y, Williams K, Lindsay M and Dair C (2012) The influence of individuals' environmental attitudes and urban design features on their travel patterns in sustainable neighbourhoods in the UK. *Transportation Research Part D* 17(3) 190–200.

Thornton A, Evans L, Bunt K, Simon A, King S and Webster T (2011) Climate change and transport choices segmentation model: a framework for reducing CO_2 emissions from personal travel, report for Department for Transport. London: Department for Transport.

van de Coevering P and Schwanen T (2006) Re-evaluating the impact of urban form on travel patterns in Europe and North America. *Transport Policy* 13(3) 229–239.

WSP and Arup (2005) Impacts of land use planning policy on transport demand and congestion, research report for Department for Transport. Cambridge: WSP Policy and Research. www.wspgroup.com/upload/documents/PDF/news%20attachments/PPG13_Final_Report.pdf, accessed 8 April 2015.

16

RETROFITTING SUBURBIA FOR HEALTH

Scenarios for neighbourhood planning

Hugh Barton and Marcus Grant

Introduction: suburban neighbourhoods

Suburbia is often sidelined in planning discussion as being neither city nor country – but the majority of people in high-income countries live in suburbia. Estimates for England vary widely, up to 86 per cent of the population (Civic Trust 2002). This high figure reflects a definition of suburb that includes all the urban areas developed since the First World War, plus the dispersed commuter villages and estates, which we will call 'exurbs'. While the concept of suburbia is rather amorphous, the image is one of staid affluence. That has led some urban commentators to disparage them. Jane Jacobs, for example, is reported as saying 'Suburbs are perfectly valid places to live, but are inherently parasitic, economically and socially.'[1]

The social reality is changing. Recent studies show the prevalence of poverty in British and American suburbs is now comparable with the population as a whole. The suburbs of thriving cities are experiencing continual growth. Older suburbs are subject to gradual intensification. Commercial and institutional investors are developing 'edge cities': low-density, car-based, campus-style developments reproducing or supplanting city centre activities. New residential suburbs and exurbs mushroom around the city. It has become a truism that many residential suburbs are very car-dependent, lack local facilities within walking distance, foster unhealthy, sedentary lifestyles and have high carbon use.

In reaction, international planning debates on urban form have been dominated by the concept of the 'compact city', intended to regenerate and intensify urban areas, fostering a more sustainable and convivial living environment. European and UK official documents have advocated the revival of neighbourhoods as part of this strategy (for example EU 1990; DoE 1998; Urban Task Force 1999). Suburban intensification is seen as a means of creating critical population levels to support more local (walkable) facilities and public transport and reduce car reliance. But the potential benefits are contested, as the 'paradox of intensification' means that extra activity will also tend to lead to extra vehicle use as well, exacerbating congestion, traffic danger and air quality, thereby discouraging active travel (Melia et al. 2012).

Neighbourhoods have been part of the lexicon of spatial planning since Howard, Unwin and Stein, early in the twentieth century. They were a dominant aspect of post-war new town design, and further developed more recently through the work of designers such as Duany and Plater-Zyberk in America (1991), Tjallingii in the Netherlands (1995), Morris and Kaufman in

Australia (1997), and Barton et al. in Britain (2010). The terminology can vary: neighbourhood, urban village, transit-oriented development – but the availability of local facilities, a pedestrian-friendly environment and the sense of local community are shared characteristics.

The growing concern for healthy urban environments, as well as for resilience in the face of climate change, has reinvigorated the debate about neighbourhoods. Low density suburbs, lacking walkable facilities, where unhealthy conditions are quite literally built into the environment, pose a particular problem. This chapter, drawing on studies in England, examines the behaviour of people in suburbs and explores the potential for retrofitting healthier neighbourhood design into suburbs as they 'densify' or extend.[2]

The chapter falls into two main sections: the first reviews research on the level of accessibility and active travel afforded by suburbs and exurbs; the second evaluates alternative planning and design scenarios in a wide range of outer city locations, tested in terms of physical practicality, effectiveness in creating healthy/sustainable environments, and market/public acceptability.[3] It draws on work reported in Barton et al. (2011, 2012).

Suburbs, health and active travel

Across Europe people are living less local lives, relying on larger, more distant facilities, normally accessed by car, especially in peripheral areas of towns and cities where low density, use-segregated patterns of development predominate (EEA 2009a). These trends come with an environmental and health cost: profligate use of energy resources and land, high carbon emissions, unhealthy air and noise pollution (Niemann and Maschke 2004), and increases in allergic reactions and lifestyle-related diseases, particularly cardiovascular disorders related to obesity, physical inactivity and stress (EEA 2009a, 2009b).

Neighbourhood renaissance would, it is held, lead to better access to key facilities, reduced social exclusion, and better physical and mental well-being (Corburn 2009). The positive view of neighbourhoods has been given added impetus by growing concern about obesity and health inequalities. Strategies to combat obesity highlight the importance of active travel as a means of increasing the physical activity of lower socio-economic groups – who typically get much of their exercise through incidental physical activity (Frank et al. 2006). Active travel also has the potential for positive impact on social networks, with benefits for mental well-being (Calve Blanco 2012). The revival of neighbourhoods could thus combat problems of isolation, inactivity and poor facility access which all contribute to health inequalities (Sugiyama et al. 2008; O'Campo et al. 2009; Van Dyck et al. 2009).

This recent, health-informed view of neighbourhoods is in line with traditional definitions of neighbourhood (except for the gender stereotypes!):

> A neighbourhood is formed naturally from the daily occupations of people, the distance it is convenient to walk for a housewife to do her daily shopping and, particularly, the distance it is convenient for a child to walk to school. He should not have a long walk and he should not have to cross a main traffic road. The planning of a neighbourhood unit starts from that.
>
> *(Boyd 1945)*

Causal relationships in complex urban systems are notoriously difficult to disentangle (Giles-Corti et al. 2007). However, there is much evidence indicating that key spatial characteristics such as land use pattern, density and accessibility pose risks to health (Croucher et al. 2007; Grant et al. 2009). The question is, can policies for neighbourhood revival and redesign halt and reverse long-term trends of sedentary car-dependent behaviour, and associated health risks and climate impacts? In academic (as opposed to policy) discourse, this is a contested matter. Studies have found complex links between neighbourhood characteristics and travel behaviour (Forsyth et al. 2009). An easy presumption is that density and 'mixed use' are key determinants, but this is by no means necessarily the case (Boarnet and Sarmiento 1998). Our own study found no clear relationship between the density of suburbs and the level of active travel (see Figure 16.1).

When we turn to the *form* of neighbourhoods, the research is fragmented. Most of the research is American and tries to compare the significance of social as opposed to environmental factors. There is consensus that residents in so-called 'traditional' localities, with a permeable network of streets, often on a grid basis, walk more than those in 'modern' layouts (Saelens et al. 2003; Handy 2005; Frank et al. 2006). Several studies have found that the most significant determinant of physical activity at the neighbourhood level was the existence, and distance, of neighbourhood facilities (Greenwald and Boarnet 2001; Lee and Moudon 2008).

Local accessibility of English suburbs and exurbs

Our study provided more precision, in the British context, of the distance, frequency and mode of trips to 'local' facilities, including superstores, convenience goods and services, schools, social and recreational facilities. It showed that most people did not have many facilities within the

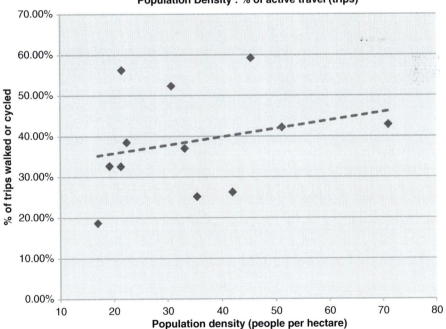

Figure 16.1   Gross neighbourhood density and the percentage of active travel trips to local facilities

Source: Barton et al. 2012.

threshold distance considered easily walkable (the 'pedshed' of 800m[4]), confirming the poor level of accessibility reported elsewhere. A striking finding was that the overall percentage of trips by foot and pedal falls very consistently with distance, across a wide range of neighbourhoods with varying social characteristics. Two thirds of respondents were willing to walk or cycle 800m to access facilities. About half walked or cycled 1000m, and around one third, 2000m. The average figures conceal the varied distances people walk to different facilities.

The results suggested two broad types of people: the more sedentary and the more active. Non-car owners, the poorest households and the very elderly were predictably more dependent on walking. Nevertheless there was some consistency of behaviour across age groups, gender, income levels and car ownership – perhaps indicating the degree to which car dependence is built into suburban lifestyle.

The most striking results concerned the difference between places. Figure 16.2 compares all the study areas. In terms of car dependence they range from 80 per cent for an exurban outlier of London down to 37 per cent for a Cambridge suburb. The newer suburbs were less 'walkable' than the older suburbs. There were significant behavioural differences between Cambridge and the other cities: the bike culture in Cambridge, and the small scale of the city, meant that even longer trips to facilities were more often than not by active means. Cultural attitudes to walking and cycling were quite similar within any given city. In Bristol, for example, active trip *distances* were similar in each neighbourhood, despite varied social patterns, but the *proportion* of walking trips was very different (see Figure 16.3). In other words there was similar behaviour in terms of how far people chose to walk, but strong contrasts in the availability of facilities within walking distance.

The conclusions to be drawn are, first, that these English suburbs conform generally to the image portrayed in the literature, but there is actually a wide range of experience, from high to

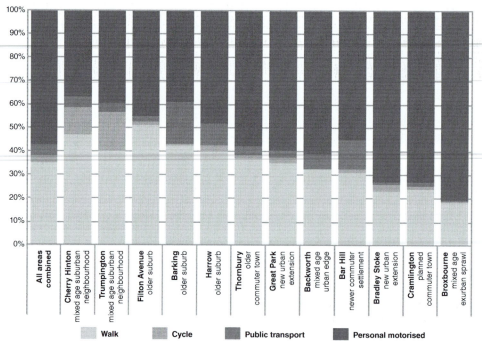

Figure 16.2   Modal split in case study areas, by active travel rank order

Source: Barton et al. 2012.

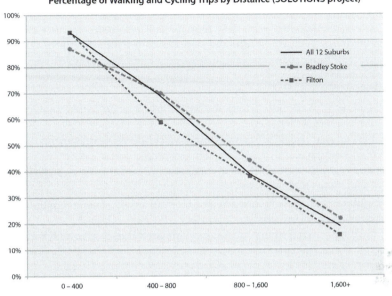

Figure 16.3   Modal choice by distance in three Bristol study areas

Source: Barton, H. and Melia, S., based on data in the SOLUTIONS study (see note 2).

moderate car dependence. Second, that cultural differences between cities and neighbourhoods are sometimes important. Third, that when there are accessible local facilities, the proportion of active travel, given a certain local culture, is quite predictable. The actual availability of facilities within walkable distance is therefore critical, varies hugely and is not simply explained by density. The question arises as to whether the physical layout of localities is a significant factor.

Evaluation of neighbourhood design scenarios

Urban form at the city scale has been the subject of extensive research and debate in recent decades (classic texts include Newman and Kenworthy 1989; Breheny 1993; Jenks et al. 1996). The same has not been true – since the post-war new towns – for the neighbourhood level. Rather, devotees of specific forms have advocated them without adequate evidence or examination. This section sets out a typology of alternative forms, building on the literature. For completeness it includes forms that are not advocated, but do occur widely.

Key variables in neighbourhood form are:

- the degree of separation or integration of neighbourhoods, estates and local areas with each other;
- the relative priority given to walking/cycling, public transport and vehicle traffic;
- the degree to which there is a road hierarchy, and the relationship of development to the main roads;
- the degree and nature of clustering of local facilities;
- the form and structure of greenspace and green infrastructure;
- density levels and variations for residential and commercial areas.

The next paragraph distinguishes five forms (four of these are illustrated in Figure 16.4), which may be combined, overlap and evolve in many ways. The first two are standard late twentieth-century patterns based on the assumption of maximum car use; the third is the classic neighbourhood unit; the fourth and fifth are both traditional forms updated for the contemporary era. From experimentation in a range of cities, it is possible to describe any part of a city using this typology.

1. Sprawl and strip – very low density residential urban sprawl, with commercial strips on some main roads (not illustrated).
2. Development pods – single use campus-style and cul-de-sac developments, hanging off the hierarchical road system.
3. Neighbourhood cells – planned community units, with local facilities at their heart, each separate and distinct with greenspace around.
4. Neighbourhood clusters – higher density groups of overlapping communities, with local facilities in each plus a central district centre.
5. Linear townships – overlapping communities clustered along a shared high street providing all facilities, backed by linear greenspace.

The following sections describe and evaluate each archetype. The research involved analysis of existing forms in the case study areas, exploratory future design scenarios, geographic informa-tion systems (GIS)-based evaluation and stakeholder workshops (see note 2). The aim was to compare, on various assumptions, the accessibility of local facilities, including greenspace, and the amount of active travel, recognising the difficulties of implementation.

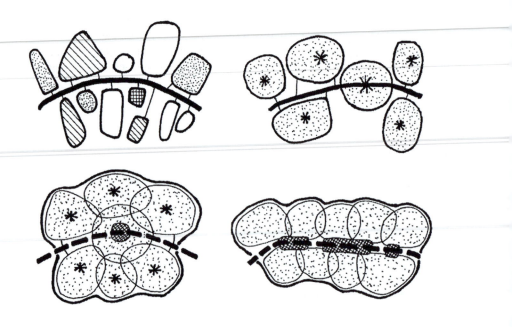

Figure 16.4   A typology of neighbourhood-scale spatial forms

Source: Barton et al. 2010, Figure 5.24.

Market-led suburban forms

Sprawl and strip

'Sprawl' is a justifiably pejorative term used to describe low density suburbs constructed on the assumption of full car ownership and use. Many cities in America and Australia have extensive 'sprawling' suburbs, lacking walkable facilities or functional neighbourhoods. The road system acts like a curvilinear or orthogonal net linking suburban developments. Retail, leisure and other activities are often clustered in 'commercial strips' along the main road, with each facility being separately accessed by vehicle, sometimes without any provision for pedestrian access between them. Such commercial strips can also be observed in some European countries – such as France – along main radials stretching out from cities and towns into the countryside. This archetype was not evident in our areas (or, generally, in England), so no evaluation was possible.

Development pods

This pattern of use-segregated development is typical of many outer city areas developed in the last 40 years: campus-style developments that are directly accessed off main distributor roads, with little or no attempt to provide pedestrian permeability. Pod development is based on a hierarchical road system serving long cul-de-sacs and loop roads, with buildings often oriented inwardly, backing onto principal and distributor roads. Pods may be business parks, retail parks, schools, universities, hospitals, residential estates or gated communities. Often there will be pods within the context of 'sprawl and strip' or other neighbourhood forms.

Pods, large and small, were almost ubiquitous in the study areas, sometimes linked to a hierarchical road system, sometimes in the context of a weak neighbourhood cell or linear form. Existing local authority policies usually discouraged pods, but with limited success. The essential advantages of pods are their ease of implementation, and the degree of control they afford to the developer. Individual landowners can bring forward sites without the complication or necessity to cooperate with neighbours. Existing residents often like them, too, because it means their own estate is not 'invaded' by strangers. Pods are flexible in terms of spatial arrangement and timing. Sites identified can be developed in any order, subject to access. This form tends to occur in market-led conditions with reactive, rather than proactive, municipality planning. Some developers and public institutions want pods because they are easier to control, conceive, design and implement.

Nevertheless, most stakeholders from public, voluntary and private sectors consider pod-based designs to be undesirable. The analysis showed that in all the cases where pods existed, or were explored through design, they performed badly. Accessibility to local centres, schools, greenspace and public transport was poor. Even with some generosity in assumptions about pedestrian connection between pods (often not provided in practice) this could not compensate for the lack of an integrated overall pattern, lack of permeability and suboptimal siting. Pods create an environment that compromises accessibility, healthy lifestyles, social equity and community cohesion.

Even when authorities have a coherent plan for sustainable development, the power of landowners and developers can sometimes undermine it. In the case of one urban extension the planners intended development to be integrated along a good public transport route. However, development actually occurred in a series of large pods, severely compromising the viability and attractiveness of the linking bus route, and giving very poor access to local facilities. This is a classic example of healthy urban environments being sacrificed on the altar of pragmatism.

Planned nucleated forms

Neighbourhood cells

The cell archetype is very different inasmuch as it derives from principles of community design, rather than from civil engineering and market pressures. The 'neighbourhood unit', as envisaged by mid-twentieth-century planners, and constructed in many suburbs, often for social housing, is a distinct, bounded residential area with a local centre (the nucleus of the cell) providing essential convenience shops and services, primary school and social facilities. Greenspace and industrial zones may separate adjacent cells. Figure 16.4 shows two types of cell: online and offline, depending on whether the local centre is hidden in the interior of the neighbourhood (a 'closed' cell) or open to passing trade (an 'open' cell). The size of the neighbourhood is determined by the catchment population (particularly for a primary school) and walkable distance. As Barton (2000) points out, the closed cell version is an inflexible design, which cannot adapt easily to changing population, catchment and behaviour. The open cell – as demonstrated in the British new town Harlow – has more potential for evolution and integration with the rest of the town (see Gibberd 1953).

The neighbourhood cell model has remarkable staying power. Apart from being the dominant (though not universal) form in the British new towns, it is advocated by urban design authors such as Calthorpe (1993) and Frey (1999). Others tacitly assume the basic form and illustrate its application in many different contexts – see for example Neal (2003) and Bullivant (2012). Contemporary thinking is that to avoid 'sink estates' every cell should be socially mixed – this also applies to the cluster and linear models (Barton et al. 2010).

Cell neighbourhoods were evident in practice when looking at a number of the study areas. But there were few evident in the official plans, and stakeholders were suspicious of them. This suspicion stemmed from the experience of earlier UK social housing estates, designed as closed, inward-looking cells, where population change and relative poverty resulted in the loss of local facilities, and they became 'sink estates'. Stakeholders were also equivocal about the idea of new mixed-tenure neighbourhoods, scaled to a primary school catchment, because of the wider choices now open to people, with high mobility and the internet, such that local facilities might not be viable.

This suspicion was supported by the evidence of existing suburbs and satellite settlements which had been carefully designed as cell neighbourhoods. They failed to reach critical mass (of population), and could not attract sufficient jobs or facilities to achieve some degree of autonomy. One such place had 81 per cent of trips by car, twice that of the city neighbourhoods (Platt 2007). The lack of scale sufficient to support a secondary school and a superstore were important factors. Such facilities are important anchors for community.

The exploratory design scenarios showed that it is normally very difficult to retrofit cell neighbourhoods into older suburbs. Established land uses, transport networks and barriers tended to preclude cell creation. However, it is often physically feasible to establish new, or to strengthen existing, neighbourhood cells in urban edge and exurban locations. Sometimes such cells could usefully integrate existing fragmented development, potentially improving access to facilities for existing residents. Key factors were the need to greatly improve connectivity and to diversify land uses and housing. In practice it was clear that implementation would not happen without strong local authority action.

Where neighbourhood cells *can* be achieved it is vital that they are 'open' – so that the neighbourhood centre is not hidden away, but visible and linked into the wider area. The cell scenarios performed better than the pods version in all ways: better levels of services, more active travel and more efficient use of land. Even so, there remains the risk that cell populations will not be sufficient to support facilities, and inequities will result. Facilities rely on very varied client or customer threshold numbers, which change over time (Barton et al. 1995). Patterns based on

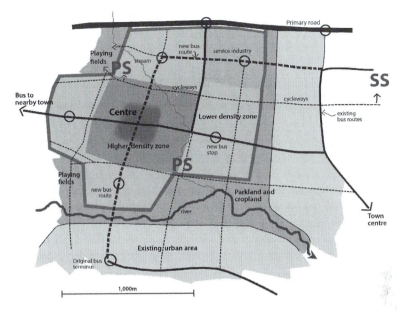

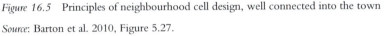

Figure 16.5 Principles of neighbourhood cell design, well connected into the town

Source: Barton et al. 2010, Figure 5.27.

separate neighbourhood units are innately inflexible, ignoring the flux of social and economic change. Figure 16.5 illustrates a new urban extension designed as a neighbourhood cell.

Neighbourhood clusters

While cell-based neighbourhoods are seen as separate units, the cluster assumes a group of over-lapping neighbourhoods – interlinked open cells that together create a small town or an urban district. This harks back to traditional pre-motor urban forms, with the size of a nucleated town defined by walkable distances, at a density sufficient to support town/township services. The neighbourhoods are fuzzy-edged, part of the urban continuum, providing 'local' services, often complementing each other because residents can reach several local centres easily by foot. The population needed to support town-level services, such as superstore, secondary school and lei-sure centre, is around 25–30,000 (in the British context) – a figure that has remained surprisingly constant over the last century and has been recommended in official documents as the minimum size for a free-standing town (Breheny et al. 1993). Within such a district/town there can be varied catchments according to the nature of a facility.

The cluster model has been powerfully advocated by the Urban Task Force (1999), as a means of achieving inclusive, sustainable, walkable suburbs. The model relies on quite high densities for its viability, so that both local and district centres are within reasonable walking distance – say 400m maximum to the nearest local centre, and 1,200m maximum to the district centre. This implies residential densities of around 100 dwellings per hectare – suggesting an inner urban rather than suburban density. The implication is also that major open spaces and industrial areas are outside the cluster.

Amongst all the study areas there were very few examples of such clusters, either existing or proposed by local authorities. In the older suburbs it was not possible to devise nucleated clusters:

densities were much too low to support walkable facilities and some areas had severe structural barriers to movement. The problems of getting from here to there were insurmountable. While urban intensification policies this century have begun to increase densities, the distribution of new development is rather random, reflecting the availability of sites through market mechanisms. As a result, many high density redevelopments are very poorly related to facilities and to public transport. Far from working towards neighbourhood clusters, new developments often form pod-like enclaves, relying on high car use.

The situation is not much more promising on the urban fringe. There is often not the land available for a new nucleated cluster of neighbourhoods because of environmental designations and physical barriers of road, rail and river. The only situation where the cluster scenario appeared feasible was as a very major urban extension where it allowed the integration of existing isolated estates, thus supporting estate regeneration.

However, local stakeholders were generally suspicious of the cluster model. They considered that the district centre, offering a wide variety of services, would be so accessible that the smaller neighbourhood centres would struggle. The more sedentary, and less mobile, members of the population, and those on the fringes of the township, would find themselves disadvantaged. The nucleated design also mitigates against easy access to major greenspace. Both the cells and linear forms have much better access to open space.

Overall the evidence from the study casts doubt on the merits of advocating the nucleated cluster on the Task Force model as means of retrofitting suburbia for health and sustainability. It is too spatially complex and inflexible to fit into most situations – at least in the UK. In countries where apartment living is the norm, and much higher densities can be achieved, it might be practicable.

The form could be modified to suit more moderate densities if cycling and bus travel as well as walking were the main means of local access. Local centres would be further apart. Lower density would allow greenspace to percolate through the town. This is similar to a scheme

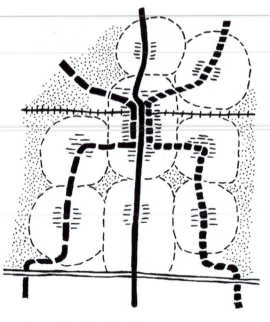

Figure 16.6   Township as a cluster of neighbourhoods

Source: Barton et al. 2010, Figure 5.30, based upon Morris and Kaufman 1997.

developed by Morris and Kaufman in Australia (1997).[5] In many ways it is intermediate between the cluster and neighbourhood cell models, and not so different from new towns such as Harlow in the UK and Almere in Holland. The question arises as to whether such 'relaxed' clusters are able to support high quality public transport and close pedestrian access to facilities to deter car dependence (see Figure 16.6).

Linear forms old and new

The linear form is evident in many older suburban areas where development occurred along main radials well served by tram or bus. In this archetype the neighbourhoods tend to merge into each other, and rather than being centred on a local centre, they are either side of the spine 'high street', which provides shared facilities. Kevin Lynch talks about the spine road as being the 'uniting seam' linking neighbourhoods together. Localities are defined more by character than separate services (Lynch 1981). The linear form (not always radial) maximises the viability and quality of public transport for both local and city-wide trips. The multipurpose high street can offer fluidity of catchment size, and is not reliant on fixed neighbourhood thresholds (Barton 2000).

Tjallingii, drawing on Dutch experience, sees linearity in relation to green/blue infrastructure as well as neighbourhood structure. The streams, rivers, woodlands and associated greenspace provide ecosystem services for the linear townships while allowing easy access from homes to major open space (Tjallingii 1995). The present writers have called this the 'twin track' approach (see Figure 16.7). The 'finger plan' of Copenhagen and the townships of the expanded city of Peterborough in the UK provide classic examples of linearity.

Linear townships centred on a tram or bus radial road were a feature of industrial towns and cities, and evident in the older suburbs examined. Two issues are obvious: the concentration of traffic can be excessive, causing congestion, poor air quality and noisy conditions; partly in consequence, and also due to social change and population decline, some older radial high streets have lost their vitality and viability. Redevelopment and intensification, rather than supporting more local facilities and walking access, could further exacerbate the situation – the paradox of intensification. Stakeholders believed that only with drastic action to rebalance the use of road space, to favour non-motorised modes and public transport, together with altered strategic priorities and cultural change, could the paradox be side-stepped.

In the urban fringe and satellite settlements the linear principle proved feasible as a long-term option. It was generally physically possible to design townships, based on the 'twin track' approach, with high street concentrations backed by green infrastructure. Often it was possible to envisage intermediate stages, first drawing together existing fragmented estates and pods into an open cell neighbourhood, then extending into a linear township. The design of optimal linear scenarios involved considerable experimentation. The art was to capitalise on existing transport and green infrastructure, integrating disparate urban elements. It was vital that the main high street was not also a key city distributor or, if it was, then there was space to widen it to boulevard standard.

Official plans and land allocations precluded effective linear designs, except where major new extensions or new settlements were envisaged. Linear development was not part of the lexicon of planning authorities. Nevertheless, the general response of stakeholders was to welcome the linear designs, because they saw them as helping to integrate disparate developments, offering easy access to open space, increasing the potential for successful local services and for good quality public transport.

What was most striking was the performance of the linear scenarios against sustainability and health criteria. The likelihood of viable local shops and services (with sufficient catchment

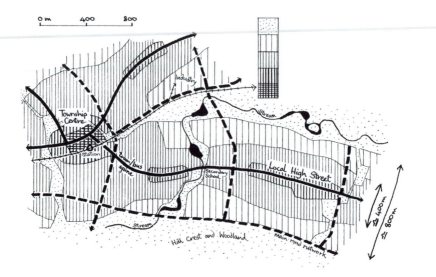

Figure 16.7　Twin-track linear township: the two tracks or networks are based on main public transport routes and greenspace respectively

Source: Barton et al. 2010, Figure 5.2.

populations) was high. Excellent accessibility for all households to facilities and greenspace could be achieved. Reduced car dependence for short and long trips was likely. Linear solutions were generally superior to both cell and cluster scenarios.

Conclusions: moving beyond rhetoric

In many situations it was clear that the allocation of land for urban expansion was driven by the categorisation of land as 'brownfield', environmental 'constraints', specific landowners or developers, and by political or community sensitivities. The tendency to rely on an incremental, often disjointed, development process was evident. What was sidelined (with some exceptions) was prior consideration of optimum urban linkage and neighbourhood form. 'Sustainable' urban environments were given 'lip service' in official reports, but often not reflected in planning and development decisions. As a result the pod model persists in many places.

Nevertheless, stakeholders from public, private and voluntary sectors were often in favour of the more healthy scenarios – and had an informed perspective on the changes necessary to achieve them. In many locations the linear designs performed best, and were physically possible to implement. In other settings neighbourhood cells were effective – always 'open' in character, and sometimes with the potential to evolve into linear forms. Nucleated neighbourhood clusters as advocated by the Task Force model were rarely feasible; the pods form could not be satisfactorily designed from the healthy environments perspective.

What then, can be done to retrofit suburbia? Undoubtedly it relies on planning authorities finding a stronger hand to play, formulating consistent and well-evidenced long-term, cross-party strategies, and working in partnership with local communities and business. Public landownership can be used to maximise leverage on public and private sector investors. Infrastructure investment should prioritise the quality of the walking and cycling environment and the viability of public transport. If health and well-being were at the heart of political, community, institutional and corporate agendas, then there is the chance that disparate interests could cooperate in creating a healthier environment. The evidence from some European cities shows what is possible.[6] If we want healthier places in the English-speaking world, we may have to countenance a more guided market.

Notes

1 Jane Jacobs quoted in Hunter (2014), p. 9.
2 The research, called SOLUTIONS (Sustainability of Land Use and Transport in Outer City Neighbourhoods), was funded by EPSRC, and undertaken by a consortium led by Cambridge University, with the University of the West of England (UWE), University College London, Leeds and Newcastle universities. The neighbourhood research undertaken by UWE involved studies of a range of localities in the city regions of Cambridge, Bristol, Newcastle and London. It had two main elements: empirical and normative. The empirical study involved household surveys and focus groups, examining current levels of active travel in relation to local facilities and neighbourhood design, and the attitudes of residents to their neighbourhoods. The normative study drew on literature to establish basic theoretical archetypes of neighbourhood design, validating these against reality, and testing their applicability in a range of outer city contexts. The website is www.suburbansolutions.ac.uk.
3 Physical practicality was assessed through the degree to which it was possible to implement them on the ground, recognising the existing development pattern, networks and local authority policy context (e.g. protection of flood plains and greenspace). Effectiveness in relation to health and sustainability was assessed in terms of the level of pedestrian accessibility afforded to existing and possible future residents, and therefore the likely level of active travel and the potential for reduced motor use. Local services (if new) – including retail centres, schools, open spaces and public transport services – were located in all scenarios so as to maximise viability and accessibility. Political, market and public acceptability were assessed through stakeholder workshops.
4 The term 'pedshed' is widely used in the UK to mean a pedestrian catchment area – derived from 'watershed'.
5 Morris and Kaufman's key diagram is reinterpreted in Barton et al. 2010, p. 272.
6 See Chapter 25 on European best practice, Chapter 37 on Kuopio and Chapter 38 on Freiburg.

References

Barton, H. 2000. *Sustainable communities: the potential for eco-neighbourhoods.* London: Earthscan.
Barton, H., Davis, G. and Guise, R. 1995. *Sustainable settlements: a guide for planners, designers and developers.* Luton: Local Government Management Board, and Bristol: University of the West of England.
Barton, H., Grant, M. and Guise, R. 2010. *Shaping neighbourhoods: for local health and global sustainability.* London: Routledge.
Barton, H., Grant, M., Horswell, M. and Rice, L. 2011. *Reshaping suburbs: a report produced as part of the EPSRC SOLUTIONS project – the sustainability of land use and transport in outer neighbourhoods.* Bristol: University of the West of England. www1.uwe.ac.uk/et/research/who/resourcesandtools, accessed 8 April 2015.
Barton, H., Horswell, M. and Miller, P. 2012. Neighbourhood accessibility and active travel. *Planning Practice and Research* 27 (2), 177–201.
Boarnet, M. and Sarmiento, S. 1998. Can land use policy really affect travel behaviour? A study of the link between non-work travel and land use characteristics. *Urban Studies* 35 (7), 1155–1169.
Boyd, J. (ed.). 1945. *Homes for the people.* London: HMSO.
Breheny, M. (ed.) 1993. *Sustainable development and urban form.* London: Pion.
Breheny, M., Gent, T. and Lock, D. 1993. *Alternative development patterns: new settlements.* Department of Environment, Planning Research Programme. London, HMSO.
Bullivant, L. 2012. *Masterplanning futures.* Abingdon: Routledge.
Calthorpe, P. 1993. *The next American metropolis: ecology, community and the American dream.* New York: Princeton Architectural Press.
Calve Blanco, T. 2012. *Analysis of local facility accessibility, social networks and perceived mental well-being in Cardiff.* Unpublished paper as part of PhD programme. Bristol: University of the West of England.
Civic Trust and Ove Arup Partners. 2002. *Sustainable suburbs: developing the tools.* London: Civic Trust.

Corburn, J. 2009. *Towards the healthy city: people, places and the politics of urban planning.* Cambridge, MA: MIT Press.

Croucher, K., Myers, L., Jones, R., Ellaway, A. and Beck, S. 2007. *Health and the physical characteristics of urban neighbourhoods: a critical literature review.* Glasgow: Glasgow Centre for Population Health.

DoE (Department of the Environment). 1998. *Planning for sustainable development: towards better practice.* London: HMSO.

Duany, A. and Plater-Zyberk, E. 1991. *Towns and town-making principles.* New York: Howard University Graduate School of Design, Rizzoli.

EEA (European Economic Area). 2009a. *About the urban environment.* European Environment Agency website: www.eea.europa.eu/themes/urban, accessed 8 April 2015.

EEA. 2009b. *Ensuring quality of life in European cities and towns.* European Environment Report 5/2009. Luxembourg: Office of Official Publications of the European Communities.

EU (European Union). 1990. *Green paper on the urban environment.* Brussels: Commission of the European Communities.

Forsyth, A., Oakes, J. and Schmitz, B. 2009. The built environment, walking and physical activity: is the environment more important to some people than others? *Transportation Research Part D: Transport and the Environment* 14 (1), 42–49.

Frank, L., Sallis, J. and Conway, T. 2006. Many paths from land use to health. *Journal of the American Planning Association* 72 (1), 75–87.

Frey, H. 1999. *Designing the city towards more sustainable urban form.* London: E & FN Spon.

Gibberd, F. 1953. *Town design.* London: Architectural Press.

Giles-Corti, B., Knuiman, M., Timperio, A., Van Neil, K., Pikora, T., Bull, F., Shilton, T. and Bulsara, M. 2007. Evaluation of the implementation of a state government community design policy aimed at increasing local walking: design issues and baseline results from RESIDE, Perth, Western Australia. *Preventive Medicine* 46 (1), 46–54.

Grant, M., Barton, H., Bird, C. and Pilkington, P. 2009. *Evidence review on the spatial determinants of health in urban settings.* Bonn: WHO.

Greenwald, M. and Boarnet, M. 2001. Built environment as a determinant of walking behaviour. *Transportation Research Record 1780*, paper no. 01–2792.

Handy, S. 2005. *Does the built environment influence physical activity: examining the evidence.* Washington, DC: Transportation Research Board.

Hunter, P. 2014. *Poverty in suburbia: a Smith Institute study into the growth of poverty in the suburbs of England and Wales.* London: The Smith Institute.

Jenks, M., Burton, E. and Williams, K. (eds). 1996. *The compact city: a sustainable urban form?* London: E & FN Spon.

Lee, C. and Moudon, A. 2008. Neighbourhood design and physical activity. *Building Research and Information* 36 (5), 395–411.

Lynch, K. 1981. *A theory of good city form.* Cambridge, MA: MIT Press.

Melia, S., Parkhurst, G. and Barton, H. 2012. The paradox of intensification. *Transport Policy* 18 (1), 46–52.

Morris, W. and Kaufman, J. 1997. *Mixed use development: new designs for new livelihoods.* Brisbane: Department of Tourism, Small Business and Industry.

Neal, P. 2003. Urban villages and the making of communities. London: Spon Press.

Newman, P. and Kenworthy, J. 1989. *Cities and automobile dependence.* Aldershot: Gower Technical.

Niemann, H. and Maschke, C. 2004. WHO LARES Final report. Noise effects and morbidity. Berlin: World Health Organization, t1.

O'Campo, P., Salmon, C. and Burke, J. 2009. Neighbourhoods and mental well-being: what are the pathways? *Health and Place* 15, 56–68.

Platt, S. 2007. *Lessons from Cambourne, Cambridge.* Cambridge: Cambridge Architectural Research Ltd.

Saelens, B., Sallis, J. and Frank, L. 2003. Environmental correlates of walking and cycling: findings from the transportation, urban design and planning literature. *Annals of Behavioural Medicine* 15 (2), 80–91.

Sugiyama, T., Leslie, E., Giles-Corti, B. and Owen, N. 2008. Association of neighbourhood greenness with physical and health: do walking, social coherence and local social interaction explain the relationships? *Journal of Epidemiology and Community Health* 62, e9.

Tjallingii, S. 1995. *Ecopolis: strategies for ecologically sound urban development.* Leiden: Backhays Publishers.

Urban Task Force. 1999. *Towards an urban renaissance.* London: Department of the Environment, Transport and the Regions.

Van Dyck, D., Deforche, B., Cardon, G. and Bourdeaudhuij, I. 2009. Neighbourhood walkability and its particular importance for adults with a preference for passive transport. *Health and Place* 15, 496–504.

17

BEYOND THE PARK

Linking urban greenspaces, human well-being and environmental health

Linda Corkery

Introduction: definitions and origins of urban greenspace

The environments in which we live, through which we travel, where we work and play all have significant, direct impacts on our health. In the context of a metropolitan region, the ecosystems which comprise the human habitat provide numerous life-supporting services including air quality regulation, clean water supply, healthy soil for food production, materials to construct our environments, and protection against natural disasters and possibly climate change. Therefore, the decisions we make in planning and designing our habitats ultimately impact not only the health of these environments, but also the health and well-being of humans and the species with which we co-exist (Millennium Ecosystem Assessment 2005; Dudley 2011).

Areas of the city where nature and natural elements predominate are increasingly valued for the ways in which they support human health, both physical and mental (Frumkin and Fox 2011; Abraham et al. 2010; Lusk 2006; Swanwick et al. 2003). Over the past 25–30 years, research has confirmed the importance of human interactions with nature in enhancing human health and well-being (Ward Thompson 2010; Maller et al. 2009; Newton 2007). In cities, these interactions mostly take place in greenspaces set aside for recreation. As urban population expands, there is an intensifying use of existing greenspace. For planners, the challenge is to ensure that greenspace provision matches the demand: how much, where and what kind to provide. For public health officials, the question is how to attract people out of their homes and into these areas to be more physically and socially active.

This chapter explores how connected, accessible urban greenspace enhances the experience of city living, and contributes to individual and collective human health, as well as the health of urban ecosystems. It opens by describing the settings that contain urban greenspace, followed by a discussion of their contribution to physical and mental health as has been established by researchers from a variety of disciplines. Major shifts in urban planning perspectives in the mid-nineteenth and early twentieth centuries foreshadowed the current thinking on this topic, particularly in relation to higher density living (Corburn 2007; Martensen 2009). The impact of research findings on practice and on some of the issues requiring further attention are addressed in the concluding section.

Defining urban greenspace

Urban greenspace is distributed across metropolitan landscapes at many scales in developed and undeveloped locations. The term 'greenspace', in this chapter, encompasses a spectrum of typologies and refers to more than just parks. Some urban greenspace is designated or formally zoned as such, including parklands, playing fields and sportsgrounds, urban agriculture and market gardens. Additionally, ecologically sensitive areas of greenspace may be categorised as conservation zones and/or nature reserves, river corridors and wetlands. These are all distinctive landscapes within the urban fabric that contribute to the health and well-being of humans and to the quality of the urban environment. In addition to these larger tracts of land, greenspace that adds amenity to the city can be found along streetscapes and transport corridors. The trees and planted verges along residential streets in the city comprise the incidental greenspaces of daily life, with which we interact most regularly and so may be the most beneficial for urban dwellers.

Metropolitan-scale systems of waterways, topography and vegetation combine with the *local* greenspaces of our everyday lives to form the urban landscape. Both scales of greenspace – macro and micro – are important; however, our experiences of them and the frequency with which we access them are considerably different. Further, they address different human and societal requirements in relation to physical and mental health. The larger scale, that is the 'green infrastructure' of the city, can impact the population health of urban residents. They provide a range of features and opportunities for programmed and unprogrammed activities, but they are likely to be located at the 'peri-urban' areas of cities, that is, 'the space around urban areas which merges into the rural landscape' (Piorr et al. 2010, p. 10). Consequently, these become places for occasional visits and so are of less relevance in the daily activities of most city dwellers.

Local greenspace is also mostly *natural*, that is, it comprises mainly open space that has some 'evidence of human presence such as walkways, paved courtyards, and roads along with a mostly natural setting' (Matsuoka 2010, p. 276). This contrasts with other civic open spaces which are 'mostly built' (ibid.), or, using Beer's criteria, mostly covered in impermeable ground surfaces. Urban plazas and gathering spots may have some vegetation and provide places for social interaction, but generally they contribute less to the environmental functioning of the city and generally provide less human–*nature* interaction (Erickson 2006, p. 16).

Local parks, public gardens, streetscapes, school grounds and playing fields distributed throughout the city are 'everyday' landscapes that can encourage incidental social contact and physical activity during our daily routines, as illustrated in Figure 17.1. In local neighbourhoods, they have the potential to enhance individual health outcomes by encouraging regular use. For example, parks with play areas co-located near places of daily commerce and retail activity work well for parents who can build in some play time with picking up groceries. Schools well connected to surrounding neighbourhoods with walkable or cycle-friendly corridors allow children to travel safely to school with parents, siblings and friends (Maller et al. 2009; Lusk 2006; Gobster 2001).

Origins of urban greenspace planning

Identifying the benefits to city dwellers of having access to nature is not a new idea (Martensen 2009; Corburn 2007; Szczygiel and Hewitt 2000). References to this 'recurring theme' extend back through the ancient history of many cultures and religions to the paradise gardens (Ward Thompson 2011, p. 187). Societal health issues were of paramount concern to the Select Committee on Public Walks in nineteenth-century England (op. cit., p. 191). Their recommendation to create the first 'public parks' originated with a shared concern for the well-being

Figure 17.1   Brooklyn Bridge Park on the East River in New York City links well to local neighbourhoods

Source: Corkery Consulting.

of growing numbers of people moving from the countryside, crowding into the cities to gain work in the factories. Urban visionaries at the time campaigned to reserve extensive tracts of undeveloped land, arguing that these areas would become great parklands that would promote improved social behaviour and a more 'civilized and salubrious' city.

Travelling in England in the 1840s, American landscape architect Frederick Law Olmsted observed the success of developments such as Liverpool's Birkenhead Park. He became a strong advocate of an approach to city design that provided abundant open spaces linked by green boulevards to optimise exposure to vegetation, sunlight and clean air. Throughout North America, Olmsted and others promoted urban parks and park systems, 'first, as a way of preventing the spread of infectious disease from the poor, and second, as a way of civilising them' (Carpenter 2013, p. 122).

Contemporary city dwellers also face increasing health challenges that are linked to environmental concerns and the design of their neighbourhoods. Rather than overcrowding and lack of sanitation infrastructure, lifestyle illnesses – such as heart disease, diabetes, mental illness and some cancers – are increasingly attributed to the character and quality of urban development of the places we inhabit. Residential environments may be in areas of *sprawl* extending into the peri-urban regions of the urban landscape, or in high density *infill* developments. Both development scenarios impact human health in various ways and can contribute, directly or indirectly, to the degradation of ecosystems, water and air quality, and productive lands as well as making it more difficult for people to access greenspace which can be the venue for active exercise, recreation and stress-relieving contact with nature.

Linking greenspace and human health: contemporary frameworks

While Olmsted and others intuitively drew a connection between greenspace and human health, contemporary decision makers in urban planning and design seek evidence of the requirements to allocate open space and associated land uses. Looking to research to provide a foundation for promoting the positive links between urban greenspace with physical and mental health and social well-being is widely accepted.

Linking nature with mental health

Early theoretical frameworks emerged from environmental psychology and focused on people's perceptions of nature derived from their experiences of specific natural settings and landscapes, initially comparing preferences for and responses to undeveloped, 'wilderness' settings. Appleton posited the 'prospect-refuge' theory, stating that human beings prefer a physical position in a setting that allows them to see – that is, to have a *prospect* – but not be seen, in other words to be in hiding, or to have *refuge* (see Figure 17.2). This 'prospect-refuge' preference, he believed, stems from humans' prehistoric origins as hunters who needed to live and travel safely through landscapes in a way that would ensure their survival (Appleton 1975).

Rachel and Stephen Kaplan's early research also focused on human experiences of wilderness landscapes (Kaplan and Kaplan 1989). Their work advanced an understanding of how exposure to nature and natural surroundings could provide feelings of 'retreat' and assist in 'restoring' mental and physical functioning. They developed the 'attention restoration theory' which suggested that people, particularly those who live and work in high stimulus environments which require extended periods of 'directed attention', suffer mental fatigue and diminished attention span, which in turn can lead to reduced physical and mental functioning (Herzog et al. 2003). In the attention restoration theory, nature is construed as offering 'restorative settings' with specific qualities and components that can be beneficial for restoring physical and mental capabilities (Kaplan 1995).

Over the years, this theory has provided a starting point for numerous investigations of urban neighbourhoods, where researchers have gauged the effects – positive, negative or neutral – of trees and landscape elements, for example, water, lawn, gardens, on human social behaviour

Figure 17.2 The dense canopy of the trees in Place des Vosges in Paris provides a 'prospect-refuge' experience for park visitors

Source: Corkery Consulting.

and/or performance, and the degree to which these landscapes provide a 'restorative' effect. Many of these later studies examined social behaviour and how the presence of urban greenspace, and tree planting in particular, enhanced social interactions, reduced crime and lifted students' academic performance in schools (Kuo and Sullivan 2001; Kuo et al. 1998), simply with views of nature from their classrooms (Taylor et al. 2001).

Ulrich's often-cited research in hospital settings (1984) established that even passive interaction with nature, such as having views out of a window to greenspace or trees, or of a landscape painting or through other sensory stimulation like sounds or smells, had measurable benefits. An indication of the effectiveness of these elements included reduced time spent in recovery, less requirement for pain relief medication, and lower blood pressure readings, etc. (Brown and Grant 2007, p. 68).

As research findings on human–nature interactions were emerging in environmental psychology, renowned biologist and theorist E. O. Wilson, together with social ecologist Stephen Kellert, originated the concept of biophilia (Kellert 1993; Wilson 1984). This theory speculates that human beings possess an inherent affinity for nature and 'a natural instinct to desire contact with nature that is evolutionary and inherited' (Newton 2007, p. 13). Hence, we can identify how individual and collective experiences of nature and life on Earth translate into values related to cultural, social and spiritual aspects of what it means to be human, which in turn can significantly impact mental health and a sense of connection to place and to other humans. While these environmental or ecological values are less easily measured and quantified, they are no less significant than physical factors when taking a holistic view of human health. The notion of biophilia has been expanded to encompass the concept of *biophilic* urbanism, or urban planning and design that incorporates the use of 'biophilic elements' that respond to the innate need for nature (Beatley 2010; see Figure 17.3).

Figure 17.3   The green wall at the Musée du quai Branly in Paris is an example of a 'biophilic' urban design element

Source: Corkery Consulting.

Physical benefits of nature

Contemporary research to understand the physical benefits of interacting with nature has verified the intuitive beliefs of nineteenth-century city planners, who were convinced that access to sunshine, clean air, and paths and streets for promenading would improve public health. However, in the past decade or so, there is again widespread concern for the general health of people in response to what has been described as 'lifestyle'-related chronic illnesses such as heart disease, diabetes and some cancers. As well, the increasing incidence of obesity among adults and children in many developed countries is also raising concern (Frumkin and Fox 2011; Frank et al. 2003). There are many factors contributing to these illnesses, but, for ones that can be improved with increased levels of physical activity, numerous research studies have focused on whether or not there is a connection between people's access to greenspace or nature, and personal levels of activity. More specifically, studies have examined how the design of the public realm, particularly in proximity to residential neighbour-hoods, encourages people to be more physically active, and if it contributes to improved health outcomes or attracts people to be more active (Ord et al. 2013; De Vries et al. 2003).

Some previous studies have found that living in proximity to urban greenspace attracts more positive health behaviours and more individual physical activity (Sugiyama et al. 2010; Giles-Corti and Donovan 2003), while other research reports a lack of association between greenspace and physical activity (reported in Ord et al. 2013). Where there is a positive association between physical activity and greenspace, the perceived quality or level of attractiveness of greenspace clearly influences people's behaviour. Research design needs to account for this, along with varying social and cultural norms, economic variances and geographic location which affects local climatic con-ditions, and thus the appeal of undertaking physical activity outdoors (Ord et al. 2013).

'Green' exercise, that is, the 'range of activities which advocate the synergistic benefits of carry-ing out physical activities whilst simultaneously being exposed to nature' has also been studied as a means of gaining physical, as well as mental, benefits (Newton 2007, p. 19). In other words, do you get more benefit from exercising in greenspace than in working out at the gym? The assumption that activities pursued in parks and other urban greenspace are all active needs to be challenged. Many park users report fairly passive or moderate activity such as walking, sitting and having picnics with family and friends as their main greenspace activities. In an effort to increase physical benefits for people, some park programmes have introduced working in nature conservation activities, community gardens or tree planting programmes to increase participants' activity levels (ibid.).

To boost the authority of their findings regarding the benefits of greenspace to human physi-cal and mental health, researchers have sought to generate more objective, quantitative data using contemporary technology. For example, studies have used accelerometers to measure actual lev-els and locations of activity (Giles-Corti et al. 2005); eye tracking devices to determine aspects of the landscape settings that attract access and activity (Nordh 2012); and geographic information systems to determine access, movement and preferences (Thwaites et al. 2005). In a significant research undertaking, Ward Thompson et al. (2012) have measured the levels of salivary cortisol in people before and after exposure to greenspace. Cortisol, in medical terms, is understood to be a 'biomarker for variation in stress levels'. An initial sample trial indicates that 'greener environ-ments may offer better opportunities for moderating or coping with stress' (p. 227).

Challenges for planning urban greenspace

Metropolitan regions around the world face the need to house millions of new residents over the coming decades. And while higher density living may appeal to singles, couples and/or retired people, families with children require access to greenspace to play, picnic and exercise the dog. As urban populations expand and residential densities increase, existing vacant land will be developed and remaining greenspaces will come under pressure as the level of use intensifies (Maller et al. 2009, p. 555). De Vries et al. (2003, p. 1729) conclude that as cities accommodate more high density residential development

> a green living environment may become a necessity rather than a luxury, as it is (some-times) considered. For example, the ongoing process of the densification of cities, in order to save the countryside from urban sprawl, may turn out to have unexpected negative health consequences.

In addition to *where* it is located, there is also the question of *how much* greenspace in a city is enough? In many countries, planners typically allocate open space on the basis of numerical standards, related to projected population numbers; for example, 1 hectare of open space per 1,000 population. Another standard is to provide one local neighbourhood park within a 500 metre radius of every household so every household is no more than a 10–15 minute walk away (Veal 2008). These sorts of open space standards of provision have been used for many years by planners, particularly in setting the amount of open space required to be allocated in new devel-opments. Over time, however, they have been open to a wide variation in interpretation and are regularly subject to local negotiations with widely varying results. Standards such as these are rarely achievable in infill, urban redevelopment contexts where a great deal of urban residential development is occurring (Searle 2011; Veal 2008).

That said, dense inner-city neighbourhoods are not the only urban areas experiencing increased pressure on greenspace. New residential development at the periphery of many cities, the 'peri-urban' region, shows evidence of the shrinking and, in some cases, *disappearing* backyard (Hall 2010). As Frank et al. note (2003, p. 154), street layouts in these new suburban developments often prevent residents from accessing local parks and public recreation areas, requiring them to travel by car, or walk and cycle in unsafe conditions throughout their neigh-bourhoods, or just not bother at all.

Equitable distribution across the metropolitan region is another dimension of concern when considering the amount of total greenspace and/or amount of natural elements, such as street trees, green walls, greenways and trails, against the socio-economic characteristics of neighbourhoods. Not surprisingly, a number of studies reveal that lower socio-economic areas are less well pro-vided for. Access to greenspace within a reasonable distance, for example a 10–15 minute walk, is increasingly considered an issue of environment justice (Wolch et al. 2014; see Figure 17.4).

In addition to how much and where greenspace is distributed, of equal concern is the *kind* of greenspace that is provided and, importantly, does it attract people to use it in ways that will contribute to improved health outcomes? As Ward Thompson notes:

> . . . there has been little such research on what it is about landscape perception and experience that elicits activity and physical exercise . . . if people are to be encouraged to engage in more active lifestyles, then better theoretical understandings about why different landscapes might elicit healthy exercise are needed.
>
> *(in Nelson et al. 2008)*

Similarly, Hitchings (2013, pp. 101–102) suggests that researchers need to discover what pre-vents people from using urban greenspace, and to target non-users on their research methodologies. Even with an understanding of nature's potentially restorative powers, many people do not take the opportunity to use greenspace daily.

Figure 17.4   The playground in Tear Drop Park in Battery Park on Manhattan's west side serves children from the immediate area and is also a regional play attraction

Source: Corkery Consulting.

As once vacant inner city parcels fill up with new residential developments, it is likely there will not much be land available for acquisition as greenspace. Cities will need to seek creative solutions to create new urban greenspace to meet their obligations to residents for open space provision. In response, many projects around the world have demonstrated the creative potential in redeveloping 'greyfields' and 'brownfields', former industrial sites and disused land left behind by extractive industries such as sand and gravel mining, shifts in industry and associated land uses and transport corridors. Parklands are being created on former landfill sites, while boardwalks provide access through wetlands along with recreation-environmental education facilities. Water storage reservoirs and urban freeways can be decked over to create new urban greenspace and deliver better connections through the city (see Figure 17.5). Disused rail line corridors have become recreation trails for hiking and cycling and, in some cases, abandoned infrastructure can be transformed into highly attractive open space assets. Good examples of the latter are the celebrated High Line on the west side of Manhattan, and the Promenade Plantée in Paris, both green linear parks constructed on abandoned elevated rail line structures (Wolch et al. 2014; Harnik 2010).

Other possibilities include rethinking the role of streetscapes by reducing space for cars, and widening footpaths to better accommodate pedestrians, bicyclists and street trees. New areas of greenspace are appearing on the roofs and walls of new and redeveloped buildings. These projects can be symbolic of a desire to improve the sustainability performance of buildings, and in some cases genuinely do provide greenspace for building residents and office workers. As contributing and functional elements of greenspace in the urban environment, their cumulative social and environmental impact is yet to be verified, and opens up another area of research to determine their true social and/or physical health benefits (Wolch et al. 2014, p. 235).

Community gardens and small-scale urban agriculture also contribute to the total greenspace resources in a city. As well as producing fresh food for local consumption, community gardeners enjoy the benefits of moderate exercise associated with the activity of tending a garden and of interacting with fellow gardeners. Shared greenspace resources such as school grounds and public sporting fields represent vast areas of greenspace that are used intermittently, or seasonally.

Figure 17.5   The Paddington Reservoir in Sydney is a city park developed in the underground space of a former water storage facility

Source: Corkery Consulting.

Rethinking how these lands could be managed to accommodate more public access would 'release' more open space into the public realm (Harnik 2010).

Greenspace benefits for specific user groups

Understanding the mutually beneficial links between humans and nature extends to the needs of specific user groups in specific physical settings. Several examples of user groups with particular needs include children, the elderly and culturally diverse urban residents.

Children and nature

Encouraging children's interactions with nature and the importance of active engagement with the outdoors was promoted in John Dewey's educational philosophies in the early twentieth century. More recently, Moore and Cosco's research on children's access to outdoor environments has widely influenced play environment design and research on nature-based play (Moore and Cosco 2010). When journalist Richard Louv (2005) assembled convincing evidence that many American children suffered from what he named 'nature deficit disorder', the issue captured the attention of a popular audience and has since prompted a sense of urgency among educators, child development experts and public health professionals.

The public health concern for increasing problems of overweight associated with poor nutrition and lack of physical exercise among the general population, and particularly with children, is rising in developed countries such as the UK, the USA and Australia. In response, there is increasing attention on the need for children to increase their daily physical activity and nearby public parks and urban greenspace, safer roads and walkable routes to school are seen as ways to facilitate this (Freeman and Tranter 2011). The design of local neighbourhoods has the potential to generate more incidental exercise throughout the day, providing play areas near where they live, safe footpaths and cycleways, reduced traffic, better public transport, as well as places to simply hang out and enjoy the company of friends (Irvine et al. 2013).

Ageing population

The ageing of urban populations is a worldwide demographic trend. Research is developing a strong evidence-based understanding of the capabilities and preferences for this segment of the population. Where 'supportive neighbourhood environments' were provided, that is, interesting, safe and comfortable areas in which to be active and socialise with others, older people were found to walk more and be in better health A combination of pathways and greenspace with appropriate facilities such as community centres, community gardens, shops and markets provide attractive destinations for people in late life who wish to 'age in place' in the neighbourhoods where they've long resided (Sugiyama and Ward Thompson 2007; see Figure 17.6).

Most of the street design considerations that enable elderly city dwellers to safely and comfortably move around also address many requirements for people with physical disabilities, and those who are temporarily incapacitated or negotiating city streets with children or infants.

Use of greenspace by different ethnic groups

As urban and suburban neighbourhoods become more culturally diverse, understanding multiple perspectives and preferences for types of greenspace and the activities they attract will inform planning and ensure social and cultural inclusion. In the seminal Park Life Study undertaken in the UK some 20 years ago (Greenhalgh and Worpole 1995), the use of urban greenspace by various ethnic groups often differed from the traditional uses of these spaces. This has been found to be the case in other countries as well (Low et al. 2005; Thomas 2001, 2002). In Australia, for example, studies revealed widely differing values about nature, sense of personal

Figure 17.6 Elderly pedestrians enjoy the convenience of clear pathways between home and local services

Source: Corkery Consulting.

Figure 17.7   Bocce players make use of a gravel-covered area at Ballast Point, an inner city park on Sydney
Harbour developed on a former oil storage site

Source: Corkery Consulting.

security in some types of landscape settings, and preferences for using open space for large community and family gatherings among people who had migrated from Vietnam and Macedonia.
Similarly, research from the Commission for Architecture in the Built Environment (CABE) in
England found that 'people from ethnic minorities were more likely than white people to visit
parks for exercise', and that 'high numbers of people from black and minority ethnic (BME)
groups have access to five times fewer public parks and good quality green space than people in
more affluent areas' (in Carpenter 2013, p. 125; see Figure 17.7).

Detailed qualitative research in Prospect Park, Brooklyn's heritage park designed by Olmsted
and Partners and constructed between 1867 and 1873, identifies distinctive usage patterns of
various ethnic groups in this major urban park (Low et al. 2005). The findings are consistent
with those cited above, that is, groups of Hispanics, blacks and whites all demonstrated culturally specific ways of using the park spaces and resources, and that non-white users represent the
majority of the numbers of people using the park. However, across the cultural groups, there
appears to be a consistency regarding *why* parks are valued and people's motivations for using
greenspace. The primary reasons people use parks, regardless of ethnicity, are to relax, be in
nature, escape from the city and be with their children (Chiesura 2004).

Conclusions: questions for research and practice

Accessible greenspace needs to extend beyond parks, across the entire public domain of metropolitan landscapes, from local sites to the periphery of the urban boundaries. Research confirms
that connected greenspaces of many sizes, offering a variety of facilities for all ages and abilities,
convenient to where people live and work, and equitably distributed, will support biodiversity and
human health in all its guises, while continuing to promote the environmental health of a region.

Much of the research referenced in this chapter identifies the increasingly complex and
'cross cutting themes' to be addressed in understanding how human health interacts with

urban change and environmental health (Bell et al. 2007). The multiple variables under investigation require multiple disciplinary perspectives to frame the research questions and interpret the findings. A number of major working groups around the world have formed to concentrate on one or a number of these subjects, and they are interdisciplinary collectives seeking to address various combinations of these matters, for example, the I'DGO/OPEN space research programme at the University of Edinburgh; the PHENOTYPE research project in the UK and Europe; and the World Health Organization's Collaborating Centre for Healthy Urban Environment.

The dissemination of research from these groups similarly must flow on to the relevant practitioners and decision makers who influence the shaping of future urban environments. Further, collaboration *across* areas of expertise – urban design, planning, landscape architecture, public health, environmental science – is fundamental to addressing urgent, interconnected issues (Jackson 2003). Such an all-inclusive approach necessitates the synthesis of research findings to inform planning and design decision making, and subsequent research that follows up on resulting developments as they are constructed and managed.

The interlinking matters of human health, contact with nature, viewpoints on urban design, concerns for environmental health and support for the needs of specific user groups, all need continuing research and investigation. Typically, in reporting their findings, researchers point out future research needs. Similarly, this chapter concludes with a number of the key questions that need further exploration to expand our understanding of the relationships between human health, urban greenspace and environmental health.

How much, where and what kind of greenspace is required to increase physical activity?

Not only how much is enough, but what *kinds* of urban greenspace will motivate people to use them for better health outcomes, be affordable to create and maintain and remain flexible to changing needs of the populations they serve?

Is green space equitably distributed across the city?

As Wolch et al. (2014) note there is a fine balance to be achieved in making cities 'just green enough' to ensure neighbourhoods offer widely affordable residential development, as well as being well-serviced by greenspace.

What methods will best determine how/if physical activity in greenspace directly benefits health?

Using new technology in research methods to generate measurable physical responses to greenspace interactions will enhance the authority of research findings and may be more persuasive in making the case for greenspace provision.

How can we identify the specific design elements and qualities of greenspace to attract, encourage and enable increased physical activity?

As above, the more that information about personal preferences for specific aspects or qualities of greenspace can be quantified and linked to increased health-supporting physical activity, the more that arguments will be easier to make for the provision of specific kinds of greenspace and associated facilities.

How can urban greenspace be planned and developed in anticipation of the effects of climate change?

Research on the urban heat island effect is one measure that is increasingly understood to be significantly affected by vegetation cover, but planting trees to provide shade is not an 'instant fix'. Significant areas of cities need to be 'greened' now to provide the required vegetative cover in another 20–30 years.

How transferable are research findings from one locale to another?

Croucher et al. (2007) ask whether or not research findings from one locale can be readily applied in other places, taking into consideration the many variables which influence health. More research needs to offer cross-cultural and cross-national comparisons, testing the universality of current research results that are predominantly from the UK, USA and/or Europe.

Finally, there are questions about how to integrate and account for the many dimensions of greenspace – such as water management, wildlife, food production, air quality – in a practical setting. Chapter 27 on green infrastructure provides insights from research and practice.

References

Abraham, A., Sommerhalder, K. and Abel, T. 2010. Landscape and well-being: a scoping study on the health-promoting impact of outdoor environments. *International Journal of Public Health* 55, 59–69.

Appleton, J. 1975. *The experience of landscape.* New York: Wiley.

Beatley, T. 2010. *Biophilic cities: integrating nature into urban design and planning.* Washington, DC: Island Press.

Bell, S., Montarzion, A. and Travlou, P. 2007. Mapping research priorities for green and public open space in the UK. *Urban Forestry and Urban Greening* 6(2), 103–115.

Brown, C. and Grant, M. 2007. Natural medicine for planners. *Town & Country Planning – Special issue: Planning for Healthy Communities* 76(2), 67–69.

Carpenter, M. 2013. From 'healthful exercise' to 'nature on prescription': the politics of urban green spaces and walking for health. *Landscape and Urban Planning* 118, 120–127.

Chiesura, A. 2004. The role of urban parks for the sustainable city. *Landscape and Urban Planning* 68, 129–138.

Corburn, J. 2007. Reconnecting with our roots: American urban planning and public health in the twenty-first century. *Urban Affairs Review* 42(5), 688–713.

Croucher, K., Myers, L. and Bretherton, J. 2007. *The links between greenspace and health: a critical literature review.* Stirling, Scotland: Scottish Natural Heritage and NHS Health Scotland.

De Vries, S., Verheij, R., Groenewegen, P. and Spreeuwenberg, P. 2003. Natural environments – healthy environments? An exploratory analysis of the relationship between greenspace and health. *Environment and Planning A* 35(10), 1717–1731.

Dudley, N. 2011. *Authenticity in nature: making choices about the naturalness of ecosystems.* London: Earthscan.

Erickson, D. 2006. *MetroGreen: connecting open space in North American cities.* Washington, DC: Island Press.

Frank, L., Engelke, P. and Schmid, T. 2003. *Health and community design: the impact of the built environment on physical activity.* Washington, DC: Island Press.

Freeman, C. and Tranter, P. 2011. *Children and their urban environment: changing worlds.* London: Earthscan.

Frumkin, H. and Fox, J. 2011. Contact with nature. In Dannenberg, A., Frumkin, H. and Jackson, R. (eds). *Making healthy places: designing and building for health, well-being and sustainability.* Washington, DC: Island Press.

Giles-Corti, B. and Donovan, R. 2003. Relative influences of individual, social environmental, and physical environmental correlates of walking. *American Journal of Public Health* 93(9), 1583–1589.

Giles-Corti, B., Broomhall, M.H., Knuiman, M., Collins, C., Douglas, K., Ng, K., Lange, A. and Donovan, R. 2005. Increasing walking: how important is distance to, attractiveness, and size of public open space? *American Journal of Preventive Medicine* 28, 169–176.

Gobster, P.H. 2001. Neighbourhood open space relationships in metropolitan planning: a look across four scales of concern. *Local Environment* 6(2), 199–212.

Greenhalgh, L. and Worpole, K. 1995. *Park life: urban parks and social renewal*. London: Comedia Association with Demos.

Hall, T. 2010. *The life and death of the Australian backyard*. Canberra, Australia: CSIRO Publishing.

Harnik, P. 2010. *Urban green: innovative parks for resurgent cities*. Washington, DC: Island Press.

Herzog, T., Maguire, C. and Nebel, M. 2003. Assessing the restorative components of environments. *Journal of Environmental Psychology* 23, 159–170.

Hitchings, R. 2013. Studying the preoccupations that prevent people from going into green space. *Landscape and Urban Planning* 118, 98–102.

Irvine, K., Warber, S., Devine-Wright, P. and Gaston, K. 2013. Understanding urban green space as a health resource: a qualitative comparison of visit motivation and derived effects among park users in Sheffield, UK. *International Journal of Research in Public Health* 10(1), 417–442.

Jackson, L. 2003. The relationship of urban design to human health and condition. *Landscape and Urban Planning* 64, 191–200.

Kaplan, R. and Kaplan, S. 1989. *The experience of nature: a psychological perspective*. Cambridge: Cambridge University Press.

Kaplan, S. 1995. The restorative benefits of nature: toward an integrative framework. *Journal of Environmental Psychology* 15, 169–182.

Kellert, S. 1993. The biological basis for human values of nature. In Kellert, S. and Wilson, E. (eds). *Biophilia hypothesis*. Washington DC: Island Press.

Kuo, F. and Sullivan, W. 2001. Environment and crime in the inner city: does vegetation reduce crime? *Environment and Behavior* 33(3), 343–367.

Kuo, F. Bacaicao, M. and Sullivan, W. 1998. Transforming inner-city landscapes: trees, sense of safety, and preference. *Environment and Behavior* 30, 28–59.

Louv, R. 2005. *Last child in the woods: saving our children from nature-deficit disorder*. Chapel Hill, NC: Algonquin Books.

Low, S., Taplin, D. and Scheld, S. 2005. *Rethinking urban parks: public space and cultural diversity*. Austin, TX: University of Texas Press.

Lusk, A. 2006. Promoting health and fitness through urban design. In Platt, R. (ed.). *The humane metropolis: people and nature in the 21st century city*. Boston, MA: University of Massachusetts Press and The Lincoln Institute of Land Policy.

Maller, C., Henderson-Wilson, C. and Townsend, M. 2009. Rediscovering nature in everyday settings: or how to create healthy environments and healthy people. *EcoHealth* 6, 553–556.

Martensen, R. 2009. Landscape designers, doctors, and the making of healthy urban spaces in 19th century America. In Campbell, L. and Wiesen, A. (eds). *Restorative commons: creating health and well-being through urban landscapes*. Newtown Square, PA: USDA Forest Service, Northern Research Station, pp. 26–37.

Matsuoka, R. 2010. Student performance and high school landscapes: examining the links. *Landscape and Urban Planning* 97, 273–282.

Millennium Ecosystem Assessment. 2005. *Ecosystems and human well-being: synthesis*. Washington, DC: Island Press.

Moore, R. and Cosco, N. 2010. Using behaviour mapping to investigate healthy outdoor environments for children and families: conceptual framework, procedures and applications. In Ward Thompson, C., Aspinall, P. and Bell, S. (eds). *Innovative approaches to researching landscape and health*. London: Routledge, pp. 33–73.

Nelson, N., Wright, A., Lowry, R. and Mutrie, N. 2008. Where is the theoretical basis for understanding and measuring the environment for physical activity? *Environmental Health Insights* 2, 111–116.

Newton, J. 2007. *Wellbeing and the natural environment: a brief overview of the evidence*. Report from the Wellbeing in Developed Countries (WeD) research group at the University of Bath.

Nordh, H. 2012. Quantitative methods of measuring restorative components in urban public parks. *Journal of Landscape Architecture* 7(1), 46–53.

Ord, K., Mitchell, R. and Pearce, J. 2013. Is level of neighbourhood green space associated with physical activity in green space? *International Journal of Behavioral Nutrition and Physical Activity* 10. www.ijbnpa.org/content/10/1/127, accessed 8 April 2015.

Piorr, A., Ravetz, J. and Tosics, I. (eds). 2010. *Peri-urbanisation in Europe: towards a European policy to sustain urban-rural futures – synthesis report*. Frederiksberg: University of Copenhagen/Academic Books Life Sciences.

Searle, G. 2011. Urban consolidation and the inadequacy of local open space provision in Sydney. *Urban Policy and Research* 29(1), 201–208.

Sugiyama, T. and Ward Thompson, C. 2007. Older people's health, outdoor activity and supportiveness of neighbourhood environments. *Landscape and Urban Planning* 83, 168–175.

Sugiyama, T., Francis, J., Middleton, N., Owen, N. and Giles-Corti, B. 2010, Associations between recreational walking and attractiveness, size, and proximity of neighborhood open spaces. *American Journal of Public Health* 100(9), 1752–1757.

Swanwick, C., Dunnett, N. and Woolley, H. 2003. Nature, role and value of green space in towns and cities: an overview. *Built Environment* 29(2), 94–106.

Szczygiel, B. and R. Hewitt, R. 2000. Nineteenth-century medical landscapes: John H. Rauch, Frederick Law Olmsted, and the search for salubrity. *Bulletin of the History of Medicine* 4(4) Winter, 708–734.

Taylor, A., Kuo, F. and Sullivan, W. 2001. Views of nature and self-discipline: evidence from inner city children. *Environmental Psychology* 21. www.idealibrary.com, accessed 1 August 2014.

Thomas, M. 2001. *A multicultural landscape: national parks and the Macedonian experience*. Sydney: NSW National Parks and Wildlife Service.

Thomas, M. 2002. *Moving landscapes: national parks and the Vietnamese experience*. Sydney: NSW National Parks and Wildlife Service.

Thwaites, K., Helleur, E. and Simkins, I.M. 2005. Restorative urban open space: exploring the spatial configuration of human emotional fulfilment in urban open space. *Landscape Research* 30(4), 525–547.

Ulrich, D. 1984. View through a window may influence recovery from surgery. *Science* 224(4647), 420–421.

Veal, A. 2008. *Open space planning standards in Australia: in search of origins*. School of Leisure, Sport and Tourism Working Paper 5. Sydney: University of Technology.

Ward Thompson, C. 2011. Linking landscape and health: the recurring theme. *Landscape and Urban Planning* 99, 187–195.

Ward Thompson, C., Roe, J., Aspinall, P., Mitchell, R., Clow, A. and Miller, D. 2012. More green space is linked to less stress in deprived communities: evidence from salivary cortisol patterns. *Landscape and Urban Planning* 105(3), 221–229.

Wilson, E. 1984. *Biophilia: the human bond with other species*. Cambridge, MA: Harvard University Press.

Wolch, J., Byrne, J. and Newell, J. 2014. Urban green space, public health, and environmental justice: the challenge of making cities 'just green enough'. *Landscape and Urban Planning* 125, 234–244.

18

HOTTER CITIES

Climate change and planning for resilient, healthy urban environments

Louise McKenzie

Introduction: an unhealthy trend

This chapter examines the impact of urban heat on health. It provides frameworks through which to view vulnerability, heatwaves and heat-related public health risk and what this means for urban planning. A number of issues are raised such as ageing and chronic illness, physical activity and community resilience, and all of this against a background of increasing global temperatures. But to begin, it starts with the real experiences and impacts of heatwaves during Australia's summer of 2013–14.

'Adelaide is the hottest city on Earth today', proclaimed headlines on 16 January 2014 (The Advertiser 2014). The title of world's hottest city was conferred on Adelaide, an Australian city of nearly 1.3 million people, when temperatures peaked at 44.2°C. Amid one of the most significant heatwaves to affect south-eastern Australia, Adelaide experienced five consecutive days of temperatures above 42.0°C, with overnight temperatures up to 29.9°C. Over the course of the 2013–14 summer, public media was saturated with news of record temperatures for Australian cities: Melbourne had seven 40°C days, against an average of one; Adelaide had 11 days of 42°C or above, against an average of one; and Canberra had 19 days of 35°C or above, against an average of 5.4 (WMO 2014; Australian Bureau of Meteorology 2014). Images of bushfires, blackouts, melting tarmac, buckling train tracks and heat-stressed players at the Australian Open Tennis Championship dominated news bulletins (Time 2014), accompanied by health messages to stay well hydrated, wear light clothing, seek out cool places and check on neighbours, especially the elderly.

As heatwave action plans were activated, a national 'Pilot Heatwave Forecast' (Figure 18.1) assisted individuals and agencies to take precautions and be prepared. City authorities opened air-conditioned bus stations and building foyers for people to sleep in, set up water-mist sprays in outdoor malls, and extended trading hours for public swimming pools. Over 1,000 homeless people were given free pool-passes, while charities donated swimming bathers and towels. A medical clinic for the homeless extended drop-in hours as clients were suffering from seizures, confusion and aggravated skin conditions caused by mite bites and poor hydration (The Age 2014). To a public generally familiar with heatwaves, the Australian Medical Association president warned, 'We don't realise how hot it is because we are used to the warmer days . . . but the reality is it is a

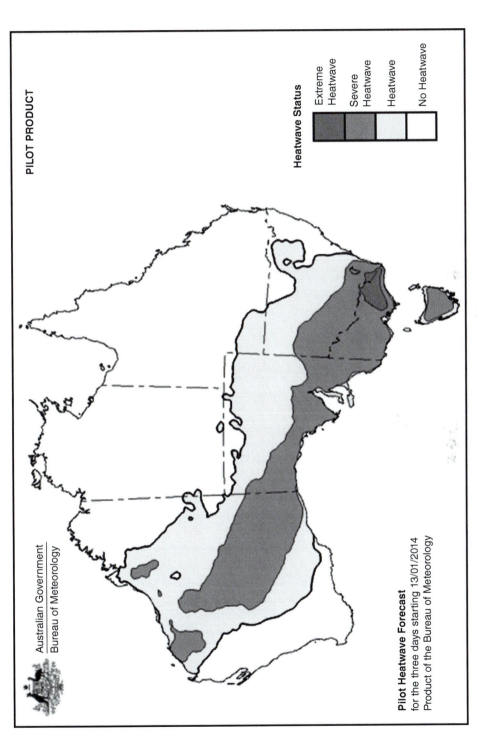

Figure 18.1 Australian Bureau of Meteorology 'Pilot Heatwave Forecast' for 13 January: one of a set of four maps forecasting the heatwave path to 16 January 2014

Source: Australian Bureau of Meteorology, Pilot Heatwave Forecast, 2014. www.bom.gov.au/australia/heatwave, accessed 13 January 2014.

© Commonwealth of Australia, Bureau of Meteorology

lot hotter than what we have experienced so far, so we need to take better precaution' (Business Insider 2014). Concurrently, the Climate Council released their new report, 'Australian Heatwaves: Hotter, Longer, Earlier and More Often' (Climate Council 2014). The impact of bushfires is also closely followed by the residents of Australia's largest cities, as described in Box 18.1.

BOX 18.1 Diary of a Sydney bushfire: 2013

Extreme heat triggers multiple and simultaneous health impacts

21st October – Springtime. Temperatures have reached over 30°C on five separate days this month. Unusually hot. Today the sky is an eerie, luminous haze. Bushfire smoke. I can see and smell the smoke although I'm more than 40 km away from the nearest of the 58 fires currently burning across the state of New South Wales. Flames have engulfed one village on Sydney's perimeter. I check the national broadcaster's 'Live Blog' – 200 homes have been lost and one person has died. The Fire Service warns this level of emergency in October is unprecedented: 'This is a feature of slowly evolving climate. We have always had fires, but not of this nature, and not at this time of year, and not accompanied by the record-breaking heat we've had' (The Guardian 2013).

Where I live, an inner city area, air quality hits 'Very Poor'. Sydney's outer suburbs strike 'Hazardous'. Health alerts recommend 'Everyone, especially people with heart and lung diseases, should avoid outdoor exertion and stay inside as much as possible' (Figure 18.5). Oddly, after a short walk, I feel breathless. Is it the pollution? I ring my elderly mother who lives nearby, to ask after her husband with heart disease. They'd finished their chores early, then played outdoor lawn-bowls. The smoke and heat hadn't worried them – except for irritated eyes. Nonchalance borne of living through many heatwaves.

22nd October – The Fire Commissioner advises that tomorrow's forecast is 'as bad as it gets'. Very high temperatures and wind speeds and low humidity. Emergency plans are outlined to 2,500 people at a local public meeting.

23rd October – I wake to a clear mid-blue sky. A gentle breeze. The sun's rays have that telling bite – it's going to be hot. Greater Sydney is on extreme fire danger alert. 1pm – a sudden wind whips tree tops. I can see and hear the wind but don't feel it. An anxious neighbour observes, 'Not looking good.'

24th October – The extreme fire danger passes without further property damage or lives lost. Public commentary turns, as it often does in response to extreme heat and bushfires, to issues of politicising disasters by connecting heatwaves to climate change and the need to reduce carbon emissions.

The summer of 2013–14 is a window to a future, hotter Australia. While Australian cities face specific climate change challenges arising from their unique physical, social, cultural, economic and political environments, they also share a range of challenges with cities across the world that are confronting a hotter future. This chapter focuses on the impact of urban heat on human health and vulnerability, and the importance of designing and planning cities and neighbourhoods to increase resilience. Urban policy and the broader issues of equity and community well-being are examined, with emphasis on the Australian context. The twenty-first-century spectre of climate change, ageing populations and epidemic levels of chronic illness presents multiple health challenges since groups most vulnerable to the negative impacts of heat include older people and those with chronic illnesses. With over half the world's population now residing in cities, increasing urban temperatures threaten the quality of urban life and exacerbate the global public health challenge.

2013 at a glance

Globally, 2013 was a warm year. Australia, the north Pacific and central Asia experienced record warming, while in northern and central Europe a hot summer followed a cold spring. Parts of east Asia endured exceptionally hot summers. South America, Scandinavia and the Middle East were exposed to large fluctuations between extreme heat and cold, including record or near-record heat and cold occurrences within days of each other. In the United States, temperatures were near normal following a record warm year in 2012 (Trewin et al. 2014).

In 2013 the Intergovernmental Panel on Climate Change (IPCC 2013) reported unequivocally that the climate system is warming, the frequency of heatwaves is likely to increase in large parts of Europe, Asia and Australia, and temperatures will continue to increase with regional and interannual-to-decadal variability. The IPCC (2007) and World Health Organization (WHO 2012) project numerous human health impacts from climate change, overall mostly adverse, including increased injury, disease and death from heatwaves, fires, droughts, storms and floods, and increased cardiorespiratory morbidity and mortality due to air pollution. For Australia, the main health impacts will result from heat exposure, extreme weather, air pollution, reduced local food production, food- and vector-borne infectious disease and mental stress. One of the most significant impacts is likely to be increased heat-related deaths amplified by the ageing population (McInnes et al. 2008; Kjellstrom and Weaver 2009).

Vulnerability to heat

Vulnerability to increasing temperatures and extreme heat results from the interactions of exposure, sensitivity and adaptive capacity (Figure 18.2). City design and planning directly and indirectly influence the vulnerability of individuals and populations.

Exposure to heat is influenced by the climate variability of a city and the environments in which people live and work. In cities located in hot climates, levels of exposure are affected by factors such as the thermal performance of neighbourhoods and housing, provision of cool public places, occupational exposures and proximity to bushfires. Groups identified as most vulnerable to heat exposure include outdoor workers, people living in poor quality housing, the homeless, people living in neighbourhoods with little greenery, and people without access to air conditioning, services and public transport (McInnes et al. 2008; Hajat et al. 2010; Walker et al. 2011; Reid et al. 2012).

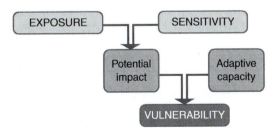

Figure 18.2   Vulnerability and its components

Source: Garnaut (2008, p. 125).

Garnaut Climate Change Review: Final Report © Commonwealth of Australia 2008

Sensitivity refers to the prevalence of heat-related health risk factors in a population, such as older age, obesity and chronic health conditions – that is, cardiovascular and respiratory diseases, mental health conditions and diabetes. These risk factors reduce an individual's ability to regulate their body temperature which, in turn, can lead to heat stress, heat exhaustion and potentially fatal heatstroke. Night-time minimum temperatures particularly impact on health as the body has little overnight relief from persistently warm temperatures, inhibiting the body from recuperating from high day-time temperatures and adding to heat stress accumulation (Hajat et al. 2010; Hansen et al. 2011).

Adaptive capacity refers to the ability to ameliorate the potential impact of heat and is influenced by socio-economic factors such as education level and income, which may affect a person's ability to live in a thermally efficient home or in a green neighbourhood; the willingness and ability of individuals, governments and other networks to deploy relevant resources; and social capital, including relations with neighbours and whether a person lives alone. Disability and mental health conditions may also restrict adaptive capacity (Preston and Stafford-Smith 2009; Brown et al. 2011; Barnett et al. 2013).

Relations between adaptive capacity, tree cover and disadvantage were revealed in a study of six Australian cities, which found trees to be less dense in areas of low income and educational status than in areas of high income and education (Kirkpatrick et al. 2011). A study in Florida, USA, found a significantly lower percentage of tree cover in neighbourhoods with a higher proportion of African-Americans, low-income residents and renters (Landry and Chakraborty 2009). Results suggest residents of wealthy neighbourhoods are able to meet the maintenance costs of trees, with associated benefits for physical and mental health, pollution moderation, thermal performance and reduced cooling costs.

Box 18.2 Building resilience to climate change

Health-supportive, age-friendly and thermally efficient built environments are critical to reducing chronic disease burden and maximising population resilience to climate change (Bambrick et al. 2011; Barnett et al. 2013).

Socio-cultural vulnerability

Vulnerability to heat may be exacerbated by social and cultural factors. Indigenous understanding of the Australian climate focuses on weather patterns of intersecting hot–cold and wet–dry contrasts and the availability of water, flora and fauna, questioning Eurocentric responses to climate (Rose 2005). While sun and sea are embedded within the national psyche, Lowe (2005) suggests European settlers and their descendants – bent on taming this 'bright and savage land' – have never realistically engaged with the Australian climate, leading to an ambivalence towards heat and the world's highest rates of skin cancer.

Migrants and tourists to Australia, particularly those from cooler countries, may lack awareness of local climate and adaptive behaviours and be unacclimatised to high temperatures. Increased exposure to gambling can result for people, particularly the elderly, seeking refuge in air-conditioned sporting and service clubs with gambling facilities (Hansen et al. 2013). Non-English speaking people are recognised amongst the most vulnerable to heat-related illness in the 'Heat-wave plan for Victoria' (Victorian Department of Health 2011). It is expected that climate change will exacerbate existing health inequalities and vulnerability (McMichael et al. 2006).

Heatwaves

While there is no standard definition, 'heatwaves' are frequently described as periods of unusually or exceptionally hot weather. The Australian Bureau of Meteorology (2014), for example, defines a 'heatwave' as 'three days or more of high maximum and minimum temperatures that is unusual for that location'.

Over the past two decades, heatwaves in parts of Europe, North America and Australia led to unprecedented death tolls. In the summer of 2003, an estimated 70,000 people died in Europe from heat-induced illnesses (Hajat et al. 2010; Stones Jnr 2012), while in 1995, 514 people died from health-related impacts of a heatwave in Chicago (Naughton et al. 2002). More recently, in early 2009, an estimated 500 people died in Victoria during a heat-wave immediately prior to the Black Saturday Bushfire in which 173 people died (Victorian Department of Health 2011). Indeed, in Australia, heatwaves cause more deaths than any other natural disaster, including cyclones, flood or bushfires – yet they are 'private, silent deaths which only hit the media when morgues reach capacity or infrastructure fails' (Australian Commonwealth 2011, p. 3). While Australians are mostly accustomed to hot summers, the number of heat-related deaths in temperate Australian cities is expected to rise significantly by 2050 due to increases in the frequency and intensity of heatwaves from climate change. The full extent of heatwave impacts are, however, yet to be realised as morbidity from extreme heat remains under-reported (Nairn and Fawcett 2013).

Geographical differences in heat-related mortality suggest that people become relatively accustomed to the climate in which they live (Bambrick et al. 2008) and this is reflected in the different threshold temperatures activating heatwave plans. For London, threshold day and night temperatures are 32°C and 18°C respectively (Greater London Authority 2011), while the heatwave plan for Melbourne nominates a threshold day temperature of 36°C and a mean temperature of 30°C (Victorian Department of Health 2011).

The health impacts of extreme heat also vary temporally due to acclimatisation. Consequently, a heatwave in spring or early summer can have greater impact than one in late summer (Hajat et al. 2010). While communities adapt to their prevailing climates through physiological, cultural, behavioural and technological responses, heatwaves often force them past their adaptation bounds (McMichael et al. 2006). Beyond discussion here, the vulnerability of natural systems to heat also differs greatly across seasons and regions.

With future susceptibility likely to increase with the growing incidence of chronic disease, ageing populations in high-income countries and rapid urbanisation in low-income countries, the health impacts of heatwaves are rapidly becoming a global public health challenge for this century (Hajat et al. 2010).

Cities: a greater human health concern

People living in cities are at greater risk from heat impacts than their rural neighbours, as cities experience hotter temperatures leading to more intense heatwaves, with hotter nights and higher levels of air pollution (McInnes et al. 2008; Hajat et al. 2010). These impacts are magnified for people living in geographically expanding or sprawling cities, cities with poor quality housing and cities with topographies that give rise to stagnant air masses and summer pollution, such as Santiago de Chile and Mexico City (Patz and Kovats 2002). Urban heatwaves may also impact on health through energy infrastructure failures, leading to blackouts, water delivery disruption and transport failures, as in Buenos Aires in 2012 (Figure 18.3).

A tree-lined street (canyon) in a high density residential area, Buenos Aires, November 2012

Heatwave in Spring 2012: unusual afternoon crowd in a shaded public plaza in a high density residential area, Buenos Aires

Figure 18.3 A heatwave in early November 2012 in Buenos Aires led to major infrastructure failures in power, water and transport, while tree-shaded parks and streets provided 'cool spaces' for residents living in high-rise apartments

Source: McKenzie.

Urban heat islands

City temperatures are amplified by the urban heat island (UHI) effect, whereby urban environments with high thermal storage capacity and poor ventilation absorb and retain heat. UHIs are essentially nocturnal phenomena since temperature elevations are largest during the night; during daytime hours temperature differences between city centres and surrounding countryside are usually much smaller (Givoni 1998). The UHI effect was especially evident during the 2003 European heatwave, when central London was up to 10°C warmer than the surrounding greenbelt (Greater London Authority 2011).

UHIs and their intensity are affected by weather conditions and urban features. The UHI effect is strongest during clear, still weather and weakest during cloudy, windy weather, since more solar energy is absorbed on clear days and heat is removed more slowly when air is still. Urban features, such as the size and density of cities, ratio of building heights to the distances between them, orientation and width of streets, thermal storage capacity and reflexivity (albedo) of building materials, permeability of surfaces, vegetation and the nature of the surrounding urban landscape have strong effects on the magnitude of UHIs and the microclimates of outdoor spaces within cities (Gartland 2008; Coutts et al. 2012; Argüeso et al. 2013).

UHIs tend to expand and become more intense as cities expand and densities increase. Argüeso et al. (2013) simulated future urban expansion in Sydney and forecast little impact on daytime temperatures but strong impact on night-time temperatures due mostly to increased heat storage capacity of urban structures and reduced evaporative cooling. Coutts et al. (2007) explored four sites of increasing density across Melbourne and observed greater night-time temperatures with increasing density, attributed to variations in heat storage release, due in part to street canyons and layout.

Although UHIs tend to exhibit typical characteristics, their intensity and timing vary according to an area's topography, weather conditions and urban design and the resulting temperature and energy flow balance (Gartland 2008). A study of high-rise quarters in Shanghai showed

Digital image   Weather clear and still
5pm Feb 2014   Air temperature 36.2°C
                Relative humidity 30%
* Data from infrared image

Infrared image   Weather clear and still
11pm Feb 2014   Air temperature 27.8°C
                  Relative humidity 32%

Figure 18.4   Infrared photography at 5pm and 11pm on a hot summer day indicates natural elements (trees and thin grass cover) have lower thermal storage capacities than built elements (asphalt road and concrete path) in a residential street

Source: McKenzie.

summertime UHI variations were influenced by site planning, building design and greenery: the daytime UHI was mostly influenced by shading from buildings or vegetation canopies; the night-time UHI, more difficult to assess due to anthropogenic heat, was significantly influenced by greenery density and cover (Yang et al. 2011). Infrared photography demonstrates the higher thermal storage capacities of built elements compared with natural elements during summer in a low density residential street in Sydney (Figure 18.4).

A major concern is that the rate at which cities are warming is significantly higher than global warming rates. Temperature data in global warming data sets is statistically adjusted to project the rate of temperature change at the scale of the planet as a whole by largely excluding city data through the selection of rural weather stations. A study of 50 large American cities (Stones Jnr 2012) indicated that the majority are warming at double the rate of global climate change. For some cities, the UHI remained unchanged or was shrinking, while still reporting higher temperatures than rural areas. This trend was commonly associated with Rust Belt cities that are slow-growing or have declining populations, possibly leading to reduced waste heat emissions and recovering urban tree cover. Land-use change and waste heat emissions were identified as playing a more significant role in ongoing urban warming trends than greenhouse gas emissions.

Box 18.3   Urban policies and practices need to address four principal features to reduce urban heat

1.   Reduction in the amount of moisture for evaporative cooling produced by the displacement of vegetation by streets, car parks and buildings, and lack of water harvesting and reuse systems.

(continued)

(continued)

2. Low surface reflexivity of materials, such as dark paving and roofing materials, enabling absorption of solar energy.
3. Reabsorption of reflected radiation by the vertical surfaces of tall buildings, compounded by diminished reflexivity.
4. Generation of waste heat from anthropogenic sources, such as vehicles, power plants, industrial operations and air-conditioning systems.

(Stones Jnr 2012; Coutts et al. 2012)

Urban heat, air pollution and aeroallergens

Air pollution, particularly ozone and particulate pollution, and aeroallergens increase as urban temperature increases, exacerbating the health risks for people with heart and lung disease, older people and children. Ground-level ozone is one of the most toxic components of photochemical urban smog and poses health risks, especially for people with heart and lung conditions. Vehicle emissions in combination with strong sunlight during hot summer months form most ozone and very high levels may be registered during heatwaves.

Particulate pollution, known as 'particulate matter' (PM), also poses health risks for people with heart and lung conditions. Natural sources of PM include volcanoes, bushfires, dust storms and living vegetation. Bushfires can produce vast amounts of particulate and gaseous pollutants with dramatic, short-term impacts on air quality. Anthropogenic sources of PM include vehicles, industrial processes and power plants (Kjellstrom and Weaver 2009; Kolbe and Gilchrist 2009; Beggs and Bennett 2011; Spickett et al. 2011)

The production, allergenic potential and distribution of aeroallergens, such as pollen, increase alongside increasing temperatures and may be augmented by the presence of air pollutants, exacerbating respiratory allergic diseases, such as asthma and hay fever. Strategies for reducing impacts include firmer management of allergenic plant species, and careful selection and use of plant species by government authorities and communities in populated areas (Beggs and Bennett 2011). In the event of high air pollution or aeroallergen levels, health alerts recommend avoiding outdoor activity (Figure 18.5).

Urban heat and urban policy

The drivers of climate operate over large geographic areas and long time frames and are consequently difficult to integrate into policy. Measuring increasing greenhouse gases in the atmosphere and the pace of climate change at the global scale are critically important (Stones Jnr 2012; Pitman et al. 2012). For cities, however, policy-relevant effects occur on regional, city and neighbourhood scales. To date, only limited climate change assessments have been in formats or at scales easily accessible to planners and designers. While unquestionably small, a single lawn, car park or residential tree may contribute to the cumulative spatial extent of land surfaces influencing regional and neighbourhood climates (Stones Jnr 2012). A study of the cooling influence of greenspaces in urban areas in Lisbon, for example, identified the 'park cool island' effect, confirming the potential contribution of even small parks to mitigating urban heat (Oliveira et al. 2011).

In Australia, accessible climate information is being developed by innovative collaborations between researchers, government and industry partners. On regional and metropolitan scales, climate projections at 10km resolution are currently under development for application by government agencies and the public in managing climate change impacts on health, infrastructure, agriculture and services (Lee et al. 2013). On a city scale, spatial heat-related vulnerability

AIR POLLUTANT	LEVEL [data reading]	PUBLIC ADVICE
OZONE	POOR	Children and adults with respiratory disease, such as asthma, should avoid exercising outdoors in the evening.
PARTICLES PM10	VERY POOR	People with heart or lung disease, older adults, and children should avoid exercising outdoors. Everyone else should reduce prolonged or heavy exertion. If you have symptoms rest and use your reliever medicine. If symptoms persist, seek medical advice.
PARTICLES PM2.5	HAZARD-OUS	Everyone, especially people with heart or lung disease should avoid outdoor exertion and stay inside as much as possible. If you have symptoms rest and use your reliever medicine. If symptoms persist, seek medical advice.

Figure 18.5 Health alert for Sydney south-west for 1pm on 21 October 2013 during a heatwave with bushfire, including advice for outdoor activity – excerpt of the complete list of alerts for that day

Source: Air quality, NSW Office of Environment and Heritage. www.environment.nsw.gov.au/aqms/aqialerts/htm. Accessed 22 October 2013.

indices for Australian cities have been developed (Loughnan et al. 2013), identifying areas most at risk and enabling adaptation programmes, such as green infrastructure and housing improvement programmes, to be prioritised (Barnett et al. 2013). On a neighbourhood scale, information is currently being collected to determine the effect of street trees and pavement colour on urban temperatures, to help reduce macro- and microclimatic heat and create thermally comfortable public spaces (City of Sydney 2014).

Designing and planning with climate

The ability of cities to modify their own climates and microclimates has been understood for centuries. Ancient Romans discerned streets became hotter after widening to accommodate growing commercial activity and prescribed narrower streets shaded by tall houses. Middle Eastern cities have long featured narrow, curving and discontinuous street patterns to curb heat and wind-blown sand. The use of shade trees, water and covered walkways in age-old public plazas continue to provide comfortable, cool retreats from the searing heat in Spain (Figure 18.6). By the late nineteenth century, the first measurement of the UHI had been calculated by Howard, an amateur meteorologist, who showed Central London to be nearly 4°F warmer than the surrounding countryside (Stones Jnr 2012).

Water from illuminated fountains cools paving at the end of a   Dense tree canopy provides a cool public place for afternoon
hot summer day – Plaza Mayor in Cáceres, Spain   activity on a hot summer day – Baños de Montemayor, Spain

Figure 18.6   Comfortable microclimates in urban public spaces created through evaporative cooling and
use of vegetation

Source: McKenzie.

A century later McHarg (1992) and Hough (1995) outlined the relations between cities and natural processes that are fundamental to urban climate and human health. Their ecology-based approach, which incorporated environmental data into landscape planning and design, remains acutely relevant to creating a place for nature and reducing heat in cities. Bioclimatic planning and design, embracing sensitivity for climate-land-flora, is showcased by architects, such as Yeang (1995), Murcutt (Drew 1996) and Givoni (1998). Agencies, such as PLEA[1] and LEED,[2] have long fostered and continue to champion integrated renewable energy and passive energy technologies, and internationally recognised rating systems for green buildings and neighbourhoods.

In the early twenty-first century, 'green infrastructure', 'water-sensitive urban design', 'cool roofs' and new generation rating systems, such as the 'Living Building Challenge',[3] promote robust integrated systems for reducing urban heat by managing urban vegetation and water, as well as providing benefits to communities, such as food production and health benefits (Ely and Pitman 2012; Coutts et al. 2012; Norton et al. 2013). Numerous industry associations, government agencies and institutions provide planning and design research and tools for mitigating urban heat and creating thermally efficient, healthy comfortable cities.

Questions around air conditioning

Factors identified as strongly protective against the impacts of extreme heat include thermally efficient housing, household air conditioning, access to cooler environments and public awareness (McMichael et al. 2006; McInnes et al. 2008; Hajat et al. 2010). In Australia, the focus has been on air conditioning with the proportion of homes with air-conditioning units increasing dramatically over a short period of time, rising from 35 per cent in 1999 to around 73 per cent in 2011 (Topp and Kulys 2012). Households have typically taken a staged approach to managing comfort during hot weather before resorting to air conditioning, including wearing light clothing, closing blinds and increasing natural cross-ventilation (Saman et al. 2013).

The expansion of residential air conditioning has, however, attracted criticism. Fabotko and Waitt (2011) argue that residential air conditioning is a 'poorly conceived technological solution' to heatwave conditions, potentially exacerbating existing inequities and increasing vulnerability. Other critics suggest that the habituation to air-conditioned homes, workplaces and vehicles and the reduced incentive to adapt may inhibit acclimatisation and even threaten behavioural adaptation (Kovats and Hajat 2008; Hajat et al. 2010). Healy (2008) argues that the 'thermal monotony' of deliberately engineered indoor environments minimises thermal stimuli, such as the invigorating effects of 'fresh air', and confuses traditional human connections with time, weather and seasons. Barnett et al. (2013) found that the thermal performance of low-income housing and surrounds has a significant impact on temperatures, impacting on air-conditioning use and energy costs. Furthermore, during heatwaves air-conditioning use increases peak loads on electricity grids, adding to the potential for blackouts and requiring upgraded power infrastructure and higher service costs (Wang et al. 2010).

Successful adaptation, as a result, requires a move from sole dependence on residential air conditioning. Access to air conditioning in non-residential public spaces, for example, should become central planks in policy. As during recent heatwaves in Australia and Argentina, public 'cool spaces', such as libraries, greenspaces and pools, may safeguard people vulnerable to heat-health impacts, including those unable to afford air conditioning. Other air-conditioned facilities, such as recreation clubs and shopping centres, also offer protection but may restrict access to non-consumers (Fabotko and Waitt 2011).

Importantly, by cooling indoor environments, air-conditioning exhaust increases external ambient temperatures. Distinguishing its effect amongst all other urban thermal emissions is not feasible, but at microclimatic scale, one representative air conditioner thermally transferred $47\,^{\circ}$C of radiant heat into a $35\,^{\circ}$C summer afternoon, as measured in a thermal emissivity study in a medium density residential precinct in Sydney (Samuels et al. 2010).

Heat and outdoor activity

Macro- and microclimates influence human thermal comfort, behaviour and everyday activity in outdoor environments (Nikolopoulou and Lykoudis 2006; Eliasson et al. 2007; Chan and Ryan 2009; Gehl 2010). Consequently, urban design and planning supporting health need to be 'climate-responsive'. Yet, limited attention is given to urban heat.

Two examples where active transport (walking, cycling and public transport) strategies consider urban heat are specific to the subtropics. Transit-orientated development (TOD) guidelines for Florida, USA recognise that heat, humidity, strong sunshine and torrential downpours negatively impact on walking environments at certain times of year and significantly shorten walking trip lengths (Florida Department of Transportation and Department of Community Affairs 2011). Aligned with TOD guidelines for south-eastern Queensland, Australia (O'Hare 2006), recommendations include landscaping, shade, shelter and air movement to mitigate discomfort and improve walking environments, and concentrating land uses to reduce walking times.

Walkability guidelines are largely produced in temperate zones and promote the 400 metre (five minute) walk as the benchmark of urban walkability. In contrast, computer-modelling using climatic, urban density and behavioural data for Miami, Florida calculated a 'comfort ped' of 240 metres (three minute walk) during which the average individual maintains thermal comfort, 'even in the stifling humidity and still air of morning commute hours' (DeVeau 2011).

A study exploring public space use during hot weather in a disadvantaged suburb in Sydney identified a significant shift on very hot days towards a 'siesta', exhibited by unusual periods of low activity in the mid-afternoon, especially by older people. Public spaces were used for socialising and exercising by significantly more people and for longer periods in the evening on hot days. Limited greenspace and low quality, medium density housing without private gardens possibly influenced this behavioural shift. Results suggest adaptation planning requires local-level understanding of communities and priorities, and modification of public space design – and possibly service hours – to support physical activity patterns and informal social networks (McKenzie 2015).

In Australia, where human behaviour responds to temperature in concert with harmful ultraviolet radiation exposure (Makin 2011), there is a great opportunity to develop public policy around shade and comfort in public areas. For example, audits for programmes encouraging walking to and from school could assess shade provision in addition to road safety to reduce exposure to high temperatures and ultraviolet levels. Audits identifying paucity of shade may inform street tree planting programmes, as well as traffic management, useful to setting local government priorities.

Box 18.4 'Co-benefit' opportunities of adaptation

Increased greening reduces temperatures and provides comfortable environments for healthy behaviours, such as walking, cycling and public transport. In turn, increased healthy behaviours lead to reduced private vehicle use, obesity and chronic conditions, greenhouse gas emissions, air pollution and urban temperatures, and a more enjoyable and healthy outdoor environment (Walker et al. 2011; Bambrick et al. 2011).

Community resilience and local agency

Building community resilience and local agency is likely to be most successful when communities themselves play a role in contextualising heat vulnerability and assessing local-level adaptation capacity. Community development and cultural resources can usefully provide accessible information and assist communities to articulate vulnerabilities, adaptation priorities and informal social capital opportunities in relation to the 'patchwork mosaics of neighborhoods and households' within urban regions (Wilhelmi and Hayden 2010). Innovative examples include public seminars exploring the role of creative arts in stimulating responses to climate change (Griffith University 2013) and community engagement works, such as artist Hiromi Tango's (2014) response to the 2009 dust storm in the city of Brisbane, and influences on psychological and physical health.

Conclusions: future challenges for hotter cities

Climate change and urban heat pose an immense health challenge to people living in cities. City design and planning are critical to meeting this challenge. With cities warming at a greater rate than IPCC projections for the globe, the reduction of heat and creation of healthy environments must be primary objectives for urban policy and strategy. From 'whole of city' to streetscape scales, the plans we make, the materials we use, the built forms we construct, and the way we manage water and vegetation fundamentally influence the extent and rate of urban warming, and the quality of life and resilience of urban dwellers. With the knowledge, skills and technology now available to model, measure and monitor urban heat, decision-makers are well positioned to assess the long-term implications of policies and proposals. To what extent will increasing densities impact on urban heat? Will stormwater harvesting and vegetation be utilised to increase evaporative cooling? Will site planning and materials maximise thermal performance? Will children be protected from heat walking home from school? Will capital works budgets prioritise funding allocation for street trees, footpaths and 'cool places'? Cities are dynamic, in constant flux, with physical, social, cultural and economic environments continually shifting. City designers and planners must have their fingers on the pulse, gaining and sharing new knowledge, identifying emerging issues, and collaborating with researchers and industry partners to transform our cities into thermally comfortable, healthy and resilient environments.

Notes

1 http://plea-arch.org
2 www.usgbc.org/leed
3 http://living-future.org/lbc/about

References

Argüeso, D., Evans, J., Fita, L. and Bormann, K. 2013. Temperature response to future urbanization and climate change. *Climate Dynamics*, May.

Australian Bureau of Meteorology. 2014. Special climate statement 48: one of southeast Australia's most significant heatwaves. Available at: www.bom.gov.au/climate/current/statements/scs48.pdf. Accessed 23 March 2014.

Australian Commonwealth Government. 2011. Protecting human health and safety during severe and extreme heat events: a national framework. Available at: www.pwc.com.au/industry/government/assets/extreme-heat-events-nov11.pdf. Accessed 4 February 2014.

Bambrick, H., Dear, K., Woodruff, R., Hanigan, I. and McMichael, A.J. 2008. The impacts of climate change on three health outcomes: temperature-related mortality and hospitalisations, salmonellosis and other bacterial gastroenteritis, and population at risk from dengue. *Garnaut Climate Change Review*.

Bambrick, H., Capon, A., Barnett, G., Beaty, R. and Burton, A. (2011). Climate change and health in the urban environment: adaptation opportunities in Australian cities. *Asia-Pacific Journal of Public Health* Supplement 23 (2): 67S–79S.

Barnett, G., Beaty, R., Chen, D., McFallan, S., Meyers, J., Nguyen, M., Ren, Z., Spinks, A. and Wang, X. 2013. Pathways to climate adapted and healthy low income housing. *National Climate Change Adaptation Research Facility*.

Beggs, P. and Bennett, C. 2011. Climate change, aeroallergens, natural particulates, and human health in Australia: state of the science and policy. *Asia-Pacific Journal of Public Health* Supplement 23(2): 46S–53S.

Brown, H.L., Proust, K., Spickett, J. and Capon, A. 2011. The potential role of health impact assessment in tackling the complexity of climate change adaptation for health. *Health Promotion Journal of Australia* 22 Special Issue.

Business Insider Australia. 2014. Heatwave sweeps east across the country, mercury set to soar to 45. 13 January. Available at: www.businessinsider.com.au/graphics-heatwave-sweeps-eastbound-across-australia-mercury-set-to-soar-to-45–2014–1#heatwave. Accessed 23 March 2014.

Chan, C. and Ryan, D. (2009). Assessing the effects of weather conditions on physical activity participation using objective measures. *International Journal of Environmental Research and Public Health* 6: 2639–2654.

City of Sydney. 2014. Urban heat island effect. Available at: www.cityofsydney.nsw.gov.au/vision/sustainable-sydney-2030/sustainability/carbon-reduction/urban-heat-island. Accessed 14 February 2014.

Climate Council. 2014. Press release: interim findings on heatwaves. 17 January. Available at: www.climatecouncil.org.au/interim-heatwaves. Accessed 23 March 2014.

Coutts, A., Beringer, J. and Tapper, N. 2007. Impact of increasing urban density on local climate: spatial and temporal variations in the surface energy balance in Melbourne, Australia. *Journal of Applied Meteorology and Climatology* 46: 477–493.

Coutts, A.M., Tapper, N.J., Beringer, J., Loughnan M. and Demuzere, M. 2012. Watering our cities: the capacity for water sensitive urban design to support urban cooling and improve human thermal comfort in the Australian context. *Physical Geography* 37(1): 2–28.

DeVeau, M. 2011. Strategies to address the climatic barriers to walkable, transit-oriented communities in Florida. Master's thesis – Georgia Institute of Technology. Advisor: Brian Stone. Available at: https://smartech.gatech.edu/handle/1853/40779. Accessed 20 March 2014.

Drew, P. 1996. *Leaves of iron – Glenn Murcutt: pioneer of an Australian architectural form*. Australia: Angus & Robertson.

Eliasson, I., Knez, I., Westerberg, U., Thorsson, S. and Lindberg, F. 2007. Climate and behaviour in a Nordic City. *Landscape and Urban Planning* 82: 72–84.

Ely, M. and Pitman, S. 2012. Green infrastructure: life support for human habitats. *Green Infrastructure Project: Botanic Gardens of Adelaide*. South Australia: Department of Environment, Water and Natural Resources.

Farbotko, C. and Waitt, G. 2011. Residential air-conditioning and climate change: voices of the vulnerable. *Health Promotion Journal of Australia* 22 Special Issue.

Florida Department of Transportation and Department of Community Affairs. 2011. A framework for transit orientated development in Florida. Available at: www.fltod.com/renaissance/docs/Products/FrameworkTOD_0715.pdf. Accessed 24 March 2014.

Garnaut, R. 2008. *The Garnaut climate change review – 6. Climate change impacts on Australia*. Melbourne: Cambridge University Press. Available at: www.garnautreview.org.au/pdf/Garnaut_Chapter6.pdf. Accessed 26 August 2014.

Gartland, L. 2008. *Heat islands: understanding and mitigating heat in urban areas*. London: Earthscan

Gehl, J. 2010. *Cities for people*. Washington, DC: Island Press.

Givoni, B. 1998. *Climate considerations in building and urban design*. New York: Van Nostrand Reinhold.

Greater London Authority. 2011. London resilience heatwave plan. Available at: www.london.gov.uk/sites/default/files/archives/London-Resilience-Heatwave-Plan-version-1.pdf. Accessed 25 January 2014.

Griffith University. 2013. Climate change public seminar series: climates that art can change. 23 May. Available at: www.griffith.edu.au/research/research-excellence/griffith-climate-change-response-program/program. Accessed 20 February 2014.

Hajat, S., O'Connor, M. and Kosatsky, T. 2010. Health effects of hot weather: from awareness of risk factors to effective health protection. *Lancet* 375: 856–863.

Hansen, A., Bi, P., Nitschke, M., Pisaniello, D., Newbury J. and Kitson, A. 2011. Older persons and heat-susceptibility: the role of health promotion in a changing climate. *Health Promotion Journal of Australia* 22 Special Issue.

Hansen, A., Bi, P., Saniotis, A., Nitschke, M., Benson, J., Tan, Y., Smyth, V., Wilson, L. and Han, G. 2013. Extreme heat and climate change: adaptation in culturally and linguistically diverse (CALD) communities. *National Climate Change Adaptation Research Facility*. Available at: www.nccarf.edu.au/publications/extreme-heat-adaptation-cald. Accessed 28 January 2014.

Healy, S. 2008. Air-conditioning and the 'homogenization' of people and built environments. *Building Research & Information* 36(4): 312–322.

Hough, M. 1995. *Cities and natural process*. London: Routledge.

IPCC (Intergovernmental Panel on Climate Change). 2007. Summary for policymakers. In: M.L. Parry, O.F. Canziani, J.P. Palutikof, P.J. van der Linden and C.E. Hanson (eds.) *Climate change 2007: impacts, adaptation and vulnerability. Contributions of Working Group II to the Fourth Assessment Report of the Intergovernmental Panel on Climate Change*. Cambridge, UK: Cambridge University Press.

IPCC. 2013. Summary for policymakers. In: T.F. Stocker, D. Qin, G.-K. Plattner, M. Tignor, S.K. Allen, J. Boschung, A. Nauels, Y. Xia, V. Bex and P.M. Midgley (eds.) *Climate change 2013: the physical science basis. Contribution of Working Group I to the Fifth Assessment Report of the Intergovernmental Panel on Climate Change*. Cambridge, UK and New York: Cambridge University Press.

Kirkpatrick, J., Daniels, G. and Davison, A. 2011. Temporal and spatial variation in garden and street trees in six eastern Australian cities. *Landscape and Urban Planning* 101(3): 244–252.

Kjellstrom, T. and Weaver, H.J. 2009. Climate change and health: impacts, vulnerability, adaptation and mitigation. *NSW Public Health Bulletin* 20(1–2): 5–9.

Kolbe, A. and Gilchrist, K. 2009. An extreme bushfire smoke pollution event: health impacts and public health challenges. *New South Wales Public Health Bulletin* 20(2): 19–23.

Kovats, R. and Hajat, S. 2008. Heat stress and public health: a critical review. *Annual Review of Public Health* 29(1): 41–55.

Landry, S. and Chakraborty, J. 2009. Street trees and equity: evaluating the spatial distribution of an urban amenity. *Environment and Planning A* 41(11): 2651–2670.

Lee, C., Lewis, B., Shankie-Williams, N. and Mitchell, D. 2013. Towards a resilient Sydney: climate change adaptation planning for Sydney. *Proceedings from State of Australian Cities Conference 2013, Sydney*.

Loughnan, M., Tapper, N., Phan, T., Lynch, K. and McInnes, J. 2013. A spatial vulnerability analysis of urban populations during extreme heat events in Australian capital cities. Available at: www.nccarf. edu.au/sites/default/files/attached_files_publications/Loughnan_2013_Spatial_vulnerability_analysis. pdf. Accessed 28 January 2014.

Lowe, I. 2005. Sunshine, social factors, solar energy and sustainability. In: T. Sherratt, T. Griffiths and L. Robin (eds.) *A change in the weather: climate and culture in Australia.* Canberra: National Museum of Australia Press, pp. 116–125.

McHarg, I. 1992. *Design with nature: 25th anniversary edition.* New York: John Wiley & Sons Inc.

McInnes, J., Ibrahim, J. and Loughnan, M. 2008. Reducing harm to older persons in Victoria from extreme hot weather: literature review. Melbourne, Victoria: Centre of Research Excellence in Patient Safety, Monash University, Medicine, Nursing and Health Sciences.

McKenzie, L. 2015. Design, context and use of public space: the influence of heat on everyday activity and implications for health and wellbeing – a Western Sydney case study. PhD thesis in progress, University of NSW. For submission in 2015.

McMichael, A.J., Woodruff, R.E. and Hales, S. 2006. Climate change and human health: present and future risks. *The Lancet* 367(9513): 859–869.

Makin, J. 2011. Implications of climate change for skin cancer prevention in Australia. *Health Promotion Journal of Australia* 22 Special Issue.

Nairn, J. and Fawcett, R. 2013. Defining heatwaves: heatwave defined as a heat impact event servicing all community and business sectors in Australia. The Centre for Australian Weather and Climate Research, Partnership between CSIRO and the Bureau of Meteorology, Australia. March.

Naughton, M., Henderson, A., Mirabelli, M., Kaiser, R., Wilhelm, J., Kieszak, S., Rubin, C. and McGeehin, M. 2002. Heat-related mortality during a 1999 heat wave in Chicago. *American Journal of Preventive Medicine* 2(4): 221–227.

Nikolopoulou, M. and Lykoudis, S. 2006. Thermal comfort in outdoor urban spaces: analysis across different European countries. *Building and Environment* 41: 1455–1470.

Norton, B., Coutts, A., Livesley, S. and Williams, N. 2013. Decision principles for the selection and placement of green infrastructure to mitigate urban hotspots and heat waves. A report for the Victorian Centre for Climate Change Adaptation Research (VCCCAR), Victoria. March.

O'Hare, D. 2006. Urban walkability in the subtropical city: some intemperate considerations from SEQ. *Proceedings from Subtropical Cities 2006 Conference.*

Oliveira, S., Andrade, H. and Vaz, T. 2011. The cooling effect of green spaces as a contribution to the mitigation of urban heat: a case study in Lisbon. *Building and Environment* 46(11): 2186–2194.

Patz, J. and Kovats, R. 2002. Hotspots in climate change and human health. *British Medical Journal* 325: 1094–1098.

Pitman, A., Arneth, A. and Ganzeveld, L. 2012. Regionalizing global climate models. *International Journal of Climatology* 32: 321–337.

Preston, B.L. and Stafford-Smith, M. 2009. Framing vulnerability and adaptive capacity assessment: discussion paper. CSIRO Climate Adaptation Flagship Working Paper No. 2. Available at: www.csiro. au/org/ClimateAdaptationFlagship.html. Accessed 28 January 2014.

Reid, C., Mann, J., Alfasso, R., English, P., King, G., Lincoln, R., Margolis, H., Rubado, D., Sabato, J., West, N., Woods, B., Navarro, K. and Balmes, J. 2012. Evaluation of a heat vulnerability index on abnormally hot days: an environmental public health tracking study. *Environmental Health Perspectives* 120(5): 715–720.

Rose, D. 2005. Rhythms, patterns, connectivities: indigenous concepts of seasons and change. In: T. Sherratt, T. Griffiths and L. Robin (eds.) *A change in the weather: climate and culture in Australia.* Canberra: National Museum of Australia Press, pp. 32–41.

Saman, W., Boland, J., Pullen, S., de Dear, R., Soebarto, V., Miller, W., Pocock, B., Belusko, M., Bruno, F., Whaley, D., Pockett, J., Bennetts, H., Ridley, B., Palmer, J., Zuo, J., Ma, T., Chileshe, N., Skinner, N., Chapman, J., Vujinovic, N., Walsh, M., Candido, C. and Deuble, M. 2013. A framework for adaptation of Australian households to heat waves. National Climate Change Adaptation Research Facility, Gold Coast. Available at: www.nccarf.edu.au/sites/default/files/attached_files_publications/ Saman_2013_Adapting_households_to_heat_waves.pdf. Accessed 22 March 2014.

Samuels, R., Randolph, B., Graham, P., McCormick, T. and Pollard, B. 2010. Final report: micro-urban-climatic thermal emissions: in a medium-density residential precinct. City futures. The University of New South Wales. Available at: www.be.unsw.edu.au/sites/default/files/upload/pdf/cf/research/ cityfuturesprojects/heatisland/Final_Report_Hassell.pdf. Accessed 22 March 2014.

Spickett, J., Brown, H. and Rumchev, K. 2011. Climate change and air quality: the potential impact on health. *Asia-Pacific Journal of Public Health* 23(2) Supplement.

Stones Jnr, B. 2012. *The city and the coming climate: climate change in the places we live.* New York: Cambridge University Press.

Tango, H. 2014. Hiromi Tango: infinity magnet. Available at: http://hiromitango.com/Insanity-Magnet. Accessed 30 May 2014.

The Advertiser. 2014. Adelaide is the hottest city on earth today – and CFS warns of extreme bushfire danger on Frida. 16 January. Available at: www.adelaidenow.com.au/news/south-australia/adelaide-is-the-hottest-city-on-earth-today-and-cfs-warns-of-extreme-bushfire-danger-on-friday/story-fnl1ee8j-1226802735418. Accessed 23 March 2014.

The Age. 2014. Melbourne lord mayor Robert Doyle backs 'oases' for homeless in heatwave. 31 January. Available at: www.theage.com.au/victoria/melbourne-lord-mayor-robert-doyle-backs-oases-for-homeless-in-heatwave-20140130–31pqx.html#ixzz2zZtnWlMJ. Accessed 23 March 2014.

The Guardian. 2013. We need to talk about bushfires and climate change – if not now, when? 21 October. Available at: www.theguardian.com/world/2013/oct/21/we-need-to-talk-about-bushfires-and-climate-change-if-not-now-when. Accessed 20February 2014.

Time. 2014. Australia is melting under a horrifying heatwave. 17 January. Available at: http://time.com/1032/australia-is-melting-under-a-horrifying-heatwave. Accessed 23 March 2014.

Topp, V. and Kulys, T. 2012. Productivity in electricity, gas and water: measurement and interpretation. Canberra: Productivity Commission Staff Working Paper.

Trewin, B., Jones, D., Braganza, K., Plummer, N. and Smalley, R. 2014. 2013 was Australia's hottest year, warm for much of the world. The Conversation, 3 January. Available at: http://theconversation.com/2013-was-australias-hottest-year-warm-for-much-of-the-world-21670. Accessed 3 January 2014.

Victorian Department of Health. 2011. Heatwave plan for Victoria: protecting health and reducing harm from heatwaves. Available at: http://docs.health.vic.gov.au/docs/doc/45C7A59BDE5B1E95CA257A360015AAB5/$FILE/Heatwave%20plan%20for%20Victoria.pdf. Accessed 28 January 2014.

Walker, R., Hassall, J., Chaplin, S., Congues, J., Bajayo, R. and Mason, W. 2011. Health promotion interventions to address climate change using a primary health care approach: a literature review. *Health Promotion Journal of Australia* 22 Special Issue.

Wang, X., Chen, D. and Ren, Z. 2010. Assessment of climate change impact on residential building heating and cooling energy requirement in Australia. *Building and Environment* 45: 1663–1682.

WHO. 2012. Atlas of health and climate. Available at: www.who.int/globalchange/publications/atlas/report/en. Accessed 23 March 2014.

Wilhelmi, O. and Hayden, M. 2010. Connecting people and place: a new framework for reducing urban vulnerability to extreme heat. *Environmental Research Letters* 5(014021).

WMO (World Meteorological Organization). 2014. Extreme weather in parts of the world. Available at: www.wmo.int/pages/mediacentre/news/ExtremeWeatherinpartsoftheworld.html. Accessed 23 March 2014.

Yang, F., Lau, S. and Qian, F. 2011. Urban design to lower summertime outdoor temperatures: an empirical study on high-rise housing in Shanghai. *Building and Environment* 46(3): 769–785.

Yeang, K. 1995. *Designing with nature: the ecological basis for architectural design.* New York: McGraw-Hill School Education Group.

Other resources

- Leadership in Energy & Environmental Design (LEED), www.usgbc.org/articles/about-leed
- WHO – Health Impact Assessment and Health in the Green Economy, www.who.int/hia/green_economy/en/index.html

19

HOUSING, ENERGY EFFICIENCY AND FUEL POVERTY

Brenda Boardman

Introduction: the problem of fuel poverty

Fuel poverty occurs when a low-income household cannot pay for the energy services that it needs from a reasonable proportion of income. All aspects of this definition are country specific: a reasonable proportion of income depends upon both the levels of income and fuel prices. In a country with high fuel prices, such as many Eastern European countries and Northern Ireland, the proportion is likely to be high. The energy services required vary with the geographical location and severity of the winter and the energy efficiency of the dwelling: an energy inefficient home in a country with short winters could cost more to heat than an energy efficient property in a country with a long, hard winter. The concept, however, is universal – even the poorest people should be able to afford the heating, lighting and other energy services that are considered a basic requirement by the average household. A useful rule of thumb is that no household should have to pay more than twice the median proportion of income on fuel. This was the basis for the original UK definition: in 1988, the average household spent 5 per cent on fuel, so twice the median and the original definition of fuel poverty was that it occurred if the required expenditure exceeded 10 per cent of income (Boardman 1991, p. 205).

The phrase 'fuel poverty' was first coined in the UK after the oil crisis in 1973 as a result of the substantial increase in fuel-related problems. These were not in themselves new, just of a greater magnitude than before. The symptoms of fuel poverty – debt and disconnections – were early indicators and demonstrated the roles of both high fuel prices and low incomes. The role of the third factor, energy inefficient housing, was the focus of the publication *Fuel poverty: from cold homes to affordable warmth* (Boardman 1991). This confirmed that poor quality housing is the real cause of fuel poverty and, hence, improving it is the only long-term solution. Anyone living in an energy inefficient home has to buy expensive warmth: most of the heat is produced in inefficient heating systems, often using expensive fuels (for example oil and electricity) and the building fabric does a poor job of retaining the warmth, so it is lost to the outside quickly. The benefit of the warmth is short-lived, despite its high cost. To obtain longer-lasting and cheaper warmth requires high levels of insulation in the fabric, an efficient heating system and the use of less expensive fuels. This implies substantial capital investment.

It is the role of capital that distinguishes fuel poverty from other forms of poverty: additional income will reduce poverty, but is a recurring and expensive solution to fuel poverty.

Only substantial capital investment to the energy efficiency of the building and its heating system will limit the extent of fuel poverty, permanently. If the aim of society is to ensure that the poorest people can afford to be warm, then the implication is that it is these people who should live in the most energy efficient properties – those that are the cheapest to heat. In most countries, the opposite is the case. This makes tackling fuel poverty particularly tough for policy makers as it requires overcoming market trends.

Fuel poverty is not only about keeping warm, though this is the largest fuel expenditure and the one most linked to keeping healthy. The other energy services – hot water, lighting, the use of appliances – are all included in reality, as they are an indistinguishable part of the household's fuel bills. These other energy services also have links to health: well-lit stairs reduce the risk of a fall; hot water for washing people and clothes is important for hygiene and keeping food cold avoids it deteriorating and causing infection. Another part of the definition, which is accepted, but is difficult to measure, is that 'adequate energy services' should be what the household needs, not just what it can at present afford. A low-income household that is economising on fuel bills and living in the cold is in fuel poverty, so its current level of expenditure is not a good indicator of what is needed. The required levels of consumption of the other energy services are poorly understood, but may equally be higher in fuel poor homes, particularly where there is a disability.

On the positive side, knowledge is accumulating from the way that fuel poverty is being tackled in different jurisdictions and what is working or not (Boardman 2012a).

International perspectives

Initially, fuel poverty was a recognised social problem only in the UK, Ireland and New Zealand. The UK has a legacy of energy inefficient buildings that justifies its title as the 'Cold Man of Europe'. On a range of measures, the UK performs worse than other European countries

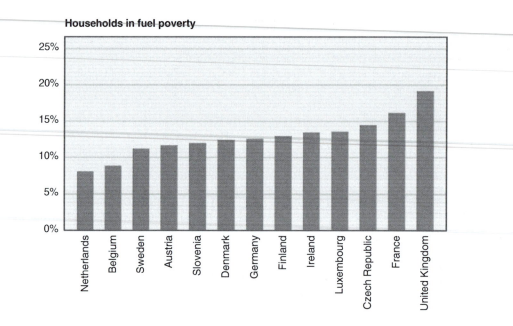

Figure 19.1 Proportion of households in fuel poverty in Western European countries, and ranking, 2011
Source: Based on EBR (2013).

and so is thought to have the greatest level of fuel poverty (Figure 19.1). Much of the developed world initially thought it was not affected. This is in the process of changing quite rapidly as shown by European projects that look at comparisons across Member States (for instance the ACHIEVE project[1]) and enable researchers to network with each other (Thomson[2]).

One of the factors that has influenced the growth of fuel poverty in the ex-communist countries of Eastern and Central Europe (ECE) has been the liberalisation of the energy market. Previously, in many of these countries, the rent for the property included the cost of heating and electricity, both at nominal prices. As a result, the properties were poorly insulated and the heating system lacked controls – these were deemed unnecessary. Since 1990, the state has been removing the subsidies and imposing prices that are closer to market costs. The result has been substantial price increases and severe hardship in many countries, coupled with limited ability to control the size of the fuel bill. Several authors have been reporting on the growth of fuel poverty in ECE (Buzar 2007; Herrero and Urge-Vorsatz 2012).

This developing situation, partly exposed when the ECE countries joined the European Union (EU), increased the pressure on the European Commission to look at fuel poverty (sometimes called energy poverty) and introduce legislation. The electricity and gas directives (2009/72/EC; 2009/73/EC) in the third energy package required EU Member States to report on fuel poverty in their country and how it is being tackled. While the official response has been limited, the mere existence of the legislation has pushed fuel poverty up the political agenda. In most cases, when researchers have started to look in their own country for the problem of fuel poverty they have found it (for example Dubois 2012; Brunner et al. 2012).

The requirement for capital investment to solve the problem of fuel poverty begs the question of who is providing the money. What should be the contribution from:

- The building owner, who has the equity in the building?
- The building occupant, who will benefit from any reduction in running costs?
- All taxpayers, via the Treasury? This is probably the most progressive approach.
- All energy-bill payers, via the utilities? It is difficult to make this progressive, that is, to ensure that the fuel poor receive more benefit than they contribute.
- When should the finance be provided as a grant and when as a loan? The latter is rarely applicable to the fuel poor, as the reduction in running costs will be insufficient to service a loan at commercial rates, as has been demonstrated in the UK with the Green Deal.

With all fuel poverty programmes there is a tension between spending money solely on the fuel poor, with all the targeting and stigma issues that this raises, or taking a more holistic view of the housing stock so that there are a range of policies for the different income groups receiving a grant. The latter can be justified in terms of climate change policy.

In France, the proceeds of the EU emissions trading scheme auctions are being targeted on energy efficiency improvements for the fuel poor (EurActiv 2012). Eight other Member States (including Germany, Italy, Romania, Czech Republic) have similar policies and this is proposed by the Energy Bill Revolution for the UK.

Some commercial approaches can be helpful to the fuel poor, for instance community heating systems and energy saving companies (ESCOs). Both involve non-domestic properties and heat networks for a whole area, with district heating widely used in areas of Europe where there is a limited gas-distribution network. Unless there is central or local government support, ESCOs involve a financial levy on the users, so have to be carefully designed to assist the fuel poor. Similarly, a national feed-in-tariff (FIT) can be utilised, where the installer puts photovoltaics on the roof of a low-income household and keeps the FIT to pay for the installation.

The householder benefits from free electricity when it is sunny and this might amount to 50 per cent of all electricity consumption.

It is clear that the appropriate policies are country specific, but that there are large sums of money being generated from energy-related activities that could provide funds. The co-benefits of investing in the infrastructure, climate change mitigation, employment creation and better health, are rarely adequately taken into account, but provide powerful additional justification.

Comfort and health

The World Health Organization has been providing guidance on the temperatures that deliver a healthy home environment since about 1968 (Ormandy and Ezratty 2012) – we are not ignorant about what is needed. There are both direct and indirect effects on well-being: physical and mental ill health are both major results of the problem of fuel poverty. Hard evidence of the links between cold homes and ill health are difficult to obtain (Tanner et al. 2013), partly because of the logistical complexity of linking temperature monitoring with someone who might get ill. The most quoted figure is the number of excess winter deaths (EWD) – that is, the number of people who died of cold-related diseases during the four winter months, who would not have died if it had stayed summer all year round. The main causes are heart attacks, strokes and respiratory disease, including flu. There is little seasonal fluctuation in the number of deaths from cancer.

In England and Wales, the exceptionally cold winter December 2012–March 2013 resulted in 31,100 EWD, a 29 per cent increase over the year before. In comparison, there were less than 2,000 deaths on UK roads in 2013. There is considerable caution about the proportion of EWD that can be linked to cold homes, partly because of the political implications, but few are due to hypothermia when the body's core temperature becomes very low, for instance as a result of a fall outside.

EWD do not increase as much in countries with colder climates that have well-insulated properties. Hence, there is a lower incidence of EWD in Scandinavia, Russia, Canada – EWD in the UK are 23 per cent higher than in Sweden (EBR and ACE 2013b, p. 4). Whereas countries with short but potentially harsh winters, such as Portugal and northern Greece, show a similar rate of EWD to the UK (Healy 2003; EBR and ACE 2013a, p. 14). The common understanding for this somewhat obverse outcome is that countries with relatively mild winters have not historically stressed the need for energy efficiency in their building stock and therefore have a legacy of homes that cannot easily and cheaply be kept warm.

Someone who is in fuel poverty has difficulty keeping warm in a normal winter, so the extra cold can rarely be met with an increase in spending on fuel. The budgeting task is exacerbated as many low-income households pay for fuel as it is used, for instance through a prepayment meter or monthly bills. They are not able to spread the expenditure evenly over the year, as wealthier individuals on a direct debit or payment plan can, either because they do not have a bank account or are not creditworthy or do not want the risk of debt.

The strain of trying to keep adequately warm while fearing the size of the energy bill causes substantial mental stress. Many people report feeling less anxiety as a result of an energy efficiency improvement, in addition to feeling warmer (Gilbertson et al. 2012). Studies show that another component in the struggle to pay the fuel bills is the sheer ignorance of what energy costs and which equipment uses the most. There are heartbreaking examples, like the woman with chronic arthritis who crawled upstairs rather than use the electric chair lift, to save money. The cost would have been at most 5p per trip (that is, 5 minutes use of a 5kW machine at 13p/kWh).

The much quoted phrase to describe the challenge faced by the fuel poor is that they have to choose between 'heating and eating'. As a generalisation, families with young children are often prepared to go into debt in order to keep the babies warm. Pensioners, on the other hand, will not risk getting into debt as their incomes will never be higher. They are, therefore, the group that is most likely to be in extreme cold. Many of the fuel poor – those with children, pensioners, the unemployed, the disabled – are at home most of the day. They do not go out to work where the employer pays for the heating. Thus, a condition of the fuel poor is to have a high demand for heating and large fuel bills if the home is energy inefficient (Boardman 2010, p. 178). The poorest households need a lot of something that is expensive, but essential for health – a terrible dilemma for them.

For every EWD in England, in the winter there are eight people admitted to hospital and 100 visits to doctors (Wookey pers comm 2014). The statistics on the costs to the NHS are limited, but patently substantial. Each local authority now has a Health and Wellbeing Board (HWB), to add to their responsibilities for housing. Many are giving priority to the Marmot Review's six policy objectives for reducing health inequalities (Humphries and Galea 2013), three of which are:

- ensure a healthy standard of living for all;
- create and develop healthy and sustainable places and communities;
- strengthen the role and impact of ill-health prevention.

It is not yet clear how this will relate to housing policies, or the links between social deprivation, poor quality housing and fuel poverty, though the HWB have increasing involvement in decisions on major health expenditure.

One of the constraints for fuel poverty policy is the absence of temperature monitoring in the home. The last comprehensive national survey was undertaken in 1996 and, since then, the temperatures being achieved in the home have been inferred from consumption data. This is totally inadequate, especially because of the large fuel price rises that have occurred since 2004 and with the continuing squeeze on incomes and benefits as a result of the recession. Large numbers of low-income households are probably living in cold homes without the ability to respond to severe weather, as demonstrated by the increase in EWD in 2012–2013.

When there are exceptionally hot summers, as in 2003, there is a peak in summer deaths. The evidence is that these are predominantly elderly people and occur when the night-time temperature does not go below 25°C. This means that the buildings cannot cool down enough at night, to limit the daytime temperature increase. In the UK it is thought that up to 2,000 people died from heat-related causes, and in France up to 15,000 (Met Office 2003; White 2004). A properly insulated home provides protection against both cold and heat, for instance by recognising the importance of the heat (or cold) stored in the thermal mass, but there is virtually no preparation in the UK for future heat waves.

Variations in residential energy efficiency

There is a range of factors that determine the energy efficiency of a property and, therefore, the cost of keeping it warm.

First, heat is lost to the cold outside, so the number of external surfaces is strongly influential. (There is a convention that there is no heat movement across a party wall.) A flat in the middle of a block of flats has only one external surface, a terraced house has three and a detached house has six. The relative heat loss through external surfaces depends not only on type of structure (roof or wall), but also on orientation and aspect relative to sun, night sky and prevailing wind. As a result, rates of heat loss for similar sized properties can vary by a factor of two, or even more. Conversely, it can be more difficult to make substantial energy efficiency improvements to some types of property, for example, flats, as the opportunities are less.

Second, the type of construction has changed over the years and is gradually becoming better at retaining heat. Several attributes of the original building are impossible to change, for instance orientation and how many external walls it has, and others are effectively fixed, such as wall type and the level of insulation (or not) in the floor. With existing homes, the opportunities and cost of improving the energy efficiency have strong links to the date of construction – an unimproved, older dwelling is almost certainly one of the least energy efficient. For instance, anything built before about 1930 probably has a solid wall, with no cavity to trap air or contain insulation. A solid wall can only be insulated internally (disruptive to decor and makes the room smaller) or externally (better, but alters the appearance of the property (Figure 19.2). External insulation to the back of a property, where it cannot be seen, solves part of this problem).

The other major component of the energy efficiency of the dwelling is the heating system and the fuel used: these are interconnected as few heating systems can use more than one fuel. In each country, the choice and cost of fuels vary, but there are major financial benefits to having an efficient, modern system using the cheapest fuels. There are also large variations in the carbon intensity of the different fuels: those using renewable sources of energy (often electricity) result in no carbon emissions, in comparison with anything derived from fossil fuels, with coal being the worst.

A final factor affecting the cost of keeping warm and fuel poverty is the relationship between the size of the dwelling, the number of occupants and the resultant income – often the fuel poor are under-occupying their home. This means that there may be only one small income with which to provide the energy services for a largish house, perhaps the original family home.

Figure 19.2 Solid wall insulation and replacement windows transform an Easington terrace in County Durham, UK

Source: Boardman.

Women are thought to be the most reluctant to move and downsize, because of their strong emotional attachment to the property (CLF 2013).

As a result of the Energy Performance of Buildings Directives (EPBD), each European Member State has a system of grading the energy efficiency of buildings, often using the familiar EU scale of A–G (where A is the best) found on appliances. It is, thus, possible to identify the worst, least energy efficient buildings in each country and to have targets to systematically improve the calibre of the stock. The speed and scale of activity needed varies, but should be substantial to comply with the needs of climate change mitigation (Boardman 2012b). Germany has one of the most successful approaches (Rosenow et al. 2013) using the rate of interest on loans to encourage greater activity.

The average energy efficiency of the stock is affected by the churn in the stock, particularly the rates of construction and demolition. As the population increases and the size of households continues to fall (less than the 2.3 people per household in the UK in 2011 – ONS 2011), there needs to be a bigger housing stock every year. All new additions should be relatively energy efficient, as they have to comply with national building regulations and the EPBD, although the standard of construction can undermine this improvement (Bell et al. 2010). In the UK, the rate of demolition is both very low and not necessarily linked to the worst, least energy efficient homes. About 20,000 properties a year are demolished (Boardman et al. 2005, p. 87), which means that the present stock of 27 million homes will not be replaced for over 1,300 years. Therefore, in the UK, up to 95 per cent of the homes that are already built will still be occupied in 2050.

In most situations it is likely that few new build homes are made available to the fuel poor, but in all cases it is important that new construction results in either minimal additional energy demands or, better still, uses renewables to produce more energy than it consumes. This requires considerable attention to detail and the involvement of planning for minimal energy use from the beginning of the design process – too often energy services are only considered at a late stage. For instance, orientation has implications for the opportunities to use roof-mounted renewables, passive solar gain and heat loss due to prevailing winds. The design of glazing and entrances is also important. Planting trees throughout a neighbourhood can reduce housing heat loss through wind chill by 5 per cent (Finbow 1988). It is also vital that the location reflects the needs of the fuel poor (good access to amenities on foot or by inexpensive public transport), as well as the relevant microclimate and the risk of flooding. The location, siting, design and landscape of new housing in order to minimise energy costs and carbon emissions is a critical planning issue. Many guides now offer information and skills advice to assist.

Where there is a slow rate of turnover in the housing stock, as in the UK, it has another effect: household size is reducing faster than the change in the size of the average home, which means that the space per person is constantly increasing. And more space implies more energy consumption – heating and lighting are usually related to the space, whereas hot water and most other uses are linked to the number of people. A focus on reducing the carbon footprint of a population should incorporate policies to ensure that smaller properties are available for these smaller households.

The UK government uses the Standard Assessment Procedure (SAP)[3] to model the energy efficiency of dwellings and this is used on the Energy Performance Certificates (EPC).[4] The SAP covers the use of energy for space and water heating (mainly gas) and fixed lighting – the regulated uses. The remaining energy is predominantly electricity for appliances – the unregulated uses. As homes become better insulated with more efficient heating systems, the proportion of energy, carbon and expenditure that is omitted from the EPC is growing and represents a substantial policy challenge (Boardman 2012b, p. 24). In a brand new home or in a passivhaus,[5]

Figure 19.3   Living in a passivhaus provides a modern standard of comfort without hurting the environment

Source: Boardman.

around 80 per cent of energy is used in the unregulated activities, depending on the calibre of the construction (Figure 19.3).

Lessons from the UK

The UK has had long experience of trying to tackle fuel poverty. While this has been of limited success, there are some lessons of relevance to other countries (Boardman 2012a). Perhaps the two most important findings are the central role of capital investment and the benefits of targeting the worst homes in the context of the whole housing stock. Thus, policies on fuel poverty and climate change are coming together: they are definitely not in conflict. There is still a political debate about the extent to which better-off households should be subsidised when making their homes more energy efficient and the extent to which the improvements should be required by regulation. Whichever approach is taken, it becomes more difficult and/or more expensive to achieve as time passes.

The situation with regard to fuel poverty in the UK is in considerable flux as the government has introduced a new definition for England – Wales, Scotland and Northern Ireland are keeping the old definition. In England in 2014, there will be 2.46m–4.82m (11–22 per cent) households in fuel poverty, depending on which definition is used (EBR and ACE 2014, p. 4): the lower figure comes with the new definition (Hills 2012). Whichever number is used, it is a substantial proportion of the housing stock that has to be upgraded. Limited progress is being made on energy efficiency improvements and is certainly insufficient to offset the drop in real incomes of the poorer households and rising fuel prices. Thus, fuel poverty is getting worse and this is likely to continue for the foreseeable future.

Note that the detailed debate about definitions usually just refers to the monitoring and modelling of the problem. While this is essential for policy makers and campaigners, it is important to also focus on the needs of the delivery agent: how to identify a fuel poor household on the doorstep. For practical purposes, a level of simplicity is required, otherwise the front door has been closed and the householder receives no help.

For a variety of reasons, tenure and energy efficiency are correlated. In the UK, there is a clear difference between the energy efficiency of social housing (belonging to a local authority or housing association) and that of the private sector (whether rented or owner-occupied). Social housing has a high proportion of flats, with a smaller floor area, that have been built more recently, been better maintained and are more likely to have had energy efficiency upgrades. They are, therefore, more energy efficient than those in the private sector. Over the ten years 2001–2011, both groups improved by 10 SAP points (Figure 19.4). The average rate of improvement of 1 SAP point per annum is what is required until 2050, if the housing stock is going to reduce carbon emissions by the amount required to comply with the 2050 target of the Climate Change Act 2008 (Boardman 2012b).

There is growing recognition that policies to provide individual measures to individual households have ceased to be effective. To use the money effectively requires accurate targeting of the fuel poor, but this in turn costs a considerable amount of money (perhaps £300–400 per targeted property), before any investment can be offered. As a result of poor targeting, most previous fuel poverty policies in the UK have only achieved an average of 20 per cent being actually available for the fuel poor (Boardman 2010, p. 66).

The debate is now switching from the installation of individual measures to the benefit provided by area-based approaches combined with substantial upgrades, where every household is visited and given the opportunity to participate in the programme. This:

- brings economies of scale at the household level, for instance where only one set of scaffolding is used to install both solar technology and insulate a solid wall externally;
- brings economies of scale at the community level, as contractors move from house to house, rather than travelling between jobs. This is especially important in rural areas;
- builds on an existing community, with neighbours providing reassurance to each other. This is of crucial importance as many of the most severely fuel poor are thought to hide and refuse help, for fear of unwanted repercussions (Boardman 2010);
- develops the involvement of the community through discussion on the design and implementation of the project, together with utilising the skills of a local workforce, as demonstrated through the Centre for Sustainable Energy's PlanLocal.[6]

Area-based approaches have been implemented in England through Warm Zones for several years (CSE 2003). In Northern Ireland, Census Output Areas (about 125 households) are being used successfully to target areas of concentrated fuel poverty and to provide generous grants for

	2001	2011
Social sector	52.1	62.9
Private sector	45.3	55.4
Average	46.7	56.7

Figure 19.4 SAP ratings by tenure, England, 2001–2011

Source: English Housing Survey (2013, Table 4.1, Annex).

improving the property for those on a low income (Liddell and McKenzie 2013). The aim is both to treat and prevent fuel poverty – a wider aim than other jurisdictions.

These practical examples from Northern Ireland and Warm Zones demonstrate that treating the homes of the fuel poor has to be set in the context of upgrading the whole housing stock. This is partly because under the Climate Change Act 2008, the UK has an extremely challenging commitment to reducing greenhouse gases by 80 per cent by 2050. While some of the carbon reduction may come from the decarbonisation of the electricity supply, it is cheaper – and possibly more achievable – to reduce demand for all fuels (Boardman 2012b). Reducing fuel poverty is only one part of the challenge of delivering on climate change commitments. A major benefit of an area-based approach in each local authority is that it generates local employment, throughout the country.

The level of demand reduction achieved in practice will depend upon the strength of policies enacted and the clarity of government vision for the whole housing stock. Some of the core elements in the proposal are:

- to ensure that energy efficient properties have greater value;
- to contribute to this by introducing mandatory minimum standards of energy efficiency, at the point of sale, that become tighter over time;
- to clarify that it is the property owner, not the occupant, that is responsible for achieving this level of energy efficiency – just as it is the owner who is responsible for maintaining the integrity of the fabric and dealing with health and safety;
- a major role for regulation and minimum standards.

Conclusions: reducing inequity, mitigating climate change

Fuel poverty is a serious social problem that exacerbates health inequalities, since the poorest people live in many of the least energy efficient homes. It undoubtedly exists in every country where there is a demand for heating in winter, but is most prevalent where there is a stock of poor quality, energy inefficient homes, such as the UK and Eastern and Central Europe. In the latter, the situation is a direct result of past communist policies on cheap heating and electricity when there was no emphasis on energy efficiency. The substantial ill-health effects that result from this legacy of energy inefficient homes are rarely brought into the policy debate and even less into calculations of costs and benefits. There is a flurry of media attention when the statistics are published on excess winter deaths, or hospital beds fill up during a cold spell. Then the focus disappears for another year.

A household on a low income has, inevitably, no capital to spend on energy efficiency improvements. So these will only occur in the home if someone else provides the funds. The perceived roles of the state, the utilities, the health service and the property owner fluctuate and are in need of clarification. What is not in dispute is that the housing stock, and indeed the entire building stock, are an extremely important part of the country's infrastructure and should be properly maintained for this reason (Boardman 2012b, p. 2). In many countries, private expenditure on buildings is usually in the form of maintenance and improvements that are thought to add value to the property, such as extra space in conservatories or a room-in-the roof. As yet, there are few links between the value of the property and its energy efficiency. If policy could engender that link, for instance through the introduction of minimum standards of energy performance, then the market would be working towards the elimination of the worst properties. This is needed both for alleviating the worst health outcomes associated with fuel poverty and for mitigating climate change. Whatever practical policies are introduced, a comprehensive housing policy is required to combat climate change and focusing this on areas of fuel poverty will be the first essential and humane step.

Notes

1 ACHIEVE (ACtion in low-income Households to Improve energy Efficiency through Visits and Energy diagnosis) is an EU wide action for practical and structural solutions that help Europeans to reduce fuel poverty. For further information see: www.achieve-project.eu
2 http://fuelpoverty.eu/contributors
3 Standard Assessment Procedure (SAP) is the British government's recommended system for energy rating of dwellings, using a scale of 1–100 for the modelled annual energy costs of space and water heating and fixed lighting. 100 is the best.
4 Energy Performance Certificate (EPC) – in the UK, the SAP (see above) is used to grade the energy efficiency of the dwelling and place it in one of the seven bands, A–G, coloured green to red. The grading is portrayed on the EPC, together with the associated Carbon Index, and recommendations for the most cost-effective improvements.
5 Passivhaus, originally a German concept, now used widely, are new buildings that are so well insulated they can be heated by passive sources of heat only (sunlight, human bodies, waste heat from appliances). A passivhaus does not require an active heating or cooling system: the house maintains a good level of thermal comfort in all seasons. For refurbishment of existing homes, the equivalent standard is EnerPHit: www.passivhaus.org.uk
6 www.planlocal.org.uk

References

Bell, M., Wingfield, J., Miles-Shenton, D. and Seavers, J. 2010. *Low carbon housing: lessons from Elm Tree Mews*. Joseph Rowntree Foundation. www.jrf.org.uk/publications/low-carbon-housing-elm-tree-mews

Boardman, B. 1991. *Fuel poverty: from cold homes to affordable warmth*. Belhaven: Wiley

Boardman, B. 2010. *Fixing fuel poverty: challenges and solutions*. Earthscan. London

Boardman, B. 2012a. Fuel poverty synthesis: Lessons learnt, actions needed. *Energy Policy*. 49, 143–148

Boardman, B. 2012b. *Achieving zero: delivering future-friendly buildings*. A report for Greenpeace Environmental Trust. Environmental Change Institute, University of Oxford

Boardman, B., Darby, S., Killip, G., Hinnells, M., Jardine, C.N., Palmer, J. and Sinden, G. 2005. *40% house*. Environmental Change Institute, University of Oxford

Brunner, K.-M. Spitzer, M. and Christanell, A. 2012. Experiencing fuel poverty: coping strategies for low-income households in Vienna/Austria. *Energy Policy*. 49, 53–59

Buzar, S. 2007. *Energy poverty in Eastern Europe: hidden geographies of deprivation*. Ashgate. Aldershot

CLF. 2013. Chesshire-Lehmann Fund Conference report. https://docs.google.com/viewer?a=v&pid=sites&srcid=ZGVmYXVsdGRvbWFpbnxjaGVzc2hpcmVsZWhtYW5ufGd4OjUwYzU4NzZhNzdiYjY1OTY

CSE 2003. *Warm zones external evaluation: first annual report*. Centre for Sustainable Energy. Bristol. www.cse.org.uk/pdf/pub1028.pdf

Dubois, U. 2012. From targeting to implementation: the role of identification of fuel poor households. *Energy Policy*. 49, 107–115

EBR. 2013. *UK suffers worst fuel poverty in Western Europe*. Press release. 28 March. www.energybillrevolution.org/wp-content/uploads/2013/03/Press-Release-UK-Suffers-Worst-Fuel-Poverty-in-Europe.pdf

EBR and ACE 2013a. *Fact file: the cold man of Europe*. Energy Bill Revolution and Association for the Conservation of Energy. March. www.energybillrevolution.org/wp-content/uploads/2013/03/ACE-and-EBR-fact-file-2013-03-Cold-man-of-Europe.pdf

EBR and ACE 2013b. *Energy efficiency and excess winter deaths: comparing UK and Sweden*. Energy Bill Revolution and Association for the Conservation of Energy. www.energybillrevolution.org/wp-content/uploads/2013/12/ACE-Research-Comparing-the-UK-and-Sweden-3.12.13.pdf

EBR and ACE 2014. *Fuel poverty: 2014 update*. Energy Bill Revolution and Association for the Conservation of Energy. January. www.e3g.org/docs/ACE_and_EBR_fact_file_(2014-02)_Fuel_Poverty_update_2014.pdf

English Housing Survey. 2013. *Homes 2011*. Department for Communities and Local Government. www.gov.uk/government/uploads/system/uploads/attachment_data/file/211324/EHS_HOMES_REPORT_2011.pdf

EurActiv. 2012. *France puts its ETS money into housing renovation*. EurActiv.com. www.euractiv.com/energy-efficiency/france-use-ets-money-fund-energy-news-515040

Finbow, M. 1988. The contribution of shelter planting. In Dodd, J.S. (Ed.) *Energy saving through landscape planning*. Volume 3. Property Services Agency, Croydon, London

Gilbertson, J., Grimsley, M. and Green, G. 2012. Psychosocial routes from housing investment to health: evidence from England's home energy efficiency scheme. *Energy Policy*. 49, 122–133

Healy, J.D. 2003. Excess winter mortality in Europe: a cross country analysis identifying key risk factors. *Journal of Epidemiology and Community Health*. 57, 784–789

Hills, J. 2012. *Getting the measure of fuel poverty: final report of the Fuel Poverty Review*. CASE, LSE, London

Humphries, R. and Galea, A. 2013. *Health and wellbeing boards, one year on*. London: King's Fund. www.kingsfund.org.uk/sites/files/kf/field/field_publication_file/health-wellbeing-boards-one-year-on-oct13.pdf

Liddell, C. and McKenzie, P. 2013. *Area-based targeting of fuel poverty: an empirical evaluation*. OFMdFMNI, Coleraine, Northern Ireland: University of Ulster

Met Office. 2003. *The heatwave of 2003*. www.metoffice.gov.uk/education/teens/case-studies/heatwave

ONS (Office for National Statistics). 2011. *Population and household estimates for the United Kingdom, March 2011*. www.ons.gov.uk/ons/rel/census/2011-census/population-estimates-by-five-year-age-bands--and-household-estimates--for-local-authorities-in-the-united-kingdom/stb-population-and-household-estimates-for-the-united-kingdom-march-2011.html

Ormandy, D. and Ezratty, V. 2012. Health and thermal comfort: from WHO guidance to housing strategies. *Energy Policy*. 49, 116–121

Rosenow, J., Eyre, N., Rohde, C. and Buerger, V. 2013. Overcoming the upfront investment barrier: comparison of the German CO_2 Building Rehabilitation Programme and the British Green Deal. *Energy & Environment*. 24 (1–2), 83–103

Tanner, L.M., Moffatt, S., Milne, E.M.G., Mills, S.D.H. and White, M. 2013. Socioeconomic and behavioural risk factors for adverse winter health and social outcomes in economically developed countries: a systematic review of quantitative observational studies. *Journal of Epidemiology and Community Health*. 67, 1061–1067. http://jech.bmj.com/content/67/12/1061.full

Tirado Herrero, S. and Urge-Vorsatz, D. 2012. Trapped in the heat: a post-communist type of fuel poverty. *Energy Policy*. 49, 60–68

White, R. 2004. A very British heatwave. *Geography Review*. September, 21–23

Wookey, R. pers comm. 2014. Public Health England, presentation at CAN conference, 5 February 2015

20

THE SPATIAL DETERMINANTS OF AIR QUALITY

Enda Hayes

Introduction: the air that we breathe

Our atmosphere is essential for life on earth. It protects us from solar and cosmic rays, with the ozone layer shielding us from ultraviolet radiation; it acts as a 'greenhouse', regulating the temperature of the earth; and it provides a transportation mechanism for water, pollen and other propagules. Most importantly, the atmosphere sustains life by providing 'air' for humans, animals and plants to breathe. Despite these, and other essential services, the atmosphere is consistently taken for granted. In recent centuries, the quality of the air we breathe has deteriorated rapidly primarily due to human activities. Energy generation, industrial productivity, road transport, domestic heating and cooking in our towns and cities all contribute to poor urban, national and international air quality and subsequently affect our health and the services our ecosystem provides.

The growth of world population will create more demands on an increasingly stressed planet with limited resources. It will be cities and the associated industrial and commercial activities that will demand the majority of the 40 per cent increase in world energy forecast by 2030. This is a recipe for continued poor air quality and illustrates the importance of careful urban planning and resource management.

Commercial interests, governments and the public implicitly chose air pollution as a consequence of the political, economic and societal choices made. The public's willingness to accept pollution is slowly changing as society becomes more environmentally conscious and health aware. There is a continuing need and responsibility for urban planners, transport planners, industrial regulators and energy policy-makers to make the hard political and economic decisions to ensure that we meet health-based standards for our air quality.

Air pollution, planning and design

What is air pollution?

Air pollution is anything not naturally present or anything out of natural proportions or any substance in air which causes 'problems'. Weber (1982) defined air pollution as 'the presence of substances in the ambient atmosphere, resulting from the activity of man or from natural processes, causing adverse effects to man and the environment.' There are three 'types' of air pollution:

1. *Primary pollution* – typically from combustion processes, primary pollution occurs when materials pass from the fuel to air usually through incomplete combustion (for example carbon monoxide, CO) or as a product of the combustion process itself (for example nitrogen oxides, carbon dioxide).
2. *Secondary pollution* – formed in the atmosphere by chemical reactions between precursors, these are pollutants that are not emitted directly into the atmosphere (e.g. ozone and nitrogen dioxide).
3. *Natural pollution* – this includes pollution from natural rather than anthropogenic sources, such as forest fires, volcanoes, Saharan dust storms etc. (for example fine particles, sulphur dioxide).

Air pollution can be thought of in a systematic way:

*   *Source* – pollution comes from a source such as transport, industry, energy generation, agriculture or natural sources.
*   *Emission* – the source can release a single pollutant or multiple pollutants at a fixed or variable rate. The emissions can come from point sources (e.g. industrial stacks), mobile sources (for example vehicles), area sources (e.g. compost facilities) or jet sources (for example aviation).
*   *Dilution/dispersion* – the emitted pollutant is released into the atmosphere where the mechanical impact of meteorology and chemical interactions with other atmospheric compounds causes dilution and dispersal by wind. The dispersion characteristics are highly dependent on variables such as wind speed, wind direction, emission release height, emission temperature and buoyancy, and structure of the surrounding environment.
*   *Deposition/absorption* – deposition and absorption of air pollutants can affect ecosystems, changing biodiversity and reducing water quality. Air pollutants are removed from the atmosphere through 'wet deposition' (rain, snow and fog), and by 'dry deposition' (direct uptake of gases and particles to land and water surfaces).
*   *Effect/receptors* – air pollutants can have an effect on humans through our respiratory or cardiovascular systems and can affect ecosystems through acidification and eutrophication.

The significance of planning and design

Fluctuations of air pollution concentrations in the atmosphere tend to be controlled more by urban design, topography and meteorological factors than by changes in actual air pollution emissions. Therefore careful urban design and planning can prevent some of the impacts. Fluctuations in air pollution concentrations can be exacerbated by urban designs such as a city's location within the surrounding topography or the physical design and alignment of a street within that city. For example, Santiago City in Chile is surrounded on all sides by the Andes mountain range which has a substantial influence on meteorological conditions, often creating stable conditions and temperature inversions over the city. This has the effect of reducing pollution dispersion and the mixing height, therefore 'holding' pollution in place in the city. At a smaller scale, the actual physical characteristics and geography at the street level can impact on how pollutants disperse, that is, the street canyon effect. For example, Bath City in the south-west of England has historical high buildings (5–8 storeys) on either side of busy streets. The historical structure and layout of the city was never designed for the volume of road traffic currently being experienced. The combination of tall buildings, narrow streets and traffic volumes result in a street canyon effect. Wind moving over the rooftops hits the windward side of the street canyon and, moving downward, 'pushes' the pollution over towards the leeward side. However, given the height of the buildings and the narrowness of the street, the air simply recirculates around the street canyon. The result is pollution staying within the street environment and not dispersing, therefore elevated air pollution concentrations are experienced.

A combination of geographic context and town planning is found in the case of Freiburg, south-west Germany. Here a daily katabatic wind sweeps down from the Black Forest, and cleanses the main trafficked streets from pollutants built up during the day. A city planning ordnance deliberately restricts the construction of large buildings that would impede this airflow. These are just three examples illustrating the need for careful urban planning and design at both the large and small scale.

While there are hundreds of known air pollutant compounds, this chapter will focus on the main anthropogenic 'traditional' pollutants of concern in urban environments, namely, sulphur dioxide (SO_2), nitrogen dioxide (NO_2), ozone (O_3) and particulate matter (PM) (Figure 20.1). Over the twentieth century we have managed to successfully address most primary sources through effective regulation but we still struggle to manage the range of problems caused by secondary pollutants. The management of these pollutants is complex because of a lack of direct control of their emissions; instead we have to try to control sources of the precursor pollutants. The management difficulties are further exacerbated due to the delays that occur in the chemical reactions and also because the reactions cause complex non-linear relationships between precursors and pollutants. These issues, coupled with the impact of meteorology, topography and urban design, have a substantial effect on fluctuations of pollutant concentrations. Our social, political and economic responses to air pollution have often lagged behind our awareness and understanding of the impact of air pollution. Additionally, while environment scientists and environmental health practitioners have a good understanding of air pollution and its impact, they are not responsible nor have the powers to regulate the sources or parameters that influence air pollution; this responsibility falls to city managers, land-use planners, transport planners and policy decision-makers.

Air pollution also has a spatial element that requires coordinated efforts not just across policy 'silos' or departments and government 'spheres' or levels. Air pollution is a local, national, pan-continental, hemispheric and global issue as air pollution does not respect administrative boundaries. Consequently, there is an equity issue at the heart of air pollution management. There is a need to consider air quality management in the context of wider environmental justice (the equitable treatment of all people regardless of their race, income and social class). Gegisian (2007) identified a link between areas of high deprivation and breaches of air quality standards in the UK. Treating air quality management in isolation does not provide for the inclusion of social impacts and therefore when considering the urban environment as the local human habitat there is a need for an integrated and holistic consideration of multiple parameters.

The health effects of poor air quality

The primary concern about air pollution is its effect on human health. Other effects include damage to crops, damage to ecosystems, harm to animals, damage to buildings and a reduction of visibility. From a health perspective, air pollution has been linked to eye and skin irritation, respiratory disorders and affects the cardiovascular system. For some pollutants the epidemiological evidence is clear and long understood (for example carbon monoxide) but for other pollutants the evidence is less clear (for example particles and nitrogen dioxide) and is still being researched. It is only recently that we have begun to understand the biological mechanisms for these effects and the size of the impact on the population.

When considering the health effect we need to understand short-term versus long-term exposure. Long-term or chronic exposure can usually be quantified as greater than 1 year. Short-term or acute exposure is 10 minutes to 24 hours. The problem is exacerbated when you contemplate the effects of repeated acute exposure to high concentrations and the cumulative effects of exposure to multiple pollutants at varying exposure periods. This bombardment on our individual respiratory systems and society's health is substantial. The World Health Organization (WHO 2014), emphasising the link

Pollutant	Description and source	Health impact	Ecosystem impact	WHO thresholds
Sulphur dioxide (SO_2)	Formed from the use of fossil fuels in combustion processes. 75% of SO_2 emissions are from human activity. Key sources – energy generation, shipping and rail.	Poisonous (more so in the presence of particles). Coughing and difficulty breathing. Respiratory tract infections.	Can rapidly form sulphurous/ sulphuric acid. Forms acid rain causing damage to crops and ecosystems.	20 µg/m³ 24-hour mean 500 µg/m³ 10-minute mean
Nitrogen dioxide (NO_2)	Formed through the combustion of fossil fuels, it is generally considered as a secondary pollutant formed by the oxidation of nitric oxide (NO) and ozone. 5–20% of all NOx (the sum of NO and NO_2) is emitted as NO_2, the remainder is created in the atmosphere due to oxidation. Key source – all transport and energy generation.	Short-term exposure to high concentrations can lead to lung irritation and potential lung damage. Long-term exposure makes humans more susceptible to respiratory infections.	Damages vegetation, damages fabrics and dyes, corrodes metals, forms acid rain, secondary particles and ozone. Reduces visibility.	40 µg/m³ annual mean 200 µg/m³ 1-hour mean
Ozone (O_3)	Ozone plays a role in the stratosphere filtering out short-wave radiation but in the troposphere it is considered a pollutant. While not directly emitted by human sources it is a secondary pollutant formed by reactions involving NOx, volatile organic compounds and carbon monoxide. Key source – any source which generates a precursor, e.g. transport, industry.	Respiratory irritant. Causes pulmonary oedema at high concentrations. Lung fibrosis and reduced lung function. Precipitates asthma attacks. Ozone precursors can also have an effect, e.g. certain hydrocarbons are carcinogenic.	Significant effect on plants and especially crop yield.	100 µg/m³ 8-hour mean
Particulates (PM_{10}, $PM_{2.5}$, PM_1, $PM_{0.1}$)	PM is not defined by its chemical composition but is most commonly defined by its size (e.g. PM_{10} – particles that pass a sample entry at 10 µm). Can be primary (direct emissions from combustion) or secondary (formed due to chemical reactions). Key sources – transport, energy generation, construction, domestic, industry.	Coarse particles (PM_{10}) affect trachea and large airways. Fine particles ($PM_{2.5}$) affect alveoli and gas exchange regions. Ultrafine particles (<PM_1) can cross into the bloodstream and affect cardiovascular systems.	Coating with PM may cause abrasion and radiative heating reducing photosynthesis. Causes leaf surface injury. Influences nutrient cycling. Impact on ecosystem through action as a climate change pollutant.	$PM_{2.5}$ 10 µg/m³ annual mean 25 µg/m³ 24-hour mean PM_{10} 20 µg/m³ annual mean 50 µg/m³ 24-hour mean

Figure 20.1 Introduction to 'traditional' air pollutants

Source: Hayes' summary, based on Air Quality Expert Group (2004, 2009a, 2009b).

between air pollution and heart disease, respiratory problems and cancer, indicates that one in eight global deaths were linked to air pollution. WHO estimate that seven million people died globally as a result of air pollution in 2012, making it 'the world's largest single environmental health risk'. The European Environment Agency (EEA 2013a) have stated that 90 per cent of city dwellers in the European Union are exposed to air pollutants at levels deemed harmful to health. The Committee on the Medical Effects of Air Pollution estimate that approximately 29,000 deaths per annum are brought forward by poor air quality in the UK and that $PM_{2.5}$ alone reduces the average life expectancy by 6 months per person (COMEAP 2010).

Not everyone is affected equally by poor air quality. Sections of society which suffer from multiple deprivation; individuals with asthma, diabetes, obesity and chronic obstructive pulmonary disease (COPD); and the more vulnerable members of society, such as the young and old, are more susceptible to the effects of poor air quality. These health inequalities and environmental justice issues add to the complexity of our understanding of air quality and subsequently our difficulty in managing its impact.

Poor air quality is projected to be the world's leading environmental cause of mortality by 2050, ahead of dirty water and lack of sanitation (Organisation of Economic Co-operation and Development 2012). Air pollution is now classified in the same category as tobacco smoke and ultraviolet radiation (International Agency for Research on Cancer 2013). In the UK, the cost to society from poor air quality is on a par with that from smoking and obesity, at an estimated £16 billion per annum (House of Commons Environmental Audit Committee Report 2011). This does not include the wider implications of climate change and the effect it can have on social and environmental determinants of health.

The high cost of treating the effects of air pollution is leading to a renewed focus on prevention rather than cure. With direct links to fitness, obesity and general well-being, air pollution has become part of the 'Healthy Cities' agenda (Pilkington et al. 2008). While air quality management is often perceived by the public health community as a success primarily because of the establishment of clear health-based standards within primary legislation, these standards do not guarantee or preserve the 'right' of everybody to clean air. Sometimes the objectives are policy intentions and are not legally binding. There is therefore a considerable need to develop knowledge and understanding on both sides, public health community and air quality practitioners, to work together towards the implementation of successful mitigation strategies.

Box 20.1 London smog, 1952

On 5 December 1952 a severe fog descended on London due to a slow moving anticyclone. The fog grew gradually thicker throughout the day and people began to experience discomfort in breathing as some one million industrial and domestic chimneys, primarily burning coal, were continually adding to the problem. On the evening of the 5th, respiratory cases were twice the normal rate. The lack of spatial separation between source and receptor, coupled with the fuel being used and the meteorological conditions, had created a 'pea-souper' which was to have a considerable effect on London. On 6 December visibility was near zero and prize animals at Smithfield Agricultural Show were taken ill and had to be destroyed. The smog encroached indoors with an opera at Sadlers Wells being abandoned due to poor visibility. The smog continued for the next five days, transport came to a standstill and respiratory problems continued to be reported. On 10 December the anticyclone lifted and an estimated 4,000 excess deaths were caused due to poor air quality. The subsequent public outcry resulted

(continued)

(continued)

in the development of the Clean Air Acts (1956) which was the first UK legislation to control domestic and industrial pollution sources by moving power stations out of cities, legislating for higher chimneys to improve pollution dispersion, allowing local authorities to create 'smokeless zones' and creating a grant scheme for households to change from coal to gas or electric.

Understanding air quality and the urban environment

No two urban environments are the same. Even within a single city or a single street there is variation in the determinants of air quality. There are three key sources of air pollution within the urban environment; these are transport, industry and housing.

Air quality and transport sources

Transport emissions in an urban environment include road transport (motorbikes, cars, buses, heavy goods vehicles), rail transport, aviation and shipping in coastal areas. Despite technological advances in engines and fuels, emissions from road transport remain the major source of air pollution. A key issue is that most urban environments were never designed for the volume of traffic that they now have to experience and the fluid nature of the traffic source makes it difficult to regulate. The EEA (2013b) notes that, excluding energy use and supply, transport in the European Member States (EU-27) is the largest contributor to NOx emissions (46 per cent), non-methane volatile organic compounds (NMVOCs; 14 per cent), fine particulate matter $PM_{2.5}$ (19 per cent) and CO (28 per cent) with road transport being the predominant source. There are a number of ways for reducing emissions from transport and these can be broadly divided into two categories: technical and non-technical measures.

Technical solutions are primarily based around strategies for reducing emissions; these include cleaner fuels, cleaner and more efficient engines and alternative fuels. Historically, it was hoped that technical fixes alone would drive improvements in air quality and to some extent they have, and we have seen a reduction in emissions over the last decade. However, the increase in the number of vehicles on the road and the number of vehicle kilometres travelled has started to outweigh the improvements brought about by technical solutions. It is the non-technical measures that will be the key to helping us achieve good air quality in the future and it is urban planners and transport planners who are in 'the driving seat' to deliver this. Urban and transport planners can encourage uptake of new vehicle technologies, promote vehicle maintenance and efficient driving and facilitate Low Emission Zones and refuelling infrastructure, as well as promoting sustainable travel and modal shift while ensuring that the urban design is fit for purpose to allow for the proactive and reactive management of air pollution from road transport sources.

Non-technical solutions are wide and varied in their quantifiable impact and success. They include initiatives such as those described below:

- *Promoting modal shift* – encouraging changed behaviour by providing the right travel information to facilitate modal shift towards public transport, cycling and walking. This can include initiatives such as travel planning, travel awareness campaigns, car clubs, car sharing and teleworking. The Department for Transport (2005) suggested that a potential reduction in peak urban traffic of up to 20 per cent could be achieved through the public switching to sustainable travel modes.

- *Development planning* – land use, urban form and locational policies designed to minimise trip frequency, trip distance and public exposure. The impact of development planning on air pollution emissions in the medium to long term can be substantial. Air quality must be a material consideration in any planning system and needs to be an integral component of any planning policies and procedures.
- *Management of urban road space* – the design and management of streets and traffic to support low energy modes, creating pedestrian- and bike-friendly environments. Computerised systems are being used in major cities to improve the flow of traffic in relation to air quality, car park management and bus priority. Where these systems are optimised, congestion has improved, and lower pollutant emissions are likely.[1]
- *Low Emission Zones* – a geographically defined area where the most polluting vehicles in the fleet are restricted or discouraged. The aim is to improve air quality by setting an emissions-based standard for the vehicles within the area. Low Emission Zones do not need to be expensive or hi-tech like London but can be simple paper permit systems such as in Berlin.[2]
- *Greenspaces* – access to greenspace can increase levels of physical activity resulting in improved fitness and health and increase resilience to the impact of air pollution (Tanaka et al. 1996; Giles-Corti and Donovan 2003). Additionally, greenspaces and green infrastructure have a role to play in acting as sinks to reduce ambient pollution levels (Pugh et al. 2012).

Air quality and industry sources

The impact of industry on urban air quality has been recognised and attempts to regulate it go back to the middle of the seventeenth century. In 1659, coal was the fuel of choice in industry and John Evelyn identified three key principles of pollution control which still stand today. These were: smokeless fuels, fuel substitution and separation of polluting source from receptors. The Industrial Revolution, or in a global context, early industrialisation, resulted in an explosion of industrial activity in the last two centuries, with urban populations and population densities growing rapidly as people gravitated to work in the coal-powered industrial enterprises. This trend continued and industrial smogs in recent decades had significant effects on public health (see Box 20.1).

In most of the developed world the impact on industry has been largely addressed through heavy regulation and substantial legislation such as the EU Directive on Integrated Pollution Prevention and Control (IPPC) (2008/1/EC).[3] Additionally manufacturing industry is spatially separated from potential points of exposure through careful town and city planning – that is, separate residential and industrial zones. The occurrence of pollution events such as the London Smog of 1952 are now rare. However, in the developing world this is not the case. A lack of legislation, planning and regulation, coupled with the overriding political drive for economic growth, has resulted in large scale industry having substantial impact on local communities and overall regional and hemispheric pollution levels. During the 2008 Olympics in Beijing, concerns were raised over the air quality and the potential effect on athletes. Beijing removed 60,000 taxis and buses and relocated 200 local factories including a large steel factory out of the city by the end of 2007. Additionally, emergency pollution control measures were introduced, such as suspending production at more factories and coal-fired power plants and introducing licence plate restrictions allowing motorists to drive on alternate days only during the Games itself. These restrictions reduced the levels of air pollutants such as carbon monoxide, ozone and carbon dioxide (Worden et al. 2012). Additionally, as air pollution reduced, markers of key biological pathways associated with cardiovascular disease also improved, demonstrating specific mechanistic links between air pollution and cardiovascular health (Rich et al. 2012). This showed the importance of the role that urban planning and industrial location can have on air quality and health.

Air quality and domestic sources

The primary sources of air quality emissions from domestic sources are a consequence of cooking and heating. In the developed world, domestic sources are not a major health or air pollution issue as our cooking and heating is largely provided through displaced energy sources, that is, electricity or gas. However, in the developing world, the WHO estimate that 3 billion people cook and heat their homes using open fires and simple stoves burning biomass (wood, animal dung and crop waste) and coal[4] and that, without major policy change, the total number of people relying on solid fuel will remain largely unchanged by 2030. The WHO (2014) states that low and middle income countries in South-East Asia and Western Pacific regions had the largest air pollution death burden in 2012 with 6 million deaths attributed to air pollution with 55 per cent linked to indoor air pollution. Studies from Asia, Africa and the Americas have shown that indoor air pollution levels in households reliant on biomass fuel or coal are extremely high: for example typical 24-hour mean levels for PM_{10} in homes using biomass fuels are around 1000 $\mu g/m^3$, compared to the current limits of 50 $\mu g/m^3$ set by the European Union.[5] With an increase in households' prosperity and development, household fuels move from solid fuels (crop waste, dung, wood, charcoal and coal) to non-solid fuel (kerosene, gas, liquid petroleum gas and electricity) and subsequently there is an increase in cleanliness, efficiency and convenience, leading to reduced negative health impacts.

The use of these polluting solid fuels has a wider sustainable development issue, particularly in terms of the inequality of its impact. Emissions primarily affect women and children: fuel gathering consumes considerable time for women and children and the practice of fuel gathering often detracts from other income generation and education. The solutions lie in improving the source of the pollution (better cooking devices, alternative fuel–cooker combinations and reducing the need for fire), addressing the living environment (improved building design and ventilation) and addressing user behaviour (education, reduced exposure, better operation of the source).

Air quality management: a risk management approach

There are various types of risk associated with air quality for public health, individual health, the environment, the economy, society, political futures and technology. Any risk framework should consider science, should be effects-based, consider cost-effectiveness and cost–benefit, consider proportionate responses, adopt a precautionary principle and consider subsidiarity. These issues are also the key drivers of policy development. In recent decades and looking to the future the key risk in air quality management in the urban environment is continued unfettered traffic growth and use of fossil fuels.

The challenge is that the judgement of risk is often based on poor air quality data and/or weak epidemiology evidence, and governments have to weigh decisions of environment versus continued economic growth. The connection between environment, health and well-being is relatively new to the decision-making processes and can influence the risk judgements that governments make based on the balance of evidence. The continued growth in the body of scientific evidence and its effective communication to the public, who are becoming more environmentally aware and health conscious, is important. All environmental practitioners, public health officials, urban planners and policy-makers have a coordinated role in ensuring that the risks, challenges and solutions are communicated effectively.

Risks can be reduced with coherent and effective engagement with transport, planning, health, climate change and other policy areas. But this engagement must move beyond the traditional processes of consultation and these stakeholders must be embedded into the management framework to ensure that there is a collective 'ownership' not only of the air quality problem but more importantly of the air quality solutions.

Risks are also evident in conflicts with other policies areas, for example, climate change. Due to the relationships between the sources of air pollutants and climate-active emissions, management strategies implemented for one will often have an impact on the other. The outcome of such can result in either a synergy (where attempts to reduce or control the emissions of air pollutants results in an associated reduction in climate-active emissions or vice versa) or a trade-off (where attempts to reduce or control emissions of air pollutants results in an associated increase in climate-active emissions or vice versa).[6] For example, flue gas desulphurisation on power stations can address SO_2 emissions but can result in an increase in CO_2 emission by 3 per cent; abatement technologies for vehicle exhaust emissions such as catalytic converters and particulate traps can address NO_2 and PM_{10} emissions but may increase CO_2 emissions by 5 per cent; bypasses can alleviate poor air quality in towns and cities but can increase the vehicle distance travelled resulting in increased fuel use and CO_2 emissions.

Conversely, many management strategies can be complementary with the obvious synergies coming from actions focused on behavioral change and demand management: modal shift to non-motorised transport which has a feedback loop in terms of health benefits; increased public transport use; more greenspaces and trees; and greater energy efficiency. Through the identification and implementation of co-beneficial and cost-effective actions, sustainable urban decision-making and active engagement of key stakeholders, sustainable and healthy urban environments can be achieved (Hayes et al. 2007).

Conclusions: knowledge, awareness and ownership

Air quality management is a complex and challenging task. Good air quality is essential to our well-being but also vulnerable to our activities and the decisions we make. The key challenge is one of knowledge, awareness and ownership of the problems and solutions.

Adverse outcomes from the health risks associated with air quality management are substantially higher without the collective engagement by all relevant stakeholders. Therefore all stakeholders, including public health practitioners, transport planners and land-use planners, must embed air quality management within their decision-making processes. These stakeholders do not need to become experts in air pollution and health but must be willing to involve the relevant experts in their planning and decision-making; to demand the highest standards from developers; and to think long term. They must employ a strategic viewpoint that can encompass the cumulative effects of urban growth and change, both temporally and spatially. Data sets have continued to develop and grow in recent years but the key challenge for all stakeholders is how to maximise the utility of this data to ensure that we make optimum decisions. For example, many countries now have excellent spatial and temporal data sets on air quality (both monitored and modelled), together with health statistics, social deprivation statistics, source characterisation and urban spatial data. But is it all being utilised to make informed planning and design decisions?

Air pollution and air quality management is not an emerging issue. It has, and continues to be, a challenge that governments and society have continually failed to successfully address. Continued growth in fossil fuel combustion plus the effect of climate change, such as atmospheric stagnation events (that is, calm weather conditions not conducive to dispersion), may result in 55 per cent of the world's population experiencing more frequent and longer air pollution episodes. All professionals with a stake in city development and transport need to ensure that air quality is considered as part of a larger systemic environmental management strategy to ensure the preservation of the health of future generations.

Notes

1 www.utmc.uk.com
2 www.lowemissionzones.eu
3 http://ec.europa.eu/environment/air/pollutants/stationary/ippc/summary.htm
4 WHO Fact Sheet 292, 2014, www.who.int/mediacentre/factsheets/fs292/en

5 WHO Briefing, 2012, www.who.int/indoorair/info/briefing2.pdf
6 Defra, 2010, www.gov.uk/government/uploads/system/uploads/attachment_data/file/69340/pb13378-air-pollution.pdf

References

Air Quality Expert Group (AQEG). 2004. Nitrogen dioxide in the UK. London, UK: Department for the Environment, Food and Rural Affairs.

Air Quality Expert Group (AQEG). 2009a. Ozone in the UK. London, UK: Department for the Environment, Food and Rural Affairs.

Air Quality Expert Group (AQEG). 2009b. Particulate matter in the UK. London, UK: Department for the Environment, Food and Rural Affairs.

Committee on the Medical Effects of Air Pollutants (COMEAP). 2010. The mortality effects of long-term exposure to particulate air pollution in the UK: HMSO, www.comeap.org.uk/documents/reports/128-the-mortality-effects-of-long-term-exposure-to-particulate-air-pollution-in-the-uk.html

Department for Transport. 2005. Smarter choices: changing the way we travel, www.gov.uk/government/publications/smarter-choices-main-report-about-changing-the-way-we-travel

European Environment Agency (EEA). 2013a. Air quality in Europe: 2013 report, EEA Report/No 9/2013. Copenhagen, Denmark: European Environment Agency.

European Environment Agency (EEA). 2013b. Air pollution fact sheet 2013: European Union (EU-27). Copenhagen, Denmark: European Environment Agency

Gegisian, I. 2007. Assessing the contribution of local air quality management to environmental justice in England and Wales. PhD thesis, University of the West of England, Bristol, UK.

Giles-Corti, B. and Donovan, R.J. 2003. Relative influence of individual, social environmental, and physical environmental correlates of walking. *American Journal of Public Health* 93(9): 1583–1589.

Hayes, E.T., Leksmono, N.S., Chatterton, T.J., Symons, J.K., Baldwin, S.T. and Longhurst, J.W.S. 2007. Co-management of carbon dioxide and local air quality pollutants: identifying the 'win–win' actions. Brisbane, Australia: International Union of Air Pollution Prevention and Environmental Protection Association Conference.

House of Commons Environmental Audit Committee Report. 2011. Air quality: a follow up report, Ninth Report of Session 2010–12, HC1024, http://archive.defra.gov.uk/environment/quality/air/airquality/panels/igcb/documents/100303-aq-valuing-impacts.pdf

International Agency for Research on Cancer. 2013. Eds. Straif, K., Cohen, A. and Samet, J. Scientific Publication No. 161 Air Pollution and Cancer, www.iarc.fr/en/publications/books/sp161/index.php

Organisation of Economic Co-operation and Development. 2012. OECD Environmental Outlook to 2050: the Consequences of Inaction. www.oecd.org/env/indicators-modelling-outlooks/oecdenvironmentaloutlookto2050theconsequencesofinaction.htm

Pilkington, P., Grant, M. and Orme, J. 2008. Promoting integration of the health and built environment agendas through a workforce development initiative. *Public Health* 122: 545–551.

Pugh, T.A.M., MacKenzie, A.R., Whyatt, J.D. and Hewitt, C.N. 2012. The effectiveness of green infra-structure for improvement of air quality in urban street canyons. *Environmental Science & Technology*. doi: 10.1021/es300826w

Rich, D., Kipen, H., Huang, W., Wang, G., Wang, Y., Zhu, P., Ohman-Strickland, P., Hu, M., Philipp, C., Diehl, S., Lu, S., Tong, J., Gong, J., Thomas, D., Zhu, T. and Zhang, J. 2012. Association between changes in air pollution levels during the Beijing Olympics and biomarkers of inflammation and thrombosis in healthy young adults. *The Journal of the American Medical Association* 307(19): 2068–2078.

Tanaka, A., Takano, T. and Nakamura, K. 1996. Health levels influence by urban residential conditions in a megacity: Tokyo. *Urban Studies* 33: 879–945.

Weber, E. 1982. *Air pollution: assessment methodology and modeling*. NATO Challenges to Modern Society. Basic Books, www.springer.com/environment/pollution+and+remediation/book/978-0-306-40997-4.

Worden, H., Cheng, Y., Pfister, G., Carmichael, G., Zhang, Q., Streets, D., Deeter, M., Edwards, D., Gille, J. and Worden, J. 2012. Satellite-based estimated of reduced CO and CO_2 emission due to traffic restrictions during the 2008 Beijing Olympics. *Geophysical Research Letters*. doi: 10.1029/2012GL052395

World Health Organization (WHO). 2014. Seven million premature deaths annually linked to air pollution, News Release, www.who.int/mediacentre/news/releases/2014/air-pollution/en

21

WATER MANAGEMENT, URBAN DEVELOPMENT AND HEALTH

Jessica Lamond

Introduction: water at risk

Water is central to health and well-being with the basic need for water supply for drinking, fishing, washing and irrigation of vital food supplies. For this reason human settlements historically formed around sources of water, often on rivers or coastal sites that offered the added benefits of ease of transportation and waste disposal. The positive practical aspects of living near water-courses and the sea in the developed world have reduced with, among other things, the advent of piped water and drainage; domination of road and air travel over canals and shipping routes; and concentration of food distribution in the hands of large retailers with international supply

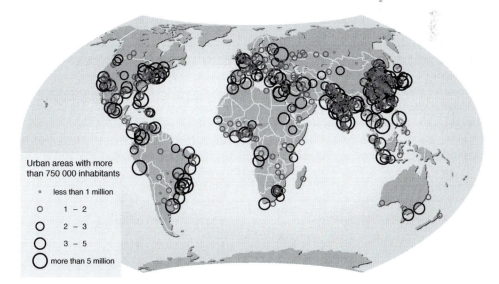

Urban areas with more
than 750 000 inhabitants

　　·　　less than 1 million

　　○　　1 – 2

　　○　　2 – 3

　　○　　3 – 5

　　◯　　more than 5 million

Figure 21.1   The urbanising world: world map of large urban areas in 2005

Source: Courtesy of Hugo Ahlenius (Nordpil) with data from the UN Population Division, http://nordpil. com/go/portfolio/mapsgraphics/world-map-of-large-cities-in-2005.

chains. However, these early settlements formed the basis of the major conurbations in which a large proportion of the world population now lives (see Figure 21.1).

As populations grow, and the climate changes, there is a higher total demand for water supply, with water footprints reaching far into food production and manufacturing processes (Hoekstra and Mekonnen 2012). As a result many developing and developed countries are subject to water shortages implying that the supply of water, often seen as a right and taken for granted, is becoming increasingly important. For example in Australia there has been a propensity to drought over the past decade that has resulted in crises for water supply and farming. Access to water may not require waterside development but ownership of rights to extract water from different sources is becoming a rural and urban planning and governance issue.

Meanwhile the disadvantages of waterside or floodplain living are becoming more apparent in an era of climate change and sea level rise. Population growth, urbanisation and high demand for new dwellings means a lot of development continues in flood prone areas, with increased density and lower permeability of the urban form, compounding flood risk (White and Howe 2002; Wheater and Evans 2009).

Flooding undeniably has a detrimental effect on human health and well-being (Tapsell et al. 2002) so that the question arises whether it would be preferable to avoid any further development in areas at risk. In some places changing climate and weather patterns have increased the risk from flooding leading to some thinkers and commentators advocating abandonment of some areas in existing settlements. A prime example is the debate around the recovery of New Orleans after Hurricane Katrina in 2005 (Glaeser 2005; Olshansky 2006). Relocation and managed retreat have become a reality in some river catchments such as Curitaba in Brazil (Tucci 2004) and coastal zones such as at Medmerry in West Sussex, UK (McGrath 2013).

However, humans harbour a deep and continuing connection to water sources so that although, in theory, modern advances in technology render it possible to move settlements away from rivers and coasts, in practice this is unlikely to be witnessed in the near future on a large scale. The sheer difficulty of the task of moving existing settlements will militate against such actions. Transport sustainability promotes the placement of new settlements close to old ones, and economics and (in some countries) planning policy positively discourages moving away from historically settled areas and perpetuates the growth and infill of existing urban areas (Echenique et al. 2012). Therefore scientists and practitioners need to temper the radical approach of risk avoidance with the realistic and integrated paradigm of risk management. Risk management rather than prevention forms the basis of evolving thinking about integrated flood and water management as outlined in this chapter. This paradigm requires a broad definition of flood and water management and also an appreciation of the health and well-being advantages, and disadvantages, of water within the urban environment. Through this the monistic and technologically driven discourse around risk avoidance can be balanced by the pluralistic and human centric view focusing on well-being, resilience and risk management.

Urbanisation and the water cycle

Unlike traditional catchment management that sought to control natural forces, new thinking seeks to mimic the natural undeveloped catchment (also known as river basin) processes (Burns et al. 2012). Many authors argue that returning rivers and catchments to a more natural state is a good thing because it is better for the environment, wildlife and biodiversity (Gilvear et al. 2012; Larson et al. 2013). It can also be seen to be a positive step with added utility if benefits to human health and well-being can be demonstrated. Understanding of the urban water cycle is therefore an important aspect of urban development planning. The natural water cycle is a well acknowledged scientific principle but often urbanisation and poor planning disrupts this natural cycle so causing problems with flood risk or water supply (Wheater and Evans 2009). The global water cycle and its links to climate and availability of freshwater are beyond the scope of this chapter. Water resources for the twenty-first century are discussed at length in Shiklomanov and Rodda (2003) where it is noted that most of the water on the planet is held in the oceans; the amount available through ground and freshwater sources at any time is less than 3 per cent of the total. The local catchment scale hydrological cycle is illustrated in Figure 21.2. Water flows within a natural catchment tend to be slow and widely distributed. Rain permeates the ground and enters rivers and groundwater at a gradual rate and then is lost to plant growth, evapotranspiration and outflow to the sea. By contrast, in a developed catchment, one in which urban centres and hinterlands have a significant impact on land use, water flows are to some extent controlled in order to maximise space for development, amenity and resource needs within the built environment and rural hinterland. However, permeability is reduced, thereby increasing the quantity and rate of surface run-off particularly within urban areas (Shuster et al. 2005).

Dams and reservoirs are often constructed to restrict flows, create storage, reduce flood risk and generate hydropower (Shiklomanov and Rodda 2003). The advantages and social and environmental impacts of dams have been widely explored, for example in Tannahill et al. (2014). Rivers are channelised or culverted, particularly within the urban area, to restrict their encroachment onto developable land or for functional reasons such as transport, flow control or wastewater disposal as shown in a US example (see Figure 21.3). As a result water flows within urban catchments can tend to be faster as channels are clearer, water is deeper, and the engineering objective is to move 'problematic' water through and out to the sea.

Containing water underground was seen in the past as a solution to overcome the drive to use surface spaces for more 'profitable' purposes (Gandy 2004). In many cities rivers were converted to drains or sewers or culverted, as for example in Melbourne where the Elizabeth Street drain, now a main street in the business district, is subject to torrential flows during intense

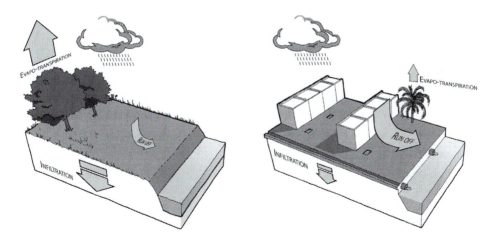

Figure 21.2 Permeability of undeveloped and developed catchment

Source: Copyright BACA Architects.

Figure 21.3   Channelised Los Angeles River in downtown Los Angeles

Source: Downtowngal under creative commons.

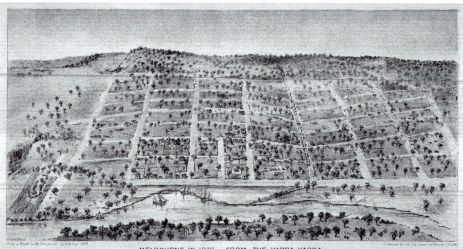

Figure 21.4   Historic map of Melbourne showing Elizabeth Street as an open channel

Source: Clarence Woodhouse, Melbourne, in 1838 from the Yarra River, c. 1888. Courtesy of the State Library of Victoria under creative commons.

rainfall as clearly shown in Figure 21.4. While the engineered piped water and urban drainage systems that resulted had large benefits and reduced disease at the time (Gandy 2004), as cities grow, the continued need to upgrade and maintain the inflexible underground systems becomes expensive and disruptive. Therefore new development, changes in density and infill can cause huge problems if their drainage requirements are not catered for.

Water supply is often piped into major urban centres but it may be sourced from the upper reaches of the catchment from reservoirs, or from groundwater. Where these sources do not suffice, wastewater may be treated, storm water harvested or desalination undertaken (Ifelebuegu et al. 2014). Many of these practices cause knock-on impacts to urban environments and ecosystems and the variable quality of the water made available can have impacts on human health and well-being. The silo thinking associated with such approaches to water supply management has not allowed for consideration of these wider impacts and led to severe problems across many different supply models. According to the World Bank and the Institute for Global Environment Strategies (Institute for Global Environmental Strategies 2008; The World Bank 2010) excessive pumping of groundwater causes problems with subsidence. As cities grow and demand increases, particularly in delta regions in Asia, the problems with land subsidence can cause further flood problems demonstrating a direct link between water shortage and flood risk. As an example in Jakarta in Indonesia some areas are observed to be sinking further below sea level at a rate of 20cm per year (Delinom et al. 2009). Rising sea levels also cause saltwater incursion into groundwater resources and heavy urban pollution can also result in contamination of this vital resource. In Ho Chi Minh City saltwater incursion seems to be escalating with increased drawdown of groundwater resources (Institute for Global Environmental Strategies 2008). In the UK polluted run-off from road surfaces is contributing to contamination of groundwater sources (Ellis 2014).

In order to protect coastal assets and indeed to increase land for building and agriculture, coastal processes have also been controlled in the past. Land reclamation, and the construction of sea walls and defences have combined to produce coastal squeeze, the disruption of coastal ecosystems such as wetlands, mangroves and coral, and the encouragement of further development in areas at risk from flooding. In the light of predicted sea level rise much of this activity may prove to be unsustainable. Considerations about making space for the return to a more natural catchment are central to the debate about urban form because higher density development, while more sustainable in terms of land use and transportation, tends to be less permeable and restrict space for water.

Water and health

Health and well-being implications of flooding

In the anticipation of increased flooding attributable to changing climates, the health impacts of flooding are increasingly being researched as recent evidence reviews demonstrate (Few and Matthies 2007; Tapsell et al. 2008; Du et al. 2010; Alderman et al. 2012). Of most concern are deaths directly attributable to catastrophic flooding, and this is the aspect about which most evidence exists. The available quantitative evidence suggests that fewer people now die as a direct result of floods as shown in disaster databases and Figure 21.5, probably as a result of human actions to limit flooding and to take emergency action to prevent deaths when floods occur (Jha et al. 2011).

Despite massive investment in warning systems and evacuation plans, even when these work as expected, deaths still occur. In essence the number of flood related deaths is highly linked to the speed of onset of flooding (Du et al. 2010), as are flood related injuries. In which context, processes that slow onset or allow systems to fail gracefully are expected to be helpful in reducing the number of direct flood related deaths and injuries. After a flood, health risk can arise from a number of different causes such as water borne disease vectors and unhealthy living conditions (Few and Matthies 2007). The prevalence and consequences of this are dependent

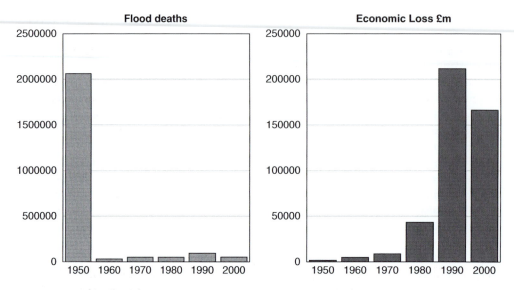

Figure 21.5 Worldwide decadal flood deaths and economic losses from flood disasters

Source: Author from EM-DAT, the International Disaster Database, Centre for Research on the Epidemiology of Disasters (CRED).

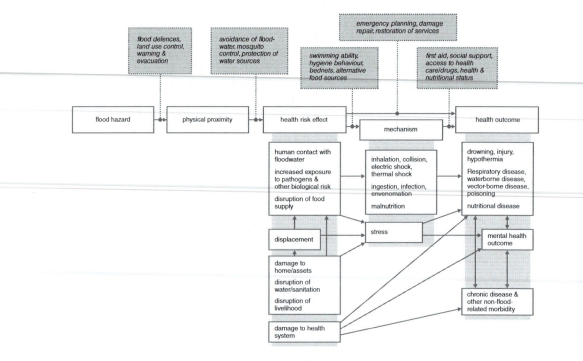

Figure 21.6 Health impact pathway for flooding, with examples of response mechanisms

Source: Few (2007).

on flood characteristics, reinstatement speed, climate, social capacity and the ability of health services to cope with raised need (see Figure 21.6).

Other health impacts from flooding include psychological effects due to the trauma of experiencing a flood and the worry that flooding may happen again (Tapsell and Tunstall 2003; Mason et al. 2010). For example Watkiss and Hunt estimate that mental health problems attributable to coastal flood risk could cost as much as 1.5 billion euros annually (Watkiss and Hunt 2012). While this is in part related to the direct flood experience, there is increasing evidence that recovery from such mental distress is also related to the length of time taken to reinstate 'normal' living conditions after an event (Du et al. 2010).

Well-being is also affected through the stress associated with loss of possessions, disruption of social activities while displaced from the home, increased family tensions and money worries. This may not result in diagnosable mental health problems but causes ill health through the stress of negative emotions, fatigue and lack of funds for other activities (Fothergill 1999; Joseph et al. 2011; Whittle and Medd 2011).

Flooding causes financial and economic loss to individuals and society. The expenditure on flood emergency and recovery diverts funds from other programmes. In Africa for example flooding is identified as one of the principal climate risks that will delay the achievement of Millennium Development Goals. This is demonstrated by a UN–Habitat study that rates flooding as a major factor standing in the way of poverty alleviation (Actionaid 2006). Food security and malnourishment have also arisen directly in the aftermath of the Pakistan 2010 and 2011 flooding as observed by the World Health Organization (Shabir 2013).

In the US, recent flood and storm damage in New Orleans, Mississippi and New York has required Acts of Congress to provide recovery funding. In the UK money was diverted from the decent homes programme to aid in flood recovery (Audit Commission 2007). Loss of critical infrastructure can spread the impacts of flooding over a wide population, particularly if key services such as hospitals and schools or energy supplies are affected by flooding and unable to operate. Transport disruption can affect local economies as well as being very inconvenient for individuals, as was seen in the Australian floods of 2011 (Chhetri et al. 2012). Livelihoods and security and financial security are impacted and the risk of flooding can deprive otherwise financially secure households of the comfort of property insurance, leaving them exposed to real financial hardship if flooding recurs (Association of British Insurers 2005; Lamond and Proverbs 2008).

Health and well-being implications of water shortage

At a very basic level supply of water is necessary to sustain life. Severe water shortage causes drought and famine and more people are affected by drought than any other natural disaster except flooding. Figure 21.7 shows drought disasters recorded over the last 30 years by continent and Figure 21.8 displays the trend in total numbers affected by flood disasters over the last century.

Water shortage affects health and well-being in a multitude of ways. Within an urban environment, shortage of clean water for drinking and cooking purposes leads to lower quality supplies being used. This can lead directly to disease, for example cholera, or it can cause longer term health issues from drinking water contaminated with iron, arsenic or other toxins (Sekovski et al. 2012). Equally if these supplies are overused then the contamination will worsen and issues such as saltwater intrusion into fresh and groundwater may ensue (Moser and

		Number of events	Number killed	Total number affected	Damage (000 US$)
Africa	total	172	2593	279,543,016	2,308,939
	per event		15	1,625,250	13424
Americas	total	101	57	28,513,476	51,475,339
	per event		1	282,312	509,657
Asia	total	99	4798	1,233,604,984	33,731,347
	per event		49	12,460,656	340721
Europe	total	34	2	10,488,769	22,426,309
	per event		0	308,493	659,597
Oceania	total	14	60	7,883,019	4,896,000
	per event		4	563,073	349,714

Figure 21.7 Numbers affected by drought by continent over the last 30 years

Source: International Disaster Database, Centre for Research on the Epidemiology of Disasters (CRED).

Satterthwaite 2008). Increased reliance on groundwater, rainwater and surface water brings into sharp focus the impact of urbanisation on the quality of run-off and groundwater quality. Some impacts from pollution in infiltrated water can last for decades (Ellis 2014). Furthermore extraction of water disrupts the natural ecological processes through establishing a new regime of abnormal low water flow, exacerbated by disposal of wastewater which adds to the concentration of pollutants; the result is that water shortage causes damage to the wider ecosystem. This can badly affect future water supply and the ecosystem services supplied by the natural landscape (Malmquist and Rundle 2002). In particular food production is heavily affected by water supply and this is true of agricultural communities (McMichael and Lindgren 2011) but also urban farms and gardeners.

However, in the urban environment the use of water, particularly surface water sources and water for irrigation, can contribute to health and well-being through the effect on use of space and feel-good factor. This well-being aspect is reflected in the higher property prices seen for properties near to attractive water bodies (Luttik 2000) or with a water view (Benson et al. 2000; Bin et al. 2008). Water shortage reduces the impact of water features and greenspaces as water is diverted from aesthetic uses such as maintaining greenspaces to more essential uses (White 2010). The potential for flash fires increases and the soil, air and water quality suffers through dehydration. Lower water levels in water features decrease the potential for leisure uses and may reduce healthful activity. Poorly maintained surface water sources may harbour disease.

An option for increasing supply is desalination, regarding which there is a current debate whether it provides a sustainable solution (Tal 2011) and whether it is acceptable to communities (Dolnicar et al. 2011). Alternative water supplies can meet considerable community opposition, for example in Redwood, California, local pressure groups opposed the use of recycled water in children's play areas on health grounds (Ingram et al. 2006), and in Toowoomba near Brisbane public opposition defeated plans to recycle water for potable uses (Hurlimann and Dolnicar 2010).

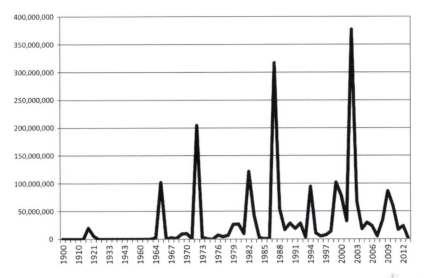

Figure 21.8   Chart showing increasing numbers reported to be affected by drought disasters 1900–2013

Source: International Disaster Database, Centre for Research on the Epidemiology of Disasters (CRED).

Figure 21.9   Water features in the urban environment, Brisbane

Source: Lamond.

Sustainable water management

Emerging trends in flood/water management

Future settlement patterns, particularly in the most rapidly urbanising areas of the world, are likely to put more and more people at the water's edge (Jha et al. 2011). Poor planning will put these people at risk of both too much and too little water and climate change will only add to the problems if weather becomes more extreme. It is clear for example that the Thames Barrier, designed to protect London from storm surges, may become inadequate in decades to come (Haigh and Fisher 2010) and the devastation caused by Hurricane Sandy illustrates that London is not alone in facing severe risk (Lamond and Proverbs 2013). Australian cities, such as Brisbane, Sydney and Melbourne, are increasingly facing a cycle of drought (and associated fire risk) and flooding (Chhetri et al. 2012) causing the introduction of desalination plants. The traditional control and supply methods are now seen as inadequate (Gandy 2004) and, as noted above, thinking in catchment or river basin management is moving towards naturalisation of the water cycle processes while continuing to supply water and prevent an increase in flood risk (Dobbie et al. 2013).

A plethora of concepts and theories are emerging at various scales that drive home this principle, for example integrated catchment (river basin) management; integrated flood risk management (Jha et al. 2012); room for the rivers; making space for water (Baca Architects with Building Research Establishment 2009); blue–green cities (Everett and Lamond 2014); water sensitive urban design (WSUD) (Ward et al. 2012); low impact development (LID)

Figure 21.10 Example of catchment management slowing flows within wetlands in the upper reaches, Iowa

Source: Lynn Betts courtesy of the USDA Natural Resources Conservation Service under creative commons.

(Dietz 2007); transition town planning (Hopkins 2008); and integrated urban water management (Sharma et al. 2008). These concepts, though often having subtle differences in emphasis, recognise that traditional solutions that attempt to control water, store it centrally and control distribution and keep water out of settlements need to work with novel approaches that redirect development to areas at lower risk, slow flows throughout the catchment, increase permeability within urban spaces and allow for local collection and distribution of water resources.

All have an interface with urban planning disciplines in terms of allocating appropriate land use and ensuring the necessary integration across spatial scales. They are summarised below under the phrase 'blue-green approach' (see Figure 21.11).

The new approach is exemplified in the LifE project (see Figure 21.12). It is described in a UK guidance document (Baca Architects with Building Research Establishment 2009) that outlines a catchment approach to living with future environments. The holistic goal is to combine appropriate zoning and risk assessment with good urban design that minimises residual risk in existing and new development within zones at risk. Wider river corridors, wetlands, building regulations and engineered defences can all be integrated as appropriate. Importantly the link between water supply and flood protection, the environment in the time between floods and

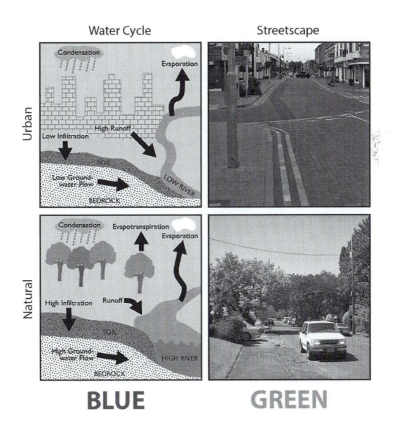

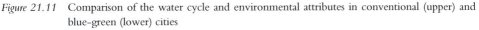

Figure 21.11 Comparison of the water cycle and environmental attributes in conventional (upper) and blue-green (lower) cities

Source: Courtesy of C. Thorne and E. Lawson, Blue Green Cities Research Consortium.

the implications of exceeding the designed protection should be given due consideration rather than focusing on flood protection alone.

In Portland, Oregon, this approach has been put into practice over 20 years so that green infrastructure catchment management, flood management, river restoration and wastewater services work together to deliver improved flood management and water supply. This is illustrated in Figure 21.13 with: naturalised water treatment facilities in the upstream areas (Figure 21.13a); river restoration to enhance urban water quality on the approaches to the city (Figure 21.13b); a green streets programme to increase infiltration that relieves surface water flooding as well as reducing the demands on the drainage and processing systems (Figure 21.13c) and novel examples

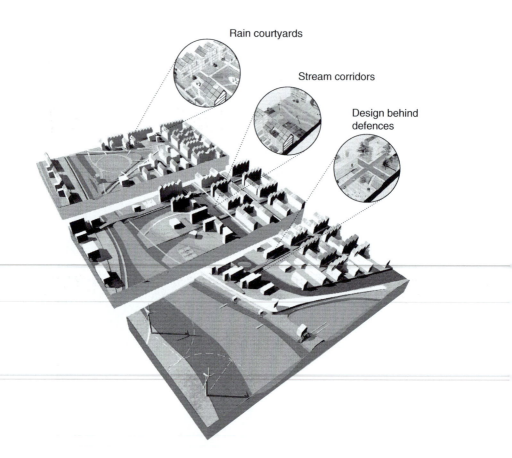

Rain courtyards

Stream corridors

Design behind defences

The LifE Principles

1. Provide space for the river
2. Provide space for rain
3. Create space for amenity
4. Integrate with community needs

5. Design to be adaptable
6. Reduce car dependency
7. Provide space for energy
8. Provide backups

Figure 21.12   LifE project concepts for the water/energy nexus

Source: Copyright BACA Architects.

of urban storm water management trains where rainwater is filtered, stored and recycled into sanitation systems (Figure 21.13d).

For all the validity of these new approaches, their successful implementation faces a number of significant barriers (Brown and Farrelly 2009). These include: the pressures to urbanise caused by growing urban populations; poor governance leading to disregard of zoning and other regulations; increased fragmentation of control structures via privatisation of core services such as water supply; high value of floodplain land in major urban centres; policies on brownfield development;

(a)
(b)
(c)
(d)

Figure 21.13 Portland green infrastructure. (a) Clearwater treatment plant, (b) river restoration, (c) street bioswale, (d) Epler Hall storm water system

Source: Lamond.

and minimum density requirements. Not only water but the water–energy nexus needs to be considered in the water sensitive city, meaning that water sensitive behaviours need to be encouraged not only for water conservation but to reduce energy demand (Brown et al. 2009). For example Kenway et al. (2013) in a study of Melbourne have advocated the combination of a compact urban form, demand management and solar hot water systems to reduce water consumption and associated energy demand. Integrated urban water management (Maheepala et al. 2010) suggests that other social and environmental goals such as carbon management can be systematically included in mainstream planning. The evaluation of who benefits from blue-green infrastructure and who pays for it or loses out becomes more complicated than when considering the engineering solutions that have fewer co-benefits. For this and other reasons, such as maintenance requirements, these approaches require a shift in thinking and wider engagement from a larger group of stakeholders (Everett and Lamond 2014), potentially leading to a need for greater participatory planning. In particular the integrated approach with inclusion of multiple co-benefits that reach broad stakeholder groups raises questions about funding.

Health and well-being co-benefits of the blue-green approach

The foregoing discussion demonstrates the importance of considering blue and green infrastructure within urban planning and as an integral part of urban design. Many planning regimes are changing to mandate water sensitive design in new settlements and it is clear that the justification for blue-green features can sometimes be made on the basis of their role in flood risk reduction, storm water control or increased water supply. It is not clear how acceptable these approaches are in respect of public attitudes to the softer side of integrated flood risk and water management (Everett and Lamond 2013). However, Kenyon (2007) found positive feelings in response to the ecological benefits of natural rather than engineered approaches to flood management.

As discussed above, the enhancement of urban capacity to supply water and prevent flooding has health and well-being benefits for society and individuals. However, the argument for incorporating blue-green infrastructure goes beyond these primary benefits and may be informed by the co-benefits that can ensue from pursuing these approaches. For example, in Malmo (Sweden) the regeneration of the neighbourhood of Augustenborg was principally driven by considerations that included flood risk management (Kasmierscak and Carter 2010). However, the associated improvements to significant amounts of green infrastructure have also helped the neighbourhood become a more pleasant place to live and work and thereby improved its reputation.

Improvements in water quality are a large incentive to install blue-green infrastructure in urban areas and the wider catchment with associated positive impact on health of residents. Permeable paving and other installations that increase infiltration can help to restore groundwater recharge, with water that would otherwise be lost to sewers or watercourses (Gilroy and McCuen 2009); the use of optimal contaminant filters can ensure that water is of high quality (although they may result in slower infiltration).

Vegetation associated with blue-green infrastructure in urban areas, such as green roof installations, can improve air quality (Stovin et al. 2012). This provides an important co-benefit since air quality in urban areas has demonstrable impacts on health and well-being, with the World Health Organization (2005) suggesting that even low levels of particulates can cause short- and long-term health issues.

Reduction of the urban heat island can prevent mortality though overheating such as occurred in France in 2003. Blue-green infrastructure can contribute to attenuation of heat islands through evapotranspiration effects from vegetated areas and water features (Vila et al.

Figure 21.14　An example of a roof garden, Brisbane

Source: Lamond.

2012; Stovin et al. 2012). Thermal insulation from green roofs also adds to the thermal comfort of building inhabitants (Bastien et al. 2011); vegetated areas can reduce noise pollution adding to well-being (Vila et al. 2012, Livingroofs.org no date).

Blue–green infrastructure can add to biodiversity through the provision of wildlife habitat (Vila et al. 2012; Stovin et al. 2012; Bowman et al. 2012); an example is the 400m² roof area of the tower block housing Barclays Bank in London (UK) which was converted into a green roof (Livingroofs.org 2005). Soon after completion, it was found that around 10 per cent of the invertebrate species identified on the roof were considered nationally rare, whilst 2 of the 20 beetle species found were very rare and had previously only been recorded six times before in the UK (Warwick 2007). It has been demonstrated by various authors (de Vries et al. 2003; Groenewegen et al. 2006; Maas et al. 2006; Bowman et al. 2012) that proximity to greenspace in an otherwise dense urban area can have a positive impact on perceptions of health and well-being. However, there may also be harmful impacts of biodiversity if, for example, mosquitoes or other disease bearing insects are attracted by water sources and vegetation.

Lessons for policy and practice

Lessons for planning practice include the need for:

- more intelligent approaches to application and enforcement of appropriate land use zoning;
- better processes for the consideration of the impact of new development on urban water services;

- creative responses to the tension between the desire to increase urban density and the need to make space for water and manage the urban water system;
- proper consideration of the urban hinterland and wider catchment processes; and
- promoting multifunctional installations that use land efficiently and provide co-benefits.

However, implementation of blue-green thinking brings with it various challenges, particularly in the range of agencies, stakeholders and communities that need to be mobilised in the process. The novel approaches such as water sensitive design are more people centred

Originating body/year	Year	Title
Building Research Establishment	2009	Life handbook. Long-term initiatives for flood-risk environments
CIRIA	2010	Planning for SuDS – making it happen
CIRIA	2013	Creating water sensitive places – scoping the potential for water sensitive urban design in the UK
City of Portland	2014	Stormwater Management Manual
City of Gold Coast	2007	Water Sensitive Urban Design (WSUD) Guidelines – section 13.11 Porous and Permeable Paving
City of San Francisco	2010	San Francisco Stormwater Design Guidelines – BMP Factsheets
CREW Scotland	2012	Sustainable urban drainage systems (SUDS) and flood management in urban areas
District of Columbia	2013	Stormwater Management Guidebook
Environmental Protection Agency (USA)	2008	Managing Wet Weather with Green Infrastructure – Municipal Handbook – Green Streets
Government of South Australia	2010	Water Sensitive Urban Design – Technical Manual
Institution of Engineers, Australia	2013	ARR Guideline 51e
Landscape Institute	2014	Management and maintenance of Sustainable Drainage Systems
New York City Department of Environmental Protection	2012	Guidelines for the Design and Construction of Stormwater Management Systems
Snodgrass	2006	Green roof plants: a resource and planting guide
State of Victoria	2014	Growing Green Guide: A guide to green roofs, walls and facades in Melbourne and Victoria, Australia
Victoria BID, London	2013	Green Infrastructure Audit – Best Practice Guide
Chelsea Green Publishing	2008	The transition handbook
Green and Blue Space Adaptation for urban areas and eco-towns (GRaBS); Interreg IVC.		Adaptation to climate change using green and blue infrastructure – A database of case studies
Maheepala, S., Blackmore, J., Diaper, C., Moglia, M., Sharma, A. & Kenway, S. 2010.	2010	Integrated Urban Water Management Planning Manual

Figure 21.15 Storm water management and green infrastructure guides

Source: Lamond.

and require participatory planning and management where town planners are part of a wider urban management team. Planners, civil engineers, flood risk managers, emergency planners, biologists, building service engineers and others must learn to speak each other's language and think outside the urban centre to the hinterland/catchment scale. More understanding of the natural processes are necessary, such as the length of time and support required to develop appropriate biodiversity corridors and the risks of introducing harmful or invasive species. The transition to blue-green approaches may involve a change in perspective that allows urban areas to evolve over longer timescales, rather than be constructed as a finished article. Resources are available to help planners (some of which are shown in Figure 21.15) but they will need training and education or support from other experts and the vision to plan for the future.

In many respects, this new thinking in flood and water management has immense synergy with approaches being developed for planning that address other aspects of health and sustainability. For example, international planning literature is exploring the benefits of localism, participation and dialogue (Boddy and Hickman 2014). However, the need to think in a catchment sense, sometimes the need to even consider national flood risk management goals and to integrate with international water supply companies, is a challenge that requires local agendas to be contextualised within the wider good and the national picture. Therefore both governance and policy changes and transformation of practice will be necessary.

Conclusions: emerging solutions

Whole system approaches in terms of flood risk, water and catchment management are more compatible with supporting health and well-being than traditional fragmented approaches. This new wave of thinking better supports co-benefits and is based on concepts of integration, holistic catchment thinking, naturalisation and blurring the urban/rural definition; it also combines both blue and green agendas to achieve better outcomes. Implementation of this thinking can be seen to contribute towards increased health of settlements through a variety of factors, including reduction of hazard, security of water supply, enhancing the quality of environments and changing of behaviours. This contrasts with past practice which detracted from healthy settlements through seeking to control natural systems by excluding them from the urban scene.

However, whole system approaches are challenging to implement and examples of truly integrated systems are hard to find. Research is ongoing towards policy, governance and engagement tools that can assist in propagating the seeds of change more widely. Questions include how it is possible to measure the multiple benefits, how to attribute these benefits to specific elements of the whole system and the distribution of beneficiaries as against sponsors of blue-green infrastructure.

Furthermore it is important to examine the performance of blue-green approaches over the longer term, seeking evidence about the ongoing maintenance requirements and the long-term impact on urban neighbourhoods, both positive and negative. As discussed, blue-green approaches form part of integrated, whole systems, flood and water management. The success or otherwise of the blue-green element will be reflected in the broader societal impact of the paradigm shift on urban discourse and public attitudes to and relationship with water that may in turn stimulate the call for more sustainable integrated systems.

References

Actionaid. 2006. Climate change, urban flooding and the rights of urban poor in Africa. Actionaid. Available: www.actionaid.org.uk/sites/default/files/doc_lib/urban_flooding_africa_report.pdf

Alderman, K., Turner, L.R. and Tong, S. 2012. Floods and human health: a systematic review. *Environment International*. 47, 37–47.

Association of British Insurers. 2005. The social value of general insurance. London: Association of British Insurers.

Audit Commission. 2007. Staying afloat: financing emergencies. *Public Service National Report*. London: Audit Commission.

Baca Architects with Building Research Establishment. 2009. LifE handbook. Long-term initiatives for flood-risk environments. Bracknell: BRE.

Bastien, N.R.P., Arthur, S., Wallis, S.G. and Scholz, M. 2011. Runoff infiltration, a desktop case study. *Water Science and Technology*. 63, 10, 2300–2308.

Benson, E.D., Hansen, J.L. and Schwartz, A.L. 2000. Water views and residential property values. *The Appraisal Journal*. 68, 260–271.

Bin, O., Crawford, T.W., Kruse, J.B. and Landry, C.E. 2008. Viewscapes and flood hazard: coastal housing market response to amenities and risk. *Land Economics*. 84, 434–448.

Boddy, M. and Hickman, H. 2014. *Planning for growth: stakeholder views on prospects for growth in the Cambridge sub-region under localism*. Bristol: University of the West of England.

Bowman, T., Tyndall, J.C., Thompson, J., Kliebenstein, J. and Colletti, J.P. 2012. Multiple approaches to valuation of conservation design and low-impact development features in residential subdivisions. *Journal of Environmental Management*. 104, 101–113.

Brown, R.R. and Farrelly, M.A. 2009. Delivering sustainable urban water management: a review of the hurdles we face. *Water Science & Technology*. 59, 839–846.

Brown, R.R., Keath, N. and Wong, T.H.F. 2009. Urban water management in cities: historical, current and future regimes. *Water Science & Technology*. 59, 847–855.

Burns, M.J., Fletcher, T.D., Walsh, C.J., Ladson, A.R. and Hatt, B.E. 2012. Hydrologic shortcomings of conventional urban stormwater management and opportunities for reform. *Landscape and Urban Planning*. 105, 230–240.

Chhetri, P., Hashemi, A., Basic, F., Manzoni, A. and Jayatilleke, G. 2012. Bushfire, heat wave and flooding: case studies from Australia. *Report from the International Panel of the WEATHER project funded by the European Commission's 7th framework programme*. Melbourne: RMIT University.

de Vries, S., Verheij, R.A., Groenewegen, P.P. and Spreeuwenberg, P. 2003. Natural environments – healthy environments? An exploratory analysis of the relationship between greenspace and health. *Environment and Planning*. A35, 1717–1731.

Delinom, R.M., Assegaf, A., Abidin, H.Z., Taniguchi, M., Suherman, D., Lubis, R.F. and Yulianto, E. 2009. The contribution of human activities to subsurface environment degradation in Greater Jakarta Area, Indonesia. *Science of the Total Environment*. 407, 3129–3141.

Dietz, M.E. 2007. Low impact development practices: a review of current research and recommendations for future directions. *Water, Air, and Soil Pollution*. 186, 351–363.

Dobbie, M.F., Brookes, K.L. and Brown, R.R. 2013. Transition to a water-cycle city: risk perceptions and receptivity of Australian urban water practitioners. *Urban Water Journal*. 11, 427–443.

Dolnicar, S., Hurlimann, A. and Grün, B. 2011. What affects public acceptance of recycled and desalinated water? *Water Research*. 45, 933–943.

Du, W., FitzGerald, G.J., Clark, M. and Hou, X.-Y. 2010. Health impacts of floods. *Prehospital and Disaster Medicine*. 25(3), 265–272.

Echenique, M.H., Hargreaves, A.J., Mitchell, G. and Namdeo, A. 2012. Growing cities sustainably. *Journal of the American Planning Association*. 78, 121–137.

Ellis, J.B. 2014. Water quality and treatment. In Booth, C. and Charlesworth, S. (eds.) *Water resources issues and solutions for the built environment*. Oxford: Wiley-Blackwell.

Everett, G. and Lamond, J. 2013. Household behaviour in installing property-level flood adaptations: a literature review. In Brebbia, C.A. (ed.) *Sustainable cities*. Kuala Lumpur: WIT Press.

Everett, G. and Lamond, J. 2014. A conceptual framework for understanding behaviours and attitudes around 'Blue-Green' approaches to flood-risk management. Flood recovery innovation and responses. Poznan, Poland: WIT Press.

Few, R. 2007. Health and climatic hazards: framing social research on vulnerability, response and adaptation. *Global Environmental Change*. 17, 281–295.

Few, R. and Matthies, F. (eds.). 2007. *Flood hazards and health responding to present and future risks*. London: Earthscan.

Fothergill, A. 1999. An exploratory study of woman battering in the Grand Forks flood disaster: implications for community responses and policies. *International Journal of Mass Emergencies and Disasters*. 17, 79–98.

Gandy, M. 2004. Rethinking urban metabolism: water, space and the modern city. *City*. 8, 363–379.

Gilroy, K.L. and McCuen, R.H. 2009. Spatio-temporal effects of low impact development practices. *Journal of Hydrology*. 367, 228–236.

Gilvear, D.J., Casas-Mulet, R. and Spray, C.J. 2012. Trends and issues in delivery of integrated catchment scale river restoration: lessons learned from a national river restoration survey within Scotland. *River Research and Applications*. 28, 234–246.

Glaeser, E.L. 2005. Should the government rebuild New Orleans, or just give residents checks? *The Economists' Voice*. 2.

Groenewegen, P.P., van den Berg, A.E., de Vries, S. and Verheij, R.A. 2006. Vitamin G: effects of green space on health, well-being and social safety. *BioMed Central: Public Health*. 6, 1–9.

Haigh, N. and Fisher, J. 2010. Using a 'Real Options' approach to determine a future strategic plan for flood risk management in the Thames Estuary. London: Draft Government Economic Service Working Paper.

Hoekstra, A.Y.A. and Mekonnen, M.M.A. 2012. The water footprint of humanity. *Proceedings of the National Academy of Sciences*. 109, 3232–3237.

Hopkins, R. 2008. *The transition handbook*. White River Junction, VT: Chelsea Green.

Hurlimann, A. and Dolnicar, S. 2010. When public opposition defeats alternative water projects: the case of Toowoomba Australia. *Water Research*. 44, 287–297.

Ifelebuegu, A., Charlesworth, S.M. and Booth, C.A. 2014. Desalination. In Booth, C. and Charlesworth, S. (eds.) *Water resources issues and solutions for the built environment*. Oxford: Wiley-Blackwell.

Ingram, P.C., Young, V.J., Millan, M., Chang, C. and Tabucchia, T. 2006. From controversy to consensus: the Redwood City recycled water experience. *Desalination*. 187, 179–190.

Institute for Global Environmental Strategies. 2008. Groundwater and climate change: no longer the hidden resource. *IGES White Paper*. Available: http://pub.iges.or.jp/modules/envirolib/upload/1565/attach/09_chapter7.pdf

Jha, A., Lamond, J., Bloch, R., Bhattacharya, N., Lopez, A., Papachristodoulou, N., Bird, A., Proverbs, D., Davies, J. and Barker, R. 2011. Five feet high and rising: cities and flooding in the 21st century. *Policy Research Working Paper 5648*. Washington: The World Bank.

Jha, A., Lamond, J. and Bloch, R. 2012. *Cities and flooding: a guide to integrated urban flood risk management for the 21st century*. Washington: GFDRR/World Bank.

Joseph, R., Lamond, J. and Proverbs, D. 2011. Property-level flood adaptation: a tool for reducing the intangible impact of floods on households in the UK. *International conference in building resilience: interdisciplinary approaches to disaster risk reduction and the development of sustainable communities*. Sri Lanka: Kandalama.

Kasmierscak, A. and Carter, J. 2010. Adaptation to climate change using green and blue infrastructure: a database of case studies. Manchester, UK: University of Manchester: Green and Blue Space Adaptation for urban areas and eco-towns (GRaBS); Interreg IVC.

Kenway, S.J., Turner, G.M., Cook, S. and Baynes, T. 2013. Water and energy futures for Melbourne: implications of land use, water use, and water supply strategy. *Journal of Water and Climate Change*. 5, 163–175.

Kenyon, W. 2007. Evaluating flood risk management options in Scotland: a participant-led multi-criteria approach. *Ecological Economics*. 64, 70–81.

Lamond, J. and Proverbs, D. 2008. Flood insurance in the UK: a survey of the experience of floodplain residents. *First international conference on Flood Repsonse Innovation and Recovery (FRIAR)*, 2–3 July 2008. London: WIT Press.

Lamond, J. and Proverbs, D. 2013. Sandy: come and gone. Rising currents: projects for New York's waterfront: a review. *Landscape Architecture Magazine*. April. American Society of Landscape Architects.

Larson, E.K., Earl, S., Hagen, E.M., Hale, R., Hartnett, H., McCrackin, M., McHale, M. and Grimm, N.B. 2013. Beyond restoration and into design: hydrologic alterations in aridland cities. In Pickett, S.T.A. and McGrath, M.L.C. (eds.) *Resilience in ecology and urban design* (pp. 183–210). Netherlands: Springer.

Livingroofs.org. 2005. *Green roof case study: Barclays HQ (London).* Livingroofs.org. Available: http://livingroofs.org/20100801224/exemplar-green-roof-case-studies/case-study-barclays-bank.html

Livingroofs.org. no date. Homepage. Available: http://livingroofs.org/2010030671/green-roof-benefits/waterrunoff.html

Luttik, J. 2000. The value of trees, water and open space as reflected by house prices in the Netherlands. *Landscape and Urban Planning.* 48, 161–167.

Maas, J., Verheij, R.A., Groenewegen, P.P., de Vries, S. and Spreeuwenberg, P. 2006. Green space, urbanity and health: how strong is the relation? *Journal of Epidemiology and Community Health.* 60, 587–592.

Maheepala, S., Blackmore, J., Diaper, C., Moglia, M., Sharma, A. and Kenway, S. 2010. *Integrated urban water management planning manual.* Denver: Water Research Foundation and Commonwealth Scientific and Industrial Research Organisation (CSIRO).

Malmquist, B. and Rundle, S. 2002. Threats to the running water ecosystems of the world. *Environmental Conservation.* 29, 134–153.

Mason, V., Andrews, H. and Upton, D. 2010. The psychological impact of exposure to floods. *Psychology, Health & Medicine.* 15, 61–73.

McGrath, M. 2013. Sea surrender plan to ease flood fears on south coast. BBC News, Science and Environment. Available: www.bbc.co.uk/news/science-environment-24770379

McMichael, A.J. and Lindgren, E. 2011. Climate change: present and future risks to health, and necessary responses. *Journal of Internal Medicine.* 270, 401–413.

Moser, C. and Satterthwaite, D. 2008. *Towards pro-poor adaptation to climate change in the urban centres of low- and middle-income countries.* London: IIED.

Olshansky, R.B. 2006. Planning after Hurricane Katrina. *Journal of the American Planning Association.* 72, 147–153.

Sekovski, I., Newton, A. and Dennison, W.C. 2012. Megacities in the coastal zone: using a driver-pressure-state-impact-response framework to address complex environmental problems. *Estuarine, Coastal and Shelf Science.* 96, 48–59.

Shabir, O. 2013. A summary case report on the health impacts and response to the Pakistan floods of 2010. *PLoS Currents.* 5.

Sharma, A.K., Gray, S., Diaper, C., Liston, P. and Howe, C. 2008. Assessing integrated water management options for urban developments: Canberra case study. *Urban Water Journal.* 5, 147–159.

Shiklomanov, I.A. and Rodda, J.C. (eds.). 2003. *World water resources at the beginning of the twenty-first century.* Cambridge: Cambridge University Press.

Shuster, W.D., Bonta, J., Thurston, H., Warnemuende, E. and Smith, D.R. 2005. Impacts of impervious surface on watershed hydrology: a review. *Urban Water Journal.* 2, 263–275.

Stovin, V., Vesuviano, G. and Kasmin, H. 2012. The hydrological performance of a green roof test bed under UK climatic conditions. *Journal of Hydrology.* 414–415, 148–161.

Tal, A. 2011. The desalination debate: lessons learned thus far. *Environment: Science and Policy for Sustainable Development.* 53, 34–48.

Tannahill, K., Mills, P. and Booth, C.A. 2014. Impacts and issues of dams and reservoirs. In Booth, C. and Charlesworth, S. (eds.). *Water resources issues and solutions for the built environment.* Oxford: Wiley-Blackwell.

Tapsell, S. and Tunstall, S. 2003. An examination of the health effects of flooding in the United Kingdom. *Journal of Meteorology.* 28, 341–349.

Tapsell, S.M., Penning-Rowsell, E.C., Tunstall, S.M. and Wilson, T.L. 2002. Vulnerability to flooding: health and social dimensions. *Philosophical Transactions of the Royal Society of London (A).* 360, 1511–1525.

Tapsell, S.M., Tunstall, S.M. and Priest, S. 2008. Developing a conceptual model of flood impacts upon human health. *Integrated Flood Risk Analysis and Management Methodologies.* London: Middlesex University, Flood Hazard Research Centre.

The World Bank. 2010. *Deep wells and prudence: towards pragmatic action for addressing groundwater overexploitation in India.* Washington: The World Bank.

Tucci, C.E.M. 2004. Integrated flood management case study – Brazil: flood management in Curitiba Metropolitan Area. WMO/GWP/APFM. Available: www.apfm.info/publications/casestudies/cs_brazil_full.pdf

Vila, A., Pérez, G., Solé, C., Fernández, A.I. and Cabeza, L.F. 2012. Use of rubber crumbs as drainage layer in experimental green roofs. *Building and Environment.* 48, 101–106.

Ward, S., Lundy, L., Shaffer, P., Wong, T., Ashley, R., Arthur, S., Armitage, N.P., Walker, L., Brown, R., Deletic, A. and Butler, D. 2012. Water sensitive urban design in the city of the future. *WSUD 2012: 7th International Conference on Water Sensitive Urban Design.* Melbourne, Australia.

Warwick, H. 2007. The garden up above. *Geographical Magazine.*

Watkiss, P. and Hunt, A. 2012. Projection of economic impacts of climate change in sectors of Europe based on bottom up analysis: human health. *Climatic Change.* 112, 101–126.

Wheater, H. and Evans, E. 2009. Land use, water management and future flood risk. *Land Use Policy.* 26, S251–S264.

White, I. 2010. *Water and the city, risk, resilience and planning for a sustainable future.* Abingdon, Oxon: Routledge.

White, I. and Howe, J. 2002. Flooding and the role of planning in England and Wales: a critical review. *Journal of Environmental Planning and Management.* 45, 735–745.

Whittle, R. and Medd, W. 2011. Living with flood: understanding residents' experience of recovery. In Lamond, J.E, Proverbs, D.G., Booth, C.A. and Hammond, F.N. (eds.). *Flood hazards, impacts and responses for the built environment.* New York: Taylor CRC Press.

World Health Organization (WHO). 2005. WHO air quality guidelines for particulate matter, ozone, nitrogen dioxide and sulfur dioxide. Geneva: World Health Organization.

PART IV

Processes and tools

Overview by Sarah Burgess

This section of the book is particularly pertinent to practitioners, policy makers and community groups. It brings together best practice approaches and case studies to identify critical tools and processes. The aim is to demonstrate the opportunities that can be created to improve the quality of the built environment. The chapters have a practical perspective, exploring the mechanisms for delivering places to support healthier and more sustainable outcomes for communities. These tools and approaches range from strategic to project specific. The first five identify concepts and tools that can be used at both the strategic and local level. The final four chapters take a different orientation, addressing the tools and approaches that are relevant to delivering specific, but critical, aspects of the built environment: housing, energy and green infrastructure. The chapters in this section all demonstrate that the interrelationship of systems within our cities mean that one sector alone cannot achieve healthy urban environments. Collaborative partnerships are of critical importance.

The co-benefits framework for understanding and action on climate change

In the first chapter, Susan Thompson and Tony Capon present a co-benefits approach to identify the interrelationship between human activity, human health and planetary health. Using climate change as a catalyst, the chapter highlights how a co-benefits framework can facilitate the identification of complex social, cultural, economic and environmental interactions and how policy interventions can have multiple benefits. This is an important tool for policy makers, developers and communities as it provides a way of addressing critical and complex issues in our urban environments.

Delivering healthy places: the role of the private sector

The importance of recognising the current economic orientation of decision-making is addressed in this chapter by James de Havilland and Sarah Burgess. The market-led system in England, like many other places, means that the private sector plays a very significant role in the location, design and delivery of development. Unless health and well-being are proactively adopted by developers, and reinforced by clear policy frameworks, it is very difficult to achieve healthy environments. Partnership with local authorities and close working with communities and stake-holders are critical to the development process. The authors provide two case studies which illustrate creative approaches for strategic planning, design and the management of development.

Building collaborative partnerships

Building on lessons identified in the previous chapters, Lynda Addison focuses on collaborative partnerships as a way of achieving healthy and sustainable outcomes. Drawing on her extensive work as a practitioner working with local authorities in England, Lynda details how collaborative partnerships can be achieved and the importance of leadership and commitment – at the right level, with the right partners, the right decision-making arrangements, and at the appropriate spatial scale. To achieve this, Lynda argues, requires a dramatic shift of attitudes, including on the part of elected members, and a shared focus on the well-being of people.

Creating healthier, smarter places: learning from European cities

In this chapter, Nicholas Falk, an economist, urbanist and strategic planner, brings his extensive experience of working in the UK and Europe to promote a model of public sector led development. He shows how, in relation to movement, work, housing and environment, European cities have created healthier places than has been possible through the Anglo-American liberal model. Two key factors common to all the exemplars are city ownership of development land and public investment banks, enabling early infrastructure provision and clear spatial frameworks.

Assessing the potential health effects of policies, plans, programmes and projects

An important tool for designers and decision-makers is that of impact assessment – identifying likely effects of an intervention or policy on social, economic and environmental outcomes. Ben Cave, a UK-based health practitioner, identifies the strengths and weaknesses of current European practice of health considerations in impact assessment, including environmental impact assessment and strategic environmental assessment. Ben's chapter highlights the importance of identifying not only how health and well-being will be affected by an intervention but, perhaps more significantly, what can be done to improve health outcomes. He argues that a systematic approach, whether through a separate health impact assessment or an integrated assessment, is needed. The goal is that health becomes a mainstream consideration of all decision-making.

A strategic approach to green infrastructure planning

In the first of the chapters addressing tools and approaches that relate to a specific aspect of the environment, Val Kirby examines the planning of green infrastructure, as a way of integrating people, landscape, networks and nature. She emphasises that for settlements to be healthy they must be planned as part of the environment, not imposed upon it. The chapter builds on analysis of the health value of greenspace in Chapter 17. Val identifies the multiple benefits of a diverse and robust green infrastructure network and reinforces the message that inter-agency working is essential to achieve, and manage, such a network.

Healthy housing

In the first of two chapters that focus on housing, Elena Marco and Sarah Burgess highlight the critical link between housing and health and provide a historic overview of the economic, social, technological and political conditions that have influenced the design and delivery of housing in the United Kingdom. The chapter analyses different tools that have been used in the past and questions whether these should be revisited in current practice to address today's challenges for housing design and delivery. The importance of providing high quality and adaptable housing solutions for a range of different household types, across the lifecourse, is highlighted. While standards can be set for new houses being delivered, it is the improvement of the existing housing stock that will provide one of the biggest challenges for the healthy housing agenda.

Community housing and place-making: narratives, forms and processes for convivial living

In this chapter, Martin Large and Hugh Barton focus on the role of community-led housing in addressing issues of housing need and overcrowding at the same time as delivering healthier, more sustainable and convivial communities. Martin and Hugh highlight the multitude of delivery models for community-led housing, including co-housing, community land trusts and self-build. They draw on a range of European, American and British case studies, emphasising the importance of affordability and user control.

Local management of energy demand and supply

And, finally, Ove Mørck an energy consultant in Denmark, continues the theme of community-focused initiatives by exploring community management of energy demand and supply in Europe. He stresses the importance of immediate action on energy efficiency and supply – a response to the problems of fuel poverty discussed in Chapter 19. Four distinctive case studies are presented, which use different tools and approaches to achieve a local energy supply, but common themes of local authority leadership, recognition of local context, use of planning regulations and the role of advocacy and promotion.

22

THE CO-BENEFITS FRAMEWORK FOR UNDERSTANDING AND ACTION ON CLIMATE CHANGE

Susan Thompson and Anthony Capon

Introduction: healthy people, healthy planet

Climate change is arguably the biggest global health challenge of the twenty-first century (Costello et al. 2009). The very survival of living organisms – humans, animals and plants – is threatened by the deterioration of the planet's health. Scientists are concerned that we have already transgressed a 'safe operating space for humanity' for a number of planetary systems including biodiversity and the climate system (Rockström et al. 2009). Governments in developed and developing nations, together with communities, private businesses and the not-for-profit sector, are beginning to mobilise to tackle this challenge. The magnitude of the threat to health is unprecedented and may imperil the future of civilisation, even the survival of the human species. There is increasing agreement that climate change is a 'wicked' problem and that to adequately and appropriately address its outcomes will require new and integrative ways of understanding, analysis and collective action. One such approach being advanced is the co-benefits framework.

Action on climate change is often seen in a negative light – the focus is on the economic costs of mitigation, potential reductions in living standards and unsettling of the foundations of our current way of life (Ganten et al. 2010). Adopting a co-benefits framework in addressing climate change means recognising potential multiple benefits from a single policy action (Smith 2013). The approach also acknowledges that low carbon ways of living are healthy ways of living – positive for both physical and mental health – provided structural inequities are addressed. One of the compelling arguments for highlighting health co-benefits is that it makes it clear that transitions to low carbon ways of living will improve personal health and will do so over a short time frame (Egger and Dixon 2010). Co-benefits provide a rationale, as well as an incentive, for individual action, urgently. An understanding of co-benefits enables people to realise the near-term and personal health benefits of transitions to environmentally sustainable ways of living.

This chapter explores the nature of health co-benefits from action on climate change. We detail the potential positive outcomes for human and planetary health from low carbon policies with a focus on actions linked to the built environment and urban planning. This is of relevance in high, middle and low income countries as they address climate change and other global environmental threats. A holistic and integrative way of thinking about and conceptualising co-benefits is presented. This framework goes beyond traditional notions of health. It facilitates creative thinking about the relationships between a comprehensive range of environmental

319

issues and similarly broadly conceived health and well-being outcomes. The emphasis is on joined-up thinking, researching and acting to bring about the global transformations needed to align the health of people, places and planetary systems.

The co-benefits framework

The co-benefits framework takes as its starting point an acceptance that global climate change is occurring and that human actions are largely responsible (McMichael et al. 2012). Further, it accepts that the human health consequences of climate change will be far reaching. The Intergovernmental Panel on Climate Change (IPCC) has identified three main ways that climate change is affecting health, and will continue to do so. These are, first, direct impacts – associated with 'different patterns in the frequency of extreme weather events including heat waves, drought, and heavy rainfall' (IPCC 2014, p. 6). Second, impacts influenced via natural systems such as 'disease vectors, water-borne diseases, and air pollution' and third, impacts significantly affected by 'human systems' such as 'occupational impacts, under nutrition, and mental stress' (IPCC 2014, p. 6).

People living in poverty, especially those in developing countries, are particularly exposed. As a result, they will most likely suffer adverse health outcomes even with modest shifts in climate, in particular for 'climate sensitive diseases' including childhood diarrhoea, malaria, under-nutrition, asthma and heart disease (McMichael et al. 2012). Thermal stress from climate change also has implications for the productivity of outdoor workers and others who do not work in air conditioned environments. For children, fear and anxiety about the consequences of climate change is a mental health concern. In all age groups there are potential mental health impacts from climate change associated extreme weather events (McMichael et al. 2012). Globally, there is potential for conflicts and 'environmental refugee flows' when populations are displaced due to their homes being destroyed or the environmental conditions of their homeland no longer able to sustain them or their livelihoods (McMichael et al. 2012).

A key premise of the co-benefits approach is the interrelationships between the health of the planet and living organisms. Early recognition of these interconnections in this context came from McMichael (Butler et al. 2014). More recently, a manifesto published in *The Lancet* takes this further by calling for a transformational reframing of how we conceptualise public health in the face of potential for collapse of contemporary civilisations. The planetary health manifesto argues for recognition, and action, on the interdependence of human and ecosystem health at every level, from the personal to the planetary (Horton et al. 2014). Unfettered economic growth is unsustainable and ignores the dependence that all life has on the health of global ecosystems (Lang and Rayner 2012).

There is no doubt that to protect our planetary system upon which all life depends, we have to put 'human and ecosystems health' at the centre of policy and decision making (Lang and Rayner 2012, p. e1). Nevertheless, we cannot deny the centrality of economic considerations in contemporary global policy and decision making. And this is what makes the co-benefits framework powerful to those yet to be persuaded by the urgency of acting on climate change. The co-benefits approach demonstrates that there are multiple benefits, including significant economic advantages, from urban design and individual decisions in support of low carbon ways of living. The costs of such mitigation will be offset by savings in the health budget, greater productivity and flow on economic benefits for society.

Low carbon policies and decision making bring various environmental, social, cultural and economic benefits. Understanding the extent of these co-benefits can help build the rationale for climate change mitigation policies, making them more politically palatable and providing a

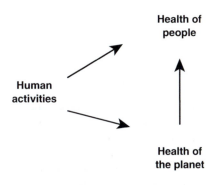

Figure 22.1 Concept of co–benefits for health

Source: Adapted from Boyden (2013, p. 153).

clear economic case for the uptake of low carbon policies. In essence, the co-benefits approach makes it clear that addressing climate change will bring additional benefits to society (see Smith 2013 for a comprehensive and detailed overview). It is important that this is acknowledged and understood by professionals in relation to policy development and practice, political decision makers, private sector developers and members of the community. The multiple benefits of action on climate change (and, more broadly, environmental sustainability) can be incentives for transitions to low carbon living.

Figure 22.1 provides a diagrammatic representation of the concept of co-benefits for health. All human activities have potential direct positive and negative human health impacts. This is through pathways such as nutrition and levels of physical activity, and indirect human health impacts through the health of the planet (for example, the climate system). It follows that there will be co-benefits for health from actions to tackle climate change. For clarity, the arrows are presented as unidirectional; however, there are relationships in both directions.

Exploring the co-benefits of climate action

There has been a growing acknowledgment across the health and built environment disciplines that action on climate change and accompanying transitions to low carbon living will result in additional benefits well beyond greenhouse gas reductions (see, for example, Smith 2013). In this section we present an overview of key co-benefits that will arise from environmentally sustainable actions.

Urban transport

The health benefits for our bodies and minds of being physically active are well researched and documented (see Kent and Thompson 2014 for an overview). Active transport is very much a part of this and if we can incorporate walking and cycling into daily life, rather than as an additional task that has to be slotted into an already busy day, there is more chance that sedentary behaviours across the generations will shift. Active transport encompasses walking and cycling, and the use of public transport. The latter usually involves walking or cycling from home to the train, tram or bus interchange, and then to the destination point following the trip (see Figure 22.2). It can also involve periods of standing which is increasingly recognised as beneficial to health (Dunstan et al. 2012; Rhodes et al. 2012).

Figure 22.2 Public transport involves physical activity which has health benefits for people and the planet: trams in Berlin

Source: Thompson.

Less car driving and more active transport will have benefits for both people and planetary health. Emissions of carbon dioxide and other pollutants will be lowered, thereby reducing human exposure to toxic air pollution and associated risks of respiratory and cardiovascular disease (IPCC 2014). Increased levels of physical activity bring physical and mental health benefits, including reducing body weight and lowering the attendant risks of heart disease, diabetes, some cancers and depression. This will have significant economic benefits as well because the health costs of physical inactivity are substantial. In Australia, for example, it has been estimated that the direct and indirect costs are AUD13.8 billion per annum (Medibank Private 2008) which is about 1 per cent of total gross domestic product (GDP). Investment in cycling and walking infrastructure is economically beneficial, something which has previously been either underrated or ignored (see Davis and Parkin, Chapter 8). A study in Australia that examined the provision of bicycle infrastructure revealed a strong economic case for investment considering factors such as reduced traffic congestion, parking cost savings, lower levels of air and noise pollution, and health benefits (RTA and DECC 2009).

Additional health benefits will accrue from lower levels of air pollution, reducing the burden of disease from cardiovascular and respiratory conditions such as asthma. Of course electric vehicles can also improve levels of air pollution (provided the electricity is derived from renewable sources) but will not render the physical and mental health improvements from being more active (Shaw et al. 2014). The most benefits will accrue from active transport – there will be less traffic congestion with fewer vehicles and this will have significant economic advantages for major cities as people and goods can move more efficiently. Tourism may also be enhanced with well-connected cycleways and ready access to bicycles in public places (see Figure 22.3). Fewer cars also means better safety from traffic accidents and with more people out and about in their neighbourhoods, walking and cycling, improvements in community safety can also be anticipated, enhancing social and cultural capital. In short, investment in infrastructure to support active transport has multiple benefits that go well beyond the reduction of carbon emissions.

Figure 22.3   Tourists on bicycles explore the city of Copenhagen

Source: Thompson.

Food

The food system is also a major contributor to climate change. Globally, it has been estimated that agricultural activities, especially those associated with the production of livestock (see Figure 22.4), are responsible for about 20 per cent of all greenhouse gas emissions (McMichael et al. 2007). This is further exacerbated by land clearing for farming (Smith 2013). To reduce greenhouse gas emissions from this source, people need to eat less meat and more plant-based foods. This shift in diet will benefit health because high dietary levels of saturated fats from meat and dairy products contribute to heart disease, diabetes and some cancers (IPCC 2014). UK research has found that a 30 per cent reduction in the consumption of meat and dairy products will lead to a lowering of heart disease risk by 16 per cent (Friel et al. 2009), although in other cultural contexts the scale of the risk reduction will differ. Increased consumption of fruit and vegetables has also been shown to reduce the risk of chronic diseases (IPCC 2014; see Figure 22.4).

Reduced consumption of processed foods and an overall reduction in food consumption and wastage also have health and economic benefits as well as lessening carbon emissions relating to food (see Dixon and Ballantyne-Brodie, Chapter 13). Highly centralised food distribution systems which perpetuate car-based access (such as large shopping centres designed for the automobile) are health depleting and have adverse economic outcomes for local economies and small businesses. This can be addressed, in part, by community led initiatives to establish vegetable gardens and producer markets which reinforce healthy eating and sustainable environmental practices, facilitate access by active transport (due to geographic proximity) and enhance social capital (Lapping 2004; Hinrichs et al. 2004; Thompson et al. 2007).

Energy

Small and large scale energy production needs to be considered in relation to reducing greenhouse gases and establishing a more distributed and diverse energy supply. This is important in addressing resilience in the face of climate change and giving communities more confidence

Figure 22.4 Diets rich in vegetables and fruit are environmentally sustainable and healthy

Source: Thompson.

about sustaining energy needs. Low carbon electricity generation will also result in health benefits and associated economic improvements from reduced exposure to air borne pollutants, which contribute to respiratory and cardiovascular diseases (Dennekamp and Carey 2010). Solar panels on rooftops across cities, for example, will improve energy security meaning people are less vulnerable to, and anxious about, a large power station being incapacitated by flooding, wild fire or other extreme weather event (see Figure 22.5).

At the domestic level, the use of solid fuel combustion stoves for cooking and the resultant air pollutants is an important global health challenge (Wilkinson et al. 2009). This is a particular burden in developing countries, contributing to ongoing and acute respiratory illnesses, cancer of the lung, low birth weight and stillbirths, and, in some cases, tuberculosis (IPCC 2014).

Figure 22.5 150 kilowatts of photovoltaic panels on the Tyree Energy Technologies building at the University of New South Wales in Sydney, Australia

Source: Robert Largent, School of Photovoltaic and Renewable Energy Engineering, UNSW, Australia.

Better building design for thermal comfort will mean less energy use, resulting in reduced greenhouse gas production, less air pollution and better health. Home insulation is an important aspect of reducing energy use that brings about health improvements, as well as reducing costs to householders (Chapman et al. 2009). This has implications for those on low incomes who cannot afford high energy bills and sometimes face having to choose to buy food rather than heat their dwelling (see Allen and Allen, Chapter 7).

Urban design

More compact cities and neighbourhoods, with nearby destinations that encourage active transport from home to work, school, shops and services are healthier for both people and the planet. With less cars comes reduced air and noise pollution, fewer traffic accidents, and more people out and about, enhancing community feelings of safety. These are all important contributors to a healthy lifestyle. Building design which incorporates energy savings, accessible stairs to encourage walking within the building and the provision of green roofs and walls will contribute to sustainable health gains.

An economic analysis by Trubka et al. (2010) suggests a combined annual health care and productivity benefit of AUD1,452 for each new dwelling built in a 'sustainable urban form' by comparison to an 'unsustainable urban form' over a two-year period. This estimate was based on analysis of a 1,000 dwelling high density, mixed use urban development that promoted both active and public transport. Over a 50-year period, the estimated benefit for 1,000 dwellings was AUD34.6 million.

The provision of greenspaces is another aspect of healthy city design. With higher densities, less land is covered by buildings and potentially more land is available for parks and gardens. Increases in green open space in cities can reduce ambient temperatures and the urban heat island effect (IPCC 2014; see also McKenzie, Chapter 18). The mental health benefits of greenspace are well known (Brook 2010; see Corkery, Chapter 17). Green walls and green roofs in more compact cities also play a role in relieving psychological stress and anxiety.[1] These are all examples of health co-benefits resulting from the provision of green infrastructure and provide good economic arguments for implementation.

Community development

Low carbon ways of living are healthy ways of living. A less materialistic and consumptive lifestyle enhances community resilience and reduces the high cost of living. More sharing of goods such as cars and gardening equipment, setting up 'walking school buses' and enjoying home-grown food together augurs well for the development of friendships and a culture of caring for the other. This enhances community safety, which in turn is positive for physical and mental health. Economically, communities can form co-operatives to enhance their buying power. This has been done in relation to the establishment of community based energy schemes (see, for example, Hicks and Ison 2011; Devine-Wright 2011; Seyfang et al. 2013).

An integrative framework for conceptualising co-benefits

Figure 22.6 provides a matrix for integrative understanding of urban sustainability and population health. The horizontal axis comprises six broad urban domains – economy and work, transport and urban form, housing and buildings, nature and landscape, media and communication, and culture and spirituality. These domains were selected because planners, policy makers and urban managers are often responsible for one or more of them. Indeed, these domains can be thought of as 'silos' of responsibility. There is no doubt that cities are 'systems' (Newman and

---

Box 22.1 Motivating low carbon and healthy decisions: calculating the co-benefits

Assessing the co-benefits of climate change mitigation policies and actions is not a straightforward task. The development of methodologies to do this is being embraced as part of the work of the Cooperative Research Centre for Low Carbon Living in Australia (www.lowcarbonlivingcrc.com. au). A proposed project is the development of a suite of calculators to assist and motivate low carbon policies and decision making. The calculators will use a co-benefits framework drawing on disciplinary knowledge from health, economics, environmental sustainability and urban planning, to quantify the multiple benefits of low carbon decisions. At its most complex, the calculator will facilitate low carbon decisions by policy makers and government officials that embrace the multiple benefits of reduced greenhouse gas emissions, enhanced economic benefits, and improved human health (both physical and mental). Use of the calculator will support better informed and more holistic urban planning decisions. As well as considering the issues typically taken into account (for example, solar access, provision of public domain and floor space ratios), a range of low carbon, human health and socio-cultural outcomes will be factored into the determination. Knowledge of the multiple benefits across sectors would assist in making the economic case for undertaking substantial environmental modifications on buildings and within precincts.

At the practice level professionals from the public and private sectors in the built environment and health could use a further iteration of the calculator to understand the benefits across multiple disciplinary areas of instituting low carbon initiatives. This could facilitate development and planning outcomes that embrace multiple benefits which are accepted and, indeed, sought by planners, developers, policy analysts and other key stakeholders to enhance the broader societal contributions of their work.

And at the third level, it is envisaged that community members would use the co-benefits calculator to allow deeper understandings about the many benefits of personal low carbon actions (such as taking the bus and walking, instead of using a motor car). In turn, this enhanced appreciation will act as an incentive for the take-up of such initiatives. The community calculator could be a mobile application on a smartphone or small computer.

Jennings 2008) and clearly urban settlements do not function as six discrete silos. On a daily basis, cities generate flows of water, energy, food and other resources which can be characterised as the 'ecological footprint' of the city (Rees 1992). The vertical axis of the matrix comprises determinants of human health and well-being. These include air quality, water quality, noise exposure, infection, chemical exposures, local climatic conditions, food security, physical activity, safety, interpersonal relationships and social capital. In aggregate, these factors – sometimes called 'risk factors' in public health – 'determine' our physical and mental health. The essence of the matrix is the cells created by the intersections between the six urban domains and the various determinants of health. In these cells, it is possible to ask planning, policy and research questions. The cells in the matrix have been populated with examples of factors that could lead to co-benefits. These examples are used for illustrative purposes only and are not a comprehensive listing. The matrix is a tool to support systematic identification of potential co-benefits of possible policy and planning interventions.

The Figure 22.6 matrix column entitled 'transport and urban form' has been expanded in Box 22.2 to serve as a useful illustration that further develops our understanding of different co-benefits for these factors.

Box 22.2 Transport, urban form and health: many interactions, many opportunities

The nature of the urban transport system – the mix of modes available and the infrastructure provided – and urban layout are key drivers of the health impacts of the urban transport 'task', and its environmental impacts, in any city. Urban transport emissions are major determinants of overall urban air quality that affect cardiovascular and respiratory health, in particular. If the city encourages walking and cycling and has a good mass transit system, local air quality will be better than in a city where the only convenient transport mode is the private motor car. During periods of heavy rain, motor vehicle pollutants are washed into storm water channels and contaminate creeks, rivers and oceans. Urban transport is also often the most important source of noise exposure in cities. People who live close to major roads can be exposed to high levels of noise during peak travel periods. Local climatic conditions are affected by both urban transport systems and urban form and layout because motor vehicle use contributes to the 'urban heat island' (see McKenzie, Chapter 18) and affects human health through heat stress, particularly during periods of hot weather. Making provision for trees and other vegetation in cities provides shade and ameliorates the urban heat island. Transport and urban form can determine where, and what, food people buy and consume. Healthy foods such as fruit and vegetables are (by definition) heavier than energy dense foods and older people, and people with disabilities, may have difficulty accessing a healthy diet unless it is available close to where they live. Growing food in the city – community gardens, nature strip plots – brings a variety of health co-benefits – physical activity, social interaction and a healthy diet. Transport systems and urban layout are important determinants of levels of activity in daily life. When planning supports walking and cycling by providing necessary safety and other infrastructure – particularly if essential shops and services are close to where people live – it is possible to get plenty of incidental physical activity in daily life. Transport systems and urban layout are determinants of the amount of time we spend commuting for work, education and recreation. In turn, this determines how much time remains for developing healthy interpersonal relationships and for community participation.

Conclusions: adopting a new paradigm

The Lancet commission on managing the health impacts of climate change finds that the ongoing change to the world's climate is the biggest global health threat of the twenty-first century (Costello et al. 2009). As well as underlining the urgent need for action, the commission's finding is an appeal to the indomitable human spirit to tackle this enormous challenge. It may well be the most complex scientific, economic, social and cultural challenge humanity has ever faced. Understanding co-benefits provides one pathway forward. It rests on an appreciation of what is driving global decision making today – the economic orthodoxy and cultural primacy of consumption and economic growth – as well as how we need to develop and grow in order to adapt and change.

For professionals working across the built environment and health disciplines, it is incumbent upon us to develop a new narrative aligning concerns about human health with planetary health. Future generations depend on this happening – we have a moral imperative to act.

Framework for urban sustainability and population health

This is a worked example of how the various urban domains relate to health determinants. For the purposes of illustration, a single example is used in each. (Box 22.2 provides some other examples for the transport and urban form column.) We encourage use of the framework to explore holistic co-benefits in a range of situations – by professionals to consider policy and planning issues; by academics to ask research questions; and by teachers to encourage students to envisage a wide range of co-benefits for environmental sustainability and health.

Urban ecological footprint →

Human health and well-being →

Economy and work	Transport and urban form	Housing and buildings	Nature and landscape	Media and communication	Culture and spirituality	
Working from home reduces VKT (vehicle kilometres travelled) and thereby decreases air and noise pollution	Infrastructure for walking, cycling and public transport reduces VKT and associated pollution	Improved building design, insulation and ventilation can improve indoor air quality and reduce energy use for heating and cooling	Greening the city with plants can reduce the urban heat island, associated thermal stress and run-off pollution in waterways	Monitors to measure household energy use and raise consciousness about energy conservation	Siesta in hot climates reduces thermal stress in the middle of the day and energy used to cool buildings	**Air, water, noise, infection, chemical exposures, local climate**
Urban and peri-urban agriculture can enhance resilience of the food system and access to healthy, fresh food	Local shops and markets reduce travel to source food, with particular benefits for older and less physically able people	Communal edible gardens in housing developments can enable access to fruit and vegetables, including cultural culinary preferences	An urban growth boundary can preserve arable land, proximity reducing food transport and enhancing food security	Fast food advertising should be restricted near schools to reduce consumption of fast food by children	Culturally diverse food landscapes enhance sense of belonging and sharing of different healthy food traditions	**Food security**
Changing rooms, showers, bike racks and lockers in workplaces make it practical to commute in physically active ways	Mixed use development can reduce commuting distances and enable active transport – walking, cycling and public transport	Improved location and visibility of stairs can encourage incidental activity for those who are able to participate	Provide greenspace (shaded in hot climates) for recreational walking and exercise in urban areas near to workplaces and residences	Signs in buildings to encourage use of stairs to move between floors thereby increasing incidental physical activity in everyday living and reducing energy used for lifts and escalators	Creating a cycling chic and greater appeal to women in countries where cycling participation rates are highly gendered	**Physical activity**

Safety	Provide standing workstations as standard workplace health and safety practice. Less sitting time counteracts our sedentary lifestyle	Provide dedicated cycle lanes to make cycling a safer activity and to reduce pedestrian injuries on shared pathways	Modify homes so that older people can continue to live safely, free from falls, in the community that they know and love	Create verge gardens in cities to increase separation between vehicles and pedestrians for a safer and more pleasant environment	Work with local communities to counteract negative media messages that give disproportionate publicity to violent and criminal activity, thereby challenging perceptions of lack of safety and encouraging outdoor activity	Revitalise streetscapes to enhance multicultural street life, bringing more people out and about, and enhancing belonging for all members of the community
Family relationships	Support telecommuting hubs as an alternative workplace closer to home. This will mean more time to be with family members and a healthier work/life balance	Create a mixed use city with work opportunities distributed across the urban area, reducing commuting stress and enhancing family relationships	Provide a diversity of housing types in residential locations to support ageing in place and extended family relationships across the generations	Provide well maintained and green local parks within easy walking distance of all residents so that family and friends can meet to play with children and have fun together	Provide high speed internet to every household to enable working at home, enabling less commuting and more time to be with family, enhancing relationships and sharing of domestic tasks	Valuing older people in the community as part of enhancing family and broader neighbourly relationships; a re-acknowledgement of the wisdom of the elders
Social capital	Enact policies that encourage decentralised urban hubs, distributing jobs, shops and services across the urban landscape and enabling civic activity throughout the day	Increases in active commuting (walking, cycling, public transport) can enhance social capital as neighbours recognise, greet and interact with each other on a daily basis	Promote active street frontages to bring people out into their neighbourhood, getting to know each other, sharing goods, and checking on older and less able folk	Provide dog parks in local residential areas, bringing people together as they have fun exercising their pets; social barriers are broken down and relationships blossom	Promote sustainability street initiatives to bring neighbours together in cooperative environmental activities	Promote work/life balance to allow time for social connection and community participation

Figure 22.6 A matrix for integrative understanding of urban sustainability and population health

Source: Thompson and Capon.

Traditional ways of working are no longer advancing understanding. We require a transcendence of disciplines. This goes beyond medical sovereignty of knowledge about health to alternate understandings that embrace traditional philosophies, indigenous knowledge and human ecology. It also demands breaking down the 'compartmentalization of scientific and professional knowledge' and the 'applicability gap' – which can be defined as the absence of 'effective collaboration between scientists, professionals, and policy decision makers' working across natural and built environments (Lawrence 2010, p. 125). Joined-up, respectful and integrative ways of working are the only way forward. And we have to learn as we go, being adaptive managers sharing our stories, reflecting on what worked well and where we did not achieve the desired outcome (Economos et al. 2013). This is no easy task, requiring a seismic shift in our values and how we operate – and a commitment to a shared future vision (Capon and Thompson 2011).

In short,

> An urgent transformation is required in our values and our practices based on recognition of our interdependence and the interconnectedness of the risks we face. We need a new vision of cooperative and democratic action at all levels of society and a new principle of planetism and wellbeing for every person on this Earth – a principle that asserts that we must conserve, sustain, and make resilient the planetary and human systems on which health depends by giving priority to the wellbeing of all.
>
> *(Horton et al. 2014, p. 847)*

This is not just about recognising the environmental risks to our survival; it is also about our responsibilities as privileged citizens in a world redolent with inequity, mistrust of those in control and intolerance. We join with Horton and colleagues in visioning a planet that 'nourishes and sustains the diversity of life with which we coexist and on which we depend'. An understanding of health co-benefits is one starting point for the necessary transformation.

Note

1 City of Sydney Council. 2014. *Green roofs and walls.* www.cityofsydney.nsw.gov.au/vision/sustainable-sydney-2030/strategic-directions/a-leading-environmental-performer/greening-the-city/green-roofs-and-walls, accessed 8 April 2015.

References

Boyden, S. 2013. Biohistory. In Singh, S.J., Haberl, H., Chertow, M., Mirtl, M. and Schmid, M. (Eds.) *Long term socio-ecological research: studies in society-nature interactions across spatial and temporal scales*, New York: Springer. Also at www.biosensitivefutures.org.au/content-images/bio-triangle-2.jpg/view, accessed 8 April 2015.

Brook, I. 2010. The importance of nature, green spaces, and gardens in human well-being. *Ethics, Place and Environment: A Journal of Philosophy and Geography* V13(3): 295–312.

Butler, C., Dixon, J. and Capon, A.G. (Eds). 2014. *Healthy people, places and planet: reflections based on Tony McMichael's four decades of contribution to epidemiological understanding.* Canberra: ANU E-Press.

Capon, A.G. and Thompson, S.M. 2011. Built environments of the future. In Dannenberg, A.L., Frumkin, H. and Jackson, R.J. (Eds.) *Making healthy places: designing and building for health, wellbeing and sustainability.* Washington, DC: Island Press: 366–378.

Chapman, R., Howden-Chapman, P., Viggers, H., O'Dea, D. and Kennedy, M. 2009. Retrofitting houses with insulation: a cost-benefit analysis of a randomised community trial. *Journal of Epidemiology and Community Health* 63(4): 271–277.

Costello, A., Abbas, M., Allen, A., Ball, S., Bell, S., Bellamy, R., Friel, S., Groce, N., Johnson, A., Kett, M., Lee, M., Levy, C., Maslin, M., McCoy, D., McGuire, B., Montgomery, H., Napier, D., Pagel, C.,

Patel, J., Puppim de Oliveira, J.A., Redclift, N., Rees, H., Rogger, D., Scott, J., Stephenson, J., Twigg, J., Wolff, J. and Patterson, C. 2009. Managing the health effects of climate change. *The Lancet* V373(9676): 1693–1733.

Dennekamp, M. and Carey, M. 2010. Air quality and chronic disease: why action on climate change is also good for health. *NSW Public Health Bulletin* 21(5–6): 115–121.

Devine-Wright, P. 2011. Renewable energy and the public: from NIMBY to participation. London; Washington, DC: Earthscan.

Dunstan, D.W., Kingwell, B.A., Larsen, R., Healy, G.N., Cerin, E., Hamilton, M.T., Shaw, J.E., Bertovic, D.A., Zimmet, P.Z., Salmon, J. and Owen, N. 2012. Breaking up prolonged sitting reduces postprandial glucose and insulin responses. *Diabetes Care* V35: 976–983.

Economos, C.D., Sallis, J.F., Keith, N.R. and Newkirk, J. 2013. The active living research 2013 conference: achieving change across sectors: integrating research, policy, and practice. *American Journal of Health Promotion* 2014; 28(3 Suppl): S1–4.

Egger, G.J. and Dixon, J.B. 2010. Obesity and global warming: are they similar 'canaries' in the same 'mineshaft'? *Medical Journal of Australia* 193(11/12): 635–637.

Friel, S., Dangour, A.D., Garnett, T., Lock, K., Chalabi, Z., Roberts, I., Butler, A., Butler, C.D., Waage, J., McMichael, A.J. and Haines, A. 2009. Public health benefits of strategies to reduce greenhouse gas emissions: food and agriculture. *The Lancet* 374: 2016–2025.

Ganten, D., Haines, A. and Souhami, R. 2010. Health co-benefits of policies to tackle climate change. *The Lancet* 376: 1802–1804.

Hicks, J. and Ison, N. 2011. Community-owned renewable energy (CRE): opportunities for rural Australia. *Rural Sociology* 20: 244–255.

Hinrichs, C., Gillespie, G. and Feenstra, G. 2004. Social learning and innovation at retail farmers' markets. *Rural Sociology* 69(1): 31–58.

Horton, R., Beaglehole, R., Bonita, R., Raeburn, J., McKee, M. and Wall, S. 2014. From public to planetary health: a manifesto. *The Lancet* V383 (March): 847.

IPCC (Intergovernmental Panel on Climate Change). 2014 human health: impacts, adaptation, and co-benefits. In *Climate change 2014: impacts, adaptation, and vulnerability*. IPCC Working Group II Contribution to AR5. http://ipcc-wg2.gov/AR5/images/uploads/WGIIAR5-Chap11_FGDall.pdf, accessed 1 May 2014.

Kent, J.L. and Thompson, S.M. 2014. The three domains of urban planning for health and well-being. *Journal of Planning Literature* 29(3): 239–256.

Lang, T. and Rayner, G. 2012. Ecological public health: the 21st century's big idea? *British Medical Journal* 345: e5466.

Lapping, M. 2004. Toward the recovery of the local in the globalizing food system: the role of alternative agricultural and food models in the US. *Ethics, Place & Environment* 7(3): 141–150.

Lawrence, R.J. 2010, Deciphering interdisciplinary and transdisciplinary contributions. *Transdisciplinary Journal of Engineering & Science* V1(1): 125–130.

McMichael, A.J., Powles, J.W., Butler, C.D. and Uauy, R. 2007. Food, livestock production, energy, climate change, and health. *The Lancet* 370(9594): 1253–1263.

McMichael, T., Montgomery, H. and Costello, A. 2012. Health risks, present and future, from global climate change. *British Medical Journal* 344: e1359.

Medibank Private. 2008. *The cost of physical inactivity*. Medibank Private, Australia. www.medibank.com.au/Client/Documents/Pdfs/The_Cost_Of_Physical_Inactivity_08.pdf, accessed 1 May 2014.

Newman, P. and Jennings, I. 2008. *Cities as sustainable ecosystems: principles and practices*. Washington, DC: Island Press.

Rees, W.E. 1992. Ecological footprints and appropriated carrying capacity: what urban economics leaves out. *Environment and Urbanization* 4: 121–130.

Rhodes, R., Mark, R.S. and Temmel, C.P. 2012. Adult sedentary behavior: a systematic review. *American Journal of Preventative Medicine* V42(3): e3–e28.

Rockström, J., Steffen, W., Noone, K., Persson, A. and Chapin, S. 2009. A safe operating space for humanity. *Nature* 461 (September): 472–475.

RTA and DECC (Roads and Traffic Authority of NSW and the Department of Environment and Climate Change). 2009. *Evaluation of the costs and benefits to the community of financial investment in cycling programs and projects in New South Wales*. www.pcal.nsw.gov.au/__data/assets/pdf_file/0008/90899/Evaluation_of_NSW_cycling_study.pdf, accessed 8 April 2015.

Seyfang, G., Park, J.J. and Smith, A. 2013. A thousand flowers blooming? An examination of community energy in the UK. *Energy Policy* 61, 977–989.

Shaw, C., Hales, S. and Howden-Chapman, P. 2014. Health co-benefits of climate change mitigation policies in the transport sector. *Nature Climate Change* 4(6): 427–433.

Smith, A. 2013. *The climate bonus: co-benefits of climate policy*. Abingdon: Earthscan from Routledge.

Thompson, S., Corkery, L. and Judd, B. 2007. The role of community gardens in sustaining healthy communities. Paper presented at the State of Australian Cities National Conference, Adelaide. http://soac.fbe.unsw.edu.au/2007/SOAC/theroleofcommunitygardens.pdf, accessed 8 April 2015.

Trubka, R., Newman, P. and Bilsborough, D. 2010. The costs of urban sprawl: physical activity links to healthcare costs and productivity. *Environment Design Guide* GEN 85: 1–13.

Wilkinson, P., Smith, K.R., Davies, M., Adair, H., Armstrong, B.G., Barrett, M., Bruce, N., Haines, A., Hamilton, I., Oreszczyn, T., Ridley, I., Tonne, C. and Chalabi Z. 2009. Public health benefits of strategies to reduce greenhouse-gas emissions: household energy. *The Lancet* 374: 1917–1929.

23

DELIVERING HEALTHY PLACES

The role of the private sector

James de Havilland and Sarah Burgess

Introduction: the private sector perspective

The private sector plays a major role in the creation of our towns and cities. It influences the location, design and quality of housing as well as the mix of land uses and public spaces in neighbourhoods. In order to achieve healthy and sustainable settlements it is important that developers take a holistic approach to place-making; one that not only provides housing but addresses the social, cultural, economic and environmental aspects of successful places (Calcutt 2007; Maliene and Malys 2009). However, in England, despite a national planning policy framework that specifically identifies the need for vibrant and healthy communities, with accessible services that support its health, social and cultural well-being (DCLG 2012), this is not a straightforward task. Like many parts of the world, including North America and Australia, there is still a question over how well good intentions are carried through by the development industry and local decision-makers.

This chapter explores the existing system of housing delivery in the United Kingdom (UK) and the role of private developers in shaping towns and cities. While there is a UK focus, the barriers for delivering healthy and sustainable outcomes as well as the opportunities to achieve high quality outcomes are not unique to the UK. Two case studies are used to highlight positive examples of health-led masterplans and to identify the tools and approaches that can be used to achieve positive outcomes. The chapter begins with an overview of the dominant housing delivery mechanism in the UK, the large 'volume' house builder, and concludes by identifying key lessons from the two case studies about how the private sector can deliver healthy, sustainable neighbourhoods.

Characteristics of the existing approach to housing delivery

In the UK, over 85 per cent of new homes are developed by the private sector (CPRE 2014). The creation of new communities is, therefore, largely dependent on the objectives and processes of the house building industry. House builders operate within a highly commercial and competitive environment and their ultimate focus is on maximising profit to deliver value for shareholders. On the whole, rather than seeking to achieve the best possible outcome, the focus of house builders will be to meet the minimum standard needed to gain planning approval.

House builders are inherently conservative and cater for a specific market that they have identified and efficiently respond to. Often, high risk and low return investments (such as mixed use) are avoided. This risk aversion is perpetuated by the planning and policy environment in which house builders operate (Gyourko and Rybczynski 2000) as well as the cyclical 'boom and bust' nature of the economic system (Crabtree and Hes 2009). This means that when demand is low, the product must have the widest appeal and when demand is high, anything will sell. Therefore, pressure to change the product and the way it is delivered is often met with resistance from the industry.

It is also worth acknowledging that in relation to the entire housing stock, new housing is a very small percentage. Often, as a society, we expect a great deal of change to be delivered from what is in effect a very narrow proportion of the market. That said, new development still offers the greatest opportunity to deliver improvements to the built environment and the lives of existing and future populations.

The modern housing industry is a relatively young industry, only recently grown after the war and the demise of mass social housing provision. During this period, there has been little evidence that high quality places have been achieved on a regular basis (CABE 2004, 2005, 2006; Williams and Lindsay 2005). It could be argued that this is due to the constant variation of regulatory controls, including government and local authority policy changes, political variance and interference, for example, the abolition of the Regional Spatial Strategies in England, and the changing requirements for meeting a minimum density (ODPM 2000; DCLG 2012). This ever changing policy background has created an uncertain housing and development market. A lack of clear thinking and decision making at a local level has further exacerbated this uncertainty. This over politicised framework has not helped a juvenile industry to set standards driven by quality or a clear framework to guide design.

A profit-driven investment

The interest of private house builders in new residential-led development is usually short term and the focus is on the sale of individual houses rather than any long-term stewardship of the neighbourhood or the community (Kriese and Scholz 2011). This is at odds with issues of health, which tend to be related to long-term outcomes. For this reason house builders' interest in health and sustainability is generally limited to what, in policy terms, they are required to provide as a minimum. The lack of sufficient incentives to deliver quality is a recognised weakness of the current model (Calcutt 2007).

That said the primary objective of the house builder is to achieve planning permission so that they may build their product and acquire the financial return. To achieve planning permission they need to fulfil planning policy agendas and objectives. In doing this, they will seek to minimise the financial risk in achieving these policies. However, up to the gaining of planning permission, a pragmatic approach will be taken to ensure that this goal is achieved. However, this is a game of two halves. The first relates to obtaining planning permission. Gaining planning permission on a piece of land creates significant additional value, therefore if 'ticking the policy boxes' allows planning permission to be achieved more quickly, then, invariably, the development proposal will accommodate these requirements. However, the second half is the delivery of the product after planning permission has been obtained. The delivery of policy requirements are often viewed as 'additional costs' and thus house builders will seek to minimise these through negotiation of planning obligations or the mitigation of costs through value engineering and cheaper alternatives (Williams and Dair 2006). Therefore, it is critical that planning policy, at the outset, explicitly identifies place-making principles and clear requirements are identified and consistently promoted for the development proposal by the local authority.

Land value and availability

There is a strong case to argue that the current manner in which land comes to the market for development makes it difficult for any developer to achieve the best development possible. In order for a development to deliver high quality housing with a sustainable provision of services in a healthy and desirable environment, it needs to be above a particular size to achieve a critical mass; be in the right location to meet demand; and have the ability to generate sufficient value from the land to pay for the development as well as return a profit for the stakeholders invested in the process. The problem with the current speculative model of land promotion in the UK is that it is heavily weighted toward the landowner in fiscal benefit terms. This, coupled with the short-term politicised housing land supply agenda required by national government (local authorities need to demonstrate five years land supply plus 20 per cent), creates a recipe for poorly planned, poorly funded and poorly designed developments.

That said, without primary legislation to fundamentally change the land model, we must work within the system that exists. Local authorities need to recognise their role in the speculative land market as they can significantly influence the market. Proactively planning for long-term housing needs and taking full account of the delays in the process as well as seeking to avoid a monopoly in any given location can go a long way in stabilising land prices. The more land available, the less likely land value will be overinflated and the better the outcomes that can be delivered within the developers' financial model.

Viability and undelivered promises

At the outset, designers are able to initiate mechanisms that can facilitate community involvement and the delivery of high quality physical structures that allow developments to maximise health benefits. However, all too often initial ambitions and proposals are watered down as the development process progresses and many features are never realised on the ground. The test comes during viability testing and negotiations about planning obligations (which, in England, can occur post-planning approval). In the absence of government funding, the developer must pay for the 'non-profit' aspects of the development (which will include important social infrastructure such as affordable housing, education and community facilities). This is the point when many of these worthy elements are 'played off' against each other in a 'competition' for funding in the limited pool of resource (accrued from the increase in land value gained by the planning permission). At this point all of the brave and bold strategic ideas that have, until now, added value to the proposal and allowed for a successful application are often no longer seen as valued items by the developer; they are seen as 'additional' costs, eating into profit margins. Designs can rapidly change during the planning and post-planning stages leading to the loss of facilities, build quality or design features. Financial grounds are more often than not the reason provided for this watering down of quality and provision; however, conflicting or weak policies and technical requirements can also significantly contribute to the degradation of a proposal. If high quality, health-orientated developments are to be ensured, a thorough understanding of the delivery mechanisms and technical issues are required at the masterplanning stage to ensure that funds are available for delivery of all that was promised in the planning application.

Case studies of alternative approaches

Two case studies are presented to highlight that best practice at the design stage through stakeholder engagement, consideration of realistic financial costs of delivery and innovative management vehicles can produce schemes with the necessary attributes of healthy developments. These two case studies are significant as they have been designed for delivery by large 'volume' house builders. A critical tool that was used throughout the iterative design process was the use of a simple checklist. This ensured that all design decisions had regard to key health and sustainability aspects and to ensure that best practice was considered. The checklist prompted stakeholders and designers to question whether the development provided:

- community space and opportunities for social interaction;
- well-connected networks for active travel;
- safe places with a focus on crime reduction;
- local facilities and services and opportunities for local employment;
- adaptable homes that meet local needs and are designed for life;
- beauty in the built and natural environment;
- a minimisation of resource use to address climate change agendas; and
- acceptable air quality and noise levels.

Both case studies represent significant masterplan developments. They are, at the time of writing, presented at the pre-planning stage. As such, both should be subject to further study at the implementation stage to ascertain the success of the proposals in delivery and the creation of healthy developments.

Case study one: consolidation of the urban boundary

A health-led masterplan has been prepared for a 23-hectare development site in the urban–rural fringe. While the site is outside the area designated for development in the local plan, it is well located in relation to existing settlements. The design approach was to create a high quality neighbourhood that reinforces the existing transport and local facilities to promote physical health and mental well-being. The masterplan includes the development of 400 dwellings as well as a new local centre that will provide a community building, local shop and doctor's surgery that will service the new and existing communities.

The existing green infrastructure has been identified as a backbone for the development concept. The existing green assets, including hedgerows that created the boundaries of the agricultural fields that make up the site at present (Figure 23.1), has been used to guide the network of connected and mature green infrastructure. This has created a series of safe and attractive open spaces, varying in size, function and character, including a community orchard and allotments for local food production, wildlife habitats and walking and cycling corridors. Dwellings have been sited into this green framework which means that each dwelling has access to a greenspace within 100 metres, providing opportunities for recreation, exercise and contact with greenery.

The house builder involved with this proposal understands the difficulties of ensuring the longevity of responsibility and governance required to sustain the community places and spaces. In response to this, the house builder is establishing a community trust to ensure that the community spaces are managed in an inclusive manner with the full involvement of stakeholders, new residents and occupiers. A community trust is a neighbourhood government vehicle that allows the developer to provide seed funding to establish the long-term management of community assets.

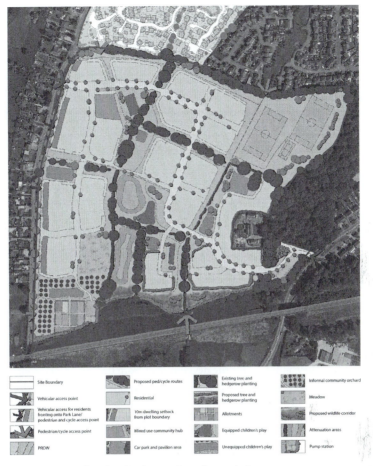

Site Boundary	Proposed ped/cycle routes	Existing tree and hedgerow planting	Informal community orchard
Vehicular access point	Residential	Proposed tree and hedgerow planting	Meadow
Vehicular access for residents fronting onto Park Lane/ pedestrian and cycle access point	10m dwelling setback from plot boundary	Allotments	Proposed wildlife corridor
Pedestrian/cycle access point	Mixed use community hub	Equipped children's play	Attenuation areas
PROW	Car park and pavilion area	Unequipped children's play	Pump station

Figure 23.1   Concept masterplan showing integration of green infrastructure

Source: Barton Willmore on behalf of Barratt Homes.

The ownership of the assets is transferred to the trust along with an ongoing management charge paid by the new community, providing a future income for the trust. This provides a mechanism to ensure that the provision of important elements within the design are realised and funded. This was a key aspect to the successful incorporation of high quality communal greenspace, natural areas and amenity assets that are critical to the delivery of a healthy neighbourhood.

This development is particularly contentious as the site is not identified within the local plan. However, the area provides a plausible location for expansion of the town and will help to meet local housing need. The masterplan has promoted health and well-being as a central concept and the design successfully reflects this aspiration. The house builder has been keen to deliver on this agenda, as promoted in national policy, as it recognises that this approach presents the greatest chance of success for planning permission.

Case study two: creating a new community

The second case study is a larger masterplan that highlights the important role of the local authority in identifying a suitable area for development. The local authority and developer both

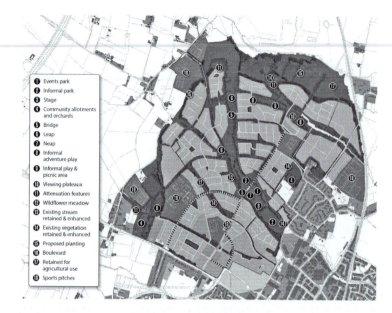

Legend:
1. Events park
2. Informal park
3. Stage
4. Community allotments and orchards
5. Bridge
6. Leap
7. Neap
8. Informal adventure play
9. Informal play & picnic area
10. Viewing plateaux
11. Attenuation features
12. Wildflower meadow
13. Existing stream retained & enhanced
14. Existing vegetation retained & enhanced
15. Proposed planting
16. Boulevard
17. Retained for agricultural use
18. Sports pitches

Figure 23.2   Masterplan showing key features of the development

Source: Barton Willmore on behalf of Persimmon & Bovis Homes.

recognised health as a key ambition for the development from the outset, and sought to embody best practice design principles to deliver a healthy place. The masterplan, which includes a major new commercial and business centre and over 4,500 new dwellings, is the culmination of an inclusive design process and the result of a number of workshops with local stakeholders and planning officers over a seven-year period (Figure 23.2). This significant urban extension is arranged in a polycentric structure, which consists of overlapping neighbourhoods where people can access key facilities for daily living on foot, bike or bus. This physical arrangement is driven by the aspiration to create a healthy neighbourhood, ensuring that it is walkable and offers a variety of activities on the doorstep for all ages.

Similar to the other case study, the scheme is structured around a multifunctional green infrastructure network. A central recreation spine forms the hub of the informal recreational space and is linked to the wider provision of formalised playing fields via green connections, which promote biodiversity as well as providing attractive routes for walking and cycling. Throughout the network are high quality community spaces such as new allotments, community orchards and active natural play spaces. This network provides opportunities for social interaction with connections between key uses within the site and to the wider area.

The masterplan supports a range of architectural styles and details, which contribute to giving the development a sense of place and identity. The proposal allows for 35 per cent affordable housing and explores the opportunity for self-build plots. The layout of buildings, streets and public spaces maximise accessibility and opportunities for natural surveillance and active street frontages. Buildings will be designed at an appropriate scale to their surroundings and to maximise solar, wind and water gains. Building heights will be varied with breaks in the building line to reduce shadowing and increase solar access within the perimeter blocks. Short distances to local shops, facilities and greenspaces provide opportunities for social interaction and reduce

Figure 23.3   The layout and high quality public realm encourages social interaction

Source: Barton Willmore on behalf of Persimmon & Bovis Homes.

feelings of isolation (Figure 23.3). An inclusive social environment is also promoted through the provision of different house types, sizes and tenures that have the capacity to expand and adapt to changing needs.

This case study highlights how large developments provide the best opportunity to deliver healthy communities, as physical elements of a healthy and sustainable neighbourhood can be designed and integrated into the built form. Funding for these elements can also be incorporated and planned for from the outset. Larger projects also offer the opportunity to test new and innovative solutions and approaches to community management and governance. But this process takes time. This masterplan design is the culmination of ten years of engagement and promotion – a considerable time given this site is identified in the local plan and has the support of the local authority. During this gestation time, the planning process has been subject to significant change both politically and from a policy perspective. These changes have served to create difficult conditions for developers resulting in costly delays and much uncertainty about delivery. But this is just the start of the process. Once consented, the masterplan will have a build delivery life of approximately 20 years. This represents a period of private sector investment of 30–40 years, before the return on investment is fully realised. This is a long time period for any investment model and thus ways of reducing these time and cost burdens need to be explored. If a new model can be delivered that enables a depoliticising of strategic sites and increased certainty this would go a long way to developing a better collaborative planning process and more funds to dedicate towards healthier and more sustainable urban environments.

Key lessons for delivering high quality, healthy places

The two case studies set a clear ambition for health and used a set of criteria to help shape the design of the masterplans. They highlighted a number of potential barriers that can act as an impediment to successfully achieving these ambitions; however, they also demonstrated that key aspects of healthy urban environments, such as the provision of multifunctional greenspaces, attractive sustainable transport opportunities and the design of the built form can be achieved. Key lessons for delivering high quality, healthy places include:

- *Local authority leadership*: delivery of high quality, healthy and sustainable places should be high on the local authority agenda in recognition of the long-term benefits that a well-designed and functional living environment can provide. If presented with policy certainty and a robust and timely application process, then quality responses can be commonly achieved. Local authorities should promote a transparent and holistic approach to development standards and requirements.

- *Health as a core planning agenda*: a proactive approach to health is needed so that it sits hand in hand with sustainability. This requires early incorporation of basic health and well-being parameters and early stakeholder involvement.

- *Viability at the outset*: local authorities should establish, at an early stage of the design process, the key design elements required through clear policies and early consultation with stakeholders. This enables developers to identify likely land requirements and incorporate essential features into their financial calculations, enabling a realistic expectation of the value of the land and a 'rebalancing' of the fiscal benefits that currently favour the landowner.

- *Local authority landownership and control*: another way of ensuring that the fiscal benefits of increased land value are relayed to the new community is for the local authority to take an active role in development and the upfront delivery of infrastructure and facilities (see chapters by Falk, Grant and Barton, and Mørck for examples of how this is done in Europe).

- *Alternative models of management*: the provision of infrastructure is a key health component and this has a significant cost implication in terms of maintenance and management of assets once delivered. The liability for this has historically fallen to the local authority to maintain. However, more cost-effective means are emerging, such as community trusts, community asset seed-funding and other neighbourhood governance tools. These models can also promote innovation and encourage a sense of local ownership and civic pride (Kriese and Scholz 2011).

- *Developing a common interest*: honest, open and ongoing engagement with the community is needed with a real commitment to developing a communal vision for the proposal. This supports the early identification of issues and problems and provides the ability to capitalise on and respond to local initiatives, harnessing the energy and resourcefulness of local stakeholders and incorporation of their agendas. This will require the establishment of appropriate new local agencies, forums and mechanisms for communication, forward thinking and decision making, capacity building debate and incorporation of feedback. Planning Performance Agreements (PPAs) are a tool used in England to agree upfront the community involvement process.[1]

- *Utilising best practice and local creative solutions*: detailed planning, design and implementation phases should create site-specific solutions that build on established practices as well as finding new ways to ensure that development meets the aspirations of the existing and new communities. This includes innovative forms of ownership and management. Professional bodies should ensure that the knowledge and experiences are shared amongst designers, developers and decision-makers, and that the right tools are available and accessible.

- *A role for small and medium sized developers*: there are a growing number of small and medium sized developers, as well as housing co-operatives, that seek to single themselves out as providers of a better product, in terms of both residential design and build quality as well as the wider neighbourhood environment and facilities. These companies have a vested interest in embracing a quality agenda as this approach allows them to appeal to a higher value market. They are also more willing to attempt more innovative approaches than the larger publically limited companies; they are often privately owned companies and thus do not have the same level of fiscal pressure exerted upon them (Kriese and Scholz 2011). Thus, these companies can bring fresh attitudes to the provision of innovative approaches given the right decision making environment.

- *Communal self-interest*: there is a growing recognition that the move towards a more individualist society in recent decades has many weaknesses and this is leading to the realisation that collaborative efforts can bring wider local benefits to the community and environment (Barton Willmore 2012). This shift in societal thinking should be capitalised on by developers to ensure that community involvement in the design of new places can overcome the established norm of a lack of interest.
- *Identifying new opportunities for engagement*: internet participation and feedback in the community, commercial and political arenas is growing as social media plays a greater role in our society. It provides a relatively accessible, wide reaching and cheap option for communication, involvement and debate. These mechanisms also have the potential to be the vehicle for localised social and community organisations, acting as information hubs and organisational tools (Barton Willmore 2012).

Conclusions: housing development for healthy communities

Health in the built environment is gradually moving to the forefront of planning policy agendas and as such will need to be addressed by all developers and their consultants when proposing schemes for new housing. Many elements of the health agenda are already being delivered, in part by other agendas and policies. However, often aspects of these are lost at the implementation stage of development due to viability reasons as they carry little weight individually and lose out to more traditionally funded elements such as affordable housing and education. This results in a reduced quality scheme and diminished health agenda. The case studies show how principles of healthy places can be practically implemented within masterplanned schemes. The bringing together of the various aspects of design of the built environment and community governance under the umbrella of healthy communities brings new vibrancy to the quality of place and well-being agenda.

The complexity of social, economic, political and environmental factors differ geographically and change over time and are a major challenge for the delivery of healthy communities by the private sector. A 'health first' approach should be adopted within the design and decision making processes which requires commitment across disciplines to ensure that health and well-being outcomes are achieved. This includes the early involvement of stakeholders to ensure a transparent and integrated approach that delivers the most beneficial scheme. Although the local authority holds the key to initiate this process and creates a strong local policy background for its implementation, the private sector has an important role in ensuring adherence to the involvement process and ensuring a high quality design is delivered.

Note

1 ATLAS (2014) *Planning performance agreements*. www.atlasplanning.com/page/ppa.cfm, accessed 8 April 2015.

References

Barton Willmore. 2012. *New market towns*. Reading: Barton Willmore. Available at: www.bartonwillmore. co.uk/resources/new-market-towns, accessed 8 April 2015.
CABE. 2004. *Housing audit: London, the South East and East of England*. London: CABE.
CABE. 2005. *Housing audit: North East, North West and Yorkshire and Humber*. London: CABE.

CABE. 2006. *Housing audit: East Midlands, West Midlands and the South West.* London: CABE.

Calcutt, J. 2007. *The Callcutt Review of housebuilding delivery.* London: Communities and Local Government.

CPRE. 2014. *Increasing diversity in the housing building sector.* London: Campaign to Protect Rural England.

Crabtree, L. and Hes, D. 2009. Sustainability uptake in housing in metropolitan Australia: an institutional problem, not a technological one. *Housing Studies.* 24(2), 203–224.

DCLG (Department of Communities and Local Government). 2012. *National planning policy framework.* London: Communities and Local Government.

Gyourko, J.E. and Rybczynski, W. 2000. Financing new urbanism projects: obstacles and solutions. *Housing Policy Debate.* 11(3), 733–750.

Kriese, U. and Scholz, R.W. 2011. The positioning of sustainability within residential property marketing. *Urban Studies* 48(7), 1503–1527.

Maliene, V. and Malys, N. 2009. High-quality housing: a key issue in delivering sustainable communities. *Building and Environment.* 44, 426–430.

ODPM (Office of the Deputy Prime Minister). 2000. Planning policy guidance 3: housing. London: ODPM.

Williams, K. and Dair, C. 2006. What is stopping sustainable building in England? Barriers experienced by stakeholders in delivering sustainable developments. *Sustainable Development.* 15, 135–147.

Williams, K. and Lindsay, M. 2005. The extent and nature of sustainable building in England: an analysis of progress. *Planning Theory and Practice.* 8(1), 31–49.

24

BUILDING COLLABORATIVE PARTNERSHIPS

Lynda Addison

Introduction: the need for joined-up working

How we plan and manage the places we create for people affects health and well-being. The issues we face – of growing health inequalities, obesity, ageing population, housing need, globalisation and climate change – are all cross-cutting in nature. They require different authorities, spatial areas, disciplines, sectors and communities to work together. From my own work undertaken with many local authorities in England, supporting them in developing their planning strategies, few members, officers or those in the community fully understand sustainable development, or the relevance of health, or their implications for planning (that is, the integration of economic, transport, housing and green infrastructure policies and actions).[1] A collaborative, joined-up policy process for health and sustainable development is still not mainstreamed in most local authorities.

It is of fundamental importance that local authorities, as part of delivering their planning and other functions, recognise the need to build collaborative partnerships, and have the expertise and tools to do so. This requires a change of culture and attitudes, and the development of skills of communication and negotiation (Forester 1989; Healey 1997, 2006).

This chapter looks at the importance of collaborative planning and decision-making to achieve healthy and sustainable places. It explores the different methods of partner engagement and joint working and the various stakeholders that could, and should, be involved. It assesses the challenges with building collaborative partnerships but also celebrates the opportunities that it presents. The approach is based on the principle that local authorities, as a whole, are responsible for planning their area, not just planning departments working independently of other services and functions of the authority. This approach is core to England's Planning Advisory Service/Innovation and Development Agency benchmark of an 'ideal planning authority' (Innovation and Development Agency, Addison & Associates 2009). Hence collaborative partnerships start within the local authority as part of everyday practice and a way of working, not an occasional task.

The chapter draws on my experience in England. Legislative frameworks, cultural attitudes and policies vary. However, the principles, tools and expertise highlighted are generic, and apply equally to other countries. The evolving situation in England offers scope for collaborative partnerships, and helps to justify this England-focused approach.

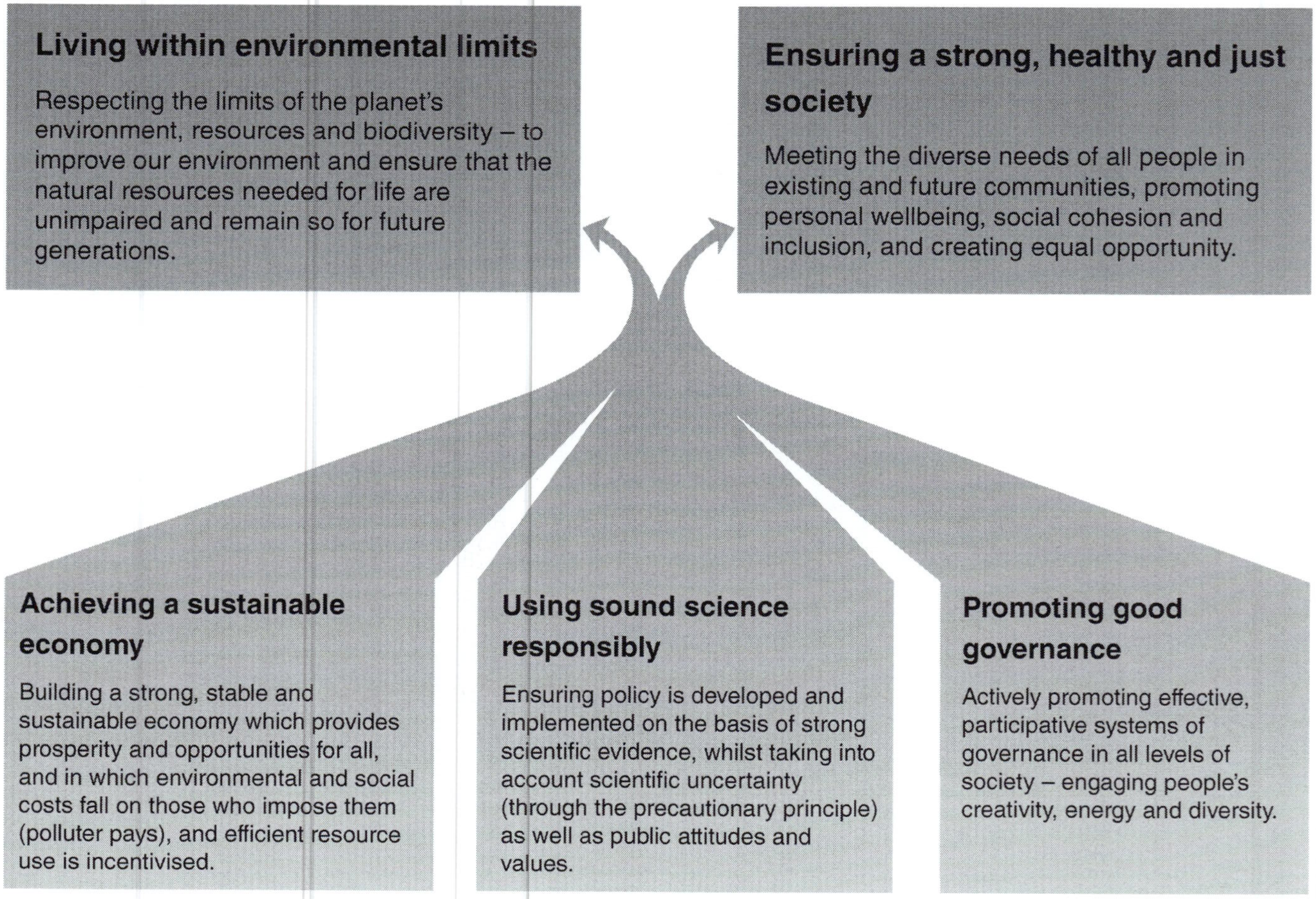

Living within environmental limits

Respecting the limits of the planet's environment, resources and biodiversity – to improve our environment and ensure that the natural resources needed for life are unimpaired and remain so for future generations.

Ensuring a strong, healthy and just society

Meeting the diverse needs of all people in existing and future communities, promoting personal wellbeing, social cohesion and inclusion, and creating equal opportunity.

Achieving a sustainable economy

Building a strong, stable and sustainable economy which provides prosperity and opportunities for all, and in which environmental and social costs fall on those who impose them (polluter pays), and efficient resource use is incentivised.

Using sound science responsibly

Ensuring policy is developed and implemented on the basis of strong scientific evidence, whilst taking into account scientific uncertainty (through the precautionary principle) as well as public attitudes and values.

Promoting good governance

Actively promoting effective, participative systems of governance in all levels of society – engaging people's creativity, energy and diversity.

Figure 24.1 Understanding sustainable development

Source: Sustainable Development Commission (2005).

Note: Acronyms refer to departments and agencies of UK government.

Meeting the challenge of sustainable development and healthy planning

The importance of taking a holistic approach to planning, highlighting the relevance of planning to health, quality of life, viability of town centres, active travel, sustainability and climate change, heritage and transport as well as the economy is central to sustainable development (for England, see Department for Communities and Local Government (DCLG) 2011 and 2012). The definition of sustainable development provided in Figure 24.1 makes clear the centrality of health and well-being.

The more recent *National Planning Policy Framework* (DCLG 2012) reinforces this alliance. The Settlement Health Map (see Chapter 1, Figure 1.2; Barton and Grant 2006), which acts as the conceptual framework for the book, shows how the determinants of health relate to all facets of sustainable development. Spatial planning influences the whole spectrum. Whether the focus is a region, a city, a town or a village, the purpose of planning is to create places where people want to live and work, where healthy lifestyles come naturally, where local and global ecosystems are robust, and what we do today does not create problems for the future.

My work with local authorities suggests that few planners use these holistic concepts of healthy spatial planning or sustainable development effectively. The terms are used in policy documents, without being followed through in any consistent way. Rhetoric is not converted into action.

If spatial planning means . . .

- considering social, economic and environmental issues together in relation to place;
- putting people's quality of life, health and well-being at the heart of planning;
- the use and management of geographical space for all activities;
- coordination and alignment of services;
- working collaboratively across all sectors and across boundaries;
- providing a framework for action on climate change and delivery of sustainable development;
- ensuring implementation is a key part of process.

. . . then spatial as well as activity-based partnerships are essential to provide for the cohesion of places and to address the complexities involved.

Research confirms that there are significant benefits in pursuing a partnership approach (Audit Commission 1998).[2] The health and well-being of communities stands to gain (Ross and Chang 2012). The Audit Commission report lists the benefits thus:

- agreeing and achieving common goals;
- achieving value for money;
- bringing in skills and other strengths;
- developing integrated strategies;
- increasing an ability to deliver a breadth of agenda;
- a louder voice and more weight (e.g. with government);
- reduced duplication of work;
- clarity of message in local area – community leadership;
- driving improvement and innovation;
- creating collaborative approach to problem solving;
- closer working with critical friends.

Governments' responses have varied over the years. Regional and subregional structures of various forms have been instituted to promote collaboration. Local strategic partnerships and community strategies were intended to embrace a wide range of agencies and departments, including health authorities. Now, in 2014, with the abolition of strategic planning authorities, local authorities have a 'duty to cooperate'. Local enterprise partnerships, transport boards, and health and well-being boards are intended to build bridges between organisations. In addition, local authorities and communities have established their own ad hoc groupings, all designed to respond to the need for joint working, but their effectiveness varies enormously.

Principles of collaborative partnerships

There are many different interpretations of the words 'collaboration' and 'partnership'. *Collaboration* is working with each other to do a task and to achieve shared goals. It is a collective determination to reach an objective by sharing knowledge, learning and building consensus. Some planning theorists have suggested that the central job of the planner is to facilitate collaboration processes between public, private and community interests, trying to make debate as honest and effective as possible. The planner is a 'kind of knowledge mediator and broker' (Healey 2006, p. 309).

Partnership (the main focus of the chapter) goes beyond this. It *is a formal arrangement in which parties agree to cooperate to advance their mutual interests*. Partnerships present the involved parties with special challenges that must be navigated to agreement. Overarching goals, areas of responsibility, lines of authority and succession, how success is evaluated and distributed, must all be negotiated.

These definitions highlight both the differences and the similarities of the two words. Collaboration is an essential part of a partnership but the reverse is not true. Collaboration tends to be task focused and more limited in scope than working in partnership – which requires a greater level of determination to tackle and overcome differences for the greater good and achievement of wider goals. They are not just 'joint' arrangements but founded on a strong building block, at the heart of which is the need to find solutions that are mutually acceptable. Partners share the risks as well as the rewards, which is not true in collaboration. There has to be 'give and take' in partnership.

A partnership may be appropriate where there is common purpose between the parties involved, the opportunity to achieve coordinated and cohesive solutions, and the potential to deliver more than the sum of the individual contributions. A key feature of all partnerships is that all parties agree to the need for the partnership.

The characteristics of a good partnership are:

- trust;
- leadership;
- mutual respect;
- united in a common purpose;
- lack of recrimination;
- clear ground rules;
- sharing skills/best practice;
- communication;
- shared costs and benefits.

In capitalist countries the power to effect spatial change is very widely dispersed amongst private, public and voluntary agencies. Without cooperation it is not possible to achieve coordinated

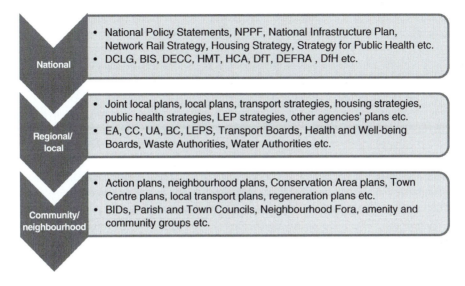

Figure 24.2   The hierarchy of planning in England

Source: Addison.

development that promotes health. Even within the public sector the problems of consistency are manifold. The remits, boundaries, attitudes and politics vary. Figure 24.2 illustrates this in relation to planning in England.

The fragmentation of roles and responsibilities (Figure 24.2) makes collaborative partnerships complex and difficult. Different areas will also have different needs and priorities. From the evidence of inspectors' reports on local plans,[3] many plans do not effectively tackle the complexities and challenges required in relation to, for example, housing delivery, enhancing accessibility, and integrating economic, housing and transport needs across an effective spatial area. Many focus on land allocations, housing numbers and road schemes. It is therefore important that delivery bodies, like the Local Economic Partnerships in England, are an integral part of preparing a local plan – a key partner not just a consultee. Where a delivery plan is included it tends to focus on known schemes and is not seen as driving the vision's implementation.

For plans to support delivering health and well-being active implementation is needed and this requires partnership working, which differs fundamentally from consultation and engagement. There is a need to think differently, develop a better understanding of spatial planning and improve methodologies, and, underpinning all of this, is ensuring collaborative working is the norm.

Partnership in practice: West London

One partnership that has successfully endured many years and engaged in a wide variety of activities is the West London Partnership. The organisation originated in 1998 as the subregional partnership for local government, business, public service and the voluntary sector. The Partnership is dedicated to strengthening the cohesion and well-being of West London's communities, enhancing their quality of life, improving the environment for business and creativity, and promoting business and employment growth. It aims to provide strategic leadership and an influential public voice to secure recognition of West London as a distinctive area – a major contributor to London's economy and a unique place to live and work. It brings together six West London Councils (Brent, Ealing, Harrow, Hammersmith & Fulham, Hillingdon and Hounslow) representing 1.8 million residents, West London Business Chamber (representing 800 businesses), Brunel University, and West London Network (West London Partnership 2014).

The key issues it seeks to influence are all relevant to the health and well-being of the area and its communities, for example, providing job security and supporting leisure activities thereby enhancing both physical and mental well-being. This remit has been successfully delivered since 1998. As an illustration of its success it has secured over £1 million in external grants as well as delivering major transport and economic strategies. For the 2012 Olympics it secured access to jobs and skills training for over 2,000 West London residents, 800 West London Ambassadors to welcome visitors, helped 180 West London businesses to secure contracts to help deliver the Games and enabled small grants for 86 West London sports clubs and organisations plus over £250,000 for capital improvements to sports facilities. This success led to consideration by the West London councils of adopting a similar cross-borough approach to public health service planning and coordination, following the move to a local authority responsibility in 2013.

This is consistent with the approach taken on transport in 1997. They produced a joint transport strategy across the authorities (Addison & Associates 1997), in addition to submitting a joint statement and funding bid to the Government Office for London/London Transport to implement the action plan. Not only did the local authorities cooperate through the West London Alliance but their consultants worked with West London Partnership and their business and transport operator members, including British Airways, the bus operators and London Transport. The consultants' approach was collaborative with the community, businesses, transport operators and authorities, both within and outside the 'partnership'. The outcome was a transport strategy and implementation plan owned, agreed and implemented by all local authorities across the political spectrum, the transport operators and reflecting the needs of the different sectors of the community.

This was the first time London authorities had cooperated to produce a transport strategy. It was entirely voluntary but its success is demonstrated in the continuation of the partnership. The process followed is equally applicable today and possibly more so especially in the context of enhancing accessibility, mobility, sustainability and improving health and well-being.

Developing effective partnerships

The United Kingdom's Home Office (2007) identified six key requirements for success in developing effective collaborative partnerships:

1. empowered and effective leadership;
2. visible and constructive accountability;
3. intelligence-led business processes;
4. effective and responsive delivery structures;
5. engaged communities;
6. appropriate skills and knowledge.

Developing effective partnerships necessitates a top-level commitment, which is more than words and is aiming for a long-term relationship. The leadership normally has to come both from principal elected representatives (such as mayors) and relevant chief officers. The leaders need to decide on the goals ensuring the whole partnership is appropriate and relevant to what is sought: that it is inclusive and all partners are equal and valued. The Audit Commission emphasises the importance of building partner participation: mutual trust, respect and support (Audit Commission date unknown)

Any partnership needs to be flexible, build on its success (e.g. West London Partnership) and provide adequate time for planning so that it has clearly articulated goals, objectives and projects. There has to be space for debate and conflict resolution, building consensus, adjusting style to relate to occasion – for example collaborative, directional, facilitative, catalytic or power sharing (Audit Commission date unknown).

It needs to exploit all partners' strengths but accept that getting to know people and developing trust takes time; it is a learning curve, which if approached positively can deliver considerable benefits. A mature partnership accepts there will be differences but ensures they do not undermine the commitment to collaborative partnership and facilitates independence. The 'culture' and 'attitudes' of all members of the partnership (at individual and corporate level) has a substantial impact on the likelihood of success. At a practical level all partnerships need terms of reference and an appropriate level of infrastructure. Someone will need to be responsible for coordination, facilitating the dialogue and establishing an evaluation mechanism.

The building blocks of partnership are illustrated in Figure 24.3.

Building effective partnerships takes effort, determination and time. Good relationships will have been developed before a decision is made to establish a 'partnership'. The various parties need to have worked together successfully before embarking on partnership working. Agreement is needed that moving towards a partnership will add value to the current practice. The process suggested is illustrated in Figures 24.4 and 24.5.

Besides the benefits of collaborative partnerships it is important to understand and address the potential dis-benefits and barriers. These include a loss of control by partners, the potential

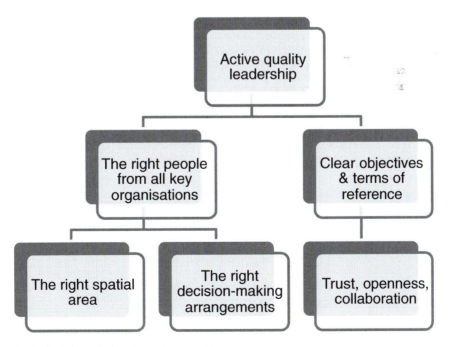

Figure 24.3   Building collaboration and partnerships

Source: Addison.

Figure 24.4 The key stages for developing a partnership

Source: Addison.

for conflicts, possibly increased costs, as well as pressure on inadequate resources and time. Unless acknowledged and acted upon it is probable that effective avoiding action will not occur. Allowing time to resolve issues, particularly if there are cultural differences, reflects the long-term nature of partnerships. Problems also occur if desired outcomes are either unclear or not agreed. Partnerships can struggle with finances or with operational issues, for example, staff, and information and communications technology. All aspects need to be debated, and a solution agreed and acted upon. Equality of effort and risk as well as responsibility is key.

From practical experience there are five main messages for building a successful partnership in the context of planning for health and well-being:

1. A common understanding of healthy and sustainable development, and commitment to real delivery, at the highest level of the lead organisation.
2. Agreement to exploit all aspects of corporate, community and planning activity holistically.
3. Coherence and consistency of policy and implementation across agencies, people, actions, time and space.
4. Being ambitious for the future (not accepting the status quo) and in for the long haul, notwithstanding any hurdles.
5. Establishing clear evidence-based holistic strategies with explicit implementation plans regularly reviewed.

Integrating health and planning

Enhancing health and well-being requires action at different spatial levels so a range of different and potentially interlocking partnerships are required:

- neighbourhood, parish, town or action area;
- local authority area;
- travel to work area, city region or other defined subregion.

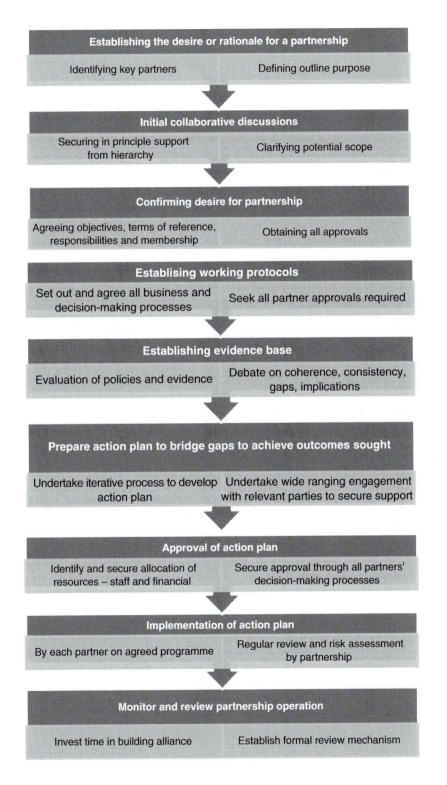

Figure 24.5 The route map for building a partnership

Source: Addison.

This hierarchy reflects the differing responsibilities of the parties involved (see Figure 24.2). Action at each level should be consistent with and reinforce those above and below. Mechanisms for ensuring this interlocking are important, demanding more than receiving minutes of meetings. Dialogue and communication is essential.

All collaborative partnerships need a clear understanding of all relevant housing, transport, health, leisure, environment and economic strategies, the way they interrelate, reinforce or pull against each other. This integrated picture needs to be informed by sound science – understanding the relationship between spatial policies and health and well-being, and a sound evidence base at the three scales. There needs to be a critical analysis of all strategies and their implications for the area, endorsed by all partners, assessing the options and cross-sector implications.

Achieving coherence and consistency is a formidable challenge. It is needed *within* plans, and *between* plans and programmes of various partners, across the different functional areas. This relies on avoiding the prime focus being on, for example, housing numbers and sites; instead, there needs to be a real focus on spatial areas and place-based evidence, which integrates across agencies and topics. There then has to be an explicit implementation plan linked to the spatial planning strategy and partners' other strategies and action plans/programmes. The means of delivery have to be borne in mind throughout, and success subsequently monitored: are health objectives, and/or proxy measures of healthy environments, being realised?

Three examples of where a collaborative partnership should be formed to effectively secure the long-term health and well-being of the community are set out below.

Contexts for health-integrated planning

Example 1: forging local partnerships for strategic coherence

In the absence of formal regional or subregional plans, the British 'local plan' performs a strategic role. But the local plan area is normally too small for effective strategic planning. It has a remit to foster health and well-being as part of delivering sustainable development. Figure 24.6 illustrates a simplified model where partnership working would be highly beneficial.

Local plans should deal with areas that make sense in terms of people's lives rather than administrative boundaries. As such, local plans should be produced by a consortium of local authorities. Together they should:

- develop a long-term spatial vision of the place with relevant partners to ensure a healthy environment and a sustainable economy;
- ensure effective collaboration with economic, transport, health, environmental and utility agencies, whose agendas interact with spatial planning and the outcomes sought, so that there is a common understanding of the issues, and a joint approach to their resolution;
- develop in locations that can enhance accessibility by active travel and public transport as well as private vehicle – working with landowners, developers and the marketing agents;
- include effective spatial policies which define what sustainability means locally supported by coherent policies in economic, transport, housing and social strategies;
- include effective delivery mechanisms for the plan via a cross sector agreement linked to each relevant organisation's own delivery programmes;
- encompass innovation reflecting the entrepreneurial role of local authorities.

Collaborative partnerships are essential to deliver the above. However, to achieve this approach is far from straightforward. Responsibilities are split both across agencies, and within agencies,

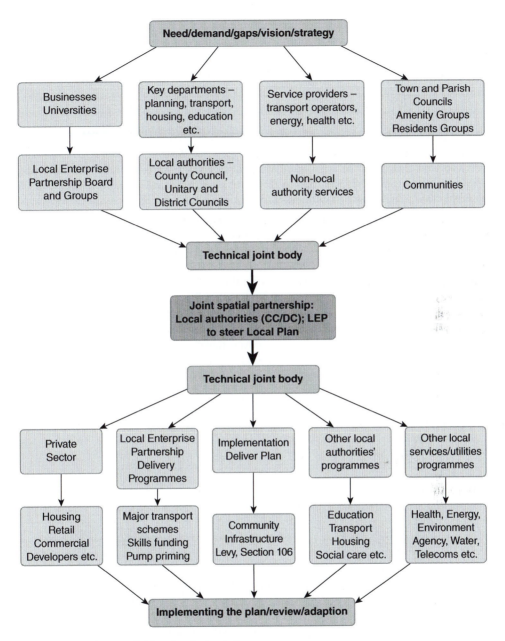

Figure 24.6   Evolving and delivering the local plan

Source: Addison.

Notes: CC – County Council; DC – District Council; LEP – Local Enterprise Partnership.

making establishing partnership with key parties extremely difficult. Apart from the fragmentation, there are, for example, attitudinal barriers, legislative requirements for competition, the tendency for organisations to think short term, financial and governance constraints. Some local authorities have managed to overcome these barriers. It is fundamental that at chief executive and leader level they understand spatial planning, sustainability and partnership working, its relationship to the local plan, including Community Infrastructure Levy and the Integrated Delivery Programme, development management, and the wider role of the authority in delivering 'place'. Without that authorities will continue to deliver housing, not places, and in ways and places that are not supporting improvements to health and well-being.

Example 2: more sustainable movement – fitter for walking

At a more local level, Living Streets established a 'Fitter for Walking' project in 2008 working with deprived areas in 12 local authorities to improve the local environment and promote walking for short journeys (Living Streets 2014). It worked in partnership with officers in the local authorities and the local communities led by a coordinator from Living Streets. An evaluation by the British Heart Foundation National Centre/Loughborough University demonstrated local authorities and communities thought it successful in delivering its objectives (Adams et al. 2012). An evaluation by the University of West of England found that Fitter for Walking is 'likely to result in significant financial savings from decreased mortality as a result of an increased number of people walking' (Sinnett and Powell 2012).

The project involved evaluating the link between small-scale capital investment and health outcomes. Partnership working was at the core: working with the communities to identify barriers to walking and investment by the authority to overcome barriers enhanced walking levels (see photos in Figure 24.7). The project won two national awards.[4] This initial partnership has led to further three-year partnerships with Blackburn with Darwen, Barking and Dagenham, and Bolton seeking to embed the benefits in local communities for the longer term.

These three-way partnerships are aimed at increasing walking in a number of ways including working with large workplaces and communities around transport corridors; with communities through street audits or walk doctors; with schools; engaging communities in seeking better streets and walking promotion; and supporting partnership development between transport and health, for example, health walks in local parks with school pupils.

(a)

(b)

Figure 24.7 a and b   Celebrating the 'Fitter for Walking' project

Source: Living Streets.

To enhance sustainable movement, partnership is essential: between different parts of local authorities', for example, public health, transport, education; sectors of the community, for example, schools, parents, residents, businesses, police; and transport operators. The work by Living Streets is dealing with one element of it. It has demonstrated such an approach can be effective but needs resources and time.

Example 3: working regionally across public and private organisations

Many assume that it is impossible to work in a collaborative partnership with a wide range of bodies. History has proved this wrong. In the ten-year period from 1985 when there was no strategic authority for London, all London boroughs, including the City, formed an alliance (that is, 33 local government bodies across the entire political spectrum), the London Planning Advisory Committee. They successfully produced three high quality and effective London Plans not by assuming 'the lowest common denominator' but by tackling key issues relevant to the future of London. The process challenged both officers and members to work together to find solutions, however difficult. A competent staff team led by a multidisciplinary steering group was crucial in driving the process forward.

Today, a similar situation arises with the establishment of Local Enterprise Partnerships (LEPs), which are city region based. Their role is to promote growth and strategic investment, including investment in housing and infrastructure. They have both resources and considerable influence in a wide range of fields relevant to the health and well-being of the community, but no explicit responsibility in that field. A number of streams of government funding are channelled to the LEPs for their decision. Recent statements indicate this arrangement will move towards a 'single pot' covering all government funding streams (HM Treasury 2011, 2012), a direction of travel being reinforced by changes in Europe (Morphet 2013).

Economic well-being is very relevant to health and well-being (Ross and Chang 2012). The role and attitude of the LEP is therefore an increasingly important health consideration and cannot be ignored. But while the local authorities have a duty to promote well-being, in part through 'health and well-being boards', LEPs have very different priorities, driven by commercial interests. They could work collaboratively with the local authorities and ensure the integration of the key aspects to deliver spatial planning and to achieve sustainable development. But the evidence available in 2014 suggests not.[5]

LEPs' effectiveness as private sector bodies working with the public sector varies substantially, particularly in their ability to evolve effective partnerships.[6] Much depends on the previous history of partnership working, the culture and attitude of individuals/key organisations, the capacity and the geography of the area.

The Coventry and Warwickshire LEP is working in partnership. The board includes businesses, representatives from two universities and councillors from Coventry, Warwickshire and two other districts. They have established a Planning Business Group[7] agreeing a protocol for the bodies commenting on planning applications. It requires all parties to sign up to commitments designed to smooth the process, including statutory consultees (the Environment Agency, Canals and Rivers Trust, Natural England and the local flood authority). Notwithstanding the number of organisations involved there is a perceived willingness to make collaboration work. There is the intention to work together on the critically important area of spatial planning, but this has yet to happen. It is proving complex and controversial.

The Coventry and Warwickshire LEP has taken an active role in promoting economic development through initiating an audit of major commercial development sites (CWLEP 2014). The work is led by staff at Coventry University, highlighting the partnership approach. What has not yet happened is collaboration across the local authorities on housing numbers and sites, the bringing together of local plans linking them to the LEP economic strategy, nor an understanding of the benefits of wider collaboration. The government focus for LEPs is housing numbers and delivery, jobs and transport. The health and well-being boards are not linked. The opportunity to bring greater benefits by integrating consideration of all elements of spatial planning through the LEP has yet to be realised.

Conclusions: learning lessons

Whatever the scope and scale of collaborative partnership working, there are some consistent challenges to be addressed if the partnership is to be effective. These are:

- It takes time to understand and develop understanding of the different players – collaborative partnership is a long-term strategy exploiting mutual skills.
- The nature and quality of the leadership is key to a successful partnership – they are the drivers of the attitude and culture as well as the process.
- Getting the correct partners related to objectives sought is critical as is agreeing the long-term objectives and outcomes.
- Collaboration and partnership encourages problem solving and innovation; it brings about new ways of working providing an opportunity to talk about issues which brings forward solutions.
- The people involved and their attitudes are crucial to creating a culture of partnership working across sectors and space.
- Experience shows that focusing on people is more likely to reflect real need and make those involved seek collaboration so that consideration of health and well-being in its broadest sense provides a unifying focus for action.
- Understanding the problems of all those in the partnership in the process of developing a long-term planning and development scenario has to consider the feasibility of, for example,

water availability, sewerage and schools: their delivery may not be possible or practical within the time frames or in the form being proposed.

- Developing the resources and skills needed for collaborative partnership is essential as they are not likely to be available initially and will take time to evolve.
- Ascertaining the priorities is a key issue, for example understanding both internal and external priorities and how they relate in the context of the provision of infrastructure.
- Developing better methodologies to assess the deliverability of spatial planning and sustainable development through collaborative partnerships, especially in the evolving field of health and well-being.
- Local government members and senior managers need to take ownership of sustainable spatial planning – that is, not just the planning service – to secure improvements in health and well-being by exploiting 'planning': they need to understand planning is about delivery of change in places for people, not just dealing with planning applications and local plan production.

To achieve all the above requires a substantial change in the attitudes of all the relevant professions as well as the politicians and the public. It is unlikely to happen quickly and will require considerable effort and perseverance by many parties. However, without this approach it is difficult to see how many of the intractable issues facing society today are going to be resolved. Global issues of poverty, health, an ageing growing population, food and energy supply, and climate change, make the challenges we are facing greater. They are cross-cutting in technical, spatial and governance terms so have to be resolved by collaboration and partnership.

Notes

1 Lynda Addison is a former Director of Planning and Transport in local government; former Managing Director of award winning planning and transport consultancy Addison & Associates advising national and local government; and Visiting Professor in Planning. She has led reviews of over 250 local authority planning services and both established and advised on partnerships.
2 From consultancy work undertaken by Addison & Associates, 1997–2010.
3 See Planning Inspectorate reports on Local Plan Examination in Public.
4 National Transport Awards – Excellence in Walking and Public Realm 2012, and the Charity Times 'Big Society' Award 2012.
5 Based on information received from Coventry and Warwickshire Local Enterprise Partnership. February 2014.
6 Information derived from personal interviews with those working with LEPs.
7 Includes representatives from energy, transport, planning, consultants, developers.

References

Adams, E.J., Goad, M.A. and Cavill, N. 2012. *Evaluation of Living Streets' Fitter for Walking project*. Loughborough: BHF National Centre for Physical Activity and Health, School of Sport, Exercise and Health Sciences, Loughborough University.

Addison & Associates. 1997. *Delivering integrated transport in West London*. West London Leadership. London: Addison & Associates.

Audit Commission. 1998. *A fruitful partnership: effective partnership working*. London: Audit Commission.

Audit Commission. (date unknown). *Building capacity through partnerships. From comprehensive performance assessment analysis: briefing 6*. London: Audit Commission.

Barton, H. and Grant, M. 2006. A health map for the local human habitat. *Journal of the Royal Society for the Promotion of Health* 126(6): 252–253.

CWLEP (Coventry and Warwickshire Local Enterprise Partnership). 2014. *Planning*. Available from: www.cwlep.com/business-group/planning?sec=bg&cat=21, accessed 7 August 2014.

DCLG (Department for Communities and Local Government). 2011. *Localism Act*. London: DCLG.

DCLG. 2012. *National planning policy framework*. London: DCLG.

Forester, J. 1989. *Planning in the face of power*. Berkeley, CA: University of California Press.

Healey, P. 1997. *Collaborative planning*. London: Macmillan.

Healey, P. 2006. *Collaborative planning: shaping places in fragmented societies*. London: Palgrave Macmillan.

HM Treasury. 2011. *2011 budget statements*. Available from: http://webarchive.nationalarchives.gov.uk/20130129110402/www.hm-treasury.gov.uk/2011budget_documents.htm, accessed 7 August 2014.

HM Treasury. 2012. *2012 budget statements*. Available from: http://webarchive.nationalarchives.gov.uk/20130129110402/www.hm-treasury.gov.uk/budget2012.htm, accessed 7 August 2014.

Home Office. 2007. *Delivering safer communities, a guide to effective partnership working*. London: Police and Crime Standards Directorate, Home Office.

IDeA, Addison & Associates. 2009. *A benchmark for the spatial planning function*. Document version 3. London: PAS.

Living Streets. 2014. *Fitter for walking*. Available at: www.livingstreets.org.uk/professionals/working-with-communities/fitter-for-walking, accessed 7 August 2014.

Morphet, J. 2013. *How Europe shapes British public policy*. Bristol: Policy Press, University of Bristol.

Ross, A. and Chang, M. 2012. *Reuniting health with planning: healthier homes, healthier communities*. London: TCPA.

Sinnett, D. and Powell, J. 2012. *Economic evaluation of Living Streets' fitter for walking project*. Loughborough, UK: BHF National Centre for Physical Activity and Health, School of Sport, Exercise and Health Sciences, Loughborough University.

Sustainable Development Commission. 2005. *Securing the future: delivering the UK Sustainable Development Strategy*. Produced by Department of Environment, Food, and Rural Affairs, March 2005. CM 6467. London: Sustainable Development Commission.

West London Partnership. 2014. *Welcome to West London Partnership*. Available from: www.westlondonpartnership.org.uk, accessed 7 August 2014.

25

CREATING HEALTHIER, SMARTER PLACES

Learning from European cities

Nicholas Falk

Introduction: problems and solutions

Despite periodic reports on urban malaise, gross health inequalities and climate change threats, local authorities complain they lack the powers and resources needed to change direction (Parkinson et al. 2006). Governments of different political colours have increasingly bought into 'free market' principles, and prefer to leave development decisions to the property markets. In the UK planning has become largely reactive in the last few decades. At the same time financial institutions have become ever more centralised and short term in their outlooks. One direct result in the UK is the unacceptably low rate of house building, at the same time as housing has become unaffordable for most people (Falk 2014). Another, experienced across the world, is rising inequalities, and reduced well-being as cities become more polarised (Wilkinson and Pickett 2010).

The problems for growing cities in emerging economies seem almost intractable. In India, for example, 180 cities experience air pollution six times higher than World Health Organization standards, and the situation is considered critical in 50 cities.[1] Rising temperatures and sea levels could turn crisis into catastrophe as the use of cars and air conditioning worsen conditions for pedestrians and cyclists.[2] Generally the lure of economic growth, and the power of elites dominates thinking, and it is the poor who suffer most because they cannot escape the worsening conditions. But is there another way?

Many cities in north-west Europe have forged a different approach after devastating wartime destruction. They have exercised greater control over land use, and have boosted their economies and environment in the process. Significantly studies into the quality of social life and children's happiness also support the European social democratic model over the Anglo-American liberal model.[3] So there is a lot to be learned not only from looking at the places that have made the most changes, but also from considering how the lessons for dealing with land and strategic planning can be transferred to the laggards.

This chapter is based on a series of study tours I have led to some of the most innovative cities in Europe.[4] The concept of smart growth is derived from the Charter of US Congress for New Urbanism (www.cnu.org). A report from the McKinsey Global Institute based on interviews with leaders of successful cities states that, 'They achieve smart growth, which means securing the best growth opportunities while protecting the environment and ensuring that all their citizens enjoy prosperity.'[5] What I call 'smarter growth' involves matching development with infrastructure through local authorities playing a more proactive role.

European cities have gone far further than their American counterparts in moderating the impacts of economic growth. *Good Cities, Better Lives* sets out the lessons from different European case studies that provide models for tackling the challenges facing our cities (Hall 2013). There is surprisingly much in common between the success stories. While it is often argued that it is impossible to change attitudes and behaviour, here are strategies for mobilising land and investment resources that have produced tangible results. My examples are organised under four themes: changing the way we move; changing the way we work; changing the way we build homes; and caring for the environment. The conclusion of the chapter shows how the lessons can be transferred through mechanisms that apply the 'ABC of place-making leadership': ambition, brokerage and continuity.[6]

Theme 1: changing the way we move

A central problem for most towns and cities is reducing the dominance of the car while improving accessibility and physical activity for all. Shifting the modal split is difficult as it depends on a number of simultaneous changes that raise the cost of using a private car while at the same time offering cheaper and better alternatives. This does not mean doing away with the car altogether, but rather 'taming' a machine that has come to dominate too many of our lives, and which requires coordinated action over a wide area.

In Lille and Roubaix, former textile towns in Northeastern France, the opportunity arose when Lille succeeded in attracting a station on the new high speed rail line linking Paris and Brussels with London. But the city went much further, when the mayor persuaded the 80 adjoining communes to work together in a 'Metropolitan compromise'. Through a historic agreement with the national government (Contrat de Ville), along with a levy on the payroll of major employers (Versement Transport) the funding was secured for an integrated driverless underground metro, and upgraded trams.

The public realm in the city centre was transformed so cars could no longer drive through, and the city won the status of European City of Culture. Importantly, investment was also directed at spreading the benefits, for example by restoring old industrial buildings in the smaller textile towns. Thus an old swimming bath in Roubaix was converted into La Piscine, now one of the most popular art galleries in the whole of France. So though unemployment is still high, attitudes and the image both inside and outside the city have been completely altered thanks to greatly improved connectivity (Cadell et al. 2008).

In Malmo and Copenhagen, a new bridge across the Oresund, which separates Sweden from Denmark, has enabled two medium-sized port cities to work together for the common good. Copenhagen had already won the title of most liveable city, thanks partly to pedestrianising its mile long main street, Stroget, which connects the railway station with the old harbour. The city has long sought to reduce car use by encouraging cycling, and 37 per cent of trips to work are now by bike. As a comparative study tour and follow-up conference discovered, the changes in behaviour are due to action on many fronts.[7] Cycling has been turned into a pleasure by providing priority for cyclists at road crossings, clearly defined cycle lanes, space on trains and at stations to store bikes, and showers in major offices. Instead of cycling being seen as for sports freaks, it is treated as the normal way for women, men and families to get about.

Helped by the missionary zeal of leading urbanist Jan Gehl, and taken up by Copenhagen's Cycling Embassy and the City Council, Copenhagen's successes in upgrading the public realm are being transferred not only to other Danish cities, but even as far as New York's Times Square (Gehl 2010). The different attitude to city movement can also be seen in the way that cafes extend on to the pavement, providing blankets and heaters for the cold, which in turn keeps streets feeling much safer and more interesting. Across the bridge in the harder circumstances of Malmo, a former shipbuilding town, sustainable principles have been used to both upgrade old housing estates like Augustenberg and build the exciting new development of Bo01 as part of an Expo, or international building exhibition in the old harbour. Varied architecture and a beautiful public realm have attracted families back to live in the centre. In both cities people spend a fraction of the time travelling to work than in the UK, which provides them with much more time to spend with their family or on leisure pursuits. Most importantly of all, despite language and cultural differences, adjoining cities and regions are working together thanks to improved connectivity.

Theme 2: changing the way we work

New sources of work are needed not just to provide income and activity for young people or the older unemployed, but to provide a sense of hope or purpose in areas affected by major economic change. Part of the answer lies in encouraging the knowledge or creative economies, and it is significant that the French state investment bank, the Caisse des Depots, has a whole division devoted to that aim. But it is also through supporting independent businesses, and it is Germany that provides the best models for what can be done, with two very different examples, Leipzig and Freiburg. We will consider a third in the Ruhrgebiet when we consider how to change the environment.

Leipzig, a medium-sized city in the former Eastern zone, suffered hugely from a loss of jobs and population after reunification. Ninety per cent of manufacturing jobs disappeared, and the city became one of the most famous 'shrinking cities'. However, as documented in *Phoenix Cities*, it has since recovered and found a new sense of purpose (Power et al. 2010). The key to the change was tapping the university's ideas on what economic clusters the city should concentrate on (Porter 2008). This led to a strategy that, among other things, restored ancient functions, such as a centre for trade fairs, but also promoted new forms of work, such as in the motor industry and creative businesses.

With Porsche already in the city, the municipality concentrated on attracting BMW's new plant against over 200 competitors. When it came down to the final six, the city agreed with the regional and federal governments to build a new stretch of motorway round the south of the city, so that parts would get to the factory on time. Only six years after the agreements were signed, both the factory and associated motorway opened on time! Creative businesses have been attracted to grow by the conversion of a vast cotton spinning mill (the Spinnerei) into studios and galleries, this time a private initiative (Figure 25.1). Tax incentives attracted investment in restoring the many grand houses, which now provide cheap places to rent. The support of both local universities, the principal one of which is located in the city centre, and also local savings banks (Sparkasse) help explain how Leipzig has rebuilt its economy after decades of domination by the Soviet Union.

In *Good Cities, Better Lives*, Freiburg is called the 'city that did everything'. From a rubble strewn wreck of a historic city, completely destroyed by Allied bombers, the city first restored its centre. It then built urban extensions on new tramlines at Rieselfeld and Vauban that are models for the rest of the world of how to apply sustainable development principles. Under the theme 'A city of short distances', children as well as adults cycle safely everywhere, and car use has declined. The ancient university has thrived in such an attractive and affordable city, but the real success has been renewable energy. A commitment to develop alternatives to atomic power has led to Freiburg becoming the 'solar capital of Europe'. Research institutes as well as manufacturing and contracting firms employ over 3,000 people.

Figure 25.1   Old mills house new enterprise in Leipzig

Source: Falk.

The spirit of local independence and self-sufficiency enthuses everything. So though incomes are significantly lower than the surrounding region of Baden Wurtemburg, the quality of life is so high it compensates. Indeed the local saying is that it is better to be unemployed in Freiburg than to have a job in Berlin! The city's success can be attributed not just to municipal leadership but also to the greater freedom German cities have to control their own destinies without state direction, thanks to a post-war constitution which makes a return to totalitarianism impossible.

Germany managed to avoid the worst effects of the recession following the bank collapses in the UK and USA because people have sought to earn their own living and to save through Sparkasse or local savings banks, not profit from inflation in house prices. This in turn creates self-respect as people have more control over their own lives. Though some still feel excluded, on the whole people seem to feel better about themselves and the cities they live in, which of course makes them healthier.

Theme 3: changing the way we build homes

Successful places attract people to them, and hence need to grow, but in a planned or thought-out way. In the UK, green belts and "Not In My Back Yard" (NIMBY) attitudes obstruct new housing, and contribute to house price inflation. Developers are free to put in proposals for any piece of land irrespective of its planning status or accessibility. However in the Netherlands, a country that is even more densely populated than the UK, and with many cultural similarities, the Dutch have succeeded in building new suburbs that are far better than almost anything built in the UK in recent years. This is the verdict of successive study tours that have cycled around the new VINEX suburbs (known by the name of the national plan that brought them into existence).[8] The plan identified the best places for growth, and set out the basic principles that should guide their development. Local authorities then drew up masterplans and set up joint ventures with developers to deliver them. One of the best places to appreciate the Dutch approach is

Figure 25.2   Dutch urban extensions

Source: Falk.

from the city of Utrecht, and its various outlying towns on the edge of the Randstadt, which forms a 'green heart' between the main cities (Figure 25.2).

Amersfoort is an ancient town to the north of Utrecht, with a population of around 150,000 and expanding fast. The town is at a crossroads on both the road and rail systems in the centre of the country, and hence is well-placed to grow. Growth started with two urban extensions promoted by the municipality at Kattenbroek and Nieuwland. The success of these enabled one of the city's aldermen to overcome local opposition to the idea of a further extension or new community at Vathorst, which when fully completed will encompass some 10,000 homes as well as a new business park and shopping centre.

Visitors are impressed by the way Vathorst has been masterplanned into five distinct neigh-bourhoods, each with its own identity or brand. There is a mix of tenures, with 30 per cent social housing. The local authority has passed over serviced sites to housing associations as well as selling off homes at a discount under an arrangement where if the house is resold, part of the uplift in values goes to the local authority. Energy has been saved by providing facilities like combined heat and power and heat pumps. This is possible because the municipality set up the Vathorst Development Company with a group of development companies. Funding from the state investment bank, BNG Bank, makes it possible to service the sites before they are sold off to a wide variety of builders thanks to a long-term loan at a low rate of interest.

Houten is a new town to the south of Utrecht of just under 50,000 residents, which has been voted one of the most attractive places to live by a popular Dutch magazine. Priority for cycling and walking has been built in from the start. New schools act as community hubs, and are designed so they can be returned to other uses when the demand for primary schools falls off. As in Vathorst, bike hire is easy, with the ground level of the new station given over to bike storage.

Figure 25.3   Custom building in Almere

Source: Falk.

Again the visitor is struck by the huge choice and variety of housing types, so that living in a new home is as popular as an old one, unlike the situation in the UK. Attractive landscaping creates a place which is a pleasure to walk and cycle around. There is a strong sense of community.

The Netherlands, or the Low Countries, have a long tradition of having to combat water in order to build anything. This 'Polders' mentality undoubtedly has helped people to work together for the common good, and has resulted in local authorities owning more land and exercising greater control over it. But what has really impressed visitors from the UK has been the way that local authorities have exercised leadership, taken on or reduced development risks, and in the process created a much less dependent society. The collaborative spirit is reinforced by the provision of sites where people can commission their own homes, which in the new town of Almere is being used to create a whole new quarter, while small builders and housing associations cater for niche markets, such as the elderly (Figure 25.3). In this way the costs of owning your own home are reduced, and the rate of development and occupation speeded up.

Theme 4: caring for the environment

The final ingredient in enjoying a better life is an environment that is both beautiful and sustainable. While many people in Britain and the USA say they prefer to live in the countryside, or away from cities, it is often a reaction to the negative aspects of city living, such as pollution, congestion and perceived crime, and a resistance to paying for the services needed to maintain high standards. Of course all cities contain poor parts, which in turn draw people in so they can better their lives, as Ed Glaeser perceptively points out; they do not make people poor (Glaeser 2011). But it is often these areas – if not demolished through slum clearance – that subsequent generations treasure. This applies not just to dense medieval quarters in cities like York, but also to waterfronts and their warehouses, and city parks. Even industrial cities can make the most of their heritage, as the following examples show.

Turin in Northern Italy came to prominence in the nineteenth century as one of the main manufacturing centres, and the headquarters of Fiat. In recent years, despite industrial set-backs and a flood of immigrants, it has reinvented itself as an attractive place to visit through an ambitious plan. Old buildings have been restored and converted to new uses, such as hotels. The old multistorey car plant is now a mixed use development with fine shops and galleries. The barriers once created by railway cuttings have been built over, creating a dense, lively and highly walkable centre. Significantly Turin has managed to attract investment despite the notorious problems facing the Italian economy and government, thanks to a clear and visionary plan that makes the most of its heritage.

Dortmund lies on the edge of the Emscher Landscape Park in the German Ruhrgebiet. Formerly the main production centre for iron and coal, a vast area became desolate as the mines closed, and steel production was lost to China. However, following a tradition of reforesting the edges of cities, an International Building Exhibition was launched in 1989 which sparked off a competition for hundreds of projects. By simply leaving structures to rust and opening them to the public, industrial relics have been turned into visitor attractions. Waterways have been restored, and are no longer taking all the region's waste. Imaginative lighting and landscaping has helped change the area's image.

Most ambitious of all, in Dortmund one part of the redundant Phoenix iron works has become the centre of a technology park, where spin-offs from the university can start and grow. On the other side of the city a vast lake of 20 hectares, a fifth of the area, has been created where the iron works once stood, providing a new leisure area for the city. The fine views have encouraged wealthier residents to build their own homes instead of living in the suburbs (Figure 25.4).

The success of the German, and perhaps even the north Italian, economies is bound up with the way they are managing the process of industrial change. The state of the physical and

Figure 25.4   A lake and new housing where the Phoenix iron foundry, Dortmund, once stood

Source: Falk.

natural environment is a visible symbol of how well we care for our cities, and undoubtedly affects the level of private investment. But subconsciously it also affects the spirit of the people, the pride they feel in where they live and work, and the sense of identity or soul of the city that outlives generations.

Transferring lessons from Europe

The institutional and cultural context of cities in much of the rest of the world is very different to the cities described above. Planning powers and funding mechanisms vary hugely, and a pre-condition for place-making leadership is some kind of state investment bank to fund the huge costs involved in assembling and preparing land for development. Nevertheless, by applying the ABC of leadership – ambition, brokerage plus continuity – cities can transform their prospects as the examples above have illustrated.

The most fundamental reason why so much more has been achieved in the European cities referred to lies in the financial system. So long as most housing and commercial development is undertaken by speculative developers, and so long as land is sold to the highest bidder, the kinds of changes described earlier will be the exception rather than the rule. It is clear that almost every European country has a more responsive financial system than the UK that makes long-term finance available for local infrastructure and that avoids land values becoming inflated by speculation. State investment banks such as KfW in Germany, BNG Bank in the Netherlands, Kommuninvest in Sweden and Caisse des Depots in France combine a number of ingredients.

First these investment banks are set up for the public good, not private profit. Second they have the expertise to evaluate complex proposals and promote innovative programmes, not simply look at the financial returns. Third they work in association with local authorities, who in turn play a much more proactive role in identifying where development is appropriate. Finally they make finance available on longer terms and at cheaper rates than private financial institutions. Though they support government policies, they are independent of the government, and do not count against public sector borrowing. This idea is transferable to countries such as the UK, where it would be possible to double the rate of house building while upgrading local infrastructure (Falk 2014).

But even without radical legislative or financial change, progress towards a healthier, more equitable situation is possible. To find ways out of the impasse created by poor past investment and planning decisions, cities need to rediscover the art of place-making leadership. Whenever changes are required that take years to produce beneficial results, as in all the examples referred to above, there need to be individuals (or teams) that can explain and justify a particular change of course. In a series of 'leadership masterclasses' in Cambridge, presentations from successful transformations in Freiburg, Amersfoort and Harlow brought out the common importance of ambition, brokerage and continuity – the ABC of place-making leadership (Falk and Munday 2014). Brief examples, largely from schemes I have worked on in England, illustrate their relevance.

Ambition

Ambition is about wanting to do better, and raising one's position. Smarter cities do not fall for unrealistic dreams, but make the most of their strengths or 'common wealth' within the wider subregion. Hence they need to be team players, and to exercise judicious and sustained leadership. Despite the obstacles created by centralised funding, a number of British cities have used examples from elsewhere to forge and implement ambitions plans.

Birmingham's city centre was blighted and largely abandoned by wealthier shoppers in the early 1980s, making redevelopment unviable. A City Centre Symposium in 1988 brought experts from around the world together with local politicians and practitioners. The resulting vision, labelled The Highbury Initiative, set out a simple strategy of promoting a series of distinct quarters connected by a high quality public realm, and dropping the 'concrete collar' of the Inner Ring Road, which has been designed to bring motorists from the suburbs into the centre. A complete reversal of the work of preceding decades, the strategy was adopted, and implemented. It is credited with turning the city centre's fortunes around, for example attracting Selfridges to become the flagship of a rebuilt Bullring shopping centre.

Cambridgeshire is a rare exception where local people saw the need to assess all the options for growth, and commissioned a study known as Cambridge Futures. Using advanced modelling techniques, different scenarios were compared before settling on the one that provided the best balance between a set of objectives. The process resulted in a shared vision, which all the local authorities in Cambridgeshire supported, backed up by a delivery body, Cambridgeshire Horizons. At the heart of the spatial plan was a new high quality rapid transit line, a guided busway to replace the old railway line from St Ives to Cambridge, and which acts as the spine and rationale for the new town of Northstowe to the north. While this development became mired in disagreements, the area on the city's southern fringe, which was taken out of the green belt, has rapidly developed into a highly attractive residential area. Significantly the principles set out in the adopted Cambridgeshire Quality Charter for Growth, and overseen by the City's Quality Panel, have been put into practice in a number of new neighbourhoods.[9] The university has decided to promote developments on land it owns rather than selling the land to developers. The results are places that look as distinctive as the Continental examples that inspired many of them.

Brokerage

Getting the resources together to regenerate or develop large areas is always difficult, and can easily be foiled by an objection or one of the stakeholders falling out. It is particularly difficult in locations that are off centre, and in times of recession and uncertainty. British cities have often ended up in the position of 'poor relations', scrambling for handouts. Municipal leadership, often focused on the figure of a strong mayor (but not necessarily as both Birmingham and Cambridgeshire illustrate), can overcome administrative divisions. There does need to be a source of capital funding, and here the local payroll tax (Versement Transport) in France provides an admirable model. Unlike the UK, where the focus is on a few grand projects such as High Speed Two, French cities have linked local transport improvements to national upgrades. Similarly the Danish approach of using the uplift in land values from associated development in Copenhagen as the main means of building a new metro shows how smarter development can also apply to finance. Much depends on brokering agreements, as the following examples illustrate.

Graylingwell in Chichester and the New England Quarter in Brighton are two examples where exceptionally high environmental standards have been achieved. In both cases, the process has been helped by agreeing a development framework before the masterplan was drawn up, in which objectives are articulated.[10] Graylingwell Park, a former mental hospital, was the subject of a community planning exercise which led to building more homes than originally conceived, and one of the first combined heat and power systems to be installed in a UK housing scheme. In the case of the Brighton scheme, strong community opposition initially to the original proposals from Sainsbury's led on to a largely car free and low energy development that has helped knit the existing shopping area and the railway station together. The masterplan divided the seven hectare site into some 20 development parcels, with codes which ensured high standards of design. Innovations included building housing over a new supermarket, and developing zero energy housing in a development by BioRegional Quintain which is a demonstration of One Planet Living.

Some of the lessons are being applied in Barton West, Oxford, which is a rare British example of a local authority selecting a property company as partner to devise an exemplary housing scheme on land it owns. Through extensive local consultations, and visits to other schemes, a masterplan was drawn up rapidly to which there was little or no opposition. The use of a joint venture company enabled the local authority to benefit from the expertise and resources of an experienced private company, while the master developer benefited from a more collaborative and speedier approach to planning. Through using the increased value created from mixed tenures around a new park to provide social housing, the objectives of each partner were reconciled.

Continuity

As large scale development, especially regeneration schemes, take a long time, a project has to outlive the politicians or officers who have may have launched it. Plans and policies are inert, and often end up lost in files or on shelves. So some kind of organisation is needed that can hold on to the vision, do all the deals, and eventually receive the awards or criticisms! There is no perfect structure, but a number of mechanisms can address the particular weaknesses and challenges identified above, and help other places replicate what we like about European towns and cities. In particular the financial backing to take a long-term perspective, as discussed earlier, is critical.

Derwenthorpe in York was one of a number of new communities that came together in the Sustainable Urban Neighbourhoods Network for a two year project to share experience and learn from the best Dutch projects (Falk and Carley 2012).[11] Promoted by Joseph Rowntree as a second 'New Earswick', it faced a decade of determined opposition from local people. The completed scheme has won many awards for its innovations, such as combined heat and power. But most important has been the commitment to employing a high calibre team that were able to apply the lessons from elsewhere in their own way. No private developer would have bothered until the risks had been overcome.

Cooperatives and community projects often have a better chance of ensuring continuity. The Coin Street project on London's South Bank is a famous example, providing affordable housing and helping to trigger wider regeneration. Springhill, Stroud, is one of a growing number of projects where people seek to commission their own homes, and work together for best results, as in many parts of Denmark. Shared facilities, including space for children to play with each other, helps build community spirit, and thus relieves the demands on social services. The obstacle to more of these is not lack of interest but lack of sites. They will often be outbid by large house builders, so local authorities need to adopt land planning policies to ensure that a diversity of builders can be involved.

Conclusions: economic models for healthier places

The central argument of this chapter has been the importance of a new business model for development in which the public sector takes the lead. This will meet a series of social, economic and environmental pressures and ensure that developments strengthen our towns and cities rather than sapping life from them. The tools are available to achieve a transformation, provided the state reforms the investment banking system. The inspiration of places that have

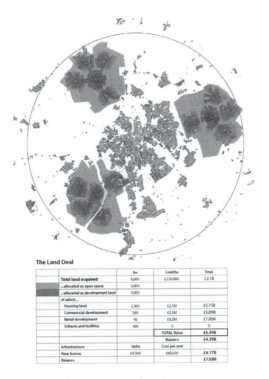

The Land Deal

	ha	Cost/ha	Total
Total land acquired	6,000	£350,000	£2.1B
...allocated as open space	3,000		
...allocated as development land	3,000		
of which...			
Housing land	2,300	£2.5M	£5.75B
Commercial development	260	£2.0M	£520M
Retail development	40	£3.0M	£120M
Schools and facilities	400	0	0
		TOTAL Value	£6.39B
		Balance	£4.29B
Infrastructure	Units	Cost per unit	
New homes	69,500	£60,000	£4.17B
Balance			£120M

Figure 25.5   Proposals for a twenty-first-century garden city

Source: Falk.

been transformed in Continental Europe, as well as the UK's own recent successes, should provide the confidence for all cities to change direction, and not expect to return to 'business as usual'. A new crop of twenty-first-century garden cities that plough land value uplift into sustainable infrastructure could turn the visions into reality (Rudlin and Falk 2014; Figure 25.5).

Notes

1   Central Pollution Control Board. 2007. www.cpcb.nic.in
2   IPCC Climate Change. 2014. Impacts, adaptation and vulnerability. www.ipcc.chin
3   UNICEF. 2013. Report card 11, child wellbeing in rich countries, UNICEF UK. www.unicef-irc.org/publications
4   For example, Learning from Lille, learning from Copenhagen and Malmo etc. www.urbed.coop
5   McKinsey Global Institute. 2013. How to make a city great. www.mckinsey.com/insights/urbanization
6   The principles emerged from leadership masterclasses held in Cambridge, and were reaffirmed in a conference organised by the Planning Advisory Service and Cambridge Architecture. The report *Backing for a big idea: consensus building for strategic planning in Cambridge* was published by PAS in 2013. www.pas.gov.uk
7   URBED. 2013. Report of Symposium Getting to Copenhagen. www.urbed.coop
8   See for example, Nicholas Falk. 2011. Learning from the Netherlands: report of the Dutch SUNN study tour (Sustainable Urban Neighbourhoods Network), URBED. www.urbed.coop
9   Nicholas Falk. 2010. Cambridgeshire quality charter for growth, URBED for Cambridgeshire Horizons.www.qedproperty.com

10 Nicholas Falk. 2012. Sustainable new communities on the South Coast. www.urbed.coop
11 Michael Carley and Nicholas Falk. 2010. How can local authorities create sustainable urban neighbour-
    hoods? www.jrf.org.uk

References

Cadell, C., Falk, N. and King, F. 2008. *Regeneration in European cities: making Connections.* York: Joseph
    Rowntree Foundation.

Falk, N. 2014. *Funding housing growth and local infrastructure: how a British investment bank can help.* London:
    The Smith Institute.

Falk, N. and Carley, M. 2012. *How can local government build sustainable urban neighbourhoods?* York: Joseph
    Rowntree Foundation.

Falk, N. and Munday, B. 2014. *The ABC of housing growth and infrastructure.* London: The Housing Forum.

Gehl, J. 2010. *Cities for people.* Washington, DC: Island Press.

Glaeser, E. 2011. *Triumph of the city: how our greatest invention makes us richer, smarter, greener, healthier and
    happier.* London: Pan Macmillan.

Hall, P. 2013. *Good cities, better lives: how Europe discovered the lost art of urbanism.* Abingdon, Oxon:
    Routledge.

Parkinson, M., Champion, T., Simmie, J., Turok, I., Crookston, M., Katz, B. and Park, A. 2006. *State of
    the English cities: volumes 1 and 2.* London: ODPM.

Porter, M.E. 2008. *Competitive advantage: creating and sustaining superior performance.* New York: Simon and
    Schuster.

Power, A., Plöger, J. and Winkler, A. (Eds.). 2010. *Phoenix cities: the fall and rise of great industrial cities.*
    Bristol: Policy Press.

Rudlin, D. and Falk, N. 2014. *Uxcester Garden City* (Winner of the Wolfson 2014 Economics Prize).
    www.urbed.coop

Wilkinson, R. and Pickett, K. 2010. *The spirit level: why equality is better for everyone.* London: Penguin UK.

26

ASSESSING THE POTENTIAL HEALTH EFFECTS OF POLICIES, PLANS, PROGRAMMES AND PROJECTS

Ben Cave

Introduction: impact assessment

This chapter looks at the way in which the potential health effects of planning can be examined at policy, plan, programme and project level. The focus is on Health Impact Assessment (HIA); however environmental assessment plays an important role in planning and as such the ways health can be addressed through environmental assessment are also discussed.

This is a reflective chapter that draws on the author's experience as an impact assessment practitioner working in the United Kingdom, across mainland Europe and elsewhere with all levels of government, with community groups and with the private and the public sectors.

First, impact assessment and HIA are defined. Second, the stages of HIA are explored to provide a sense of the process. The chapter concludes with a look at the ways in which health is considered in Strategic Environmental Assessment (SEA) and in Environmental Impact Assessment (EIA).

The International Association for Impact Assessment (IAIA) tell us that 'Impact Assessment simply defined is the process of identifying the future consequences of a current or proposed action. The "impact" is the difference between what would happen with the action and what would happen without it' (IAIA 2010).

Impact assessment has a dual nature (IAIA 2010):

- it is a technical tool for analysing the consequences of a planned intervention (policy, plan, programme or project) and providing information to stakeholders and decision makers; and
- it is a legal and institutional procedure linked to the decision-making process of a planned intervention.[1]

Impact assessment aims to (IAIA 2010):

- provide information for decision-making that analyses the biophysical, social, economic and institutional consequences of proposed actions;
- promote transparency and participation of the public in decision-making;

- identify procedures and methods for the follow-up (monitoring and mitigation of adverse consequences) in policy, planning and project cycles; and
- contribute to environmentally sound and sustainable development.

Impact assessment in general covers many sectors and topics. Health is addressed in other impact assessments and there is variation within HIA itself: thus Fehr et al. (2011) introduce the notion of a family of health-related impact assessments and consider ways in which the different forms can work together. Harris-Roxas and Harris (2011) provide a typology of HIA which seeks to explain the different ways in which HIA is used. On a practical note there are also specialist approaches to HIA that seek to correct perceived omissions from the more general approach: for example there are guides that focus on mental health (Cooke et al. 2011) and those that emphasise the role of HIA in examining the effects of a proposal on equity (Aldrich et al. 2005; Heller et al. 2013).

Health in impact assessment

Lee et al. (2013) and Winkler et al. (2013) provide a global overview of the countries and regions where HIA is either formally required or where guidance exists. It has been practised in the European Union, in diverse forms, since the 1980s. It is one of the assessments that project proponents are required to conduct as a condition of the loans provided by multilateral lenders such as the World Bank and the International Finance Corporation (IFC 2009). Industry bodies have also developed guides for HIA in mining (ICMM 2010) and for oil and gas infrastructure (IPIECA 2005). Its use is growing in the United States (Jackson et al. 2011; Health Impact Project 2014).

How is it defined?

IAIA (Quigley et al. 2006) define HIA as

> a combination of procedures, methods and tools that systematically judges the potential, and sometimes unintended, effects of a policy, plan, programme or project on both the health of a population and the distribution of those effects within the population. HIA identifies appropriate actions to manage those effects.

It is worth unpicking this definition. HIA can use a range of different methods and approaches (see the assessment section later in this chapter). HIA can be applied across the policy process unlike SEA, which is used on plans and programmes, or EIA, which focuses on projects. From now on, unless otherwise stated, the term 'policy' will be used to cover policy, plan, programme or project. The definition also shows that HIA is carried out in advance of a particular policy intervention: early writers on HIA used terms from epidemiology to describe the temporal relation of the assessment to the policy being assessed. Thus HIA could be prospective, concurrent or retrospective (see for example Kemm and Parry 2004: 1–2). At the time of writing these terms are still in use but should be abandoned. As we saw in the opening statement of this chapter impact assessment looks at the *future* effects of a *current* or proposed action (IAIA 2010) and thus is always prospective. The IAIA definition talks about current action so there might be a glimmer of hope for *concurrent* impact assessment but this is best described as monitoring, or maybe even adaptive monitoring. Retrospective impact assessment is evaluation.

HIA is a systematic inquiry. This systematic approach is important and provides the integrity for the findings. The IAIA definition tells us that the findings of an HIA are judgements on the potential effects. This judgement takes into account the effect on health for the whole population as well as potential effects on population groups. Health tends to be defined broadly and to follow the definition in the constitution of the World Health Organization (WHO): namely as being 'a state of complete physical, mental and social well-being and not merely the absence of disease or infirmity' (WHO 1948). This encompasses mental and physical health and inequalities in health. It also positions health as a positive concept. The impact assessment advises policy-makers on steps that can be taken to manage any effects that are identified: this includes enhancing beneficial effects as well as mitigating adverse effects.

The Gothenburg Consensus Statement identifies four values for HIA (WHO Regional Office for Europe and European Centre for Health Policy 1999):

1. democracy: providing people with the opportunity to contribute to decision-making;
2. equity: ensuring that the distribution of effects is examined and that advice is given so as to protect and improve health for people who are vulnerable and marginalised;
3. sustainable development: short- and long-term effects as well as direct and indirect effects; and
4. ethical use of evidence: HIA is an evidence-based approach which seeks to present a full picture to the policy-maker. This might include for example a analysis of contrary and conflicting information and a consideration of the degree of uncertainty attached to any findings.

All assessments will be specific to a time, a place and a proposed policy. They will generally use a broad and all-encompassing model of health.

Human health has long been considered in planning but HIA allows a formal consideration of health issues and, through its focus on stakeholder engagement, it brings a wider range of analysis to bear on the decision. Some authors have made the case that HIA, with its focus on stakeholder engagement, can play an important role in a project proponent achieving a social licence to operate (Viliani 2009). Public health typically has three components; each of these is shown below along with its link to planning:

1. health services: the development of health services can be a matter for planning while health services themselves have a vital role in dealing with all manifestations of ill health including acute and chronic illness and injury;
2. health protection: making sure 'bad things do not happen' by keeping emissions to air, water, noise etc. below certain limits – these are mostly covered through planning but it must be borne in mind that while the limits used are deemed safe it does not mean that they prevent adverse effects from happening – all emissions to air, no matter how small, cause changes in health; and
3. health improvement: the most challenging aspect for assessment and for planning.

The insight into health that HIA provides depends upon the way in which the assessment is set up (see the scoping stage). Kemm (2000) suggests that assessing effects on health can:

- identify health effects beyond issues typically examined;
- enable a more precise quantification of the magnitude of health effects;
- clarify health trade-offs;

- provide for better mitigation or enhancement of health effects (depending on their direction);
- enhance the transparency and openness of decision-making; and
- change the culture of policy-makers to consider health.

For health to be satisfactorily considered and for the findings of an HIA to be taken into account, there are both technical issues and political, or strategic, issues to address (Ison 2009; Harris et al. 2014). Technical aspects include the ways in which health effects of changes in air quality, noise, social capital, employment etc. can be described, or modelled. Political aspects cover the ways in which relationships between different sectors are handled: how is health and well-being, and by extension HIA, located in the policy process? Many of the decisions made in the course of an HIA require a mixture of these two aspects. By and large technical challenges can be overcome but the assessment will be of little, or no, importance if the political issues are not addressed. Our focus in this chapter is on health but the observations apply to any topic that cuts across sectors. Successful impact assessment relies on the different actors in the policy process working together.

Health impact assessment

Mindell et al. (2008) reviewed HIA frameworks. They found agreement in:

- the stages of HIA;
- the use of a socio-economic or socio-environmental model of health;
- recognition of the need to integrate research evidence, local data and the knowledge of stakeholders, particularly members of affected communities; and
- the need to consider the distribution of effects as well as the potential overall impacts.

Hebert et al. (2012) revisited and updated this review. They looked at 45 guidance documents and found both variety and convergence. While the procedure of conducting an HIA was similar throughout the range of documents surveyed, Hebert et al. found variety in the number of stages in the process, the name of each stage and the activities included under each stage. There was convergence around issues such as the importance of reducing inequalities and importance of community engagement. In the chapter the process is divided into five stages:

5. screening;
6. scoping;
7. assessment;
8. reporting/feedback; and
9. monitoring and evaluation.

These are considered in turn below. In essence, each of these stages consider the same questions:

- Will this proposal have an effect on health?
- Who will be affected?
- What can we do about it?

As the HIA process progresses, it can become more focused and involve a wider range of people in answering the above questions.

Screening

All guidance documents identify screening as the first stage. This is where the decision is made about whether to request an HIA. Inclusion is easy – exclusion is harder. Planning policies need to be clear as to when an HIA is required. Some spatial planning policies in England state that an HIA should be conducted alongside an EIA. Bond (2004) notes that less than 0.1 per cent of planning applications in the UK are subject to EIA (after Weston 2002) and that tying the screening decision for health to the EIA process is to suggest that 99.9 per cent of development has no significant health implications.

Screening does not feature greatly in the literature so we rarely hear about decisions not to proceed to an HIA. Slotterback et al. (2011) provide a rare example. They describe how seven municipalities, in the USA, screened housing and transport proposals for health effects and subsequent HIA. They each determined that no additional analysis of health effects was needed. The users valued a screening tool that was quick and easy to use and this enabled them to decide how to move forward in the planning process and which health issues might be most relevant. Slotterback et al. tell us that in six of these seven examples the screening was led by planning staff. The seventh example was led by public health and, from the summary provided, this was the only screening process to result in recommendations to modify the design to promote and protect health.

It is clear that in screening, a conclusion is reached about potential health effects of a proposed policy, even if the decision is not to proceed with an HIA. It also suggests that there should be some level of health involvement in the screening process.

For this stage, it is recommended that a screening checklist/process is used so that the decision is robust and defensible and also so that across an organisation a measure of consistency regarding HIA can be achieved.

Scoping

Scoping is a very important stage. If done well it saves time, work and resources in the subsequent stages of the HIA (Harris et al. 2007). In the scoping stage the parameters of the study need to be established, including the temporal and geographic parameters of analysis, the populations of interest and the determinants of health that will be considered. The time and resources that are needed, the key decision points and the personnel who will do the HIA work also need to be identified.

Many guides recommend establishing a steering or an advisory group: this establishes a formal link between the proponent and the wider stakeholders. It allows for formal oversight of the process and is particularly beneficial in the absence of established, tried and trusted relationships as might exist between planning departments and planning consultants and/or a legislated process with established precedents (Kemm 2013). Membership of the steering group is likely to include a senior representative of the Ministry of Health for the area (in the United Kingdom this role is typically filled by the Director of Public Health), the proponent and their consultants (see, for example, ERM 2008). Other parties may be invited to join, with membership being informed by the policy that is being assessed, for example, environmental health officers, police, non-governmental organisations. At project level this also serves to develop a working relationship between the proponent and the public health stakeholders and enables consensus to be reached: see, for example the report of an HIA of a proposed underground gas storage facility (Ben Cave Associates Ltd 2011) and the Statement of Common Ground that was agreed with the chair of the steering group after the assessment had been completed (Thompson 2012).

This stage is often marked by a scoping report.

During this stage, it is important to be clear about what you are 'scoping out' as well as what you are 'scoping in' and establish well-defined terms of reference for the steering group.

Assessment

In the assessment stage different types of information are used to analyse the policy and identify the potential effects on health. This will include qualitative and quantitative evidence. The sources are mainly academic literature, grey literature[2] and, gained through consultation and engagement, the lived experience of people who will be affected by the policy. Policymakers and others often give greater weight to quantitative analysis, and where possible this should be done. There are, however, challenges in quantifying predictions for small populations in small areas. Note also that quantitative analysis will include value judgements and may give a false impression of objectivity (O'Connell and Hurley 2009; Bhatia and Seto 2011).

As in all cross-sector work it is sensible to check how partners are defining the aspects of the study. HIA is an evidence-based approach: evidence, to public health officers, may mean information from peer-reviewed studies, whereas for planning officers it might mean information from national and local statistics. Jackson et al. (2011) focus on the characterisation of effect and the use of evidence to show how health effects can be described.

- Nature: the description of the effect and pathway through which it would occur.
- Intensity: the severity of the effect (for example, fatal, disabling or no disability).
- Distribution: delineates the extent of the impact across the population and on various groups, communities or subpopulations that are likely to bear differential effects.
- Direction: whether the effect is adverse or beneficial to health. In some cases the direction of the effect may be unclear, or conflicting influences on a given health outcome may be identified.
- Magnitude: the anticipated burden of disease attributable to the effect being described.
- Likelihood (probability): are the effects qualitative, estimable or calculable? The effects can be analysed as definite, probable or speculative, or according to frequency in similar settings.
- Timing and duration: at what phase(s) of the proposed activity (such as construction versus operation of a new power plant) will the impact occur and how long will it last? How rapidly will the changes occur? Are expected effects reversible or permanent?
- Strength of evidence: the evidence base for public health ranges from local stakeholder input to studies that can be generalised to the proposal under consideration. Literature on related situations often forms the foundation for analysis; systematic reviews are available on some topics. Expert opinion plays a central role in HIA analysis.

In the assessment stage be consistent and clear about the way evidence is assembled and provide a transparent description of how it is analysed (Fredsgaard et al. 2009; North American HIA Practice Standards Working Group 2010).

Reporting and feedback

Reporting and feedback should occur throughout the assessment process. If this continuous feedback has taken place, that is, health input has been provided, and heeded, from the early conceptual stages to the final stages, then the assessment should not be reporting any large (potential) adverse effects.

The findings of the assessment are formally documented in the final report.

Recommendations can be presented as a public health management plan whereby timelines and actors are identified for each action.

The HIA team and the advisory group should also consider how the results will be shared and whether there are different audiences for the findings of the HIA.

Monitoring and evaluation

Evaluation involves focusing on, and untangling, a specific strand of analysis (in our case HIA) and identifying its effect on a complex and political process (Bekker et al. 2005). There are, typically, three forms of evaluation: outcome, process and effectiveness. Outcome evaluation involves identifying what actually happens to health as a result of a policy, plan, programme or project. While this form may be the most desirable it is also the most challenging given that many of the health changes will take place over a long time and the causal pathway by which health might be expected to change is long with many intervening factors. Lessons from follow-up of EIAs are instructive: while seen as important, follow-up is conducted more often on the physical environment than on the socio-economic outcomes (Morrison-Saunders and Arts 2005). In a similar way, when considering monitoring health effects it is easier, and cheaper, to focus on changes to the physical environment, for example, noise, water or air quality than on the social environment or on actual changes in health outcomes. Changes to noise, water and air quality, etc. might be considered as proxy indicators for health, and readings collected as part of routine monitoring. The HIA should flag up potential exposure of vulnerable groups, whereas an environmental assessment will indicate whether regulated standards are likely to be exceeded.

That leaves us with evaluation of process and of effectiveness. Process evaluation is an examination of the actual outputs of the process against the intended outputs. This can involve headcounts of number of people involved, surveys of the experiences of people involved and reflection on the part of the HIA team and the steering group: for a specific example of a process evaluation see Opinion Leader Research (2003) and for an evaluation of practice across the USA see Schuchter et al. (2014).

How effective is HIA? Writing with regard to EIA Morgan (2012) places discussions of effectiveness into two broad groups according to the way in which the assessment process is understood to operate: the first group sees assessment as an information processing model (rationalist) and the other a variant of the symbolic politics model (using terms proposed by Bartlett and Kurian 1999). Thus Gray et al.'s (2011) examination of the ways in which the results of the HIAs are reflected in the plan and development process belongs to the information processing model. Analyses that are closer to the symbolic politics model focus on the context in which decisions are made and the actors who take those decisions. Thus impact assessments, HIAs included, are seen as sources of information that are used by decision-makers and that are likely to be used for political goals (Bekker et al. 2005); Harris et al. (2014) focus on the values held by stakeholders as a way to understanding the ways in which HIAs are part of the policy-making process. Cashmore et al. (2010) argues persuasively that all aspects of impact assessment are political, from the identification of issues, to data gathering, assessment and methods for establishing effectiveness. Morgan (2012) poses some questions for EIA effectiveness. In the bullet points below, I have adapted Morgan's questions so they relate to effectiveness for HIA.

- Has the process opened opportunities for local people to be more involved in decision-making?
- Have project proponents and other stakeholder become more aware of health issues through HIA and modified their practices accordingly (in the case of the private sector this is likely to be to gain competitive advantage)?
- Has change been brought about in government bodies dealing with, say, vulnerable population, to internalise HIA thinking?
- Do decision-makers, and other stakeholders, understand and use the HIA information provided to them?

It is important that during this stage the types of monitoring and evaluation that are required and the sources of funding for this work are specified. Details about who will collect and interpret the data and what will happen if the results suggest that changes are required should also be established.

Quality assurance

Quality assurance has been added to the end of this summary of evaluation. This is critically important to the process of impact assessment and thus far more than a topic to 'bolt on'. Quality assurance can look at:

- the skills and competencies of the organisations that conduct assessments (IEMA 2012);
- the individuals who practise assessment – Birley (2011: p. 113) provides a person specification for a competent HIA consultant;
- the conduct of the assessors – IAIA encourage their members to sign a professional code of conduct and ethical responsibilities (IAIA 2009); or
- the completed report – processes and checklists are available to enable those paying for, using or doing HIA to check its quality (see, for example, Fredsgaard et al. 2009; Ison 2012).

Expectations of an assessment should be established well before assessment work begins. This simple point is often overlooked. Anecdotal evidence suggests that planning authorities that fail to do this are disappointed with the HIAs issued by project proponents (Cave 2013; McAteer 2014).

A review package (Fredsgaard et al. 2009) has been adopted as planning policy on HIA by some English authorities (South Cambridgeshire District Council 2011; Bristol City Council 2013) and it is used by the Wales Health Impact Assessment Support Unit (Green, L. personal communication 2013). The process is based upon similar documents for EIA (Lee and Colley 1992; Lee et al. 1999), which were instrumental in identifying areas of weakness in, and thus improving, EIA practice. The process involves two reviewers who work through a set of questions about the HIA report. They then compare their results and reach a consensus decision. The HIA team are provided with a final score and a detailed set of comments about their HIA. This set of comments is useful in enabling the HIA team to improve the report. However, determining quality is not a straightforward, cut and dried, affair. It involves judgement and negotiation and it is therefore important that the reviews are conducted by a minimum of two people. Haigh et al. (2013) used the Fredsgaard et al. review process (2009) to examine 55 HIAs in Australia and New Zealand.

It is important that quality is considered as early as possible and that it is clear what is required from the assessment process. It is therefore useful to establish a benchmark for the authority or organisation to achieve and to use this as a way to improve standards. One way of achieving this is to ensure that any document that establishes a requirement for HIA (for example, as a formal step within policy or guidance) also considers how quality will be assured.

Other forms of assessment

Can health be integrated into other forms of impact assessment? This question is considered by looking, from a predominantly European perspective, at the way in which health is addressed in SEA and EIA. As noted earlier, these forms of assessment are conducted on plans, programmes and projects that lie within spatial planning. The question is sometimes posed as to whether health can be addressed in an *integrated appraisal*. This is a catch-all term to describe any bundle of impact assessments that are conducted or, more often, simply reported together. The lessons from health in SEA and EIA can equally be applied to health in an *integrated appraisal*.

Strategic Environmental Assessment

The SEA Directive (European Parliament and Council of the European Union 2001) refers to public plans and programmes but not to policies. The idea is to identify issues at a strategic level so that they do not arise at project level. In practice the link between strategic assessment and project assessment has proved problematic (Arts et al. 2005). SEAs are most commonly carried out for land-use plans and programmes, but are also applied to other sector-specific plans, such as for energy, water, waste, transport, agriculture and industry (UN Economic Commission for Europe 2010). The SEA Directive explicitly requires the consideration of 'the likely significant effects on the environment, including on issues such as . . . human health . . .' (European Parliament and Council of the European Union 2001). In 2010, the SEA Protocol (UN Economic Commission for Europe 2003) was ratified. This goes further than the SEA Directive as it uses the term 'environment and health' throughout and it indicates that health authorities should be consulted at the different stages of the process.

The SEA Directive does not provide a detailed definition of these aspects: thus, within SEA practice, health is addressed in different ways and in ways that do not systematically require the input of public health or even formal sign-off from health authorities. This has implications for the analytical processes in SEA but also for the accountability of the health input (Jackson et al. 2011). Ensuring that significant health effects are satisfactorily identified and considered is challenging, and the SEA directive has not led to widespread involvement of public health experts in the assessment process or in planning: the health sector tends to be external to the plan-making process (Cave et al. 2007). In Denmark, health is a formal component in the assessment of spatial plans: noise, drinking water, air pollution, recreation/outdoor life and traffic safety are considered with regard to health (Kørnov 2009). A review in England and Germany found that all SEAs, in a sample of eight, considered aspects of physical and natural effects on health, such as noise, emissions, pollution and similar, while four SEAs out of the sample also considered social and behavioural aspects (Fischer et al. 2010). Bond et al. (2013) examined whether there is active planning for health improvement in the English spatial planning system. The spatial planning profession was found to be ill-equipped to consider the health and well-being implications of its actions, whilst health professionals are rarely engaged and have limited understanding and aspirations when it comes to influencing spatial planning. For their part, health professionals have insufficient knowledge and understanding of planning and how to engage with it to be able to plan for health gains rather than simply respond to health impacts. HIA practice is patchy and generally undertaken by health professionals outside the statutory planning framework. Thus, whilst appropriate assessment tools exist, they currently lack a coherent context within which they can function effectively.

Environmental Impact Assessment

The EIA Directive (Council of the European Union 1985) states that the effects of a project on the environment are assessed in order to take account of concerns to protect human health.[3] However, human health is not currently specified in the direct and indirect effects of a project that must be identified, described and assessed. These include: human beings, fauna and flora, soil, water, air, climate and the landscape, the interaction between these factors, material assets and the cultural heritage. Noise is covered by a separate directive but is typically covered in EIA. In 1998, the British Medical Association (1998) found that this absence of health from the list of effects that must be considered led, somewhat unsurprisingly, to a poor coverage of human health. The British Medical Association (1998) reviewed 39 Environmental Impact Statements. They found that 72 per cent did not list human health in the table of contents; 49 per cent contained no analysis of potential effects on human health and 67 per cent did not enable an estimation of the population size that might be affected by particular impacts. Bond (2004) argues that it is the interpretation of 'human beings' that often determines the extent to which health is explicitly considered in EIA. This may be true from a legal viewpoint. However, it is likely that it is as much to do with the actions of public health stakeholders, who lobby and advocate for health to be included, as it is to do with the existence of a policy requirement.

National governments have interpreted the EIA Directive differently: the English ministry responsible for planning has resisted calls to include health explicitly within EIA. In contrast, Germany has sought to address health within EIA and, in 1992, passed a resolution on HIA in the context of EIA (Fehr et al. 2004; Fehr and Mekel 2013).

Calculations about safe exposure levels are included in the environmental limits for noise, air emissions and water quality so environmental assessment does contain consideration of health protection. However, EIAs:

*   rarely conduct consultation wider than liaison with statutory authorities;
*   do not look in detail at the populations likely to be exposed and can thus be less able to suggest adequate mitigation;
*   focus on compliance with the environmental limit values which does not mean that there will be no health effect, for example, the smallest increase in air emissions will have an effect on health; and
*   focus on ensuring that the project does not change the baseline, thus opportunities to improve the situation are not considered.

A survey of the application of the EIA Directive found that all new member states of the European Union report that human health aspects are assessed as part of the EIA reports (COWI 2009). The majority of new member states, that were surveyed, define health in environmental terms. Public health authorities are involved but mainly on environmental health matters. Procedures for assessing human health impacts vary between the member states. Few of the new member states have produced guidance documents on these issues (COWI 2009). Common elements for the new member states were found to be:

*   human health effects are identified in the scoping stage of EIA;
*   consultations take place with health authorities or experts within the field on human health; and
*   assessment of effects on human health is part of the environmental documentation submitted by the developer.

An earlier study found agreement that, wherever possible, human health effects of a project should be assessed within an EIA rather than through a separate HIA (Hilding-Rydevik et al. 2005). Once again differences emerge in the types of health effects that should be assessed. The authors concluded that health should be integrated into EIA; they acknowledged that best practice for including health in EIA remains undefined, and that it is dependent on a number of contextual factors, not least the way in which health is defined, that is, whether it is predicated on environmental impacts or on a broader range of human health determinants (Hilding-Rydevik et al. 2005).

Recent EIA Directive changes (to be transposed into national legislation by spring 2017) require that 'human health' is included in the scoping of all EIAs (European Parliament and Council of the European Union 2014). The changes require that EIA shall identify, describe and assess in an appropriate manner, in the light of each individual case, the direct and indirect significant effects of a project on population and human health.

Conclusions: raising the health agenda through assessment

As we have seen impact assessment, and HIA in particular, has a dual role: it provides advice to policy-makers and it is part of a legal and institutional procedure linked to a decision-making process. This chapter has demonstrated how each stage of an HIA provides answers to the simple questions 'how will this policy affect health and what can be done?' and it has identified the importance of screening and scoping, two early stages that decide whether or not to proceed and then delineate the boundaries of the study. The importance of public health officers building relationships with other stakeholders, and advocating for health, has also been highlighted.

In its short history HIA has been seen as one of the main ways by which health advice can be provided to planning. This has sometimes been interpreted as meaning that HIA is the only way that health advice can be provided. This is manifestly not the case. HIA is one of the techniques recommended by the WHO (2010) in its Health in All Policies approach and is thus just one approach in a wider palette. Other authors within this publication report ways in which they seek to streamline the consideration of health so that health issues receive more frequent consideration. This chapter notes that a full HIA is not always required. Where HIA has been used consistently, health issues play a greater role in mainstream policy development (Mindell et al. 2010; Bhatia and Corburn, 2011), so the process of looking at a particular policy raises the awareness of health and well-being across and within organisations and the capacity to look at health issues quickly. Delany et al. (2014) find that the methods used in HIA and Health in All Policies overlap considerably. If done properly, HIA remains one of the most complete articulations of Health in All Policies: it identifies the effects of a policy on all aspects of health and well-being and health inequalities and it suggests ways to adjust the policy and to manage the potential effects.

Advocacy and legislation are both important: any approach, for considering effects on health, that relies for its implementation on relationships and advocacy will be prey to changes in political administration or changes in personnel. Legislation plays a role in ensuring that health is considered, but as the examples of SEA in Europe and of quality in HIA show we also need public health officers to step forward and to assist planning colleagues in defining what is meant by properly addressing health and in ensuring that quality standards are met.

Notes

1 In their definition IAIA also note that impact assessment is used to inform responses to events, which are unplanned. As examples they cite natural disasters and war and conflict. The degree to which war and conflict are unplanned is a moot point.
2 Grey literature includes: government reports, committee reports, academic papers, theses, bibliographies, conference papers and abstracts, discussion papers, newsletters, PowerPoint presentations, conference proceedings, programme evaluation reports, standards/best practice documents, technical specifications and standards, and working papers (Alberani et al. 1990).
3 The EIA Directive states that ' . . . the effects of a project on the environment must be assessed in order to take account of concerns to protect human health, to contribute by means of a better environment to the quality of life, to ensure maintenance of the diversity of species and to maintain the reproductive capacity of the ecosystem as a basic resource for life'.

References

Alberani, V., De Castro, P.P. and Mazza, A.M. 1990. The use of grey literature in health sciences: a preliminary survey. *Bulletin of the Medical Library Association.* 78(4), 358–363.

Aldrich, R., Mahoney, M., Harris, E., Simpson, S. and Stewart-Williams, J. 2005. Building an equity focus in health impact assessment. *N.S.W. Public Health Bulletin.* 16(7–8), 118–119.

Arts, J., Tomlinson, P. and Voogd, H. 2005. *EIA and SEA tiering: the missing link.* International Association of Impact Assessment, position paper for the conference on international experience and perspectives in SEA. 26–30 September, Prague. Available at http://bit.ly/1eJAYPh

Bartlett, R.V. and Kurian, P.A. 1999. The theory of environmental impact assessment: implicit models of policy-making. *Policy and Politics.* 27(4), 415–433.

Bekker, M.P.M., Putters, K. and van der Grinten, T.E.D. 2005 Evaluating the impact of HIA on urban reconstruction decision-making: who manages whose risks? *Environmental Impact Assessment Review.* 25(7–8), 758–771.

Ben Cave Associates Ltd. 2011. *Preesall underground gas storage facility, Lancashire: Health impact assessment.* Pyper, R. et al. eds. Halite Energy Group. Available at http://bit.ly/1pwu0xk

Bhatia, R. and Corburn, J. 2011. Lessons from San Francisco: health impact assessments have advanced political conditions for improving population health. *Health Affairs (Millwood).* 30(12), 2410–2418.

Bhatia, R. and Seto, E. 2011. Quantitative forecasting in health impact assessment: opportunities and challenges. Draft. *Environmental Impact Assessment Review.* 31(3), 301–309.

Birley, M. 2011. *Health impact assessment: principles and practice.* London: Earthscan.

Bond, A. 2004. Lessons from EIA. In *Health impact assessment: concepts, theory, techniques and applications.* Kemm, J., Parry J. and Palmer, S. eds. Oxford: Oxford University Press. pp. 131–142.

Bond, A., Cave, B. and Ballantyne, R. 2013. Who plans for health improvement? SEA, HIA and the separation of spatial planning and health planning. *Environmental Impact Assessment Review.* 42, 67–73.

Bristol City Council. 2013. *Planning a healthier Bristol: assessing the health impacts of development.* Practice Note (draft). Available at http://bit.ly/1aChZ0R

British Medical Association. 1998. *Health and environmental impact assessment: an integrated approach.* London: Earthscan.

Cashmore, M., Richardson, T., Hilding-Ryedvik, T. and Emmelin, L. 2010. Evaluating the effectiveness of impact assessment instruments: theorising the nature and implications of their political constitution. *Environmental Impact Assessment Review.* 30(6), 371–379.

Cave, B. 2013. *Reviewing the quality of an HIA.* Montreal, Canada: Course unit: National Collaborating Centre for Healthy Public Policy. HIA online training course. Available at http://bit.ly/1p0UIxF

Cave, B., Bond, A. and Coutts, A. 2007. Addressing health in strategic environmental assessment. *Town and Country Planning.* 76(2), 59–61.

Cooke, A., Friedli, L., Coggins, T., Edmonds, N., Michaelson, J., O'Hara, K., Snowden, L., Stansfeld, J., Steuer, N., and Scott-Samuel, A. 2011. *Mental well-being impact assessment: a toolkit for well-being.* Members of the National MWIA Collaborative (England). Available at http://bit.ly/1k7DLTR

Council of the European Union. 1985. *Council Directive of 27 June 1985 on the assessment of the effects of certain public and private projects on the environment.* 85/337/EEC. Official Journal No. L 175, 05/07/1985. Available at http://bit.ly/1pFTwTw

COWI. 2009. *DG ENV study concerning the report on the application and effectiveness of the EIA Directive.* European Commission. Final report, June. Available at http://bit.ly/1npJUse

Delany, T., Harris, P., Williams, C., Harris, E., Baum, F., Lawless, A., Wildgoose, D., Haigh, F., MacDougall, C., Broderick, D. and Kickbusch, I. 2014. Health impact assessment in New South Wales & health in all policies in South Australia: differences, similarities and connections. *BMC Public Health.* 14(1), 699.

ERM. 2008. *The Stansted generation 2 project: a health impact assessment.* BAA Ltd. Available at http://bit.ly/u8lYFk

European Parliament and Council of the European Union. 2001. Directive 2001/42/EC of the European Parliament and of the Council of 27 June 2001 on the assessment of the effects of certain plans and programmes on the environment. *Official Journal of the European Communities.* L19730-37.

European Parliament and Council of the European Union. 2014. Position of the European Parliament adopted at first reading on 12 March 2014 with a view to the adoption of Directive 2014/. . ./EU of the European Parliament and of the Council amending Directive 2011/92/EU on the assessment of the effects of certain public and private projects on the environment (Text with EEA relevance). *Official Journal of the European Communities.*

Fehr, R. and Mekel, O. 2013. Health impact assessment in Germany. In *Health impact assessment: past achievement, current understanding and future progress.* Kemm, J. ed. Oxford: Oxford University Press. pp. 156–167.

Fehr, R., Mekel, O. and Welteke, R. 2004. HIA: the German perspective. In *Health impact assessment: concepts, theory, techniques and applications.* Kemm, J., Parry, J. and Palmer, S. eds. Oxford: Oxford University Press. pp. 253–264.

Fehr, R., Martuzzi, M. and Gulis, G. 2011. Family of health-related impact assessments. Poster displayed at the 11th International HIA Conference, Granada. Available at http://bit.ly/1wheucb

Fischer, T.B., Martuzzi, M. and Nowacki, J. 2010. The consideration of health in strategic environmental assessment (SEA). *Environmental Impact Assessment Review.* 30(3), 200–210.

Fredsgaard, M.W., Cave, B. and Bond, A. 2009. *A review package for health impact assessment reports of development projects.* Ben Cave Associates Ltd, Leeds, UK. Available at http://bit.ly/k63NtC

Gray, S., Carmichael, L., Barton, H., Mytton, J., Lease, H. and Joynt, J. 2011. The effectiveness of health appraisal processes currently in addressing health and wellbeing during spatial plan appraisal: a systematic review. *BMC Public Health.* 11(889).

Haigh, F., Harris, E., Chok, H.N.G., Baum, F., Harris-Roxas, B., Kemp, L., Spickett, J., Keleher, H., Morgan, R., Harris, M., Wendel, A.M and Dannenberg, A.L. 2013. Characteristics of health impact assessments reported in Australia and New Zealand 2005–2009. *Australian and New Zealand Journal of Public Health.* 37(6), 534–546.

Harris, P., Sainsbury, P. and Kemp, L. 2014. The fit between health impact assessment and public policy: practice meets theory. *Social Science and Medicine.* 108, 46–53.

Harris, P.J., Harris-Roxas, B.F., Harris, E. and Kemp, L.A. 2007. Health impact assessment and urbanisation. Lessons from the NSW HIA project. *N.S.W. Public Health Bulletin.* 18(9–10), 198–201.

Harris-Roxas, B. and Harris, E. 2011. Differing forms, differing purposes: a typology of health impact assessment. *Environmental Impact Assessment Review.* 31(4), 396–403.

Health Impact Project. 2014. HIA in the United States: supporting healthier communities in all regions of the country. Washington, DC: Pew Charitable Trusts. Available at http://bit.ly/1rBtf9A

Hebert, K.A., Wendel, A.M., Kennedy, S.K. and Dannenberg, A.L. 2012. Health impact assessment: a comparison of 45 local, national, and international guidelines. *Environmental Impact Assessment Review.* 34, 74–82.

Heller, J., Malekafzali, S., Todman, L.C. and Wier, M. 2013. *Promoting equity through the practice of health impact assessment.* California and New York: PolicyLink. Available at http://bit.ly/WakFQZ

Hilding-Rydevik, T., Vohra, S., Ruotsalainen, A., Pettersson, A., Pearce, N., Breeze, C., Hrncarova, M., Lieskovska, Z., Paluchova, K., Thomas, L. and Kemm, J. 2005. *Health aspects in EIA.* Österreichisches Institut für Raumplanung for the European Union, Sixth Framework Programme. D 2.2 Report WP 2. Improving the Implementation of Environmental Impact Assessment. Available at http://bit.ly/MpuV2v

IAIA. 2009. *Vision, mission, values, professional code of conduct and ethical responsibilities.* International Association for Impact Assessment, Fargo, ND, USA. Available at http://bit.ly/Zfqyuf

IAIA. 2010. *What is impact assessment?* International Association for Impact Assessment, Fargo, ND, USA. Available at http://bit.ly/XHuar6

ICMM. 2010. *Good practice guidance on health impact assessment*. London, UK: International Council on Mining & Metals. Available at http://bit.ly/W09Cdn

IEMA. 2012. *EIA quality mark: applicant guide*. Lincoln: Institute of Environmental Management and Assessment. Available at http://bit.ly/14TmXcn

IFC (International Finance Corporation). 2009. *Introduction to health impact assessment*. Washington, DC: International Finance Corporation. Available at http://bit.ly/wz8BkV

IPIECA. 2005. *A guide to health impact assessments in the oil and gas industry*. Eds. Krieger, G. and Balge, M. International Petroleum Industry Environmental Conservation Association, International Association of Oil and Gas Producers. Available at http://bit.ly/XzJAKq

Ison, E. 2009. The introduction of health impact assessment in the WHO European healthy cities network. *Health Promotion International*. 24(Suppl 1), i64–i71.

Ison, E. 2012. *Peer review of health impact assessment: a process for learning and developing skills*. Ben Cave Associates Ltd for the Equity Action Programme, Leeds, UK. Developed with the WHO European healthy cities sub-network on health impact assessment (2008). Adapted for the training programme: Learning. Reflection. Action. Health Impact Assessment in the Equity Action Programme – building capacity. Available at http://bit.ly/13CB1mk

Jackson, R.J., Bear, D., Bhatia, R., Cantor, S.B., Cave, B., Diez Roux, A.V., Dora, C., Fielding, J.E., Zivin, J.S.G., Levy, J.I., Quint, J.B., Raja, S., Schulz, A.J. and Wernham, A.A. 2011. *Improving health in the United States: the role of health impact assessment*. Committee on Health Impact Assessment. Board on Environmental Studies and Toxicology, Division on Earth and Life Studies. Washington, DC: National Research Council of the National Academies.

Kemm, J. 2013. Screening and scoping. In *Health impact assessment: past achievement, current understanding and future progress*. Kemm, J. ed. Oxford: Oxford University Press. pp. 15–24.

Kemm, J. and Parry, J. 2004. What is HIA? Introduction and overview. In *Health impact assessment: concepts, theory, techniques and applications*. Kemm, J., Parry, J. and Palmer, S. eds. Oxford: Oxford University Press. pp. 1–14.

Kemm, J.R. 2000. Can health impact assessment fulfil the expectations it raises? *Public Health*. 114(6), 431–433.

Kørnøv, L. 2009. Strategic environmental assessment as catalyst of healthier spatial planning: the Danish guidance and practice. *Environmental Impact Assessment Review*. 29(1), 60–65.

Lee, J.H., Röbbel, N. and Dora, C. 2013. *Cross-country analysis of the institutionalization of health impact assessment*. Geneva: World Health Organization. Social Determinants of Health Discussion Paper 8. Available at http://bit.ly/1atIZRj

Lee, N. and Colley, R. 1992. *Reviewing the quality of environmental statements*. University of Manchester. Manchester: EIA Centre, Department of Planning and Landscape. Occasional paper No. 24 (second edition). Available at http://bit.ly/ZanCOw

Lee, N., Colley, R., Bonde, J. and Simpson, J. 1999. *Reviewing the quality of environmental statements and environmental appraisals*. University of Manchester. Manchester: EIA Centre, Department of Planning and Landscape. Occasional paper No. 55. Available at http://bit.ly/17eVrWh

McAteer, S. 2014. *Halton: health impact assessment*. Presentation at Health: the challenge of mainstreaming. Manchester: RTPI North West.

Mindell, J., Boltong, A. and Forde, I. 2008. A review of health impact assessment frameworks. *Public Health*. 122(11), 1177–1187.

Mindell, J., Bowen, C., Herriot, N., Findlay, G. and Atkinson, S. 2010. Institutionalizing health impact assessment in London as a public health tool for increasing synergy between policies in other areas. *Public Health*. 124(2), 107–114.

Morgan, R.K. 2012. Environmental impact assessment: the state of the art. *Impact Assessment and Project Appraisal*. 30(1), 5–14.

Morrison-Saunders, A. and Arts, J. 2005. Learning from experience: emerging trends in environmental impact assessment follow-up. *Impact Assessment and Project Appraisal*. 23(3), 170–174.

North American HIA Practice Standards Working Group. 2010. *Minimum elements and practice standards for health impact assessment (HIA)*. Eds. Bhatia, R. et al. Oakland, CA: North American HIA Practice Standards Working Group. Version 2. Available at http://bit.ly/XviXqZ

O'Connell, E. and Hurley, F. 2009. A review of the strengths and weaknesses of quantitative methods used in health impact assessment. *Public Health*. 123(4), 306–310.

Opinion Leader Research. 2003. *Report on the qualitative evaluation of four health impact assessments on draft mayoral strategies for London*. London Health Commission, Greater London Authority and the London Health Observatory. Available at http://bit.ly/1nVUOsU

Quigley, R., den Broeder, L., Furu, P., Bond, A., Cave, B. and Bos, R. 2006. *Health impact assessment.* International Association for Impact Assessment, International best practice principles. Special publication series No. 5. Available at http://bit.ly/X2iOxM

Schuchter, J., Bhatia, R., Corburn, J. and Seto, E. 2014. Health impact assessment in the United States: has practice followed standards? *Environmental Impact Assessment Review.* 47(July), 47–53.

Slotterback, C.S., Forsyth, A., Krizek, K.J., Johnson, A. and Pennucci, A. 2011. Testing three health impact assessment tools in planning: a process evaluation. *Environmental Impact Assessment Review.* 31(2), 144–153.

South Cambridgeshire District Council. 2011. *Health impact assessment SPD.* Available at http://bit.ly/1hCnuqg

Thompson, J. 2012. *Health impact assessment of proposed underground natural gas storage facility, Preesall, Lancashire. Statement of common ground.* NHS North Lancashire. Available at http://bit.ly/1nyjlVV

UN (United Nations) Economic Commission for Europe. 2003. *Protocol on strategic environmental assessment to the convention on environmental impact assessment in a transboundary context.* Geneva, 12. Available at http://bit.ly/1bf6wIp

UN Economic Commission for Europe. 2010. New international treaty to better integrate environmental and health concerns into political decision-making. Geneva, Switzerland: UNECE website. Available at http://bit.ly/1o8QswV

Viliani, F. 2009. HIA and extractive industry: relevance for the CSR agenda. Presentation at the 29th Annual Meeting of the International Association for Impact Assessment, Accra, Ghana. Available at http://bit.ly/1yLPoVU

Weston, J. 2002. From Poole to Fulham: a changing culture in UK environmental impact assessment decision making? *Journal of Environmental Planning and Management.* 45(3), 425–442.

Winkler, M.S., Krieger, G.R., Divall, M.J., Cissé, G., Wielga, M., Singer, B.H., Tanner, M. and Utzinger, J. 2013. Untapped potential of health impact assessment. *Bulletin of the World Health Organization.* 91(4), 237–312.

WHO (World Health Organization). 1948. *Preamble to the constitution of the World Health Organization; signed on 22 July 1946 by the representatives of 61 States and entered into force on 7 April 1948.* New York: Official Records of the World Health Organization, no. 2, p. 100. Available at http://bit.ly/1cgnJ3S

WHO. 2010. *Adelaide statement on health in all policies: moving towards a shared governance for health and well-being.* Adelaide, South Australia: World Health Organization and Government of South Australia. Report from the International Meeting on Health in All Policies. Available at http://bit.ly/18hiI8v

WHO Regional Office for Europe and European Centre for Health Policy. 1999. *Health impact assessment: main concepts and suggested approach. Gothenburg consensus paper.* Brussels: WHO Regional Office for Europe, ECHP. Available at http://bit.ly/XyA89L

27

A STRATEGIC APPROACH TO GREEN INFRASTRUCTURE PLANNING

Val Kirby

Introduction: green infrastructure – origins and scope

In recent years 'green infrastructure' has become a politically acceptable and professionally popular term to use in the context of environmental planning. Sometimes it is scattered, like confetti, across policy documents, leading to the suspicion that green infrastructure might be just a superficial greenwash, with little deep meaning. But, properly done, it is much more than that.

Green Infrastructure is the latest answer to an old question: how to convince policy and decision makers of the need to do joined-up, long-term planning, in ways that benefit people *and* the environment. Green infrastructure works at a range of scales, from city region to site, always accepting the principles that the world is a system of networks and that everything connects to everything else. It's about making the most of both natural and human connections between places. It's about improving existing networks and creating new ones. It also requires an insight into system dynamics, so that we understand how wildlife, water and people move through landscapes, and how environmental networks change over time.

Definitions

Green infrastructure has many, varied definitions. The variation is particularly evident when comparing USA and European definitions. In the USA the federal Environmental Protection Agency (EPA) defines green infrastructure as large-scale watershed management. In Europe multifunctionality and green networks are the usual focus.

Landscape is one of the big ideas that lie behind green infrastructure. Landscape, as defined by the European Landscape Convention,[1] neatly encapsulates the intimate links between places, whether largely natural or much modified, and people. Another key idea is *infrastructure*, familiar from its association with essential services such as piped water, electricity supply and road and rail systems. The third idea is *network*, where each element is in some way connected to and impacts on every other element. The final idea is *multifunctionality*: this has greatest currency in small, crowded countries, where it is easy to justify the principle that each piece of land (and water) should perform more than one function. Although of course it doesn't matter where you are: a multifunctional approach is an important aspect of sustainable planning everywhere.

Natural England (2009), the UK's Landscape Institute (2013a) and the European Commission (EC) all have definitions that include networks and multifunctionality, and imply landscape and

386

infrastructure. The EC's definition is the most comprehensive of these: it describes green infrastructure as 'a strategically planned network of high quality natural and semi-natural areas with other environmental features, which is designed and managed to deliver a wide range of ecosystem services and protect biodiversity in both rural and urban settings' (European Union 2013).

England's National Planning Policy Framework (NPPF) contains one of the rare definitions that includes health: it defines green infrastructure as 'a network of multi-functional green space, both new and existing, both rural and urban, which supports natural and ecological processes and is integral to the health and quality of life of sustainable communities' (DCLG 2012).

In contrast the US EPA emphasises green infrastructure's role in managing water and creating healthier urban environments. Some of the EPA's guidance recognises the potential for recreation and well-being benefits, but the management of storm-water is central.[2]

Evolution

The years after World War II saw rapid urban expansion and agricultural industrialisation in Europe, North America and Australasia. Understanding the huge environmental impacts of these changes grew during the 1950s and 1960s, but public policy changed slowly. In Britain, for example, post-war forward planning only applied to major settlements, excluding both the countryside and ecological issues. But over time environmental awareness did emerge, and by the late 1960s the British planning system was extended to rural areas. It took longer for ecological issues to be reflected in planning policy. Writers such as Rachel Carson (1962), Ian McHarg (1969) and Nan Fairbrother (1973), criticised the narrow approach and proposed new ways of working. From the 1970s support grew for embedding ecological thinking into planning and design, and a systems based, multiple objective approach to planning both urban and rural areas was widely advocated.

In the UK early environmental projects that influenced evolving practice included the Bollin Valley Urban Fringe experiment;[3] and the Community Forests initiative.[4] They worked not just with environmental networks and multifunctionality, but with cross-sectoral partnerships. The partnership theme was picked up in the sequence of Single Regeneration Budget programmes of the 1990s, though these emphasised local economies more than the environment (Rhodes et al. 2007). The Accessible Natural Greenspace Standard (ANGSt) is also worth mentioning. Developed in England in the early 1990s, ANGSt is relevant to green infrastructure because of the way it links people and recreational greenspaces at different scales (see Figure 27.1).[5]

Accessible Natural Greenspace Standard

The recommendation is that everyone, wherever they live, should have an accessible natural greenspace:

- of at least 2 hectares in size, no more than 300 metres (5 minutes walk) from home;
- at least one accessible 20 hectare site within two kilometres of home;
- one accessible 100 hectare site within five kilometres of home; and
- one accessible 500 hectare site within ten kilometres of home; plus
- a minimum of one hectare of statutory Local Nature Reserves per thousand population.

Figure 27.1 Accessible National Greenspace Standard

Source: Natural England (2010, p. 12).

In the early years of this century the United Nations Millennium Assessment (MEA) introduced the concept of ecosystem services to a worldwide audience, seeking to raise global awareness of the importance of the connections between ecological networks, mult-functionality and people's needs (MEA 2005). Although the term ecosystem service can appear opaque, the underlying concept is simple: the natural world provides people with many services that are often under-appreciated and under-valued. A recent assessment (Costanza et al. 2014) puts the value of total global ecosystem services in 2011 as $125 trillion/year, while confirming that many of these services are best considered public goods – the kind of goods with which green infrastructure is often associated (Simpson 2011). Green infrastructure provides a useful hook to help explain what ecosystem services are all about (although ascribing monetary value to services such as open space, which are often assumed to be freely available, is still problematic (Simpson 2011)).

The World Health Organization's (WHO) report on the health implications of the MEA focuses on the big issues facing the world's poor – access to clean water, sanitation and food, services that are essential to survival (MEA 2005). It is not surprising that green infrastructure is not mentioned. Neither does the UK's own National Ecosystem Assessment mention green infrastructure specifically, although it does say that 'observing nature and participating in physical activity in green spaces play an important role in positively influencing human health and wellbeing' (Pretty 2011).

Connections to health and sustainability
Green infrastructure and health

You can't use laboratory conditions and controlled experiments to prove causal relationships between the physical environment and benefits to people's health. But there is enough evidence to support the positive connections between them (Landscape Institute 2013b). Tzoulas et al. (2007) reviewed many sources before devising a conceptual framework linking green infrastructure with ecosystem health and human health and well-being. The beneficial green infrastructure elements range from green corridors to churchyards, and from domestic gardens to open water. The human health issues that benefit from access to green infrastructure range from physical ailments such as cardiovascular, respiratory and digestive conditions to relaxation from stress, positive emotions and a sense of community identity.

The WHO's Healthy Cities programme has long accepted the link between environment and health: the European Healthy Cities network has about 90 members, all working to bring health and sustainable development to local people. But just providing greenspaces, footpaths and cycleways does not necessarily make people healthier. The things that people do are influenced by other variables, particularly those concerning social and economic conditions: people who suffer deprivation need positive support to change their lifestyles (Commission on Social Determinants of Health 2008). But if opportunities are provided, and are backed up with incentives targeted at specific groups of people, then it is reasonable to assume that health benefits will follow. These can include increased life expectancy, reduced health inequalities, and improvements in health and well-being (Forest Research 2010).

Other potential benefits include reductions in the costs of health care. The cost of reducing cardiovascular mortality through clinical interventions is claimed to be 27 times more than the cost of achieving the same result through local public health spending (Mays 2011; Milstein et al. 2011). The Landscape Institute's position statement, *Public Health and Landscape*, comments that 'interventions in the landscape can, and indeed should, play an important role in delivering these cost-effective improvements in public health and wellbeing' (Landscape Institute 2013b).

All local planning authorities in England are required to build a green infrastructure strategy into their local plans, in line with the NPPF (DCLG 2012).

| | Policy priorities | | | | | | | |
| | Economic | Environmental | | | | | Social | |
	Economic growth and employment	Protect and enhance cultural heritage	Protect and enhance the landscape, geodiversity and natural environment	Biodiversity conservation and enhancement	Climate change mitigation and adaptation	Promoting sustainable transport and reducing the need to travel by car	Community cohesion and life long learning; volunteering	Healthy communities; health and well being
Access, recreation, movement and leisure								
Habitat provision and access to nature								
Landscape setting and context for development								
Energy production and conservation								
Food production and productive landscapes								
Flood attenuation and water resource management								
Cooling effect								

Figure 27.2   Green infrastructure and policy priorities

Source: Natural England (2009).

Natural England's green infrastructure guidance has many references to health. It advocates the use of green infrastructure to bring the natural world into every neighbourhood, supporting healthier lifestyles by providing green routes and spaces and helping to reduce the urban heat island effect. Figure 27.2 summarises the links between green infrastructure and a range of policy priorities, including health and well-being.

Although it is widely accepted that there is enough evidence to satisfy policy makers, there will always be gaps in our knowledge. A recent review of practice and evidence by the Landscape Institute and the Town and Country Planning Association (2012) acknowledges this.

Green infrastructure and sustainability

For green infrastructure to work properly, it needs to be done sustainably. This means ensuring that what is done now does not compromise options for future generations (WCED 1987). Early sustainable development rhetoric emphasised the need to think about the environmental and social impacts of development, as well as economic benefits. There has been much debate and critique about how to integrate these very different elements (see for example Sneddon et al. 2006). In some places the financial crisis of 2008 has resulted in a reordering of the priorities: for example, to the UK government, 'Sustainable development means encouraging economic growth while protecting the environment and improving our quality of life – all without affecting the ability of future generations to do the same.'[6]

A growing awareness and understanding of global climate change has reinforced the need to find more sustainable ways of managing and developing our environments. Although at the time of writing the final synthesis reports of the 5th Assessment Cycle are still being finalised, the urgency of taking more action to enhance mitigation and support adaptation is clear from the documents produced so far.[7]

Sustainable Urban Drainage Systems (SUDS) are a good example of the kind of initiative that works well in a green infrastructure context. SUDS can provide cost effective alternatives to traditional grey infrastructure, whilst also benefiting the environment and people's health and well-being, through increasing the number and area of greenspaces for wildlife and passive and active recreation.[8, 9]

Green infrastructure can contribute towards all three pillars of sustainable development, and can help address the issues created by climate change. It focuses on the joined-up, cost-effective planning of the more natural elements of the physical environment, in ways that benefit both the environment and people.

Green infrastructure in practice

In the United States the EPA has supported green infrastructure since 2007, emphasising its potential to *manage wet weather*. Green infrastructure is also supported by the US Department of Agriculture, professional bodies such as the American Society of Landscape Architects (ASLA) and organisations with specific remits such as parks, or wildlife and nature conservation, or mitigating the effects of climate change. Although the EPA's key focus is water management, benefits to people and open space networks are acknowledged. In 2013 the EPA produced a strategic agenda, committed to make green infrastructure part of *business as usual* across government, at all levels (EPA 2013).

ASLA takes a wider approach, defining green infrastructure as a framework for understanding and working with ecosystem services throughout cities, park systems and wildlife corridors.[10] ASLA's website lists many organisations, from federal to local, with an equally great range of ways of doing green infrastructure, from green roofs, to green walls, urban forests and river catchment planning.

In the United Kingdom the range of applications is also considerable. For example the Scottish Government endorses green (and blue) infrastructure as a way of working at all spatial scales with *the services that the environment can provide*. It makes a clear case for developing green infrastructure at a range of spatial scales: thus buildings connect to the street, which connects to the neighbourhood, which connects to strategic places (Scottish Government 2011). It also emphasises the potential health and well-being benefits (mental as well as physical), through opportunities for increased general physical activity, active travel, healthy food production and healthy eating.

Two of the Landscape Institute's three publications on green infrastructure focus on the strategic scale (Landscape Institute 2009, 2013a); the third is aimed at local decision makers (Landscape Institute 2011). The 2013 statement links the benefits of green infrastructure with a fully integrated approach to land use. Health and well-being benefits are mentioned throughout. This document also argues that green infrastructure helps provide joined-up, cost-efficient solutions to issues such as housing, flood management, food growing and biodiversity.

Across the EU green infrastructure is practised at a range of scales and in many different contexts: the EU-wide commitment appears set to last until at least 2020. The EC's 2013 strategy is a key step in achieving Europe's 2020 Biodiversity Strategy target of maintaining and enhancing ecosystems and their services by establishing green infrastructure and restoring at least 15 per cent of degraded ecosystems (remembering that ecosystem services include human health and well-being). Although it is still early days, the EC has an ambitious, cross-sectoral commitment to green infrastructure, and aims to affect a wide number of policy areas (EC 2013).

Case studies

These four case studies deal with green infrastructure at the strategic scale, although what 'strategic' means is different in each case.

London's Green Grid

The 2012 Olympic Games were held in London. The *East London Green Grid* (ELGG) was a response to the selection of a depressed part of East London as the site for the games. Siting high profile, international events in such areas is common practice, but it can be hard to ensure that they experience long-term benefits. Using green infrastructure in this context has the potential for long-term environmental and social benefits, making sure that each piece of land performs different functions and using partnership working to bring together a wide range of public and private organisations. The sports focus of the Olympics gave the ELGG an added attraction, in its emphasis on helping ordinary people – not just the sporting elite – develop healthier ways of living.

The ELGG was launched in 2007, five years before the games, as a strategic partnership project between local and central government. The overall scheme was ambitious: it aimed to shape and support growth, by providing a richly varied, high quality landscape and better connections between places where people live and work, public transport, London's Green Belt and the River Thames. It also aimed to help East London's communities adapt to the challenges of climate change. The ELGG is a network of multifunctional open spaces, based around the area's natural systems. Six smaller areas nest within it, each with its own grid or network, and action plans contain detailed projects, down to the scale of neighbourhood open spaces (see Figures 27.3 and 27.4).

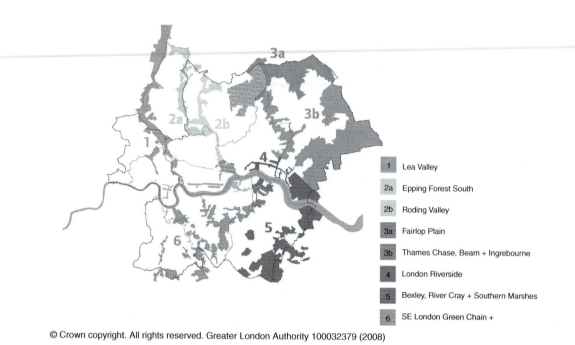

Figure 27.3   East London Green Grid Areas

Source: Greater London Authority (2008).

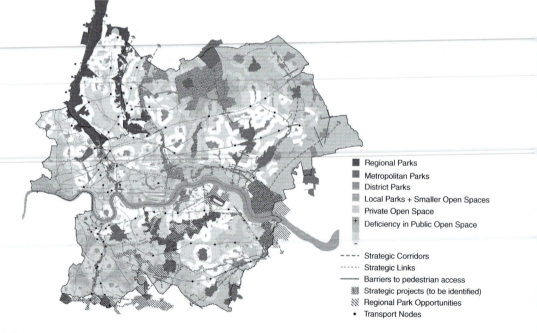

Figure 27.4   East London Green Grid, Strategic Framework

Source: Greater London Authority (2008).

(1) Protect, conserve and enhance London's strategic network of green and open natural and cultural spaces, to connect the everyday life of the city to a range of experiences and landscapes, town centres, public transport nodes, the countryside in the urban fringe, the Thames and major employment and residential areas;

(2) Encourage greater use of, and engagement with, London's green infrastructure; popularising key destinations within the network and fostering a greater appreciation of London's natural and cultural landscapes; enhancing visitor facilities and extending and upgrading the walking and cycling networks in between to promote a sense of place and ownership for all who work in, visit and live in London;

(3) Secure a network of high quality, well designed and multifunctional green and open spaces to establish a crucial component of urban infrastructure able to address the environmental challenges of the 21st century – most notably climate change.

Figure 27.5   Aims of the All London Green Grid

Source: GLA (2011).

The ELGG became legally enforceable in 2008, as Supplementary Planning Guidance which stressed the connections with public health and well-being (GLA 2008). The approach was soon extended to the whole of London (GLA 2011), with 11 green grid areas. Figure 27.5 shows the three aims of the All London Green Grid – everyday life is mentioned, but health and well-being are not made explicit at this high level (although there are 45 mentions of one or other of these terms in the All London Green Grid Supplementary Planning Guidance document).

Central Scotland

Central Scotland has long been affected by degraded landscapes and townscapes, a legacy of the decline in heavy industry. Here is another example of green infrastructure developing in two stages. The focus here is on several towns and cities, plus the landscapes between. Green infrastructure is linked to the potential for long-term environmental improvement, multifunctionalism and the essential use of partnerships. The need to tackle Scotland's health inequalities also influenced the adoption of green infrastructure, as it increases opportunities for healthy outdoor activities. The Central Scotland Forest (CSF) began more than 20 years ago, and so predates the green infrastructure movement. The CSF covered 620 square miles (1606 sq km) in the area bounded by Glasgow, Edinburgh, Falkirk/Stirling and Lanark and was a mosaic of many woodlands.

Since March 2014 the CSF has been absorbed into the Central Scotland Green Network (CSGN), covering 10,000 sq km across the whole of central Scotland, where 3.5 million people live. Like London's Green Grid, it has legal standing. Although green infrastructure is only mentioned once in the core document, it clearly is green infrastructure on a strategic scale, with an implementation programme lasting until 2050. Figure 27.6 shows the five themes of the network.[11]

Philadelphia

Philadelphia Water Department's Green City, Clean Waters programme is a US example of the federal EPA's focus on managing catchments and storm-water. The programme came into force in 2011 and will last for 25 years: it aims 'to protect and enhance our watersheds by managing

Central Scotland Green Network – The Vision

Five themes

1   **A Place for Growth**
    Creating an environment for sustainable economic growth
2   **A place for balance**
    Creating an environment more in balance, one that will support Central Scotland to thrive in
    a changing climate
3   **A place to feel good**
    Creating an environment which supports healthy lifestyles and good physical and mental
    wellbeing
4   **A place to belong**
    Creating an environment that people can enjoy and where they choose to live and bring up
    their families
5   **A place for nature**
    Creating an environment where nature can flourish

Figure 27.6   The five themes of the Central Scotland Green Network

Source: CSGN (2011).

stormwater with innovative green infrastructure' (Philadelphia Water Department 2011). The focus on watershed management reflects a core function of the EPA, and the language used to describe the programme focuses on the benefits of implementing a more cost-effective kind of drainage system, replacing traditional grey infrastructure. The programme includes large-scale projects to improve rivers and streams and enhance the ability of the wider landscape to retain water and reduce run-off, and greening storm-water infrastructure at the level of the street. Potential health benefits are mentioned many times, although they are not headlined. A multi-sectoral partnership approach, led by the city but involving private as well as public sector partners, is key to the large financial investment that the programme requires.

European Community

Green Infrastructure for Tomorrow! (GIFT-T!) is funded by the EU's INTERREG IVB programme, to support the development of the EU's Green infrastructure Action Plan in North West Europe.[12] GIFT-T! runs from 2010 to 2015, and focuses on showing how green infrastructure can help deliver benefits to biodiversity and ecosystem services, in close cooperation with other policy measures related to agriculture, urban development, transport, recreation and climate change adaptation. There is a strong emphasis on working with the business sector, making links between green infrastructure and economic prosperity; on partnership working at the level of individual communities; and on finding ways of coping with reduced public sector budgets, since the 2008 financial crisis.

There are seven partners, two each in Belgium and the UK and three in the Netherlands. The province of Antwerp is one of the Belgian partners. The province is developing a green infrastructure project in the Campine region, which will focus on the role and potential of local and regional spatial planning for developing green infrastructure on inland dunes and small watercourses.

Doing green infrastructure properly: joining everything up

Doing green infrastructure properly means acting in a joined-up way, both in physical places and in the world of strategies, plans and organisations, both now and in future.

Connecting places

Wherever you are in the world you are in a landscape system, connected to other places by natural and cultural networks. Green infrastructure strategies should be based on an analysis of present and potential connectivity of all the land and water within the area concerned and the air above. Figure 27.7 lists the range of systems and networks that should be considered.

Every place is also nested within a hierarchy of places at different scales, from regional to local, like a set of Russian dolls. Green infrastructure programmes must reflect this, showing how each community is connected to the programme at the regional or subregional scale. This is a key issue if health and well-being benefits are to be achieved.

Landscape systems are not just inhabited by people: attention has to be given to other living things. Soil microfauna, bacteria and fungi are as important as more instantly attractive wildlife species, such as birds and butterflies. Air and water quality are crucially important. Planning for biodiversity and making connections between desired species, the conditions that they require to thrive and the habitats that are actually available, are essential to good green infrastructure.

The important links vary with each situation. If, for example, freshwater systems are an important element in a green infrastructure network, then the network must present no gaps or barriers to the movement of fish. If a particular range of bird life is desired, then habitats are required that will support those birds, either from the start, or through appropriate management strategies. Further, there has to be enough habitat to support breeding populations.

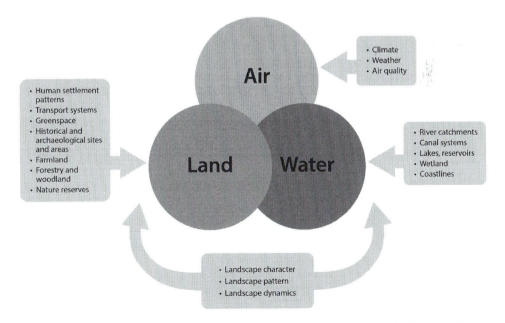

Figure 27.7   Green infrastructure strategy: systems and networks that contribute to health and well-being

Source: Kirby.

If intense human activities (such as housing, education, employment, farming or play) are to co-exist with wildlife, then we must understand the sensitivity of different species to distur-bance, whether this is caused by noise, or light, or a concentration of people, or by regular or irregular cropping, or a combination of factors.

Different activities can take place in the same part of a green infrastructure network. For example people use roads, paths, railways and waterways to move through landscapes, and these – and their margins – can be wildlife habitats and part of a SUDS network as well. But such multiple uses must be considered from the start, and careful assessments made of the ways different functions interact, both before a green infrastructure programme starts and as it matures, so that potential problems can be dealt with.

Connecting organisations and communities

Full policy integration at all levels of government is hard to achieve. But for green infrastruc-ture to fulfil its potential, integration is needed across all areas of policy and strategy, in central, regional and local government.

The links between local government, non-government organisations and local communities are also vitally important. Partnership working is a prerequisite for the effective integration across all policy areas. Figure 27.8 shows some of the essential organisational connections.

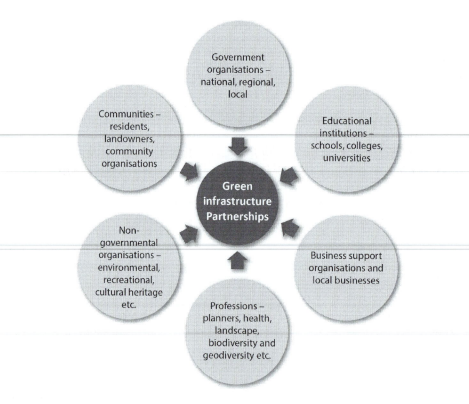

Figure 27.8 Green infrastructure: connecting organisations

Source: Kirby.

Connecting across time

Green infrastructure has to be done strategically and consistently, over appropriate time periods. Political time frames are usually short: typical electoral cycles are three, four or five years. Business planning cycles are short too. Achieving comprehensive and long lasting change through green infrastructure takes a long time. So agencies committed to doing green infrastructure properly have to find ways of working across business planning and electoral cycles.

Green infrastructure simply won't work if attempted in an incremental way. It requires a strategic, phased approach. Long-term green infrastructure strategies should be managed in shorter delivery phases so that they align with business and political cycles. It is also important to build monitoring, evaluation and learning lessons into the delivery timetable.

Green infrastructure networks need long-term, sustainable management strategies: different elements of the network need different approaches to management, led by a range of organisations from the public, private and voluntary sectors, over different timescales. A wide range of management approaches is needed for both the physical and the organisational aspects of green infrastructure. For example, maintaining and renewing play equipment in playgrounds in housing areas requires a different approach, over different timescales, from managing urban forestry, or improving water quality in a river catchment.

The UK Landscape Institute's Five Principles of Healthy Places (see Figure 27.9) summarise the range of health and well-being benefits that can be built into green infrastructure strategies. Putting these into practice means:

- building a Health Impact Assessment[13] into green infrastructure planning, to provide a strategic overview of the opportunities to achieve health and well-being benefits throughout the network;
- adopting a multi-agency partnership approach from the start;
- contributing to improvements in air quality and reducing the urban heat island effect, through tree and shrub planting, and green walls and roofs;
- commissioning river catchment management plans, including measures to clean up polluted streams and rivers and improve flood defences;
- adopting a policy to clean contaminated land and restore it to active use;
- planning walking and cycling path networks that are convenient, safe and attractive for people to use, as part of strategies to build active travel into people's lives;
- adopting standards for local open space provision (such as England's ANGSt). Prioritise the creation of new greenspaces in socially deprived areas, designing facilities to attract people of all ages and abilities;
- involving local residents in planning, restoring and creating open spaces, for example by involving them in cleaning up derelict sites, or getting school children in planting schemes;
- linking green infrastructure with local health services, so that the network provides paths and outdoor gyms for people who are prescribed outdoor activity for either physical or mental health conditions;
- designing community gardens for people with mental health problems, disabilities or simply poverty;
- designing open space hubs close to where people live, with shelters, seats and play equipment for children and teenagers;
- designing open spaces that are visible and legible (where users can easily 'read' how to move about and use) to users, to increase people's sense of security;
- building new business and education opportunities into green infrastructure strategies – for example community plant nurseries and horticulture enterprises, training and educational facilities.

> **Connecting GI with Health and Wellbeing**
>
> **Principle 1**   Healthy places improve air, water and soil quality, incorporating measures that help us adapt to, and where possible mitigate, climate change
>
> **Principle 2**   Healthy places help overcome health inequalities and can promote healthy lifestyles
>
> **Principle 3**   Healthy places make people feel comfortable and at ease, increasing social interaction and reducing antisocial behaviour, isolation and stress
>
> **Principle 4**   Healthy places optimise opportunities for working, learning and development
>
> **Principle 5**   Healthy places are restorative, uplifting and healing for both physical and mental health conditions

Figure 27.9   Five Principles of Healthy Places

Source: Landscape Institute (2013b).

Connecting green infrastructure with sustainability

We have already seen that green infrastructure, if done well, can contribute to sustainable development, where the environmental, social and economic aspects are in balance.

If achieving improvements in people's health and well-being is made a high priority in green infrastructure strategies, and if local communities are directly involved in planning how this will be done, the social aspect of sustainability will be covered.

As for the environmental side of sustainability, green infrastructure is built around the idea of environmental networks, where habitats are linked and the opportunities for wildlife movement are optimised. Green infrastructure also incorporates the full range of ecosystem services. To make the most of the environmental sustainability of green infrastructure, programmes must take account of relevant strategic biodiversity assessments, priorities and targets. Green infrastructure partnerships need to include organisations that specialise in wildlife conservation and management.

A recent review of green infrastructure's contribution to economic growth cites inward investment, visitor spending, environmental cost-saving, health improvement, market sales and employment generation as the main benefits (Gore et al. 2013). Some of these benefits arise directly from green infrastructure itself, for example by reducing flood risk. Practical steps can range from changing land management strategies across a whole catchment so that natural percolation increases, to implementing SUDS in built up areas. Some benefits are more indirect: building quality greenspace into green infrastructure can have a positive impact on land and property markets, creating settings for investment and acting as a catalyst for wider regeneration. Examples of the positive connections between economic development green infrastructure are growing: for example, in the UK, the design of Crewe's Business Park is based on ecological principles.[14]

Conclusions: making green infrastructure work

Doing green infrastructure properly is a large scale, long term and complex exercise. Good green infrastructure has multiple objectives, which should incorporate environmental, social (including health and well-being) and economic aspects of sustainability. Green infrastructure managers need a broad understanding of the breadth of disciplines involved. The political system under which green infrastructure operates must be capable of making long-term commitments, so that green infrastructure does not suffer from a 'stop–start' approach as administrations, and sources of funding, change.

It therefore follows that green infrastructure programmes require a partnership approach; expert, multidisciplinary teams; and the consistent use of project planning and management methods that can deal with complexity. Effective green infrastructure delivery needs a governance structure that reflects the partnership of public bodies (national, regional and local); non-governmental organisations and communities; and an approach to funding that is consistent over a number of years.

Exactly how to do green infrastructure depends, of course, on where you are in the world, and on the prevailing organisational, political, community and economic contexts. Given that sensitivity to local context is essential, there is an increasing body of guidance about how to do green infrastructure well. Figure 27.10 summarises Natural England's seven steps for developing a strategic approach to green infrastructure.

The UK's Town and Country Planning Association, with the Wildlife Trusts, also provides good practice guidance, focusing on green infrastructure and biodiversity (TCPA and Wildlife Trusts 2012). It summarises six principles of good practice. In summary these are:

1. plan green infrastructure strategically, to create a comprehensive and integrated network;
2. have wide partnership buy-in;
3. demonstrate 'multifunctionality';
4. ensure that funding supports both creation and maintenance of sites;
5. green infrastructure must be central to all designs; and
6. green infrastructure should reflect and enhance locally distinctive character.

The Landscape Institute's principles include monitoring: it is important to emphasise this. Effective monitoring and evaluation are needed in order to close what is probably the biggest knowledge gap affecting green infrastructure, finding out how effective green infrastructure strategies actually are. No one has yet answered this question – it is too soon, given that green infrastructure is such a recent phenomenon.

Doing green infrastructure properly is a practical and organisational challenge, wherever it is attempted. Three additional challenges merit particular attention:

1. The green infrastructure message needs to be more effectively communicated to decision makers across the whole spectrum of policy.
2. Effective monitoring and evaluation of large-scale green infrastructure strategies is essential and should include explicit questions about the links between green infrastructure and health and well-being benefits.
3. Securing effective funding from a combination of public and private sources.

Green infrastructure is an attractive label for a complex approach to environmental planning and management that brings together landscape, networks, infrastructure and multifunctionality. It is an internationally popular approach to working across landscapes, at a range of scales from strategic to local, using an understanding of the dynamism inherent in natural and cultural networks and systems to bring benefits to the environment, to the economy and to people – especially to their health and well-being.

Partnering and vision

- Develop and define a vision relevant to the area, commanding wide support.
- Identify geo-spatial extent of the project at landscape scale, unconstrained by political and administrative boundaries.
- Establish cross-cutting steering group with authoritative leadership and key stakeholder and community representation, supported by appropriate expertise.
- Promote collaborative working across political and organisational boundaries, multiple landowners, disciplines and scales.

Contextual review

- Review and co-ordinate the national, local and community policy framework to provide a sound basis for formal planning intervention, development management, infrastructure provision and funding applications.
- Use Landscape Character Assessment to understand and identify the features that give a locality its 'sense of place'.

Data audit and resource mapping

- Record green assets and identify ownership, primary uses and potential viability, using Geographical Information Systems (GIS) where appropriate.

Needs and opportunities assessment

- Identify local issues, challenges, risks and community needs using data audit and consultation.
- Evaluate and where possible quantify current and potential ecosystem services benefits from existing and proposed GI.
- Establish the resources and costs for successful, sustainable implementation and long-term management.

Design planned interventions

- Prepare and communicate a draft strategy, plan or design, incorporating the vision and objectives.
- Use responses to refine and improve the plan, strategy or design and its delivery.
- Ensure that the plan, strategy or design meets requirements for function, durability and beauty.

Implementation

- Set design and management standards by establishing locally relevant criteria.
- Ensure the provision of adequate funding mechanisms for ongoing management and maintenance.
- Build the project, launch the strategy and adopt the policies.
- Set milestones, targets and programme.

Management and maintenance

- Monitor delivery against objectives, using key performance indicators and stakeholder consultation.
- Deliver aftercare, management and maintenance.

Figure 27.10   Seven steps for developing a strategic approach to green infrastructure

Source: Natural England (2013a).

Notes

1 The European Landscape Convention (ELC) defines landscape as 'an area, as perceived by people, whose character is the result of the action and interaction of natural and/or human factors' (Council of Europe 2000).
2 http://water.epa.gov/infrastructure/greeninfrastructure/gi_what.cfm, accessed 17 February 2014.
3 Website of the Bollin Valley Partnership: www.cheshireeast.gov.uk/leisure,_culture_and_tourism/ranger_service/countryside_sites/macclesfield_area_countryside/bollin_valley/the_bollin_valley_partnership.aspx, accessed 5 May 2014.
4 Website of England's Community Forests: www.communityforest.org.uk/aboutenglandsforests.htm, accessed on 5 May 2014.
5 ANGSt is based on research into the minimum distances people would travel to visit greenspaces. The current standard has five different levels, from the very local to the regional. The most local standard is for everyone to have 2 hectares of open space within 300 m (5 minutes walk) from home (Natural England 2010).
6 www.gov.uk/government/policies/making-sustainable-development-a-part-of-all-government-policy-and-operations, accessed 25 May 2014.
7 IPCC website: www.ipcc.ch/news_and_events/press_information.shtml
8 In the US the EPA talks about 'sustainable stormwater practice' and Low Impact Development, rather than SUDS.
9 See more about SUDS benefits on Susdrain's website: www.susdrain.org/delivering-suds/using-suds/benefits-of-suds/SuDS-benefits.html, accessed 25 May 2014.
10 ASLA green infrastructure web pages: www.asla.org/greeninfrastructure.aspx, accessed 5 May 2014.
11 Central Scotland Green Network website: www.centralscotlandgreennetwork.org/about
12 www.gift-t.eu/files/file/download/id/229
13 Health Impact Assessments are widely referenced: see the WHO's advice on www.who.int/hia/en and Public Health England's advice on www.apho.org.uk/default.aspx?QN=P_HIA
14 See website: www.cheshireeast.gov.uk/business/employment_sites_and_premises/employment_sites/crewe_business_park.aspx, accessed 5 May 2014.

References

Carson, R. 1962. *Silent spring*. Boston, MA: Houghton Mifflin.
Commission on Social Determinants of Health. 2008. *Closing the gap in a generation: health equity through action on the social determinants of health. Final Report of the Commission on Social Determinants of Health*. Geneva: World Health Organization.
Costanza, R., de Groot, R., Sutton, P., van der Ploeg, S., Anderson, S.J., Kubiszewski, I., Farber, S. and Turner, R.K. (2014) Changes in the global value of ecosystem services. *Global Environmental Change*. 26: 152–158.
Council of Europe. 2000. *European Landscape Convention*. Strasbourg: Council of Europe.
CSGN (Central Scotland Green Network). 2011. *The vision*. CSGN Brochure.
DCLG (Department of Communities and Local Government). 2012. *National planning policy framework*. London: DCLG.
EPA (Environmental Protection Agency). 2013. *Green infrastructure strategic agenda*. Washington, DC: United States Environmental Protection Agency.
EC (European Commission). 2013. *Technical information on green infrastructure*. Commission staff working document SWD (2013) 155 final. Brussels: European Commission.
European Union. 2013. *Building a green infrastructure for Europe*. Luxembourg: Publications Office of the European Union.
Fairbrother, N. 1973. *New lives, new landscapes*. London: Architectural Press.
Forest Research. 2010. *Benefits of green infrastructure*. Report by Forest Research, Forest Research, Farnham.
GLA (Greater London Authority). 2008. *East London green grid framework*. London: GLA, Supplementary Planning Guidance.
GLA. 2011. *Green infrastructure and open environments: the all London green grid*. London: GLA, London Plan Implementation Framework, Supplementary Planning Guidance.

Gore, T., Ozdemiroglu, E., Eadson, W., Gianferrara, E. and Phang, Z. 2013. *Green infrastructure's contribution to economic growth: a review*. EFTEC and CRESR, Final Report for Defra and Natural England. London: Defra.

Landscape Institute. 2009. *Green infrastructure: connected and multifunctional landscapes*. London: Landscape Institute position statement.

Landscape Institute. 2011. *Local green infrastructure: helping communities make the most of their landscape*. London: Landscape Institute advisory booklet.

Landscape Institute. 2013a. *Green infrastructure: an integrated approach to land use*. London: Landscape Institute position statement.

Landscape Institute. 2013b. *Public health and landscape: creating healthy places*. London: Landscape Institute position paper.

Landscape Institute and Town and Country Planning Association (TCPA). 2012. *Green infrastructure scoping study: theme 1 – current condition of green infrastructure*. Contract for Department for Environment, Food and Rural Affairs: WC 0809. London: Defra.

Mays, G. 2011. Evidence links increases in public health spending to declines in preventable deaths. *Health Affairs*. 30(8): 1585–1593.

McHarg, I. 1969. *Design with nature*. Philadelphia: Natural History Press.

MEA (Millennium Ecosystem Assessment). 2005. *Ecosystems and human well-being: synthesis*. Washington, DC: Island Press.

Milstein, B., Homer, J., Briss, P., Burton, D. and Pechacek, T. 2011. Why behavioral and environmental interventions are needed to improve health at lower cost. *Health Affairs*. 30(5): 823–832.

Natural England. 2009. *Green infrastructure guidance*. NE 176. Sheffield: Natural England.

Natural England. 2010. *Nature nearby: accessible natural greenspace guidance*. NE 265. Sheffield: Natural England.

Philadelphia Water Department. 2011. *Green city, clean waters*. City of Philadelphia Program for combined sewer overflow control – program summary. Philadelphia: Philadelphia Water Department.

Pretty, J.N. 2011. *Health values from ecosystems*. UK EA technical report. Chapter 23. Living with environmental change programme. Defra.

Rhodes, J., Tyler, P. and Brennan, A. (2007). *The single regeneration budget: final evaluation*. Consultancy report. Cambridge: University of Cambridge Department of Land Economy, for the Office of the Deputy Prime Minister.

Scottish Government. 2011. *Design and placemaking*. Edinburgh: Scottish Government.

Simpson, R.D. 2011. *The 'ecosystem service framework': a critical assessment*. Ecosystem Services Economics Working Paper Series: paper number 5. Nairobi: UNEP.

Sneddon, C., Howarth, R.B. and Norgaard, R.B. 2006. Sustainable development in a post-Brundtland world. *Ecological Economics*. 57: 253–268.

TCPA (Town and Country Planning Association) and the Wildlife Trusts. 2012. *Planning for a healthy environment: good practice guidance for green infrastructure and biodiversity*. London: TCPA and Wildlife Trusts.

Tzoulas, K., Korpela, K., Venn, S., Ylipelkonen, V., Kazmierczak, A., Niemela, J. and James, P. 2007. Promoting ecosystem and human health in urban areas using green infrastructure: a literature review. *Landscape and Urban Planning*. 81: 167–178.

WCED (World Commission on Environment and Development). 1987. *Our common future* (Brundtland Report). United Nations.

28

HEALTHY HOUSING

Elena Marco and Sarah Burgess

Introduction: the context and challenge

The importance of good quality housing for health and well-being has been recognised since the nineteenth century (Carmona et al. 2003). While the health outcomes might be different today, the importance of connecting architecture and the built environment to health are just as relevant. Good design can do more for public health than the medical profession (Jencks and Heathcote 2010). While the role of neighbourhood design is critical in supporting good health and well-being, this chapter explores the role of housing and the tools and approaches that can be used to improve design quality of homes.

However, compared to the rest of Europe, the United Kingdom (UK) is one of the most densely populated countries and has one of the oldest housing stocks (Williams 2009; DCLG 2010). The UK has 6.8 million homes (nearly one third of the existing housing stock) in substantial disrepair, suffering from serious damp or a 'category 1' Housing Health and Safety Rating System hazard such as mould growth or asbestos, or that fail the Decent Homes Standards by which a house should be warm, weatherproof and with reasonable modern facilities (DCLG 2006, 2011). According to the Building Research Establishment this poor quality housing costs the National Health Service (NHS) approximately £600m per year (Nicol et al. 2010). And so the spiralling cost of deteriorating health highlights the importance of introducing and promoting health and well-being when designing places (Wanless 2004; Murray 2009; CABE 2009). It is therefore imperative ill health is prevented in the first place.

Demographic trends and the traditional family unit in the UK, as well as many other parts of the world, are also changing, showing an increase in one-person households and an ageing population (ONS 2005; Bennett and Dixon 2006; DCLG 2013). This not only has implications for the quantity and typologies of housing needed but also the quality, as people in these two groups are also more likely to live in poor conditions, especially those over 80 (Revell and Leather 2000). The latest population projections show that the number of people over 65 in the UK will have almost doubled to 19 million by 2030, and the cost to the health service from retired households is double that of non-retired households (Cracknell 2010). One million vulnerable people over the age of 75 live in poor housing conditions but yet spend around 80 per cent of their time at home (Department of Health 2013). Health and housing are therefore inextricably linked.

The domestic sector accounts for 30 per cent of the UK's energy consumption and contributes to almost 30 per cent of the UK's carbon dioxide (CO_2) emissions (Zero Carbon Hub 2014), which shows the importance of building energy efficient homes. Different UK governments have used different tools to try to reduce energy consumption and emissions from the residential sector by delivering 'Zero Carbon Homes'. These include setting benchmark standards through the Code of Sustainable Homes and then the progressive tightening of the building regulations (DCLG 2014; Zero Carbon Hub 2014). However, these approaches have a focus on new residential development and given the significance of the domestic sector, there is still a need improve the energy efficiency of the existing housing stock if CO_2 emission targets are to be met.

This chapter illustrates the connection between housing design, health and the policy approaches that can be used to achieve good quality homes. It considers the health aspects of housing design and how some past initiatives might be revisited to future proof 'healthy housing' with a focus on the existing housing stock as an urban legacy. First, health is examined in the context of housing design, and how housing design influences the wider determinants of health. The chapter then provides an overview of past and contemporary approaches to addressing housing issues, highlighting how the impact of rapidly changing demographics and technologies have influenced housing design. The final section then identifies the key challenges for housing design in regards to meeting the needs of a healthy and sustainable lifestyle. In addressing this, the tools and approaches to best achieve quality outcomes are considered.

The relationship between housing and health

As outlined in the other chapters of this book, health and well-being are influenced by the 'wider determinants of health', including social, cultural and environmental factors. Household income, education, housing and the environment all have an effect on our lifestyles and therefore our health and well-being. Whilst built environment and public health professions often recognise the importance of these wider determinants of health (Butland et al. 2007; National Heart Forum 2009; RTPI 2009) and the role of good quality housing to meet basic human needs, in practice, the importance of housing and neighbourhood quality are often not prioritised (Carmona et al. 2003). In the past, the quality of housing could be assessed directly through spatial or utility provision, such as having access to sanitation, hot water or heating. Modern housing needs are more complex, especially considering the loss of the traditional family unit and rapidly changing demographic trends (Bennett and Dixon 2006). Figure 28.1 presents a diagram illustrating the link between the physical environment and health outcomes.

A home needs to provide 'adequate space' for people to undertake basic daily functions such as cooking, eating, relaxing and storing (Mayor of London 2010). Having sufficient personal

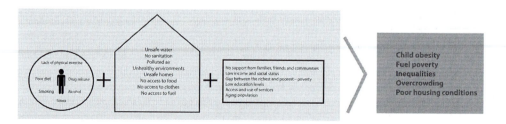

Figure 28.1 The interlinked nature of health and housing

Source: Marco.

space has been shown to reduce stress, anxiety and depression (Reynolds 2005). And a good home learning environment has been linked to better educational performance (Cassen and Kingdon 2007). It is also important that living spaces in the home are well lit, well ventilated and 'delightful' spaces to be in (CABE 2003).

Fuel poverty has also been shown to be a determinant of health (Department of Health 2012). Globally, there is a growing concern of the scale of the fuel poverty challenge and the inadequacy of society to address it, especially when annual fuel bills continue to rise (Fuel Poverty Advisory Group 2013). The energy efficiency of our homes is critical to reducing the need for the heating and cooling. Where possible, housing should maximise opportunities for renewable energy production. Infrastructure that facilititaes community energy supply and demand for housing also needs to be considered (see Ove Mørck's chapter in this book about this issue). Furthermore, there is an equality issue with fuel poverty, as one third of households in fuel poverty also have someone with a disability or long-term illness, whilst 20 per cent have a child under 5 and a further 10 per cent contain someone over 75 (Hills 2012). So fuel poverty, as with poor housing, disproportionately affects the most vulnerable sectors of society.

Both mental and physical illness have been related to poor housing quality, leading to more frequent and longer hospital admissions, and in some cases even death. Winter deaths due to the cold are exacerbated by poorly heated or insulated homes, and children living in colder homes are more than twice as likely to suffer respiratory problems (Royal College of Nursing 2012).

It is clear that housing needs to be thought of holistically in relation to future adaptation from an economic, social and environmental perspective (Figure 28.2). Society needs inclusive and environmentally responsible neighbourhoods and communities in order to tackle the challenges of the wider determinants of health (National Heart Forum 2009). Therefore, house designers must take into account the wider determinants of health when designing and building new homes, especially for low-income and vulnerable occupants, with a view to removing some of the health problems associated with poor design. They also need to take into account

HOME

Figure 28.2   Holistically designing 'healthy housing'

Source: Marco.

changing climatic conditions and future demographic projections, as current house designs and standards may not be suitable for a future, ageing population, living with global warming and more extreme weather events. Designers need to consider the immediate spatial needs of the average occupant and beyond this to take into consideration the impact of their design decisions on reducing health inequalities.

In the same way that Gething (2013) suggested for climate change, healthy housing should also be seen 'as a constantly moving target', which needs to take into consideration more than just projected changes in demographics. Housing needs to be adaptable and resilient to change.

Past approaches to improve housing quality in the UK

Since the nineteenth century, the quality of housing in the UK has been a persistent social problem and continues to be so. There has been a constant tension between providing good quality housing and providing enough housing to cope with the demands of rapid population growth. Legislative measures inevitably have an impact on the way houses are designed. This section analyses how key UK housing policies over the past 100 years have considered the health aspects of housing design.

The Industrial Revolution

The Public Health Act of 1848 was the first major milestone in public health history (WHO 2005). Responding to the health challenges of the poor housing and slum conditions generated by the Industrial Revolution in cities, and triggered by the cholera epidemic of the 1830s, it aimed to improve housing quality for all. The filthy living conditions created by a lack of sanitation, water supply and waste as well as overcrowding were causes of ill health for the working population and this had an impact on the economy of the nation (Royal Commission for Inquiry into the State of Large Towns and Populous Districts 1844). Following the Public Health Act, several other pieces of legislation[1] pertaining to workers' dwellings were enacted, demonstrating the state's involvement in new housing provision. But it wasn't until the 1909 Housing and Town Planning Act that the first legislative measures defined standards of repair and habitation, such as proper sanitary conditions and lighting, as well as forbidding the building of 'back-to-back' houses[2] (Thompson 1909).

The Industrial Revolution forced a major rethink about the relationship between land use and the quality of the built environment. Factory-led housing developments, such as Port Sunlight and Bourneville, built by factory owners, emerged with the provision of higher quality housing and neighbourhood amenities (Swenarton 1981). Around the same time, Ebenezer Howard (1898) published his 'Garden Cities of Tomorrow' report and promoted his theory of urban growth (Ray and Cresswell 1970). This revolutionary approach to city design was ahead of its time in relation to concepts of health and happiness in the home and neighbourhood (Reade 1913). The garden city vision was articulated through the development of Letchworth, the first of a small number of garden cities in the UK and Europe (Reade 1913). Despite being viewed as an exemplar of good town planning, the theory was criticised at the time for only satisfying a small proportion of the high demand for housing (Edwards 1913). In particular, when compared to existing affordable terraced houses available in cities it was suggested that the money would be better spent improving the existing housing stock and creating better places and communities in urban areas rather than in satellite settlements (Edwards 1913). Regardless of the debates, for theorists like Howard and Unwin, the Garden City Movement played a key role in improving people's lives, focusing the design of homes and neighbourhoods on improving health and well-being, even if it was seen as too expensive for the common worker (Swenarton 1981).

Interwar period

During the interwar period, housing became a political issue and state involvement was notable, as was scrutiny and evaluation by the media (Short 1982). Unwin (1924) commented on the cramped conditions of housing, especially workers' housing, and the lack of space generally. Space in Unwin's words is 'what needs to be kept clean and tidy from mess'. He also acknowledged that the quality of living depended on the production of comforts and necessities in life, but more importantly he highlighted the need for sufficient space in the home, the street and the neighbourhood. As Girardet (1992) noted, 'buildings have to be seen as organic processes that can be adapted, reshaped, redecorated or re-plumbed to accommodate the changing needs of their inhabitants'.

It was the 1918 Tudors Walter Recommendations that played a pivotal role in the raising of housing standards during this period (Wilding 1973; Swenarton 1981). The 1919 Housing and Town Planning Act, known as the Addison Act, converted some of these recommendations, along with some of the Garden City Movement ideas, into law (Short 1982). The Addison Act made local authorities major providers of housing (Wilding 1973; Swenarton 1981). It required the consideration of functional space and layout of the home through the use of model house plans. However, these standards were mandated only for use on publicly funded housing developments and did not need to be followed by private developers. This disconnect between standards for public and privately funded housing is still evident in today's policies and practice.

The Addison Act showed a clear shift in housing policy, especially in relation to health and well-being, using housing standards as a tool to improve the size and quality of housing (Wilding 1973). The model house plans were generous in terms of the size of rooms, but the imposition of these standards was criticised as being too costly for the working class and as a result few houses were built. Even those houses which were built sometimes only paid lip service to these standards – for example, a bathroom was required, but this was often sacrificed and the requirement was 'satisfied' by placing a bath within the kitchen (HATC 2006). The 1924 Housing and Town Planning Act, also known as the Wheatley Act, was introduced to address these challenges. However, the high standards of the Addison Act were watered down in the Wheatley Act, allowing the housing demand to be met, but resulted in the development of smaller and 'less healthy' houses (McKibbin 1998).

During the interwar period, housing expectations had been raised thanks to the private and publicly funded housing developments of the pre-war era. Concerns over basic housing provision began to be replaced with a growth in immense suburbs and 'one-class housing estates', which created a physical separation between the working and middle classes (Schoffham 1894). Technological advances during this period also had a huge impact on homes, especially after the introduction of mains electricity (Chapman 1955).

Post-war period

The huge task of post-war reconstruction led to two publications that gave guidance on space standards, the 1944 and 1949 *Housing Manuals* (Ministry of Works 1944, 1949). Both of these *Housing Manuals* recognised progress in technology of the time, identifying that prefabricated kitchen–bathroom equipment was available for installation in the home, and recognising the need to allocate space for a fridge.

However, once again due to cost implications, the ambitious standards of the 1940s were progressively watered down during the 1950s, especially in 1958 when new standards were set by the Ministry of Housing and Local Government (Ministry of Housing and Local Government 1958). The 1950s saw a phenomenal rise in electrical goods (Chapman 1955) and by the time the Parker Morris Report was published in 1961, washing machines, televisions, vacuum cleaners and refrigerators were readily available. The importance of the machine within the household was clear.

The Parker Morris Revolution

1961 saw the publication of the Parker Morris Report, *Homes for Today and Tomorrow*, still the most cited benchmark for healthy housing in the UK (RIBA 2011) and a standard that wholeheartedly took into consideration the wider determinants of health. At its time of writing, as now, patterns of living were rapidly changing. It presented a 'guidance' approach to housing design, which contrasted with the legislative approach that had been used up until this time.

The Parker Morris Report identified 'space and heating' as the major changes required for healthy housing design (Parker Morris 1961), sentiments just as relevant today. It acknowledged the need for spaces where families could come together, but also acknowledged the need for privacy (Figure 28.3). The standard recognised the importance of the activities that take place in the home and, instead of simply prescribing minimum sizes for rooms, it allowed the designer to experiment (see Figure 28.4). For example, it took into consideration the 'strong medical evidence about the importance of providing facilities immediately adjacent to the WC for washing the hands' (Parker Morris 1961). At the time private houses were already being marketed by the 'number of rooms', which was leading to the (still current) problem of being small and overcrowded. The Parker Morris Report noted the disproportionate amount of

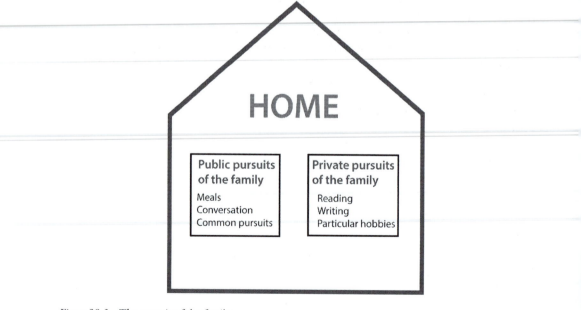

Figure 28.3   The pursuit of the family

Source: Marco.

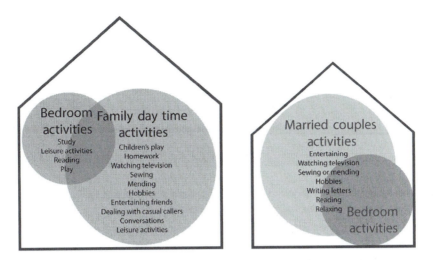

Figure 28.4 Example activities within the home for different households identified in the Parker Morris standard

Source: Marco.

space taken by bedrooms which are only used for sleeping and instead favoured fewer rooms but bigger and flexible spaces.

By removing labels from rooms, designers were able to focus on what was needed in the house, whilst at the same time ensuring it was flexible enough to be adapted by future genera- tions. Whilst understanding that better homes cost more, the approach was to provide adaptability that took into consideration what we nowadays call the 'lifecourse approach'. Parker Morris takes into consideration health in relation to quality housing and proposes an approach that encourages innovative design that is adaptable as people age and circumstances change.

Parker Morris is seen as the highpoint of housing quality in relation to space standards, although it was only ever applied to social housing (Towers 2005). Milner and Madigan (2004) argue that the concept of flexibility in the Parker Morris Report is constrained when thinking about inclusive design, but as Karn and Sheridan (1994) demonstrate, even modern houses built by housing associations, which are usually more sensitive to inclusive design, do not meet the requirements of Parker Morris standards. The alternative argument is that over-regulating the size of space in the home can restrict its use and occupants' behaviour (Schneider and Till 2007). However, as has been demonstrated in the UK, when left unregulated the overall amount of space reduces, which also restricts behaviour and has been linked to health problems (Carmona et al. 2010).

Contemporary approaches to improve housing design

Since the Parker Morris standard, there have been a range of different approaches adopted in the UK aiming to improve the size and quality of new homes. Four of these are discussed in this section as examples of the range of tools used. First, the Building Research Estab- lishment (BRE) *Design Handbook* (BRE 1993) sought to provide guidance to practitioners and developers with a mix of non-statutory guidance, and regional and local planning policy requirements. Second, the inclusive design agenda, closely linked with the lifecourse approach, led to Lifetime Homes (Brewertin and Darton 1997) being adopted nationally, but provision decided locally. Third, the National Housing Federation (NHF) *Good Practice Guide* (NHF 1998) focused on improving the size and quality of social housing by linking the use of design guidance to funding requirements. And finally, the Greater London Authority have adopted the *London Housing Design Guide* (Mayor of London 2010), which sets out minimum space standards for new homes.

The BRE *Housing and Design Handbook* (BRE 1993) provides detail with regard to the functions and roles of different rooms in the house. It distinguishes 'primary' and 'occasional' activities, and physically separates the quiet/noisy and tidy/untidy activities within the house, since they are not compatible in the same space (Figure 28.5). Adaptability and flexibility within the home, as per the lifecourse approach, is also taken into consideration through current and future user requirements.

Also in the 1990s, the Lifetime Homes standards (Brewertin and Darton 1997) provided design criteria related to the lifecourse approach and population inequalities. The idea of developing a series of inclusive housing standards to support the inhabitants throughout the whole of their lives aims to future-proof our homes and is a clear example of a healthy housing initiative. The overarching principles were inclusivity, accessibility, adaptability, sustainability and value for money, which demonstrates a holistic approach to space design. Contrary to Parker Morris, the Lifetime Homes standards give sizes of rooms required and furniture that might be needed. It is a prescriptive set of standards and limits the scope of the design. However, it does cater for the needs of a wider section of society as the standards are more generous (Carmona et al. 2010) and it is the most used standard above Part M (DCLG 2013).

In 1998, the NHF first published the *Standards and Quality in Development: A Good Practice Guide* for those involved in the design of new affordable housing. The guide gives a general overview of good practice, and although it can be overly procedural, it is nevertheless an important guide considering that social housing landlords manage 20 per cent of all housing in the UK (Drury 2008). For internal spaces, the guide gives minimum dimensions for activities and furniture, but without specifying the activities that take place within the home. This is a very different approach to Parker Morris, which explicitly identifies how people live in their homes and the activities that needed to be accommodated at the time.

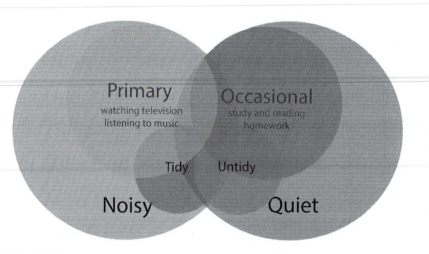

Figure 28.5   BRE home activities

Source: Marco.

By the new millennium, an emerging sustainability agenda and drive for energy efficiency requirements led to the development of EcoHomes, a design and assessment method for sustainable housing. EcoHomes was replaced by the Code for Sustainable Homes (CSH) in 2006, which raised the minimum levels of performance required. Later editions of the BRE guide, the Lifetime Homes standards and the NHF guide embraced the ethos of the CSH, with the NHF actually requiring schemes with social housing funding after 2008 to achieve CSH Level 3, with indications that this would increase to Level 4 in time (see BREEAM 2014 for further details on CSH standards).

The *London Housing Design Guide* (Mayor of London 2010) includes the Lifetime Homes standards, but broadens the remit to look at creating good places that are entwined with the city and its infrastructure. It highlights the importance of designing for a diverse city where shared spaces are part of the community. The guide aims to become an 'enabler' for the home to be more than a dormitory and, as encompassed by Parker Morris, places importance on the activities taking place within the home. Whilst the *Design Guide* advocates flexibility to manage the life-course of the home and its inhabitants, the specified activities are very similar to those identified by Parker Morris 50 years earlier (Figure 28.6). The relevance of these activities to modern day life is likely to have changed significantly through factors such as new technologies and increased commuting distances. These daily activities might need to be updated to reflect current trends and, where necessary, addressed in order to promote more sustainable and healthy lifestyles.

As at 2014, the UK government is currently analysing feedback from the Housing Standards Review launched in 2013, which proposes to introduce housing standards across the country, eliminating the CSH and any other minimum space standards and replacing them with a national standards framework that will be integrated into the building regulations (DCLG 2013). The incorporation of housing standards into building regulations should be seen as a positive step towards improving housing quality nationally; however, in the review it is clear that a balance needs to be found between housing quality (and the long-term benefits of this) and the upfront cost of a higher quality design and build.

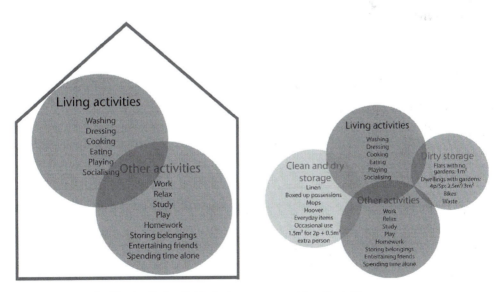

Figure 28.6   London Housing Design Guide: the home as an enabler of activities

Source: Marco.

Challenges for the design of healthy housing

Designing and retrofitting for 'healthy housing' means to look beyond the boundaries of the home, engaging with the neighbourhood and the wider community as means to improve the vital infrastructure that will make the 'healthy home' possible. The adaptability and flexibility of the home then becomes the key challenge for designers as they will have to think beyond the fabric of the building and take into consideration the social and economic needs and changes ahead, such as demographic trends and future health projections.

Design considerations

- Housing design cannot be considered in isolation. The wider design of the neighbourhood and the community also need to be engaged in these debates in order to have a positive impact on health and social capital.
- The consideration of the complex aspects of living in the twenty-first century, changes in demographic trends and a lifecourse approach will influence house design and will challenge designers to think about the adaptability and flexibility of the home. Designers should consider the form and function of the building and how design decisions might have a particular influence at different points during an occupant's life.
- The need to think about health equity and the integration of vulnerable groups within the society will not only affect the physical fabric of the building and its design and repair, but this also highlights the importance of understanding the wider determinants of health.
- The development of social capital within family structures and the wider community should be encouraged through housing design, by providing spaces that bring the family and the wider community together for shared benefits. The design of the home needs to take into consideration the emotional relationship of the inhabitants with the home.
- While the space for living should remain flexible, it should accommodate the current and future needs of the inhabitants. Entertaining, cooking, eating, sleeping, playing, studying and washing are some of the functional space requirements that have to be considered when designing homes (Figure 28.7).

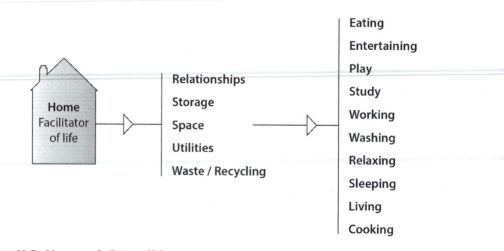

Figure 28.7   Home as a facilitator of life

Source: Marco.

The effect of technology within the home

From the 1930s onwards, technological advances have had a huge impact on homes, especially after the introduction of electricity (Chapman 1955). The home, inundated by commodities, has become a 'temple of consumption' (Lury 1996). The rise of the machine has increased generally accepted standards of living, but at the cost of a detrimental effect on our physical well-being (Goodall 2010). When designing or retrofitting, the designer will have to carefully consider the effects of the machines against healthy and sustainable behaviours.

Space for storage

As stated in the Parker Morris Report (1961), 'space and heating' are critical to the design of healthy housing, and this is just as relevant today. The role of the machine within the home, and the need to store possessions as a way of expressing affluence, are an important part of how we live. Designers need to better understand the 'lifecourse of the home' (Norton and Novy 1991) in relation to space requirements and living patterns.

The retrofit agenda

The majority of the tools and policies that have been used in the past have focused on the development of new housing. Given that the majority of our future housing stock already exists, simply designing new housing to be healthier and of a better quality will not be enough to address the health problems outlined earlier. The real challenge ahead for 'healthy housing' is the adaptation of existing housing stock: ensuring it is fit for purpose, energy efficient, inclusive and adaptive to the changing demographic and technological trends.

Conclusions: responsibility and legacy

Housing needs to be seen as an organic enabler, adapted, reshaped and rearranged to accommodate the changing needs of society. Nowadays, the quality of living depends more and more on the production of comforts and necessities in life. However, this needs to be balanced by a design that enables sustainable and healthy behaviours within the home and takes into consideration the wider community infrastructure that supports those behaviours.

Designing 'healthy housing' goes beyond the physical, psychological, economic, environmental and cultural dimension of the house. The design of the home is therefore intimately linked to its contents and its inhabitant's lifestyles. The role of the machine within the home, and the need to store possessions as a way of expressing affluence, has become central to achieve a quality of life but does not necessarily address healthy and sustainable behaviours within the home.

The creation of new healthy homes and neighbourhoods will not be enough to address the urban legacy that needs to be retrofitted and repaired. If we are serious about future proofing for 'healthy housing', a managed programme of healthy retrofitting becomes an imperative, especially considering that the vast majority of the housing stock that will be available in 2024 already exists (Whitehead 2004). Ownership and funding are huge hurdles to the implementation and management of wide-scale retrofitting and, to date, incentive schemes have had mixed success in stimulating action.

This chapter highlighted that the Parker Morris Report is still the most visionary policy document in British history in regard to space standards and health and well-being. The report saw investment in space as a key part of adaptive design and the consideration of the function of the home was paramount. It also recognised the role of technology in the home and the need to store possessions as a part of modern life. Whilst adopting other policy documents, like the Lifetime Homes standards, across the country intended to result in a better built environment and healthy living for all, the reality is that not enough new houses are being built to these standards, and therefore will have a minimal impact in meeting the needs of what is already an ageing population (Barlow and Venables 2004; Carmona et al. 2010).

Whilst history shows that issues relating to housing design appear again and again, there are some lessons that can be learned in terms of the tools and approaches that we use to address them. When designing for 'healthy housing' it is imperative that the proposals promote inclusion not segregation, that they take a lifecourse approach to adaptable and flexible solutions, understand and balance the use of the machine in the home versus sustainable and healthy behaviours and don't consider space as a value, but as a healthy tool for future-proofing our housing stock.

'Healthy housing' embraces overarching principles of inclusivity, accessibility, adaptability, sustainability and value for money, demonstrating a holistic approach to space design. As Parker Morris suggested, space in the home is about focusing on what is needed socially, environmentally and economically within the home while ensuring that there is enough flexibility for the home to be adapted by future generations.

Notes

1 The 1868 Artisans' and Labourers Dwellings Act (Torrens Act), the 1875 Artisans' and Labourers' Improvement Dwellings Act (Cross Act) and the 1885 and 1890 Housing of the Working Class Acts.
2 'Back-to-back' houses were high density houses that shared three out of four walls with other buildings. They therefore had limited access to daylight, were poorly ventilated and generally had poor sanitation.

References

Barlow, J. and Venables, T. 2004. Will technological innovation create the true lifetime home? *Housing Studies*, 19(5), 795–810.

Bennett, J. and Dixon, M. 2006. *Single person households and social policy: looking forwards*. York: Joseph Rowntree Foundation.

BRE (Building Research Establishment). 1993. *BRE housing design handbook: energy and internal layout*. Watford, UK: BRE Press.

BREEAM. 2014. *Code for sustainable homes*. Watford: Building Research Establishment.

Brewertin, J. and Darton, D. 1997. *Designing lifetime homes*. York: Joseph Rowntree Foundation.

Butland, B., Jebb, S., Kopelman, P., McPherson, K., Thomas, S., Mardell, J. and Parry, V. 2007. *Tackling obesities: future choices. Project report*. London: Government Office for Science.

CABE (Commission for Architecture and the Built Environment) 2003. *Creating excellent buildings: a guide for clients*. London: CABE.

CABE. 2009. *Future health: sustainable places for health and wellbeing*. London: CABE.

Carmona, M., Carmona, S. and Gallent, N. 2003. *Delivering new homes: processes, planners and providers*. London: Routledge.

Carmona, M., Gallent, N. and Sarka, R. 2010. *Housing standards: evidence and research. Space standards: the benefits*. London: University College London for CABE.

Cassen, R. and Kingdon, G. 2007 *Tackling low educational achievement*. York: Joseph Rowntree Foundation.

Chapman, D. 1955. *The home and social status*. London: Routledge and Kegan Paul Ltd.

Cracknell, R. 2010. *The ageing population. Issues for the New Parliament 2010*. London: House of Commons Library Research.

DCLG (The Department for Communities and Local Government). 2006. *A decent home: definition and guidance for implementation*. West Yorkshire: DCLG Publications. Available from: www.gov.uk/government/uploads/system/uploads/attachment_data/file/7812/138355.pdf, accessed 12 May 2014.

DCLG. 2010. *English housing survey: household report 2008–09*. London: Department for Communities and Local Government.

DCLG. 2011. *English housing survey: homes 2011*. London: Department for Communities and Local Government.

DCLG. 2013. *Households interim projections 2011 to 2021 England: housing statistical release 24*. London: Department for Communities and Local Government. Available from: www.gov.uk/government/uploads/system/uploads/attachment_data/file/190229/Stats_Release_2011FINAL DRAFTv3.pdf, accessed 15 August 2013.

DCLG. 2014. *Housing standards review: summary of responses*. London: Department for Communities and Local Government. Available from: www.gov.uk/government/uploads/system/uploads/attachment_data/file/289144/140225_final_hsr_summary_of_responses.pdf, accessed 15 June 2014.

Department of Health. 2012. *Public health outcomes framework for England, 2013–2016*. London: Department of Health.

Department of Health. 2013. *Improving outcomes and supporting transparency*. London: Department of Health.

Drury, A. 2008. *Standards and quality in development: a good practice guide*. 2nd Edition. London: National Housing Federation.

Edwards, A.T. 1913. A criticism of the garden city movement. *The Town Planning Review*, 07/1913, 4(2).

Fuel Poverty Advisory Group. 2013. *Fuel Poverty Advisory Group (for England), 11th annual report*. Available from: www.consumerfutures.org.uk/files/2013/12/FPAG-11th-annual-report.pdf, accessed 15 June 2014.

Gething, B. 2013. *Design for climate change*. Technology Strategy Board. London: RIBA Publishing.

Girardet, H. 1992. *The Gaia atlas of cities: new directions for sustainable urban living*. London: Gaia Books.

Goodall, C. 2010. *How to live a low carbon life*. London: Earthscan.

HATC. 2006. *Housing space standards*. London: Greater London Authority.

Hills, J. 2012. *Getting the measure of fuel poverty: final report of the Fuel Poverty Review. CASE Report 72*. London: CASE.

Jencks, C. and Heathcote, E. 2010. *The architecture of hope*. London: Frances Lincoln.

Karn, V. and Sheridan, L. 1994. *New homes in the 1990s: a study of design, space and amenity in housing association and private sector housing*. Manchester: Joseph Rowntree Foundation and the University of Manchester.

Lury, C. 1996. *Consumer culture*. Cambridge: Polity Press.

Mayor of London. 2010. *London housing design guide*. London: London Development Agency.

McKibbin, R. 1998. *Classes and cultures: England 1918–1951*. Oxford, New York: Oxford University Press.

Milner, J. and Madigan, R. 2004. Regulation and innovation: rethinking 'inclusive' housing design. *Housing Studies* 19(5), 727–744.

Ministry of Housing and Local Government. 1958. *Ministry of Housing and Local Government in the flats and houses: design and economy*. London: His Majesty's Stationery Office.

Ministry of Works. 1944. *Housing manual 1944*. London: His Majesty's Stationery Office.

Ministry of Works. 1949. *Housing manual 1949*. London: His Majesty's Stationery Office.

Murray, R. 2009. Danger and opportunity: crisis and the new social economy. London: NESTA.

National Heart Forum. 2009. Building health: creating and enhancing places for healthy, active lives. London: National Heart Forum.

NHF (National Housing Federation). 1998. Standards and quality in development: a good practice guide. London: National Housing Federation.

Nicol, S., Roys, M., Davidson, M., Ormandy, D. and Ambrose, P. 2010. *Quantifying the cost of poor housing*. Watford, England: IHS BRE Press.

Norton, A. and Novy, K. 1991. *Low income housing in Britain and Germany*. London: Anglo-German Foundation for the Study of Industrial Society.

ONS (Office for National Statistics). 2005. General household survey series. London: TSO. Available from: www.ons.gov.uk/ons/rel/ghs/general-household-survey/2005-report/index.html, accessed 15 August 2013.

Parker Morris. 1961. *Homes for today and tomorrow*. London: Ministry for Housing and Local Government.

Ray, T. and Cresswell, P. 1970. *The new town idea*. London: Open University Press.

Reade, C. 1913. A defence of the garden city movement. *The Town Planning Review*, 10/1913 4(3).

Revell, K. and Leather, P. 2000. *The state of UK housing: a factfile on housing conditions and housing renewal policies in the UK*. 2nd Edition. Bristol: The Policy Press and Joseph Rowntree Foundation.

Reynolds, L. 2005. *Full house? How overcrowded housing affects families*. London: Shelter.

RIBA (Royal Institute of British Architects). 2011. *The case for space*. London: Cantate.

Royal College of Nursing. 2012. *Health inequalities and the social determinants of health*. London: Royal College of Nursing.

Royal Commission for Inquiry into the State of Large Towns and Populous Districts. 1844. *Reports*. London: Clowes.

RTPI (The Royal Town Planning Institute). 2009. *Delivering healthy communities (GN5)*. London: RTPI.

Schneider, T. and Till, J. 2007. *Flexible housing*. London: Architectural Press.

Schoffham, E.R. 1894. *The shape of British housing: George Godwin*. Essex and New York: Longman Group Limited.

Short, J. 1982. *The post-war experience: housing in Britain*. London and New York: Methuen.

Swenarton, M. 1981. Homes fit for heroes: the politics and architecture of early state housing in Britain. London: Heinemann Educational Books.

Thompson, W. 1909. *Handbook to the Housing and Town Planning Act 1909*. London: National Housing Reform Council.

Towers, G. 2005. *An introduction to urban housing design: at home in the city*. Oxford: Architectural Press.

Unwin, R. 1924. The influence of housing conditions on the use of leisure. *International Labour Review*, 9, 815–828.

Wanless, D. 2004. The Wanless report: securing good health for the whole population. London: HM Treasury.

Whitehead, C. 2004. The economic framework for housing. *Housing Futures 2024*. London: CABE and RIBA.

WHO (World Health Organization). 2005. Bulletin of the World Health Organization. Vol. 83, n. 11. Geneva Nov. Print version ISSN 0042-9686. Accessed from: www.scielosp.org/scielo.php?pid=S0042-96862005001100017&script=sci_arttext&tlng=enen, accessed 15 June 2014.

Wilding, P. 1973. The Housing and Town Planning Act 1919: a study in the making of social policy. *Journal of Social Policy*, 2, 317–334.

Williams, K. 2009. Space per person in the UK: a review of densities, trends, experiences and optimum levels. *Land Use Policy*, 26S, S83–S92.

Zero Carbon Hub. 2014. Zero carbon homes and nearly zero energy buildings: UK building regulations and EU directives. London: Zero Carbon Hub. Available from: www.zerocarbonhub.org/sites/default/files/resources/reports/ZCHomes_Nearly_Zero_Energy_Buildings.pdf, accessed 15 June 2014.

29

COMMUNITY HOUSING AND PLACE-MAKING

Narratives, forms and processes for convivial living

Martin Large and Hugh Barton

Introduction: the potential of community-led housing

The purpose of this chapter is to present and analyse some examples of tools and processes for community building, homes and place-making. Housing is recognised as a key determinant of health – in terms of availability, quality and user control (Barton and Tsourou 2000; Kreiger and Jacobs 2011). In some countries, such as the UK, the cost of housing to buy or rent, shortage of supply and lack of security in the rented sector, greatly exacerbates health inequalities. The results in terms of relative poverty, mental stress and low social capital are key factors in health inequalities (Marmot 2010).

The seminal World Health Organization report about health inequity, *Closing the gap in a generation*, makes three overarching recommendations. The first is: 'improve daily living conditions', including the availability of good quality affordable housing. The second is 'tackle the inequitable distribution of power, money and resources', referring to the need for all groups to be empowered in decision-making, and civil society to be enabled to organise and act to support political and social rights. The third is to measure and understand the problem of health inequity and assess the impact of action (Commission on Social Determinants of Health 2008).

Community housing offers a way of making progress in relation to these aspirations. According to Lang and Novy (2014), co-operatives help fill the gap left by the withdrawal of the state from the provision of social housing, they build strong social bonds and shared place-identity that contribute to cohesive neighbourhoods, and promote a culture of 'bottom-up' participatory processes. Research in Vienna suggests the strong linkages forged by co-operative initiatives with public decision-makers at varied levels helps leverage the wider interests of residents (Lang and Novy 2014, p. 1744).

This chapter explores the potential of community-led housing to achieve the first two recommendations: improving living conditions, especially access to housing, and empowering less affluent households and enabling civil society to take a dynamic role in creating healthy places. The scientific evidence of effectiveness in health improvement (the third requirement) is so far thin on the ground.

Some hard evidence does exist in relation to community housing. For example Redditch Co-operative Homes in the UK has developed five tenant co-ops comprising 400 homes.

Research shows that residents in these co-ops have high levels of civic engagement, are very satisfied with their homes, like managing their co-ops, feel a strong community spirit and there is practically no crime.[1] The benefits of co-op tenant management include volunteering; higher levels of performance such as reduced voids; reduced arrears; tenant satisfaction; increased income for the co-op; as well as community building, co-production and co-design.

Community housing initiatives often involve close collaboration between public and voluntary sectors. Redditch Co-operative Homes is a social business, and works in partnership with Redditch Borough Council as its new build partner and the communities of people in tenant housing co-operatives. In Stockholm, a cohousing community was built by Stockholm City Council and co-designed from the start with the future residents – a public–social partnership. The many communal facilities are managed by the residents, who also comment on the active social life and mutual support that they enjoy.

This chapter is primarily based on the evidence of experience and personal research into a wide range of initiatives. It also draws on the 'Back to the Future Conference' at Letchworth Garden City, England, on scaling up community-led housing, food and renewable energy, in November 2012, and the subsequent report (Conaty and Large 2013). It aims to provide professionals working in different organisational and professional silos in both the statutory and business sectors with an introduction to the landscape of community-led housing.

A typology

The term 'community-led housing' encompasses a huge diversity of arrangements, distinguished by the fact that they are neither public sector nor market housing. Some of the common models for community-led housing are listed here:

- *Ownership housing co-ops* are owned, managed and controlled democratically by members and tenants, who are usually members of the co-op. They can be fully mutual where all residents are co-op members, or partially mutual with a wider membership base.
- *Tenant management co-ops* have a management agreement with their landlord, such as a local authority or housing association.
- *Short life housing co-ops* lease empty properties on a short-term lease.
- *Self-build co-ops* comprise tenants who help build their houses, with their labour giving them a 'sweat equity', that is, they own a percentage of the property based on the amount of labour put in, with the tenant renting the remaining proportion of the property.
- *Community Gateway* housing provision offers a wide range of tenant and community empowerment opportunities, so people are involved in decisions about homes and neighbourhoods.
- *Tenant controlled housing associations*, or *community based housing associations* are tenant led, making up the majority of the governing body.[2]
- *Community land trusts* are owned and controlled by members of a geographical community of place, with one member one vote. They capture land value for community benefit, secure land into trust and develop various forms of affordable co-op, self-build, tenant and part ownership, homes and community facilities.[3]
- *Cohousing*, short for co-operative housing, was a form of community-led housing invented in Denmark with design features including shared facilities such as a common house, laundry, kitchen, garden and communal pay areas, and again tenures can range from freehold, to long leasehold, part ownership and rental.
- *Ecovillages*, now a global movement, are intentional communities designed by inhabitants, where they use innovative technologies for sustainable living, building relationships and caring for the environment.

Challenge and response

So what housing challenges do we face? Countries vary in their population trajectory. In the UK, by way of example, the number of households is predicted to grow to 27.5 million, with the growth mainly in older households; 1.7 million households are currently on the social housing waiting list; over half a million are living in overcrowded conditions; poor housing costs the National Health Service at least £600 million a year. The problems of housing affordability are getting progressively worse, especially in the south of the country.

In Britain civil society and ordinary people have little voice in the creation of housing and neighbourhoods. The house builders and the state (central and local) have a near monopoly of power. Indeed the housing sector and the state planning system has been so thoroughly captured by business that some housing developers are capturing upwards of 75 per cent of the land value uplift from getting planning permission for housing.[4]

Paradoxically, in the UK, the housing market and state failure are key drivers of civil society movements such as the cohousing and community land trust movements. These are made up of early innovating people who say, 'So, let's do it ourselves!' In 2005–2006 there were only five community land trusts in Britain, now there are over 160. Even Persimmon Homes, a volume house builder, has started marketing cohousing.

The practical benefits of community-led housing are of course considerable. People and communities will engage constructively around building the desirable future of their communities and housing if the conditions are right, and this builds social capital. The most important benefit is that co-operative and community-led housing can offer a viable alternative to both market and state housing. Provided that such community-led housing is done well, then health and well-being benefits for people can be secured.

A shift is needed from provider-led housing to co-designed homes and neighbourhoods that start with customer, citizen, locality and community needs. However, for community-led housing to succeed and scale up from small schemes, there needs to be enabling partnerships between civil society, the state and business, each playing to their strengths. Housing is a complex, risky undertaking. But there are many global examples of successful community-led housing. There are also valuable experiments from the past that we can learn from now. The following section details a number of forms of community-led housing, starting with a classic historic example.

Community housing, community land

A strategic approach: Letchworth Garden City

Ebenezer Howard's Garden Cities Association established the Town and Country Planning Association in 1899. The mission was to develop new, healthy, human scale cities to solve overcrowding, poor health and urban blight in ways that united the best of urban and the best of rural life. Letchworth was a town designed for healthy living, with employment opportunities that made a full measure of social life possible, a green environment and accessible countryside around. All the town land was held in trust for the community and leases sold to households and businesses.[5] The ground rents were critical to the provision of physical and social infrastructure, and enabled the Letchworth Trust to achieve an enviable quality of urban environment.

Letchworth originally encouraged a diversity of housing provision, with housing competitions in the early days to encourage innovation. The diversity has not been maintained, however. Since the 1980s, as a result of government policy, the excellent social housing has been progressively sold off to residents, and become unaffordable except to the relatively rich. The sell-off included the freehold of the land, so the Letchworth Trust has lost much of its income, and can no longer provide the same level of community investment. This illustrates the vital importance of establishing community rights in perpetuity.

So what 'garden city principles' can be drawn on to underpin community-led housing? Philip Ross, a former Letchworth mayor, considers that garden cities are a radical proposition, with a transformative mission, with common ownership of the land through community land trusteeship, and a leasehold system capturing land value for community benefit rather than for private gain. The values of common ownership and citizenship make a town, not just the buildings and green spaces. Philip Ross writes: 'To us the consensus is that a Garden City is not about charity and paternalism but about empowerment and citizenship' (Conaty and Large 2013; see also Id22: Institute for Creative Sustainability: experimentcity 2012).

A key point from the planning perspective is that there needs to be a body, whether it be a planning authority, a new town corporation or a garden city organisation, that holds a strategic vision of the desirable future of a city, town, area and neighbourhood. This vision is needed as a facilitating framework for community-led initiatives. Freiburg, in south-west Germany, is a much-quoted exemplar (see Chapter 38).

Current forms: cohousing

Cohousing now comprises 8 per cent of Denmark's housing. Short for co-operative housing, the movement was started by single parents advertising an invitation for others to share housing and then to design convivial ways of living. The proven social, health and practical benefits are such that there is Danish state funding and support for developing, building and running cohousing communities. Cohousing is a way of living, which brings individuals and families together in groups to share common aims and activities whilst also enjoying their own self-contained accommodation and personal space. Cohousing encompasses the ideas of intentional community and a neighbourhood that people have designed and where they choose to live in a supportive way with each other. People live in their own dwellings but there is a common house where people meet regularly and socialise, with rooms where guests can stay, and common facilities such as a laundry, a community kitchen and where shared equipment can be stored.

Co-determination, sustainability and support are important cohousing principles. Dwellings are designed to be low carbon, using sustainable building materials, renewable energy and offering food growing space. What attracts people is certainly not the long hours it takes to get a cohousing group off the ground. Rather it's the promise of a better quality of life, a sustainable way of living, a safe place to live and a village-like friendliness.

Typically, it takes a cohousing group between three and five years to go from a first meeting to a new build or renovated cohousing community ready to move into. Members have to be prepared to work hard to develop their group, to get used to talking through ideas and taking decisions together. In the USA cohousing development companies and housing associations acting as developers help speed up the process. In the UK currently about 43 cohousing groups are working together to develop cohousing communities through the UK Cohousing Network[6] (Figure 29.1).

Some cohousing schemes are only for owner-occupiers while others are mixed tenure. Cohousing can be developed for any tenure but development partners, like community land trusts and housing associations, are needed for rental models involving public subsidy. Most cohousing is aimed at intergenerational groups of people or families, but the first older people's only cohousing community is now being developed in London. Recent research commissioned by Newcastle University, the Quality of Life Partnership and Newcastle Elders Council explored

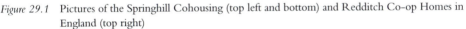

Figure 29.1   Pictures of the Springhill Cohousing (top left and bottom) and Redditch Co-op Homes in England (top right)

Source: Large.

the interest amongst older people for developing cohousing groups. The research demonstrated that older people are keen on cohousing and the processes involved for self-determination attract them. Older people are particularly keen on having a range of housing and living alternatives and commented that talking through ideas about cohousing helped them free up their minds so they could think more broadly and imaginatively about the lives they wanted to have.[7] Amersfoort City housing department in the Netherlands has helped enable cohousing development of at least 12 communities for the over 50s around specific interests such as crafts and food growing.

Co-operative homes

Co-operative homes are another tried and tested housing option for low-income households. A housing co-operative is a group of people who live in properties and work together to manage and maintain them, so each co-op arranges for repairs, rent to be paid and resolves any problems collectively. Coin Street Community Builders, for example, located near the OXO Tower and Gabriel's Wharf on the South Bank in London, are a leading example of a tenant housing co-operative with 220 homes and community facilities. These give control to tenants in human scale neighbourhoods, which are managed by residents.[8]

Coin Street Community Builders is a social enterprise with a fascinating history. In 1977, Coin Street Action was formed by local residents to campaign on the South Bank in London against plans for office blocks that would replace their neighbourhood, which was then in decline, and clear it of low-income people. Seven years later after a relentless campaign the residents were supported by the Greater London Council to acquire a 13-acre site of mainly derelict buildings and to implement a grassroots plan to regenerate their community. The campaign attracted widespread support and a group of companies were formed in 1984 to take on the daunting challenge. The Coin Street Community Builder companies included a social enterprise trading company, a non-profit charitable organisation and a secondary housing co-operative. Working collaboratively, these three companies have both achieved their mission and demonstrated the untapped potential for community land stewardship approaches in big cities.

Essentially, Coin Street Community Builders is a community land trust. The land is owned by a development trust and a range of housing co-operatives have been established; the Oxo Tower and other derelict industrial and commercial buildings have been transformed into shops, galleries, cafes, restaurants, bars, a riverside walk and a vibrant park; and the non-profit company manages and operates a range of services for the community including childcare, family support and learning, enterprise support programmes, a community and sports centre and is currently developing a public swimming pool and leisure centre. There are many sources of commercial income captured for community benefit. Only local residents can become members of Coin Street Community Builders and any profits are ploughed back into the meeting of public service objectives.

Redditch Co-operative Homes (RCH) is the largest provider of new-build co-operative housing in Britain, with over 400 homes built to date for five neighbourhood tenant co-operatives. Since 2001 RCH has pioneered the design of socially cohesive and environmentally friendly homes with co-op residents. Co-op members help plan their neighbourhoods and then manage them, resulting in dynamic, active communities. The varied low-carbon homes are manufactured offsite using the Norwegian Hedalm timber-framed eco-home system. Space inside the homes is very generous, of Parker Morris and Scandinavian standards, and the quality shows.

The RCH board comprises Redditch Council, Accord Housing Association and the community, that is, the residents. The mission is to develop affordable co-operative housing for people in housing need. RCH prides itself on creating vibrant, healthy, environmentally aware and safe communities that are empowered to manage and control their own housing. Community-led architecture and design are ways to realise co-op values, for example concern for the community, member economic participation, self-responsibility, equal opportunities and education.

Carl Taylor, the general manager of RCH, considers that, 'Mutuality is the forgotten solution for meeting Britain's housing needs as an effective way of increasing community ownership and resident control, of building trust, community and garden neighbourhoods.'[9]

Community land trusts

A community land trust is defined as a not-for-private-profit, democratic, open membership body that secures land and property into trust for affordable homes, workspace, farmland and community facilities. Removing landownership from homeownership enables community interests to be embedded for the long term.

The Champlain Housing Trust in Burlington, Vermont, is the largest community land trust in the USA and is a good example of community self-help. Burlington Council aimed to set up a civil society land trust, distinct from the government and business partners. It was founded as Burlington Community Land Trust in 1984 when the Federal government programmes to fund affordable housing were cut back. Taking land out of the market was pursued as an alternative subsidy strategy through a community land trust that emerged from a partnership between community groups and the city council. With active support from the mayor of Burlington, strategic funding was mobilised. This included a core revenue grant to set up the community land trusts and a $1 million line of credit from the city employees' pension fund to provide investment.[10] The USA community land trusts movement is now scaling up from small towns to cities.

The Champlain community land trust has expanded steadily and manages over 2,000 affordable homes including part-equity homeownership and apartments to rent. The community land trust also supports on its land an additional 115 limited equity homes with five housing co-ops. It provides a full technical assistance service to support the development of new housing co-ops. In addition to housing, the community land trust has developed a day centre for the elderly, a nursery facility, managed office space for social enterprises and non-profits, a city centre shopfront for the community development credit union, an office for the Legal Aid Service and a multi-unit housing and enterprise workspace in a redundant bus depot. The trust operates as a democratic and mutual enterprise. It currently has over 2,500 members that range broadly from local businesses to social investors and they contribute gift capital regularly to the development of the community land trusts. Member rates include: the carpenter rate of up to $50, the community developer rate of $250–500 and the Visionary rate of over $1,000. These community investment funds are used to leverage additional capital to acquire land and loans for development finance.

A ground rent charge of $25 per month from leasehold members is another source of revenue for the community land trusts. Over 26 years, even during the credit crunch, no land or homes have ever been lost from the community land trust's portfolio. The ground rent system acts like a canary in a coalmine as non-payment flags up leaseholder money problems and enables the community land trusts to intervene early. The Champlain Housing Trust and its Homeownership Centre services have led good community land trust practice in the USA and won the United Nations World Habitat Award in October 2008.

The community land trust model had to be reinvented in Britain in 2004/2005, drawing on the USA movement, whilst learning from such forgotten pioneers as Letchworth. It was defined in English law by the 2008 Housing and Regeneration Act. Innovative community land trusts and cohousing tenures are being pioneered, such as mutual home ownership at LILAC in Leeds. LILAC (Low Impact Living Affordable Community) is a new urban ecovillage in Bramley, Leeds. The group of founding members are developers of a cohousing scheme with 20 homes. LILAC is pioneering Mutual Home Ownership as a limited equity co-operative. It has devised a unique funding model, which offers new possibilities for social renters. Finance has been provided by Triodos Bank, and the Co-operative Housing Finance Society has provided loan guarantees to new members for the first 12 months. Ethical investment has also been raised by the successful promotion to the public of co-operative loan stock. The lease payments that build equity shares are affordable as they are based on 35 per cent net household income. The housing has been designed to high ecological standards using permaculture design principles, renewable technologies and natural building. The common areas for co-operative members includes shared cooking and eating facilities, a meeting room and play area. The gardens and outdoor common spaces maximise opportunities for food production and social interaction.

London Citizens, one of the most radical social movements to have arisen recently in the UK, has successfully pioneered community organising methods. One of the basic concepts that they, and many community-led housing groups, adhere to is that a home is a home, not a commodity. The East London Community Land Trust was established in 2007 by London Citizens. The trust was established as part of a campaign to secure affordable housing from the 2012 London Olympic Games legacy. After almost a decade of campaigning, this now independent community land trust is a partner in the redevelopment of St. Clement's Hospital in Mile End, East London, after a lengthy tender process overseen by site owner, the Greater London Authority. One of the community land trust's key objectives is to restore a sensible balance between housing costs and actual incomes in the area served by the community land trusts. The cost of a mortgage and the service charge will be no more than a third of median local incomes. Shared owners will be able to on sell their fixed equity share, but with any uplift in value set by rises in local incomes. This will break the link with house price increases related to the investment value of housing (in London) as a speculative commodity. The freehold of the whole site will be owned by a newly formed community foundation that will use the annual ground rental income from all 200 homes within the development to support local charitable activities.[11]

By mobilising the community around the development site over three years before the tender, and undertaking their own community planning activities, St Clement's community land trust has created a positive climate of local opinion that is in favour of the development. The current development partner is benefiting from this community support and informed interest as the scheme goes forward for planning approval. The community, the trust, developer and planning authority all have mutually reinforcing objectives to create value for each other by making the project a long-term success.

Community land trusts can ensure a wide variety of affordable housing remains available indefinitely. Affordability can be greatly helped through self-build housing, where the sweat equity of prospective users allows prices to be low. Dwellings in a scheme in Cornwall, England, are held in perpetuity for qualifying local people at less than a third of their open market value.[12]

Self-help housing and empty houses

Whereas self-build involves constructing permanent homes from scratch, self-help housing involves local people bringing empty properties into use that are awaiting redevelopment or are otherwise in limbo. As there are a large number of such empty properties, the potential is vast. One outstanding example that started with self-help housing, now a worldwide model of green, healthy, convivial housing, is the old French army barracks at Vauban in Freiburg, Germany. The conversion of the barracks contributed to the creation of a new low carbon, pedestrian friendly neighbourhood. Such a project as Vauban shows what can be done when there is partnership between civil society activists, the statutory and the private sectors.

The benefits of self-help housing include those that come from community organising, active participation, self-help solutions, improved self-confidence and greater control over important aspects of often socially excluded people. Street level initiatives and place-making improve security, health and well-being.[13]

Convivial housing can also be secured through developing bodies that manage properties for landlords who would otherwise leave them empty. There are hundreds of thousands of empty properties in the UK. These include flats, houses and offices. Imported from Holland, Ad Hoc provides a service that benefits both the property owner and those looking for low cost accommodation by putting these buildings back into use. Anyone looking for affordable accommodation that is 'responsible and employed' can apply to become a Property Guardian. Guardians are allocated a room or property. Prices range from £150 to £500 per month. Areas such as kitchens are shared. People live in the building as their home, effectively house-sitting for the owner.

This tenure differs from a tenancy and the rights and responsibilities are different, as detailed in a Guardian Handbook containing Ad Hoc house rules. Ad Hoc uses a licence agreement and can terminate this with only 28 days' notice, but claims to try their best to rehouse Guardians.

Such innovative housing options are likely to keep developing with the Internet facilitating networking and mutual solutions as updated alternatives to squatting.[14] AirBnB is another example of such an innovation in what is becoming known as the sharing economy.[15]

Community processes and tools

The above case studies and examples do not happen by accident, but are the outcome of skilled design and careful facilitation. They are people and community led, though a fruitful partnership with the statutory and business sectors helps greatly. There are seven principles.

First, a key organising concept is the three-way contribution of civil society, government and business – each playing to their strengths. For example, Redditch Co-operative Homes is clear about its work as a social business, working in partnership with Redditch Council as the planner, landowner and regulator, and with the civil society organisation of tenant co-ops.

Second, community-led housing is a client- or customer-led process, rather than a statutory or private business producer model. Ideally, the delivery of housing and neighbourhoods should be a co-production process.

Third, the processes involved in community organising include facilitation, process design, social learning, leadership development, communication, relationship building, social analysis, problem solving, participative planning and design. Better health and well-being comes from putting people in control of their lives.

Fourth, the assumptions behind participative planning and design and facilitation are that people want to co-create desirable futures such as decent housing and neighbourhoods, that people are prepared to take responsibility and that they will contribute if they see that their efforts will lead to valued outcomes. The participative paradigm is quite different from the top down bureaucratic and expert-led paradigms.

Fifth, good facilitation is essential, as well as effective technical assistance with finance, law, building design, construction, planning and more. The technical system needs to support development of the social system.

Sixth, civil society has given birth to a series of social housing movements. The advocacy of the human right to decent, green, well designed housing in convivial neighbourhoods has recently been articulated across Europe by the cohousing movement as a challenging alternative, and globally via the ecovillages networks.

Seventh, there needs to be a set of agreed planning principles, such as the garden city principles, and an overall, shared vision of the desired future for a settlement that can facilitate various types of community-led housing.

According to Ross, former mayor of Letchworth, the garden city principles, updated for today, are as follows:

1. Residents are Citizens of the Garden City.
2. The Garden City owns itself under a form of community land trust.
3. Energy efficient and carbon neutral.
4. Provides access to land for living and working to all.
5. Fair Trade principles are practised.
6. Prosperity is shared (e.g. participatory budgeting; local currencies).
7. No special privileges for anyone.
8. Fair representation and direct democracy.
9. Participatory design and public spaces.
10. A city of rights and the right to the city.
11. Knowledge is held in common, shared and enhanced.
12. Wealth and harmony measured by happiness and health.[16]

(Ross and Cabannes 2014)

Conclusions: an open source, experimental movement

Community-led housing offers responses to current economic, environmental, political and cultural challenges, and also ways of realising people's dreams of sustainable and convivial life-ways. The varied and growing community-led housing landscapes are not just a scattering of fragmented buildings and housing schemes. Rather, they are a developing network of enterprising residents, housing experts, planners, health professionals, local government officials, architects and builders who are working together across Europe and elsewhere in an open source, convivial, experimental movement.

One the one hand the case studies and examples presented in this chapter can be seen as action research labs. There have been many study visits to Freiburg, Stockholm, Letchworth and even Redditch by housing professionals and city planners from all over the world. So why is convivial, community-led housing not happening more? What are the blockages and the ways round them?

To conclude, a shift from business and/or state-led housing to community- or civil society-led housing could help build more resilient places to live. Ideally three-way partnerships between civil society, business and state working to their strengths can work best for housing. Approaches to co-operative place-making include cohousing, co-ops, self-build, self-help housing, sharing options and community land trusts at the neighbourhood level, and respect for 'garden city design principles' at the city level. Convivial place-making can help achieve more inclusive access to appropriate housing, reduce inequality, build social capital and increase health and well-being.

Notes

1 See www.ccmh.coop/publications
2 See Mark Simmons, *Simply legal*, Co-ops UK, Manchester 2009; www.uk.coop
3 See www.communitylandtrust.org.uk
4 Conversation with Maurice Glasman, House of Lords, February 2014, and with UK based property developers who don't want to be named. By definition, researching this question accurately would be hard.
5 See Conaty and Large (2013).
6 www.cohousing.org.uk
7 See www.qualityoflife.org.uk
8 See Conaty and Large (2013), Coin Street Community Builders case study 1.
9 Large (2010).
10 Taken from Conaty and Large (2013, p. 14). See www.champlainhousingtrust.org
11 Conaty and Large (2013, p. 40).
12 See www.communitylandtrust.org.uk
13 See report by the BSHF: Pattison, B., Strutt, J, and Vine, J. 2011. *Self-help housing: supporting locally driven housing solutions.*
14 www.adhoc.eu/great-britain/property-guardian
15 www.airbnb.co.uk
16 www.newgardencitymovement.org.uk, Conaty and Large (2013, p. 64).

References

Barton, H. and Tsourou, C. 2000. *Healthy urban planning*. London: Routledge.
Commission on Social Determinants of Health. 2008. *Closing the gap in a generation*. Geneva, World Health Organization.
Conaty, P. and Large, M. 2013. *Commons sense: co-operative placemaking and the capturing of land value for 21st century garden cities*. Manchester: Co-operatives UK.

Id22: Institute for Creative Sustainability: experimentcity. 2012. *Cohousing cultures*. Berlin: Jovis Verlag.

Kreiger, J. and Jacobs, D. 2011. Healthy homes. In Danneburg, A., Frumkin, H. and Jackson, R.J. (eds) *Making healthy places*. Washington, DC: Island Press.

Lang, R. and Novy, A. 2014. Co-operative housing and social cohesion: the role of linking social capital. *European Planning Studies* 22(8), 1744–1764

Large, M. 2010. *Common wealth*. Stroud, UK: Hawthorn Press.

Marmot Review. 2010. *Fair society, healthy lives*. London: Institute of Health Equity.

Ross, P. and Cabannes, Y. 2014. *21st Century garden cities of to-morrow*. New Garden City Movement. Stroud, UK: Hawthorn.

30

LOCAL MANAGEMENT OF ENERGY DEMAND AND SUPPLY

Ove Christen Mørck

Introduction: community energy management

The demand of household energy and the way it is supplied determines the amount of greenhouse gas (GHG) emissions a specific house, community or city generates to provide thermal comfort to its inhabitants. The demand for energy is typically dependent on the age and state of the building(s) and the user behaviour. The supply of energy, however, is typically influenced by external (to the house owner or tenant) factors, such as the availability of different forms of fuel (for example natural gas or biomass), presence of technologies or potential for them (for example district heating or geothermal supply), influence of financial measures and subsidies or factors such as sufficient land available for a ground-coupled heat pump or the aspect of a roof for solar panels. Therefore, there is a degree of control that an individual can have over the demand for energy (a house owner can decided to energy renovate their home) but the supply is often limited by external factors or is community dependent.

This chapter investigates the possibilities and aspects of community management of energy demand and supply in relation to the individual. It demonstrates that community management of energy demand and supply is a 'win–win' solution. It provides a more efficient energy service (resulting in higher levels of thermal comfort) and community supply systems are also more flexible, which allows for the introduction of future clean energy supply technologies as they arise. It is also important to health and well-being as community managed energy is based on renewable resources, which makes it more environmentally friendly, resulting in fewer pollutants in the atmosphere. Therefore, communities and municipalities need to integrate this approach into urban agendas and make efforts to plan for community management of energy.

The chapter is based on four case studies of municipal local planning; each very different in nature and context. The four studies have been reported as part of a research project exploring municipal efforts to promote energy efficient settlements in Europe. The research was carried out in the framework of an EU CONCERTO project, 'Cost-effective Low-energy Advanced Sustainable Solutions – Class1', that was conducted in the period 2007–2013 (Concerto 2014a).

The case studies highlight different tools and approaches that have been successfully used in planning for community energy management. These tools can be summarised as four key areas for potential action: local (municipal) regulation; promotion of initiatives and information campaigns; energy supply systems for common heating supply; and utilisation of governmental initiatives.

Four case studies from four European countries

The case studies are drawn from municipalities that participated in a European project promoting energy efficient buildings (Concerto 2014a). They represent a variety of different planning and regulatory conditions, building types and technologies, ownership arrangements and energy efficiency focus (Figure 30.1).

Stenloese South, Egedal, Denmark: creative use of alternative local regulations

In the Danish town of Stenloese South, the municipality of Egedal actively sought to challenge both existing planning and building practices in order to promote community management of demand and supply on ordinary market terms. More specifically, the planning and regulatory process was challenged in order to facilitate changes in local building projects by rethinking the role of the municipality and operationalising new types of planning instruments. Through this process the municipality of Egedal has succeeded in convincing ordinary building developers to construct residential buildings with higher energy efficiency standards. This represented a change of local building regulation and process as most building projects today tend to only comply with the energy efficiency levels prescribed by the national building regulation (Quitzau et al. 2009).

In this approach the municipality played an active role as a facilitator of change. The urban development project in Stenloese South illustrates a municipal attempt to promote more energy efficient building standards within ordinary market conditions.

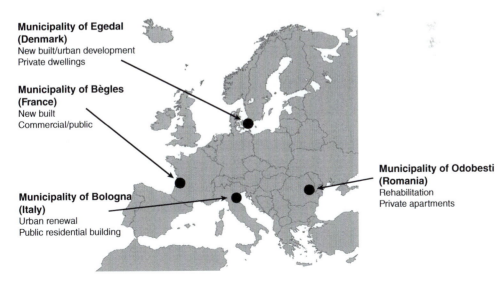

Municipality of Egedal (Denmark)
New built/urban development
Private dwellings

Municipality of Bègles (France)
New built
Commercial/public

Municipality of Bologna (Italy)
Urban renewal
Public residential building

Municipality of Odobesti (Romania)
Rehabilitation
Private apartments

Figure 30.1 Overview of cases from the four European municipalities

Source: Department of Management Engineering (2009).[1]

Box 30.1 Stenloese case study summary

The town of Stenloese offers a combination of urban and rural elements within close proximity to the Danish capital, including connection to the Copenhagen railway system.

The proposed development is an urban extension (750 dwellings) constructed on farmland configured in a ring around a central recreational area (Figure 30.2). The dwellings will consist of a combination of one-family low-rise buildings, such as detached houses and terraced houses, and of blocks of apartments. The area will also provide a childcare centre, a small store and a recreational area.

Figure 30.2   Aerial photograph of Stenloese South in 2007. The area is situated south of the boundaries of the city of Stenloese

Source: The Municipality of Egedal.

The municipality of Egedal used local plans as instruments to regulate the energy efficiency of buildings in the urban development area. In Demark, like many other countries, the regulation of land use is a strong tool for local municipalities. Local plans are used as the common land use regulation instrument that provides the primary means for municipalities to regulate the built environment. However, the municipality experienced deficiencies in this regulation instrument as clauses regarding energy efficiency were not legally binding through normal planning processes. As such the implementation of the energy efficiency requirements in the local plan were proving to be ineffective.

In response to the inability for the local plan to regulate energy efficiency, the municipality devised an alternative strategy that drew upon civil laws concerning rights of property. In Denmark, an owner of land has extensive property rights, one being the right to incorporate legally binding easements that regulate specific elements of the area or buildings. By enacting easements on each plot of land in the Stenloese South expansion, the municipality was able to ensure that the municipal energy efficiency requirements were legally binding for those buying and building on each of the offered plots. This required the municipality of Stenloese to make some significant investments since it had to first acquire the land in order to have the right to implement the easements. This step is no longer necessary as the Building Regulation and Planning Act has since been reformed and municipalities are now able to set legally binding low-energy classifications stated in the Building Regulation in the local plan. This means that it is now possible to implement their low-energy requirements through the planning system, without imposing actual easements on the lots. Although the legal limitations of local planning instruments still hinders other sustainable requirements for development, the initiative and creative approach taken by Egedal demonstrates how local municipalities can utilise non-traditional tools and processes to achieve better outcomes.

Odobeşti, Romania: improving the existing building stock

The promotion of community management of demand and supply in the municipality of Odobeşti in Romania originated through local building rehabilitation projects aimed at modernising the existing building stock. The integration of energy efficiency measures in such projects represented somewhat of a challenge for the municipality, as most of the rehabilitation projects involved privately owned building stock. This meant that the municipality was reliant on the voluntary involvement of stakeholders to implement the measures. To address this, the municipality initiated a certification process which highlighted the benefits of energy efficient measures. House owners were invited to carry out energy audits and thermal rehabilitation projects to obtain building certification. An important element of this process was that the municipality could draw upon a national funding scheme to support the thermal rehabilitation of buildings. During the process, the municipality acted as a promoter of the national scheme as well as coordinator of the specific thermal rehabilitation projects, in dialogue with local stakeholders, such as private residents, the local building industry and building experts.

Box 30.2 Odobeşti case study summary

Odobeşti is a middle-sized town of 10,500 inhabitants in Romania.

The project aimed to modernise existing building stock in Odobeşti in a sustainable way to improve the quality of life for residents, promote environmental protection and attract new investment and business. The municipality sought to improve the energy efficiency of the existing building stock, with a specific emphasis on apartment blocks, while essential improvements were being made to buildings in the city. Promoting national funding schemes for energy efficiency projects enabled local builders and residents to undertake the additional works. The municipality of Odobeşti is responsible for spatial planning within the town. It acts under the jurisdiction of the Romanian State and the County of Vrancea.

Existing buildings in Odobeşti represent a major opportunity for promoting energy efficiency as there is a great need for modernisation in the city. Approximately 80 per cent of the existing building stock was constructed between 1960 and 1989, when Romania was still an Eastern Bloc country. Buildings constructed in this period typically have low levels of thermal comfort (mainly due to poor insulation of windows and doors and lack of thermal insulation of

Figure 30.3   Typical apartment block in Odobeşti city

Source: The Municipality of Odobeşti.

roofs), primitive heating systems (based on a fireplace with the combustion of wood for each apartment[2]) and a lack of a supply of hot water from the distribution network (Figure 30.3). Particularly in the historic centre of Odobeşti, there are also some buildings in an advanced stage of degradation. Improving the energy efficiency of the existing building stock represents a major issue, not only in Odobeşti, but in Romania in general, where the energy consumption in apartment blocks is 65 per cent for heating, 15 per cent for hot water, 10 per cent for electric appliances and 10 per cent for lighting (Quitzau et al. 2009).

The municipal strategy is to promote the integration of energy efficient solutions into the modernisation and rehabilitation projects being undertaken within the city. This strategy aligns with the overall aim of the municipality to increase the quality and value of the built environment, raising the dwellings to modern living standards. The strategy also addresses some of the dwellers' complaints regarding the experience of having cold and uncomfortable apartments and complies with their interests in lowering energy consumption bills.

A key challenge for the implementation of the strategy is to convince and motivate apartment owners and the local building industry to address the issue of energy rehabilitation. This is especially difficult in Romania, since societal and cultural conditions for carrying out energy rehabilitation prove to be difficult. Most importantly, energy savings have not been widely articulated in the country, resulting in low awareness and limited knowledge and expertise regarding energy rehabilitation among both users and professionals. Also, in terms of motivation, incentives have so far been limited due to the relatively low prices of energy. However, it seems that a strong motivation for energy rehabilitation is the widespread need among owners to update and modernise dwellings. Furthermore, there is a growing commercial enthusiasm to boost green market development in Romania in order to stimulate local economies.

The municipal initiative to integrate energy efficiency in local rehabilitation projects is heavily dependent on national initiatives to support the promotion of energy efficiency in privately owned buildings. Such initiatives are provided by the Romanian government, which recognises the need to motivate municipalities, apartment owners and the building industry to integrate energy efficiency into rehabilitation projects (Quitzau et al. 2009). One of the more general initiatives from the Romanian government has been the energy performance certification scheme within the Energy Performance of Buildings Directive, which entered into national law on 1 January 2007 (Concerted Action 2011). The programme provides financial funding for municipal projects that are aimed at increasing the energy performance of buildings, reducing thermal energy bills (and implicitly decreasing the foreign exchange effort for the import of energy), improving the quality of life for particular sectors of the population, and improving the aesthetic aspect of buildings and localities.

Bègles, France: optimising urban renewal programmes

The municipality of Bègles in France has promoted sustainable development in urban planning for many years. The municipality is currently involved in a number of urban planning projects where a range of different models for community management of energy demand and supply are demonstrated. One of these projects involves the renewal of an urban neighbourhood which includes both the construction of new buildings and renovation of existing housing stock. The municipality engaged with local residents to achieve a socially diverse and mixed use area that protects the local environment (Quitzau et al. 2009).

Box 30.3 Bègles case study summary

Bègles is a small city of (25,000 inhabitants) in the south-west of France, in the Bordeaux region. The municipality is currently undergoing a process of urban renewal, with a large number of urban planning projects launched in order to develop the town in a sustainable way. The municipality of Bègles is responsible for the spatial planning of the city.

The project is a 20 hectare urban renewal project, *Opération de Renouvellement Urbain* (ORU), a major area of social housing (32 per cent of the building stock) in the north-east Yves Farge/Terres Neuves district of the municipality. This district accommodates 14 per cent of the town's social housing and consists of 448 apartments built in the 1960s.

The municipality aims at improving the energy efficiency of the built environment in all urban planning projects. One major initiative in this regard is to implement energy performance requirements that are superior to the French thermal regulation, RT2005 (see Rogers 2007, for an overview of RT2005). For example, the new social housing buildings in the ORU project aim to be 10 per cent more energy efficient than what is required by RT2005 (80 to 100 kWh/m²/year, compared to 110 to 130 kWh/m²/year), with higher standards as well for hot water and heating (reaching 50 kWh/m²/year). Such requirements are also set with regards to rehabilitated buildings (improving from 180 kWh/m²/year at present for heating, hot water and ventilation to 110 kWh/m²/year).

These environmental initiatives were adopted in 2010 through the city's own Agenda 21, a political programme that also includes a local climate policy called *Plan Climat Territorial*. This was updated in June 2012. An important element of the planning activities in the municipality includes different forms of communication and dialogue with residents and citizens in order to ensure their participation in the projects and their awareness on energy, GHG emissions and environmental issues. One example of this is that Bègles has set up citizen's councils (*conseils 'arrondissement*) in some areas. These councils have their own budget (€10,000) which can be used for whatever the citizen council decides. Another example is the use of community work-shops to engage communities with many issues including education, culture and sustainable development (for example, a 'Begles 2030' workshop was held for the citizens to discuss what they wanted for the future development of their city).

As well as considering the energy efficiency of buildings, the municipality also considers how to make the individual and collective energy systems more efficient. Consideration is also given to transport patterns and how to encourage active travel through the layout and structure of the urban area.

Bologna, Italy: an integrated sustainable energy programme

The municipality of Bologna in Italy works strategically to integrate community management of demand and supply of energy in local building projects. One important initiative is the implementation of minimum requirements regarding energy performance in a redevelopment programme to improve social housing standards and conditions in the historic part of the city. The municipality acts as a project leader in the planning process for the redevelopment programme, where selected buildings are partly demolished and reconstructed in cooperation with a social housing company. The municipality has implemented ambitious energy performance requirements through the local building regulations.

Box 30.4 Bologna case study summary

The city of Bologna (377,000 inhabitants) is situated in Northern Italy. It acts under the jurisdiction of the Italian government and the Region of Emilia-Romagna.

In 2007 the municipality initiated an Energy City Programme with the purpose of upgrading the first urban energy plan, developed in 1999, and in response to new international and national requirements regarding the promotion of energy efficiency. Some of the key ambitions of the new energy programme are to:

- establish an energy qualification programme for the urban system;
- integrate the energy programme into the municipal structural plan and its operational tools (for example municipal operative plans and building regulations); and
- identify a means of applying initiatives from the European Union (EU) energy performance of buildings directive in future district buildings and renewal projects with special emphasis on public buildings.

In order to introduce policies to reduce GHG emissions, Bologna developed an Energy Urban Plan in 2007 and an action plan, updated with the Sustainable Energy Action Plan in 2012, with the goal of a 21 per cent reduction target. The energy saving measures and promotion of renewable energy sources identified in the plan were based on the close integration of the analysis of energy issues in the city and the development of appropriate urban planning tools. A spatial analysis of GHG emissions was undertaken, using census data and information about energy consumption in individual buildings available through geographical information systems databases. The data is collected in an Energy Atlas. The atlas can be used to identify: (a) urban areas with the highest energy intensity; (b) specific areas and buildings that may be the object of direct improvement; and (c) energy-related impacts of new urban developments. By using the spatial energy analysis, areas affected by highly significant urban transformation have been organised in clusters, called Urban Energy Basins. These form homogeneous areas in which the city applies specific energy policies. A set of building rules provides a comprehensive technical tool for professionals working on city development projects to integrate energy savings measures. The energy standards contained in these rules have been set at even higher levels in the Urban Energy Basins according to their characteristics. This project won the Sustainable Energy in Cities prize in 2008, promoted by the Italian Ministry for the Environment and the National Institute of Urban Planning within the Sustainable Energy Europe campaign.

Bologna's Sustainable Energy Action Plan promotes a wide energy refurbishment of existing buildings to high energy performance standards. The plan encourages redevelopment within existing building envelopes, with particular attention to historic buildings, and contributes to the transformation of the city towards sustainable mobility through the pedestrianisation of parts of the city centre and development of the public transport network, including interconnection with neighbouring municipalities. Key facilities in the city, such as the airport, university, BolognaFiere (an exhibitions and fairs area) and hospitals, together with main commercial areas, are recognised as important actors in the plan and specific roles have been assigned to them.

The implementation of the Sustainable Energy Action Plan began with the signing of a protocol between the mayor and 32 associated bodies representative of the city's main stakeholders. The protocol aims to promote partnership to enable a low rate rebate to house owners, through a special agreement between the associated companies and several regional and national banks.

A major area of focus in the municipality of Bologna concerns the improvement of the energy performance of residential buildings, which represents the most important and increasing sector of the municipality (62 per cent) in terms of energy consumption (ICLEI 2011). A redevelopment programme concerning public residential buildings in Bolognina, a historic part of the city, was launched by the municipality in order to integrate the improvement of energy efficiency with the general need to improve housing and social conditions in the city. This programme, called 'District contracts II – Bolognina', is based on a national initiative aimed at renewing social housing buildings in Italy, while simultaneously improving the environmental conditions and the provision of services, development works and social integration (Urban Center Bologna 2013). These district contracts are not generally aimed at promoting energy efficient buildings, but projects that experiment with improvements in energy performance have a greater probability of obtaining funding. The redevelopment programme of Bolognina represents a total net area of more than 11,000 square metres, with a historic consumption for heating and hot water of 2,700,000 kWh per annum (Grow and North East South West INTERREG IIIC 2007).

Tools and approaches

In this section some of the key tools and approaches in relation to community management of energy demand and supply are summarised based on experiences from the four case studies.

Municipal local regulations: local plans

In all four case studies the municipalities have been very active in demonstrating leadership in this field. They have identified targets and made plans and regulations to support the achievement of these targets. This includes setting minimum standards for new buildings as well as renovation projects. The spatial analysis that informed the Bologna Sustainable Energy Action Plan provides accurate information for monitoring and future modelling of energy requirements. Alternative options were found when local regulation proved insufficient. This was the case for Stenloese South in Denmark, where the municipality had to buy the plots for new construction and sell them with easements stating the requirements. One interesting experience from Stenloese South was that the house owners, when facing the more stringent requirements for energy efficiency as defined by the municipality, accepted these as they were consistently applied to everyone. User enquiries have indicated that residents are generally happy with their new houses and appreciate the improved thermal comfort compared to their previous homes.

Promotion of initiatives

In all four case studies promotion of the overall targets were considered very important and information campaigns were launched to reach the different stakeholders. The concept of constructing a demonstration project to illustrate the energy efficiency concepts in practice were utilised by the Romanian, French and Italian municipalities. The Municipality of Egedal has also constructed the new town hall in accordance with the best energy and indoor environment class in the Danish Building Regulations. Bologna is improving available tools and assessment methods in their aim to promote the implementation of energy efficient technologies.

Energy supply systems for common heating supply of communities

In one of the case studies, Stenloese South, influencing the energy supply system was possible from the very beginning of the design process as the project was a new settlement. Here the choice was a bio-fuelled district heating system for the dense low-rise areas and individual heat pumps for the single family houses. A large solar thermal plant was installed for the district heating system and individual solar heating systems were required on the individual houses to supplement the heat pumps. In this way a mix of rational use of energy and renewable energy systems was introduced to minimise the total GHG emissions. The reason why district heating wasn't chosen for the single family houses was that it wasn't financially justifiable, as the installation costs and the heat loss from the pipes would be relatively high compared to the low-energy consumption of each house. The Municipality of Egedal also improved energy efficiency during the renovation projects of seven public buildings through the installation of photovoltaic cells, thereby reducing the total primary energy consumption and carbon dioxide (CO_2) emissions by 67 per cent for the buildings included in the EU project, Class1 (Concerto 2014b). In Bègles, the municipality worked to improve both the individual and collective energy systems. In some projects, they have introduced wood burning furnaces – again to minimise total GHG emissions.

Capitalising on government initiatives

The municipality of Odobeşti has taken on the role of local coordinator of a national programme. This enables them to facilitate energy efficient initiatives in the existing building stock by getting national financing to the municipal projects, which both aims to reduce energy costs and improve the quality of life for the population. In France, a concept of 'contracts' is used to engage responsible stakeholders. The contract is made between the government, the local authorities, unions, companies and associations in France. The contract specifies the objectives in order to meet the targets of the future.

Conclusions: local action

From the analysis of the four case studies presented a few general conclusions can be drawn.

Municipalities can successfully act as front-runners: in all four examples, the municipality has taken on the responsibility to make 'things happen'. And they have succeeded with their initiatives. This is an encouragement to other cities, municipalities and communities not to hesitate, but get started with their own initiative to promote efficient community management of energy demand and supply

Local specific energy requirements work: in three of the case studies, the municipality has strengthened the building energy requirements in relation to the national level. This proved to be an efficient approach, which is straightforward to copy by local authorities elsewhere.

Local supply systems should be planned for: in Egedal and Bègles the municipality planned and implemented local supply systems based on collective wood-burning furnaces and solar heating systems. This can and should be taken up by other local authorities with the responsibility for local energy planning as this provides the means to make a quick shift to a CO_2-neutral energy supply to a large number of buildings. At the same time, it presents the possibility for an optimisation of the energy efficiency measures in the buildings reached and in the energy supply system – enabling a 'most value for the money spent' scenario.

Promotion seems to help – but a combination of sticks and carrots work better: communities and local authorities in general may promote energy efficient supply and demand by information campaigns, workshops, etc. However, the above examples show that direct involvement by the municipalities in the form of setting requirements or helping local builders or owners to get government subsidies has a stronger impact and produces immediate significant results.

The promising results of the four case studies presented in this chapter makes one think of an 'old' phrase: 'Think globally, act locally.' The local initiatives matter not only for the health and well-being of the people directly influenced by the actions, but it also inevitably leads the way towards a more sustainable society. So, communities and municipalities should start implementing local energy efficient demand and supply actions as soon as possible – it matters! Inspiration may be taken from the examples above and numerous other similar examples (International Energy Agency 2013).

Notes

1 Department of Management Engineering at the Technical University of Denmark – TUD, Lyngby, Denmark.
2 Due to lack of resources Odobești is the only city in Vrancea County where the central heating company has been declared bankrupt. For this reason most citizens are forced to produce heat in the dwelling by burning wood.

References

Concerted Action. 2011. Implementation of the EPBD in Romania: status in November 2010. Available at: www.epbd-ca.org/Medias/Pdf/country_reports_14-04-2011/Romania.pdf, accessed 26 August 2014.
Concerto. 2014a. Class1 website. Available at: www.class1.dk, accessed 26 August 2014.

Concerto. 2014b. The completed low-energy building projects: new buildings and energy renovated public buildings. Available at: www.class1.dk/fundanemt/files/Class1_wp1_Completed_building_projects_D4_rev1.pdf, accessed 26 August 2014.

Grow and North East South West INTERREG IIIC. 2007. Local involvement at the former fruit and vegetable market, Bologna, Italy: 'Bologna: a changing city'. Available at: www.laboratoriorapu.it/Plans_Project/Download/Lezioni/Lezione%203/bologna_market_paper.pdf, accessed 29 August 2014.

ICLEI (International Council for Local Environmental Initiatives). 2011. Sustainable NOW: ways to successful sustainable energy action planning in cities. Available at: www.iclei-europe.org/fileadmin/templates/iclei-europe/files/content/ICLEI_IS/Publications/SustainableNOW_Final-Brochure_www_SKO.pdf, accessed 26 August 2014.

International Energy Agency. 2013. EBC annex 63 implementation of energy strategies in communities. Available at: www.iea-ebc.org/projects/ongoing-projects/ebc-annex-63, accessed 29 August 2014.

Quitzau, M.-J., Hoffmann, B., Elle, M., Munthe-Kaas, P. and Lilliendahl-Larsen, J. 2009. Municipalities as promoters of energy efficient buildings: idea catalogue for proactive planning practices. Department of Management Engineering. Available at: www.class1.dk/fundanemt/files/Class1_wp2_Report_Proactive_Planning_Practise_D8_2010.pdf, accessed 26 August 2014.

Rogers, M.-C. 2007. Energy performance of buildings: public buildings. Available at: http://energycodesocean.org/sites/default/files/ECF9AFDD02AE46EA97F0C452BDA805DB.pdf, accessed 29 August 2014.

Urban Center Bologna (2013) Contratto di Quartiere. Available at: www.urbancenterbologna.it/strategie-progetti-urban-center-bologna/progetti-mostra-urban-center-bologna/310-contratti-di-quartiere-ii-bologna, accessed 29 August 2014.

PART V

Healthy planning in global practice

Hugh Barton and Laurence Carmichael

Part V of the book includes 11 chapters examining the way health issues and well-being strategies are being pursued through spatial planning in a wide variety of countries and settings. The sequence moves from East to West, starting with Oceania, then Asia, Europe and North America. The purpose is to illustrate planning solutions and effective processes, drawing out general principles and transferable policy approaches.

The degree to which health issues and well-being strategies are being pursued through spatial planning varies widely according to culture, economic conditions, governance and the sophistication of planning policy instruments. In particular, the situation will be different in low, middle and high income countries. Amongst our set of chapters are one low income country (India), two middle income countries (Taiwan and Turkey) and six high income countries (Australia, New Zealand, England, Finland, Germany and the USA). Despite the contrasts, however, there is much common ground.

Australia and New Zealand

Kent and Thompson's chapter 'Healthy planning in Australia' gives a view of the way a critical new goal is being progressively incorporated in a whole country, with major implications for the direction of spatial change. It highlights some of the challenges of integrating health into planning, focusing on the changing political priorities and difficulties of cross-sector working in Australia's complex and multi-layered regulatory system. Kent and Thompson identify the opportunities for integration thanks to key policy contributions by the non-government sector, in particular the National Heart Foundation and the Planning Institute of Australia.

By contrast, Vallance's chapter on Christchurch and the wider Canterbury region of New Zealand deals with the response to a very specific catastrophic situation: the devastating earthquake of 2010 which destroyed much of the city, and many livelihoods and communities. The resilience of cities and their planning systems must be reassessed in view of the growing threat of climate change, the occurrence of more extreme weather events, as well as other natural disasters. Vallance introduces new thinking around the reuniting of disaster management and peacetime planning, drawing out lessons from the process of recovery and rebuilding. She shows how inter-agency coordination and engagement with communities is useful to define the meaning of recovery and tackle timely and adaptive action at the right scale.

Taiwan, India and Turkey

Chao's chapter on Taiwan deals with an issue which affects countries across the globe: ageing populations. The healthy ageing programme in Taiwan, launched in 2010, latched onto the WHO Age-Friendly Cities Project, and by the end of the time of writing this chapter, 22 cities had joined. The development of the programme was informed by scientific studies, and continues to be linked to university researchers. Chao emphasises the key principles of active, independent living and 'ageing in place'. She explores how bringing key stakeholders together and involving citizens is a crucial aspect for successfully building age friendly cities.

Population trends are very different in India, still with a pyramidal age structure (though changing), and very rapid urbanisation. The basic health problems of poverty, housing and sanitation persist. With a fifth of the world's population, 40 per cent of which is predicted to live in cities by 2030, Indian cities must plan for the future. Thapar and Rao's chapter on the city of Hyderabad details the methods and evidence used by town planners to inform the masterplan of the city. This chapter demonstrates how strategic approaches to reduce urban sprawl, improve infrastructure and create open space that will improve the well-being of residents, must be supported by reforms in urban planning, governance and management to ensure cross-sector working and public engagement.

Turkey is still experiencing rapid urban growth, with resulting pressures on land, housing and infrastructure. Health has been a key motivator for more effective planning. Fidan and Yilmaz's chapter on integrating health into planning in Turkey explains how, with the moral support of the WHO Healthy Cities network, Turkish cities have been developing programmes to improve quality of life and contribute to physical and mental health, in some cases targeting specific constituencies of residents. Infrastructure improvements for physical activity also assist the creation of low carbon environments. Projects promoting pedestrianisation, active travel, public transport and the development of urban greenspaces, have enhanced urban and historic centres like Bursa. A key lesson for city planners has been to build up cooperation with outside organisations from the private and community sectors.

England, Finland and Germany

Population trends, average income levels and governance systems in Western Europe offer considerable opportunities for creating healthy cities. However, difficulties persist in relation to working in a pluralistic and neo-liberal decision-making context. Kurth and her colleagues in the English Midlands describe the recent positive shifts in professional and governmental guidance, then evaluate progress in Stoke-on-Trent, Sandwell and Lincolnshire. They suggest that success in delivering results on the ground relies on a *dogged and pragmatic pursuit of the 'art of the possible'* at local level. The chapter shows how an assessment tool, Integrated Impact Assessment, can support cross-sector working between planning and public health professionals, and the creation of a shared understanding of health and planning amongst stakeholders.

Finnish local authorities have greater autonomy than the British. Although Kuopio, in the heart of the country, has grown up as a largely car dependent town, it is now implementing a radical strategy of change. Kosonen, former chief planner, describes his 'three fabrics' approach to transport, land use and community planning. This is based on progressively extending the zones of the city accessible by walking and public transport, sometimes together with the regeneration of poorly served neighbourhoods. The result is increased active travel, improved accessibility, higher environmental quality and reduced greenhouse gas emissions. The measurement of the 'three fabrics' gives simple public indicators of policy success.

Germany has a very developed hierarchical planning system that gives extensive powers to city authorities. Grant and Barton's chapter on the south-western city of Freiburg shows that it is possible to have multidimensional approaches to quality of life and environmental sustainability that will support healthy urban living. Freiburg has become an iconic beacon of urban sustainability, based on long-term, cross-party commitment to a coherent social, economic and physical strategy. Central to this is the integration of transport, land use and development planning, combined with the delivery of a high quality people-friendly urban environment. Implementation has been achieved through effective city leadership and strong community and stakeholder engagement.

The USA and Canada

The cities of North America are known for their low density sprawl, very high level of car use and the disinclination of people to walk. Partly as a result, the USA has the highest level of obesity of any country. Some cities in the USA and Canada are responding with energy to this challenge. McVean and Saunders explore the way Chicago, Montreal, New York, Portland, Seattle, Vancouver and Washington are reshaping their streets and public realm to facilitate active travel. Schemes include protected bike lanes, cycle streets, tree planting, and re-appropriation of on-street parking for pedestrians and street community activity. The authors point to multiple benefits flowing from these initiatives: healthy physical activity, flourishing social networks and economic regeneration. A key ingredient has been political leadership, in particular the vision of strong mayors to address contentious issues and secure the speedy delivery of large projects.

A few cities in North America have taken the integration of health into planning practice at a much more overarching level. Portland is a case in point. Abbott and McGrath emphasise the importance of the right institutional and cultural contexts to deliver a whole city or metropolitan spatial strategy. Their chapter retraces the progress made by Portland since the 1970s. A critical factor has been the existence of Metro – the only elected regional government in the USA. Public health concerns have been a driver for change, leading to the integration of public health into urban and transport planning. Restrictions on excessive outward sprawl, and investment in public transport rather than freeways, with neighbourhood renewal and intensification along main public transport routes, have begun to turn the city from its previous unhealthy trajectory. The changed priorities have found a welcome response from residents and the housing market.

Tillett then illustrates the application of the broad strategy within a particular Portland neighbourhood. The Pearl District, close to the city centre, was a dying commercial zone. Tillett describes how a strong planning and urban design strategy has focused on recreating attractive streets and mixed uses to generate local human activity, healthy behaviour and a vibrant sense of community. He shows that rigorous public design regulations and programming, far from inhibiting the market, have released investment from landowners and private sector developers. This has facilitated the rapid transformation of The Pearl District into a highly successful neighbourhood where active travel is the norm and car ownership not essential. The tools and design processes are in theory transferable, but rely on creative professional responses to specific needs and situations, political commitment, together with sustained clarity of vision. This exemplar of neighbourhood regeneration and the creation of a health-supporting environment is a fitting finale to the book.

31

HEALTHY PLANNING IN AUSTRALIA

Jennifer Kent and Susan Thompson

Background

There is widespread acceptance in Australia that chronic disease is a major economic and social issue. Rates of overweight and obesity continue to rise, increasing from 44 per cent of adults in 1989 to 63 per cent in 2012 (National Health Performance Authority 2013). It is projected that in 2025 over 80 per cent of Australian men and 75 per cent of women will be overweight or obese (Department Human Services Victoria 2008). This has serious consequences for life expectancy, rates of disability and quality of life. The financial burden for the Australian economy will be massive. In 2012, expenditure on health was estimated as over AU$130 billion annually, representing 9.4 per cent of the nation's gross domestic product (GDP). This has increased from 8.2 per cent ten years earlier (Australian Institute of Health and Welfare 2012). Australian governments are understandably concerned about this burgeoning health care bill and are looking to preventive measures to halt the growth in chronic disease.

The potential for the built environment to support human health and well-being is also gaining acceptance. Urban planning is increasingly recognised as an effective mechanism to shape and manage built environments so that they encourage and support physical activity, social connection and access to healthy food (Kent and Thompson 2014). The not-for-profit sector has been a particularly strong advocate of healthy built environments in Australia, and there is engagement across health and the built environment academic disciplines. Private sector developers have also started to see healthy planning as providing a market edge and local communities are increasingly demanding healthier places to live and work. Nevertheless, while there is a keen acknowledgement of the importance of healthy planning across national, state and local government jurisdictions, political commitment remains somewhat uncoordinated and inconsistent. Our chapter engages with these issues to present an overview of the status of healthy built environments in Australia. We provide examples of, and opportunities for, healthy planning in a nation working to tackle health problems that are relatively common, yet highly complex. The chapter concludes with a discussion of ongoing challenges. While Australian governments and associated stakeholders regularly acknowledge the potential for built environments to promote health, changing political priorities, complex regulatory systems and difficulties associated with working across disciplines continue to threaten realisation of this potential.

Early history

Australian town planning legislation and practice has its origins in the British system (Williams 2012). Concerns for people's health in the eighteenth and early nineteenth centuries, particularly the scourge of contagious diseases (Cullingworth and Nadin 2006), lay the foundations for the creation of fundamental planning concepts such as land-use zoning and the garden suburb. This enabled the separation of dirty and polluting land uses from residential neighbourhoods, in turn idealising the suburban environment as essential for healthy and happy families (Freestone 2012; Figure 31.1).

Post-World War II housing programmes boosted suburban development and the greater availability of the motor car reinforced this trend (Mumford 1961). Australian cities today are characterised by low residential densities and segregated uses, now the hallmarks of sedentary and unhealthy lifestyles (Dannenberg et al. 2011; Figure 31.2). The lower-density urban form of the nation's cities is a marked contrast to rural and regional areas, which are characterised by vast areas of unpopulated land interspersed with townships of various sizes. While the majority of the Australian population live in urban areas, the health needs of rural dwellers cannot be ignored. This unique population geography provides interesting challenges for the promotion of healthy built environments.

Healthy planning emerged in Australia largely as a result of the efforts of public health professionals and their growing awareness of the influence of the built environment on health outcomes. These developments reflected what was happening on the global stage with the commissioning of Health21 by the World Health Organization (WHO) (Barton and Tsourou 2000; Baum 2008). This 1970s initiative was followed with the declaration of the Ottawa Charter for

Figure 31.1   Mural celebrating Haberfield in Sydney's Inner West as an example of the garden suburb
Source: Thompson.

Figure 31.2   Low density suburban development found in cities across Australia

Source: Thompson.

Health Promotion in 1986 and the establishment of the WHO Healthy Cities. Healthy Cities projects in Australia include Onkaparinga (formerly Noarlunga) in South Australia (Baum 2008) and the Illawarra in New South Wales (NSW) (Healthy Cities Illawarra 2014).

More recently, a series of major public inquiries in Australia have been driven by the increased incidence of preventable diseases and the need to look beyond individual behaviours in the promotion of health and well-being. These reviews included the *National Parliamentary Inquiry into Obesity* (House of Representatives Standing Committee on Health and Ageing 2009) and *Australia: The Healthiest Country by 2020?* (Australian Government Department of Health and Ageing 2010). The latter culminated in the release of the National Preventative Health Strategy (Commonwealth of Australia 2009) which included specific recommendations about the built environment's role in supporting healthy behaviour as part of everyday living.

From these foundations, built environment professionals and related organisations are increasingly embracing a health promotion role. A key barrier to better coordination is undoubtedly the complex structure of governance underpinning Australia's planning and land-use systems. Our chapter now progresses to provide a brief introduction to this system and describe some of the ways it supports the provision of healthier built environments.

Healthy planning and the Australian government sector

A note on Australia's governance structure

Urban governance in Australia is a product of the division of political power and functions of national (also referred to as commonwealth and federal), state and local governments. Australia's Constitution details this three tier division, and generally deems that matters relating to the planning and regulation of land-use are the responsibility of the nation's six state and two territory governments. Over time, each of these jurisdictions has developed its own planning system which, while administered by the state, often defers many of the day-to-day practices of planning to local government. Adding to this complexity is the constitutionally enshrined retention by the federal government of the power to intervene in matters of 'environmental significance', which can, quite appropriately, include aspects of the way places are planned. There are, therefore, multiple potential points of intervention in the Australian land-use planning system where principles of healthy built environments can be activated.

National scale governance for healthy built environments

The extent of federal intervention in Australian planning has fluctuated through different periods of political leadership. Establishment of a national Major Cities Unit in 2007, however, signalled an upsurge in commonwealth government interest in the planning and management of significant urban centres. The subsequent release of a National Urban Policy (Commonwealth of Australia 2011), with both a direct focus on interdisciplinary and sectoral engagement, and a specific appeal to 'liveable' cities, heralded a new federal commitment to the pursuit of community well-being through urban planning. Attempts to embed the consideration of planning matters into a wide array of federal and state agencies reflect a relatively contemporary conceptualisation of urban planning as important in the management of matters beyond the regulation of development. This is aligned with a healthy planning agenda because it paves the way for health to be recognised as a relevant issue for land-use planning. Further, the specific inclusion of 'liveability' as a major goal for the National Urban Policy, with a key objective to 'support community wellbeing' (Commonwealth of Australia 2011, p. 18), signals a clear intention for Australian national urban policy to assume responsibility for its relationship with issues of human health and well-being.

From federal to state

In 2009, the emergent federal focus on both urban affairs and inter-sectoral collaboration was further augmented in a resolution by Australia's combined council of state, territory and local governments (COAG). This resolution included criteria for better integration and standardisation of strategic land-use planning frameworks around Australia. Various state governments have subsequently used this opportunity as the catalyst and mode of delivery for a reorientation of their planning systems towards human health and well-being.

South Australia's 'Health in All Policies' model

The state of South Australia provides an excellent case for the inclusion of health in its strategic intent. Although not developed directly under the COAG mandate for metropolitan and regional planning, this state's pursuit of a Health in All Policies (HiAP) approach has directly influenced development of the seven objectives underpinning its State Plan (Public Health Bulletin SA 2010). One of these objectives is the creation of 'Safe communities; healthy neighbourhoods'. It articulates an inspiring vision of urban areas characterised by their ability to enable healthy practices. A key mechanism in the South Australian HiAP model is a process termed Health Lens Analysis which draws on health impact assessment methods. This process has been used successfully across a range of projects, including development of a guide for the pursuit of transit-oriented development (TOD) in South Australia's largest city, Adelaide (Department of Health, Government of South Australia 2011). The document provides a consistent set of principles for TOD and is used as a resource by state and local government agencies.

South Australia's ambitious HiAP process is a highly commendable approach. It is an exemplar of the kind of vision and strategic intent that is essential to the activation of health in urban planning processes. As an instrument for change, however, it lacks the more direct power afforded to legislatively enforceable statutory planning arrangements.

The New South Wales healthy planning legislative objective

Each Australian state and territory has a unique statutory planning system which represents an enforceable legislative framework for urban land-use planning. These systems are generally underpinned by a single primary piece of legislation, which in turn dictates key land-use planning objectives. Objectives include matters such as the promotion of orderly economic development, public participation and, more recently, protection of the natural environment. These objectives are extremely significant in that they articulate how planning legislation is to be interpreted. Indeed, any land-use decision made contrary to an act's objective can be deemed unlawful (Gurran 2011). Inclusion of the promotion of health and well-being as an objective of planning legislation is therefore a powerful tool to guarantee that health is considered when determining a planning matter.

While the time frames and politics associated with legislative amendment deem this a slow and arduous process, recent developments in Australia's largest state, NSW, provide a positive example of the way planning legislation can be changed to better support human health. In July 2011, the NSW government commenced the first comprehensive review of the state's planning system in over 30 years. The process was launched with extensive consultations and at each stage, a consortium of healthy built environment stakeholders provided detailed responses. This sent a clear and consistent request for inclusion of health as a planning objective in the state's new planning legislation. Providing the ultimate endorsement of urban planning's embrace of health as a planning concern, the draft legislation tabled in the NSW Parliament in October 2013 included health as a primary matter for consideration under the new planning act.

Local government

Local government in Australia relates to a specific area or locality, the geographical borders of which are defined by each state. The day-to-day practices of Australian planning are often deferred to these local authorities, which are overseen by elected representatives who form a local council. In reality, constraints to funding and influence deem that health and well-being are one of many concerns to be addressed by land-use planning at this scale. There is, however, evidence of increased awareness and action in local jurisdictions, indicating a degree of latent potential for local land-use authorities to contribute to healthy built environments in Australia.

Some of the most successful examples of local government action for healthy built environments rely on innovative collaborations between land-use planning authorities and local health agencies. An example is the creative partnership between Bellingen Shire Council and the North Coast Area Health Service in northern NSW. The council had already identified goals relating to community well-being, sustainable growth and enhanced quality of life in its plan of management. The local health authority became involved specifically to assist with realisation of these goals. In an exemplar of cross-sectoral partnerships, the link between the area health service and the council was initially facilitated by one of Australia's most proactive non-government organisations (NGOs) in this field – the National Heart Foundation (discussed further below). The collaboration was initiated during a review of the region's primary planning framework and controls for land use. As a result of the collaborative process the revised plans emphasised a comprehensive array of key healthy planning principles.

Awareness of the link between the built environment and health is undoubtedly growing across Australia's local authorities. Professionals working at this scale commonly identify a need for education on ways to use the various systems and processes within which planning operates to enact positive change. A number of tools have been developed to fill this demand. In NSW, for example, the state government department responsible for health developed a *Healthy Urban Development Checklist* (NSW Department of Health 2009) to support both health and built environment professionals evaluating and commenting on urban development policies, plans and proposals in relation to health. This exceptionally comprehensive checklist is available in both hard copy and online, where users can record and review evaluations, as well as obtain feedback from other professionals. The checklist not only provides a series of evaluative questions to be answered in relation to a specific development proposal or plan, but also supplies users with information on how to engage relevant stakeholders and inform decision-makers.

Healthy planning and the Australian non-government sector

Various NGOs have made significant contributions to policy initiatives which facilitate collaboration between health and built environment professionals in Australia.

The National Heart Foundation

The National Heart Foundation of Australia has taken a leading role in this area. It remains at the vanguard of thinking about, and building relationships between, the built environment and health sectors. Since the launch of a suite of simple yet effective Healthy by Design Guidelines in 2004, the Foundation has developed other valuable assistance for planners, designers, developers and communities. These include strategies for food sensitive urban design and advice for property developers on consumer preferences for healthy built environments. The Foundation has also developed a walkability checklist for communities to lobby for more walkable neighbourhood streets. All tools are available free to download from the Heart Foundation's website.[1]

The Planning Institute of Australia

Australia's professional planning body, the Planning Institute of Australia, has also made a substantial contribution to the promotion of healthy built environments. In 2009, the Institute launched Healthy Spaces and Places – a web-based resource which includes practical tools, case studies and guidelines for planning and developing sustainable communities to encourage healthy ways of living.[2] The resource is the outcome of cross-disciplinary and cross-sector collaboration between the Australian Local Government Association and the National Heart Foundation, with funding from the Australian Government's Department of Health and Ageing. The Institute has subsequently embarked on a series of professional workshops to educate planning professionals, particularly local government employees, about the design principles and development types that promote healthy and active living.

The Cancer Council

The Cancer Council of Australia works in conjunction with state-based Cancer Councils to address the complex issues associated with the prevention and treatment of cancer. Sun exposure is a particular concern given that Australia has the highest melanoma rate in the world (Australian Institute of Health and Welfare and Australasian Association of Cancer Registries 2012, p. 21).

Figure 31.3   A typical shade structure in an Australian park ensuring sun protection for children

Source: Thompson.

The built environment has a significant role to play here – as do planners, designers, engineers and local government officials. Of particular importance are shade guidelines from the Cancer Council NSW (2013). Their aim is to increase the provision of user friendly, quality shade in the community (Figure 31.3). Not only is this of relevance to local councils, it is a further demonstration of how built environment and health professionals need to work together.

Healthy planning and the Australian private sector

The Australian private sector is increasingly interested in healthy built environments. The potential to link health and sustainability is appreciated by some developers, as are the possibilities of marketing environments that support healthy living. At the national level, the Green Building Council of Australia has a 'Green Star Communities' pilot rating tool that defines benchmarks for best sustainability practice.[3] Developments are assessed under the categories of governance, design, economic prosperity, environment, innovation and liveability (including components of healthy and active living).

Also at the national level, the Urban Development Institute of Australia (UDIA) via its Queensland Office and EnviroDesign[4] has a set of criteria to rate residential developments in terms of environmental and community standards. The latter embrace significant healthy planning criteria including safety, accessibility and public transport, as well as specific facilities for residents to be active and easily access healthy food. These types of rating tools can offer a degree of confidence for the consumer who is keen to live in a sustainable and healthy environment. Developers can also use a good rating to promote how their projects support healthy lifestyles – for example, the Greater Ascot Development in one of Australia's most northerly regional cities – Townsville (Figure 31.4).[5]

Figure 31.4   Rouse Hill is another example of a new suburb in Sydney designed with healthy built
environment principles

Source: Thompson.

Inter-sectoral work in Australia

Our chapter has thus far focused on various healthy planning activities initiated and maintained by a series of different sectors and agencies around Australia. The ongoing success of this increasingly active movement, however, will depend on strong collaboration between these various sectors and agencies. Productive alliances are emerging, and we now discuss some of the key forums for, and outcomes of, these collaborations.

The NSW Premier's Council for Active Living

Established in 2004, the NSW Premier's Council for Active Living is a state funded initiative with the specific aim to enhance access to opportunities for physical activity and healthy food in day-to-day community life. The Council comprises senior representatives from across government, industry and the community sector. It has played a leading role in workforce development, policy integration and advocacy for legislative change. One of its key accomplishments has been a comprehensive assessment checklist for use by urban planners in NSW – *Development and Active Living: Designing Projects for Active Living* (Premier's Council for Active Living 2009). The Council is currently working on a further set of guidelines to assist local governments to incorporate support for active living and healthy eating into an array of standard planning and reporting requirements. These various guidelines and checklists, as well as case study material and the Council's newsletter, can be downloaded from their website.[6]

The role of tertiary institutions

Collaboration between tertiary institutions and state government agencies is consistently identified as critical to the progression of the healthy planning agenda in Australia. These alliances are increasingly popular, and have developed to advance healthy built environment research, domestic capacity building, education and advocacy.

The Healthy Built Environments Program (HBEP) in the Faculty of the Built Environment at the University of NSW is an example of this type of cross-sectoral engagement. In 2009, the state department of health established this five year initiative, bringing together an interdisciplinary team from academic, government, private sector and NGOs with expertise across health, urban planning and design. An innovative feature of the HBEP is that it is situated in one of Australia's largest faculties of the built environment (Thompson et al. 2013).

Situating a health funded programme in a university built environment faculty sends a strong message about the importance of interdisciplinary approaches in this field. A related initiative in Victoria involves the McCaughey VicHealth Centre for Community Wellbeing at the University of Melbourne. While administratively positioned within the University's public health faculty, the centre is involved in collaborations and research on the way built environments influence health. One example of the centre's cross-sectoral collaboration involves a large consortium of local government institutions – the North and West Metropolitan Regional Management Forum (RMF). This forum engaged the University of Melbourne to undertake an array of support functions for the Forum's work in implementing the state's health plan, including the provision of data and the execution of evaluative research (Butterworth 2011).

Figure 31.5   Students from a healthy built environment class undertaking field work auditing environments for health supportive infrastructure

Source: Thompson.

Planning for healthy built environments in Australia benefits from positive collaboration between government organisations and the tertiary sector. University involvement can assist with providing an evidence base for policy, as well as ensuring that the contemporary policy context informs research. Furthermore, such collaborations enhance both the content and delivery of tertiary and professional education, contributing to the critical need for interdisciplinary learning. Undergraduate and postgraduate healthy planning courses at the University of NSW in Sydney are examples of practice-based education that uses an interdisciplinary approach to understand and address increasingly common lifestyle-related health problems. These courses engage students from a range of built environment and health/medical disciplines in fieldwork and theory related to urban planning and health (Thompson and Capon 2010; Figure 31.5).

Combining sectors and agendas

The healthy built environment challenge in Australia has been assisted through the formation of alliances with other related agendas. An obvious opportunity for such cross-agenda collaboration is presented by acknowledgement of the co-benefits for human health from actions to address climate change. For example, in 2008 a consortium of local government authorities in metropolitan Sydney was awarded a government grant to develop an Agenda for Sustainability and Wellbeing (WSROC 2008). The subsequent framework innovatively draws on a view that cities are 'human ecological systems', acknowledging that the health of the population and the biophysical environment are co-dependent. Successful implementation of the agenda requires commitment from a range of government and non-government agencies. These include local and state health and environment authorities, representatives from tertiary institutions, schools, local retailers and community organisations.

Challenges into the future

Healthy planning has clearly come a long way in Australia. There is a growing collection of cases where concern for human health has changed the way built environments are planned and managed. Many of these examples are discussed above, with further information accessible from each organisation's website.

Nevertheless, healthy planning continues to vie for legitimacy and is vulnerable to the shifting sands of legislative reform. In many quarters the rhetoric reinforcing the need for an increased focus on preventive health is loud and consistent. However, there are some significant challenges to the adoption of healthy planning policy and practice. In this final section of the chapter we outline these difficulties and discuss emerging possibilities for strengthening healthy planning in Australia and elsewhere.

There are debates around the types and adequacy of research 'evidence' needed to underpin Australian policy and practice. In health, epidemiological studies and randomised control trials have traditionally been accepted as the most appropriate ways of undertaking research. These methods underscore the desire for consistent, repeatable and objective measurements of the relationship between the built environment and healthy behaviours. This approach is in sharp contrast to the appreciation of the complex interplay between people and place that built environment professionals typically embrace. These understandings are based on practice wisdom and design principles, together with observational and case study research. As healthy planning evolves, these different ways of thinking need to be respected and increasingly synthesised.

Changing political priorities, often following the election of a new government, are a continuing challenge for the institutionalisation of healthy planning. The multiple scales of governance in Australian planning can make these changes particularly disruptive. Even if healthy planning is embedded in legislation, as we hope will occur in NSW (see previous discussion), acts can be modified and replaced. The ways that built environment and health professionals work together, sharing knowledge and understanding across their disciplines (see for example, Kent and Thompson 2012 and Thompson and Kent 2013), will be key to ensure that healthy planning becomes core Australian policy and practice. The escalating costs of chronic disease will no doubt further persuade governments to consistently support healthy planning.

Transferability of the approach

This chapter has presented an overview of the status of healthy built environment initiatives in Australia. We have provided examples of how different levels of government, NGOs and the tertiary and private sectors are embracing and championing this potential. While there is an increasingly robust and active network of professionals advocating this complex agenda, it remains vulnerable. This is particularly so in relation to uncoordinated and inconsistent political commitment. Turning the advocacy, enthusiasm and evidence into real change in Australian built environments is a continuing challenge.

Australia has a unique population geography, and maintains a series of complex political and land-use planning systems. The challenges faced by professionals working in healthy planning, however, have relevance for other jurisdictions where preventable disease is problematic and urban areas are dispersed and car-dependent. In the Australian experience, the crucial ingredient for successful translation of enthusiasm into action is the development of genuinely interdisciplinary working relationships. These must be based on mutual understanding and respect, where key champions are encouraged, and political support is realised. We propose that this understanding and respect are universal characteristics of healthy planning practice and the evolution of healthy communities. We look forward to the time when Australian urban environments are consistently characterised by both.

Notes

1 www.heartfoundation.org.au
2 www.healthyplaces.org.au
3 www.greenstarcommunities.org.au
4 www.envirodevelopment.com.au
5 www.greaterascot.com
6 www.pcal.nsw.gov.au

References

Australian Government Department of Health and Ageing. 2010. *Australia: the healthiest country by 2020?* National Preventative Health Taskforce. Canberra: National Preventative Health Taskforce.

Australian Institute of Health and Welfare. 2012. *Health expenditure in Australia 2010–11.* www.aihw.gov. au, accessed 21 January 2014.

Australian Institute of Health and Welfare and Australasian Association of Cancer Registries. 2012. *Cancer in Australia: an overview, 2012.* Cancer series no. 74. Cat. no. CAN 70, Canberra: AIHW.

Barton, H. and Tsourou, C. 2000. *Healthy urban planning: a WHO guide to planning for people.* London: Routledge.

Baum, F. 2008. *The new public health.* Melbourne: Oxford University Press.

Butterworth, I.A. 2011. Regional health and wellbeing implementation strategy for Melbourne's North and West Metropolitan Region: harnessing the capability of the Regional Management Forum. *Proceedings of the Fifth State of Australian Cities Conference,* Melbourne, 2011.

Cancer Council NSW. 2013. *Guidelines to shade.* Sydney: Cancer Council NSW.

Commonwealth of Australia. 2009. *Australia: the healthiest country by 2020. A national preventative health strategy.* Canberra: National Preventative Health Taskforce, Australian Government.

Commonwealth of Australia. 2011. *Our cities, our future: a national urban policy for a productive, sustainable and liveable future.* Canberra: Commonwealth of Australia.

Cullingworth, B. and Nadin, V. 2006. *Town and country planning in the UK.* London: Routledge.

Dannenberg, A.L., Frumkin, H. and Jackson, R.J. (Eds) 2011. *Making healthy places: designing and building for health, well-being, and sustainability.* London: Island Press.

Department of Health, Government of South Australia. 2011. *Transit-oriented developments . . . through a health lens: a guide for healthy urban developments.* Adelaide: Government of South Australia.

Department Human Services Victoria. 2008. *Future prevalence of overweight and obesity in Australian children and adolescents 2005–2025.* Melbourne: HSV.

Freestone, R. 2012. An historical perspective. In: Thompson, S. and Maginn, P.J. (Eds) *Planning Australia: an overview of urban and regional planning.* 2nd ed. Melbourne: Cambridge University Press, pp. 73–97.

Gurran, N. 2011. *Australian urban land use planning: principles, systems and practice.* Sydney: Sydney University Press.

Healthy Cities Illawarra. 2014. *Healthy Cities Illawarra.* www.healthyillawarra.org.au/healthycities, accessed 4 March 2014.

House of Representatives Standing Committee on Health and Ageing. 2009. *National parliamentary inquiry into obesity.* Canberra: Commonwealth of Australia.

Kent, J.L. and Thompson, S. 2012. Health and the built environment: exploring foundations for a new interdisciplinary profession. *Journal of Environmental and Public Health,* May.

Kent, J.L. and Thompson, S. 2014. The three domains of urban planning for health and well-being. *Journal of Planning Literature,* published online before print 19 February 2014. doi:10.1177/0885412214520712.

Mumford, L. 1961. Suburbia and beyond. In *The city in history: its origins, its transformations, and its prospects.* Harmondsworth: Penguin Books.

National Health Performance Authority. 2013. *Healthy communities: overweight and obesity rates across Australia, 2011–12.* www.nhpa.gov.au, accessed 21 January 2014.

New South Wales Department of Health. 2009. *Healthy urban development checklist.* Sydney: New South Wales Department of Health.

Premier's Council for Active Living. 2009. *Development and active living: designing projects for active living.* Sydney: Premier's Council for Active Living.

Public Health Bulletin SA. 2010. Health in all policies: Adelaide 2010 international meeting. *Public Health Bulletin SA,* 7(2).

Thompson, S. and Capon, A.G. 2010. Designing a healthy and sustainable future: a vision for interdisciplinary education, research and leadership. Paper presented to Connected: 2nd International Conference on Design Education, 28 June–1 July 2010, University of New South Wales, Sydney, Australia.

Thompson, S. and Kent, J.L. 2013. Healthy built environments supporting everyday occupations: current thinking in urban planning. *Journal of Occupational Science,* 1–17. doi:10.1080/14427591.2013.867562

Thompson, S., Kent, J.L. and Lyons, C. 2013. Planning and health: forging new alliances in building healthy and resilient cities. In *Proceedings of the Joint European (AESOP) and American (ACSP) Congress.* Dublin.

Williams, P. 2012. Statutory planning. In Thompson, S.M. and Maginn, P.J. (Eds) *Planning Australia: an overview of urban and regional planning.* 2nd ed. Melbourne: Cambridge University Press, pp. 98–123.

WSROC. 2008. *An agenda for sustainability and wellbeing in Western Sydney.* Blacktown: Western Sydney Regional Organisation of Councils Ltd.

32

PLANNING FOR RESILIENT CITIES

Lessons from post-earthquake Canterbury

Suzanne Vallance

Natural hazards

As I write this chapter, people living and working along the Thames in the United Kingdom are battling severe flooding and now, unfortunately, have something in common with victims of Hurricane Sandy (United States), Typhoon Haiyan (in the Philippines) and the Tohoku tsunami (Japan). The world seems more hazardous. This may be because the climate is changing more rapidly, and bringing more extreme weather events (IPCC 2013). It is possibly because urbanisation makes us more vulnerable to everything from microbes (Patel and Burke 2009) to an overdependence on (increasingly) privatised critical infrastructure (Klein 2007). Or maybe the world has always been risky but the *quality* of risk has changed (Beck 2009) with our knowledge that some of those 'acts of God' or so-called 'natural' disasters have very human causes, including inadequate planning.

Planners profoundly shape the urban exoskeleton that supports city life. Although avoiding calamity is often *implicit* in peacetime planning, actual disasters have long been regarded as unwelcome intrusions (Montgomery 2014) that then require a dedicated field of scholarship and practice of 'disaster recovery'. Nonetheless, forensic analysis of several high profile disasters, including Hurricane Katrina in New Orleans, has highlighted ways in which catastrophe could have been avoided or mitigated through more appropriate land uses and better deployment of infrastructure. Dedicated recovery plans, on the other hand, can be dominated by attempts to reduce the risk of exposure to similar events, ignoring or marginalising important peacetime concerns. In these ways distinctions between 'disaster management' and 'peacetime planning' can be unhelpful, and an explicit rapprochement seems overdue. The concept of 'urban resilience' has the potential to weave together these two strands of scholarship and practice.

In this chapter, I identify some of the key issues around urban resilience that have resulted from this cross-pollination of disaster management and peacetime planning, before testing some of those debates as they have played out in a particular context. Beginning on 4 September 2010, the Canterbury region of New Zealand was rocked by an ongoing sequence of earthquakes that has caused 185 direct fatalities, numerous injuries and inflicted widespread damage to land, infrastructure and utilities, town centres, community facilities and services. The social, economic and environmental effects have been considerable, affecting all who live and work in the region.

As a result of this disaster, numerous plans of varying scope and scale have been developed. The second part of this chapter therefore provides an overview of some of the more influential of these before assessing them in terms of the key debates.

Urban resilience: bouncing back, bouncing forward

Urban resilience is configured in numerous ways (see, for example, Walker and Salt 2006 for a socio-ecological systems perspective) but, following disaster, the emphasis tends to be on 'bouncing back' to normal or resuming some steady, functional state that may be described as 'coping'. Yet many see disasters as also providing opportunities to 'bounce forward', or 'build back better', not least by reducing the risk from future events by retreating from vulnerable areas, adopting new technologies or stronger building codes, and upgrading dilapidated infrastructure.

The prospect of bouncing forward is compelling and, from a distance, perhaps resembles the simple aggregation of rational decisions, informed by expert evidence, shaped by professional best practice, but it is not always that easy. 'Stronger building codes' can increase the cost of rebuilding and cause affordability problems. 'Retreating from vulnerable areas' can feel like forced eviction to residents whose livelihoods and lifestyles are connected with particular places. In some cases, like New Orleans post-Katrina, resettlement strategies based on scientific assessments of flood-prone areas looked, to some residents, more like racial cleansing than reducing vulnerability (Olshansky and Johnson 2010).

Indeed, New Orleans post-Katrina has served as particularly fertile ground for research, highlighting important connections between the *substance* of recovery plans and the *processes* through which these plans are developed (although see Allmendinger 2002 for a discussion of a post-positivist take on substantial versus procedural issues). Consequently, rather than the number of houses rebuilt, or roads repaired, the extent to which those affected by the disaster are able to participate in decision-making processes has been mooted as fundamentally underpinning the idea of recovery (Lorenz 2011). Unfortunately, disasters are often accompanied by a discourse of urgency that helps create a certain 'state of exception' (Agamben 2005). This can then be used to justify the suspension of more deliberative and inclusive participatory processes (Gotham and Greenberg 2008; McClennen 2012). Consequently, it is only through a better understanding of process that important questions about 'building back better *for whom*' may be answered.

The Canterbury case study

I turn now to an overview of how some of these literary threads identified above – distinctions between peacetime planning and disaster management, timeliness and transparency, substance and process – have played out in a particular context. Due to fairly frequent low magnitude earthquakes, New Zealand is often referred to as 'the Shaky Isles'; however, strong building codes around structural seismic strengthening mean that fatalities from earthquakes have been uncommon. In fact, the first magnitude 7.2 earthquake on 4 September 2010 caused no casualties, although there was widespread damage to land, infrastructure and housing in Kaiapoi (in the Waiamakariri District) and in the eastern suburbs and central business district (CBD) of Christchurch city. But then, six months later, a 6.8 magnitude earthquake occurred almost directly under the city of Christchurch. Although 'smaller' in magnitude than the first quake, the peak ground acceleration of 2.2 (over twice that of gravity) was one of the highest ever recorded and would have 'flattened' most world cities.[1] This time, 185 people lost their lives and thousands were injured. The inner city was cordoned off for two years and numerous schools, community and leisure facilities, businesses, and other services were closed (some permanently). Over 400 hectares of residential land under approximately 8,000 homes was 'Red Zoned'; that is, deemed too expensive and disruptive to remediate at this time (Figure 32.1).

The extended Canterbury earthquake sequence caused damage (Figures 32.2 and 32.3) across three different local councils' jurisdictions – the Canterbury Regional Council (ECan),

Figure 32.1   Damage to housing and infrastructure led to the 'Red Zoning' of over 8,000 homes

Source: Vallance.

Figure 32.2   Earthquake damage to inner city housing blocks

Source: Vallance.

Christchurch City Council (CCC) and Waimakariri District Council (WMK). Because of this and a rebuild cost of over $40 billion, an external coordinating body was seen as necessary to manage the 'the political and fiscal risks involved' (Brookie 2012, p. 28). Whilst some countries have standing organisations that undertake this role (e.g. the Federal Emergency Management

Figure 32.3 'Greening the Rubble' puts temporary parks on vacant sites

Source: Vallance.

Agency (FEMA) in the US) the New Zealand government established the Canterbury Earthquake Recovery Authority (CERA), answerable to the Minister for Earthquake recovery, Gerry Brownlee.

CERA is a controversial entity because, through the CER Act of 2011, the minister has extraordinary decision-making powers. The CER Act gives the minister the ability to suspend, amend, cancel (or) delay ECan, CCC or WMK plans or policies. These local councils' recovery plans must be consistent with CERA's recovery strategy and signed off by the minister (Brookie 2012). While this *may* have expedited rapid decision-making, some are concerned about the suspension of citizens' rights and the lack of a layer of governance between CERA and the right-leaning central government National party. CERA's practice has been described as 'top-down, centralised, and highly bureaucratic' (Brookie 2012, p. 29), with public involvement limited to token consultation rather than empowered or delegated decision-making as seen in various typologies (for example the IAP2's *Spectrum of Participation* (www.IAP2.org) as used by CERA 2012a, p. 16).

Within this rather controversial context, CERA has taken responsibility for either the development, or final approval, of numerous recovery plans and strategies including the Central City Recovery Plan, the regional Land Use Recovery Plan and the Greater Christchurch Recovery Strategy as detailed below.

The Greater Christchurch Recovery Strategy

The Recovery Strategy (CERA 2012a) is a high level document setting out how the recovery of greater Christchurch (including Waimakariri) will be achieved, primarily by establishing principles guiding how CERA and other agencies (such as the affected local councils) will work together. It describes the pace and phases of recovery; identifies work programmes, and which organisations will lead to specific projects; identifies priorities for recovery efforts; sets up governance structures to oversee and coordinate the work programmes and links them to wider initiatives; and commits to measuring and reporting on progress towards recovery.

The strategy identifies five recovery components – cultural, social, built, natural (including geotechnical considerations) and economic – that link together, with a sixth component – community – at the centre. The recovery process is divided into immediate (repair, patch, plan), short-term (rebuild, replace and reconstruct) and medium to long-term phases (construct, restore and improve) phases, each with attendant milestones (for details, see CERA, 2012a, p. 9).

While this provides strategic oversight, the actual implementation of the strategy is to be enacted through a series of other plans.

The Land Use Recovery Plan

Pre-quake, from 2004 to 2007, ECan facilitated the creation of the Greater Christchurch Urban Development Strategy ('the UDS') to guide regional growth over the next 30 years. Based on over 3,250 submissions and collaboration between ECan, CCC, WMK and neighbouring Selwyn District Council, the UDS vision, guiding principles, strategic direction and a framework for implementation had been given statutory weight in Chapter 12 of ECan's Regional Policy Statement in 2010, just prior to the first earthquake.

While the UDS enabled a fairly rapid appraisal of available land to be made, widespread land damage and the discovery of fault lines demanded some refinements. In November 2012, the Minister for Canterbury Earthquake Recovery directed ECan (at their request) to prepare a draft Land Use Recovery Plan ('the LURP', CERA 2012b). Consultation identified some key areas of initial concern including tensions around market-led development and appropriate regulation, council land-use consent processes, greenfield versus brownfield development, housing affordability, infrastructure, public transport and suburban centres (AERU 2012).

The difficulties and politics of 'building back better' pervade this document. As noted above, while CERA provides oversight on recovery, much of the implementation falls to local councils and they have different views of 'betterment'. As an example, tension has been particularly high between CERA over their new 'design-led' Comprehensive Development Mechanisms (CDMs) which would see high density housing throughout the city, and the CCC who believe the public have not been adequately informed. Given even medium density housing has a controversial history in Christchurch (Vallance et al. 2005) the CCC has argued for better consultation over the issue and for CDMs to be limited to certain zones. As another example, integrating various plans documenting where, when and how to build back better has been difficult for, although the LURP guides regional recovery, it explicitly does *not* address the CBD of Christchurch.

The (Christchurch) Central City Recovery Plan: the blueprint

Following the 22 February earthquake which led to the demolition of over 60 per cent of building stock in the CBD, the CCC began developing a draft Central City Plan (CCP) for the central city. In May 2011, the CCC initiated the six week *Share an Idea* campaign in order for 'the public to tell us their ideas about how the Central City should be redeveloped to be a great place again . . .'[2] Combining a weekend of on-site opportunities and an online crowdsourcing tool, the campaign generated more than 106,000 ideas from over 60,000 participants. These ideas were analysed so as to inform the draft CCP and guide inner city development for the next 10–20 years.

Following this and a number of other, smaller workshops, the draft CCP was signed off in August 2011 before being sent to the Minister for Earthquake Recovery for approval. The minister's view (as outlined on the council's website[3]) was that 'taking into account its impact, effect and funding implications, [the Plan] could not be approved without amendment . . . given insufficient information . . . on how the Recovery Plan would be implemented and changes to the District Plan that [are] unnecessarily complex.'

Consequently, the minister established a special unit within CERA, the Christchurch Central Development Unit (CCDU) which, working with a 'professional consortium', was given 100 days to finalise the Plan and take a lead role in its implementation. The Central City Recovery Plan (CCDU 2012) is based on a masterplanned blueprint of the CBD providing street layout, the location of 'anchor' projects (including a convention centre and sports facility), and various precincts which, they hope, will stimulate further development.

Despite a lack of public involvement in the CCDU's 100 Day Plan and controversial compulsory land acquisition to enable the anchor projects to go ahead, the Plan's executive summary states that, 'The city centre [will be] . . . a reflection of where we have come from, and a vision of what we want to become.' Yet, the tension between substantive public involvement and timeliness is evident as it is claimed that 'the experience of other cities after a natural disaster shows that substantial redevelopment must start within three years if recovery is to be successful. One year has passed. Speed is of the essence . . .' (CCDU 2012, p. 4).

So pervasive is the tension between timeliness and the lack of public participation in Christchurch's recovery, questions are raised about what engagement 'best practice' might look like, how best practice should be evaluated, and by whom. To address this question, I turn now to an example of where this tension was addressed with more success.

The Waimakariri District Council's integrated and community-based Recovery Framework

The Waimakariri District is adjacent to the city of Christchurch with a population of about 50,000 people. It has traditionally been described as agricultural with large farms, lifestyle blocks and smallholdings devoted to horticulture; however, a few settlements have grown rapidly and now form a commuter corridor of townships, with many residents travelling to work in Christchurch each day. After the September 2010 earthquake, parts of the Kaiapoi township suffered extensive land damage with over 1,000 homes and the town centre severely affected. The damage, *proportionally*, was similar to that experienced in Christchurch, but their recovery strategy has been quite different (see Vallance 2013 for details).

Within two months of the first quake, three new recovery manager positions (general, social and infrastructure/engineering) were established and deployed to 'the Hub'. The Hub was designed to be a 'one-stop recovery shop' at the coalface, in Kaiapoi. The Hub housed the council's pre-quake Kaiapoi Service Centre staff, some of the council's Building Unit and Community Team usually located in Rangiora, and a dedicated earthquake communications manager. The Hub also accommodated many different non-council services ranging from the Inland Revenue Department (IRD) dealing with tax, to the 15 Waimakariri Earthquake Support Service Co-ordinators who, in the first two years, assisted between 400 and 600 cases with accommodation, and helped with earthquake claims, legal aid and counseling for earthquake stress. This co-location was fundamental to their integrated, community-based recovery strategy. It facilitated communication between the Social Recovery and Infrastructure Recovery Managers which, in turn, helped the engineering and utilities teams to appreciate the positive and negative impacts of their work, and for residents to better understand what engineers and other experts were doing, and why. It also enabled community intelligence to inform infrastructural recovery. This became important in the face of both the neighbourhood infrastructure rebuild programme (involving approximately 1,200 households, broken down into smaller clusters for rebuild in different stages) and the Kaiapoi Town Centre recovery plan.

While it is difficult to make direct comparisons between Christchurch and Waimakariri given the different contexts, satisfaction with the WMK's recovery framework is high with endorsements from the Minister for Earthquake Recovery, Residents' Association representatives and an evaluation from an independent working group (as reported in Vallance 2013). Population movements are also telling: Waimakariri is now one of the fastest growing regions in the country, with many of the District's new residents emigrating from Christchurch. Residents' confidence in the two councils may also be reflected in the most recent local government elections of October 2013. In the Waimakariri District, nine of ten councillors were re-elected with the mayor unchallenged. In Christchurch only four of thirteen were re-elected (with the mayor and two others resigning).

Lessons from Canterbury

The Canterbury earthquake case study highlights some important lessons, not only for those involved in recovery planning, but for *all* planners whose activities implicitly seek to reduce risk in order to build a more resilient city. Indeed, the first 'lesson' may be to challenge, or at least more carefully interrogate, the supposed distinction between 'peacetime planning' and 'disaster management' more specifically. Whether we are looking at land use, urban form or the location of infrastructure (above and below ground), a good deal of planning practice is directed at reducing, mitigating or eliminating risk. Even pre-quake urban growth and development strategies – like the UDS – can be seen as usefully informing recovery plans, particularly if hazard assessments are included.

Although it is tempting to now embark on a discussion of the implications for the correct scale of such plans and their implementation, the range of hazards and their potential impacts indicates a need for more comparative research across different settings and disaster contexts before drawing firm conclusions. Instead, a second lesson we might tentatively draw from the Canterbury case study is that there are likely to be issues around the integration of recovery plans over different scales, and that there may be tension between the recovery agencies who implement them. The capacity, capability and coordination of potential mixes of different actors therefore deserve as much attention as the identification of hazards.

If the inference from all this for planners generally is 'start planning for disaster risk reduction in peacetime', an implication for recovery planners is to look beyond disaster management scholarship to better understand the 'politics of planning' (e.g. Flyvbjerg 1998). Plans are the result of *process* but there is perhaps no other time when planning is so dominated by a rational, technical, expert discourse than in the post-disaster context. While recovery plans should, no doubt, be informed by expert volcanologists, geotechnical engineers, or nuclear physicists, depending on the type of disaster, this can be used to privilege some approaches to recovery over others . . . Or give the appearance of doing so as it did in New Orleans post-Katrina.

So what can the Canterbury case study add to this emerging strand of more critical disaster management around the process underpinning plans? First, relying on ad hoc entities like CERA may result in delays while the organisation builds capacity and capability. There may also be delays while the recovery authority builds participatory pathways that enable adequate public involvement in decision-making. This situation can be made worse if the ad hoc authority assumes some of the roles of pre-existing organisations, like local councils, to which residents might naturally turn for decisions and information.

Second, the decision-making powers – *including the authority to define what recovery means* – needs very careful thought. Whilst placing decision-making authority in one person – in this case the Minister for Earthquake Recovery – has made decision-making pathways clearer, it has also created a bottleneck and may be impeding broader recovery. Ironically, too much clarity (e.g. in the form of the CCDU's masterplanned blueprint for the CBD) may stifle organic, grassroots attempts to recover. It is currently unclear as to whether or not the minister/CCDU's vision for Christchurch and the CBD resonates sufficiently with the wider public and potential investors. A lack of confidence in the plan has led to suggestions that the recovery of the CBD – or, rather, implementation of the blueprint – has stalled (McCrone 2014).

Finally, the best practice seen in the Waimakariri District raises interesting questions about whether or not their approach can be *upscaled* to larger metropolitan areas. Or perhaps it may be more appropriate to ask how larger cities might effectively *downsize* their recovery frameworks to a scale that seems to work well. Or perhaps, once again, an emphasis on form and scale detracts from more fundamental issues around process. The Hub, and the management structure that supported it, facilitated good communication flows between community and council, and enabled synergistic decision-making to be enacted both at head offices in Rangiora and at the coalface in Kaiapoi. This 'distributed' style of decision-making and communication helped address the challenge that plagues, and often stalls, recovery; that is, striking the balance between timeliness and transparency.

In parallel with suggestions above that recovery plans can begin before an event (through growth strategies like the UDS, inventories of physical assets including infrastructure, and information about geotechnical, industrial, atmospheric or coastal hazards, etc.), so too can recovery planning processes, by gaining experience with deliberative and inclusive participatory processes and a working relationship with potential partners.

As Hayward (2013) has noted, based on her experience as a social scientist and resident of Christchurch, the axiomatic question of resilience thinking – the 'resilience of what, to what' – ought to be recast as the 'resilience of what, *for whom*'. The Canterbury case study certainly indicates a need to look more closely at what a resilient city might entail, in terms of both form *and* process, that speaks to risk reduction *and* recovery.

Notes

1 www.stuff.co.nz/national/christchurch-earthquake/4711189/Tuesday-quake-no-aftershock
2 www.ccc.govt.nz/homeliving/civildefence/chchearthquake/ShareAnIdea.aspx
3 www.ccc.govt.nz/homeliving/civildefence/chchearthquake/centralcityplan.aspx

References

AERU. 2012. *Land use recovery plan consultation report*. Lincoln University, PO Box 85084, Lincoln 7647, Christchurch, New Zealand.

Agamben, G. 2005. *State of exception*. Chicago: Chicago University Press.

Allmendinger, P. 2002. Towards a post-positivist typology of planning theory. *Planning Theory* 1, 77–99.

Beck, U. 2009. *World at risk*. Cambridge: Polity Press.

Brookie, R. 2012. *Governing the recovery from the Canterbury earthquakes 2010–11: the debate over institutional design*. Institute for Governance and Policy Studies, Victoria University, Victoria University of Wellington, PO Box 600, Wellington, New Zealand.

CCDU (Christchurch Central Development Unit). 2012. *The plan*. Available at: http://ccdu.govt.nz/the-plan, accessed December 2013.

CERA (Canterbury Earthquake Recovery Authority). 2012a. *The Greater Christchurch recovery strategy*. Available at: http://cera.govt.nz/sites/cera.govt.nz/files/common/recovery-strategy-for-greater-christchurch.pdf, accessed December 2013.

CERA. 2012b. *The land use recovery plan.* Available at: http://cera.govt.nz/recovery-strategy/built-environment/land-and-land-use/land-use-recovery-plan#view, accessed December 2013.

Flyvbjerg, B. 1998. *Rationality and power.* Chicago: University of Chicago Press.

Gotham, K. and Greenberg, M. 2008. From 9/11 to 8/29: post-disaster recovery and rebuilding in New York and New Orleans. *Social Forces* 87(2), 1039–1062.

Hayward, B. 2013. Rethinking the politics of resilience. A paper presented at the New Zealand Political Studies Association conference, Christchurch, 2–3 December.

IPCC. 2013. *Climate change 2013: the physical science basis.* Contribution of Working Group I to the Fifth Assessment Report of the Intergovernmental Panel on Climate Change. T.F. Stocker, D. Qin, G.-K. Plattner, M. Tignor, S.K. Allen, J. Boschung, A. Nauels, Y. Xia, V. Bex and P.M. Midgley (eds.). Cambridge, UK and New York: Cambridge University Press.

Klein, N. 2007. *The shock doctrine: the rise of disaster capitalism.* Picador: New York.

Lorenz, D. 2011. The diversity of resilience: contributions from a social science perspective. *Natural Hazards,* online first, www.springerlink.com/content/jp68pv2185320301

McClennen, S. 2012. Neoliberalism as terrorism; or state of disaster exceptionalism. In J. Di Leo and U. Mehan (eds.). *Terror, theory and the humanities,* pp. 178–195. University of Michigan Library, Ann Arbor: Open Humanities Press.

McCrone, J. 2014. Christchurch rebuild: a city stalled. *The Press.* Available at: www.stuff.co.nz/the-press/business/the-rebuild/9805314/Christchurch-rebuild-A-city-stalled, accessed March 2014.

Montgomery, R. 2014. Bringing natural hazard and disaster management planning into mainstream urban and regional planning. In *UHPH_14: Landscapes and ecologies of urban and planning history.* Proceedings of the 12th conference of the Australasian Urban History, University of Wellington.

Olshansky, R. and Johnson, L. 2010. *Clear as mud: planning for the rebuilding of New Orleans.* Chicago and Washington: APA Planners Press.

Patel, R. and Burke, T. 2009. Urbanization: an emerging humanitarian disaster. *New England Journal of Medicine,* 361, 741–743.

Vallance, S. 2013. *The Waimakariri District Council's integrated, community-based recovery framework.* Available at: http://hdl.handle.net/10182/5512, accessed 8 April 2015.

Vallance, S., Perkins, H.C. and Moore, K. 2005. The results of making a city more compact: neighbours' interpretation of urban infill. *Environment and Planning B: Planning and Design* 32(5), 715–733.

Walker, B. and Salt, D. 2006. *Resilience thinking: sustaining people and ecosystems in a changing world.* Washington, DC: Island Press.

33

THE DEVELOPMENT OF A HEALTHY AGEING PROGRAMME IN TAIWAN

Tzu-Yuan Stessa Chao

The ageing phenomenon and healthy ageing issues

The rapid increase in the ageing population has become a global phenomenon. Over the next three decades, the 'baby boomers' will enter their 60s, and, by 2050, the global population will reach a peak of 20 billion (WHO 2007). According to the United Nations (UN), this increase will be greatest and most rapid in developing countries, where the older population is expected to quadruple. Rapid declines in both the fertility and mortality rates also result in disproportionate changes within the population. These demographic trends are creating new challenges for our urban and rural environments. To address these challenges, cross-disciplinary research between medical, social and spatial sciences is required.

The ideas of 'healthy ageing', 'active ageing' and 'ageing in place' (Figure 33.1) have been strongly advocated by the World Health Organization (WHO) and the UN in order to promote better living situations for older population since the late 1990s. In 2007, the WHO officially initiated the Age-Friendly Cities Project and published *Global Age-Friendly Cities: A Guide* which identified eight key domains for establishing an 'age-friendly city'. The goal is to deliver a living environment that supports active ageing. As such the eight domains include issues regarding outdoor spaces and buildings, transportation, housing, social participation, respect and social inclusion, civic participation and employment, communication and information, community support and health services. Since December of 2009, the 'Global Age-Friendly Cities Network' has officially operated. In 2014, over 100 cities in the world have participated in the network. Taiwan initiated its involvement in this project in April 2010. Based on the WHO's active age-friendly city model, each city has developed its own framework and action plans. By the end of 2013, all 22 city mayors in Taiwan had announced their political commitment to this movement.

Towards a silver society in Taiwan

In Taiwan, as is the case in many Asian countries, the presence of high-density and mixed-use urban areas makes the environment not particularly age-friendly. In 2008, the population aged over 65 exceeded 10.3 per cent of the total population and, according to projections, by 2017 the population over 65 will exceed 14 per cent (Figure 33.2). As many studies have indicated, the rapid population ageing in developing countries results in serious issues, including causing tremendous pressure on medical systems, social welfare systems and contributing to overall socio–economic conflicts (WHO 2007; Council for Economic Planning and Development, Taiwan 2008).

According to Taiwan's demographic data, the speed at which the population reaches an 'ageing society' will be much faster than expected. Figure 33.3 illustrates a population projection done by the Council of Economic Planning and Development in Taiwan. Accordingly, it is clear that it will only take 25 years for Taiwan to become an 'aged society' (for comparison it

Term	Definition	Determinants
Healthy ageing	'Healthy aging is the development and maintenance of optimal mental, social, and physical well-being and function in older adults. This will most likely be achieved when communities are safe, promote health and well-being and use health services and community programs to prevent or minimize disease' (Minnesota Department of Health 2006: 2).	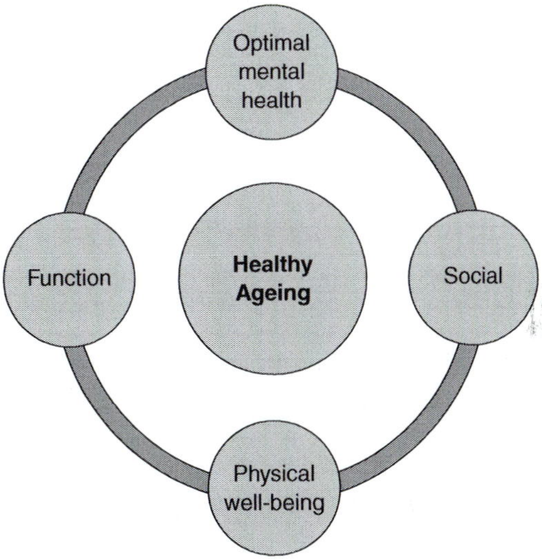 *Source*: Chao.
Active ageing	'Active ageing is the process of optimizing opportunities for health, participation and security in order to enhance quality of life as people age' (WHO 2002).	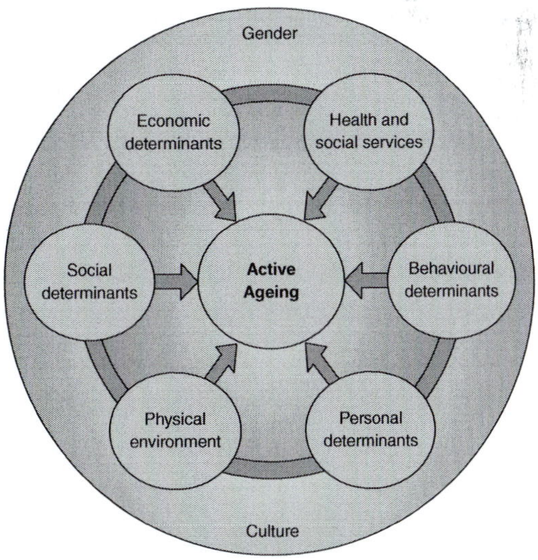 *Source*: Chao.

Figure 33.1 (continued)

Figure 33.1 (continued)

Ageing in place	'The ability to live in one's own home and community safely, independently, and comfortably, regardless of age, income, or ability level' (Centers for Disease Control and Prevention 2013).	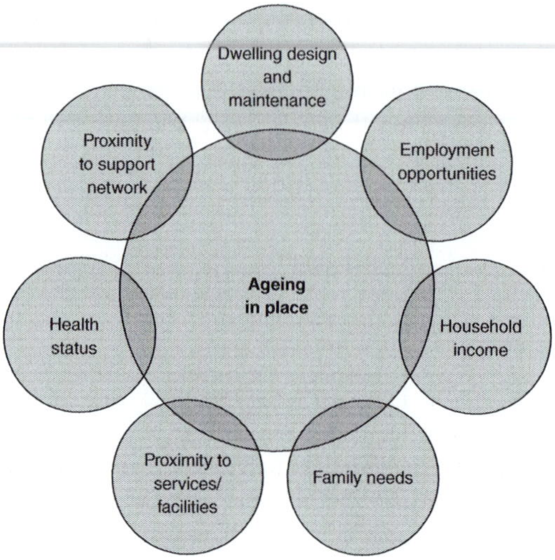 Source: Adapted from Public Health Agency of Canada 2012 by Chao.
Ageing society	7–14% of the population are 65 years or older (Coulmas 2007: 5)	
Aged society	14–21% of the population are 65 years or older (Coulmas 2007: 5)	
Hyper-aged society	21% or more of the population are 65 years or older (Coulmas 2007: 5)	

Figure 33.1 Key terms and definitions relating to healthy ageing

Source: WHO (2002); Minnesota Department of Health (2006); Coulmas (2007); Public Health Agency of Canada (2012); Centers for Disease Control and Prevention (2013).

will take 115 years for France and 73 years for the UK). The rapid ageing situation in Taiwan suggests that socio-economic resource distributions and spatial development patterns will need to change in the near future. The majority of the population in Taiwan will not have pensions after retirement, which means that many older people will be faced with stressful lives in their old age. More concerns also arise regarding the burden of such a large number of older people on Taiwan's health care and social welfare systems.

Coupled with these challenges, Taiwan is a small country, but there are significant differences between urban and rural areas. As has been the case with most prospering countries in Asia, rapid urbanisation, large migration of young people to cities in search of jobs, and more women entering the formal workforce has further resulted in unbalanced population distributions between the urban and rural areas. For example, according to the latest census, the overall old-age dependency ratio (i.e. the population aged 0–14 and that aged 65 or over, divided by the population aged 15–64) in Taiwan reached 0.65 in 2009, while in a rural area, Chia-Yi County, the old-age dependency ratio had already reached 0.79, which is the highest in Taiwan (Ministry of the Interior Taiwan 2009). In comparison with another Asian country, the UN has stated that by 2025, the overall old-age dependency ratio in Japan will be only 0.70 (United Nations 2002; Ogawa and Matsukura 2007).

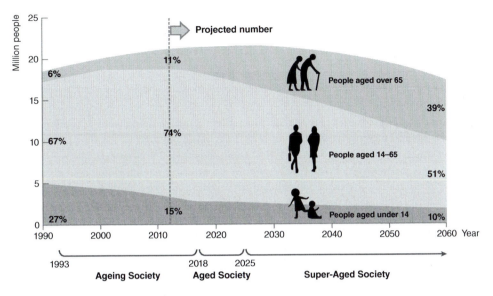

Figure 33.2   The population trend in Taiwan

Source: Council for Economic Planning and Development, Taiwan, 2012. Image: Tzu-Yuan Stessa Chao.

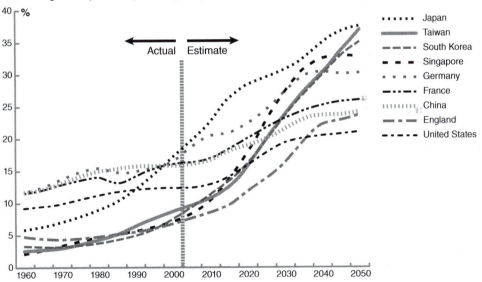

Figure 33.3   The rate of ageing populations in different countries

Source: Council for Economic Planning and Development, Taiwan, 2012. Image: Tzu-Yuan Stessa Chao.

While it is clear that the older population in urban areas will encounter different difficulties from those populations in the rural areas, the ageing phenomenon in rural areas has posed more serious challenges environmentally and socio-economically for public sectors where resources are fewer.

Ageing in place

The concept of 'ageing in place' is derived from the theory of environmental gerontology, which was conceptualised half century ago and was intended to research and optimise the inter-action between the elderly and their living environment (Wahl 2001; Schwartz and Scheidt 2013). Environmental gerontology usually is concerned with environmental arrangements for the elderly, from indoor housing spaces to outdoor settings. In the past two decades, both the research and practical experience in the field of environmental gerontology have confirmed that in order to address the real-world issues of older individuals and their environment, there must be an awareness of a variety of social-physical conditions faced by older individuals focused at the local level (Schwarz and Scheidt 2013). Furthermore, many studies undertaken in the field of public health have also indicated that there is an urgent need for promoting ageing in place in Taiwan in terms of reducing costs for caretakers and enhancing community support mechanisms (Chang et al. 2002). Also, Lin indicated the importance of enhancing community social care services and channelling with local medical resources in order to satisfy the needs of the elderly at the community level (Lin 2003, 2010).

Researchers on this topic have acknowledged that the ultimate goal for the age-friendly society in Taiwan should be to encourage older people to stay healthy, independent, and stay in the same community for as long as possible. Accordingly, one of the national major studies conducted from 2010 to 2011 by the Health Promotion Administration, Ministry of Health and Welfare in Taiwan, started to explore and analyse the issues of the interactions between the elderly and living environments from the perspective of the eight domains proposed by the WHO Age-Friendly Cities Project. Figure 33.4 indicates the most important of these issues.

The Age-Friendly Cities framework and policy in Taiwan

In response to the ageing phenomenon, the Ministry of Health in Taiwan recognised the impor-tance of the Age-Friendly Cities Project and establishing a cross-sector framework to promote this project. As part of a broader concept, the central government has also acknowledged that it is essential to create a more suitable and coherent living environment rather than only creating living units for the elderly.

Age-friendly city domain	Importance to age-friendly city	Key local issues	Photos
Outdoor spaces and public buildings	As key features of a city's physical environment, these three domains have a strong influence on individual mobility, safety from injury, security from crime, health behaviour and social participation.	1. Urban outdoor spaces are not friendly to older people. 2. Most public spaces are suitable for younger users and seldom consider older people's needs, such as stairs, lighting and size of signage, etc. 3. Poor walking environment. 4. Public facilities below expectations.	*Source*: Tzu-Yuan Stessa Chao.

Transportation		1. Lack of reliable public transportation provision in rural areas. 2. Poor public transportation services in urban areas. 3. Very high dependency on private vehicles and scooters. 4. Lack of choice of transportation in mid-size cities.	 Source: Tzu-Yuan Stessa Chao.
Housing		1. Affordability issue. 2. Lack of choice: over two thirds of the elderly stay with their families. 3. Lack of supportive interior equipment such as handrails, safety facilities and elevators.	 Source: Tzu-Yuan Stessa Chao.
Social participation	Social participation refers to the engagement of older people in recreation, socialisation, and cultural, educational and spiritual activities.	1. Opportunities for social participation are not evenly distributed. 2. Lack of a variety of activities. 3. Lack of sufficient information about activities.	 Source: Tzu-Yuan Stessa Chao.
Respect and social inclusion	Respect and social inclusion deals with the attitudes, behaviour and messages of other people and of the community as a whole towards older people.	1. Ageism usually occurs in poor communities with lower educational levels. 2. Public servants fail to give special attention to the older population. 3. Neglect of the importance of cross-generational activities.	 Source: Tzu-Yuan Stessa Chao.

Figure 33.4 (continued)

Figure 33.4 (continued)

Civic partnership and employment	Civic participation and employment addresses opportunities for citizenship, unpaid work and paid work; it is related to both the social environment and to the economic determinants of active ageing.	1. Ageism in the work environment. 2. Lack of equal opportunities and payment. 3. Lack of job training or lifetime education systems to maintain an ageing population with up-to-date work skills.	 *Source*: Tzu-Yuan Stessa Chao.
Communication and information	Communication and information and community support and health services involve both social environments and health and social service determinants.	1. Information availability varies in urban and rural areas. 2. Low percentage of older PC users. 3. High victim rate from information fraud.	 *Source*: Tzu-Yuan Stessa Chao.
Community support and health service		1. Rural county governments often fail to spend 80% of the annual budget in the health service sector due to manpower shortages. 2. Affordability of medication. 3. Difficulties with connecting health care resources to each community.	 *Source*: Tzu-Yuan Stessa Chao.

Figure 33.4 Age-friendly domains and local issues in Taiwan cities

Sources: WHO (2007) and Ministry of Health and Welfare (2010). Images: Tzu-Yuan Stessa Chao.

The programme comprised three phases. The first phase was focused on understanding and promoting the age-friendly concept to stakeholders, including the elderly, the public sector, academics and non-profit departments. A thorough study of the overall ageing issues was also conducted. In the second phase, a general assessment checklist, based on the WHO age-friendly city checklist, was developed through a series of studies. And in the third phase, cities in Taiwan were recruited to participate in this project to explore their own tasks at the local level by first developing a local assessment checklist and then developing age-friendly initiatives.

The national vision of the age-friendly city programme is to reemphasise traditional Confucianism, in which the elderly are respected, and to create a city where every elderly citizen is treated like the parent of all younger city residents (see Figure 33.5).

In the meantime, a series of research projects began from April 2010 at both national and local levels. Both qualitative and quantitative methods were used, including focus group interviews, and over 3,200 telephone interviews were conducted with the elderly in Taiwan. The

Figure 33.5   The national vision of an age-friendly city in Taiwan

Source: Ministry of Health and Welfare (2010). Image: Tzu-Yuan Stessa Chao.

Taiwan indicator system provides a tool to assess the level of age-friendliness and identifies the level of urgency for improvements in addition to assisting in the development of age-friendly cities in Taiwan.

The age-friendly framework and policy in Chia-Yi City

In order to establish a comprehensive framework for age-friendly promotion, in March 2011 Mayor Huang of Chia-Yi City, a city in southern Taiwan, announced this city as the first age-friendly model city in Taiwan. After working in conjunction with an academic research team, the Healthy City Research Center, and National Cheng-Kung University for three years, the city of Chia-Yi won the 'Best Age-Friendly City Practice Award 2013' in Taiwan and was considered to be one of the best comprehensive models following the WHO age-friendly city framework. The major achievements of this city are as follows:

1. *Establishment of local framework*: over 400 older citizens from different age cohorts were involved in the community meetings, focus group interviews and questionnaire surveys during the research phase (Figure 33.6). The city also established the Age-Friendly Chia-Yi City Task Force led by the mayor. This task force invited dozens of older representatives to continue their participation in the following phases to make sure the implementation met the expectations of older citizens. It included directors of all the departments in the city, important local non-government organisations (NGOs), non-profit organisation groups, political representatives and academic experts. The task force forms a strong information exchange platform and serves an executive role in promoting age-friendly city initiatives.

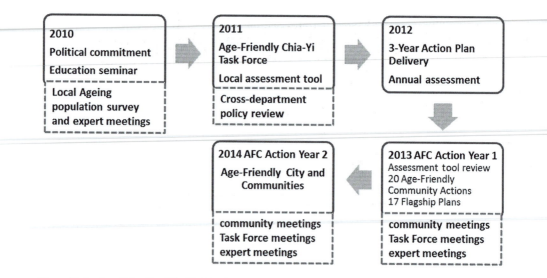

Figure 33.6   Age-Friendly Chia-Yi City Program

Source: Tzu-Yuan Stessa Chao.

2. *The bottom-up mechanism*: recognising the importance of understanding the local characteristics of the ageing population in terms of age, background, household structure
and socio-economic status, the research team undertook 1,600 telephone interviews.
These interviews explored the satisfaction level of older citizens towards the eight age-
friendly domains in Taiwan. This was followed by dozens of community meetings at
the local level in Chia-Yi City, four focus group meetings and questionnaire surveys
involving over 600 local older participants. This local, bottom-up approach is important to the task force and the age-friendly city initiative. Empowering the elderly is a
process and should be part of a changing strategy (Tseng 2003). In 2013, this approach
was further extended to an additional 20 communities in Chia Yi City. Each led by
community leaders, the 20 communities sought to identify and understand their own
age-friendly tasks and to develop and implement unique action plans focusing on different
age-friendly city domains. Over the two-year collaboration, over 50 age-friendly
pharmacy stores, over 20 age-friendly restaurants and 4 age-friendly hospitals participated in the programme (Figure 33.7).

3. *The local self-assessment and action plans*: community meetings, interviews and surveys were
conducted to identify local issues in accordance with the recommendations in the WHO
(2007) age-friendly cities guide. This informed the local checklist developed in 2011. In
order to facilitate the best possible response to the self-assessment, Mayor Huang ensured
that all action plans secured funding from the annual city budget. Resources from central
government and the private sector have also been utilised. After three years, in 2013, the
task force initiated a review process to revise the checklist. The revision reflected the annual
local demand survey results and the policy implementation outcomes.

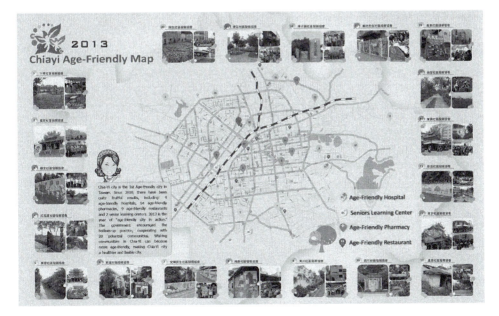

Figure 33.7   Chia-Yi Age-Friendly Map

Source: Healthy City Research Center (2013). Image: Tzu-Yuan Stessa Chao.

A total of 36 three-year action plans were first proposed in 2011, and until 2013, 17 have been selected as flagship projects.

Age-friendly places local design tool

In order to understand the needs of the elderly and their perceptions of public spaces, an age-friendly and barrier-free environment research project was conducted in 2013. Data was collected to gain a clear idea of the needs of the elderly and the results were used to develop design guidelines. According to the *Taiwan age-friendly city evaluation system and implementation project* (Ministry of Health and Welfare 2010), the average satisfaction level for three age-friendly city domains (outdoor spaces and buildings, transportation and housing) was very high. Within each domain, specific issues with higher and lower satisfaction levels were also specified (Figure 33.8).

In 2012, the Ministry of the Interior published *Regulation on the accessible housing design basis and incentives* to regulate the scope and design of accessible housing. This was intended to correspond with the major structural changes occurring in the population at that time. However, in terms of establishing an age-friendly environment, these regulations are limited to buildings and interior design and lack consideration of the larger spatial scale (Figure 33.9).

The idea of an age-friendly city contains concepts that take into consideration both the physical and the psychological needs of the elderly. Hence, three concepts were adopted, namely age friendly, barrier-free and universal design in the process of developing the design guidelines. Different from existing spatial design guidelines, this research aimed to establish design guidance that could reflect the real physical condition of the elderly in local communities that may vary from place to place. Six universal principles for inclusive design were used to

Domain	Issues with higher levels of satisfaction	Issues with lower levels of satisfaction
Outdoor spaces and buildings	The amount of outdoor open space provided, such as parks, green spaces and town squares.	Accessible road designs, traffic signs and lighting facilities provided.
Transportation	Public transportation services provided, such as the frequency of buses.	The bicycle lanes provided.
		Nice transportation environment provided, such as environments for walking, cycling and taking buses.
		Services provided for the purpose of linking urban and suburban areas.
Housing	Convenience of living facilities, such as the level of suitability to elderly individuals.	Care and services provided by groups or organisations inside the community
	The amount of medical institutions inside the community, such as hospitals and clinics.	

Figure 33.8   Issues with higher levels of satisfaction

Source: Ministry of Health and Welfare (2010). Image: Tzu-Yuan Stessa Chao.

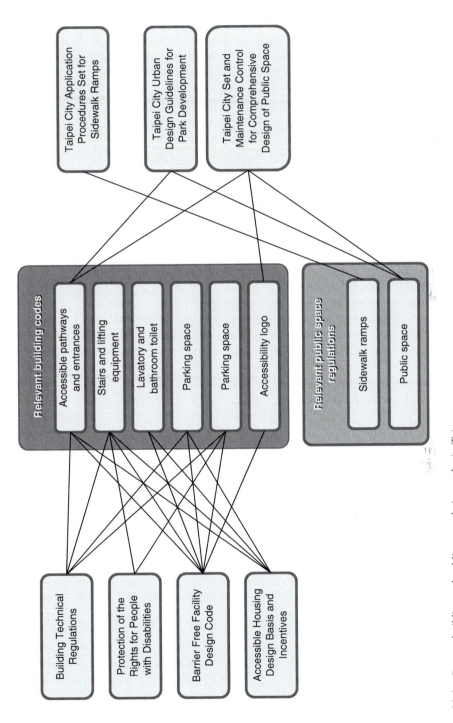

Figure 33.9 Current building and public space design codes in Taiwan

Source: Architecture and Building Research Institute (2013). Image: Tzu-Yuan Stessa Chao.

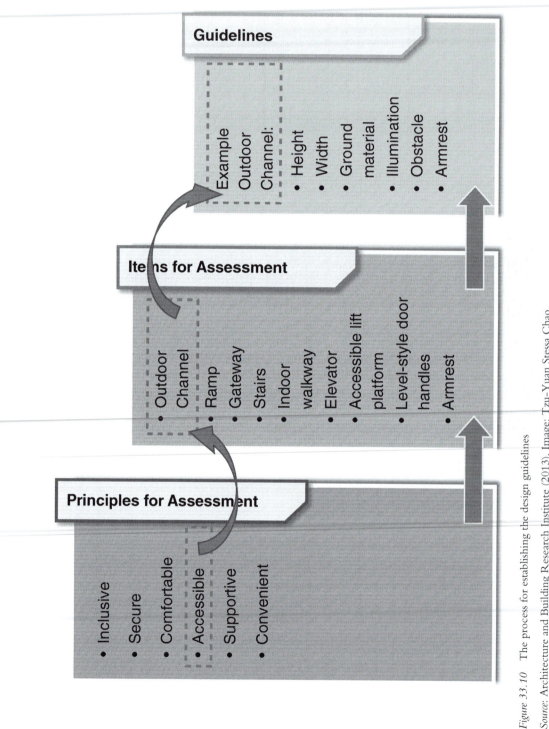

Figure 33.10 The process for establishing the design guidelines

Source: Architecture and Building Research Institute (2013). Image: Tzu-Yuan Stessa Chao.

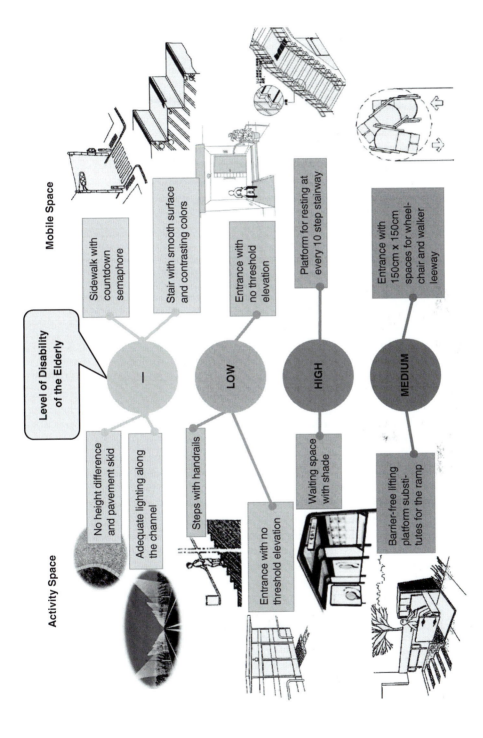

Figure 33.11 A paradigm for barrier-free public spaces improvement levels referring to the physical condition of the elderly

Source: Architecture and Building Research Institute (2013). Image: Tzu-Yuan Stessa Chao.

identify local and relevant items for assessment in public spaces with higher elderly use rates. From these assessments, specific design guidelines were established based on the local types and spatial characteristics of different public spaces (Figure 33.10). In addition, the different degrees of physical disability of elderly individuals were also taken into consideration in the guidelines. These guidelines were then tested with experts and in the local community. This ensures that local conditions are considered and addressed whilst maintaining the universal principles for inclusivity.

A self-assessment framework was also developed from the Barthel Index of Activities of Daily Living (Mahoney and Barthel 1965) and the Physical Activity Scale for the Elderly (Washburn et al. 1993). By undertaking the community self-assessment, elderly people could reflect their own level of disability and the convenience level of public spaces. This helps the elderly to quickly and easily specify their needs and the areas that need improvement. The research differentiated between community open spaces that were used for activity ('activity space') and those spaces that were used for mobility ('mobile space'). The design guidelines for both of these categories also identify design features that correspond to the average levels of disability of the elderly in the community (Figure 33.11).

The positive contribution of empowerment

This chapter introduced the ageing phenomenon in Taiwan and how the issue is addressed from different perspectives. The involvement of all stakeholders is paramount to achieving age-friendly cities and active ageing. The evaluation tools and design principles not only provide a great standard to identify the key determinants of achieving active-ageing environments but also promote a global context of health and sustainability. Policy makers and planners must acknowledge the two-way contribution that an older population and sustainable cities can provide for each other and must endeavour to develop ageing-friendly city agendas. The positive contribution that older people can make to society should be recognised, as well as the efforts they have made for their own old age, through pension provision, savings and investment in their homes, as well as the valuable contribution they make, both within their own families and in the wider society, through volunteering in and caring about their communities.

In conclusion, adopting bottom-up 'community empowerment' and 'empowerment of the elderly' approaches has proved an effective method by which to achieve age-friendly communities in Taiwan. By empowering both the elderly and communities, older individuals are able to have their needs met, a fact which encourages them to participate in wider community affairs. During the participation process, they acquire the power to change their local environment and can in turn use this power to both change and fulfil their requirements. Thus, an age-friendly community led by the elderly can be achieved.

Acknowledgements

Some materials adopted in this chapter are from different research projects individually funded by the Health Promotion Administration, Ministry of Health and Welfare; Chia-Yi City Government, Architecture and Building Research Institute, the Ministry of the Interior, and National Cheng Kung University in Taiwan. The contributors include Ms. Tsai-Ling Shih, Ms. Hui-Wen Huang, and Ms. Yu-Wei Chang.

References

Architecture and Building Research Institute, Ministry of the Interior Taiwan. 2013. *Taiwan age-friendly public space design guidance research project final report*. Taipei: Architecture and Building Research Institute, Ministry of the Interior Taiwan.

Centers for Disease Control and Prevention. 2013. Healthy places terminology. Available at: www.cdc.gov/healthyplaces/terminology.htm, accessed 29 August 2014.

Chang, R., Lin, W.I. and Wang, Y.T. 2002. *Compare the social work systems in every country of the world and survey assessment study for social work manpower demand in Taiwan*. Taipei: Ministry of Internal Affairs Taiwan.

Coulmas, F. 2007. *Population decline and ageing in Japan: the social consequences*. Oxon: Routledge.

Council for Economic Planning and Development, Taiwan. 2008. *The population projection from 2008 to 2056 in Taiwan*. Taipei City: Council for Economic Planning and Development, Taiwan.

Gin-Chyn Tseng. 2003. Exploitation and operation of elder's man-power resources from empowerment point. *Community Development Journal*. 103, 266.

Healthy City Research Center, NCKU. 2013. *2013 Age-Friendly City Chia-Yi project final report*. Chia-Yi City: Chia-Yi City Government.

Lin, W.-I. 2003. On the social housing policy and social care in Taiwan. *National Policy Quarterly*. 2(4), 53–82.

Lin, W.-I. 2010. The coming of an aged society in Taiwan: issues and policies. *Asian Social Work and Policy Review*. 4(3), 148–162.

Mahoney, F. and Barthel, D. 1965. Functional evaluation: the Barthel Index. *Maryland Medical Journal*. 14, 61–65.

Ministry of Health and Welfare. 2010. *Taiwan age-friendly city evaluation system and implementation project final report*. Taipei: Health Promotion Administration, Ministry of Health and Welfare.

Ministry of the Interior Taiwan. 2009. *Elderly survey report*. Taipei: Ministry of Internal Affairs Taiwan.

Ministry of the Interior Taiwan. 2012. *Regulation on the accessible housing design basis and incentives*. Taipei: Ministry of the Interior Taiwan. Available at: www.cpami.gov.tw/chinese/index.php?option=com_rgsys&view=detail&id=65&Itemid=202, accessed 8 April 2015.

Minnesota Department of Health. 2006. Creating healthy communities for an aging population: a report of a Joint Rural Health Advisory Committee and State Community Health Services Advisory Committee Work Group. Available at: www.health.state.mn.us/divs/orhpc/pubs/healthyaging/hareportnofs.pdf, accessed 29 August 2014.

Ogawa, N. and Matsukura, R. 2007. Ageing in Japan: the health and wealth of older persons. In Proceedings of the United Nations Expert Group Meeting on Social and Economic Implications of Changing Population Age Structures. New York: United Nations.

Public Health Agency of Canada. 2012. The Chief Public Health Officer's report on the state of public health in Canada 2010. Available at: www.phac-aspc.gc.ca/cphorsphc-respcacsp/2010/fr-rc/cphorsphc-respcacsp-07-eng.php, accessed 29 August 2014.

Schwartz, B. and Scheidt, R.J. 2013. *Environmental gerontology: what now?* London: Routledge.

United Nations. 2002. World population ageing: 1950-2050. Available at: www.un.org/esa/population/publications/worldageing19502050/pdf/preface_web.pdf, accessed 8 April 2015.

Wahl, H.-W. 2001. Environmental influences on aging and behavior. In Birren, J.E. and Schaie, K.W. (Eds.). *Handbook of the psychology of aging*. San Diego, CA: Academic Press.

Washburn, R.A., Smith, K.W., Jette, A.M. and Janney, C.A. 1993. The physical activity scale for the elderly (PASE): development and evaluation. *Journal of Clinical Epidemiology*. 46(2), 153–162.

WHO (World Health Organization). 2002. Active ageing: a policy framework. Available at: http://whqlibdoc.who.int/hq/2002/WHO_NMH_NPH_02.8.pdf, accessed 8 April 2015.

WHO. 2007. Global age-friendly cities: a guide. Available at: www.who.int/ageing/publications/Global_age_friendly_cities_Guide_English.pdf, accessed 8 April 2015.

Other sources

Age-Friendly City New York www.agefriendlynyc.org

Alliance of the Elderly Welfare Promotion in Taiwan www.pilio.idv.tw/logo/old.htm

Annual Statics Report, Ministry of Interior http://sowf.moi.gov.tw/stat/year/list.htm

Department of Health, Executive Yuan, Taiwan www.bhp.doh.gov.tw/bhpnet/portal/Default.aspx

Department of Social Affairs, Ministry of Interior http://sowf.moi.gov.tw/04/01.htm

HelpAge International website www.helpage.org/global-agewatch/data/global-agewatch-data

MAREP http://afc.uwaterloo.ca/index.html

Official Census in Taiwan www.stat.gov.tw/ct.asp?xItem=11280&CtNode=2374&mp=4

Shanghai City Government www.shanghai.gov.cn/shanghai/node2314/node3766/node3851/index.html

Taiwan Legal Database http://law.moj.gov.tw/LawClass/LawAll.aspx?PCode=D0050037

WHO www.who.int/en

34

MANAGING CITY DEVELOPMENT FOR HEALTH IN INDIA

The case of Hyderabad city

Maheep Singh Thapar and Mala Rao[1]

Urbanisation and health

The year 2008 was an important milestone in the history of human civilisation, when, for the first time, urban areas became home to more than half the world's population (Martine 2007). The twenty-first century has been referred to as the 'Century of the City'. It is anticipated that most regions of the developing world, which have the highest urban growth rates, will be predominantly urban by the middle of the century and home to an estimated 5.3 billion people of whom approximately 63 per cent will live in Asia (UN Human Settlements Programme, 2008).

Against this background of staggering growth, it is becoming evident that rapid urbanisation is resulting in a range of negative impacts on health and well-being. Although for some, urbanisation has brought great personal wealth, weakened global economies have also increased health and socio-economic inequalities, with rising levels of urban poverty, insecurity, unemployment, homelessness and crime (Commission on Social Determinants of Health 2008). In the developing world, environmental degradation associated with rapid urbanisation is exacerbating inadequate access to basic services such as water, sanitation, garbage collection, water drainage, paved footpaths and lighted streets, and is posing significant health risks to people (UN Human Settlements Programme 2009).

Many developing world cities face very severe levels of urban air pollution – higher than developed world counterparts (HEI International Scientific Oversight Committee 2010). In India the transport sector is contributing more than 50 per cent of the air pollution in most of the metro cities, and in some cases it is even up to 80 per cent (Goyal et al. 2006). Adverse health outcomes of urban air pollution include increased mortality due to cardiorespiratory diseases and cancer (Chuang et al. 2010). An additional health impact of increased vehicles is increased mortality and morbidity due to road traffic collisions (World Health Organization 2004). Heat waves associated with climate change can also lead to increased health risks such as an increase in cardiovascular disease and mortality (Fouillet et al. 2006; Griffiths et al. 2009). Urban centres may be particularly affected by the urban heat island effect where the potential health impacts of increased temperatures pose a significant challenge.

The built environment has also been shown to have direct and indirect effects on mental health (Rao et al. 2007). Poor-quality housing, residential overcrowding, insufficient daylight, noise pollution from sources such as airports and the stench from sewage and poor sanitation can affect mental well-being (Evans 2003). In addition, urban migrants and jobseekers from rural areas may live in isolation in urban slums, and without the benefits of socially supportive relationships. The harsh physical and social conditions of urban slum life lead to chronic stress in slum dwellers and an increased risk of violence and crime, as well as depression (National Academy of Sciences 2003).

Of all the health impacts of urbanisation, obesity has emerged as one of the most important public health challenges, particularly in the socially disadvantaged urban populations of the world (Rao et al. 2011). Urbanisation has created conditions in which people adopt a less physically active lifestyle and are at higher risk of obesity, which is itself a risk factor for non-communicable diseases such as diabetes and hypertension. Unplanned urban growth and a focus on motorised transport have led to a decline in safe footpaths, public and greenspaces as well as the disappearance of other popular and important street features and landmarks, leading to a diminished sense of community, decreased opportunities for physical activity and social interaction and lower levels of mental well-being.

The situation in India

India's urbanisation story has begun to pick up steam rapidly in the last two decades. It is projected that in the future Indian cities will account for nearly 70 per cent of the country's gross domestic product (GDP) and are likely to house 40 per cent of India's population by 2030 (Mckinsey Global Institute 2010), but the current performance of India's cities is poor across key indicators of quality of life. The water supplied is 150 litres per capita per day (LPCD) and even less in many cases compared with the basic service standard which is 220 LPCD. Huge deficiencies in the system lead to large losses in the supply and leakages add to the risk of contamination. Worryingly, only 30 per cent of sewage is treated even in large cities compared with a standard of 100 per cent. Approximately 24 per cent of the total population lives in slums. On average parks and usable open spaces make up around 3–6 sq m per person against a standard of 9–16 sq m (Mckinsey Global Institute 2010). Clearly, any growth in urban prosperity in India is not being translated into improved health and social well-being.

Urban planning in India is complex. An inadequate system of governance compounds the challenges of delivering civic services and of addressing the pressures on basic amenities. Nevertheless, planning is undertaken not just on a platform of appropriate theoretical principles, but is also influenced by history, tradition, and political, economic, demographic and political contexts. It must also balance the needs of the growing urban population, the services necessary to keep cities functional and manageable, and the standards necessary to ensure a reasonable quality of living. Aiming for a 'Healthy City' in the Indian context remains a gargantuan challenge.

Hyderabad: sixth city of India

Hyderabad is one of the largest and fastest growing cities in India and its economic resurgence has led to its emergence as a globally important city. Rapid urbanisation has, however, come at a cost. A growth in personal wealth and technology contrasts sharply with a rise in urban poverty, increasing stress on housing, water and sanitation, and widening health and social inequalities. Obesity has also emerged as an important public health challenge and in Hyderabad, in common with many cities of the developing world, the overall picture is one of epidemiological polarisation, a scenario in which disease patterns typical of poor living conditions and human insecurity coexist with chronic diseases more typical of developed societies and with high mortality from accidents and violence, magnifying the persistence of significant health gaps.

A climate change study undertaken by Humboldt University of Berlin and Potsdam Institute for Climate Impact Research-PIK with the help of the Federal Ministry of Education and Research (BMBF), Germany, for Hyderabad Metropolitan Region used the results of a complex modelling exercise to show the high risks of an increase in temperatures and pattern and intensity of rainfall in the region in the coming decades. Such events have serious implications on the lifestyle disease patterns, health and productivity of citizens. Recent reports in the press have also highlighted that there is a sharp increase in the number of vector borne diseases associated with poor hygiene and sanitation as well as a rise in pulmonary diseases attributed to the increasing air pollution[2] in the city.

Purpose of the chapter

This chapter describes the process and findings of a review of the Masterplan of the Core City of Hyderabad, during the period 2008–2010. The purpose of that review was to assess how best the 'plan' (process as well as the output) would be able to meet the socio-economic, health and well-being needs of the population.

The review used a spectrum of methods including the collection of wide ranging primary and secondary data, field surveys, updating of base maps, integration of cross-sectoral data, collation and synthesis of information collected through a variety of inter-departmental projects undertaken by the government and knowledge sharing workshops and focus group discussions attended by a number of key stakeholders and civil society groups.

Hyderabad city: the historical context
Transition of Hyderabad from a fort town to a sprawling metropolis

The original settlement in the region under the Kakatiya dynasty was taken over by the Qutb Shahi kings in the latter half of the sixteenth century and strengthened as a fort town spread across 3 sq km. Under the Qutb Shahis, the Golconda fort town became a wealthy and popular centre for commerce, art and culture. But this growth led to congestion and water scarcity and in the late sixteenth century Mohammed Quli Qutb Shah (the fifth Qutb Shahi King) built the new city on the southern banks of the river Musi and named it Hyderabad (Figure 34.1). The iconic monument of Charminar was built in 1591 symbolising the end of the dreaded plague and is a landmark even today. At the heart of the city is the Hussain Sagar lake built in 1562 by Ibrahim Quli Qutub Shah; this predates the development of the city of Hyderabad. Used as a drinking water source until the early twentieth century, this lake is the nerve centre of recreational activity for the citizens of Hyderabad and adds a natural balance to the growing city. The river Musi, which is mostly dry, flows from east to west and cuts through the city to join the river Krishna further downstream.

Through the centuries Hyderabad continued to grow and by the end of the eighteenth century had come under the control of the British, who influenced the architecture and shape of the city significantly. They were responsible for developing the city's cantonments, and giving it a unique character with large greenspaces and colonial style bungalows.

Following India's independence in 1947, the Hyderabad State became part of the Indian Union. Hyderabad city was retained as the capital when the state of Andhra Pradesh was created in 1956. Post-independence and between the 1950s and 1990s the city saw a steady growth of public sector undertakings and central government agencies, which resulted in people migrating to the city from all over the country.

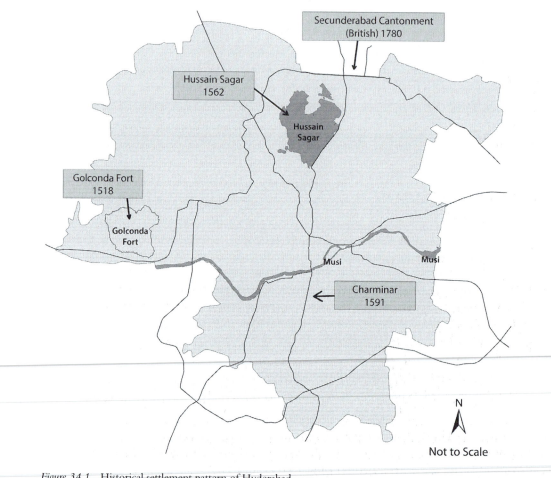

Figure 34.1 Historical settlement pattern of Hyderabad

Source: ADAPT.

Modern Hyderabad

By the end of the twentieth century Hyderabad was again positioned to take centre stage, as the global economy energised its citizens to lay the foundation of a new type of industrial growth. Hyderabad witnessed a massive transformation economically, physically and culturally. What was known to be a historic city with an amenable climate, Paleolithic rock formations and numerous lakes, became a hub of information technology, commercial and research activity with multinational corporations and 'Non-resident Indians' fuelling the economy. Hyderabad started expanding rapidly and the economic boom had a direct impact on real estate which led to an increasing demand for land, housing and urban facilities. Today Hyderabad is the sixth largest city in India and a globally recognised destination for business. The annual GDP of the city is estimated to be around 12 billion USD and Hyderabad accounts for around 15 per cent of the total software exports of India.[3]

Hyderabad city structure

The spatial pattern of Hyderabad is a radially outward spread with the 'main urbanised agglomeration' called the Greater Hyderabad Municipal Corporation (GHMC) surrounded by an 'outlying area' consisting of peri-urban and rural character. The GHMC is spread over 650 sq km and has a population of around 7 million as per the Census of India (2011). The outlying area is around 6,550 sq km with an estimated population of 1 million. The combined area of GHMC and the outlying areas admeasuring around 7,200 sq km is known as the Hyderabad Metropolitan Region (Figure 34.2).

At the heart of GHMC is the 'Core City Area' (the erstwhile Municipal Corporation of Hyderabad (MCH)) of 172 sq km and a total population of around 4.1 million (Census 2011) (Figure 34.3).

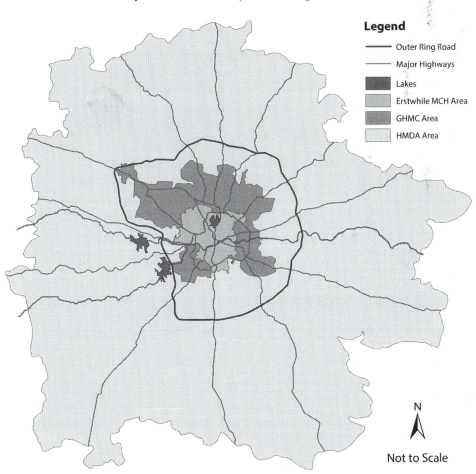

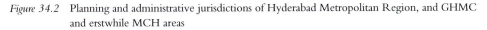

Figure 34.2   Planning and administrative jurisdictions of Hyderabad Metropolitan Region, and GHMC and erstwhile MCH areas

Source: HMDA.

Greater Hyderabad Municipal Area

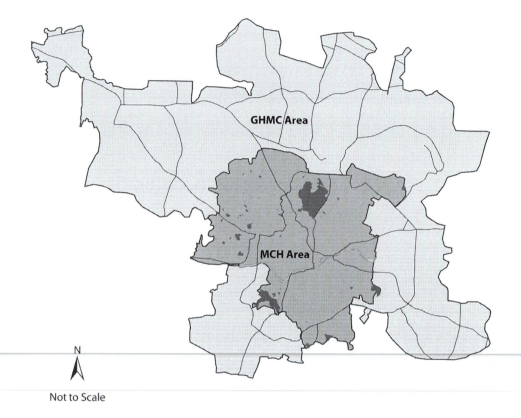

Not to Scale

Figure 34.3 Administrative jurisdictions of the erstwhile MCH area and the GHMC area

Source: GHMC.

The radial roads connect the core city with the outer development areas and the outer ring road encircles the city. The core city area, which is almost totally built up, grew at 1.15 per cent per annum compared to the 4 per cent annual growth rate of the GHMC area between 2001 and 2011 (Census 2011). The core city area remains significant as it accommodates more than 50 per cent of the total GHMC population and around 40 per cent of the total population of the Metropolitan Region.

It is striking that such a concentration of population resides within just 2 per cent of the land mass of the metropolitan region.

The revised masterplan for Hyderabad

The masterplan for the core city area was first prepared in 1975. In the last four decades the city has witnessed a major transformation, which necessitated the updating, revision and consolidation of the city's Development Plan and Zonal Development Plans. The Hyderabad Metropolitan Development Authority (HMDA) in consultation with GHMC undertook this exercise with the assistance of consultants. This complex task was completed in a record time of two years and the final statutory plan was notified in August 2010. The overall objective was to develop a plan for better quality urban living. Improved health and well-being of Hyderabad's citizens were central to this concept.

The process was supported by a rapid assessment of the shortfalls in terms of the existing situation, use and leverage of appropriate technology, and an emphasis on public participation.

The 'Mission' statement for the plan was to make Hyderabad 'The Most Livable City' in India and the review of the masterplan was underpinned by the strategic objectives of making Hyderabad a modern metropolis and a world-class city, with a high quality of life and a sustainable environment. The intent of the plan was to invigorate and strengthen five facets of Hyderabad – to be Harmonious, Humane, Hitech and Healthy, and to preserve its Heritage.

For the first time extensive public consultations were undertaken by the planning authorities with the assistance of the consultants. Stakeholder workshops were held at the various government departments and civic agencies so that essential data could be collected. These exchanges also instigated better coordination and cooperation between departments performing vital roles in managing the city. Preliminary interactions with the civil society groups and non-governmental organisations (NGOs) also resulted in critical feedback for preparing the draft plan (Figures 34.4 and 34.5).

Subsequently the draft plan was notified, in keeping with the statutory requirements, and the general public was given six months to offer feedback. A series of well publicised public consultations in the form of open house sessions were organised at various locations in the city. Meetings were held with the municipal councillors to enhance their understanding of the plan.

Major findings from the masterplan analysis

The main conclusion that could be drawn from the assessment and review was that urban sprawl and scattered growth are both undesirable types of urbanisation. Change in overall drainage and land use pattern had affected the overall environmental balance, leading to

Figure 34.4   Municipal officials explaining the plan to the citizens

Source: HMDA/ADAPT.

Figure 34.5   Citizens studying the maps on display in prominent public places

Source: HMDA/ADAPT.

degradation of air, water, land and soil. A combination of various factors leading to health problems had resulted in a substantial burden of economic costs on the city and had impacted on the lives of citizens (Figure 34.6).

Deterioration of the basic civic services and of the social and physical infrastructure like open spaces, parks, playgrounds, water bodies, pedestrian facilities and public transportation systems, as well as water, sewage, solid waste and storm water drainage had also impacted on the health of the residents.

An analysis of public opinion and feedback gathered during the consultation revealed that most of the problems were related to the lack of proper physical infrastructure and deficiencies in the physical planning of the city, specifically with respect to spatial distribution, especially open space and recreational facilities.

Critically, social imbalances due to economic inequalities, gaps in planning and inadequate inclusion of the poorer sections of society in mainstream planning were leading to both camouflaged and also latent urban conflict adding to overall urban stress.

Important headlines from the analysis of the masterplan were that there were deficiencies in civic governance and management, and inadequacy, obsolescence and interoperability related to poor data usage. There was a lack of evidence-based planning. Interdepartmental coordination and integration remained a key challenge for comprehensive planning. Although a start had been made to address these issues, much more needed to be done, especially involving citizens in the planning, implementation and monitoring of city development so that cities can be managed better and made healthier.

Apart from industrial pollution, one of the major contributors to air pollution is the increase in motorised traffic in the city. There is increasing evidence of the insidious health effects of air pollution in Hyderabad. Scientists have found high levels of oxidative stress, lung function impairment and respiratory ailments due to air pollution. Studies have estimated significant

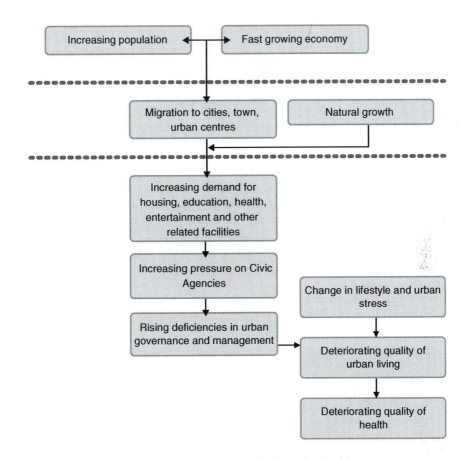

Figure 34.6 Interlinkages between the various aspects related to urban health

Source: ADAPT.

savings in terms of lives if air pollution is controlled (Centre for Science and Environment 2011). The city therefore needs assertive and sustained action to protect public health.

The physical infrastructure in the city needs a major overhaul. The percentage access to piped water supply in the erstwhile MCH area is around 70 percent (at 162 LPCD). There are serious concerns regarding the quality of water and the consequent health risk in many localities of the city. The existing sewerage system covers only 70 percent of the erstwhile MCH area and is overloaded due to the growth of population (GHMC 2006). Within the MCH area only a part of the total sewage is treated and the rest is discharged into water bodies, particularly the river Musi and lakes and natural drains, resulting in the natural storm water drains carrying a mix of domestic sewage and industrial effluent (HMDA 2010). The pollution of the water bodies poses serious health hazards.

The core city area generates more than 2,000 metric tonnes of solid waste every day and an estimated 91 per cent of this quantity is collected from the streets, garbage bins and other tertiary collection points (GHMC 2006). The civic agency faces enormous difficulties in transportation and final disposal of waste and despite substantial efforts to manage solid waste it poses a constant health hazard for the citizens and remains a management challenge for GHMC.

It is estimated that at the city level, pedestrian trips account for around 34 per cent of all trips but only 8 per cent of the total road network has pedestrian facilities. This highlights a huge shortfall in the provision of adequate pedestrian facilities. There are no exclusive cycle tracks (HMDA 2013). The main issue is the lack of dedicated space for these pedestrian and cycling facilities. It is obvious that availability of such infrastructure can have a positive impact on the health of the citizens.

Studies carried out in 2008 showed that not more than 7 per cent of the area of the core city of Hyderabad is made up of parks and playgrounds (Figures 34.7 and 34.8) and around 1.5 per cent is vacant open lands or rocky areas. For a population of around 4 million people this translates to around 3 sq m per capita of parks, which is much less than the required standards.

Spatial analysis of the core city area highlighted that almost 50 per cent of the citizens do not have access to a park of reasonable size and quality within half a kilometre of their homes.

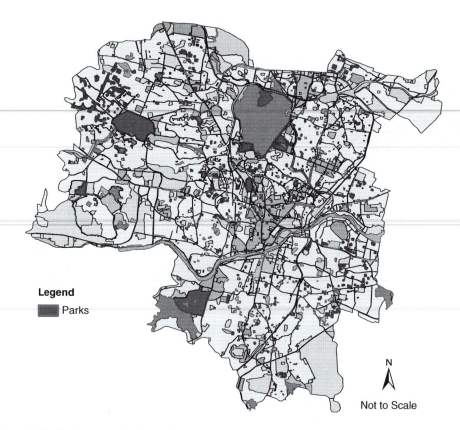

Figure 34.7 The location of parks within the core city area

Source: HMDA/ADAPT.

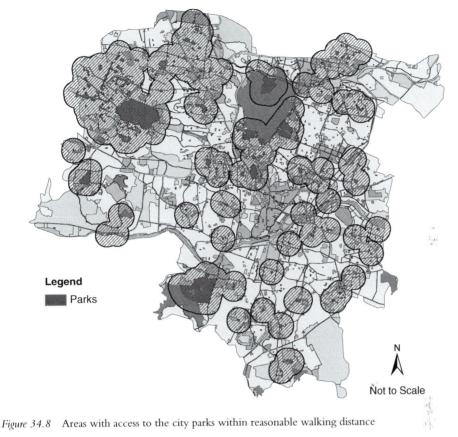

Figure 34.8   Areas with access to the city parks within reasonable walking distance

Source: HMDA/ADAPT.

Recommendations: city core, infrastructure, planning system

The authors are of the view that this analysis offers an opportunity to assess the outcomes of the masterplanning exercise from the perspective of the needs of a 'Healthy City and Healthy Citizens'. Keeping in view this objective the following recommendations are made.

Rejuvenation of cities

For core city areas, physical planning needs to focus on infusing fresh energy into promoting healthy living through supporting local activity, low carbon transport and through targeted redevelopment. There needs to be concerted action to reduce the travel trip lengths within the city. This would reduce the pressure on the transportation infrastructure and directly help in reducing pollution. Providing public facilities of basic minimum standards, at appropriate locations and within shorter distances, provision of open spaces, and improvement of existing lakes and ponds coupled with *in situ* redevelopment of government lands to create parks and open spaces can rejuvenate inner city areas and give options for the citizens to undertake recreational activity. 'Mixed Use Zoning' and 'Transit Oriented' development should be encouraged so that activity centres can be dispersed and decentralised. This would have multiple benefits in terms of reduced vehicular pollution and encouragement of physical activity with associated health benefits for the population.

Infrastructure upgrading

Efficient management and delivery of basic civic services like water, sewage, solid waste and storm water drainage are essential steps to ensure a reduction in overall health risks. Despite severe deficiencies, the city authorities have made significant progress in the last decade and tried to improve the underground sewerage system, develop new sewage treatment plants and channelise the storm water drains. But there is still a long way to go to mitigate this serious urban health issue.

Rainwater harvesting is now gaining popularity, more out of necessity than just environmental concern. This augurs well and Hyderabad Municipal Corporation gives property tax incentives for people who employ rainwater harvesting structures.

In the last few years the GHMC has been recognised and rewarded for its improvement in solid waste management under the Jawaharlal Nehru National Urban Renewal Mission supported by the Government of India. The advantages of the process include increased transparency and accountability as the information is available for anyone to verify without scope for public officials to manipulate the data. The outcome of this has been the introduction of an efficient system of garbage management.

The government of Telangana has risen to the challenge of providing pedestrian and cycling facilities for its citizens. As part of a combined initiative, various government organisations are now developing a 'Bicycle Movement Plan' for Hyderabad. The Telangana State Industrial Infrastructure Corporation (TSIIC) has built a bicycle track in the new precinct of Cyberabad and actively promotes cycle rallies and walk-to-work programmes. The HMDA is undertaking a Comprehensive Transportation Study (CTS) for Hyderabad Metropolitan Region to identify stretches for implementation of Non-Motorised Transport (NMT), continuous sidewalks (pedestrians/footpaths), bicycle routes and cycle tracks.

Supported by the Government of India the city has embarked upon the Rajiv Awas Yojana Slum Improvement programme aiming to improve slum conditions *in situ*. Considering the fact that around 30 per cent of the city population resides in slum-like conditions this initiative can go a long way to improving public health and sanitation in the city.

Reforms in urban planning, administration and management

An important step towards healthy urban planning would be to reform the Urban Planning, Administration and Management Framework. It is suggested that regional environmental plans be prepared for cities and their hinterlands together, and that they should mandatorily include the cohesive planning of watersheds and catchments, slope and drainage, public health, regional economics and transportation connectivity.

With a step change approach, the State Government simplified the building byelaws of Hyderabad in 2006 and subsequently revised them in 2012. With a series of checks and balances in place, Hyderabad city moved into a more liberalised regulatory framework and the concept of Floor Space Index (FSI)/Floor Area Ratio (FAR) as a restricting mechanism for building construction was removed. One of the main objectives that this step aims to achieve is a more compact form of city. Enabling provisions were made in the zoning control regulations for developing urban nodes/clusters and creation of more open space around buildings, ideally leading to redevelopment and rejuvenation of city areas in line with a healthier and more sustainable urban form. This approach can be explored for other cities as well (Figure 34.9).

High levels of participation of the staff of various government departments and local bodies in the plan consultation, setting clear responsibilities among the departments and facilitating sharing of work are useful steps to better urban management. Efficient and effective methods to involve the public in the planning process and increase their awareness about the importance of a good quality urban environment to health and well-being are crucially important means for improving the physical quality of the city.

The first public consultations held during the masterplan preparation set a useful and important precedent. It is hoped that this will encourage a regular cycle of reviews to be routinely instituted for all future plan preparations at various levels.

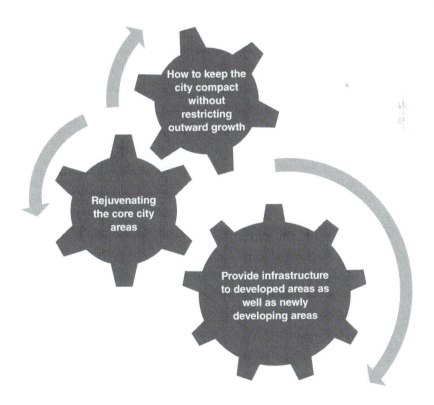

Figure 34.9 How to make Indian cities healthy: key urban planning challenges

Source: ADAPT.

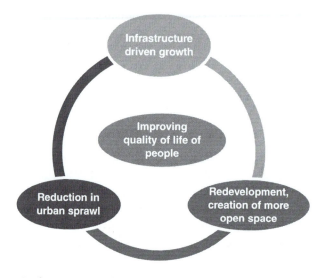

Figure 34.10 Strategies for improving urban health

Source: ADAPT.

A possible model for rapid urbanisation

Indian cities are transforming fast. It is estimated that the urban population will constitute 40 per cent of the total by 2030 (Mckinsey Global Institute 2010). This sets an enormous challenge for urban planners and city managers in attempting to maintain a desirable quality of life. In the globalised world it will be all the more important for cities, whilst being economically productive and remaining competitive, to also provide an environment conducive to public health and well-being (Figure 34.10).

Based on the results of national strategies including the Jawaharlal Nehru National Urban Renewal Mission, the Government of India is supporting the piloting of new methodologies in various Indian cities to try to regenerate them and to ensure more inclusive development. There is no doubt that the recent initiative of Smart Cities is inextricably linked to Healthy Cities.

Today Hyderabad stands at a crossroads again after the bifurcation of the erstwhile state into Telangana and Andhra Pradesh. Due to its inherent strength as an economic powerhouse it is poised to enter a new era of growth and stabilisation. This provides further impetus for the government to aim for the status of a Healthy City. The review of Hyderabad's masterplan has provided an opportunity to reflect on the successes and failures of the process in terms of supporting healthier urban development. This could provide a useful model of development and important lessons to share with urban planners involved in advising on urban planning across the rest of the country and rapidly developing cities across the globe, many of which face similar problems.

Notes

1 The authors acknowledge their appreciation of the Hyderabad Metropolitan Development Authority and Greater Hyderabad Municipal Corporation and the useful information extracted from its official records available in the public domain.

2 www.timesofindia.com, 2013: http:// timesofindia.indiatimes.com/city/ hyderabad/Hyderabad-records-rise-in-pulmonary-diseases /articleshow/19156458.cms

3 www.timesofindia.com, 2013: http://timesofindia.indiatimes.com/city/hyderabad/Andhras-ITeS-exports-outstrip-Indias-average/articleshow/22593530.cms

References

Census of India. 2011. Government of India Ministry of Home Affairs. Office of the Registrar General and Census Commissioner. Available at: http://censusindia.gov.in

Centre for Science and Environment. 2011. *Right to clean air campaign. Citizens' report. Air quality and mobility challenges in Hyderabad 2011*. Delhi: Centre for Science and Environment. Available at: http://cseindia.org/userfiles/Hyderabad%20Report.pdf

Chuang, K., Yan, Y.H. and Cheng, T.J. 2010. Effect of air pollution on blood pressure, blood lipids, and blood sugar: a population-based approach. *Journal of Occupational and Environmental Medicine*. 52(3): 258.

Commission on Social Determinants of Health. 2008. *Closing the gap in a generation: health equity through action on the social determinants of health*. Geneva: World Health Organization. Available at: http://whqlibdoc.who.int/publications/2008/9789241563703_eng.pdf?ua=1

Evans, G.W. 2003. The built environment and mental health. *Journal of Urban Health*. 80(4): 536–555. Available at: www.ncbi.nlm.nih.gov/pmc/articles/PMC3456225

Fouillet, A., Rey, G., Laurent, F., Pavillon, G., Bellec, S., Guihenneuc-Jouyaux, C., Clavel, J., Jougla, E. and Hémon, D. 2006. Excess mortality related to the August 2003 heat wave in France. *International Archives of Occupational and Environmental Health*. 80(1): 16–24.

GHMC (Greater Hyderabad Municipal Corporation) 2006. *Hyderabad City Development Plan (CDP)*. Available at: www.ghmc.gov.in

Goyal, S.K., Ghatge, S.V., Nema, P. and Tamhane, S.M. 2006. Understanding urban vehicular pollution problem vis-à-vis ambient air quality: case study of a megacity. *Environmental Monitoring and Assessment*. 119: 557–569.

Griffiths, J., Rao, M., Adshead, F. and Thorpe, A. (eds). 2009. *The health practitioner's guide to climate change*. London: Earthscan.

HEI International Scientific Oversight Committee. 2010. *Outdoor air pollution and health in the developing countries of Asia: a comprehensive review*. Special Report 18. Health Effects Institute, Boston, MA. Available at: http://pubs.healtheffects.org/getfile.php?u=602

HMDA (Hyderabad Metropolitan Development Authority). 2010. *Core city area (erstwhile MCH area) revised master plan, draft final report*. Available at: www.hmda.gov.in

HMDA. 2013. Comprehensive transportation study for Hyderabad metropolitan area: draft final report volume I. Available at: www.hmda.gov.in

Martine, G. 2007. *State of the world population 2007: unleashing the potential of urban growth*. New York: United Nations Population Fund. Available at: www.unfpa.org/webdav/site/global/shared/documents/publications/2007/695_filename_sowp2007_eng.pdf

McKinsey Global Institute. 2010. India's urban awakening: building inclusive cities – sustaining economic growth. Available at: www.mckinsey.com/insights/urbanization/urban_awakening_in_india, pp. 19–21.

National Academy of Sciences. 2003. *Cities transformed: demographic change and its implications for the developing world*. Washington: National Academies Press.

Rao, M., Prasad, S., Adshead, F. and Tissera, H. 2007. The built environment and health. *Lancet*. 370: 1111–1113.

Rao, M., Barten, F., Blackshaw, N., Lapitan, J., Galea, G., Jacoby, E., Samarth, A. and Buckley, E. 2011. Urban planning, development and noncommunicable diseases. *Planning Practice and Research*. 26(4): 373–391.

United Nations Human Settlement Programme. 2008. *State of the world cities 2008/09: harmonious cities*. London: Earthscan. Available at: http://sustainabledevelopment.un.org/content/documents/11192562_alt-1.pdf

United Nations Human Settlement Programme. 2009. *Planning sustainable cities: global report on human settlements*. London: Earthscan. Available at: www.google.co.in/url?sa=t&rct=j&q=&esrc=s&source=web&cd=1&ved=0CB0QFjAA&url=http%3A%2F%2Funhabitat.org%2F%3Fwpdmact%3Dprocess%26did%3DNTQzLmhvdGxpbms%3D&ei=BffxU8m6H7GS0QW2rIHYAg&usg=AFQjCNFmZu3j_axu794dbRw3NeUfg_TjqA&bvm=bv.73231344,d.d2k

World Health Organization. 2004. *World report on road traffic injury prevention*. Eds Peden, M., Scurfield, R., Sleet, D., Mohan, D., Hyder, A.A., Jarawan, E. and Mathers, C. Geneva: World Health Organization. Available at: http://whqlibdoc.who.int/publications/2004/9241562609.pdf

Other resources

www.ap.gov
www.aphb.gov.in
www.ghmc.gov.in
www.hmda.gov.in

35

THE INTEGRATION OF HEALTH INTO PLANNING IN TURKISH CITIES

Nalan Fidan and Ercüment Yilmaz

Context

As discussed in earlier chapters of this book, there are various determinants of health such as environmental conditions, socio-economic conditions, quality of life, housing quality, well-being and lifestyle. Many of these determinants are directly relevant to the responsibilities of local governments or are directly affected by the actions taken by local governments. In this chapter, projects from three Turkish municipalities that put health into the heart of planning are examined. These projects each have a different focus. In Bursa, environmental improvements increase active transport and social opportunities. In Karşıyaka, a bicycle based transportation system (KARBİS) has been used as a method to reduce motorised traffic and create an environmentally friendly and recreative transportation system. The final example in Kocaeli is the transformation of an old paper mill into a public park (SEKA PARK). All of the examples have the potential to affect a large number of people, support healthier lifestyles and transform unhealthy settings to healthier places that may improve human health.

History of planning in Turkey

Urban planning in Turkey started during the second half of the nineteenth century. In this period the focus was on the durability of building stock, cleaning roads, preventing fire and ensuring that buildings were fit for human habitation. These efforts were later followed by a new focus on establishing clean, attractive and modern cities that provide suitable municipal services. Similar to other countries, the urban planning process in Turkey is composed of research, preparation, approval and implementation phases. The first urban plans in Turkey were prepared by development directorates established by a special law passed in 1928. These plans are required to consider 20-year population projections, the socio-economic structure of cities and the location and speed of development. However, the fast population growth in cities, which was beyond control, has shown that population projections had a high margin of error as the migration of populations from rural to urban areas was drastically underestimated. In the 1950s only 15 per cent of the population of Turkey was living in cities; this rate increased to 75 per cent in 2009.

Rapid urbanisation is common in many places throughout the world. The negative impact of this trend on health requires new ways of thinking in planning and local governance. The global Healthy Cities movement, which is also implemented in Turkey, seeks to find and share solutions to such problems. It aims to put health high on the agenda of local governments and support systematic approaches and comprehensive policies to improve health. In Turkey, municipalities that adopted this approach have united under the umbrella of the Turkish Healthy Cities Association and work together to find solutions to mutual problems.

The Turkish Healthy Cities Association

The Turkish Healthy Cities Association was established in 2005 by ten founding cities to provide a formal platform that could support cities in improving urban health and creating better settings for their citizens. Shortly after its establishment, the Turkish Healthy Cities Association was accredited by the World Health Organization (WHO) as a National Network under the European Healthy Cities initiative. In line with its strategic goals to strengthen the Healthy Cities movement in Turkey, the Association continuously increased its member cities and in 2014 it reached 49 members covering a population of almost 30 million. The goals of the Turkish Healthy Cities Association are to reduce urban and environmental inequities; to combat poverty; to assist members by representing them at the national and the international levels; and to contribute to creating cities that are pleasant, have a high quality urban infrastructure, and respect the environment, human health and cultural assets (Turkish Healthy Cities Association 2005, 2013).

Bursa: planning for heritage and healthy transportation

Bursa Metropolitan Municipality has a population of over 2.4 million people and is Turkey's fourth biggest city (ADNKS 2012). Bursa is a historical city, which was a home to Bithynians, Romans, Byzantines and Ottomans. It was Bursa where the Ottoman State was first established. History is felt and seen all over the city with khans, city walls, castles, bathhouses, mausoleums and historical fountains, which are all preserved and exist today. The historical Bazaars and Khans Area of the city has been an urban centre since the fourteenth century.

One of the priorities of Bursa Metropolitan Municipality is to ensure the sustainability of the historical identity of the city and the functions of the historical centre of Bursa (Bursa Metropolitan Municipality 2014a; Figure 35.1). Because the urban areas has enlarged 20 times in 50 years, the distance from the edge of the city to the city centre has grown, creating various difficulties for the sustainability of the historical centre. To address this, Bursa Metropolitan Municipality, taking a holistic approach, initiated various projects related to transportation, accessibility, social and commercial relations, and aesthetics to increase the quality of life in the historical city centre, to sustain daily activities and to preserve and transfer it to future generations.

Landscaping, façade improvements and pedestrianisation of city centre streets

One of the goals of Bursa Metropolitan Municipality was to improve the general landscape and façades in the city centre. This was to ensure that the historical city centre remained an attractive and pleasant place for visitors and inhabitants, which supported local businesses and provided possibilities for leisure and recreation.

Initial landscaping and façade improvement implemented by Bursa Metropolitan Municipality changed the look and feel of the city centre. This created a demand from the people and businesses in the area for other similar projects to be undertaken. One example of this demand-led project

Figure 35.1   Historical Bazaars and Khans Area

Source: Bursa Metropolitan Municipality.

is Cumhuriyet Street, a 1.5 km street through the Historical Khans and Bazaars Area. The project was initiated after pressure from the local business association, CUMSİAD, which was formed by the business people of the street. The Municipality held open meetings with CUMSİAD and users of the street and worked to discuss each phase of the project.

Cumhuriyet Street was previously open for motorised traffic and had limited possibilities for walking and socialising (Figure 35.2). However, it was at the heart of the Historical Khans and

Figure 35.2   Cumhuriyet Street before pedestrianisation and improvements

Source: Bursa Metropolitan Municipality.

Bazaars Area and was parallel to one of the longest open bazaars in the area. To increase the attractiveness of the street it was decided to close it to vehicles, improve the façades of buildings, install urban furniture and landscape elements and a nostalgic tramway that connected outer areas to the city centre (Figure 35.3). After the completion the street became a recreation zone, where thousands of people visit to walk, shop, eat and meet friends. This improvement also dramatically increased the usage of the street at night-time.

In 2013, satisfaction with the landscaping and public realm improvement, historic building preservation and the new functions of buildings was between 80 and 90 per cent (Bursa Metropolitan Municipality 2013).

Supporting active travel and transit systems in the historical city centre

Due to the dense structure of the historic centre of Bursa and the high number of visitors for touristic activities, recreation, shopping and business purposes, heavy traffic and parking was a big problem in the city. To address this issue, masterplans were developed which promoted new transport solutions such as modern tramways connecting the city centre with transportation hubs (Bursa Metropolitan Municipality 2014b).

Figure 35.3   Cumhuriyet Street after improvements and the tram

Source: Bursa Metropolitan Municipality.

The T1 tramway line is the first of these tramway routes. The 6.5 km line encircles the historical centre and provides a connection between the light rail lines and the bus hubs (Figure 35.4a). This line was an important step for reducing motorised traffic to the city centre, reducing air pollution and creating a pleasant mode of transportation in the city centre. It will be further supported with the T2 and T3 lines which will connect the whole city with a tram network (Figure 35.4b). The tramline was intended mostly for recreational use but it has proved a popular means of transport for locals – so much so that the T1 tramline has been extended to neighbouring districts.

Figure 35.4a   T1 tramway encircling the historical city centre and connecting it with transportation hubs

Source: Bursa Metropolitan Municipality.

Figure 35.4b   Light rail system, T1 tramline and other tramlines planned in the city centre

Source: Bursa Metropolitan Municipality.

Lessons learned from Bursa city centre and transport improvements

Cumhuriyet Street is a main route between the Historical Khans and Bazaars Area, which strongly reflects the historical identity of the city. The unsustainable use and deteriorating appearance of the street prompted local businesses and the Municipality to recognise that improvements to this central street, Cumhuriyet Street, would have a positive impact to the whole region.

Alongside local concern for the area, the Khans and Bazaars Area was nominated to the United Nations Educational, Scientific and Cultural Organization (UNESCO) World Heritage List. One of the actions developed for the area in the management plan for the nomination was to reduce air pollution created by motorised vehicle traffic. Closing Cumhuriyet Street to traffic both protects the historical heritage from pollution and reduces the negative impact on health. Vehicle traffic in the city centre was further reduced by the introduction of the T1 tramline.

During the pedestrianisation of Cumhuriyet Street and construction of T1 tramline Bursa Metropolitan Municipality worked in cooperation with various stakeholders. The Cumhuriyet Street Industrialists and CUMSİAD represented shop and business owners and provided their views and suggestions on the projects throughout the process. Bursa Metropolitan Municipality also regularly met with the people living and working in the region to ensure their views and suggestions were taken into consideration. The Municipality also worked closely with Bursa Cultural and Natural Heritage Preservation Board to ensure that the construction activities in the historical area were in line with the preservation laws.

The façade improvement project carried out on Cumhuriyet Street sought to improve the visual amenity of the area by removing air conditioning devices and signboards from buildings and improving poorly maintained buildings. These activities required cooperation from private property owners to invest in improvements and maintain the buildings. This included apartment buildings, which had multiple owners. As such, the Municipality agreed to undertake and coordinate all work in apartment blocks and provided the upfront payment that was paid back by the property owners in instalments. The Municipality also invested in the social success of the area by opening a café as a pioneer for other food and drink establishments. It also organised various events after the opening of the pedestrianised Cumhuriyet Street, for example Fotofest open air photography exhibition, liberation of Bursa parade, and fast breaking meals during Ramadan. All these activities supported the new pedestrianised use of the street and created new opportunities to socialise. The pedestrianisation has reduced air and sound pollution due to removal of motorised traffic.

The positive results and feedback received from the project have triggered similar projects in other streets in Bursa. This project was embraced by citizens and has created positive changes in the silhouette of the city. The project renovated the old fabric of the city, created better transportation opportunities and also increased the quality of life for the local population.

Bursa: planning for multifunctional greenspace

The Hüdavendigar City Park in Bursa is a result of the transformation of a passive green area into a lively, active park. The site was previously closed to the public as it formed part of the flood plain of the Nilüfer River. The area is surrounded by dense residential development that lacked access to green recreational areas.

The aim of the project was to create a large park that would open this non-usable area for public usage and provide citizens with green areas, children's playgrounds, picnic areas, a pool and various sports fields such as basketball, volleyball, tennis courts, skateboard and roller skate parks, climbing walls, mini golf fields, swimming pools, bicycle roads and running tracks (Figure 35.5). The project would add one million square metres of active greenspace to the city.

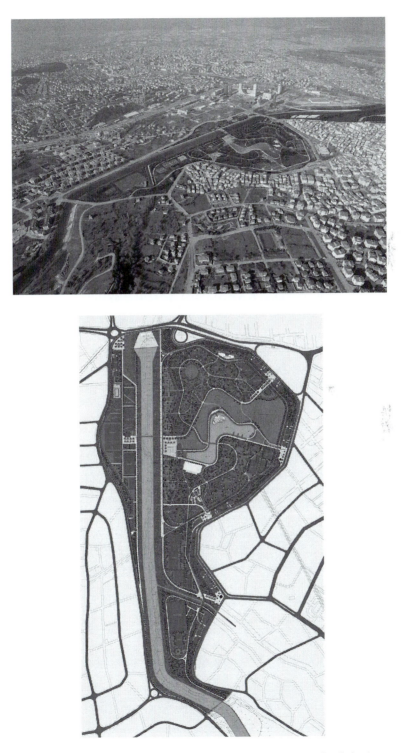

Figure 35.5   Hüdavendigar City Park under construction (above) and layout plan (below)
Source: Bursa Metropolitan Municipality.

Lessons learned

The Municipality recognised the opportunity to create natural green areas and air corridors in the city at the same time as improving the quality of the existing streams. The Municipality worked in partnership with the State Hydraulic Works, Bursa Water and Sewerage Administration, Bursa Cultural and Natural Heritage Preservation Board and the local community to find design solutions, achieve the relevant permissions and implement the project.

For the long-term sustainability of the project and to prevent flood risk, meteorological data was used to determine maximum water flows so that the stream beds could be designed and constructed accordingly. Importantly, the project was also seen as an excellent opportunity to improve the city centre and create natural places for socialising, recreation and physical activity. The Bursa Metropolitan Municipality is responsible for ongoing maintenance of these new green areas.

The Hüdavendigar City Park gives many benefits to the city, including eliminating flood risks; removing illegal buildings; increasing recreational and healthy living areas (parks, walking, bicycling roads and physical activity areas); and increasing safe urban areas.

Karşıyaka: KARBİS bicycle rental system

Karşıyaka Municipality is located at the north of the İzmir Bay with 7 km of coastline (Figure 35.6) (Karsiyaka Municipality 2012). It is made up of 25 neighbourhoods and two villages (approximately 50 km²) and in 2014 had a population of 312,213 (ADNKS 2012).

Like many cities, Karşıyaka faces problems created by an increasing population. One of these problems is transportation. The negative impact of traffic on people requires solutions to reduce the dependency on private motorised vehicles. With this in mind, Karşıyaka Municipality has developed the bicycle rental system, KARBİS (Figure 35.7). This project aims to: provide an

Figure 35.6 General view of Karşıyaka

Source: Karşıyaka Municipality.

Figure 35.7   Bicycles produced for KARBİS

Source: Karşıyaka Municipality.

alternative transportation method between metro stations and ferry ports, making transportation easier; reduce motorised traffic and environmental pollution; raise awareness of the use of bicycles to support active living; and increase the usage of the coastline.

In 2011, the Karşıyaka Municipality was the first municipality in Turkey to sign the Covenant of Mayors. The Municipality has prepared a sustainable energy action plan and carbon dioxide inventory. By implementing the projects in the energy action plan Karşıyaka Municipality aims to reduce carbon emissions by 35 per cent by 2020. The bicycle rental system is an important part of the sustainable energy action plan.

Learning from other European cities who had implemented similar bicycle rental projects was critical. The project team visited Brussels (Belgium) and Seville (Spain) to see how the successful VILLO and Sevici bicycle systems were built and operated. The locations for the bicycle stations and creation of the transportation network were also carefully considered. Seven KARBİS stations and bicycle roads were created to maximise the bicycle route along the coastline, the ferry ports and metro stations.

In designing the bicycles, portability factors such as weight and ease of usage were taken into consideration. A total of 65 bicycles and 98 bicycle stands were implemented in the project pilot. The bicycles have 26-inch wheels and three-speed transmissions. Handlebars were made with non-slip materials and the bicycles are fitted with front and rear lights for safety and use after dark. Instructions were also written on to the bicycles for ease of use and safety.

The KARBİS project was an important step for creating a healthy environment and supporting active travel and active living. The project had several partners including Municipality Kent Inc (the operator), Dokuz Eylül University, Bisan Inc, Urban Planners Chamber and Civil Society Institutions and received political support (Figure 35.8). The system currently has 145 bicycles in use and 2,800 members registered with the system. The aim is to extend the project along the coastline in partnership with neighbouring municipalities.

Figure 35.8   Cevat Durak, mayor of Karşıyaka riding a KARBİS bicycle

Source: Karşıyaka Municipality.

Lessons learned from KARBİS

It has been seen that the number of people doing sports increases if they are encouraged and are given the opportunity. It has been seen that for short distances people tend to prefer bicycles over other methods of transportation. These short journeys were targeted by locating bicycle stations near mass transportation hubs. The project has also increased private bicycle ownership in the city.

Kocaeli SEKA PARK project

The highways and railways between Asia and Europe intersect at Kocaeli Metropolitan Municipality, making this city one of the most important industrial centres of the Marmara Region and Turkey. It is a metropolitan area with 12 district municipalities and 243 villages. The city is one of the most important cities in Turkey. It is the sixth largest city in Turkey with a population of 1.6 million people and the third largest city in the Marmara region after İstanbul and Bursa (ADNKS 2012). In addition to the visions of Kocaeli as a city of science and industry, the city also attracts many tourists to the 'Kartepe Mountain and Winter Tourism Project' (Kocaeli Metropolitan Municipality 2014).

Kocaeli is primarily an industrial city with over 7,000 enterprises. The city has undertaken many industrial transformation projects to become a more liveable city. The SEKA PARK has been instrumental in this transformation. Located on an old paper mill site, the SEKA PARK was the first industrial transformation project in Turkey and has reconnected the people of Kocaeli with the İzmit Bay (Kocaeli Metropolitan Municipality 2008).

The SEKA PARK project has transformed the disused and burdensome SEKA paper mill site (Figure 35.9) into a green recreational area where people are able to spend time on the beach, relax and be with their friends (Figure 35.10). The ownership of SEKA PARK was transferred in 2004 to Kocaeli Metropolitan Municipality, after the SEKA paper mill, which was founded in 1936, was closed by the central government. In this period there was

Figure 35.9 SEKA paper mill before transformation

Source: Kocaeli Metropolitan Municipality.

Figure 35.10 SEKA PARK after transformation

Source: Kocaeli Metropolitan Municipality.

a need for greenspace in the city so the Municipality decided to transform the area into a recreational field.

At first the people of Kocaeli opposed the idea, fearing that closing the factory would create high unemployment. But after the employees of the old paper mill were reemployed with the municipality and the details of the park project were shared with the people of Kocaeli, both the people and civil society organisations fully embraced it. During the transformation of the paper mill to a recreational area the Governorship, Scientific and Technological Research Council of Turkey, Municipality and the University of Kocaeli all worked in partnership, which resulted in a unique and successful recreation area. As a result, SEKA PARK has become one of the most popular places in the city.

SEKA PARK is part of a wider programme of implementing recreational spaces near İzmit Bay. It includes an artificial grass hill, a climbing wall, an artificial beach, a concert platform with a capacity of 10,000 people, grass fields, walking and bicycling roads and cafes. In addition, the SEKA Science Centre, which is the first science centre in Turkey, is located in the park. The SEKA Paper Museum was also established which celebrates the industrialisation efforts in Turkey and the contribution of SEKA paper mill.

After the completion of the 0.58 km^2 project, the green area per capita increased four-fold in the city. The park provides a venue for social interaction and hosts large events. The project also provides access to the coastline which was previously inaccessible. The removal of the industrial uses and a clean-up of the coastal environment have meant that the water quality in the Bay has improved, providing people with a place for recreational activities. Another secondary benefit of the project has been shifting the perception of Kocaeli as an industrial city to a healthy city. In ten years, 60 km of the İzmit Bay coastline has been planted with trees. The coastline now provides a popular setting for 'Healthy City Walks' which also contribute to increased social connections between people.

Lessons learned from SEKA PARK

The first phase of the project was done in cooperation with civil society institutions, the university and central government. In the second and third phases the Municipality has developed joint projects with industrial facilities and the Scientific and Technological Research Council of Turkey. The SEKA PARK project has shown the city that positive results can be obtained if projects are developed and implemented in cooperation and partnership.

Putting health at the top of the agenda

There are many things that can contribute to supporting better integration of health and planning and putting health at the top of the agenda of local governments. Increasing public and institutional awareness about the wider determinants of health and giving an increased voice to citizens is a critical starting point. National and international movements such as the WHO Healthy Cities programme greatly assist in improving understanding.

Today, local governments benefit from voluntarily taking part in networks such as the Healthy Cities Network, participating in training, symposia, workshops and similar events where they can share their experiences. Being a part of a network aiming to improve health and quality of life has a positive influence on outcomes in Turkish cities as learning can be adapted to the circumstances of each city. In the 2013 evaluation of the Turkish Healthy Cities Association, 70 per cent of the members had started health improving actions directly because

	Bursa Metropolitan Municipality	Karşıyaka Municipality	Kocaeli Metropolitan Municipality
Natural environment (natural habitats, air, water, land)	✔	✔	✔
Built environment (buildings, places, streets, routes)	✔	✔	✔
Activities (working, shopping, moving, living, playing, learning)	✔	✔	✔
Local economy (wealth creation, resilient markets)	✔	✔	✔
Community (social capital, social networks)	✔	✔	✔
Lifestyle (diet, physical activity, work–life balance)	✔	✔	✔

Figure 35.11   Impact of the projects on the determinants of health and well-being

Sources: Adapted from Barton and Grant (2006).

of their involvement in the network. Examples include improving environmental conditions, implementation of bicycle routes and open-air sports facilities, and creation of parks and other facilities for children, the elderly and people with disabilities. The evaluation also indicated that 37 per cent of members have increased cooperation with other sectors and are more conscious of health issues.

When taken as a whole, the actions of the three case study municipalities consider the wider determinants of health. Figure 35.11 illustrates how these influence the different layers of the Settlement Health Map (see Chapter 1, Figure 1.2; Barton and Grant 2006). Recognition of the wider determinants of health is spreading across Turkish municipalities. However, coordination and cooperation is needed with communities and other organisations outside the municipality. Therefore these groups need to work in partnership to develop and achieve common goals.

References

ADNKS. 2012. Address based population registration system. Available at: www.tuik.gov.tr, accessed 1 September 2014.

Barton, H. and Grant, M. 2006. A health map for the local human habitat. *The Journal for the Royal Society for the Promotion of Health*, 126 (6), 252–253.

Bursa Metropolitan Municipality. 2013. *Bursa Metropolitan Municipality citizen satisfaction survey*. Bursa: Bursa Metropolitan Municipality Strategy Development Directorate.

Bursa Metropolitan Municipality. 2014a. *Bursa*. Available at: http://en.bursa.bel.tr, accessed 1 September 2014.

Bursa Metropolitan Municipality. 2014b. *Cumhuriyet Street becomes Bursa's showcase with the nostalgic tramway route*. Available at: http://en.bursa.bel.tr/projects/cumhuriyet-street-becomes-bursa's-showcase-with-the-nostalgic-tramway-route-986.html, accessed 1 September 2014.

Dahlgren, G. and Whitehead, M. 1991. 'The main determinants of health' model. In Dahlgren, G. and Whitehead, M. 2007. *European strategies for tackling social inequities in health: levelling up part 2*. Copenhagen: WHO Regional Office for Europe. Available at: www.euro.who.int/__data/assets/pdf_file/0018/103824/E89384.pdf, accessed 8 April 2015.

Karsiyaka Municipality. 2012. *Karsiyaka*. Available at: www.karsiyaka.bel.tr, accessed 1 September 2014.

Kocaeli Metropolitan Municipality. 2008. SEKA PARK. Available at: www.kocaeli.bel.tr/images/content/3dsanaltur/kocaeli360sanaltur/seka/index.html, accessed 1 September 2014.

Kocaeli Metropolitan Municipality. 2014. *Kocaeli Buyuksehir Belediyesi*. Available at: http://en.kocaeli.bel. tr, accessed 1 September 2014.

Turkish Healthy Cities Association. 2005. *Turkish Healthy Cities Association 2005–2020 strategy plan, mission and vision statements*. Available at: www.skb.org.tr/wp-content/uploads/2010/06/SKB_2005-2020_ Strateji_Plani.pdf (Turkish), accessed 25 April 2014.

Turkish Healthy Cities Association. 2013. *Turkish Healthy Cities Association constitution*. Available at: www. skb.org.tr/english/about-us/association-constitution, accessed 25 April 2014.

36

HEALTH-INTEGRATED PLANNING AND APPRAISAL IN THE ENGLISH MIDLANDS

*Judy Kurth, Zafar Iqbal, Paul Southon, Chris Weston
and Charlotte Robinson*

The British context

This chapter outlines three practical examples of uniting health and planning at a local authority or municipality level with a view to sharing learning that may be useful to other practitioners globally. It captures the experiences of public health practitioners from the Midlands area of the United Kingdom (UK) of working with planning authorities to develop a joined up response to healthy urban planning. That is, 'health-integrated planning and appraisal' as a mechanism for improving the population's health and well-being. It has not sought at this stage to capture the same experiences from a planning perspective; however, this is an interesting challenge for the future.

There is a growing 'healthy urban planning' movement in the UK and the complexity of the work has resulted in a plethora of networks for sharing good practice and learning which have more recently joined up to form a 'network of networks'. Key organisations include Spatial Planning and Health Group (SPAHG), the Town and Country Planning Association (TCPA), the UK National Healthy Cities Network (UKHCN) and more recently the West Midlands Health and Planning Network. The authors of this chapter were amongst the founding members of both the West Midlands Healthy Urban Planning Network and the UK Healthy City Network which affiliates to the World Health Organization (WHO) European Healthy Cities Movement. This movement has contributed significantly to raising awareness of the impact of the natural and built environment on incidence of non-communicable disease in recent years (www.euro.who.int/en/home).

Recognition of the importance of 'place' as a social determinant of health has never been stronger in the UK. The English review of health inequalities, *Fair Society, Healthy Lives* (Marmot et al. 2010), provided compelling evidence of the impact of social determinants on health inequalities and the important role of local authorities in addressing these social determinants. The Health and Social Care Act (Department of Health 2012) shifted accountability for public health away from the National Health Service (NHS) and into local authorities with the intention of ensuring greater join up and a deeper understanding between public health and the wider local authority functions, including planning and development and regeneration. The National Planning Policy Framework (NPPF) (Department of Communities and Local Government 2012) was designed to make the planning system less complex and more accessible. Its key aims are to protect the environment and promote sustainable growth. Health is recognised as an important element of sustainability; for the first time, the planning system is required to 'take account of and support local strategies to improve health, social and cultural well-being for all, and deliver sufficient community and cultural facilities and services to meet local needs' (Department of Communities and Local Government 2012, paragraph 17). In 'plan-making':

> Local planning authorities should work with public health leads and health organisations to understand and take account of the health status and needs of the local population . . . including expected future changes, and any information about relevant barriers to improving health and well-being.
>
> *(Department of Communities and Local Government 2012, paragraph 171)*

The NPPF requirements have recently been strengthened further, through the *National Planning Practice Guidance* (Department of Communities and Local Government 2014) which provides the detailed guidance to the NPPF. Furthermore, the Localism Act (Department of Communities and Local Government 2011) introduced a 'Duty to Co-operate', which places a legal duty on local authorities to work with other local authorities and other bodies, including 'health' bodies, during preparation of local plans. Local authorities must demonstrate, with evidence, 'co-operation' throughout the plan-preparation process.

This chapter will focus on lessons learnt in three areas of the Midlands: Stoke-on-Trent, Sandwell and Lincolnshire. Within this changing policy landscape, it recognises that there is no blueprint for how to embed health into planning, and that success in this area to date has been due to a dogged and pragmatic pursuit of the 'art of the possible' within each local context. A purely rational approach which relies on public health recourse to evidence base as a lever for change is not possible in relation to healthy urban planning and development as whilst a range of guidance is available, the evidence base is still developing (Glasgow Centre for Population Health 2013). Uniting health and planning is therefore contingent on developing a shared understanding and belief about why uniting planning and health matters, taking joint action, learning together and identifying what works within each local context. It is about relationship building to better understand where public health and planning can add value to each other's agendas and about providing the opportunity for a shared journey and shared learning to improve health and well-being and inform a more systematic approach to healthy urban planning and development over time.

Networking and coordination in the West Midlands

Developing networks of practice is one way in which learning and joint action can be shared across a range of partners and areas and this approach was adopted in the West Midlands. The West Midlands region in England has a long history of effective public health networks. Over the past decade much of this activity has been coordinated through the West Midlands Public Health Teaching Network and, more recently, through Learning for Public Health West Midlands (a regional network funded through levy from local government). In 2011–2012 Public Health Sandwell, working with the Learning for Public Health West Midlands, established the West Midlands Health and Planning Group (WMHPG), in recognition of the need to join up on local and national policy consultations, as well as to share good practice about 'health-integrated planning and appraisal'. The objective of the group is to share learning and experience, and coordinate joint work across the West Midlands. The overarching model for the work is drawn from the Marmot review of health inequalities in England (Marmot et al. 2010) and the vision is: 'to create and develop healthy and sustainable places and communities'.

Membership of the group has expanded beyond public health considerably. The success of the group comes from maximising the benefits of the breadth of experience across the West Midlands, providing a forum for discussion between a range of disciplines from planners, architects, public health practitioners to academics. This helps in developing a shared understanding of the different perspectives across the statutory, voluntary and private sectors. It also helps those involved to learn some of the many different professional 'languages'. The group meets quarterly but only a proportion of members attend any meeting. Some of the networking is done virtually, and weekly emails and policy updates are sent out to all members.

Establishing the network was an iterative process. It was developed at a time of considerable structural and political change and significant financial challenge across all participants. The WMHPG remained a constant during this time, taking a pragmatic approach, continuously reviewing what worked and what made it useful to members and adjusting accordingly. This included purely practical issues such as maintaining an up to date email list whilst working to develop a longer term vision for the group.

Within the WMHPG a number of people are members of more than one network, linking up across these networks and disseminating information to many people with just a few emails or phone calls. In terms of network theory these people act as 'supernodes' or connectors (Gladwell 2000). Zinoviev (2011) characterised these people as 'influential spreaders'. Mislove et al. (2007) discussed how they are critical for the connectivity and flow of information in a network. This swathe of joining up activity reflects the level of need that practitioners have to learn and share best practice in relation to health and planning as a relatively new field of public health practice and endeavour.

Whilst the WMHPG operates within the context of English spatial planning and health policy, many of the challenges it has faced will be common across different areas and in different political and policy environments:

- different professional environments, perspectives and languages;
- working across different sectors that have different drivers and incentives which can appear to be contradictory;
- different understanding of what constitutes evidence and what evidence is applicable within different spheres, for example public health and planning;
- what is needed to support a planning decision, possibly in a court of law;
- differing operating timescales: health funding, 3 years: planning, a much longer timescale.

The measure of success, however, is the extent to which the WMPHG can support local areas to take action, working through challenges and delivering change together. An example of such a challenge, which cuts across local and national networks, is around shisha bars.[1] Sandwell had community support, political support and a partnership agreement to stop shisha bar developments in Sandwell. The local government planning committee refused an application based on this local support; however, the national planning inspectorate overturned this decision.

In this case the problem was raised across the various networks. Through the UKHCN a national teleconference was arranged with interested areas and organisations. This has led to work to influence changes at a national level to enable councils to tackle the problem. This is an example of how the 'network of networks' can help to address challenges that cannot be resolved at a local level. It also demonstrates how important the networks are to support taking learning into action.

An incremental approach in Stoke-on-Trent

As a relatively new field for collaboration, it can be difficult for local government to find a start point for developing 'health-integrated planning and appraisal'. In 2009, with support from the WHO European Healthy Cites Urban Planning network, Stoke-on-Trent public health department took on the challenge of finding a practical and yet challenging approach to engaging with planning colleagues. The approach taken was incremental and pragmatic with 'shared learning' as the key lever for taking action.

Stoke-on-Trent is a unitary authority that was built upon large-scale industry including the potteries, coal mining and steel production. The decline of these industries has had severe economic, health, social and environmental consequences for the city. It is now ranked sixteenth out of 326 English authorities on the indices of multiple deprivation (Department of Communities and Local Government 2010). As a result Stoke-on-Trent has attracted a number of regeneration funds including becoming one of nine housing market renewal pathfinders set up by the government to carry out large-scale housing regeneration programmes. Called RENEW the aim was to transform local neighbourhoods into successful and environmentally sound places where local people – and newcomers – would want to live, work and play.

Motivated by the need to ensure positive health was built into the regeneration of the city, public health opened up dialogue with planning. Prior to the NPPF initial discussions were amicable but difficult as uniting planning and health was not a national imperative. There was evidence of very different use of language between the two disciplines and competing national and local priorities. Colleagues in planning were seeking to finalise their core spatial strategy as a matter of urgency, and required evidence of clear, practical ways in which public health could support them to both deliver on this and the wider healthy urban planning agenda. The 'early win' was to make a health contribution to the core spatial strategy. The longer term result is that 'health' now forms one of the principle aims of the core spatial strategy, recognising its input into the long-term vision.

The next step was to broaden out the relationship between public health and planning to include regeneration and the local university as key stakeholders. It was agreed to use Health Impact Assessment (HIA) as a learning tool for all stakeholders and to assess if it could support the city in building health into planning over the longer term. An HIA learning programme was jointly commissioned between the city council and the NHS (which was then the accountable body for public health) which focused on delivering four HIAs on areas of major intervention. An experienced and facilitative consultancy was engaged to run this process, and the value of both these qualities in gaining the confidence of partners to take this unknown journey together cannot be underestimated. Out of this work commitment was made to HIA at city council level. Further we produced a 'Planning Concordat & Memorandum of Understanding' between NHS Stoke-on-Trent and Stoke-on-Trent City Council which set out a joint commitment to support healthy urban planning. This was signed off at executive level in 2011, giving a mandate to proceed further.

Focusing on a programme of joint learning, with practical outcomes and benefits for all partners, has enabled planning and public health in Stoke-on-Trent to 'unite'. Some of the key outputs have included an increased awareness and understanding of HIA through a number of means including staff training and mentoring and also the production of a guide to health proofing masterplans by the Healthy City Partnership (Vohra 2010). This guide has been useful in helping partners to understand the impact of planning on health in a very practical way (Figure 36.1).

A number of HIAs were delivered, for example on the local Transport Strategy, Draft City Centre Area Action Plan and the Housing Support Strategy. Public health was a consultee on an

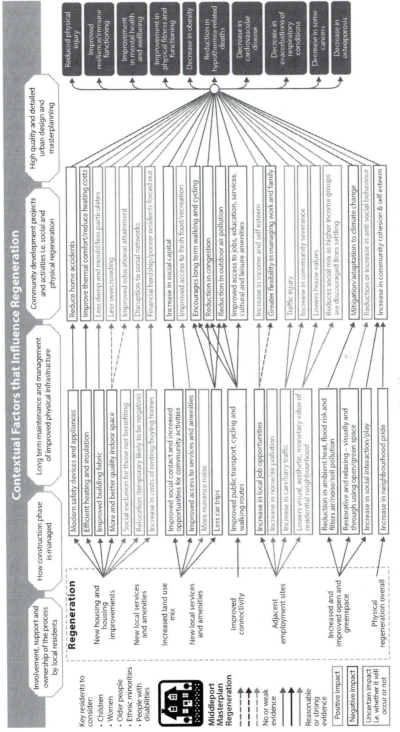

Figure 36.1 Pathways by which health and well-being can be affected by developments proposed in masterplan designs

Source: Vohra (2010).

Urban Design Supplementary Planning Document (SDP) which was adopted by the city council in 2010, and which promotes healthy urban design principles. In 2013 the council adopted a Health Urban Planning SPD enshrining its commitment to ensure that health is a consideration in all planning decisions. This SPD introduces a healthy urban planning checklist to be applied to future development proposals and introduces a requirement for an HIA to be undertaken for all large-scale major development proposals and future planning policy documents. Finally the city council consulted on a draft Hot Food Takeaway SPD from May to July in 2013, which establishes school exclusion zones to be applied to future planning decisions and encourages takeaways to adopt 'healthy eating options'.

The commitment of the city council to healthy urban planning and development continues to deepen, and much has been achieved over the past five years. A focus on HIAs as a practical tool to bring partners together for a common goal was a pragmatic move, but one which generated a lot of learning for the city. There remain some issues yet to be resolved which will continue to be addressed. The requirement for all significant developments in the city to have an HIA has resource implications for developers but this has not proved to be a barrier to date. Public health have commissioned Staffordshire University to quality assure developer-led HIAs in a way which is supportive to both developers and the development management process.

More recently it has been recognised that often HIAs are carried out at too late a stage of the planning process, and consideration is being given as to how to introduce HIA at the pre-planning phase. We are seeking to give detailed advice to developers about the scope of the HIA which they will need to carry out based on the site and type of development proposed at the pre-planning application phase, which is an alternative to the quality review which is currently carried out.

Future plans include the recruitment of a healthy urban development officer post within the council which will work between planning, public health and the local university. Based on the experience of other areas, such as Coventry, this approach will enable health to be embedded into the wider determinants such as transport planning and food sustainability. In Coventry there is evidence of uniting health not just with planners but also developers through this model.

Finally, in line with NPPF, Stoke-on-Trent City Council is developing a local plan. Health has been invited to contribute at the outset with a number of key areas identified whereby public health can add value, including developing the evidence base on health statistics and deprivation area mapping, undertaking an HIA for the draft local plan and inclusion of health into the sustainability appraisal and site selection process.

Integrated Impact Assessment in Lincolnshire

Illustrating a practical mechanism for engaging public health in planning

The recent health and social care reforms have created significant challenges for both public health and planning. However, the example from Lincolnshire demonstrates how assessing the potential impact of local planning policy on health and well-being has fostered better working relationships between public health and planning professionals and led to a shared understanding of the key health issues facing the area.

In Lincolnshire, the county council is the responsible local authority for public health, but most of the responsibility for developing planning policies and determining planning applications sits with seven district councils, each with their own planning department. By placing public health in a separate body to local planning departments, public health professionals have fewer opportunities for informal, casual dialogue and conversations to 'win' local planners' hearts and minds and promote the health agenda. This was the situation that confronted Public Health Lincolnshire in April 2013 when the department formally joined the county council from the NHS. In seeking a solution and mechanism for engagement with planners locally, public health uncovered a methodology being attempted by three district councils (through a combined Central Lincolnshire Joint Planning Unit (JPU)). The methodology was itself innovative and would allow public health the formal 'in' to the local planning world that was sought by the local public health team.

At the time, the JPU were preparing a local plan for the Central Lincolnshire area, which covers the administrative boundaries of City of Lincoln, West Lindsey and North Kesteven District Councils. Central to the preparation of the local plan is the sustainability appraisal. This is a legal requirement (Office of the Deputy Prime Minister 2004) and assesses the extent to which an emerging plan meets locally derived economic, social and environmental sustainability objectives. The sustainability appraisal must also incorporate the requirements of Strategic Environmental Assessment (SEA), as set out in the Strategic Environmental Assessment Directive (European Commission 2001) and implemented in England through the Environmental Assessment Regulations (Great Britain, Parliament 2004). This ensures environmental considerations are integrated into the consideration of the impacts of the emerging local plan. Under the SEA Directive, an environmental report must be prepared which, in the case of land use planning documents, is normally incorporated into a sustainability appraisal report to accompany the local plan when it is published.

In order to meet the requirements of other impact assessments, in producing a sustainability appraisal report to accompany the local plan, the JPU combined SEA, sustainability appraisal, equalities analysis and HIA into one Integrated Impact Assessment (IIA). IIA is an approach that assesses the potential impact of proposals (strategies, policies, programmes, projects, plans or other developments) on issues that previously may have been assessed separately, such as economic, environmental, sustainability, equal opportunities and health.

Practically, to support the JPU in undertaking the IIA and bring a range of independent expertise to the process, the JPU established an expert panel. Membership of the panel included representatives with skills and expertise in health, equality and sustainability. This helped ensure that these issues were adequately identified, and provided independent verification of the IIA appraisals and methodology. The objectives of the panel were set out in a terms of reference and included:

- a review of draft appraisals of local plan policies produced by JPU officers;
- commenting on the scope and content of the appraisals, including coverage of effects and nature of effects;
- making recommendations on mitigation measures and reviewing and advising on the IIA report that will accompany the local plan.

To assist with integrating the findings of the IIA into the local plan decision making process, a formal record of recommendations of how the policy performed against each IIA objective was completed at each panel meeting and was fed back to the policy writer. Policy writers then documented how the recommendations from the panel had been incorporated into policy and, if they had been rejected, the reasons why. This provided a clear audit trail as to how the IIA informed the development of the local plan. An extract of the record of IIA recommendations is shown in Figure 36.2.

Core Strategy Policy			
IIA/Sustainability Objective	Support Appraisal? Yes/No/Partially	Comments	Suggested Amendments and Mitigation Measures
1. Housing			
2. Health			
3. Access to Cultural Facilities			
4. Crime			
5. Biodiversity and Green Infrastructure			
7. Landscape & Townscape			
8. Heritage Assets			
9. Natural Resources: Water			
10. Natural Resources: Air & Light			
11. Natural Resources: Soil Land & Minerals			
12. Waste			
13. Climate Change Effects & Energy			
14. Climate Change Adaptation Design & Flood Risk			
15. Transport			
16. Employment			
17. Innovation and Training			
18. Economic Structure			

Figure 36.2 Record of IIA panel recommendations

Source: Central Lincolnshire Joint Planning Unit.

The benefits of this approach locally have been various. For Public Health Lincolnshire, it has allowed public health expertise to sit as a formal champion for health and to ensure it is effectively incorporated into local planning policy. Further the IIA process has led to greater opportunity to influence the local plan through consideration of health impacts early in the decision making process. For planners, the IIA has been an important tool to reconnect with public health and ensure that health impacts are considered and addressed throughout the local plan. It has also resulted in a shared understanding of the local plan policies by the JPU and its partners. For local organisations and members of the local community with an interest in the local plan, the IIA ensures the statutory requirement to assess the impacts of the local plan is presented in a user friendly format as the integrated approach avoids the need to undertake and report on separate assessments. The IIA process has provided the springboard for Public Health Lincolnshire to extend their engagement with planning beyond Central Lincolnshire to other districts in the county.

Drawing out the lessons

The three case studies above aim to illustrate that there is no blueprint for 'health-integrated planning and appraisal' but there are tools which can support any local area to get started, including HIAs and IIAs.

There are also enormous benefits in networking with a wide range of colleagues at a national, local and regional level to identify what has worked elsewhere, seek advice, and explore what it is possible to achieve locally and what needs to be done nationally. The key learning point from the West Midlands experience is that success comes from investing time and effort in understanding the people you are working with. This includes their priorities and their perspective.

Getting started and taking action within a learning framework has been a key lesson which each case study has described. Public health needs to get 'practical'; it needs to work with planners and developers to understand their world, their pressures and their language in order to identify practical opportunities for adding value. In Lincolnshire the focus was on an IIA tool, which enabled public health to influence the core strategy; in Stoke-on-Trent it was HIA, which enabled a joint approach to wider planning and health issues within both policy and development management.

All this needs a detailed and comprehensive understanding of the local context, the existing priorities, partnerships and relationships and the political dimension to the work. Success is about playing the long game, having a shared understanding of where you are trying to get to and a reasonable idea of what needs to happen to get you there. The work in Stoke-on-Trent started a number of years prior to the NPPF and so was not well supported by national policy. Taking a practical approach based on joint learning, however, has meant that an initially difficult and awkward relationship has become highly productive and planners now proactively seek opportunities to enhance health through its statutory responsibilities.

It is hoped that the NPPF will facilitate much wider and deeper joint work between health and planning on a national scale. However, the learning from the Midlands experience will still be relevant as there remains no blueprint for turning policy into practice.

Note

1 Shisha bars (also called a *hookah lounge* or *den*) is an establishment where patrons share shisha (flavoured tobacco) from a communal water pipe (hookah or nargile) which is placed at each table.

References

Department of Communities and Local Government. 2010. *Indices of multiple deprivation.* London: The Stationery Office.
Department of Communities and Local Government. 2011. *Localism Act.* S.110. London: The Stationery Office.
Department of Communities and Local Government. 2012. *The planning policy framework (NPPF).* London: The Stationery Office.
Department of Communities and Local Government. 2014. *National planning practice guidance.* http://planningguidance.planningportal.gov.uk

Department of Health. 2012. *Health and Social Care Act.* London: The Stationery Office.

European Commission. 2001. *European Union Directive 2001/42/EC on the assessment of the effects of certain plans and programmes on the environment.* http://ec.europa.eu/environment/eia/sea-legalcontext.htm

Gladwell, M. 2000. *The tipping point: how little things can make a big difference.* New York: Little Brown.

Glasgow Centre for Population Health. 2013. *The Built Environment and Health.* Concept series 11. Glasgow: Glasgow Centre for Population Health. www.gcph.co.uk

Great Britain, Parliament. 2004. *The environmental assessment of plans and programmes regulations 2004.* SI 1633. London: The Stationery Office.

Marmot, M., Allen, J., Goldblatt, P., Boyce, T., McNeish, D., Grady, M. and Geddes, I. 2010. *Fair society, healthy lives: strategic review of health inequalities in England post 2010.* London: Public Health England.

Mislove, A., Massimiliano, M., Gummadi, K., Druschel, P. and Bhattacharjee, B. (2007). *Measurement and analysis of online social networks.* Internet Measurement Conference. 24–26 October 2007. San Diego, California, USA.

Office of the Deputy Prime Minister. 2004. *Section 19 of the UK Planning and Compulsory Purchase Act 2004.* London: The Stationery Office.

Vohra, S (2010). *A guide to health proofing masterplans.* www.hiagateway.org.uk

Zinoviev, D. (2011). Information diffusion in social networks. In *Social networking and behaviour modelling: qualitative and quantitative measures.* Maytham, S. and Mahdi, K. (eds). Hershey, PA: IGI Global.

37

THE THREE FABRICS
STRATEGY IN FINLAND

Leo Kosonen

The Kuopio Model

In Finland, a unique tool has been developed which combines healthy urban planning and design. The 'Kuopio Model' was developed in the Finnish City of Kuopio. This strategic approach to city planning promotes the recognition, respect and regeneration of three different systems of the urban fabric: walking, transit and car city fabrics (Kosonen 2007).

The strategic concept behind the model is to use the three identified urban fabrics (previously called 'city fabrics') as the basis for developing a masterplan and related plans to guide future development areas and patterns across an urban area, as well as identifying how existing urban fabric can be improved. A fabric in this concept is a product of certain lifestyles and functions that have needed certain physical elements and environments. It has a certain land use pattern, which is based on certain transportation priorities. Each of the three fabrics has different characteristics and benefits for health and well-being. The walking and transit city fabrics are recognised as a good basis for healthy urban planning and provide an environment that promotes healthy lifestyles. The car city fabric is clearly different. Even if it can offer aesthetically pleasant environments that are popular with many citizens, it is inherently less healthy because of the dependence on private motor vehicles, which has negative impacts both on global warming and the living conditions of the residents of the other fabrics.

This chapter explains the rationale and concepts behind the 'three fabrics' approach as well as how this has been implemented in Kuopio, Finland. The remainder of the chapter provides observations and conclusions concerning healthy urban planning and the application of the 'three fabrics' approach across Finland, as well as outlining the ongoing work towards a global theory for this model.

New way of thinking: three fabrics of a city

City planning in Kuopio has been using a unique approach to urban planning and managing development since the early 1990s. This different way of thinking recognises that there are different 'fabrics' which each contribute to the urban form and qualities of a city (Figure 37.1). This local way of thinking has led to a new focus for guiding urban change in the city, new urban planning practices (Mäntysalo and Kanninen 2013) and development outcomes which promote sustainable development and a healthy city.

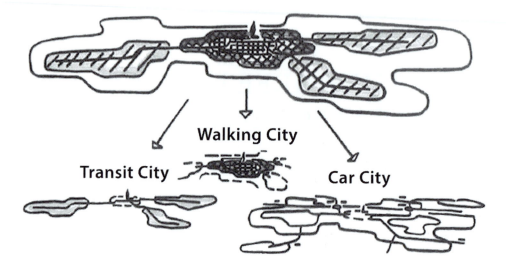

Figure 37.1 A city is a combination of three urban fabrics: walking fabric, transit fabric and car fabric

Source: Kosonen (1996, p. 3).

Walking, transit and car city fabrics have been identified as the basic overlapping systems that make up the urban environment of Kuopio (Kosonen 1994). However, these same systems can be found in any Finnish city (Kosonen and Siivola 1996; Ristimäki et al. 2013) or indeed in any other city in the world. There has not been any comprehensive theory used as the basis of these concepts but they are based on extensive professional experience and observations of daily life. This makes it a tangible and understandable tool that is easy to communicate but also provides a different approach to identify alternative solutions, which can lead to the implementation of better urban solutions.

The three fabrics approach has been referred to as the 'Kuopio Model' since 1993 (Figures 37.1, 37.3 and 37.4). This is parallel to the conceptual work by Peter Newman in Australia on city types and stages of urban development, which identified three global city types: Walking City, Public Transport City and Automobile City (Newman and Hogan 1987, pp. 14–22). Newman's illustration of the automobile city includes the areas of the transit city and the walking city as previous stages of city development (Newman and Kenworthy 1999). This recognition reinforces the representation of the three urban fabrics as the basic systems of present cities. One of the main outcomes of the Urban Fabrics Project (Kosonen 2013) was a Conceptual Combination of Three Urban Fabrics (Figure 37.2). This was compiled in Australia with Peter Newman's involvement and is based on maps and data of the International Sourcebook as well as the information of maps of more than a hundred cities (Newman and Kenworthy 1989; Kenworthy et al. 1999). A comprehensive Theory of Three Fabrics is under compilation.

Despite the lack of a comprehensive theory behind the development of the Kuopio Model, the application of the concept has been decisive and systematic. It has become a tool of communication, both in scientific and daily discussions. This has been noticed clearly in the analysis of Professor Raine Mäntysalo from Aalto University, Helsinki, who wrote about the Kuopio Model:

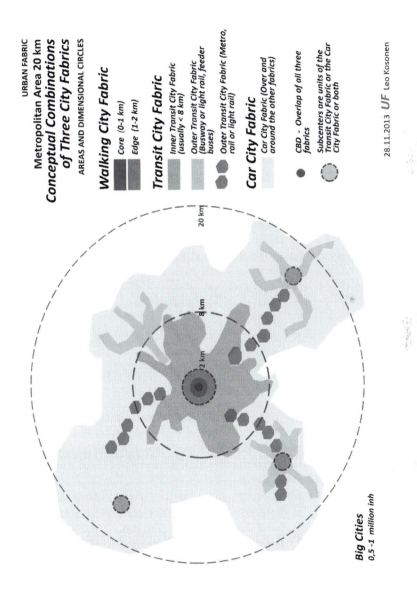

URBAN FABRIC

Metropolitan Area 20 km

**Conceptual Combinations
of Three City Fabrics**

AREAS AND DIMENSIONAL CIRCLES

Walking City Fabric

Core (0-1 km)

Edge (1-2 km)

Transit City Fabric

Inner Transit City Fabric
(usually < 8 km)

Outer Transit City Fabric
(Busway or light rail, feeder
buses)

Outer Transit City Fabric (Metro,
rail or light rail)

Car City Fabric

Car City Fabric (Over and
around the other fabrics)

CBD - Overlap of all three
fabrics

Subcenters are units of the
Transit City Fabric or the Car
City Fabric or both

28.11.2013 **UF** Leo Kosonen

20 km

8 km

2 km

Big Cities
0.5 -1 million inh

Figure 37.2   Conceptual combinations of three urban fabrics of a big city

Source: Kosonen (2013).

the Kuopio Model is well tested for policy and decision making prowess, yet rather less trialled for emancipatory use. However, the simplicity of the Model, its correspondence with everyday urban living and mobility, and dialogue-evoking capabilities regarding them – and its indifference to statistical or other administrative territorial divisions – make it a potential vehicle for increased power symmetry in urban planning practices.

(Mäntysalo and Kanninen 2013, p. 68)

Emergence and development of the Kuopio Model

Kuopio is a city of 100,000 inhabitants and functions as the regional centre of Eastern Finland. The national analysis of cityscapes by the Finnish Environment institute (Ristimäki et al. 2013) shows that Kuopio is the smallest of Finnish transit cities (meaning the cities that have a comprehensive transit city fabric). The impact of private motor vehicles on the urban development patterns has been fast, like in all Finnish cities, which has led to a dominance of the car city fabric. This dominance of the car city fabric over the other fabrics led to the recognition that the traditional approaches to city planning were ineffective and new tools were needed.

The turning point was at the end of the 1980s: city planning had been attempting to control and limit the growth of the car city fabric, but containment policies were not being properly implemented. In contrast to the adopted masterplan and planning policies, a political decision was made to allow the construction of two out-of-town hypermarkets. This led to the deterioration of the network of local shops across the city. It also contributed to the failure of the neighbourhood centre of a new precinct of 10,000 inhabitants called Petonen Garden City. The shopping street, which was under construction at the time, was unable to attract retailers. Coupled with the large out-of-town retailing development, political decisions were duplicating the growth of the low density housing areas in the belief that this form of development was needed to compete with other cities and neighbouring municipalities. This led to the abandonment of projects and development that characterised the transit city fabric.

The focus on reinforcing the car city fabric made it clear that the old way of planning, which was based on good examples, professional skills and incremental thinking, was not strong enough to ensure appropriate and healthy urban development. This traditional approach was not only insufficient in guiding new development but it was also proving to be inadequate to analyse the existing situation. Therefore, a new orientation and new tools were needed. In 1992, the three fabrics approach was developed as a response to this realisation (Figure 37.3). This change in approach meant the policy of limitations and control in the car city fabric were replaced by a new policy of recognition and renovation of the walking and transit city fabrics.

Areas of the fabrics have been acting as not only the framework for the management and analysis of urban development but for data collection as well. For instance, the data on car ownership in each of the fabrics (Figure 37.3) is used for programming, planning and management of urban development. The recognition of the walking and transit city fabrics was the start of a new discussion in the city. At first, the Kuopio Model was simply a tool used by the masterplan architect but it was soon adopted as a common concept of new thinking across the municipality, including as the basis of the new planning policy, Strategic Plan 2005, which was approved by the city council in 1993.

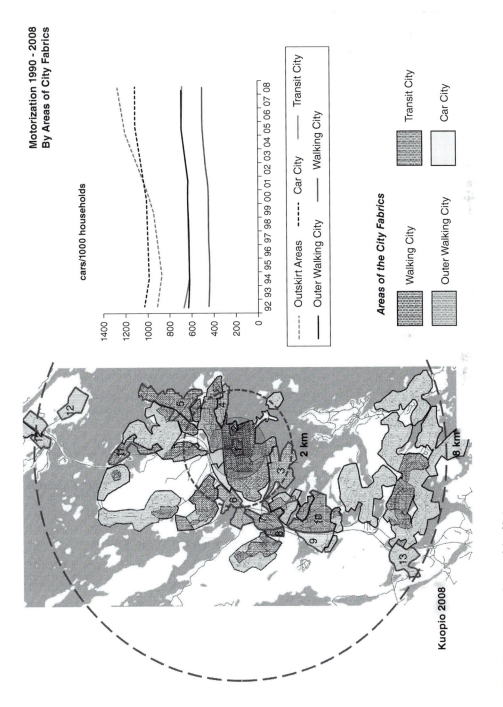

Figure 37.3 Recognition of areas of the fabrics

Source: Leo Kosonen, City of Kuopio, 27 January 2014.

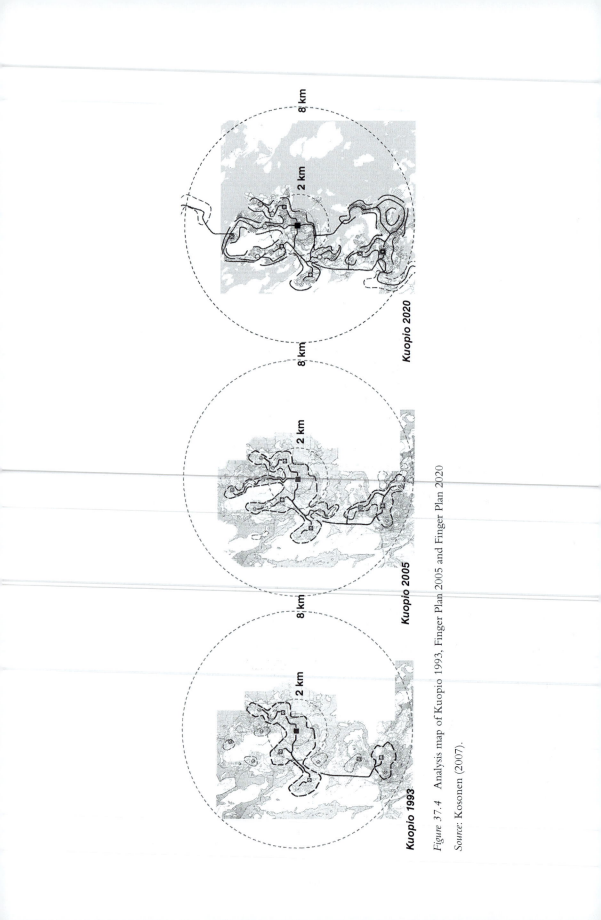

Figure 37.4 Analysis map of Kuopio 1993, Finger Plan 2005 and Finger Plan 2020

Source: Kosonen (2007).

Creating a strategic plan on the basis of the model

The Strategic Plan 2005 was developed using the Kuopio Model, which resulted in a 'Finger Plan' of growth for the city (Figure 37.4). The analysis of the plan illustrated the state and the problems of the transit city fabric in 1993. In addition to the main neighbourhoods of the transit city fabric, the plan also identified five neighbourhoods that were too small and isolated to maintain a suitable level of services and facilities to qualify as part of the transit city fabric. The strategic plan for 2005 illustrated the potential of renovation and supplementary housing in areas, which would reinforce these small outer neighbourhoods. This was achieved by strengthening and extending the 'fingers' from the city centre to combine with the small outer neighbourhoods, thereby expanding the existing transit city fabric area. *The focus was on keeping the transit city fabric livable and large enough to maintain a good network of local public transport.* This would reinforce the walking and transit city fabrics as a positive alternative, which would slow down the growth of the car city fabric. The second plan, Kuopio 2020, was approved by the city council in 2000. This plan illustrates the goals of the next phase of the strategic plan up to year 2020.

It is important to note that the Strategic Plan 2005 was not just an illustration of the future city. Together with the Kuopio Model it was a tool for promoting all kinds of new ideas, alternatives, practices and cooperation. New alternatives were needed because there were no proper development plans of the walking and transit city fabrics as the resources of city planning had been directed to addressing the problems and growth of the car city fabric. As well as the strategic plan, the model has also been supported by city-wide programmes of plans, investments and maintenance.

The City of Kuopio joined the World Health Organization (WHO) Healthy Cities Healthy Urban Planning sub-network in 2006, which reinforced the Kuopio Model as a good basis for healthy urban planning. Healthy urban planning objectives (Barton and Tsourou 2000), the Settlement Health Map (Chapter 1, Figure 1.2; Barton and Grant 2006) and the outputs of the WHO Healthy Cities network were applied relative to each of the fabrics, which led to outcomes that were combined with local practice and the international findings.

Application of the Kuopio strategy

Several renovations and extensions of the walking and transit city fabrics have been implemented in Kuopio. This section of this chapter illustrates some of the main outcomes of the approach to date. These include the pedestrian area of Kuopio city centre, renovation of the walking city fabric as well as the renovation and extension of the transit city fabric.

Pedestrian centre of Kuopio: a symbiosis of three fabrics

The commercial centre of Kuopio has been transformed into a pleasant pedestrian centre. This centre is a combination of all three urban fabrics. Previously, cars dominated the streets of the city centre; however, they now give way to walking and social life, with the central streets and squares prioritising pedestrians and social activities. Local buses are allowed in the central area and cars, while restricted in the streets, have direct access to underground car parking (the biggest car park is under the main square, hosting 1,300 cars).

It was important to recognise that all three urban fabrics function in the city centre, in particular the role of the car city fabric in ensuring viability of central shops and services. In Kuopio, like many other cities in the world, hypermarkets and malls in the car city fabric had been increasing. This was having negative consequences on the services within the walking and transit city fabrics and the city centre. Whilst carless residents of the walking and transit city fabrics were still shopping in the centre and at local shops, this was insufficient to maintain a good level of service. Therefore, to ensure viability and vibrancy of the town centre (in particular the centre of a small city like Kuopio) it was important that the centre functions as an effective element of the car city fabric as well as the more desirable transit and walking cities. So, in the city centre the fabrics have been combined into one entity, which is easy to access for all. However, it was imperative to ensure that the design and functioning of the city centre prioritises walking and cycling and lifestyles that favour local services and public transport ahead of private vehicles.

Renovation of the walking city fabric

Within the city centre, the recognition of both the problems and potentials of the walking city fabric has led to renovation of the areas surrounding the pedestrian core. This has included the construction of new houses, the introduction of a network of pedestrian streets and the removal of the one-way system of traffic in the central streets.

New housing construction

Some 2,000 apartments have been constructed in the brownfield sites of the walking city area. The Strategic Plan 2005 defined these areas as housing instead of commercial use. As a result the central population, which had declined to 13,000 in 1995, has grown to 16,000 inhabitants.

The design of the blocks in the city centre is conducive to a good walking environment. The blocks have convenient closed courtyards. Conventional parking requirements were revised 15 years ago and one third of the new apartments are for carless households instead of providing a parking place for each dwelling. Parking is provided under the buildings therefore allowing courtyards to be car free.

Network of pedestrian streets

Kuopio has a special network of narrow laneways dating from the 1700s. The total length of the laneway network is 10 kilometres and it covers the main areas of the walking city fabric. The laneways had previously been crowded by parking and car traffic in the beginning of the 1990s, but this new orientation towards the walking city fabric has led to the renovation of the whole network. As such, all of the laneways were turned to pedestrian streets.

More than half of the network has been renewed using new surfaces, greenery and environmental art (Figure 37.5). The network has gained popularity and it promotes walking and cycling. It can offer good walking routes for the population, especially for elder citizens with walkers because of the high quality surfacing and maintenance.

Renovation of the traffic systems

The traffic systems of the whole centre have been renewed. The one-way streets of the 1970s have been returned to two-way streets and the waves of green lights for traffic movement have been abandoned. Now the streets are calmer and there is more space for pedestrians, cyclists and buses. People feel the streets are now more safe and comfortable. Car drivers also find it easy to enter the parking facilities but are restricted in using the streets for through traffic.

Figure 37.5 A laneway for pedestrians and cyclists is an element of the walking city fabric

Source: Kosonen.

Renovation of the transit city fabric

The new orientation of the strategic plan has led to the renovation of six small neighbourhoods of the transit city fabric. The projects have been carried out with the residents involved. Public spaces, schools and other buildings have been renovated. Services and social activities have been improved. Supplementary housing construction has brought new residents, which has improved the level of bus transit and services.

Särkiniemi is a small neighbourhood. It previously had 2,500 inhabitants before the renewal project. A new detailed plan was compiled and public spaces were improved in close cooperation with the residents. Buildings were renovated and several new high quality apartment blocks were built to get new residents and to raise the status of the neighbourhood.

Simultaneously with the renewal, a new precinct, Särkilahti, was designed and built in the vicinity of the neighbourhood. The two areas are connected together by a special bus street and bridge and together the renovated Särkiniemi and the new area, Särkilahti, combine to form a new 'finger' of the transit city fabric. This area now has 4,000 inhabitants. The bridge is joining parks in the two areas, promoting cycling, active living and the recreational activities of the residents on both sides of the bay. The bus bridge is also a manifestation of the permanence of the transit city fabric (Figure 37.6).

In Särkilahti, the bus street has been built in the middle of the area to maximise access for residents to the bus network and the apartments are located within a short distance from the bus stops. A small pleasant square with a children's playground, a local shop and the bus stops are the core meeting place of the area. Parking is located mostly in the outskirts of the area and there is no through traffic.

Figure 37.6   Särkilahti is a new unit of the transit city fabric

Source: Kosonen (2007). Photo: City of Kuopio 2004.

The renovation and reinforcement of the transit city fabric has resulted in the older neighbourhood gaining a new respect amongst the residents and a growth in the use of local shops and services. The bus service has also been doubled, with a bus every 15 minutes instead of the old interval of 30 minutes. People are using buses more than the average in Kuopio and private vehicle use is moderate. Särkilahti has become a popular place to live. The inhabitants use the bridge as direct access for walking or cycling to the services of the main neighbourhood, the university and the central parts of the city.

New transit city fabric of Lehtoniemi

The population in the transit city fabric was declining due to the increased number of smaller households. While the decrease in household size was partly compensated by supplementary housing construction, this was not enough to curb the population decline. New growth areas were needed to maintain the proper functions of the transit city fabric as a whole.

The Urban Fabrics Project of the Finnish Environment Institute came to the conclusion that the inner transit city fabric, based on basic bus lines, should be inside a dimensional circle of eight kilometres from the city centre (Kosonen 2013). However, this potential area is very limited in Kuopio because of lakes, hills, slopes and areas of nature conservation. This meant that opening a new growth direction of the transit city fabric was not an easy task. Significant infrastructure, such as bridges and a new canal, were needed.

A bus oriented 'string of pearls'

Lehtoniemi is a new area of bus-based transit city fabric. The neighbourhood is a combination of five separate precincts. These precincts are in a queue, forming a corridor or 'a string of

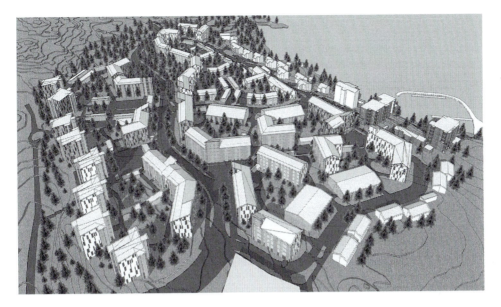

Figure 37.7   Helmi, a new precinct of the bus oriented transit city fabric, is under construction

Source: City of Kuopio.

pearls' around bus stops. Each of these precincts will have more than 1,000 inhabitants, so the total number of residents will be 8,000. This should be enough to maintain a good level of bus service and basic local services.

Concepts of the precincts have been designed by different architects or consortiums, including the winner of a Europan 8 competition for young architects. Helmi (Figure 37.7) has been designed so that the bus stop is on a small square and access to the bus stop is less than 250 metres for every resident. The buildings have peaceful courtyards with good access to greenspace and the lake. The main street runs through the middle of the area. The street is peaceful, because it is serving only local traffic and it will have a bus service once every 15 minutes. The school, kindergarten, a main square with shops and several parks with good playgrounds are already serving the residents of Lehtoniemi as well as the bus network, cycling routes and green areas.

A 'Street of Islands': a new element of three fabrics

The Street of Islands (Figure 37.8) was opened in 2008. It facilitates all three fabrics: the residents of the walking city fabric now have access to new green areas by the lake and the previously car city fabric on the other side of the lake has now become part of the transit city fabric with easy access by bus, walking or cycling to the city centre. The street has several bridges and is not a conventional road but a narrow landscaped street for slow driving (there is a 40 km/hr speed limit). A conventional road of the car city fabric was not acceptable, because it would have destroyed the value of this group of small, beautiful islands.

The lanes on the northern side of the road are for cars and buses and the lane of the southern side is for cyclists and pedestrians. The lanes are separated by a fence made of local stone. This reduces the noise of the vehicles and protects the recreational activities. The bicycle lane has been designed for recreational purposes. The bridge weaves along the northern sides of the islands creating a pleasant linear recreational area. To fit with the landscape, the bridges are low;

Figure 37.8   Street of Islands is an element of three fabrics

Source: City of Kuopio.

however, access was also needed for local boats, so a new canal with a high bridge was also provided.

In addition to the new transit city fabric that the Street of Islands provides, the street provides a new connection to 6,000 inhabitants in the car city fabric to the south. The whole area has 14,000 inhabitants and is called the 'District of Islands'. It is a combination of both the transit and car city fabrics, and both of these fabrics benefit from each other (Figure 37.9).

The areas of the car city fabric have a good level of bus transport use, which is attributable to the high number of young families and youth in the area (Kosonen 2007). These buses are now also serving the first residents of the transit city fabric created by the Street of Islands. In the future, the buses of the new transit city fabric can replace the present lines and also serve the residents of the car city fabric.

The Street of Islands and the transit city fabric of Lehtoniemi are not just a new growth direction but more like a large infill development combining areas of the car city fabric with the city centre. The Environmental Impact Assessment of the Street indicated (Figure 37.10) that, in 50 years, a 50 per cent reduction of greenhouse gas emissions from the traffic of the urban fabric based on the Street could be achieved, compared to a conventional alternative without the Street (Halme and Harmaajärvi 2003). These positive impacts will be improved even more if the good qualities of the urban fabric lead to healthy lifestyles and behaviours, such as walking and cycling to schools, using buses and local services, and families managing with just one car or even no car.

Health benefits, political risks and the wider application of the model

It is important to recognise the differences between the three fabrics in terms of how well they meet different health objectives. Tools such as the Settlement Health Map (Barton and Grant 2006) can be used to identify qualities and functions of these fabrics and how these

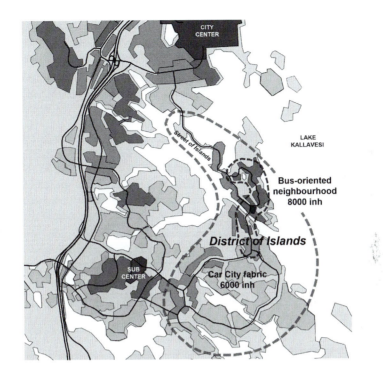

Figure 37.9   District of Islands is a symbiosis of the transit and the car city fabrics

Source: Leo Kosonen.

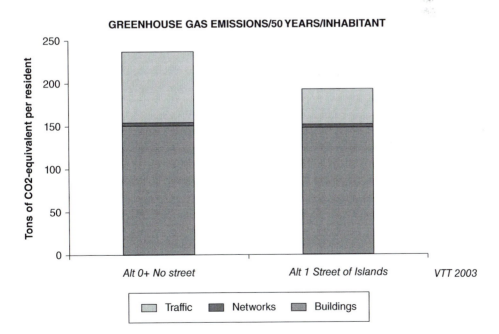

Figure 37.10   Positive impacts of the Street of Islands

Source: Halme and Harmaajärvi (2003).

relate to the wider determinants of health. Figure 37.11 shows an analysis of how each of the three fabrics performs against some example health objectives. This analysis illustrates that while health objectives can be seen as being clear and straightforward, they need to be applied in recognition of the different characteristics and functions of the three fabrics. For example, aspects of the car city fabric can be seen as healthy (e.g. opportunities for healthy exercise) and, equally, areas of the walking and transit city fabrics can be potentially unhealthy (e.g. road safety). However, what is often not recognised when analysing the impacts of the car city fabric is that this fabric is contributing to the poorer road safety in the walking city fabric. So it is important to consider the wider aspects of health and sustainability as well as the potential negative 'side effects' on the other fabrics. Therefore, the car city fabric has been assessed to be mainly unhealthy, not so much because of the physical qualities within the fabric itself, but because of the impact on the global climate as well as the negative impacts, or 'side effects', on the areas in the other fabrics. The car city fabric is also unsuitable for car-free living and discriminates against residents who cannot use cars.

Identifying the urban fabrics

The spatial distribution of the three fabrics can be identified using a combination of the theoretical concept of the three fabrics model and on the ground observations of the characteristics and features in different areas of the city (Figure 37.11). The theoretical concept provides the basic classifications of areas by using dimensional circles (Figures 37.2 and 37.12) that indicate the potential areas for different fabrics. Areas of the walking city fabric can be found within the dimensional circles of one (the inner walking city fabric) and two kilometres (the outer walking city fabric). The inner transit city fabric (based on trams or basic bus lines) can be found within eight kilometres. This can be seen from the information from basic maps (Open Street Map, Google maps) and the series of maps of several surveys (Newman and Kenworthy 1989; Kenworthy and Laube 1999; Hass-Clau and Crampton 2002; Jenks and Jones 2010; Ristimäki et al. 2013; SNAMUTS Cities 2014; Gordon 2013; Kosonen 2013). The outer transit city fabric, which is based on rail transit and feeder buses or fast bus routes, can be found up to 20–30 kilometres from the city centre. The car city fabric is around and over the other fabrics. The features of each fabric can be identified through an analysis of the physical elements of the urban areas and how the area functions, as well as the qualities and lifestyles for the residents. These 'habitats' are described below.

The habitats of the walking city fabric are centrally located neighbourhoods, which need high quality housing that is suitable for carless households and has good access to private courtyards as well as parks and public places. This habitat is likely to need a reduction of disturbances like noise and pollution.

The habitats of the transit city are neighbourhoods and smaller precincts, which need a good location, viable population size, public transport options and elements of the built environment that promote sustainability and healthy lifestyles. The transit city habitat requires a focus on safety, high quality housing, the availability of services, access to nature as well as promoting active living and opportunities for social interaction.

The habitats of the car city fabric are often large areas of housing located outside the public transport network. This habitat needs cycling routes that provide safe access to local facilities and networks of green areas for healthy exercise. It is important to try to promote active travel and reduce reliance on private cars by trying to reduce the distance to the transit city fabric.

Many habitats are combinations of fabrics, 'habitats in between'. Lifestyles and functions of the car city fabric are common in all habitats. That is problematic but on the other hand it can be seen as a challenge to change behaviours across all three fabrics.

Kuopio			
Healthy objectives	Inner City /	Urban fingers /	Urban sprawl /
28.8.2006/Leo Kosonen	Walking City	Transit City	Car City
• opportunity for healthy exercise	good	excellent	good
• social cohesion	fair	fair	segregative
• equity	yes	yes	no
• access to employment and facilities	yes	yes	by car only
• road safety	fair	good	problems / cars
• an attractive environment	good	good	good
• acceptable noise levels	fair	good	problems / cars
• good air quality	fair	good	problems / cars
• climate stability	yes	yes	no / cars

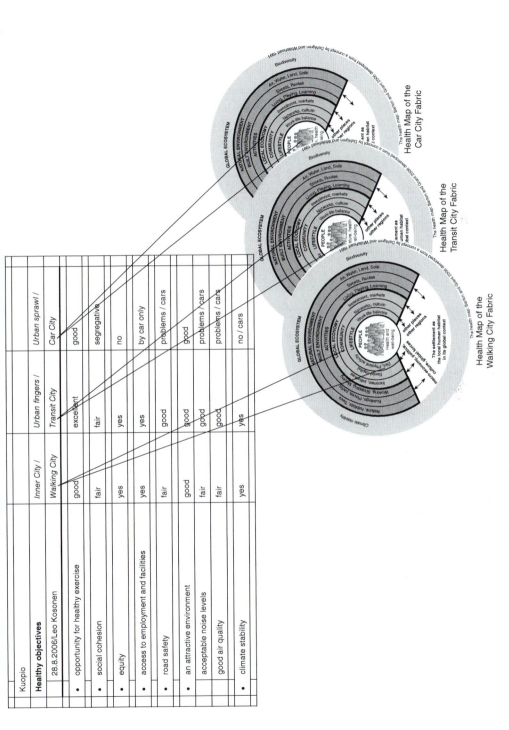

Figure 37.11 Healthy objectives and Health Maps of the fabrics

Source: Leo Kosonen, 2014. Adapted from a table by Leo Kosonen, City of Kuopio, 28 August 2006, and Barton and Grant (2006) based on Whitehead, M. and Dahlgren, G. (1991).

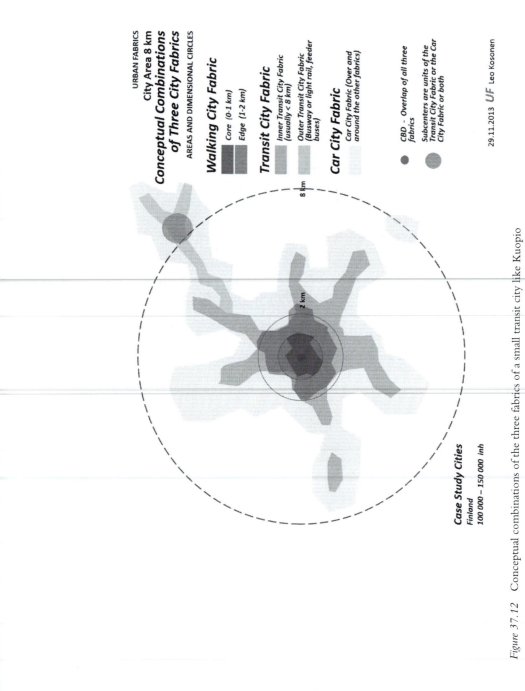

URBAN FABRICS
City Area 8 km
Conceptual Combinations
of Three City Fabrics
AREAS AND DIMENSIONAL CIRCLES

Walking City Fabric

Core (0-1 km)
Edge (1-2 km)

Transit City Fabric

Inner Transit City Fabric
(usually < 8 km)
Outer Transit City Fabric
(Busway or light rail, feeder
buses)

Car City Fabric

Car City Fabric (Over and
around the other fabrics)

● CBD - Overlap of all three
fabrics

● Subcenters are units of the
Transit City Fabric or the Car
City Fabric or both

29.11.2013 *UF* Leo Kosonen

8 km

2 km

Case Study Cities
Finland
100 000 – 150 000 inh

Figure 37.12 Conceptual combinations of the three fabrics of a small transit city like Kuopio

Source: Kosonen (2013).

Barriers to implementation

The main barrier to using new concepts such as this is that for some the car city fabric is not seen as an unsustainable pattern. This means that politicians and other stakeholders could continue to direct resources and investments that reinforce the car city fabric, even if this causes the deterioration of the other fabrics. There is always a risk that despite a strategic plan that embraces the three fabrics methodology, stakeholders may apply conventional concepts which can divert programmed plans and investments from the walking and transit city fabrics to the car city fabric.

Another potential limitation is the impact of national level legislation and taxation. These are often focused (partly inadvertently) on promoting car city fabric development like out-of-town shopping centres, car dependent housing and fast roads for the cars of commuters.

Other applications of the Kuopio Model

The Kuopio Model has been used in Finland as the basis of several national level analyses. The 'Urban Zone' project by the Finnish Environment Institute, SYKE, undertook an analysis of the changes in urban structure of 34 Finnish cities from 1985 to 2010 (Ristimäki et al. 2013). National Travel Surveys from 2004 and 2010 also used the model, as did several other cities and national projects. The concept for the Finnish Intermediate Cities (see Figures 37.12 and 37.13) is the latest application of the Kuopio Model, produced by the Urban Fabrics Project (Kosonen 2013).

Some horizon scanning for the future

The Kuopio experience shows that the new way of thinking is possible and it can lead to good results. It is a good framework for healthy urban design and programmes of healthy urban development, because it helps to combine the efforts of various groups into a series of conclusions, decisions and implementations which are complementary and lead to more or less comprehensive renovations and regeneration of the environment and the activities that can take place with it.

The easiest way to start is to concentrate on one of the fabrics at a time. The work becomes more effective when all three fabrics are recognised and addressed using a comprehensive concept. It is obvious that this way of thinking and the concepts are a good basis for a new comprehensive theory of cities (Newman et al. 2015).

References

Barton, H. and Tsourou, C. 2000. *Healthy urban planning*. London: Spon Press.

Barton, H. and Grant, M. 2006. A health map for the local human habitat. *Journal of the Royal Society for the Promotion of Public Health*. 126 (6), 252–253.

Gordon, D. 2013. Canada: a country of suburbs. www.canada.com/news/infographics/suburbs/suburbs. html, accessed 29 August 2013.

Halme, T. and Harmaajärvi, I. 2003. Kuopion yhteiskuntatalousselvitys. Eteläisten osien kaupunkirakenne-vaihtoehdot. (Urban economic study on town structure alternatives of City of Kuopio. VTT Technical Research Centre of Finland and City of Kuopio – in Finnish.) Kuopion kaupunki YK 2003: 10.

Hass-Clau, C. and Crampton, G. 2002. Future of urban transport. Learning from success and weakness: light rail. Brighton: Environmental and Transport Planning.

Jenks, M. and Jones, C. (eds) 2010. *Dimensions of the sustainable city*. Dordrecht, Heidelberg, London, New York: Springer.

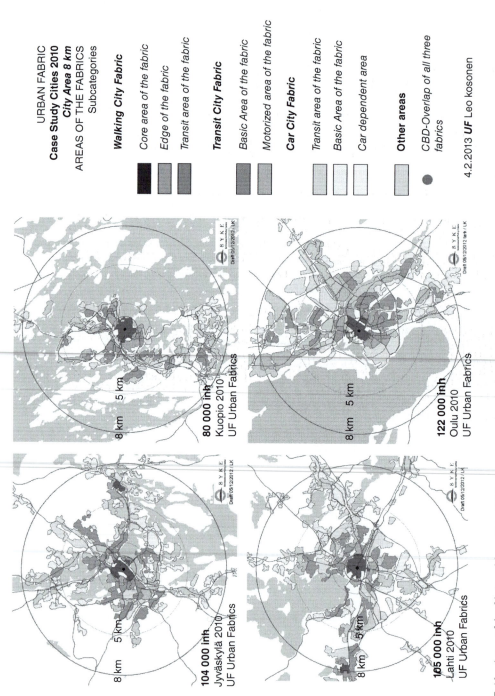

Figure 37.13 Areas of the fabrics of four cities, 2010

Source: Kosonen (2013).

Kenworthy, J., Laube, F., Newman, P., Barter, P., Raad, T., Poboon, C. and Guia, B. 1999. *An international sourcebook of automobile dependence in cities 1960–1990*. Boulder, CO: University Press of Colorado.

Kosonen, L. 1994. Kaupunkirakenne 2005. (Urban structure of Kuopio 2005 – in Finnish.) Selvitys 6/1994, Ympäristöministeriö.

Kosonen, L. 1996. Transit city: a balancing alternative. A proposal of the City of Kuopio for Urban Pilot Project of EU/DG XVI. City of Kuopio.

Kosonen, L. 2007. Kuopio 2015: Jalankulku- joukkoliikenne- ja autokaupunki. (Kuopio 2015 – A walking, transit and car city – in Finnish.) Suomen ympäristö 36/2007, Rakennettu ympäristö. Helsinki: Ympäristöministeriö. https://helda.helsinki.fi/bitstream/handle/10138/38432/SY_36_2007.pdf?sequence=5, accessed 8 April 2015.

Kosonen, L. 2013. Model of three urban fabrics: adapted for finnish intermediate cities. A net based document. The Finnish Environment Institute. http://urbanfabrics.fi, accessed 10 April 2014.

Kosonen, L. and Siivola, M. 1996. Joukkoliikennekaupunki (Transit cities – in Finnish). Kuopion kaupunki.

Mäntysalo, R. and Kanninen, V. 2013. Trading between land use and transportation planning: the Kuopio model. In Balducci, A. and Mäntysalo, R. (eds), *Urban planning as a trading zone*, 57–73. Springer Urban and Landscape Perspectives 13. Dordrecht: Springer.

Newman, P. and Hogan, T. 1987. Urban density and transport: a simple model based on three city types. Murdoch, Western Australia: Murdoch University.

Newman, P. and Kenworthy, J. 1989. *Cities and automobile dependence*. Aldershot, England: Gower Publishing Company Limited.

Newman, P. and Kenworthy, J. 1999. Sustainability and cities: overcoming automobile dependence. Washington, DC/Covelo, CA: Island Press.

Newman, P., Kosonen, L. and Kenworthy, J. 2015. Theory of urban fabrics: planning the walking, transit and automobile city. Submitted to Town Planning Review.

Ristimäki, M., Tiitu, M., Kalenoja, H., Helminen, V. and Söderström, P. 2013. Yhdyskuntarakenteen vyöhykkeet Suomessa: Jalankulku-, joukkoliikenne- ja autovyöhykkeiden kehitys vuosina 1985–2010. (Walking transit and car zones of Finnish cities 1985–2010 – in Finnish.) Reports of the Finnish Environment Institute 32/2013. https://helda.helsinki.fi/handle/10138/41574, accessed 8 April 2015.

SNAMUTS Cities. 2014. Spatial network analysis for multi-modal urban transport systems: a net based document. www.snamuts.com/snamuts-cities.html, accessed 28 August 2014.

Whitehead, M. and Dahlgren, G. 1991. 'The main determinants of health' model, version accessible in: Dahlgren, G. and Whitehead, M. (2007) *European strategies for tackling social inequities in health: levelling up part 2*. Copenhagen: WHO Regional Office for Europe.

38

FREIBURG

Green capital of Europe

Marcus Grant and Hugh Barton

The city that does it all

In the last book written before he died in 2014 at the age of 85, planning guru Peter Hall reviewed cities across Europe and identified Freiburg and Stockholm as the two best planned on the continent (Hall 2014). Freiburg, he says, is 'the city that did it all'. It has become a place of pilgrimage for planners and city leaders from across the world. In 2009 and 2010 we – the current authors – joined the throng, leading a mixed group of chief public health officers and planners from South West England. What impressed all those who went was not only the quality of the urban environment and the positive social atmosphere, but the fact that the principles of healthy urban planning were here made visible, and they worked (Figure 38.1).

Figure 38.1   View of Freiburg city centre with the Munster in the middle ground
Source: Grant.

The irony is that 'health' has not been a prime driver of policy in Freiburg. Rather the goals have been environmental sustainability and a good quality of life for all. The resulting principles include the promotion of active travel, social inclusion, a vibrant and innovative economy, a green, biodiverse and productive landscape, sustainable water and energy strategies, and a city of education, culture and co-operation. All the spheres of the Settlement Health Map (see Chapter 1, Figure 1.2; Barton and Grant 2006) are addressed in a highly synergistic way, through decision-making processes that are exemplary.

Freiburg is a town of some 200,000 inhabitants in south-west Germany, a regional centre of administration, services and education. It is situated 20 km east of the Rhine river, almost equidistant from Strasbourg in France and Basel in Switzerland. The city has a marvellous climate, with long, balmy summers and crisp winters. It is located in a bifurcated flat bottomed valley with forested slopes rising around where urban development gives way to the Black Forest on one side, the villages and hamlets of the plain on the other (Figure 38.2).

This chapter examines the spatial configuration of Freiburg, and asks how land use, transport and design policies have been developed that have achieved a good quality of life across the lifecourse, whilst also minimising global footprint.

Historical background

The city was bombed during World War II, culminating in an air raid in November 1944 that destroyed 80 per cent of the city centre, sparing only the cathedral, or Munster. Across Europe, in many such bombed cities, damaged old quarters were then comprehensively cleared and adapted to motorised traffic. In Freiburg, enlightened planners saw that the former medieval-based pattern based

Figure 38.2   Satellite image of the Freiburg urban area in its Black Forest setting

Source: Google Earth.

on the organic growth of small irregular plots and a reticulation of a variety of streets and alleys had served both commerce and city life well. They decided to rebuild the centre on the old street pattern, with modern commercial needs expressed behind the frontages in terms of the original plots being often combined to form the larger accommodation demanded by modern offices and retail. The street scene, including active frontages, massing and form was kept very close to how the centre had evolved prior to the bombing. Later, in the 1970s, the whole central area was pedestrianised, excepting for tram routes and bicycles.

Progressive green policy had its roots in the early 1970s, when the state of Baden–Württemberg's plan to build a nuclear power plant in the town of Wyhl, just 30 km away, provoked intense protest and common cause among Freiburg residents and the adjoining rural and farming communities. With widespread civil disobedience, the protesters saw a positive response was needed – solar energy and less reliance on fossil fuels (Gregory 2011). Since that period, Freiburg has become known as a city with strong green leadership and has set quality of life as a municipal objective. This economic, political and technical triumvirate for change was strongly supported, over a sustained period of time, by an academic activist and action research community from the university (Figure 38.3).

1111	Important regional marketplace is given the status of a free market town/city
1200	New Munster construction commences, proceeds in several phases
1513	Final phase of Munster construction completed
1944	Majority of the town centre razed to the ground by air raid bombing
1950s	Initiation of rebuilding of the centre to the medieval street plan
1960s	First commitment to link land use change to the retained tram system
1969	First integrated traffic management plan and cycle path network
1972	Threat of nuclear power plant in the town of Wyhl
1973	Entire city centre converted to a pedestrian zone
1975	Nuclear plant plan dropped
1984	The Municipality of Freiburg through its stakeholding in the transport authority supports the introduction of a City-wide Environmental Card giving unlimited travel on the urban tram and bus network
1985	The Municipality of Freiburg sets up an urban energy collaboration with the municipal energy utility. Emphasis on renewable energy and energy savings
1986	Energy and environmental shocks with the Chernobyl disaster and concern over acid rain damaging the Black Forest
1991	Environmental Card replaced with a RegioCard, allowing unlimited use of not only Freiburg's urban transit but also public transport in the whole region
1992	Freiburg's building design standards amended to require that all new houses built on city land use no more than 65 kWh/m2/yr heating energy, 10 kWh/m2/yr less than the national standard
1995	Vauban begun as a 'sustainable model district' collaboration between the council and Forum Vauban to house 5,000 people on a 41 hectare site, 3 km from the centre
1995	Freiburg city council resolution to permit construction only of 'low-energy buildings' on municipal land, and all new buildings to comply with 'low energy' specifications

1996	City council adopts a global climate protection plan with integrated assessment and promotion of a concern for ecology
2001	Federal renewable energy law requires utilities to buy power from independent producers
2005	Rieselfeld planned to house 12,000 on a 78 hectare site
2008	Traffic development plan 2020 further consolidates the transport approach
2008	Revisions to move new housing even closer to the 'passive house' standard of just 15 kWh/m2/yr
2010	Rieselfeld has approximately 9,000 inhabitants
2010	Freiburg declared European City of the Year, in the Urbanism Awards

Figure 38.3   Key events in a trajectory of change to a healthier urban environment: Freiburg im Breisgau

Sources: Gregory (2011), Melia (2006), Energie-Cités (1999).

Changed trajectory in behaviour, culture and impacts

The example of Freiburg contradicts those who believe that habitual behaviour and local 'culture' change so slowly that policy innovation is problematic. Older citizens in Freiburg remember when it was a conservative place with a growing traffic problem, following the general pattern of European cities (Melia 2006). But consistent policy innovation, broad-based political commitment and strategic public transport investment has enabled dramatic changes in behaviour. In the early 80s, public transport use was modest, with 29 million annual journeys and a running cost (subsidy) of €10.3 million. This issue was addressed and the situation transformed. By 2007 there were over 70 million annual journeys and subsidy had dropped to some €6 million in what had become a more efficient, frequent and extensive network (Verkehrs AG, Freiburger undated). Fares accounted for almost 90 per cent of running costs – the highest of any city in Europe (Hall 2014). Passenger numbers continued to grow, with 75 million in 2012. Modal shift between 1982 and 1999 can also be seen through the changing mix of the city's volume of traffic. During this period cycling increased from 15 per cent to 28 per cent of trips, and public transport from 11 per cent to 18 per cent, while the proportion of car trips fell from 38 per cent to 30 per cent of the total (Gregory 2011).

At the same time – unlike the general European pattern – car ownership did not increase, so that by 2006 it was 23 per cent below the German average, and carbon dioxide (CO_2) transport emissions have fallen, despite the buoyant economy and population growth (Buehler and Pucher 2011). Car ownership in the new urban extension of Vauban is a mere 150 vehicles per thousand population, equivalent to one car for every third household (ibid.). Car use is down to around a tenth of trips. There are 'sticks and carrots' involved in this transformation. Car owners have to buy a space in a communal multistorey car park on the periphery of the residential area, at a hefty one-off cost. But the essential reason is that the quality of non-car options is so good, and the car-free residential environments – policed by the residents themselves – so friendly, that most people find that cars are unnecessary

These facts give just a flavour of the lifestyle change. Increased levels of active travel have been paralleled by the reinforcement of local neighbourhood provision, the cultivation of community social capital, especially through active citizen participation, and progressive improvement in environmental conditions, so that now it is a delight to walk or cycle anywhere in Freiburg. The streets feel safe, and traffic is not intimidating. All these characteristics are – from the wider evidence literature – associated with positive health outcomes (Grant et al. 2009). Unfortunately direct health outcomes in Freiburg have proved unobtainable.[1]

The discussion below will draw out elements of the approach to change, which has always been systemic, through examining the response to four problems which many cities face:

1. How can a holistic and integrated approach to the overall planning of a city be achieved?
2. How can cities integrate transport and land use planning to ensure excellent accessibility to a range of facilities by low carbon and active modes?
3. What type of development approach is needed to support mixed and inclusive communities, and how are residents' creative energies involved in this process, supporting healthy lifestyles?
4. How can high quality, legible and characterful new neighbourhoods be delivered whilst also allowing bottom-up ownership in the design process?

Taking the long view, and seeing the city region as a whole

People make cities. In the case of Freiburg, the city has been very lucky in the people who have guided development. An integrated approach to environmental, economic and social goals has been accepted as the priority by whichever party was in power. Instead of planning policy being a 'political football', with priorities being subject to the whims and prejudices of elected representatives, there has been remarkable consistency at city and state levels. Urban planning was recognised as a long-term endeavour. This was helped because one inspirational mayor – Dr Rolf Bohme – was in office for 20 years from 1982 to 2002, and one chief planning officer – Wulf Daseking – masterminded the physical development of the city from 1984 to 2012, gathering around him a team of able and talented planners and designers. They provided a 'long-term vision allied to sustained delivery' (Hall 2014 p. 251).

The vision encompassed all facets of city life, each facet synergistically reinforcing the overarching strategy. In the economic field, the city lacked industrial strength, but had the benefit of a large research–oriented university. When the political mood was galvanised by the threat of a nuclear power station close by, the city seized the initiative by investing in the production of solar cells, at the same time creating the local market for them, so that the need for nuclear electricity was removed. It became the solar capital of Europe. More broadly the city cultivated partnerships between private firms and the university, building a post-industrial, knowledge-based economy which could compete in the global economy. University graduates found enticing local work opportunities, so the educational investment and the social connections made while at university strengthened the dynamic of the city.

Environmental, social and economic goals were combined to underpin the energy strategy. Buildings were constructed to very high energy-efficiency specifications, combined heat and power stations provided cheap heat, and with the solar investment have allowed the city to generate much of its own electricity. Fuel poverty (and attendant health problems) is banished. Excessive summer heat (with global warming a growing health hazard) is moderated by greenspaces, tree planting along streets, and well-planted private and communal gardens. Together with the surface water drainage features of swales, streams and ponds, the greenery gives the feeling of the country in the town, providing yet another clutch of health promoting urban design approaches (Sugiyama et al. 2008).

The commitment to innovative commercial opportunities has not meant that the market is allowed to dictate the fabric of the city. On the contrary, the vision was of a compact city, with people given space to enjoy the environment, and traffic tamed. Thus out-of-town development was forbidden. Instead there has been reinvestment in the city centre, encouraging a flourishing tourist industry. Other businesses and institutions are located along tram lines, as described below.

The most impressive aspect of the strategy is the way it has been implemented consistently across scales: the city region – including the hinterland of rural settlements – is seen as functionally interdependent, and adjacent authorities collaborate to bring services to all; the city itself is planned as a whole, with every development contributing, not diluting, the overall plan: the city of short distances and of neighbourhoods; the detailed design and construction of buildings and spaces enhance the vision. And throughout all the processes of change, the active partnership between communities, business and the city authority is critical.

Integration of transport and land use planning

At the heart of planning in Freiburg is a long-term, consistent spatial strategy. Transport and land use planning have always been carried out in concert, since the very first steps in rebuilding the bombed centre. Although the original street pattern was largely replicated in the rebuilding, an allowance was made for future tram provision. This integration of transport and land use planning can be seen time and again.

- Commercial and residential development and tram network development are entwined by a single ambition. The goal is to have the maximum number of people, at home, at work or at the local and central shops, within 500 m of a tram stop. This guides both permissions about where development is allowed and investment decisions for extending the tram network. Currently over 80 per cent of the city's population lives within 500 m of a stop, and the remainder have good bus access. There are no out-of-town retail or business parks only easily accessible by car.
- A transport hub has been developed at the railway station close to the centre of town. Within a few hundred metres' walk there are national and regional train platforms, a bus station, all major city tram lines, car parking and car-sharing facilities, a protected space for the parking of 1,000 bikes and a cycle hire and travel centre.
- Across the city region, tram and bus routes have been carefully designed to provide seamless integration. This has been achieved through co-ordination, both in terms of spatial configuration (network and termini) and service (ticketing, timing, frequency and first and last service times). This has given the residents of the city itself and of the surrounding hamlets and villages a good quality of city–countryside access. Responding to local need is key to the approach. For example, rural parishes contribute to a special subsidised Friday and Saturday night service which sees specially commissioned communal taxis taking young revellers back to their rural homes from the final bus terminus where required.
- The extension of the tram line into the major new neighbourhood of Rieselfeld (see below) was constructed as enabling infrastructure. The fully commissioned line was operational so early in the development programme that it was able to the carry construction workers who built the new neighbourhood. Moreover, its existence made it easy for even the first waves of residents to establish a public transport-based lifestyle. Moving house is a major life transition where people make significant decisions, such as places of work or education, where they shop and how much access they need to a car (Allender et al. 2008).

Collaborative design for inclusive communities

Freiburg demonstrates the validity of a twin approach, with the 'people side' of social engagement and 'place side' of effective technical solutions needing to work hand in hand. The 'people side' builds social capital and this influences long-term neighbourhood stability and success (Temkin

Figure 38.4   Integration of transport and land use planning at all scales: bicycle garage as part of the
central integrated city and regional transport hub; trams bravely integrated into the narrow
pedestrianised historic city core; aerial view of tramlines along the main Rieselfeld high street

Source: Grant.

and Rohe 1998). Freiburg shows how citizen engagement can occur prior to, during and after
construction. The 'technical' side, provided by the city, sets the context of land purchase, infrastructure framework and design codes.

Many urban renewal projects and two major urban extensions on brownfield sites have
demonstrated the power of the Freiburg approach. Vauban is a new locality of some 5,000 people, closely tied into the older structure of the city, and served by a new extension of the tram
system. Rieselfeld is larger, designed as a free-standing neighbourhood on the periphery, linked
by tram to the city as a whole, with major employment opportunities within walking distance.
It will grow to a population of 12,000. The city takes a hard-headed commercial approach to
development. In both cases it purchased the land from the previous users, created a masterplan
in discussion with potential residents, and invested up-front in the physical and social infrastructure. Subsequently plots are sold to a wide range of small private and community developers,
which allows all the loans to be paid off. The approach works superbly. Good location, investment in local amenity and attention to quality design has ensured high demand. By engaging
future residents from the start, many of the development risks are removed, mutual trust is built
alongside the physical building process, and social capital accumulated (Hall 2014).

Key to success is holding the big house builders at bay, thereby creating multiple options for
local people. The city enforces a maximum number of units that can be held by any one firm or
group in a perimeter block, ensuring diversity of control, design and occupation. In Rieselfeld
the maximum is one twelfth of the total units in the block. The city specifies the housing mix.
Typically a development block will include town houses and apartments, and opportunities for
commercial activity on the ground floor. Small builders, individual households, social providers
and housing co-operatives collaborate in construction. The housing co-operatives – known as

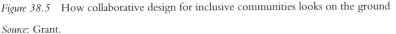

Figure 38.5   How collaborative design for inclusive communities looks on the ground

Source: Grant.

Baugruppe – comprise future residents of a development that come together for a joint building project and then disband. In Vauban the council made the decision to sell the majority of plots to Baugruppe. Bids were assessed against criteria favouring Freiburg residents, older people and families with children.

As a way of achieving a mixed community, criteria were used to ensure that Baugruppe reflected diversity. So they then built dwellings that reflected those diverse needs. The celebrated 'Wohnen and Arbeiten Passiv Haus' apartment block contains four offices, 16 apartments (ranging from one bed to two-floor family-size units), communal areas and an artist's studio. Equivalently Baugruppe have a powerful interest in the long-term quality of the environment and ongoing costs of occupation (including energy costs). These examples illustrate the care that a Baugruppe can supply but which a developer would not (Little 2007).

Following construction and occupation, a high level of social capital is already preconditioned through the shared Baugruppe development process. Ongoing interactions within and between Baugruppe are supported through the provision and maintenance arrangements of external communal space, often in the form of a shared garden. This is in addition to small private gardens or terraces for ground floor properties. It is not uncommon to see shared communal facilities such as outdoor pizza ovens, children's wigwams or other play features in the semi-private areas, reflecting the degree to which friendly communities have evolved.

Building design freedom within firm layout guidelines

The diversity of owners leads to an extraordinary variety of design, with many different architects and builders involved, giving visual vitality to the urban scene. The elevations of buildings in Vauban use every trick in the book to achieve individual expression. However, it is not a free-for-all. To ensure functional efficiency and co-operation between neighbours, the planning department specifies the layout and scale of development (Figure 38.6). The general pattern – of renewal projects as well as new neighbourhoods – is intended to ensure a highly permeable, convivial, mixed development that supports an excellent public transport service. Medium densities (normally three to five storeys) and a pedestrian-friendly public realm ensure that local facilities and tram routes are viable. Shared provision of services is normal. For example in Rieselfeld a multi-denomination church is also a community event space, the library is also a leisure and social centre with provision for a market outside and the green roof of the local sports hall is a small park.

The spatial frameworks of the new extensions are straightforward and logical. The main street leading towards the city centre is also the tram route, principle cycleway and pedestrian route, with facilities clustered along it. In Vauban play streets, where cars can unload but not park, loop away from the main route. In the bigger neighbourhood of Rieselfeld a grid of streets defines perimeter blocks. Green fingers percolate through and around the development, often combined with sustainable drainage systems. The design guide specifies the general scale, and frontage line of housing, but leaves other variables open. Many terraces have small front gardens, overflowing with greenery, where hard surfaces (for example for parking) are forbidden, allowing rain to percolate into the ground. The form of rear gardens varies hugely, according to the wishes of the residents – some opting for private space, some for patios plus shared space.

In some cultures the level of civic planning involved in Freiburg would be viewed with suspicion, but in fact it delivers extra freedoms to households, co-operative groups and small businesses. The outcome is superb – a highly liveable and inclusive community where air pollution, traffic danger and car dependence are rare, and where contact with nature and local amenities is supported; healthier lifestyles are a natural consequence this kind of urban environment (Figure 38.7).

Figure 38.6   A variety of frontages within a design code promoting a compatible aesthetic, Vauban
Source: Grant.

Figure 38.7   Good quality design ensures an interesting and highly useable public realm

Source: Grant.

Eight challenges for cities

Freiburg presents quite a challenge to other cities. It has a special history that has accelerated its journey to becoming a unique icon of urban sustainable development. But is Freiburg unique in a non-repeatable sense? Are the lessons transferable? Could this 'island of sustainability' (Wallner et al. 1996) inspire cities across the globe?

Politically, many elements have combined that have supported the outcome seen today. The continuity of a strong triumvirate of radical green policies, creative technical approaches (including from the academic community) and willing financial backers has been essential. The following lessons build upon those of Buehler and Pucher (2011) and Hall (2014).

1. *Set clear long-term goals and pursue them consistently.* A city's political and professional leaders have to accept their responsibility to set a logical long-term course which is likely to deliver their aspirations. Freiburg has been pursuing consistent strategies since the 1970s.
2. *The city has to take control, enlisting the support of all.* A radical (health) agenda will not be achieved without strong central policies and implementation. Equivalently it relies on full-hearted support from communities, business and institutions.
3. *Work subtly and flexibly to achieve co-operation with investors and communities.* Finding the funds, strategies and persuasive arguments to convince people means seizing opportunities, making deals, implementing clear winners first.
4. *Fully integrate transport and land use planning.* Policies promoting public transport, walking and cycling rely on a settlement structure that keep distances short, routes safe and direct and destinations close to public transport stops. This applies at local, urban and city region scales.
5. *Win support from central or state authorities.* Unstable state policies and excessive central control are fatal to effective city management for sustainability and health. Cities have to have sufficient autonomy to implement coherent strategies.
6. *Allow municipalities to buy development land, and shape urban form.* The lesson not only from Freiburg, but examples across Europe, is that real quality in terms of healthy, human scale development is only achieved when authorities have the power to buy well-located land without undue legal or financial penalties, and set the spatial context for private sector and community investment.

7. *Work with civil society and potential residents/businesses from the start.* This applies whether renewal or new-build schemes. The development of mutual trust and understanding is critical to successful implementation, and sows seeds for community cohesion.

8. *Support continuity and quality of staff.* Planning departments need real authority and a willing-ness to take a positive lead to achieve stated political goals. This relies on staff with staying power and real competence across all aspects of the profession: sound understanding of the evidence (e.g. in relation to healthy behaviour), spatial and design skills, market analysis, community engagement and implementation skills.

How transferable these lessons are will no doubt depend on context. There remains a question about the relevance of the Freiburg experience to health and well-being. From personal visits and the available literature it appears that Freiburg has achieved an exemplary, world leading healthy urban environment, without highlighting health as a key issue. A degree of humility is appropriate. A belief in sustainable development and quality of life has motivated consistent healthy policies. This is to be celebrated. It means that health is not a contradictory aspiration that cuts across existing priorities. Health and well-being melds precisely with the kind of social, economic and environmental goals achieved in Freiburg.

But of course, the vast majority of places fail to achieve these goals. Even if the rhetoric is fine, reality is at odds with it. What the addition of health can do is provide a widely accepted integrating principle, and impressive evidence of what works and what does not. Using health as the touchstone for urban development provides a powerful political, professional and public motive for planning a people-orientated environment – an essential counterpoint to past and current market failures.

Note

1 We were told that health statistics were treated as confidential and held in a central store in Berlin, inaccessible to the planning department.

References

Allender, S., Hutchinson, L. and Foster, C. 2008. Life-change events and participation in physical activity: a systematic review. *Health Promotion International* 23(2): 160–172.

Barton, H. and Grant, M. 2006. A health map for the local human habitat. *Journal of the Royal Society for the Promotion of Health* 126(6): 252–253.

Buehler, R. and Pucher, J. 2011. Sustainable transport in Freiburg: lessons from Germany's environmental capital. *International Journal of Sustainable Transportation* 5(1): 43–70.

Energie-Cités. 1999. Thermal solar energy Freiburg (Germany). Available from www.cidadessolares.org.br/downloads/boas_praticas/freiburg.pdf, accessed 31 December 2013.

Grant, M., Coghill, N., Barton, H. and Bird, C. 2009. *Evidence review on environmental health challenges and risks in urban settings: for WHO European Centre for Environment and Health.* Technical Report. WHO Collaborating Centre for Healthy Cities and Urban Policy, University of the West of England (UWE), Bristol.

Gregory, R. 2011. The eco-tipping point project. Models for success in a time of crisis: our time: Germany – Freiburg – Green City. Available from www.ecotippingpoints.org/our-stories/indepth/germany-freiburg-sustainability-transportation-energy-green-economy.html, accessed 31 December 2013.

Hall, P. 2014. *Good cities, better lives: how Europe discovered the lost art of urbanism.* Abingdon: Routledge.

Little, J. 2007. Baugruppe: lessons from Freiburg on cooperative housing. Available from www.joseph-littlearchitects.com/articles/baugruppe-lessons-freiburg-cooperative-housing, accessed 9 April 2014.

Melia, S. 2006. On the road to sustainability: transport and carfree living in Freiburg. Available from www. stevemelia.co.uk/vauban.htm, accessed 31 December 2013.

Sugiyama, T., Leslie, E., Giles-Corti, B. and Owen, N. 2008. Association of neighbourhood greenness with physical and health: do walking, social coherence and local social interaction explain the relationships? *Journal of Epidemiology and Community Health*, 62: e9.

Temkin, K. and Rohe, W.M. 1998. Social capital and neighborhood stability: an empirical investigation. *Housing Policy Debate* 9(1): 61–88.

Verkehrs, A.G., Freiburger. undated. pers comm.

Wallner, H.P., Narodoslawsky, M. and Moser, F. 1996. Islands of sustainability: a bottom-up approach towards sustainable development. *Environment and Planning A* 28: 1763–1778.

39

PUBLIC REALM AND PUBLIC HEALTH IN NORTH AMERICAN CITIES

Reshaping cities to encourage and enable active travel

Bruce McVean and Lucy Saunders

Context

This chapter explores the ways in which some US and Canadian (Chicago, Detroit, Montreal, New York, Portland, Seattle, Vancouver and Washington) cities are reshaping their streets and public realm to meet a broad range of goals. These include creating sense of place, encouraging sustainable travel, tackling environmental challenges and improving the health of their population. City living is growing in popularity and there is increasing recognition of the importance of quality urban environments to attracting and retaining businesses, residents and visitors (Leinberger 2008). Cycling culture is also growing and this is being nurtured partly to tackle obesity and other public health challenges, but also reduce inequalities that arise in car dependent societies, and cut carbon emissions (Mapes 2009).

Many North American cities face significant challenges in shifting travel patterns and habits, not least the relative ease of accessing cities by car from surrounding suburbs. Once in the city, drivers benefit from a high capacity street network with multi-lane highways. However, rapid progress has been made in recent years, and the approaches North American cities are taking to address this challenge can serve as an inspiration to cities around the world.

Common approaches

Protected bike lanes on heavily trafficked streets to provide safe routes for cyclists

For decades the 'vehicular cycling' tradition dominated the approach to catering for cyclists on US streets. This considers that the best way for cyclists to avoid conflict with motor vehicles is to cycle as if they were part of traffic, taking a dominant position in the centre of the lane and cycling at speed. Champions of this approach have argued that it protects cyclists' right to the road and reduces the risk of collisions at junctions. The American Association of State Highway and Transportation Officials (AASHTO) *Guide for the Development of Bicycle Facilities* (AASHTO 1999) reflected the dominance of the vehicular cycling approach with no criteria for when cyclists should be physically separated from traffic, a preference for cyclists sharing the road and a reliance on cyclists having the necessary confidence and skills to cope with traffic (Furth 2012).

The limitations of vehicular cycling, particularly as a means of enabling mass cycling, are increasingly recognised. As Pucher and Buehler (2012, p. 351) note, 'separate cycling facilities are a crucial first step toward increasing cycling and making it socially inclusive' (see also Pucher and Buehler 2008; Furth 2012). However, national policy is taking time to catch up with best practice approaches to catering for cyclists of all preferences and abilities.

In response to this policy lag the National Association of City Transportation Officials (NACTO) published its *Urban Bikeway Design Guide* in 2012. The guide draws on international best practice as well as NACTO member cities' own experiences to 'help create complete streets that are safe and enjoyable for bicyclists' (NACTO 2012, p. 5). The majority of the approaches set out in the NACTO guidance are not referenced in the current version of the national cycle design guidance issued by AASHTO (NACTO 2014).

All US cities in this chapter are members of NACTO (Washington, New York, Chicago, Detroit, Seattle and Portland) and are actively installing bike lanes to provide dedicated space for cyclists, as are the Canadian cities of Vancouver and Montreal. The degree of separation from motor traffic varies – within as well as between cities – but there is clear recognition of the role that bike lanes can play in enabling the growth of cycling.

At their most basic level bike lanes are simply delineated by painted lines, often running down the outside of parked cars – derogatorily referred to by campaigners and advocates as 'car door lanes' as they pose the risk of injury to cyclists by a car door being opened (Figure 39.1). Painted lanes are sometimes enhanced by the addition of painted buffers, placing the bike lane far enough away from cars to avoid the danger from the opening of car doors and providing a degree of separation from passing traffic.

Figure 39.1   A painted bike lane in Washington DC, derogatorily referred to by campaigners as 'car door lanes'

Source: McVean/Saunders.

While not best practice, these approaches are often adopted for expediency. In Chicago for example, a State imposed moratorium on building physically separated bike lanes due to safety concerns over potential conflict with right turning vehicles at junctions has resulted in the city installing painted lanes that can be upgraded at a later date. In Detroit, where traffic volumes on many streets are currently low, painted lanes are helping to establish cycling as a transport mode of choice rather than necessity and claim space for cycling in anticipation of a future increase in traffic volumes as the city recovers.

In cities such as Washington, New York and Chicago buffers on the traffic side of the bike lane have been augmented with bollards, offering a higher degree of separation, increasing subjective safety and preventing motor vehicles parking in bikes lanes. This light protection has the advantage of being quick and cheap to install, and allows cycle infrastructure to be easily adapted should future demand require wider lanes. Additional protection from passing vehicles is provided by the positioning of car parking on the outside of the bike lane (Figure 39.2).

Many of New York's lightly protected lanes are now being upgraded to provide kerb separation from traffic, along with cycle only phases at junctions and pedestrian islands. A similar approach has been taken on Chicago's flagship Dearborn Street barrier-protected, two-way bike lane and on a number of streets in Vancouver and Montreal.

Quietways and cycle streets

As well as providing bike lanes on busier streets North American cities are expanding their cycle network by establishing alternative routes that allow cyclists to avoid heavily trafficked streets, for example Portland and Seattle's 'Neighbourhood Greenways' and Vancouver's 'Local Street Bikeways'.

These routes typically run through residential areas on streets with traffic flows of less than 2,000 vehicles per day, providing links to schools, neighbourhood high streets and other local services, as well as forming part of city-wide cycle networks. Key features of these routes include:

Figure 39.2 A protected bike lane in New York; parked cars provide protection from passing vehicles

Source: McVean/Saunders.

- Modal filtering to reduce traffic volumes and prevent rat running by motor vehicles by closing streets to through traffic without restricting access for pedestrians and cyclists.
- Clear and often branded signage to highlight routes and for ease of wayfinding; this can include on-carriageway markings and is essential to ensuring routes are easy to follow.
- Cycle priority at junctions requiring vehicles entering the cycle street to give way, making routes quick and convenient for cyclists and improving safety.
- Cyclist controlled crossings where routes cross main roads (Figure 39.3). At main road junctions that are not traffic light controlled, cyclists are given facilities to activate pedestrian crossings. If there is no traffic then cyclists are free to cross without waiting for lights to change.
- Reduced speed limits (usually to 20 mph or 30 kmh) and physical measures to reduce speeds such as planted mini-roundabouts and build-outs at junctions. State law in Oregon, for example, allows speed limits to be set 5 mph below the current limit on routes carrying less than 2,000 vehicles per day.
- Wider public realm improvements and integration of planting and sustainable drainage systems (see below).
- Cycle contraflows on one-way streets. Usually these are only signed and do not require any physical separation of cyclists from oncoming traffic.

Reappropriation of on-street car parking

Removal or conversion of on-street car parking is a contentious issue, particularly on high streets where local traders often view parking as essential for enabling customers to easily access shops and restaurants. Officials and campaigners often expressed frustration that a small number of local retailers can delay or prevent schemes to improve the public realm or

Figure 39.3 A dedicated cycle crossing at the end of a Local Street Bikeway in Vancouver

Source: McVean/Saunders.

introduce protected bike lanes despite evidence of the relative importance of customers who arrive on foot, bike or public transport compared with those that drive (Clifton et al. 2013).

In response, a number of cities have introduced 'parklet' programmes to temporarily (and in some case permanently) convert parking spaces to public spaces, usually incorporating seating, planting and bike parking. First trialled in San Francisco in 2009, parklets have spread rapidly to other cities: Montreal, Chicago, Vancouver and Seattle all had parklet programmes in place in 2013, with Portland and New York having operated schemes in previous years.

Parklets generally take the form of a wooden platform the length of one or more car parking spaces. Platforms are usually level with and open to the pavement, separated from the carriage-way by both a level change and fencing or planting. Reflecting the desire to create additional public space, parklets are usually open to all, even if they have been requested, paid for and maintained by an individual business, and often operate for the summer months only due to the adverse winter weather conditions. Permanent parklets, such as those on Montreal's Saint Denis, provide external seating areas for individual restaurants.

Temporary parklets often have a strong design element, for example all of Chicago's 'People Spots' (as their parklets are known) are bespoke designs by local architectural practices, creating unique public seating areas that are not necessarily associated with an individual business and are paid for by a not-for-profit organisation (Figure 39.4).

Figure 39.4   A 'People Spot' temporary parklet in Chicago

Source: McVean/Saunders.

Another popular method of reclaiming parking spaces is to convert them to 'bike corrals' providing parking for 5–10 bikes without taking space away from pedestrians. Bike corrals are typically installed at the request of local businesses.

Parklets and bike corrals help to reframe the debate around parking and how valuable public space should be used. They also serve an additional benefit beyond creating public space: limiting the opportunity to park conveniently can result in people choosing alternative modes of transport if they are available and seem like viable options.

Municipal bike-share

Public bicycle sharing systems are fast becoming a marker for cities wanting to demonstrate a new approach to transport and how their streets are used. All cities in this chapter either have a bike-share system in place (Washington, New York, Montreal, Chicago), are at advanced stages of planning for bike-share (Vancouver, Seattle, Portland) or have longer-term aspirations (Detroit).

Campaigners and officials hope that the introduction of bike-sharing will help 'normalise' cycling as an activity that doesn't require specialist equipment or clothing and is accessible to all. A study in the *American Journal of Public Health* found that people exposed to public bike-share were more likely to cycle than those who were not (Fuller et al. 2013). This may reflect the influence of the visual cues of regular bicycle docking stations and easily identifiable bicycles being used by others (Figure 39.5).

Street planting: an integrated approach to street improvement and traffic calming

Street planting is incorporated into street improvement schemes across many North American cities and can be seen as a key element to a rounded and sustainable street environment.

Figure 39.5   A CitiBikes docking station in New York incorporated into a 'paint and planters' plaza

Source: McVean/Saunders.

Planting can be used to deliver a range of outcomes, but it is vital to deliver landscape schemes to a high standard of design and secure ongoing maintenance. Approaches to integrating planting included:

- New public spaces – in New York and Washington DC large planters placed on what was formerly the carriageway demarcate the space for public plazas (see New York spotlight).
- Barriers to protect cyclists – in Vancouver planters serve as a green buffer to protect the cycle lane from moving traffic (Figure 39.6).
- Attenuation for storm water run-off – in Portland and New York rain gardens are incorporated into pavement extensions to manage storm water run-off and support the local wildlife (see Portland spotlight).
- Junction build-outs – also referred to as 'bulb-outs' or 'neck-downs' – these extensions to the pavement at junctions narrow the carriageway and force drivers to slow on approaching the junction.
- Resident and business planting – in many cities residents and businesses use the space at the base of street trees to plant flowers and shrubs.
- Enhancing new infrastructure – planting and other public realm improvements are often incorporated into new cycle infrastructure as a visible demonstration of the wider benefits delivered.

Traffic-free trails

In most North American cities only a tiny minority of the population cycle regularly for utility purposes – commuting, shopping, visits to friends and family, etc. Recent investment in on-street

Figure 39.6 Planters alongside this Vancouver bike lane provide protection from passing vehicles and enhance the street environment

Source: McVean/Saunders.

cycle infrastructure, as outlined above, aims to encourage a broader use of bikes as part of their daily routine.

Off-road traffic-free trails, by contrast, are typically aimed at providing routes for leisure cycling, but they can play an important role in growing cycling. Traffic-free trails provide a pleasurable and unintimidating introduction to cycling for those who have not previously taken part in the activity, acting as 'nursery slopes', allowing new and occasional cyclists to become more confident and potentially converting them to regular, utility cyclists (Figure 39.7).

Traffic-free trails can also potentially build demand for more cycling infrastructure as users want to experience similar feelings of safety and convenience on other routes. This is particularly the case with traffic-free trails in urban areas, which people cycle rather than drive to. Many traffic-free trails are also popular with commuters, particularly those with longer commutes, and can form part of a wider cycle network when they connect with on-street facilities.

Traffic-free trails are therefore a useful tool in building enthusiasm for cycling, but they alone cannot deliver the scale of modal shift to cycling required for population health benefits. By their nature they are often relatively isolated routes that lack the 'natural surveillance' of street environments, and as a result are unlikely to attract people travelling alone or after dark. Reflecting this, Seattle, which historically centred their cycling strategy around traffic-free trails, is now investing in on-street infrastructure and 'bicycle boulevards' to broaden the appeal of cycling.

Temporary street closures

Temporary closure of streets to traffic for community activities has been taking place in many North American cities for decades. New York's Play Streets programme, which closes streets to motor vehicles to allow children to play out, began in 1914. The programme has grown in

Figure 39.7   The traffic-free Capital Crescent Trail in Washington DC

Source: McVean/Saunders.

popularity in recent years, partly as a result of strong support from the city's health department as part of their efforts to combat childhood inactivity and obesity. While promoted and enabled by city government, initiatives such as Play Streets rely on local community members to request street closures. These are typically small scale events limited to one or two streets and only closing those streets for a couple of hours at a time.

A number of cities also organise much larger scale, day-long street closures to create a walking and cycling route several miles long and host a range of complementary activities. Examples include Summer Streets (New York), Open Streets (Chicago), Sunday Parkways (Portland) and Bicycle Sundays (Seattle).

Such events promote walking and cycling and help to get local residents active, at least for a day. But a more important role is the potential for temporary closures to show how street spaces can be used differently, reinforcing the role of streets as public spaces and challenging the norm of streets dominated by moving and parked vehicles. Campaigners hope that this will help to build support for permanent changes to streets.

Political leadership, strong vision, effective strategies

The political imperative to deliver real improvement within relatively short election cycles can fit well with making changes to street environments, where projects can be delivered relatively quickly. But significant changes to street environments, particularly those that aim to reduce accessibility for private motor vehicles, is usually a contentious issue, and often it is the politics rather than the practicality of change that limits the pace and scale of delivery. Unsurprisingly then, strong political leadership is a consistent theme amongst those North American cities that are doing the most to reshape streets and their built environments to encourage walking and cycling, for example:

- From 2007 Mayor of New York Michael Bloomberg, working with his transport commissioner Janette Sadik Khan, pushed through a series of ambitious projects to reallocate road space away from motor vehicles to create new public spaces and provide protected cycle lanes. In 2008 New York produced its first detailed transportation strategy for the city, *Sustainable Streets*, which included proposals for introducing Bus Rapid Transit, doubling cycle commuting and halving road deaths (City of New York 2008).
- In Chicago Mayor Rahm Emanuel and transport commissioner Gabe Klein are closely identified with the Make Way for People initiative – a progamme of parklets, plazas and alley improvements that aims to create new 'public dwelling spaces' throughout the city; the Bike2015 strategy which aims to make cycling a mainstream transport mode in a few years by installing 500 miles of cycle tracks (City of Chicago 2006); and a commitment to eliminate road deaths in ten years in their 2012 *Chicago Forward* action plan (City of Chicago 2012).
- Likewise the mayor of the Montreal borough Plateau-Mont-Royal, Luc Ferrandez, since his election in 2009 has introduced a number of changes as part of his ambitious 49 point *Plan de Deplacement*, the borough transport plan, which includes more bike hire stands, lower speed limits on secondary streets, more pedestrian only streets, cycle tracks and public realm improvements (see Montreal spotlight) (Plateau-Mont-Royal 2009).

City spotlights

Portland: wider benefits of sustainable urban drainage systems

Portland, like many cities, is short of funding for street improvements to benefit cyclists and pedestrians, but joint working between the parks, transport department and environment departments enables street environment improvements as part of a wider programme of installing sustainable urban drainage systems (SUDS) to manage storm water and minimise run-off (Figure 39.8).

The city's sustainable drainage projects aim to address localised flooding, avoid the need to expand drainage and sewerage infrastructure as the population grows and prepare the city for the effects of climate change. Portland's green infrastructure-led approach to managing storm water delivers a range of other benefits. For example, rain gardens are often incorporated into curb extensions and build outs at junctions to reduce vehicle speeds. Greening neighbourhoods also helps to make them more attractive, provides shade and cooling and creates habitat for wildlife.

New York: paint and planters

Since 2007 New York has been pioneering the use of paint, planters and boulders to convert road space to plazas, creating 59 new public spaces out of traffic lanes, with a total area of 39 acres (NYCDOT 2013). This approach allows temporary changes to streets to be delivered almost instantly; the results of the intervention can then be assessed with designs refined as necessary before being made permanent.

The benefits of this approach go beyond low cost, reduced bureaucracy and speed of implementation. The temporary nature of the materials allows the local community to see how the street could look and feel, and therefore facilitates community buy-in. Once the temporary

Figure 39.8   Rain gardens in Portland, part of a city-wide sustainable urban drainage system

Source: McVean/Saunders.

interventions have been shown to work and are accepted by the local community they can be made permanent (Figure 39.9).

This approach by New York has now been incorporated into the NACTO Urban Street Design Guidance that was published in September 2013. The NACTO guidance notes that

> Interim public plazas . . . transform underutilized areas of roadway into public spaces for surrounding residents and businesses. Using low-cost materials, such as epoxied gravel, movable planters, and flexible seating, interim public plazas reconfigure and revitalize intersections that might otherwise be unsafe or underutilized.
>
> *(NACTO 2013)*

Detroit: funding partnerships

Since 2007 the Detroit Greenways Coalition, which is facilitated by the Michigan Trails and Greenways Alliance (MTGA), has been developing proposals and advocating for a network of greenways and on-street cycle routes in Detroit. As a result of their work, the length of greenways and bike lanes in Detroit grew from 12 miles in 2006 to nearly 68 miles in 2012, with another 102 miles constructed in 2013 (MTGA 2014).

This investment is made possible, despite Detroit's well documented financial difficulties, through innovative public/private partnerships – bringing together leading businesses, city government and non-profit organisations to secure funding (often through the use of donations from charitable foundations and other donors as match-funding for state and federal grants).

Figure 39.9　One of 59 new public spaces created in New York using paint and planters to convert carriageways

Source: McVean/Saunders.

Montreal: public realm improvements

The borough of Le-Plateau-Mont-Royal is situated on the northern edge of downtown Montreal and has the highest mode share for cycling in the city. In 2009, Projet Montreal, a young political party founded in 2004, took control of the borough council. A key element of their campaign was the need to invest in the public realm and improve conditions for pedestrians and cyclists. They argued for a focus on delivery rather than prolonged public consultation, which was perceived to have delayed previous initiatives.

A number of projects at a range of scales have been delivered, from planted build-outs at junctions of residential streets to significant investment in *coeur du village* locations such as transit hubs and neighbourhood retail centres, incorporating traffic calming, public plazas and seating areas (Figure 39.10). Other initiatives include improvements to bike lanes to increase separation from traffic and the closing of a number of roads that cut through parks.

Seattle: reconnecting waterfront and downtown

For more than 50 years the waterfront of downtown Seattle has been severed from streets, businesses and shops by an elevated highway known as the 'Alaskan Way Viaduct', part of State Route 99. In 2001 an earthquake damaged the viaduct and in 2013 work began to build a two mile long tunnel allowing the viaduct's downtown section to be dismantled and replaced by a new street along the waterfront.

Figure 39.10   A *coeur du village* public realm project in Montreal's Le-Plateau-Mont-Royal, incorporating planting, seating and traffic calming

Source: McVean/Saunders.

This scheme is part of the Waterfront Seattle project that aims to open up access to the waterfront, on which the city has historically turned its back. Waterfront Seattle combines major infrastructure projects with a range of other measures to open up the waterfront as a leisure space, particularly to people on foot and bicycle, such as a new pedestrian promenade, two-way cycle track and rebuilt public piers.

Supporting strategic transformation

Safe and attractive walking and cycling environments are essential to encouraging and enabling people to incorporate physical activity into their daily routine. The approaches outlined above are likely to have a significant positive impact on individual travel habits. Realising the full potential to grow active travel will require ongoing investment for decades, for example cycle networks remain patchy and few cities yet have a comprehensive city-wide cycle network. However, there will be long-term budgetary reward through co-benefits across transport, health, social inclusion and low carbon agendas. Transport and planning professionals are well placed to create the collaborations required to join up these sectors, but significant challenges remain. Investment in cycle infrastructure and efforts to restrain motor traffic remain controversial (see for example Del Signore 2011; Robbins 2011; Cherone 2014) and long-term investment will require ongoing political support, which is by no means guaranteed.

Given the social, environmental and economic challenges facing cities, it is likely that efforts to promote sustainable and active travel will continue and will intensify over time. The approaches outlined will remain key to future efforts, but they will need to be supplemented by a range of other measures if the scale of necessary change is to be achieved, including:

- reductions in the amount of parking available and higher charging for the parking that remains;
- lower motor-vehicle speeds via measures such as city-wide 20 mph speed limits;
- measures to reduce traffic volumes to allow road space to be reallocated to other users;
- planning policies to increase the density of suburbs particularly around existing or new public transport corridors; and
- removal of remaining urban freeways.

Despite differing urban, political and fiscal contexts the approaches being taken by North American cities are transferable to cities in other countries and regions. In rapidly urbanising cities and those that are yet to fully urbanise into motor traffic dominated places, these examples can serve to illustrate alternative and healthier routes for city development. They demonstrate how those seeking to grow walking and cycling from a relatively low base, or to retain it, need to deliver radical changes to their streets and public realm in a relatively short timescale.

References

AASHTO (American Association of State Highway and Transportation Officials). 1999. *Guide for the development of bicycle facilities*. Washington DC: AASHTO.

Cherone, H. 2014. *Northwest siders spar over plan for new bike lanes on Milwaukee Avenue*. DNAinfo Chicago. www.dnainfo.com/chicago/20140130/gladstone-park/northwest-siders-spar-over-plan-for-new-bike-lanes-on-milwaukee-avenue, accessed 12 April 2014.

City of Chicago. 2006. *Bike 2015 plan*. Chicago, IL: City of Chicago.

City of Chicago. 2012. *Chicago forward: Department of Transportation action agenda*. Chicago, IL: City of Chicago.

City of New York. 2008. *Sustainable streets: strategic plan for the New York City Department of Transportation 2008 and beyond*. New York: City of New York.

Clifton, K., Muhs, C., Morrissey, S., Morrissey, T., Currans, K. and Ritter, C. 2013. *Examining consumer behaviour and travel choices*. Portland, OR: Oregon Transportation Research and Education Consortium.

Del Signore, J. 2011. *Group demands citywide bike lane moratorium*. Gothamist. http://gothamist.com/2011/02/23/group_wants_bike_lane_moratorium_am.php, accessed 12 April 2014.

Fuller, D., Gauvin, L., Kestens, K., Daniel, M., Fournier, M., Morency, P. and Drouin, L. 2013. Impact evaluation of a public bicycle share program on cycling: a case example of BIXI in Montreal, Quebec. *American Journal of Public Health* 103(3), e85–e92.

Furth, P.G. 2012. Bicycling infrastructure for mass cycling: a transatlantic comparison. In: Pucher, J. and Buehler, R. (eds). *City cycling*. Cambridge, MA: MIT Press.

Leinberger, C.B. 2008. *The option of urbanism: investing in a new American dream*. Washington, DC: Island Press.

Mapes, J. 2009. *Pedaling revolution: how cyclists are changing American cities*. Corvallis, OR: Oregon State University Press.

MTGA (Michigan Trails and Greenways Alliance). 2014. www.michigantrails.org/about-us/our-work, accessed 23 February 2014.

NACTO. 2012. *Urban bikeway design*. New York: NACTO.

NACTO. 2013. http://nacto.org/usdg/interim-design-strategies/interim-public-plazas, accessed 23 February 2014.

NACTO. 2014. http://nacto.org/cities-for-cycling/design-guide, accessed 23 February 2014.

NYCDOT. 2013. *World class streets*. www.nyc.gov/html/dot/downloads/pdf/2013-dot-sustainable-streets-4-worldclassstreets.pdf, accessed 23 February 2014.

Plateau-Mont-Royal. 2009. *Premier plan de deplacement urbain du Plateau-Mont-Royal: Plan D'Action 2009–2010*. Montreal: Le Plateau-Mont-Royal.

Pucher, J. and Buehler, E. 2008. Making cycling irresistible: lessons from the Netherlands, Denmark and Germany. *Transport Reviews* 28(4), 495–528.

Pucher, J. and Buehler, E. 2012. Promoting cycling for daily travel. In: Pucher, J. and Buehler, R. (eds). *City cycling*. Cambridge, MA: MIT Press.

Robbins, L. 2011. *In Brooklyn, divided opinion about a bike lane by a park*. New York Times. www.nytimes.com/2011/03/09/nyregion/09bike.html?_r=1&, accessed 27 February 2014.

40

PLANNING A HEALTHY CITY

Progress and challenges in Portland, Oregon

Carl Abbott and Moriah McSharry McGrath

Starting points

Portland is a mid-sized metropolitan region with an outsized reputation for good urban planning. The starting points were city-level initiatives in the early 1970s that defined a symbiotic relationship between urban core and older neighbourhoods (Abbott 1983); a coeval set of decisions to prioritise public transportation and rail transit over freeways; and creation of the statewide Oregon land use planning system in 1973–1974 (Abbott 1983; Adler 2012). In the ensuing decades, Portland has maintained a professional reputation for 'smart growth' and a popular name as an epicenter of hipness.

We briefly outline the institutional and cultural context for city and regional planning in Portland and explore the incorporation of health into planning processes with case studies of two initiatives: (a) the health element of the Environmental Impact Statement in planning for a new highway bridge across the Columbia River, and (b) the role of Health and Equity Working Groups in the development of a new comprehensive plan for the City of Portland. We find that there remain challenges in incorporating public health concerns in traditional land use and transportation planning.

Portland: city and metropolitan region

The Portland region consists of a seven-county metropolitan area spanning the Columbia River in the states of Oregon and Washington (Figure 40.1). Total metropolitan population was 2,289,000 in 2012 (1,853,000 in Oregon and 436,000 in Washington), making the Metropolitan Statistical Area the 24th largest in terms of size in the United States. The core City of Portland was 588,000 in 2012.[1] Historically one of the whitest cities in the United States, the Portland area has paralleled national trends with increasing ethnic diversity over the last two decades, led by Latinos and Asian Americans. Nevertheless, 81 per cent of metropolitan area residents identified as non-Hispanic whites in the 2010 census.

For the last three decades, Portland has been a 'brain sponge' or net importer of college educated migrants. This holds true both for the highly desirable demographic of people aged 21–40 who ride bicycles a lot and for a second group of retirees and empty nesters who also cultivate healthy lifestyles. This has created a feedback loop in which well-educated people support

Figure 40.1 The seven-county Portland, OR–Vancouver, WA metropolitan area. Much of the area
included in these large areal units is farm and forest land. The City of Portland occupies
roughly the western quarter of Multnomah County

Source: Meg Merrick, Portland State University.

institutions and policies that make Portland attractive to more people like themselves (Jurjevich
and Schrock 2012). One result has been a growing repute for coolness and hipness, skewered
in the quirky cable television series, *Portlandia* (2011–), but Portland has also more than its share
of planning nerds and policy wonks (like this chapter's authors, who arrived in 1978 and 2006,
respectively).

Land use planning operates under the framework of the Oregon planning system, which
requires that each city and county prepare a comprehensive plan that responds to statewide
goals that address inclusive housing, efficient transportation and similar planning objectives.
Most notorious is Goal 14, which requires the definition of urban growth boundaries (UGBs)
around metropolitan areas. Intended to encompass developed land plus additional land supply sufficient for 20 years of growth, a UGB is like a skin that can expand as needed but
which requires compact and efficient development. The UGB that encompasses the City of
Portland and the urbanising parts of three core counties is managed by Metro, the only elected
regional government in the United States. The UGB (Figure 40.2) has had important positive
effects in focusing real estate development and community energy on central Portland. That
same effect, however, has led to high demand for housing and gentrification of older, close-in
neighbourhoods, leading to displacement of poorer residents and the attendant public health
consequences.

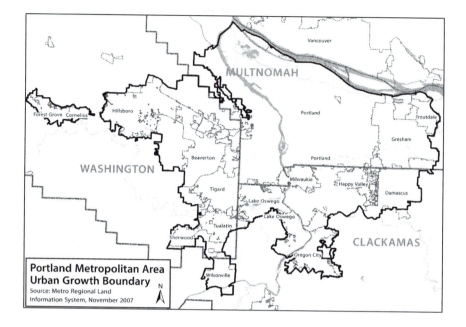

Figure 40.2   The Portland Area Urban Growth Boundary

Source: Metro Data Resource Center.

Portland in the later twentieth century shared in Oregon's particular political style, what Daniel Elazar (1972) deems moralistic political culture in which politics is conceived as a public activity centred on ideas of the public good or public interest. The moralistic political culture (contrasted with traditional and individualistic cultures) places issues ahead of individuals and accepts that government can legitimately regulate private activities. This political orientation also supports what we can call rational policy making, meaning the definition of a problem, consideration of alternatives and choice of a solution. The state land use planning system is an example of this approach, as is the Oregon Health Plan mentioned below (Abbott 1994).

Portland's progressive, prevention-oriented public health environment can be seen as another expression of this rational political culture. The Portland area was one of the initial service areas for the Kaiser Permanente Health Maintenance Organization (HMO), an innovative health care model created during World War II to serve tens of thousands of Kaiser Corporation shipyard workers.[2] Kaiser Northwest now has 480,000 enrollees and Oregon ranks fifth among the states in the proportion of residents in HMOs. On a smaller scale, but equally innovative, was the syringe exchange programme that the Portland non-profit Outside In implemented in 1989 to curb the spread of HIV/AIDS – the first such programme in the country to be developed and the third to become operational (Oliver et al. 1994; Oliver 2014). The state also received national attention in adopting the Oregon Health Plan in 1993, which increased federal Medicaid coverage for low income Oregonians by 50 per cent within one year, in part by rationing state medical spending according to effectiveness of treatments.

There are, however, contradictions within this political culture. Oregonians and Portlanders have a strong individualistic bent that may express itself as political libertarianism, hipster entrepreneurship or Occupy movement distrust of government in the public health arena – Oregon has a relatively strong anti-vaccination movement which has reduced childhood immunisation rates.[3] Even more egregious was the defeat of an effort to fluoridate Portland's water supply that had been initiated by public health advocates and medical professionals.[4] City of Portland residents voted overwhelmingly against fluoridation in a 2012 referendum in which radical environmentalists, distrustful lefties and anti-government right-wingers combined to disregard medical science in favour of a myth of Edenic purity.

Health in Portland planning

City planning is a profession and practice that centres on shaping the physical city through land use regulation, environmental protection and transportation programming with the implied purposes of protecting public health and welfare. The result is that issues of individual health tend to be secondary, albeit important, consequences of planning for other goals. Twenty-first-century Portland's strong sustainability ethos brings health closer to the surface. The city consistently ranks at or near the top of 'sustainable city' and 'green city lists' and the Portland Planning Bureau became the Bureau of Planning and Sustainability in the new century (Figure 40.3). Within this regime, health concerns have been linked most directly to efforts to reduce fossil fuel use and to increase opportunities for individual physical exercise and consumption of healthy foods. These healthy foods are understood as fresh produce from the region's small farms, which owe their continued existence to the innovative Oregon land use planning system – which protects farmland by limiting scattershot suburbanisation. The state system is augmented by the Portland Urban Food Zoning Code Update, which updated local regulations to lessen barriers to integrating community gardens, community-supported agriculture distribution sites and greenmarkets into residential zones. Similarly, conservation land is seen as an essential resource for encouraging physical activity.

Bureau of Planning and Sustainability
Innovation. Collaboration. Practical Solutions.

Figure 40.3   Logo for Portland Bureau of Planning and Sustainability

Source: City of Portland, Bureau of Planning and Sustainability.

The Portland region stopped building freeways in the early 1980s, having eliminated one that was about to be built in the 1970s and killed a quarter-circumferential highway through western suburbs in the 1990s. These efforts fed into the state's adoption in the early 1990s of a transportation rule that mandated that jurisdictions in the Portland area plan for a 20 per cent reduction on vehicle miles travelled (VMT) per capita. Although the goal was not realistic, VMT per capita indeed fell by 8 per cent from 1997 to 2011. The shift from single-occupancy vehicles to 'active transportation', whether biking or walking to mass transit, is seen as a valuable opportunity to increase Portlanders' level of physical activity.

At least some of the credit goes to the vigorous promotion of bicycling. Oregon law requiring cities to spend 1 per cent of highway funds on bike and pedestrian infrastructure was neglected until activists sued Portland in 1993. The city responded by co-opting activists as participants in bicycle planning (Johnson nd) and adopting a Bicycle Master Plan in 1996 calling for 630 miles of bike roads, lanes and trails. Over the next 15 years the city invested $100 million on bicycle infrastructure, and riders now account for roughly 10 per cent of commuters into the central business district. In 2010, the city adopted a Portland Bicycle Plan for 2030 with an extremely ambitious target of a quarter of all trips being made by bike in 2030 (City Club of Portland 2013). Building on two decades of success, advocates would like to see as many people pedalling around Portland as do so around Amsterdam or Copenhagen – although neither city has barriers comparable to Portland's 250-metre hills (Figure 40.4).

Portlanders have long valued those hills and the larger regional landscape of Pacific Ocean beaches and headlands 90 minutes to the west and snowcapped mountains 90 minutes to the

Figure 40.4   Each year thousands of Portlanders take to the city's largest public spaces – its streets – to bike, walk and roll on events called Sunday Parkways. The events encourage active transportation and community by closing long loops to automobile traffic

Source: Patrick Findler/Portland Bureau of Transportation.

east. However, attitudes toward the natural environment within the urbanised area underwent substantial change in the 1980s. After more than a century when dredge spoils from the Willamette River were used to fill riverside wetlands for developable land, the City of Portland made a U-turn in 1988 in designating Oaks Bottom, the last remaining natural area along the Willamette River within the city limits, as a wildlife refuge and park, having previously used the site for disposing of construction debris (Figure 40.5). The decision marked a new effort to preserve and promote natural landscapes within the urban fabric and to emphasise ecological services from undeveloped land (Houck and Cody 2011). Over the next 20 years, voters passed bonds that have supported $60 million in local parks and $300 million for acquiring 5,000 hectares of open space and natural areas.

The themes of mobility and open space come together in the Portland Plan, a goals-and-aspirations plan with a 25-year time horizon adopted by the City of Portland in 2012 (City of Portland 2012a). The document defines three overarching strategies: thriving educated youth; economic prosperity and affordability; and healthy connected city. The discussion tilts heavily toward protecting the health of the natural environment and encouraging individual physical activity through pedestrian and bicycle facilities, stronger neighbourhood centres, and more local attractors such as well-placed libraries and senior centres to help create the so-called '20-minute neighbourhood'. The idea updates the neighbourhood unit concept that has been central in city planning since articulated by Clarence Perry in 1929.

Case study: Portland Plan and Portland Comprehensive Plan

The development of the Portland Plan and the follow-up Portland Comprehensive Plan represent two major urban planning activities in the city. The Portland Plan laid overarching policy directions, creating a vision for the city's future. Development of 'the Comp Plan' has followed,

Figure 40.5   Mural overlooking Oaks Bottom Natural Area, a key natural area three miles from downtown

Source: Mike Houck, Urban Greenspaces Institute, Portland.

creating an implementation strategy for the Portland Plan's goals by fixing development types to certain locations in the city. As the name suggests, the Comp Plan will assign every area of the city a land use designation. The zoning code adopted in the Comp Plan will direct the location and character of development in Portland for years to come.

While it is difficult to trace the lineage of individual ideas within the Portland Plan, some features of the published plan suggest how the plan's conceptualisation of health evolved. 'Public health people' had input in the plan as individual members of the plan advisory committee, chairs of technical advisory groups and participants in an externally convened health-focused workgroup. Identifying and being identified as public health stakeholders, as opposed to clinicians or health care administrators, indicates that these groups and individuals took a broad, holistic view of health that emphasises social determinants of health and equity among population groups as pathways for improving community health. The emphasis on plan language on public health as opposed to clinical medicine signalled that the city's understanding of health went beyond the notion of health care as an economic driver. Likewise, the plan's more expansive conception of sustainability as a 'three-legged stool' with the pillars of economy, environment and (social) equity is foreshadowed by the city's creation of its Planning and Sustainability Commission in 2010 in the midst of the Portland Plan process.

For the plan itself, 2 of the 65 people appointed to the Portland Plan's Advisory Committee in 2010 represented public health organisations (City of Portland 2010). Parallel to this formal appointment, an informal group of health stakeholders formed to advocate for the integration of health issues to the Portland Plan process in 2008 (OPHI nd). This Healthy Portland Plan Workgroup urged the Bureau of Planning and Sustainability (BPS) to incorporate not just health ideas but also health experts in the development of the Portland Plan. Health experts went beyond serving on advisory committees to directly advise BPS staff on health assessments incorporated in Plan Background Reports provided to decision-makers discussing the 'Health, Food and Public Safety' action area of the Plan. Their ongoing participation was funded by public and private grants, including $7.5 million awarded to the Multnomah County Health Department as part of the federal stimulus programme intended to counter the effects of the economic downturn.

Ultimately, health rose to the top as one of four 'pillars' of the Portland Plan, along with equity, prosperity and education (Figure 40.6). The metrics the city chose to measure progress on these abstract concepts illuminate how the pillars are understood by local planners. The Healthy Portland Plan Workgroup crows that background reports written by the city during the planning process 'fram[e] health as a result of social conditions and built environments, rather than a result of solely individual behavior choices and disease outcomes' (OPHI nd),

Figure 40.6   Icons used to illustrate the Portland Plan action areas: Prosperity, Business Success & Equity; Education & Skill Development; Sustainability & the Natural Environment; Human Health, Food & Public Safety; Design, Planning & Public Spaces; Neighborhoods & Housing; Transportation, Technology & Access; Quality of Life & Civic Engagement; Arts, Culture & Innovation

Source: City of Portland, Bureau of Planning and Sustainability.

yet the implementation section of the Portland Plan uses the city's obesity rate as its benchmark for success in promoting population health through urban planning (City of Portland 2012b). Notably, obesity is seen from a public health perspective as a 'proximal' determinant of health: a person who is obese is at higher risk of multiple health problems, through causal pathways that are somewhat well understood. Such an indicator, however, gives no information about the *behaviours* that influence people's health, in turn affecting health *outcomes* (for example, obesity-related disease). And it in no way addresses the larger social determinants of health, including fundamental social causes (Link and Phelan 1995) of disease that operate through multiple pathways to create many poor health outcomes – poverty being one of the largest examples.

The Portland Plan's use of a clinical outcome to measure the city's progress on promoting health, despite the availability of data measuring health behaviours more directly influenced by the built environment – for example, physical activity rates and fruit and vegetable consumption – suggests that BPS was capitalising on America's obesity panic in order to garner support for their planning efforts, or that they had not fully internalised the more holistic view of population health and its determinants touted by the Healthy Portland Plan Working Group. At the same time, performance measures in other parts of the plan *do* represent important drivers of health: increased economic self-sufficiency, increased use of active transportation, reduced carbon emissions and increased proportion of residents living in 20-minute neighbourhoods. Health benefits are expressly mentioned for the latter three. These metrics more closely align with a public health perspective on healthy cities, for example the health principles of the World Health Organization's Healthy Cities programme's emphasis on addressing inequality by promoting health through social and economic measures along with environmental change (WHO nd).

After identifying policy directions in the Portland Plan, in 2012 the city set to updating its Comprehensive Plan adopted in 1980. Health issues have been integrated into the process in structures similar to those used during the Portland Plan. A Health and Equity in the Comp Plan Network (HECPN) was founded by staffers from advocacy group Oregon Public Health Institute (OPHI), Multnomah County Health Department and the local chapter of the Urban League – an African American advocacy group. The addition of the term equity to the workgroup's name echoes the importance of the idea in the Portland Plan as well as the growing trendiness of the term 'health equity' in the public health community. This addition of one word prompted something of an identity crisis for the HECPN, limiting the HECPN's ability to work as a cohesive group and provide unified recommendations related to the Comp Plan. Some public health practitioners assumed that the profession's emphasis on combating health disparities, which in the US are most visible along racial lines, made them qualified to address racial equity. Other stakeholders were less confident, citing the limited visibility of people of colour in the HECPN and the heavy representation of government agencies distrusted in many communities of colour in the US.

The HECPN did work hard to get its members and allies into positions where they could conceivably influence the plan. Health stakeholders leveraged the capital they had gained through participating in the Portland Plan to highlight their preferences for advisory group members to BPS. These health allies strategically targeted their applications to advisory groups that would address topics traditionally seen as detached from public health concerns – such as the Economic Development advisory group. Some HECPN allies also worked with staff from the city's Office of Equity and Human Rights to create training sessions for the advisory groups. In this way, health stakeholders were able to educate other participants about the health and racial equity implications of planning processes.

The Comprehensive Plan drafted in the months following these collaborations identifies human health as one of six 'integrated goals'. The notion of health as a cross-cutting goal seems appropriate, given the wide breadth of policies that are aligned with health issues. They include housing condition and site design (to encourage physical activity and discourage crime), as well as an environmental justice framing of watershed health that emphasises public health benefits of ecosystem services. However, the plan's contributions to health will only become clear in the ensuing years as the city develops within its strictures.

Case study: Columbia River Crossing

While the case above addresses planning for the city as a whole, public health practitioners have also participated in conversations about the health ramifications of specific projects. The Columbia River Crossing, a proposal to replace the large highway bridge on Interstate 5 that carries passengers between Portland and Vancouver, Washington, is one such example. During years of debate about the wear and traffic to this bridge, part of the main west coast highway between Mexico and Canada, many health concerns arose. In 2007, as a draft environmental impact statement (DEIS) was being prepared, the Multnomah County Health Department led the formation of a workgroup interested in adding a Health Impact Assessment (HIA). HIAs, just then getting their start in the US, are a systematic methodology for projecting the health impacts of a project in a non-health sector and formulating recommendations for policy makers about how to maximise the health benefits of the decision, minimise health harms and support an equitable distribution of project benefits and burdens.

The HIA was released as comment on the DEIS, and cited contributions from nine organisations including county and state government, Kaiser Permanente and health advocacy organisations. It focused on the impacts of additional vehicle travel, the effects of a large-scale construction project and the presence of vulnerable populations such as older adults and low-income people residing in the project area. To mitigate these impacts, the workgroup proposed including light rail in the bridge design and assuring that vulnerable populations would be served by transit routes in the vicinity of the bridge; incorporating bike and pedestrian facilities in the project; and tolling and other strategies to discourage single occupancy motor vehicle trips. While none of these mitigation measures is radical in its own right, the fact that they were presented by a public health group was novel.

The release of the DEIS was followed by years of squabbling over the project, which included a delayed, over-budget final Environmental Impact Statement three years later and myriad complaints about the proposal from all political corners. As of 2015, the project appears dead in the water and the HIA seems lost in the shuffle, rarely mentioned in conversations about the Columbia River Crossing even by groups who participated in producing it.

However, the HIA had a catalytic effect in seeding a Portland HIA community which has risen to national prominence. While the application of HIAs in the US began in San Francisco, Portland as a city and Oregon as a state rapidly outpaced their southern counterparts in HIAs per capita. Of the organisations who signed on to the Columbia River Crossing HIA, at least half have completed successive HIAs, most of them funded by prominent national agencies and foundations. Two of the non-profit groups began providing fee-for-service HIA consulting. Among government agencies, the Oregon Health Authority created an HIA programme and designated HIA one of its strategic priorities in 2012, and Multnomah County funded two full-time HIA analysts in the County Health Department. The regional HIA community has since conducted assessments of planning projects including a corridor rezoning, greenhouse gas reduction scenarios, parks development and mass transit expansion.

Perhaps due to these efforts, public health expertise has been integrated to some planning institutions in the city and region. The Metro regional government created a seat designated for representatives of public health and urban form and its planning and policy advisory committee and has called on public health practitioners to serve on project advisory committees and added health department staff to its project teams for regional economic development and transportation projects. Portland's BPS appointed the county's long-time health officer to its Planning and Sustainability Commission – which advises the city council – and now regularly seeks technical assistance from the health department on projects such as a proposed port expansion.

Institutionalising healthy planning

Portland-area planners and public health advocates are working together more frequently today than ten years ago. It remains to be seen what the tangible effects of these collaborations will be, and the early efforts reveal several inefficiencies. While mild-mannered public health people would be loath to admit to turf battles, their eagerness to participate in each new opportunity to work on planning issues can result in stepping on each other's toes, or at least confusion over the appropriate roles for government employees, advocacy organisations and academic researchers in the various projects.

Interjurisdictional relations present an additional wrinkle. While planning is almost exclusively conducted by the City of Portland, the health department operates at the county level. In a complex Venn diagram, 80 per cent of Multnomah County's population is made up of Portland residents, but some Portland residents live in neighbouring Washington and Clackamas Counties. The county has limited political pull with the city, particularly since the jurisdictions agreed in the 1970s put the county in charge of human services and give the city responsibility for planning. Furthermore, the county's willingness to be assertive with the city on health issues varies widely based on the composition of the elected county commission. Among its many duties, the commission serves as the county's board of health, a responsibility that falls to a different body in many other jurisdictions.

Despite the undoubted accomplishments, many of the actions and approaches summarised here have tended to favour the well-educated/well-off who are already likely to access health care and maintain healthy lifestyles. A cynical interpretation would suggest that health is used as a feel-good add-on when it is convenient for these officials to use it as a rallying cry. For example, the Comprehensive Plan is likely to continue in the same direction that BPS has been taking in recent years, favouring dense infill development and active transportation amenities. Citing health and equity as the reasons for these approaches may genuinely reflect the motivations of the bureau, yet the relatively high housing costs and low salaries in Portland mean that these vibrant neighbourhoods are likely to be inhabited by residents with the level of socio-economic advantage that allows them to remain in or relocate to these desirable areas. And, of course, this socio-economic advantage also decreases the likelihood of suffering from chronic diseases such as asthma and diabetes that healthy planning purports to prevent.

Disparities in health inputs and outputs have been documented in the Coalition for a Livable Future's *Regional Equity Atlas* (2007; revised edition 2013) and by Greater Portland Pulse (2014), a data consortium led by Portland State University and Metro. These disconnections suggest that coupling equity analysis with plan implementation is essential to realising the health promoting effects of Portland's Healthy Connected Neighborhoods. For example, the Climate Action Plan adopted by the City of Portland and Multnomah County in 2009 called for increasing tree canopy county-wide, yet gave no overt attention to disparities in green resources (City of Portland and Multnomah County 2009). An equity analysis of the climate plan (McGrath and Lyons-Eubanks 2011) highlighted this and other ways that a plan that serves health well at the metropolitan level can also serve to aggravate health disparities and place inequity, even if unintentionally. Some promising tools exist to highlight these aspects of decision-making – such as Multnomah County's Equity and Empowerment Lens, whose purpose is to make decision-makers aware of policy options that reduce race-based disparities.

In summary, Portland in the last decade has made public health concerns an explicit element in comprehensive land use planning, building on a 40-year history of progressive planning. This history embodies a uniquely Portlandian vision of health, planning and sustainability that is 'fun and cool', to use BPS Director Susan Anderson's summation of her approach to promoting healthy communities (Meunier 2009). While city planning is linked in many minds with power brokers and massive construction projects, BPS adopted a new logo that eschews bulldozers in favour of a blue and green peacock shape whose undulations suggest a soothing journey toward an easy Portland lifestyle for all, no messy construction projects required. This breezy vision of a healthy city is echoed in photos of frolicking children that splash across Portland Plan documents. These saccharine representations may be understandable as a way to pull the public into dense and often-dry documents. Further, it's much more challenging to graphically represent the difficult choices necessary for a planning agenda that changes the underlying inequities that structure human health.

However, the city's cheery urbanism also hints at ulterior motives for its healthy planning agenda. Anderson admits that planning for health and sustainability decreases affordability for some city residents; a major driver is 'branding' the city as healthy in order to woo technology and lifestyle companies. She explains that, 'most of these things are things we want to do to create better, healthier places anyway – but by doing that, you create a place where people want to live and have businesses' (Minow Smith 2012).

There is little doubt that the concern for health is sincere among the civic leadership, especially when it is coupled with the potential for economic development that is welcomed by business interests sometimes seen as resistant to the costs of health-related initiatives. At the same time, there are challenges to integrating such concerns into regular planning activities and project planning. Equity analysis, while being the keystone of planning for health, may also be one consideration too many for the complex planning process, where addressing health may already be seen as adding another layer of review to an already byzantine endeavour. When the political and economic feasibility of a decision is being considered, health can be perceived as too heavy an add-on. Similarly, leaders who advocate for sunny playground moments may be less comfortable leading the charge for health-promoting strategies that do more to upset the sociopolitical order. This said, however, we are encouraged to hope for continued progress locally and for Portland's example to provide useful ideas and guidance for other cities that face the common challenges of community health.

Notes

1 Because political environments differ substantially from state to state, we confine our discussion of planning and health policy to Oregon, with particular emphasis on the City of Portland and Multnomah County.
2 An HMO is a health insurance organisation to which subscribers pay a predetermined fee, either as individuals or members or a workplace group, in return for comprehensive medical services from physicians and health care workers contracted with or employed by the organisation. HMOs have incentives to stress preventive care to reduce total costs. Since 1973, federal law has required employers of more than 25 workers to offer an HMO option. Other than medical insurance programmes for the indigent and elderly and health services provided to members of federally recognised Native American groups, there is no national programme of health insurance or medical care in the United States.
3 The movement echoes a strong grassroots anti-vaccination movement from the early twentieth century (Johnston 2003).
4 The US Public Health Service has recommended water fluoridation to prevent dental decay since the 1940s (Lennon 2006) and by 2012, 72 per cent of Americans consumed fluoridated water from public systems (Zernike 2012).

References

Abbott, C. 1983. *Portland: planning, politics and growth in a twentieth century city.* Lincoln, NE: University of Nebraska Press.

Abbott, C. 1994. The Oregon planning style, in C. Abbott, D. Howe, and S. Adler, eds., *Planning the Oregon way: a twenty-year evaluation.* Corvallis, OR: Oregon State University Press.

Adler, S. 2012. *Oregon plans: the making of an unquiet land-use revolution.* Corvallis, OR: Oregon State University Press.

City Club of Portland. 2013. No turning back: a city club report on bicycling in Portland. www.pdxcityclub.org/2013/Report/Portland-Bicycle-Transit

City of Portland. 2010. Portland plan advisory group. www.portlandonline.com/portlandplan/index.cfm?c=51747

City of Portland. 2012a. Portland plan. www.pdxplan.com

City of Portland. 2012b. Portland plan documents: Portland plan final (pp. 98–139). www.portlandonline.com/portlandplan/index.cfm?c=45722,

City of Portland and Multnomah County. 2009. Climate action plan. www.portlandoregon.gov/bps/article/268612

Coalition for a Livable Future. 2007. (Revised edition 2013.) *The regional equity atlas: metropolitan Portland's geography of opportunity.* Portland, OR: Coalition for a Livable Future.

Elazar, D. 1972. *American federalism: a view from the States.* New York: Thomas Crowell.

Houck, M. and Cody, M.J. 2011. *Wild in the city: exploring the Intertwine, the Portland-Vancouver region's network of parks, trails, and natural areas.* Corvallis, OR: Oregon State University Press.

Greater Portland Pulse. 2014. www.portlandpulse.org

Johnson, S. nd. The bicycle movement. www.stevenreedjohnson.com/stevenreedjohnson/civicpdxbikes_files/Bicycle%20Movement.pdf

Johnston, R. 2003. *The radical middle class: populist democracy and the question of capitalism in progressive era Portland, Oregon.* Princeton, NJ: Princeton University Press.

Jurjevich, J. and Schrock, G. 2012. Is Portland really the place where young people go to retire? Migration patterns of Portland's young and college educated, 1980–2010. http://mkn.research.pdx.edu/wp-content/uploads/2012/09/JurjevichSchrockMigrationReport1.pdf

Lennon, M.A. 2006. One in a million: the first community trial of water fluoridation. *Bulletin of the World Health Organization* 84: 759–760.

Link, B. and Phelan, J. 1995. Social conditions as fundamental causes of disease. *Journal of Health and Social Behavior* 35: 80–94.

McGrath, M.M. and Lyons-Eubanks, K. 2011. *Portland/Multnomah County climate action plan (CAP) health assessment: public health co-benefits and health equity in our local climate plan.* Portland, OR: Multnomah County Health Department.

Meunier, A. 2009. 24 July. Portland's Susan Anderson promotes sustainability by making it 'fun and cool.' *Oregonian.* www.oregonlive.com/environment/index.ssf/2009/07/portlands_susan_anderson_promo.html

Minow Smith, D. 2012. 12 November. Breaking: Portland sustainability chief admits 'Portlandia' isn't really a parody. *Grist.* http://grist.org/cities/breaking-portland-sustainability-chief-admits-portlandia-isnt-really-a-parody

Oliver, K. 2014. Personal email communication. 3 January.

Oliver, K., Maynard, H., Friedman, S.R. and Des Jarlais, D.C. 1994. Behavioral and community impact of the Portland syringe exchange program. *Proceedings of a Workshop on Needle Exchange and Bleach Distribution Programs* (pp. 35–64). Washington, DC: National Academies Press.

OPHI (Oregon Public Health Institute). nd. HPPW timeline. www.ophi.org/strategic-projects/healthy-community-planning-overview/the-portland-plan

WHO (World Health Organization). nd. Healthy cities. www.euro.who.int/en/health-topics/environment-and-health/urban-health/activities/healthy-cities

Zernike, K. 2012. 2 March. In New Jersey, a battle over fluoridation, and the facts. *New York Times.* www.nytimes.com/2012/03/03/nyregion/in-new-jersey-a-battle-over-fluoridation-and-the-facts.html

41

DESIGNING FOR CONVIVIALITY AND CITY VITALITY IN PORTLAND

Paddy Tillett

A changing city

Healthy and sustainable cities depend as much on the sustainability of businesses, services and of social structures as they depend on design of the physical environment. The key is to recognise interrelationships between these three provinces, and to use physical design in ways that support economic and social success over time. Related yet separate is the issue of the health of those who use the city. Three generational maladies of our era are obesity in children, sedentary adults and isolated seniors. All three classes benefit from urban environments in which almost everything that one needs is within walking distance, and from circumstances that make walking the preferred way to get around. Mixed age communities are being rediscovered as marketable options, with a burgeoning population of capable seniors taking a more active role in the well-being of others – and incidentally enriching their own lives. These are simple values that Ebenezer Howard strove to recover from pre-industrial living patterns. The perversion of his garden city concept into vehicle-centric urban monocultures remains a caustic lesson to every urban planner.

The thesis presented here is that by closely observing what has worked (and failed) over time in an established urban setting where similar values are held, desirable qualities can be emulated in a new neighbourhood. Emulated but not copied, for times, needs and values all change. The era in which Portland's Northwest Neighborhood was built was one in which natural resources were used as if they were limitless, climate change was unknown and cars were just beginning to outnumber horses. Changes just as great are likely to overtake urban environments that we build today. We cannot know what those new considerations will be, but we can design a flexible and adaptable urban framework, and we can build with the certainty that natural resources will become scarcer. And it is a safe bet that *homo urbens* will remain curious, gregarious and acquisitive – all strong clues to how we should shape the built environment so that it will continue to sustain conviviality and vitality in the city.

Context

Portland's River District is a new mixed use neighbourhood built on a 50 acre (20 hectares) brownfield site north of the Central Business District (CBD). It is more commonly referred to as part of The Pearl District, which includes warehouses to the west and a mixed use area extending south to Burnside Street.

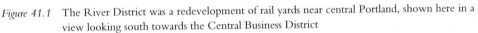

Figure 41.1   The River District was a redevelopment of rail yards near central Portland, shown here in a view looking south towards the Central Business District

Source: Tillett.

Portland, with a population of 585,000 in the city itself and 2.3 million in the whole Metro area, is Oregon's largest city. It is 650 miles north of San Francisco and 300 miles south of Vancouver BC. Portland came into being as a seaport in the mid-nineteenth century, and was as far inland as ocean-going shipping could safely navigate: a hundred miles from the ocean. Portland is on the Willamette River, a tributary of the largest river flowing into the Pacific from the Americas: the Columbia River.

The River District plan was prepared independently from the city's elaborate planning machinery. New owners of the brownfield site commissioned a local firm of architects and urban designers to develop a plan that aligned with their vision of what could be achieved as opposed to modest, low-rise uses prescribed by established City plans. Owners and consultants were attuned to relevant political obstacles: one being that much of the land was designated as an 'industrial sanctuary' in which housing and most other non-industrial uses are expressly precluded.

Essential parts of the plan for the new district reflected characteristics of the nearby Northwest Neighborhood, a mixed use and socially diverse community nearby that predated the city's planning ordinances. First, a small street grid that would make it eminently walkable; second, a mix and density of uses that have succeeded financially and socially; and third, strong connections to established employment and recreation destinations. These have engendered a vital and gregarious urban community, and give a clue as to how new development can similarly succeed.

A working model neighbourhood

Beginning in the 1980s, successful professionals with the means to live where they pleased chose the inner city instead of following their senior colleagues to a suburban spread. Most found their way to deteriorating inner city neighbourhoods, rescuing noble but neglected houses from further decline. Old ladies and cats gave place to energetic young professionals who invested cash and sweat in 'bringing back' their newfound homes. With the younger population and their disposable income came a resurgence of local retail. Throughout the region people began to drive less; public transport ridership grew and commuting by bicycle gained popularity. The reality of a '20-minute neighborhood' began to emerge: communities in which almost everything one needs is within 20-minutes' walk of one's home.

This tidal change from suburbs to inner city is certainly not unique to Portland, but here there were some relevant differences. Most of the components of a completely serviced community were still in place. Businesses responded to a resurgent population. The Northwest Neighborhood had large and small houses, town houses and apartment buildings, workplaces and retail all jumbled together, often on one block. It had always had a diverse social mix. Its inhabitants had learned to live with little off-street parking. New arrivals boosted the population of the neighbourhood to make it one of the densest in the state. Not surprisingly, retail within walking distance on NW 23rd Avenue flourished to the extent that it soon became a destination for people who lived miles away.

What had emerged was a compact, mixed use neighbourhood with streets full of people strolling between their homes and shops, restaurants, services and workplaces. It predated development regulations that for half a century have enforced segregation of uses. Benign neglect had enabled this neighbourhood to maintain its eclectic mix, finally blossoming with the new millennium as a model mixed use neighbourhood.

A new neighbourhood from scratch

Between the Northwest Neighborhood and the river lay a broad expanse of railway yards with its curtilage of old brick warehouses and small factories. The railway company sold about 50 acres (20 hectares) to local developers who set about planning a future for it that would satisfy both return on investment and civic responsibility – most had deep roots in the community. The city had zoned the land for modest redevelopment consistent with one- and two-storey employment uses that had recently been developed nearby. The new owners aimed higher, commissioning a more ambitious plan from a local architecture and urban design firm.[1]

The resulting concept plan extended the Downtown street grid of 200 foot × 200 foot (61 metre square) blocks to be occupied by mid-rise, mixed use development configured around a series of public parks. Heights had been restricted to 75' (23 m) in adjacent Old Town to discourage the practice of demolishing historic buildings in anticipation of attracting a high-rise developer. The same limit was placed on the River District.

The developers took their plan directly to the mayor and city council with a proposal that in 15 years they would create 4,500 homes and 3,000 jobs where none exists today. To achieve this, they would need carte blanche to move their development plan swiftly through the public approval process. The owners would contribute about $750 million, provided that the city council would commit about $125 million to improve and extend existing infrastructure. This compared very favourably with the cost of locating as many homes and jobs elsewhere in the city. The city council agreed.

The River District covers an area of approximately eight blocks from north to south and four blocks from east to west. Projecting circulation through the area, it soon became apparent that traffic demand on east–west dead-end streets would be limited. So some could be built as linear parks, extending the reach of more formal open space throughout the district and enhancing the walking environment – and reducing development costs.

Meanwhile, former warehouses that had served the rail yards in their heyday were being occupied by artists, galleries, some loft housing, offices for architects and photographers – anything that could use large, rough-hewn but inexpensive spaces. These helped to sustain what little retail existed along the southern fringes of the River District, and this is where the first 'toe in the water' new development began. A modest four-storey building of one- and two-storey flats with a central landscaped courtyard neatly answered the problem of efficient development of a 200 foot (61 m) square block, and quickly drew buyers.

Trading under the 'Arts District' brand, more housing soon followed, this time including street-level retail space and one level of underground parking. These were of more solid masonry construction, and were rewarded with a flurry of purchases by 'empty nesters' who appreciated what the central city had to offer in the way of arts, entertainment and fine dining. The pace of development in the River District quickened.

However, to many the depth of the market for housing looked limited. What would attract people to live in a place with no waterfront that is just too far on foot from Downtown jobs or Northwest Neighborhood retail? To some the answer was obvious: light rail had been the genius move that had put Portland on the livability map in the 1980s. But light rail is for mile-apart stations and is expensive to build. Why not build a modern streetcar like those in many European cities? It would be cheaper and would suit the scale of our 60 foot (18 m) streets. The City of Portland recognised that a streetcar route could also revive the under-served west edge of the CBD. Its function would essentially be to extend the range of those on foot, complementing the light rail and bus system, and providing an attractive alternative to driving. A 2.5 mile (4 km) line was conceived with a major destination at each end: a hospital in the Northwest Neighborhood, and Portland State University at the far end of Downtown. For residents of the River District, the shops, restaurants, cafes and pubs of Northwest would be five minutes' ride, and Downtown jobs ten minutes away.

The emerging new district possessed three key features: a scale and public realm that would make it friendly to pedestrians; a mix and density of uses that had put promenaders on the streets and filled the restaurants in the Northwest Neighborhood for generations; and third, strong connections to Downtown jobs, theatres, galleries, retail, health care and the university. Here was a formula for a new neighbourhood that would be fully connected to the rest of the central city, in which use of a car would be less convenient for most trips than walking, biking or riding transit. Increasingly, active retirees and young professionals invested in the district. As the resident population grew, so the buzz of sidewalk cafes, restaurants and knots of people strolling the parks and lanes increased. The district became a self-advertisement for healthy living in a place rich in options for shopping, relaxing, recreating – and with ready access to almost every other need. Spas and gyms multiplied, organic food merchants and a farmers' market soon followed.

Birth of The Pearl

The rate of growth of both homes and jobs in the River District was far swifter than expected. In part this was because of a national boom in real estate, but in the River District it was aided by two things. One was the notion that it was a cool place to live, another was the arrival of prestigious tenants in existing and remodelled buildings nearby. The Pacific Northwest College of Art left the confines of the Art Museum to establish a vibrant presence in a former industrial building next to the River District. Then five blocks including a handsome decorated brick brewery building just south of the district were redeveloped with mid- to high-rise offices, apartments and condominiums, including a wholesome foods supermarket. These were developed as a showpiece of sustainable architecture replete with district energy systems. On the heels of this success came accelerated investment in properties between the Brewery Blocks and the River District. A critical link was forged between the River District and the CBD. Increasingly people referred to 'The Pearl District' to include the River District, the railroad era buildings around it, the Brewery Blocks and everything in between. 'The Pearl' had a cachet that continued to draw investment in redevelopment throughout the economic bust years.

As the population of the new neighbourhood grew, so the range and quality of retail and services improved, increasing the attractions of The Pearl as a place to live. The active and wealthy population drew commercial investment, and the streets became more animated. Getting out and walking in The Pearl was more fun than most had ever imagined. Faces became familiar, since so many now lived nearby. A farmers' market opened in the forecourt of a restored warehouse building. More bars and restaurants put tables and chairs outside. People got to know one another; conviviality flourished.

As the population grew with a preponderance of well-educated and articulate residents, so their voices became more audible in City Hall. Instead of the usual 'Not In My Back Yard (NIMBY)' cries of 'no zone changes in our neighbourhood', the sentiment was to allow taller buildings and greater densities. As new development marched north across the former rail yards,

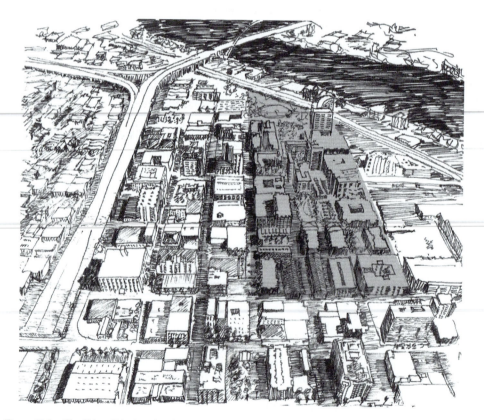

Figure 41.2 The River District, developed on vacated rail yards, is outlined here on a view looking north. It has merged with renovated and infill buildings around it to become The Pearl District: a walkable mixed use neighbourhood bordering the Central Business District to the south, and the Northwest Neighborhood to the west – connected to both by streetcar

Source: Tillett.

so buildings became taller. At a workshop arranged by city planning staff to discuss build–out of the remaining parcels in the north near Fields Park, there was consensus that residential point towers like those 100 metre spires in West Vancouver, British Columbia, should be allowed. After all, there were no significant views that would be blocked or great shadows cast by slim towers. The backdrop was the massive, mile-long Fremont Bridge – so scale was not a problem.

However, within the neighbourhood there was great sensitivity to scale and historic value. 13th Street, until recently an unpaved street with a rail spur that fed barley to the old brewery, should keep its industrial character of low-rise buildings and loading docks. Public open spaces are already protected from overshadowing by tall buildings in the city's zoning code. With bigger buildings, the eventual population of the River District may be triple the original 'ambitious' target of 4,500 households. Established rates of traffic generation in the district were far below normal, and the engineers found no capacity problem if residential point towers were permitted on remaining northern blocks.

Opening of the streetcar loop through the district in 2001 had brought the Northwest Neighborhood and the CBD within easy reach of The Pearl. Subsequently the streetcar line was extended south of the university to the South Waterfront District, and next across the Willamette River to serve the Eastside, so The Pearl became one of the best connected places in the city. Walking and using the streetcar became the most convenient ways of getting around. New residents who had been accustomed to isolated trips by car found themselves thrust into a social milieu that was friendly and stimulating.

For many if not most trips, a short walk is most convenient. Few households have more than one car so parking demand has dropped. Some developers no longer include parking with a housing purchase or rental rate, instead leasing spaces to those who want them. This has lowered the cost of housing and thus broadened the market, helping sales. The first Zip Car (then Car2Go) arrived and was quickly adopted. Car ownership has continued to fall.

Portland has a notoriously rainy climate for half the year, which might be expected to undermine the virtues of a walkable neighbourhood. Although it rains often, it rarely rains heavily. Turning again to the experience of the Northwest Neighborhood, retail and services there flourish through the winter months, depending on year-round walk-in trade. Even the city's cadre of bicycle commuters ride year round, dressing for foul weather as necessary (they represent 8 per cent of downtown commuters, a figure astonishing to most North American cities).

Street design

As North America embraced the automobile and began massive suburban expansions in the mid-twentieth century, hundreds of thousands of miles of new roads and streets were built without provisions for walking. Where sidewalks were built, they often ended abruptly. Suburbs were built under 'model' codes that segregated land uses, creating monocultures of housing separated by an automobile trip from retail and services, from work and leisure destinations. Children were of necessity driven to school, there being no practical walking or bike route.

Like most pre-World War II neighbourhoods, Portland's Northwest Neighborhood was built when most people made almost all trips on foot or by streetcar. Every street had sidewalks, and this being a timber-based economy, most sidewalks on residential streets were built wide enough to accommodate a cord of wood[2] next to the curb. Nowadays, those strips are mostly planted, often with street trees that contribute to the urban forest canopy covering more than a quarter of the city, helping to reduce heat island effects and extending habitat between parks and countryside. Another consequence is that the pedestrian realm claims 12 foot (3.66 m) on each side of the 60 foot (18 m) streets, leaving 36 foot (11 m) for two-way traffic with parking on both sides. Outside shops and restaurants, the space between street trees fills with street furniture or makes space for tables and chairs.

Two hundred foot city blocks are typically divided into 100 foot deep lots. This is spacious enough for houses to be set back from the property line, with vegetation giving some privacy from the street. But for apartments, commercial and light industrial buildings, a 100 foot deep lot can be a tight fit, so almost all build up to the property line, giving a uniform street edge. In retail blocks this is important, because pedestrians maintain awareness of the storefronts as they walk. The blocks being short, there is the visual relief of a cross street and the need to refocus on crossing safely before becoming engaged with the next series of storefronts. This pleasant rhythm draws thousands to stroll the neighbourhood shopping streets and fill the tills of the merchants and restaurateurs.

The width of the street adds another interesting dynamic. Two-way traffic is repeatedly slowed by drivers manoeuvring in and out of parking spaces, or coasting slowly in the hope of finding one. As a consequence, pedestrians can safely (though illegally) zig-zag across the street enabling retail on both sides to flourish. Elsewhere, shopping streets with faster traffic confine shoppers to one side of the street, so retail succeeds on one side or the other, not both.

A third behaviour that results from street configuration arises from the obstacle course that promenaders must navigate. Street trees, tables and chairs, moored bicycles and leashed dogs result in a narrow and winding path along the 12 foot sidewalks. In contrast to the big city sidewalks of New York or Chicago where one walks straight and avoids eye contact, here eye contact is essential to determine how approaching pedestrians are to pass one another. That contact may not elicit a smile, but it establishes a social connection and increases one's comfort level.

These three observations may seem trivial, but together they begin to explain why streets with these dimensions prompt convivial behaviour. Mature street trees are limbed up high enough for delivery vehicles and buses to clear, so looking ahead along the sidewalk, a space is defined by storefronts, overhead foliage and an irregular colonnade of tree stems, lamp posts and poles. What happens above that space is visible if one looks for it, but attention is focused at storefront level where the people are.

When this street model was recreated in the former rail yards, the sidewalks lacked their leafy roof. But trees grow quickly in Portland, and most streets are now fully fledged. Most new buildings display a clearly delineated base of storefronts, lobbies and other active uses. Because of the small city blocks, almost all properties are built up to the sidewalk, giving a continuous frontage line that effectively engages the interest of passers-by. As in the old Northwest Neighborhood, the chaotic arrangement of sidewalk obstacles soon became established. Of course only a small proportion of frontages are occupied by retail, but the same principles apply to any frontage: lots of visual interest and variety and frequent social encounters. No blank walls and consistently equitable use of the public realm.

Density, design and vitality

In both the century-old Northwest Neighborhood and the brand new Pearl District, equity in use of the public realm has been fundamental to success. This contrasts sharply with new communities that for 60 years have been shaped by the car, with sterile streets designed solely around vehicular needs. Buildings in The Pearl District come in all shapes and sizes; they give the impression of organic growth, not careful planning. A common purpose has been to focus on how our built environment can enable its residents to get the most out of life and all that an urban lifestyle can offer. Having most of the things one wants within a 20-minute walk of home is a measure of this, but it depends on a certain density of development to support all those services in a limited area. So how dense is dense enough, and when does density become too great? Residents of Manhattan have access to some of the best jobs and cultural assets anywhere. Theirs is among the densest (and costliest) developments in the country, and many would never choose to live anywhere else. But for others that lifestyle is too confined and too far removed from the natural landscape.

Perceptions of density have changed significantly in a generation. Flight to the suburbs last century was driven in part by a wish to get away from urban poverty and the foul air associated with closely packed housing and industry. In the minds of many, dense housing and slums were synonymous. Those places have little in common with today's urban living environments, yet there are lingering misgivings about density; there remains an echo in the minds of many that there is something intrinsically evil about dense development.

In reality, density is no more than a useful measurement. What determines quality of life has more to do with degree of social interaction, exposure to cultural stimuli and other existential factors. If buildings become very tall, they can function like gated communities where chance encounters are rare. Low- and mid-rise housing relies on the mixing bowl of the streets and open spaces for access, imposing a degree of social friction on everyone. But this only works well if there are many destinations within easy walking distance, and here Portland's small city blocks are a boon. By contrast, Salt Lake City has blocks ten times the size of Portland's, and wide streets with multiple lanes of moving traffic. People on foot often have a long and lonely walk to get anywhere; Salt Lake City is best navigated by car or public transport. In that case, separation, not density, is the defining factor.

The century-old Northwest Neighborhood has proved to be resilient for many reasons, but seven are noteworthy for being reproducible as demonstrated in the newly developed parts of The Pearl District:

1. a fine-grained network of streets that makes walking convenient;
2. narrow streets with generous sidewalks, two-way traffic and parking;
3. a diversity of destinations within a few minutes' walk for all residents;
4. uses and activities to meet the needs of all ages;
5. continuous, active frontages on commercial streets;
6. sufficient density of jobs and housing to attract and support a full range of retail and services;
7. a pervasive green infrastructure that includes parks, planted walkways and street trees.

It is not unusual to find the walkability score attached to advertisements of houses and apartments. People who choose to live in these neighbourhoods have learned to recognise the freedom of movement that one gains by living in a place where everything from hairdresser to health care is within a short walking distance. They have also rediscovered the small town phenomena of recognising many people on the street and impromptu meetings with friends at the grocery. It is this gregarious behaviour that is largely responsible for the resurgence of coffee houses and Portland's famous pub culture (there are 60 independent breweries within the city limits); that and the proliferation of home based businesses that need somewhere nearby for business meetings.

The lessons drawn from the birth and rapid maturity of a new community to replace an old rail yard are not of strong-arm policies, but rather of careful understanding of what has worked for this particular community in the past. Much of it echoes Ebenezer Howard's quest to recreate the comfortable muddle of pre-industrial urban settlements. It does this by putting the values of curious and gregarious people ahead of automobiles and infrastructure engineering. The seven qualities cited above relate to how we choose to behave. Although the new district was designed within the Euclidian strictures of a uniform grid of streets, every design decision was informed by human dimensions and observed preferences. Precise design has achieved a comfortable muddle.

Notes

1 ZGF Architects LLP.
2 Firewood is still sold by the cord: a unit of closely stacked firewood measuring 4' wide, 4' high and 8' long. A 4' wide strip along the curb outside most houses was provided to accommodate one such unit. A cord is probably named for the method of measuring the stacked wood.

Resources

North Pearl District Plan, City of Portland, Oregon: www.portlandoregon.gov/bps/article/268304
Pearl District Neighorhood Association: www.portlandoregon.gov/oni/48511
River District Design Guidelines, City of Portland, Oregon: www.portlandoregon.gov/bps/article/58869
River District Urban Renewal Area, Portland Development Commission: www.pdc.us/our-work/urban-renewal-areas/river-district.aspx

EPILOGUE

Hugh Barton, Susan Thompson, Sarah Burgess
and Marcus Grant

After quite a journey, we come to the final commentary in this book. We look first at the nature of the whole field of knowledge and action dealt with across all chapters, then review the research progress made, drawing on Parts II and III. This is followed by reflections on practice as illuminated by Parts IV and V. Finally, we present some trenchant thoughts on the way forward.

The field of knowledge and action

The central message of the book is that human health and well-being depends on the environment we live in, and that depends, in the broadest sense, on our planning and development policies. We separate concern for health from our spatial strategies and development management at our peril. Countries across the world face a health time bomb as populations age and sedentary lifestyles predominate, yet we are quite literally building unhealthy and unsustainable conditions into our physical environment. We complain about the escalating financial cost of caring for those struggling with disease and disability, while actively making decisions both in and well beyond the planning sphere that exacerbate the situation. There is a widespread absence of coherent, joined-up debate and action. Like the Emperor Nero in Rome, we are fiddling while population health is sacrificed – or at least seriously compromised – by silo decision-making and vested interests.

Current dominant drivers of urban form and planning have a large 'centripetal' component. The market conspires to outcomes whereby physically things are flung apart, social classes are separated and policies formulated as if they have no bearing on each other. With the prevailing Cartesian view of the world, assumptions are made about linear relationships between cause and effect. There are strong technological, institutional and financial dynamics at work. The neo-liberal political philosophy offers freedom and choice to those who can pay, rather than freedom and health for all.

Life, society, cities and earth ecology are not so simple. This book calls for an opposing force of a more *centrifugal* nature. It recognises the fundamental scientific reality, that each apparently distinct issue is a window onto a complex, interactive system. If we are to create a healthier world, then we need to break down topic silos; solve problems in partnership; bring communities together with private and public sectors; and avoid the spatial dispersal and segregation which undermines health. We need to talk about causal webs, not causal chains, and adopt holistic conceptual frameworks that encourage recognition of complexity, and ways of embracing it.

The Settlement Health Map (see Chapter 1, Figure 1.2; Barton and Grant 2006) presents one way of linking health to environment, encouraging a systematic and integrated approach. It encompasses all facets of human settlements. Individual health and well-being is related to the physical fabric of town and city regions through every layer of the map. These layers are explored by chapter authors as they discuss and evaluate the significance of lifestyles, communities and social networks, economic opportunities, access to facilities and urban activities, the aesthetics of the environment, air and water quality, and climate threats. The map can be used in multiple ways, and has been translated into many languages. It can shape the evaluation of a new planning policy or development proposal, encouraging understanding of knock-on effects; it can help analysis of health, social or ecological impacts; it can assist with understanding the needs of an urban activity (Barton et al. 2010). The point always is to see specific issues or questions in light of the whole. If we are to tackle the health crises of post-industrial society, nothing less will do.

Figure E.1   The Settlement Health Map translated into many languages (Barton and Grant 2006 based on a concept by Whitehead and Dahlgren 1991)

Research progress

It is no longer valid, if it ever was, for politicians and academics to claim that people make their own lifestyle choices, with concomitant health implications, untrammelled by broader spatial patterns. The depth and breadth of evidence linking health, the environment and planning is becoming more impressive by the year. Locational choice of households and businesses is restricted by what is available through the market and planning system. Behaviour is affected by opportunity – economic, cultural and spatial. The rich can adopt behaviours which fulfil their aspirations, though often still exposed to environmental risks. As Chapter 7 shows, the poor have much less freedom, constrained by unequal housing markets, environmental poverty, transport and access inequities, all reinforced by the sense of low status, leading to grotesque health inequality and economic inefficiency.

Nevertheless, the *degree* of planning's influence on human health and well-being continues to be contested – not only in terms of the familiar nature versus nurture debate, but also in terms of the relative significance of social, economic, cultural and environmental influences. The interactions between planning decisions and environmental conditions, and between those conditions and health, are complex. Research that tries to build a bridge right across from planning decisions to health outcomes is difficult. The problem is that many intervening variables confuse the issue, and people and places change unpredictably over time. Traditional research practices in the medical field – with controlled and randomised populations, double-blind procedures and longitudinal studies to distinguish cause and effect – are rarely possible in the social/environmental field (as argued in Chapter 31). So empirical research conclusions are tempered with caution, and systematic reviews fail to find definitive causal factors.

There are also issues of transferability. Much of the research available to English speakers has been done in the USA, but the conventional attitudes and behaviours there – for example in relation to walking and cycling – are different from, say, the Netherlands, or Britain or India. It is not necessarily appropriate to assume conclusions from a study in one country apply equally elsewhere. Academic literature reviews tend to mix varied studies and contexts, giving equivocal messages.

Having said that, there is nevertheless a surprising consistency in the research findings (see the chapters in Parts II and III). The thumbnail sketch of a healthy urban environment given in the Introduction is underpinned by research from all sides, whether in relation to physical or mental well-being, social capital, health equity or climate resilience. The only significant disagreement is in relation to crime (Chapter 12). The crime and community safety analysis challenges the consensus on density, mixed use and permeable street patterns. It highlights the fact that the conventional way cities have evolved in most places up to now has been counterproductive. The fashion for gated communities (for the rich) reflects that failure. So the way we plan and design higher densities, mixed uses and streets has to be much smarter.

Overall, despite the necessary caution of researchers, looking for general patterns, we find an increasingly comprehensive research platform that can support the argument for healthy environments. The question arises: what priorities should shape future research?

The prime focus should be on research that helps to build constituencies of support for action. A four pronged approach is suggested. First, since economic potential is the motivator for investors and many politicians, it is necessary to link the arguments for healthy urban environments to long-term economic outcomes. Second, more research needs to involve those communities who will become advocates for, and demand, a better relationship between healthy environments and their own quality of life. Third, to catch other constituencies, more research could examine the relationship between healthy environments and social justice, and between healthy environments and human ecology.

Fourth, there are questions about the reasons for practical success or failure from which academia sometimes shies away. Reading much of the research one could be forgiven for adopting a very cautious approach to policy. Yet the evidence from practice is that boldness pays off. Chapters 25 and 36 provide dramatic examples of plans being implemented with courageous consistency, triggering positive behaviour change. The research challenge is to develop a systemic approach which reveals the causal web, and points of entry for transformative implementation. A useful methodology involves the comparative study of 'natural experiments' (Diamond 2004). As with the WHO review of health inequalities (CSDH 2008), these studies need to be high profile if they are to influence politics.

Searching for good practice: people, processes and powers

Decision-makers cannot afford to wait for absolute proof of what is effective before taking action. Best practice in creating healthy places is ahead of the researchers. It involves mutually reinforcing strategies in relation to social and cultural change, economic innovation, and spatial and aesthetic characteristics. It is fair to say that sustainable spatial characteristics are well understood by many professional planners and designers across the world. What the experience in some cities shows is that the principles of sustainable development can be consistent with planning for social inclusion, economic development and health and well-being. The classic case of a holistic approach in Freiburg, Germany, is reinforced in many chapters, including theoretical perspectives (Chapters 6 and 22), integrative topics such as green infrastructure (Chapter 27), and cities such as Portland, Oregon (Chapters 40 and 41).

Achieving integrated health-seeking strategies relies on people, processes and powers. All the examples in this book, where communities, cities or regions have blazed new paths towards healthier environments, rely on the people at the top, those in the middle and at the bottom. Leadership is critical – often local authority decision-makers, but also commercial, institutional and community leaders. However, leadership without building partnerships of understanding and co-operation across districts, agencies and sectors is doomed to frustration. Neighbouring authorities have to reinforce each other in good practice (Chapter 24). Businesses and institutions, through their investment, make many of the critical environmental decisions and have to be fully engaged (Chapter 23). Civil society can promote radical alternatives that reduce inequities, and need to be supported (Chapter 29).

The problem of achieving healthy decision-making processes is to combine this collaborative approach with logic and consistency. There are specific techniques such as Health Impact Analysis which can assist, combining stakeholder interchange and scientific enquiry (Chapter 26). There are traditional rational planning processes which try to link aspiration and implementation. There are innovative appraisal tools, such as the three fabrics in Kuopio, which can act as drivers of technical, public and political endeavour (Chapter 37). But the most compelling message from the case studies is the value of co-operation between public health, planning and environmental sectors. This is especially the case in the earlier stages of policy revision towards healthy urban planning. The WHO Healthy Cities programme has been the exemplar. Whether in Australia, Taiwan, India, Turkey or the English Midlands, health professionals have acted as catalysts for change (Chapters 31, 33, 34, 35, 38). Viewing urban planning policy through a health lens offers new perspectives.

Nevertheless, goodwill and co-operation are not sufficient unless there are also the powers available to shape healthy development decisions. This is politically the most controversial area. In countries experiencing very rapid urbanisation the sheer momentum of change can overwhelm the most carefully considered plans. The following section suggests a way forward, proposing three levels of aspiration, depending on the economic, cultural and political contexts.

Three levels of healthy urban planning

The ability to engage with the health and sustainability impacts of spatial decisions, and to take action, depends on national income, culture, legal frameworks and organisational structures. Some countries have more difficulties to overcome than others. The argument of this book is that all authorities, even those in poorer countries, should attempt to engage with the full agenda of healthy urban planning, so that population health is improved, health services are more affordable, productivity is higher, and the sense of well-being widely shared.

Based on the experience of the Healthy Cities movement, there are three distinct levels (or phases) of integration of health and planning (Barton and Grant 2011). The first level is basic. It recognises the essential *life-support role* of settlements: the provision of shelter, access to food and clean water, fresh air, effective sewage treatment. It was the realisation that the industrial cities of the nineteenth century were inimical to health that led directly to modern planning. Health was seen as dependent on good settlement design. The early design codes established the sanitary systems, the separation of polluting industry from homes, and the daylight and space standards that transformed the living conditions of urban dwellers.

In the developed world we now take this primary level of planning/health dependency so much for granted, so fully institutionalised, with dedicated professionals, that it is almost sub-liminal. It is often not thought of as 'planning'. But elsewhere in the world the sheer pace of urbanisation often swamps attempts to achieve effective healthy planning through well-designed settlements. Nevertheless, city authorities and governments are far from powerless. Their investments in infrastructure, services and housing are critical. If, for example, they see the future of transport in terms of motorised mobility and road building, rather than active travel and public transport, then costly health impacts – pollution, accidents, exclusion, inequality and a rise in non-communicable diseases – are inevitable.

The second level goes beyond basic life-support into *quality of life projects*. There is the recognition that many facets of settlement planning and design affect health and well-being – and hence, from the economic viewpoint, productivity. The WHO 'healthy urban planning' initiative has many examples of good practice, some reported in Part V:

- New parks inserted into dense cities, giving opportunities for physical activity, contact with nature, fresher air and aesthetic delight.
- New allotments in urban areas, supporting access to fresh food, physical activity and social connection.
- Retrofit of comprehensive cycle networks, encouraging healthy activity (particularly amongst children), a safer environment, reduced car reliance, equity in access and combating the rise in greenhouse gas emissions.
- Housing renewal programmes that not only improve living conditions for poorer households but facilitate community cohesion through the planning process; create opportunities for play, work and education; reduce exposure to excessive cold or heat; and ensure good accessibility to essential services.
- Economic development programmes where retaining and creating sustainable job opportunities for marginalised or unskilled people is high priority, recognising that poverty and joblessness are two prime causes of illness.

Many cities have such projects (for example see Chapter 35). The addition of *health* as a motivator for action gives an extra dimension and sharper perspective. It draws in an additional constituency of political support. It provides clear criteria for success. However, it must be recognised that such projects – while admirable in themselves – do not add up to a real shift in the environmental/social determinants of health. Their effectiveness is limited by scale, and by the whole structure of economic and spatial development.

It is only when authorities start thinking (and are able to act) strategically and in an integrated way about the whole city or urban region – how it is going to evolve and how that will impact on the health and welfare of people – that the third level can be achieved. Level three is where *health is fully integrated into the planning system and in all spatial decision-making.* Health is treated not as a bolt-on extra, with a separate chapter in the strategic plan, but as a core goal. Planning for health becomes a fundamental purpose of plans at local, city and regional levels. It meshes with other core themes, like environmental sustainability, social justice and economic development.

Moving from level two to three is difficult. It is likely to challenge the organisational status quo, embedded assumptions about the role of the state, as well as the inertia of existing physical structures. Several of the case studies in Part V (English Midlands and Portland, for example) are testament to the struggle. It is necessary to have a coherent, integrated strategy across agencies and sectors, and implementation processes capable of realising it on the ground, and in people's hearts. The conclusion of comparative studies in the developed world (see Chapters 25 and 36) is that public ownership of land, public investment banks and strong planning systems are important.

Conclusion: planning and planners

What this book does is provide the evidence and arguments that can be used to convince decision-makers of the need for change, together with inspirational examples that demonstrate how health-supportive environments can be achieved in a range of contexts. If planners are to play the pivotal role necessary to make this happen, then their own attitudes will need to change. Levy (1992, p. 81) has observed that planning in the 1990s 'does not seem to have any guiding principles or central paradigm' – and many have echoed that since. We hope the book shows that planning for health and well-being does provide a new paradigm for planners, urbanists and designers of all kinds. Planning for health establishes professional criteria, drawing on research and good practice, which can give strength and clarity to planners' advice.

If this is accepted, then the education of planners and related professions will have to change course. Rather than espousing instrumental values, simply fulfilling the instructions of clients and politicians, the emphasis has to shift to fundamental values of promoting human well-being. The knowledge base then has to work from that starting point, and the skills base adapted to enable progress in relation to spatial, design and process outcomes. Skills including behavioural assessment, land market analysis, strategic thinking, spatial frameworks, community engagement, collaborative decision-making and advocacy are critical.

A common people-oriented philosophy across all built environment professions is needed, and can be greatly strengthened by a revived alliance with public health professionals. In that context, specialisation can occur without compromising coherence. There are many signs that give hope. For example, in the last few years the major professional planning/design/landscape bodies in the UK have promoted population health as an important professional goal, producing best practice guidelines. The Australian planning body has made health a touchstone of good policy. Perhaps more unexpectedly, in America the Urban Land Institute – consisting mainly of people in real estate and development industries – has produced a hard-hitting publication linking health and the built environment (ULI 2013). And Healthy Cities networks in Europe and Asia have been forging alliances between planning and health, powerfully influencing professional orientation.

The hope is that this is an idea whose time has come. That planners and designers can seize the opportunity; that planning, as viewed by politicians, investors and people in general, gains a new legitimacy – devoted to making the human habitat healthier and more sustainable – devoted to making people's lives better.

References

Barton, H. and Grant, M. 2006. A health map for the local human habitat. *Journal of the Royal Society for the Promotion of Health* 126 (6), 252–253.

Barton, H. and Grant, M. 2011. Urban planning for healthy cities. *Journal of Urban Health* 90 (1), S130–141.

Barton, H., Grant, M. and Guise, R. 2010. *Shaping neighbourhoods, for local health and global sustainability: 2nd edition.* Abingdon: Routledge.

CSDH (Commission on the Social Determinants of Health). 2008. *Closing the gap in a generation: health equity through action on the social determinants of health. Final report of the Commission on Social Determinants of Health.* Geneva: World Health Organization.

Diamond, J. 2004. *Guns, germs and steel: the fates of human societies.* New York: W. W. Norton and Co.

Levy, J. 1992. What has happened to planning? *Journal of the American Planning Association* 58 (1), 81–84.

ULI (Urban Land Institute). 2013. *Intersections: health and the built environment.* Washington, DC: Urban Land Institute.

Whitehead, M. and Dahlgren, G. 1991. 'The main determinants of health' model, version accessible in: Dahlgren, G. and Whitehead, M. (2007) *European strategies for tackling social inequities in health: levelling up part 2.* Copenhagen: WHO Regional Office for Europe.

ACRONYMS

ANGSt	Accessible National Greenspace Standard
APHA	American Public Health Association
ASLA	American Society of Landscape Architects
BMA	British Medical Association
BMI	body mass index
BPS	Bureau of Planning and Sustainability (Portland)
BRE	Building Research Establishment
CABE	Commission for Architecture and the Built Environment
CBD	central business district
CCDU	Christchurch Central Development Unit
CERA	Canterbury Earthquake Recovery Authority
CIEH	Chartered Institute of Environmental Health
CO	carbon monoxide
CO_2	carbon dioxide
COPD	chronic obstructive pulmonary disease
CPTED	Crime Prevention Through Environmental Design
CSF	Central Scotland Forest
CSGN	Central Scotland Green Network
CSH	Code for Sustainable Homes
DCLG	Department for Communities and Local Government
DCMS	Department for Culture, Media and Sport
DCSF	Department for Children, Schools and Families
DEIS	draft environmental impact statement
DFC	Design-led Food Communities
DfT	Department for Transport
EC	European Commission
ECE	Eastern and Central Europe
EIA	Environmental Impact Assessment
ELGG	East London Green Grid
EPA	Environmental Protection Agency
EPBD	Energy Performance of Buildings Directives

EPC	Energy Performance Certificates
EU	European Union
EWD	excess winter deaths
FIT	feed-in-tariff
FSPUD	Food-sensitive Planning and Urban Design
GDP	gross domestic product
GHG	greenhouse gas
GHMC	Greater Hyderabad Municipal Corporation
GIFT-T!	Green Infrastructure for Tomorrow!
GIS	geographic information systems
GPS	Global Positioning System
HBEP	Healthy Built Environments Program
HECPN	Health and Equity in the Comp Plan Network
HIA	Health Impact Assessment
HiAP	Health in All Policies
HMDA	Hyderabad Metropolitan Development Authority
HMO	Health Maintenance Organization
HWB	Health and Wellbeing Board
I'DGO	Inclusive Design for Getting Outdoors
IAIA	International Association for Impact Assessment
IIA	Integrated Impact Assessment
IMD	Index of Multiple Deprivation
IPCC	Intergovernmental Panel on Climate Change
JPU	joint planning unit
LEP	Local Enterprise Partnership
LILAC	Low Impact Living Affordable Community
LNG	Liveable Neighbourhoods Community Design Guidelines
LPCD	litres per capita per day
MCH	Municipal Corporation of Hyderabad
MEA	Millennium Ecosystem Assessment
MIT	Massachusetts Institute of Technology
MoT	Ministry of Transport
mph	miles per hour
NACTO	National Association of City Transportation Officials
NGO	non-governmental organisation
NHF	National Housing Federation
NHS	National Health Service, UK
NICE	National Institute for Health and Care Excellence
NO_2	nitrogen dioxide
NO_x	the sum of NO and NO_2
NPPF	National Planning Policy Framework
O_3	ozone
OPHI	Oregon Public Health Institute
PLEA	Passive Low Energy Architecture
PM	particulate matter
RCH	Redditch Co-operative Homes
RCT	randomised controlled trial
RCT	Rational Choice Theory

RESIDE	RESIDential Environments
SAP	Standard Assessment Procedure
SEA	Strategic Environmental Assessment
SES	socio-economic status
SO_2	sulphur dioxide
SPD	supplementary planning document
SUDS	Sustainable Urban Drainage System
TCPA	Town and Country Planning Association
TOD	transit-orientated development
UDIA	Urban Development Institute of Australia
UDS	Urban Development Strategy
UGB	urban growth boundary
UHI	urban heat island
UKHCN	United Kingdom Healthy Cities Network
UN	United Nations
UN CRC	United Nations Committee on the Rights of the Child
UNEP	United Nations Environment Programme
USDA	United States Department of Agriculture
WHO	World Health Organization
WMHPG	West Midlands Health and Planning Group
WWF	World Wide Fund for Nature

INDEX